PREFACE

In 1958 it was proposed that various juridical studies I had written on ancient Indian law, which had been published, starting from 1937, in a number of Journals, Magazines and Commemorative Volumes, should be assembled and reprinted in one or two volumes.

I accepted this proposal with enthusiasm and gratitude and began to prepare the *Studies* for publication. I felt, however, that many of them needed re-editing and that reference material should be inserted, but because my publishers in the Netherlands wanted the manuscript as early as possible, I was able to make only the most necessary changes.

After this partial editing was done and my publishers had received permission from the editors of the various journals, magazines and commemoration volumes for the reprinting of my *Studies*, the manuscript was sent to the Netherlands. After a lapse of about four years, however, the publishers informed me that for technical reasons they were unable to publish my *Studies* "at the present time."

Graciously, Motilal Banarsidass in Delhi agreed to publish them in two volumes. I wish most heartily to thank this Company, which is well-known for its interest in spreading Indian culture, for this gesture. It has taken some three years for the present volume to be published. I hope that the second will appear soon.

I must apologize to the readers of the first volume for all its imperfections and weaknesses. Most of the *Studies* reprinted therein and also in the first part of the second volume, were written before the encyclopaedic work of P.V. Kane entitled "History of Dharmaśāstra" appeared. I was therefore unable to take advantage of this monumental work. I also would like to say that if I were to have written the *Studies* now, I would have probably used a different approach. I would also probably have used better English. Most of the *Studies* were, in fact, originally written in my mother tongue, and translated afterwards into imperfect English.

I must also apologize to the readers for the fact that the first volume is appearing without a subject index. An index covering both volumes will be included at the end of the second volume of the *Studies.*

Although I have recently devoted most of my time to the study of Cāṇakya's aphorisms, the Sanskrit *kathā* and *kāvya* literature and the gnomic literature of India, I have also written and published some additional Juridical studies in ancient Indian law, but because of the size of the present volume, they will not be reprinted in the present work.

It is now my pleasant duty to express my most grateful thanks to Professor A. V. Kunst and Professor E. Sluszkiewicz, with whom I discussed some of my *Studies*, for their advice and very helpful suggestions which I always followed. I also wish to express my thanks to the Editors of the Journals, Magazines and Commemoration Volumes, who so kindly gave their permission for the re-publication of my *Studies* and to M/s. Motilal Banarsidass for agreeing to publish them.

New York *Ludwik Sternbach LL. D.*
April 1965

TABLE OF CONTENTS

OF VOLUME I

G. Prajāpatya-vivāha.

45. Definition. *Essentialia negotii.* 46-7. Participation of the father or guardian of the girl. Wedding ceremony. 48. Legitimacy of this form of marriage. 49-50. Sons, father and guardian. 51. Place in the general list of forms of marriage.

H. Gāndharva-vivāha

52. Definition. *Essentialia negotii* 53. Two subdivisions of the *gāndharva-vivāha.* 54. Legitimacy of this form of marriage. 55. Place in the general list of forms of marriage.

I. Svayaṁvara

56. Festive and ordinary *svayaṁvara* 57. Definition. *Esentialia negotii.*

J. Legal consequences of the Forms of Marriage.

58. Order of the forms of marriage in the general list. 59. Orthodox and other forms of marriage. 60-1. Special rules. *Strīdhana.* 62. Legal consequences of the orthodox and other forms of marriage. 63. Children born of orthodox and other forms of marriage.

III. SOCIOLOGICAL ASPECTS OF THE FORMS OF MARRIAGE

64. Simultaneous description of various forms of marriage. 65. Principal stages of the development of forms of marriage.

A. Marriage by capture

66. In the so-called lower stage of civilisation. 67-8. In the ancient civilized world. 69. In modern times among certain so-called primitive people. 70-1. Development of the marriage by capture in comparison with Indian sources; transition of the marriage by capture to marriage by purchase.

B. Marriage by purchase

72-4. Definition of marriage by purchase. 75. In the ancient civilized world. 76 In ancient India.

C. Marriage by Sham-purchase

77. Symbolical purchase. 79. In the ancient civilized world. 80. In modern times among certain so-called primitive people. 81. In ancient India.

ABBREVIATIONS.

ABORI — Annals of the Bhandarkar Oriental Research Institute.

Agn. P — Agni-Purāṇa in Bibliotheca Indica, Calcutta 1873-4.

AiS — The Anvār-i Suhailī or the Lights of Canopus, being the Persian Version of the Fables of Pilpay or the book "Kalīlah and Damnah" rendered into Persian by Ḥusain Vā'iz u'l-Kāshifī, trans. by E. B. Eastwick, Harford 1854.

AKM — Abhandlungen für die Kunde des Morgenlandes.

AlR — Alaṁkāraratnākara of Śobhākaramitra, POS 77.

Amar. — Amarakośa, ed. by Loiseleur Deslongchamps, Paris 1839.

An. — Anaṅgaraṅga, publ. in the Doaba Educational Press, Anarkali, Lahore.

Aṅg. — Āṅgiraḥ Saṁhitā, in "The Dharmaśāstra Text", Vol. I., ed. by M. N. Dutt, Calcutta 1908, or in Vīr. *Also* Āṅgira Smṛti.

ĀnSS — Ānandāśrama Sanskrit Series.

AOS — American Oriental Series.

AP — Agni-Purāṇa in Ān. SS.

Āp. — Āpastambīyadharmasūtram. Āpastamba's Aphorisms on the Sacred Laws of the Hindus. Ed. by G. Bühler. BSS 44 & 50. Bombay 1932.

Apar. or Aparar. — See Y.

Āp.-Gṛh. — Āpastambīya Gṛhyasūtra, ed. by A. M. Śāstri, Mysore 1893.

AsBh — Asahāyabhāṣya, as quoted in Dh

Āśv. / Āśv.-Gṛh. — Āśvalāyana-Gṛhyasūtra, ed. by A. F. Stenzler, Leipzig 1864.

B — Das Baudhāyana-Dharmasūtra, herausgegeben von E. Hultzsch. Zweite verbesserte Auflage, Leipzig 1922. AKM 16.2

Bāl.	=BBh
Baudh.	=B
BBh	Bālambhaṭṭi, being a commentary by Bālambhaṭṭa Pāyaguṇḍe on the Mitākṣarā of Śrī Vijñāneśvara on the Yājñavalkya Smṛti. Ed. by J. R. Gharpure. Bombay 1914. CHLT 5. *Also* ed. by Pt. Nityānand Pant Parvatiya (Pariṣkṛtya), Benares 1914 in ChSS 173-82, 204
BBh	in study 24=BhB
BD	Bahudarśana in IS.
Bhār.	Bhāratīya Nāṭyaśāstra.
BhB	*The Bhojaprabandha of Ballāla.* Ed. by Paṇśikar. 10th ed. Bombay 1932
Bhav. P	Bhaviṣya Purāṇa, in Vīr.
BhP	*Le Bhāgavata Purāṇa*...traduit et publié par M.E. Burnouf, Paris 1884-98
BhŚ	*The Epigrams attributed to Bhartṛhari*, including the three centuries. For the first time collected and critically edited, with principal variants and an introduction by D. D. Kosambi, Bombay 1948. Siṅghī Jain Series 23.
BhV	*Bhāratīya Vidyā* (monthly).
BIS	=IS
Boltz	=Ausgewählte Fabeln des Hitopadeśa im Urtexte nebst metrischer deutschen Übersetzung von August Boltz, Leipzig 1868
BP	*Brahmavaivartapurāṇam*...Ed. by Jīvānanda Vidyāsāgara. (Calcutta, 1888)
Brahmapur.	Brahma Purāṇa
BrDh	*Brāhmadharma* in Pratnakamranandinī Banaras
Bṛh	Bṛhaspati-Smṛti reconstructed By K. V. Rangaswami Aiyangar. GOS 85. Baroda 1941.
BṛKath	Bṛhatkathāmañjarī of Kṣemendra in KM 69.
B.S.S.	Bombay Sanskrit Series.
C	Cāṇakya, Cāṇakya's Aphorisms
Car	Caraka Saṁhitā
Cār	Cārudattam, a Sanskrit Drama in Four Acts Attributed to Bhāsa. Ed. by C. R. Devadhar, 2nd edition. POS 65, Poona 1943

CB	V. Chauvin, Bibliographie des ouvrages arabes... Liège 1892-1922
CHLT	The Collections of Hindu Law Texts
ChSS	Chowkhamba Sanskrit Series
CKl	J. Klatt, *De trecentis Cāṇakyae poetae Indici sententiis*, Halis Saxonum.
CKr	O. Kressler, Stimmen indischer Lebensklugheit. Frankfurt a/M, 1904.
CL	Laghucāṇakya version.
CLA	CL; Agra edition 1920, as quoted in CKr
CLB	CL; E. Bartoli. *Un secondo codice fiorentino inedito di Cāṇakya* RIGI 3. 3-4, 151-66. Also E. Bartoli. *Il codice napolitano di Cāṇakya* RIGI 4. 3-4, 129-33; 5.3-4, 115-9 (if divided in *adhyāyas*. If not divided in *adhyāyas* =CNN)
CLC	=CLP II
CLD	=CLP IV
CLE	=CLP V
CLI	MS No. 2411 in the Library of the India Office in London
CLL I	CL; MS A 455 in the Karl-Marx Universität, Universitätsbibliothek, Leipzig.
CLL II	CL; MS A 466 in the Karl-Marx Universität, Universitätsbibliothek, Leipzig.
CLLd	CL; MS Cod. Or. 8859; UB/123 in the University Library in Leiden.
CLM	=CLTb
CLP II	CL; MS 17072-2 (C) in the Université de Paris. Institut de Civilisation Indienne
CLP IV	CL; MS 17072-4 (D) in the Université de Paris. Institut de Civilisation Indienne
CLP V	CL; MS 17072-5 (E) in the Université de Paris. Institut de Civilisation Indienne
CLṢ	CL; Śrī-atha-ṣoḍaśa-Cāṇakya-prārambhaḥ (Bhāvanādāsa-kṛta-Hindī-vyākhyā-sahita-) Mumbaimaiṁ paṇḍita śrī Dhāra Śiva Lāl. Jñāna-Sāgara Press. Saṁvat 1932.
CLT	CL; Laghucāṇakyam. Sentenze Indiane pubblicate da E. Teza. Annali delle Università Toscane. Tomo XVI. Pisa 1879, p. 352 - 404.

CLTb	CL; MS or. fol. 1037 in the Universitätsbibliothek in Tübingen.
CM	E. Monseur. Cāṇakya. Recension de cinq recueils de stances morales......Paris 1887
CN	Cāṇakya-nīti-śāstra version
CND	=CVND
CNF	CN; Cāṇakyam. Codice indiano edito dal Dre Emilio Bartoli. Napoli 1911.
CNG	CN; The Recension of Cāṇakya used by Galanos for his 'Εκ διαφορῶν ποιητῶν by George Melville Bolling in Studies in Honour of Maurice Blomfield. New Haven 1920.
CNH	See CNJV (in KSH)
CNHU	CN; MS H. 250 in the Harvard University Library in Cambridge, Mass.
CNI	=CNI I
CNI I	CN; MS 1518a (Eggeling 3990) in the Library of the India Office in London.
CNI II	CN; MS Keith 7204 (Tagore 40b) in the Library of the India Office in London.
CNJV	CN; Cāṇakyaśatakaṁ. Ed. by Jīvānanda Vidyāsāgara. Calcutta 1926. The same text is reprinted in at least seventy eight editions, in particular in KSH 312 and KSG 2. 385.
CNL	CN; MS A 477 in the Universitätsbibliothek of the Karl Marx Universität, Leipzig.
CNM	CN; Rājanitau Cāṇikya-mūni-viracitaṁ. No place; no date.
CNMN	CN; Cāṇikya-mūni-kṛtaṁ (sic'.)-nīti-sāra. Allahabad 1880.
CNN	CN; E. Bartoli, Un secondo codice fiorentino inedito di Cāṇakya. (See CLB; first part).
CNNM	CN; Cāṇakya-nīti-māla. Ed. by Śrī Upendra Mohana Caudhurī Kavibhūṣaṇa sampādita. Bengal Art Printing Press. Calcutta 1324.
CNP I	CN; MS 17072-3 (A) in the Université de Paris. Institut de Civilisation Indienne.
CNP II	CN; MS 17072-1 (B) in the Université de Paris. Institut de Civilisation Indienne.

CNPh	CN; MS 1566 in the University of Pennsylvania Library, Philadelphia, Pa.
CNPN	CN; MS Sanskrit 684 (Cabaton 684) in the Bibliothèque Nationale in Paris.
CNS	CN; Cāṇakya-nīti-vyavahāra-sāra-saṁgrahaḥ. Ed. with a Marāṭhi translation by G.S. Sardesai, Kolhapur; POS 71.
CNŚ	CN; Cāṇakya-ślokaḥ...Śrī-rāma Śāstri Bhaṭṭa-cāryyeṇa saṁpāditaḥ Ghose Press. Calcutta 1319.
CNŚC	CN; Cāṇakya-śloka-saṁgraha...Publ. by Tārā-rasanna Mṛtyunjay. Calcutta 1915. *Also* Cāṇakya-śloka-saṁgrahaḥ...Śrī N. C. Caṭṭopādhyāya. Rudra Printing Press. Calcutta 1918.
CNŚK	CN; Cāṇakya-śloka. New Sanskrit Press. Calcutta 1887.
CNŚL	CN; Aṣṭottara-śata-Cāṇakya-ślokaḥ. Lakṣmī Printing Works. Calcutta 1322.
CNŚT	CN; Cāṇakya-śatakaṁ...Svarṇa Press. Dacca, Calcutta 1319.
CnT	etc. See below.
CNT IV	CN; MS No 5119, as quoted in CKr as TjD.
CNW	CN; A Weber. Über 100 Sprüche des Cāṇakya. In Monatsberichte der kön. Preuss. Akademie der Wissenschaften zu Berlin aus dem Jahre 1864. Berlin 1865, pp. 400-31
CnT	Note-book MSs
CnT I	CnT; MS No. 5031, as quoted in CKr as TjA.
CnT II	CnT; MS No. 5117, as quoted in CKr as TjB.
CnT III	CnT; MS No. 5118, as quoted in CKr as TjC.
CnT V	CnT; MS No. 5120, as quoted in CKr as TjE.
CnT VI	CnT; MS No. 5121, as quoted in CKr as TjF.
CnT VII	CnT; MS No. 5122, as quoted in CKr as TjG.
Col.	Digest of Hindu Law on Contracts and Successions with a commentary by J. Teracapancanana, transl. by H. T. Colebroke, Vol. I., London 1801.
CR	Cāṇakya-rāja-nīti-śāstra version.
CRB	CR; MS sansk. f. 15 in the Bodleian Library in Oxford.
CRBh I	CR; MS 347 of 1892-95 in the Bhandarkar Oriental Research Institute Collection in Poona.

CRBh II	CR; MS 348 of 1892-95 in the Bhandarkar Oriental Research Institute Collection in Poona.
CRC	CR; Cāṇakya-rāja-nīti-śāstram ed. by Pt. Iśvara Chandra Śāstri......Calcutta. Calcutta Oriental Series, No. 2
CRCa I	CR; MS Add. 2525 in the University Library in Cambridge.
CRCa II	CR; MS Add. 1040 in the University Library in Cambridge.
CRP	CR; MS 1559 in the Library of the Pennsylvania University in Philadelphia, Pa.
CS	Cāṇakya-sāra-saṅgraha-version.
CSB I	CS; MS or. fol. 598 in the Universitätsbibliothek in Tübingen.
CSB II	CS; MS or. fol. 599 in the Universitätsbibliothek in Tübingen.
CSBD	CS; Bodhi Cāṇakyam. athavā Cāṇakya-sāra-saṅgrahaḥ......by Bh. C. Dutt. Calcutta 1888.
CSC I	CS; MS Add. 1539 in the University Library in Cambridge.
CSC II	CS; MS Add. 1346 in the University Library in Cambridge.
CSJ	CS; MS belonging to professor J.W. de Jong in Leiden.
CSLd	CS; MS Cod. or. 8857; Lub/D 122 in the University Library in Leiden.
CŚ	=CN. In JSAIL 22 also identical with CM
CŚF	=CNF
CŚH	=CNH
CŚlB	=CNP II
CŚN	=CNS
CŚP	=CNPN
CŚW	=CNW
CV	Vṛddha Cāṇakya, *textus ornatior* version. In JSAIL 22 also identical with CVND.
CVA	=CvA
CVB	=CSB I and CSB II, as quoted in IS.
CVF	=CvP IV
CVG	=CvP V
CVGt	=CvGt

CVK	=CvI
CVM	CV; Vṛddha-Cāṇakhyanuṁ Bhaṭa Bālakarāma Māṁdarāma Māṁḍavīkara, Nirṇaya-sāgara Press. Bombay 1874.
CVN	=CvTb
CVND	CV; śrīḥ Cāṇakyanītidarpaṇaḥ. Bhāṣāṭīkā-sahitaṁ. Prakāśakaḥ bhārgava pustakālaya, gāyaghaṭ. Banāras. Brāñca-kacauḍīgalī, Banāras. The same text is reprinted in at least sixty-four editions and a great number of MSs contains the same text, e.g. MS Cod. Or. 8855; Lub-D 167 in the University Library in Leiden.
CVT(a)	=CnT I
CVT(b)	=CnT II
CVT(c)	=CnT III
CVT(d)	=CNT IV
CVT(e)	=CnT V
CVT(f)	=CnT VI
CVT(g)	=CnT VII
CVV	see CVND (other editions).
CVW	=CNW
Cv	Vṛddha Cāṇakya, *textus simplicior* version.
CvA	Cv; Rāja-nīti, Cāṇakya-Muni-viracitam. Agra 1920
CvGt	Cv; MS Cod. ms. sanscr. 64 in the Niedersächsische Staats-und Universitätsbibliothek in Göttingen.
CvH	Cv; MS H 250 in the Harvard University Library, Cambridge, Mass.
CvI	Cv; MS 2411 in the Library of the India Office in London.
CvL I	Cv; MS A 445 in the Karl-Marx Universität, Universitätsbibliothek in Leipzig.
CvL II	Cv; MS A 446 in the Karl-Marx Universität, Universitätsbibliothek in Leipzig.
CvLd	Cv; MS Cod. Or. 8859; UB/123 in the University Library in Leiden.
CvP IV	Cv; MS 17072-4 (D) in the Université de Paris. Institut de Civilisation Indienne.
CvP V	Cv; MS 17072-5 (E) in the Université de Paris. Institut de Civilisation Indienne.

CvṢ	Cv; Śrī-atha-ṣoḍaśa-Cāṇakya-prārambhaḥ (Bhāvanādāsa-kṛta-Hindī-vyākhyā-sahita-) Mumbaimiṁ paṇḍita Śrī Dhāra Śīva Lāl. Jñāna Sāgara Press. Saṁvat 1932.
CvTb	Cv; MS or. fol. 1037 in the Universitätsbibliothek in Tübingen.
CvW	Cv; MS Walker 205c in the Bodleian Library in Oxford.
CW	=C NW
Dak.	Dakṣa Saṁhitā, in "The Dharmaśāstra Text", Vol. I., ed. by M.N. Dutt, Calcutta 1908,or in Vīr.
Daś	Daṇḍin's Daśakumāracarita, ed. by H.H. Wilson, London 1876.
DBh or DBH	Dāyabhāgaḥ of Jīmūtavāhana. Asiatic Society of Bengal, Calcutta.
Dev.	Devala in Vīr.
Dh	*Dharmakośa*, ed. by Lakṣmaṇaśāstrī Jośī, Prājñapāṭha-śālā-maṇḍala-grantha-mālā, Wai 1937-47.
DhNP	*Dharmattvanirṇayapariśiṣṭam*, ĀnSS 98
DhSP	The Parāśara-dharma-saṁhitā or Parāśara Smṛti, with the commentary of Sāyaṇa Mādhavācārya. Ed. by Pt. Vāman Śāstri Islāmapurkar. Bombay 1911-9. BSS. 47-8, 59, 64, 67, 74.
DhV	Halāyudha's *Dharmaviveka* in KSG 1. 381
DK	Dīpakalikā, Commentary on Y. by Śūlapaṇī. IO. MSS Library, as quoted in Dh.
DN	Dāyabhāga-nirṇaya by Bhaṭṭijīdīkṣitaḥ. MS in the Bhandarkar O.R. Institute, Poona, as quoted in Dh.
DT	Dāyatattvam by Raghunandana, ed. by Jīvānanda Vidyāsāgara, Calcutta.
DV	Daṇḍaviveka of Vardhamāna critically edited by Mm. Kamala Krsṇa Smṛtitīrtha, Baroda 1931. GOS 52
G	The Institutes of Gautama, ed.......by A.F. Stenzler, London 1876. Sanskrit Text Society. (See GM).
GhN	Ghaṭakarpara's Nītisāra. In KSG I, 374
GM	Gautama-praṇīta-dharmasūtrāṇī. Ed. by G. Śāstri Gokhale. ĀnSS 61.

GMBh Goutama-dharmasūtra with Maskarī Bhāṣya. Ed. by L. Srinivasacharya. OLPSS 50. Mysore 1917.

GMH *Gautama; Mitākṣara, Haradatta.* ĀnSS, as quoted in Dh.

GMit =GM

Gobh.-Gṛh. Gobhila-Gṛhyasūtra, ed. by C. K. Tarkālaṅkāra, Calcutta 1908.

GOS Gaekwad Sanskrit Series.

Gov. Manuṭīkā. Govindarāja on Mn. in MnM. (See GR)

GP Garuḍa-purāṇa. Ed. by Jīvānanda Vidyāsāgara. 1st ed. Calcutta 1890.

GR Govindarājīyā. Ed. by V.N. Mandlik. Bombay. (See Gov.).

Gṛh Gṛhyasūtra

H Hitopadeśa

HAIS L. Sternbach, *Hitopadeśa and its Sources*, American Oriental Series, No. 44

Hal. Halāyuddha's Abhidhānaratnamālā, ed. by Th. Aufrecht, London 1861.

Har. Haradatta.

Hār. Hārīta Saṁhitā, in "The Dharmaśāstra Text", Vol. I., ed. by M.N. Dutt, Calcutta 1908.
In JSAIL 22, 25, 26 *Vyavahārādhyāya aus Hārīta's Dharmaśāstra* nach Citaten zusammengestellt von J. Jolly. Muenchen 1889. Abh. d. k. Bay. Akad. d. Wiss. I.Cl. 18, Bd. 2. Abth.

HC *Hitopadeśa, or salutary instruction, in the original Sanskrit* ...Ed. by H.T. Colebrooke, Serampore, 1804.

HDh Halāyuddha's *Dharmaviveka* in KSG 1. 381

Hem. Hemacandra's Abhidhānacintāmaṇī ed. by O. Boehtlingk and Ch. Rieu, St. Petersburg 1847.

Hit. =H. *Also* Hitopadeśa of Nārāyaṇa, ed. by M. R. Kale, Bombay 1924.

HH *The Hitopadeśa in the Sanskrita Language* (A. Hamilton). London 1810.

HJ *Hitopadeśa.* The Sanskrit text with a grammatical analysis alphabetically arranged by F. Johnson. 2nd. ed. Hartford London 1864.

HK *The Hitopadeśa of Narāyaṇa.* Ed. with a Sanskrit

Commentary and Notes.....by M.R. Kale. 5th ed. Bombay 1924.

HKS — *Kāvyasaṁgraha*. A Sanskrit anthology being a collection of the best 37 smaller poems in the Sanskrit language by Dr. J. Haeberlin, Calcutta 1847.

HL — =HH

HM — The first book of the *Hitopadeśa*. Skt. text. *Also* Second, third and fourth books of *Hitopadeśa*. Skt. text. (both) ed. by M. Müller. London 1865.

HN — Nārāyaṇa. *Hitopadeśa* nach d. nepalischen HS. neu herausgeg. von H. Blatt. Berlin 1930.

HOS — Harvard Oriental Series.

HP — *Hitopadeśa* by Nārāyaṇa. Ed. by P. Peterson. BSS 33.

HPet. — Hitopadeśa. Petersburg MS, quoted in HS

HS — Hitopadeśas, id est Institutio Salutaris. Textum codd. mss. collatis recensuerunt, interpretationem latinam et annotationes criticas adiecerunt A.G. Schlegel et Ch. Lassen, Bonn 1829-31.

HSer — =HC

IO — India Office Library, *or* MS in IO.

IS — *Indische Sprüche*. Skt. u. Deutsch herausg. von O. Böhtligk. 2nd ed. St. Petersburg 1870-3.

Jāt. — Jātaka, ed. by V. Fausböll, London 1877.

JHP — J. Hertel, Das Pañcatantra, seine Geschichte und seine Verbreitung. Leipzig und Berlin 1914.

JHTVH — J. Hertel, Über Text und Verfasser des Hitopadeśa. Leipzig 1897.

JSAIL — Juridical Studies in Ancient Indian Law by L. Sternbach. See below p. 24 sqq.

K — Kauṭilīyam Arthaśāstraṁ revised and edited by Dr. R. Shama Sastry. Mysore 1924. OLPSS 37/64. *Also* Kauṭilīyam Arthaśāstram. A new edition by J. Jolly & R. Schmidt. Lahore 1923-4. PSS 4. *Also* Kauṭilīyam Arthaśāstram with the commentary Śrīmūla of Mm. T. Gaṇapati Śāstri. Trivandrum 1924. TSS 79, 80, 82.

Kām — Kāmasūtra of Vātsyāyana with the Commentary of Jayamaṅgalā, Bombay, Nirṇaya Sāgara Press, 1900.

Kaś·	Kāśyapa Saṁhitā, in Vīr.
Kash.	See MnM
Kath.	Kathāsaritsāgara, ed. by H. Brockhaus, Leipzig 1839. See KSS.
Kāty.	Kātyāyana-smṛti-sāroddhāraḥ. Text (reconstructed), translation, notes and introduction by P.V. Kane. Reprint from the Indian Law Quarterly, Bombay 1933.
Kātyay.	=Kāty.
Kaut	=K.
KB	The Bṛhatkathāmañjarī of Kṣemendra, ed. by Pt. Śivadatta......and K. Pāṇḍuraṅg Parab, Bombay 1901. KM 69
KD	Kalila and Dimna or the Fables of Bidpai translated from the Arabic by Rev. W. Knatchbull. Oxford 1819.
KM	Kāvyamālā. Nirṇaya Sāgara Press, Bombay
KN	*Kāmadankīya-nītisāraḥ*. Ed. by Rājendralāla Mitra Bibl. Ind. 4
KR	Kathāratnākara by Hemavijaya, Jamnagar 1911. In JSAIL 22 see Rāj.
KṣB	The Bṛhatkathamañjarī of Kṣemendra. Ed. by Pt. Śivadatta and K. P. Parab. KM. 69
KSG	*Kāvyasaṁgrahaḥ pañcasaptati-saṁskṛta-kāvyātmakaḥ*. Ed. by Jīvānanda Vidyāsāgara. 3rd ed. Calcutta, 1888.
KSH	*Kāvya-saṅgraha. A Sanskrit anthology, being a collection of the best smaller poems in the Sanskrit language*. By Dr. J. Haeberlin. Calcutta, 1847.
KSS	Kathāsaritsāgara *Die Märchensammlung des Śri Somadeva Bhaṭṭa*. Ed. by H. Brockhaus, Leipzig-Paris 1839 and AKM 2.5 & 4.5
KSV	=KSG
Kul.	=Kull.
Kull.	Kullūka. Commentator on Mn. See MnK, MnM and MnM
Kuṭṭ.	Dāmodaragupta's Kuṭṭanīmata, KM 3. Bombay 1887.
La.	Lalla-Saṁhitā, in Vīr.
MaBh	*Goutama-dharmasūtra with Maskaribhāṣya*, ed. by L. Śrīnivasacharya, OLPSS 50, Mysore 1917.

Mahān	*Mahānāṭaka*, as quoted in IS
MBh or MBH	*Śrīmahābhāratam*, śrimaharṣi Vedavyāsaviracitam, ed. by P. C. Roy, 3rd ed. Calcutta 1886-8. *Also* ed. by P. R. Kinjawadekar, Poona 1933.
MBh(Bh)	The Mahābhārata for the first time critically edited by Vishnu S. Sukthankar. Poona, Bhandarkar Oriental Research Institute. Poona 1927—
Medh.	Medhātithi's Commentary on Mn., see MnJh.
Meyer	J. J. Meyer, Das alt-indische Buch vom Welt- und Staatsleben, Leipzig 1926.
Mit.	See Y.
MMu	Manuṭīkā by Kullūka (Manvartha-muktā-valiḥ in MnM and MnN)
Mn	Mānava-dharmaśāstra. See MnJh.
Mn.-Gṛh	Mānava-gṛhyasūtra, in GOS 35. Baroda.
MnH	Mānava-dharma-śāstra; or the Institutes of Menu. Ed. by G. Ch. Haughton. London 1825.
MnJ	Mānava-dharma-śāstra, the code of Manu. Text critically edited by J. Jolly. London 1887. TOS
MnJh	Manu-smṛti with the Manubhāṣya of Medhātithi (Medh.) Ed. by Mm. G. Jhā. Calcutta 1932-9, Bibl. Ind. 256
MnK	The Manusmṛti with Manvartha Muktāvali, commentary by Kullūka Bhaṭṭa (Kull.). Benares 1935. KSS 114
MnL	Lois de Manou, publiées en sanscrit, aves des notes contenant un choix de variantes et de scholies par A. Loiseleur Deslongchamps. Paris 1830
MnM	Mānava-dharma-śāstra with the commentaries of Medhātithi, Sarvajñanārāyaṇa (Sarv.), Kullūka, Rāghavānanda (Rāgh.), Nandana and Rāmacandra (Rām.), by V. N. Mandlik. Bombay 1886
MnN	Mn with the Commentary...of Kullūka. 10th ed. by Nārāyaṇa Rāma Ācārya Kāvyatīrtha. Nirṇaya Sāgara Press. Bombay 1846.
MnP	The Manusmṛti with the commentary of Kullūka, various readings, footnotes, indices, etc. tenth edition. Ed. by Nārāyaṇa Rāma Ācārya Kāvyatīrtha. Publ. by S. Pāṇḍuraṅga. Bombay 1946.

MP — The Mārkaṇḍeyapurāṇa. Ed. by Rev. K. M. Banerjee. Calcutta 1862. Bibl. Ind. 29

MPā — Madanapārijāta by Viśveśvara. In Asiatic Society of Bengal. Calcutta

MR — Madanaratnam, Bikaner Sanskrit MSS. Library as quoted in Dh.

Mṛ — Mṛcchakaṭika by Śūdraka in Nirṇaya Sāgara Press, Bombay 1950

Mṛcch. — Mṛcchakaṭika, ed. by N.B. Godabole, Bombay 1896

MRP — *Madanaratnapradīpa* (*Vyavahāravivekoddyota*). Ed. by P. V. Kane. Gaṅga Oriental Series 6. Bikaner 1948.

MS — Manuscript

MŚ — The Śiśupālavadha of Māgha. Ed. by Pt. Durgāprasāda and Pt. Sivadatta. 11th ed. Bombay 1940.

MV — Manuṭīkā, Manvarthavivṛtiḥ. Sarvajñanārāyāṇaḥ, in MnM

N — The Institutes of Nārada, together with copious extracts from the Nāradabhāṣya of Asahāya and other standard commentaries. Ed. by J. Jolly. Calcutta 1885. Bibl. Ind. 102

Nand. — Nanda's commentary on Vi., called Vaijayanti. See Vi.

Nar. — =N

Nār. — =Manuṭīkā. Nārāyaṇa's Commentary on Mn.

NIA — *New Indian Antiquary.*

NM — *Nīti Mañjarī of Dyā Dviveka.* Ed. by S. J. Joshi. Banaras 1933

NMS — *The Nāradīyamanusaṁhitā* with the Bhāṣya of Bhavasvāmin, ed. by K. Sāmbaśiva Śāstri, Trivandrum 1929. TSS 97.

NP — *The Nāradapañcarātra*, ed. by Rev. K. M. Banerjee, Calcutta 1865. Bibl. Ind. 38.

NPr — Nītiprakāśika. Ed. by G. Oppert. Madras-London 1882

NPR — =NP

NṛP — *Nṛsiṁhaprasādaḥ*, Sarasvatībhuvan, Benares, as quoted in Dh.

NŚ — *Nītiśāstra* in Telugu Characters, quoted in IS.

NV — Nītivākyāmṛta by Somadevasūri. Ed. by Pt.

	Pannālāla Soni. Māṇikacandra Digambara Jaina Granthamālā 22
OLPSS	Oriental Library Publications. Sanskrit Series. Mysore
P	Pañcatantra. See, in particular in JSAIL 20, The Pañcatantra Reconstructed by Prof. F. Edgerton in the "American Oriental Series", Vol. 2 and 3, published by the American Oriental Society, 1924.
Pa.	Pancasāyaka, published in "Punjab Sanskrit Book Depot."
Paith.	Paiṭhīnasi-smṛti
Pañc.	Pañcatantra
Pañcas.	Pañcasāyaka in IO, as quoted by Schmidt.
Par.	Parāśara Saṁhitā, in "The Dharmaśāstra Text", Vol. II., ed. by M.N. Dutt, Calcutta 1909.
PB	Th. Benfey, Pantschatantra; Fünf Bücher indischer Fabeln, Märchen und Erzählungen. Aus dem Sanskrit übersetzt mit Einleitung und Anmerkungen. Leipzig 1859.
PBK	=Pts
PD	P of Durgasiṁha by A. Veṅkatasubbiah. Zeitschrift fur Indologie und Iranistik 6.255
PDhS	=DhSP
PHP	=PP
PKS	J. Hertel, Über einige HSs von Kathāsaṁgraha-Strophen, in ZDMG 64.62
PHT	=PT
PK	=PtsK
PM	Mēghavijayas Auszug aus dem Pañcatantra von J. Hertel. Verein für Volkskunde. Zeitschrift 1906. In JSAIL 24 J. Hertel. *Eine vierte Jaina Recension des Pañcatantra* (*Meghavijaya*). ZDMG 51, 639
PN	*Pañcatantra Nepali text* as quoted in PS LXXXIX, PT 1. 153; 104-26 and PRE 2.192 sqq.
PO	*Poona Orientalist* (quarterly).
POS	Poona Oriental Series
PP	*The Pañcatantra. A Collection of Ancient Hindu Tales in the Recension , called Pañcākhyānaka...of the Jaina*

	Monk Pūrṇabhadra. Critically ed. by J. Hertel. HOS 11-2
PPP	The Pañcatantraka of Viṣṇuśarman, ed. by K. P. Parab and W.L.S. Paṇśīkar, published by P. Jāwajī, in Nirṇaya Sāgara Press, Bombay 1930
PR	*Pañcaratna* in KSG 1.277
Pras	*Śrīmatkavikulatīlakoktiḥ prasaṁgābharaṇam* (no place, no date).
PrC	*Prabandha Cintāmaṇi of Merutuṅgācārya.* Critically ed. by Jinavijaya Muni...SJS 1
PRE	The Pañcatantra reconstructed. An attempt to establish the original Sanskrit text of the most famous of Indian story-collections on the basis of the principal extant versions. Text, critical apparatus, introduction, translation by F. Edgerton. New Haven, Conn. 1924. AOS. 2. *Also* The Pañcatantra I-V. The text in its oldest form. Ed. by F. Edgerton. Poona 1930
PS	Pañcatantra (southern). Das südliche Pañcatantra. Sanskrit Text der Recension β mit den Lesarten der besten HSs der Recension α. Herausg. von J. Hertel, Leipzig 1906. Abh. der Phil.-hist. Klasse der kön. sächs. Gesellschaft der Wiss. XXIV. 5 In JSAIL 23=DhSP
PŚ	The Paddhati of Śārṅgadhara, a Sanskrit anthology. Ed. by P. Peterson. Bombay 1888... BSS 37
PSDh	=DhSP
PSo	=PS
PSS	Punjab Sanskrit Series
PT	Über das Tantrākhyāyikā, die Kaśmīrische Rezension des Pañcatantra mit dem texte der HS. Decc. Coll. VIII, 145 von. J. Hertel. Abh. d. phil.-hist. Kl. d. kön. Sächs. Gesell. d. Wiss. XXII. 5. Leipzig 1904. Also in JSAIL 23 PTem
PTem	The Pañcatantra. A collection of Ancient Hindu tales in its oldest recension the Kashmirian, entitled Tantrākhyāyikā. The original Sanskrit text, *editio minor*, reprinted from the critical *editio major* which was made for the Kön. Gesell. der Wiss. zu Göttingen by Dr. J. Hertel., Cambridge Mass.

	1915. HOS. 14. *Also* Tantrākhyāyikā; die älteste Fassung des Pañcatantra aus dem Sanskrit übers. mit Einleitung u. Anmerkungen von J. Hertel, Leipzig u. Berlin 1909.
PTs	=Pts
Pts	Pañcatantra (textus simplicior). Ed. with notes by F. Kielhorn (I), by G. Bühler (II-V). Bombay 1891-6. BSS 1, 3, 4
Ptsh.	Pañcatantra. Hamburg MS, quoted in PT
PtsK	Pañtschatantrum (*textus simplicior*) *sive quinquepartitum de moribus exponens. Ex codicibus manuscriptis editio, Commentari is criticis auxit* by 10. Godofr. Ludov. Kosegarten. Bonn 1848.
PX	Pañcatantra. *Xi* MS. Quoted in PT.
R	Rāmāyaṇa, Bombay edition reprinted. *Also* : *Śrīmad Vālmīki Rāmāyaṇa*, a critical edition with the commentary of Śrī Govindāraja and extracts from many other commentaries and readings, ed. and publ. by T.R. Kṛṣṇācārya and T. R. Vyasācārya of Kumbakonam, Bombay 1911. (In JSAIL 22) Cf. RB, RG, RV, VRK
Ragh.	Raghuvaṁśa, ed. by A.F. Stenzler, London 1832.
Rāgh.	in Mn. Manuṭīkā. Manvarthacandrikā by Rāghavānandaḥ in MnM
Rāj.	Kalhaṇa's Rājataraṅginī, ed. by M.A.Stein, Bombay 1892. *Also* ed. by M. A. Troyer, Paris 1890.
Rām	=R
RB	*Srī Vālmīki Rāmāyaṇa*. Mumbayyaṁ, śeṣaṁ gopaḷa Nārāyaṇa Prabhṛti, Maṁḍasya Mudrāyaṁtre samāptiṁ nītam 1891.
RDhK	*Rājadharmakaustubhaḥ*. Ed. by K. K. Smṛtitīrtha. GOS 72
RG	Rāmāyaṇa, poema indico di Valmici. Testo sanscrito...della scuola Gaudana per G. Gorresio. Parigi 1843-50
Ṛg.	Ṛgveda, ed. by F. Rosen, London 1838
RIGI	Rivista Indo-greco-italica di Filologia
RO	Rocznik Orientalistyczny
RR	Rājanīti-ratnākara by Caṇḍeśvara. Bihar and Orissa Research Society. Patna 1936.

RRK	=RR
RT	H. v. Wlislocki, Beiträge zu Benfey's Pañcatantra, ZDMG 42.113 sqq. The tale of Gullible Husband as known in Romanian Transylvania. See also Rāj.
RV	=R in VR
Ś	Śukasaptati. See also Śts and Śto. (in JSAIL 23)
Ś	Dipakalikā, Commentary on Y. by Śūlapāṇi, ed. by J.R. Gharpure, in CHLT 26, Bombay 1939 (See DK.). In JSAIL 23=Śuk.
Śa	*Śaṅkha Saṁhitā*
Śāk.	Kalīdāsa's Śākuntala, ed. by O. Böhtlingk, Bonn 1842
Sam.	Kṣemendra's Samayamātṛkā. KM 10, Bombay 1888
Saṁs.	Saṁskārakāṇḍa. See Vīr.
Saṁv.	Saṁvartta Saṁhitā, in "The Dharmaśāstra Text", Vol. I., ed. by M.N. Dutt, Calcutta 1908 or in Vīr.
Śaṅkh.	=Śa
Śāṅkh.	Śāṅkhāyana
Śaṅkh.Likh.	Śaṅkha-Likhita
Śānt.	*Das Śāntiśataka mit Einleitung, kritischem Apparat......* von K. Schönfeld. (Leipzig, 1910)
Sar.	Sarasvatī-Vilāsa, ed. by Rev. Th. Foulkes, London 1881.
Śāt.	Śātātapa-Saṁhitā, in "The Dharmaśāstra Text", Vol. I., ed. by M.N. Dutt, Calcutta 1908, or in Vīr.
SB	Subhāṣitārṇava as quoted in IS
ŚB	*The Budhabhūṣaṇa of King Śaṁbhu.* Ed. by H. D. Velankar. Gov. Or. Ser. C. 2 (Poona, 1926)
SBE	Sacred Books of the East
SBH	Sacred Books of the Hindus
SC	*Smṛticandrikā by Devaṇṇabhaṭṭa.* Ed. by J.R. Gharpure CHLT 11.
SCGh	=SC
Schmidt	R. Schmidt, Beiträge zur indischen Erotik, Berlin 1922.
SCi or SCM	Smṛticintāmaṇiḥ India Office MSS. Library, as quoted in Dh.
SCS	Smṛticandrikā by Devaṇṇabhaṭṭa. Ed. by R.

	Shama Sastry and L. Śrinivasacharya. Mysore 1914-21. OLPSS 43-5, 48, 52, 56
SCt	=SCM
Sewell	R. Sewell, A Forgotten Empire, London 1900
ŚGṛh	Das Śāṅkhāyanagṛhyasūtram, herausg. von H. Oldenberg, in Ind. Studien 15. (1878).
SH	Slovakisches Märchen aus Herzlova, Gömörer Comitat. H. von Wlislocki, Beiträge zu Benfey's Pañcatantra. ZDMG. 42. 113 sqq.
SJS	*Siṅghī Jaina Series*
SK	Somadeva's Kathāsaritasāgara. Die Märchensammlung des Śrī Somadeva Bhaṭṭa aus Kaśmīr, Sanskrit und Deutsch von Dr. H. Brockhaus, Leipzig-Paris 1839-63 (I-V), in AKM 2.5 (VI-VIII) and in AKM 4.5 (IX-XVIII)
SKD	*The Kathāsaritsāgara* of Somadevabhaṭṭa, ed. by Paṇḍit Durgāprasād and Kāśīnāth Pāṇḍuraṅg Parab, fourth edition, Bombay 1930.
ŚL	Śaṅkha-Likhita-dharmasūtra
Śl.S	Buddhasvāmin, Bṛhat-kathā-ślokasaṅgraha, ed. by F. Lacôte, Paris 1908-24
Smṛ.C	=SCS
ŚP	*The Paddhati of Śarṅgadhara, a Sanskrit Anthology.* Ed. by P. Peterson, BSS 37
ṢR	*Ṣaḍratra* in KSG 1.280
SRBh	Subhāṣita-ratna-bhāṇḍāgāra. Enlarged and re-edited with sources, etc. by Nārāyaṇa Rāma Ācārya Kāvyatīrtha, eighth edition, Bombay 1952.
SRK	Subhāṣitaratnākara. A collection of witty and epigrammatic sayings in Sanskrit, compiled and edited with explanatory notes by Kṛṣṇa Śāstrī Bhāṭavaḍekar, Bombay 1872
SS	*Smṛtisāraḥ*, India Office MSS. Library, as quoted in Dh
ŚŚ	*Śukranītisāraḥ, śrīmat śukrācāryaviracitaḥ* 2nd ed. Calcutta 1890.
Śto	*Die Śukasaptati, textus ornatior,* herausg. von R. Schmidt. Abh. d. Bay. Ak. d. Wiss. 21.2
STS	Sanskrit Text Society

Śts.	Die Śukasaptati, *textus simplicior*, herausgegeben von R. Schmidt. Leipzig 1893. AKM. 10.1
ŚtsA	Der *textus simplicior* der Śukasaptati in der Recension der Handschrift A von R. Schmidt. ZDMG 48
ŚtsM	Die Marāṭhi-Übersetzung der Śukasaptati. Marāṭhī und Deutsch von R. Schmidt. Leipzig 1897. AKM 10.4
Śuk.	in JSAIL 17. Śukasaptati. See Śto (t.o.), Śts (t.s.)
Śuk.	in JSAIL 23. See Śukr.
Śukr.	Śukranītsāra. Text, *variae lectiones*, etc. by G. Oppert. Madras 1882.
Suś.	Suśruta-saṁhitā in Bibl. Indica 1897. *Also* ed. by Kunja Lal Bhishagratna, Calcutta 1907
SV	The Sarasvatīvilāsaḥ of Śrī Pratāparudra Mahādeva Mahārāja. Ed. by R. Shāma Sāstry. Mysore 1927. OLPSS 71
ŚV	*Die Vetālapañcaviṁśatikā* in den Recensionen des Śivadāsa und eines Ungenannten mit kritischen Commentar, herausg. von H. Uhle, Leipzig. AKM. 8. 1.
SVez	Seven Vezirs quoted in CB.
Tant.	*The Tantrākhyāna, a Collection of Indian Tales*...by C. Bendall. JRAS XX, 465: See TN
Tar.	Taraṅga
TN	Tantrākhyāna. The Tantrākhyāna, a Collection of Indian Folklore, from a unique Sanskrit MS. discovered in Nepāl by C. Bendall. JRAS NS XX. 465. See Tant.
TOS	Truebner Oriental Series
TSS	Trivandrum Sanskrit Series
Ṭṭ.	Ṭūṭī-nāmah. Das Persische Papageienbuch. Deutsche Übersetzung von C.J.L. Iken. Berlin und Leipzig 1905. *Also* Tuti-Nameh. Das Papageienbuch...Nach der türkischen Bearbeitung... übers. von G. Rosen. Leipzig 1858.
U	Ujjvala. Āpastamba Dharmasūtra with the commentary by Śrī Haradatta Miśra. Ed. with notes, introduction by Pt. A. Chinnasvāmī Śāstrī and Pt. A. Rāmanātha Śāstrī, Benares 1932. **ChSS; KSS 93**

Uś. — Uśanaḥ-Saṁhitā, in "The Dharmaśāstra Text", Vol. I., ed. by M. N. Dutt, Calcutta 1908, or in Vīr.

Va — =Vās.

VA — The Alaṅkāra-kaustubham of Viśveśvara Paṇḍita Ed. by Pt. Śivadatta. KM 66

Vān — Vānayaṣṭaka in HKS.

Vānary — Vānaryyaṣṭaka in KSG. 1. 324

Vās. — The Vāsiṣṭha-dharmaśāstram. Aphorisms of the sacred law of the Āryas as taught in the school of Vasiṣṭha by Rev. A. A. Führer. Poona 1930. BSS 23.

Vāts. — Vātsyāyana. Kāmasūtra with Yaśodhara's Commentary (Yaś.) ed. by Paṇḍit Durgāprasāda, Bombay 1900

VBh. — Vivādabhaṅgārṇavaḥ by Jagannātha (Tarkapañcānāna). See VJT.

VC — *Vivādacintāmaṇiḥ.* Śrīvācaspatimiśraḥ, Veṅkateśvara Press, Calcutta. (See below VCsr)

VCa — Vivādacandraḥ. Maithil Nibandha Mala. Patna, as quoted in Dh

VCi — =VC

VCsr — Vikrama's Adventures or the thirty-two tales of the throne. A collection of stories about king Vikrama, as told by the thirty-two statuettes that supported his throne. Edited in four different recensions of the Sanskrit original (Vikramacarita or Siṁhāsana-dvātriṁśakā) : Southern (VCsr). Metrical (VCmr), Brief (VCbr), Jainistic (VCjr). Ed. and transl. by F. Edgerton, part 2. Text, in four parallel recensions, Cambridge, Mass. 1926 HOS. 27.

Vet — Die Vetālapañcaviṁśatikā in den Recensionen des Śivadāsa und eines ungenannten mit kritischem Commentar. Herausg. von H. Uhle. AKM 8.1

Vi. — The Institutes of Viṣṇu, (Viṣṇu Smṛti), together with extracts from the Sanskrit commentary of Nanda Paṇḍita called Vaijayantī. Ed. by J. Jolly. Calcutta 1881. Bibl. ind. 91

Vij.	See Y.
ViR	Viśvarūpa. Commentary on Y. See Y. in TSS 74, 81
Vīr.	See Y.
Vīr. Saṁs.	Vīramitrodaya-Saṁskāraprakāśa. ChSS 103, 108, 114, 122, 128, 137
Viv.	Vivādacintāmaṇi by Vācaspati Miśra, ed. by Rāmacandra Vidyāvāgīśa. Calcutta 1837. *Also* in Veṅkateśvara Press, Bombay.
Vivā	Vivādārṇavasetuḥ, by Vāreśvara. Veṅkateśvar Press, Bombay, as quoted in Dh. See VV
Vivād.	=VR
VivS	=Vivā
VivT	=VT
VJT	Vivādabhaṅgarṇava compiled by Jagannātha Tarkapañcānāna of Triveṇī. A Digest of Hindu Law and Successions with a commentary by Jagannātha Tarkapañcānana. Transl. by H. T. Colebrooke. Calcutta-London 1804. See VBh
VK	=VyK. In JSAIL 23=VKK
VKK	*Varṣa Kriyā Kaumudī by Govindānanda Kavikaṅkanācāryya.* Ed. by Pt. K. K. Smṛtibhūṣaṇa. Bibl. Ind. 149.
VM	=VyM. In JSAIL 22. *Vīramitrodaya* by M. M. Paṇḍit Mitramiśra, ed. by Parvatīya Nityānanda Śarmā Pant and Paṇḍit Viṣṇu Prasāda Śarmā Bhāṇḍārī, Benares 1906-32. ChSS. 30.
VN	Vararuci's *Nītiratna* in KSG 1. 305
VR	*Vivāda-ratnākara, a Treatise on Hindu Law by Caṇḍeśvara Ṭhakkura.* Reissue. Ed. by MM. Kamalakṛṣṇa Smṛtitīrtha. Bibl. Ind. 103
VRĀ	*Vīramitrodaya by* Pt. Mitra Miśra, Vol. II, Āhnika Prakāśa. ChSS 1913.
VRK	=VR. In JSAIL 23: Śrīmad Vālmīki Rāmāyaṇa, a critical edition with the commentary of Śrī Govindarāja and extracts from many other commentaries and readings. Ed. and publ. by T. R. Kṛṣṇācārya and T.R. Vyāsācārya of Kumbakonam. Bombay 1911-3
VRL	*Vīramitrodya* by Pt. Mitra Miśra, Vol. XX. *Lakṣaṇa Prakāśa.* ChSS 1916.
VRN	=VRV

VRR	Vīramitrodaya by Pt. Mitra Miśra, Vol. VI Rājanīti Prakāśa. ChSS.1916.
VRV	=In JSAIL 22 and 24=VV. In JSAIL 25 and 26 *Vīramitrodaya* by Pt. Mitra Miśra. Vol. VII. *Vyavahāra Prakāśa*. ChSS 1932.
VS	*The Subhāṣitāvali* of Vallabhadeva, ed. by P. Peterson and Paṇḍit Durgāprasāda, Bombay 1886. BSS 31.
VT or VTV	*Vivādatāṇḍavam*, Kamalākaraḥ, Lakshmī Vilāsa Press, Baroda, as quoted in Dh.
VV	*Vivādārṇavasetuḥ*. Veṅkateśvara Press. Bombay, as quoted in Dh. See Vivā. In JSAIL 22 and 23 Vivādavyavahāraḥ, gopalasiddhāntavāgīśaḥ, Bhandarkar C.R. Institute, Poona, as quoted in Dh.
VVCa	Vivādacandrikā by Anantarāma, Wai, as quoted in Dh.
VVy	*Vivādavyavahāraḥ*, Bhandarkar Or. Res. Institute, Poona, as quoted in Dh.
Vy or Vyās.	*Vyāsa Smṛti*
VyB	=BBh
VyC	Vyavahāracintāmaṇi by Vācaspati Miśra. MS in the Baroda Oriental MSs Library, as quoted in Dh.
VyCi	=Viv. Veṅkateśvara Press
VyK	Vyavahārakalpataru, Lakṣmīdharaḥ, Prājñapāṭhaśālāmaṇḍala, Wai, as quoted in Dh.
VyM	The Vyavahāra Mayūkha, a treatise on positive law by Bhaṭṭa Nīlakaṇṭha, part I. Ed. by J. R. Gharpure. Bombay 1914, CHLT 6. *Also* in BSS 80 (ed. by P. V. Kane)
VyMā.	The Vyavahāra Mātṛkā of Jīmūtavāhana. Ed. by Hon. Mr. Justice Asutosh Mookerjee. Memoirs of the Asiatic Society of Bengal 3. (1910-14).
VyMGh.	See VyM. (Gharpure edition)
VyN	Vyavaharānirṇaya of Varadarāja. Ed. by K.V. Rangaswami Aiyangar and A. N. Krishna Aiyangar, Adyar Library, Adyar 1942. *Also* MS in IO. Library, London, as quoted in Dh.
VyP	Vyavahāraprakāśaḥ, Śarabhojī, Saraswati Mahal Library. Tanjore, as quoted in Dh. See VyPr. In JSAIL 22=VM

VyPr	Vyavahāraprakāśaḥ, Mitramiśraḥ in ChSS, as quoted in Dh
VyS	*Vyavahārārthasamuccaya*. Saraswati Mahal Library. Tanjore, as quoted in Dh.
VySau	*Vyavahārasaukhyam*. Bhandarkar Or. Research Institute. Poona, as quoted in Dh
VyT	Vyavahāratattvam in Smṛtitattvasya 2.197. Ed. by Jīvānanda Vidyasāgara. Calcutta 1895.
VyU	Vyavahārodyotaḥ, dinakarbhaṭṭaḥ, Prājñapāṭhaśālāmaṇḍala, Wai, as quoted in Dh.
Westermarck	E. Westermarck, The History of Human Marriage, London 1925.
Wilken	G. A. Wilken, Over de verwantschap en het huwelijks- en erfrecht bij de volken van het maleische ras (Reprinted from De Indische Gids 1883, May) Amsterdam.
Y	Yājñavalkya-Smṛti. Yājñavalkya's Gesetzbuch, Sanskrit und Deutsch. Herausg. von A. F. Stenzler. Berlin-London. *Also* Yājñavalkyasmṛti Yogīśvara Yājñavalkya, with the commentary Mitākṣarā (Mit.) of Vijñāneśvara (Vij.). Ed. by V. L. Śāstri Paṇaśikar. Fourth ed. Bombay, 1936. *Also* Yājñavalkya-Smṛti with Vīramitrodaya (Vīr.). the Commentary of Mitra Miśra and Mitākṣarā the Commentary of Vijñāneśvara (Vij.) Ed. by Pt. Nārāyaṇa Śāstri Sāhityācārya and Pt. Jagannātha Śāstri Hośiṅga Sāhityopādhyāya. Benares, 1930. ChSS. *Also* the Yājñavalkyasmṛti with the commentary Bālakrīḍā of Viśvarūpācārya. Ed. by Mm. T. Gaṇapati Śāstri. Trivandrum 1922. TSS 74, 81. *Also* Aparārkāparābhidhāparādityaviracitaṭīkāsametā; Yājñavalkyasmṛti. Ed. by Pts. of the Ānandāśrama, 2 vols. Poona 1903-4. ĀnSS. 46 (Apar.)
Ya. or Yam.	Yama-Saṁhitā, in "The Dharmaśāstra Text", Vol. I., ed. by M. N. Dutt, Calcutta 1908, or in Vīr.
Yaś	See Vāts.
ZDMG	Zeitschrift der Deutschen Morgenländischen Gesellschaft

List of Juridical Studies in Ancient Indian Law and other connected Studies

JURIDICAL STUDIES IN ANCIENT INDIAN LAW

1. Reciprocal responsibility for Debts Contracted by Married People. In "Annals of the Bhaṇḍarkar Oriental Research Institute". Vol. XXIV. Part III. pp. 165-174.

   Reprinted as study XII.

2. Legal relations between Employers and Employees in Ancient India. In "The Poona Orientalist". Vol. VIII. Parts I-II. pp. 100-109; Vol. VIII. Parts III-IV. pp. 1-24.

   Reprinted as study XIV.

3. The Rākṣasa-vivāha and the Paiśāca-vivāha. In "New Indian Antiquary", Vol. VI. Nos. 8-9. pp. 182-185.

   Incorporated in JSAIL 21.

4. The Āsura-vivāha and the Ārṣa-vivāha. In "The Poona Orientalist". Vol. IX. Nos. 1-2. pp. 43-57. Submitted to the 6th session of the Indian History Congress, Aligarh 1943 and published in the "Proceedings of the Indian History Congress, 6th session, Aligarh". pp. 52-61.

   Incorporated in JSAIL 21.

5. Legal protection of Plants in Ancient India. In "Annals of the Bhaṇḍarkar Oriental Research Institute." Vol. XXV. Part IV. pp. 231-238.

   Reprinted as study X.

6. Legal Responsibility of Physicians in Ancient India for their Carelessness in Medical Treatment. In "New Indian Antiquary". Vol. VII. Nos. 5-6. pp. 101-105. Submitted to the 7th Session of the Indian History Congress, Madras 1944 and published in the "Proceedings of the Indinn History Congress, 7th session, Madras". pp. 112-119.

Incorporated in JSAIL 14.

7. Pledge. In "Bhāratīya Vidyā". Vol. VI Nos. 7-8. pp. 157-164; Vol. VI. No. 9. pp. 179-194.
Reprinted as study IV.
8. Infanticide and Exposure of New-born Children. In "The Poona Orientalist". Vol. XIII. Nos. 1 and 2. pp. 79-87.
Reprinted as study XV.
9. Juridical Aspects on the Gandharva Form of Marriage. In "The Poona Orientalist". Vol. X. Nos. 3-4. pp. 69-78. Submitted to the 12th Session of the All India Oriental Conference, Benares 1943-44.
Partly incorporated in JSAIL 21.
10. Different Types of Deposits. In "Annals of the Bhaṇḍarkar Oriental Research Institute". Vol. XXVI. Parts III-IV. pp. 263-282. Submitted to the 8th Session of the Indian History Congress, Annamalainagar 1945.
Reprinted as Study I.
11. Law of Deposits. In "Supplement to Bhāratīya Vidyā". Vol. VII. Nos. 3-4. pp. 1-22.
Reprinted as Study II.
12. Suretyship. In "Supplement to Bhāratīya Vidyā". Vol. VII Nos. 3-4. pp. 23-50.
Reprinted as Study V.
13. Legal Rules in the Pañcatantra; A. Obligation of the Father to Marry His Daughter at Proper Time. In "Supplement to Bhāratīya Vidyā". Vol. VII. Nos. 3-4. pp. 51-70.
Incorporated in JSAIL 20.
14. Legal Position of Physicians in Ancient India. In "Annals of the Bhaṇḍarkar Oriental Research Institute". Vol. XXIX. Parts I-IV. pp. 21-42; Vol. XXX. Parts I-II. pp. 1-22.
Reprinted as Study VIII.
15. Legal, Fiscal. Social and Penal Privileges Accorded to Infants, Aged, Diseased, Helpless and Distressed Persons According to Ancient Indian Law. In "The Dr. L. Sarup Memorial Volume". Published by the Vishveshvaranand Vedic Research Institute, pp. 326-41. Submitted to the 159th meeting of the American Oriental Society 1949, New Haven.

Reprinted as Study IX.

16. Legal Rules in the Pañcatantra (Book III, kathā 4). In "Prof. T. Kowalski's Commemoration Volume". Rocznik Orientalistyczny. Vol. XVII pp. 220-239.
Incorporated in JSAIL 20.

17. Legal Position of Prostitutes According to Kauṭilya's Arthaśāstra. In "Journal of the American Oriental Society". Vol. 69. pp. 25-60. Submitted to the All-India Oriental Conference in Bombay, 1949.
Reprinted as Study VI.

18. Legal Position of Women whose Husbands Live on their Earnings. In "Siddha-Bhāratī, being the Dr. Siddeshwar Varma Presentation Volume". Part 2. pp. 295-305.
Reprinted as Study VII.

19. Contract of Deposit in some Non-juridical Sources in Classical Sanskrit. In "Journal of the American Oriental Society". Vol 72. pp. 145-154; Vol. 73. pp. 16-26. Submitted to the 162nd meeting of the American Oriental Society, Cambridge and Waltham, Mass., 1952.
Reprinted as Study III.

20. The Pañcatantra and the Smṛtis. In "Bhāratīya Vidyā". Vol. XI. Nos. 3-4. pp. 222-309.
Reprinted as Study XIX.

21. Forms of Marriage in Ancient India and their Development. In "Bhāratīya Vidyā". Vol. XII. pp. 62-138.
Reprinted as Study XI.

22. The Tale of the Young Wife and the Old Husband. In "Professor P. K. Gode Commemoration Volume"; POS 93. pp. 396-425. Submitted to the 163rd meeting of the American Oriental Society. Washington 1953.
Reprinted as Study XXI.

23. The Tale of the Gullible Husband and his Cunning Wife. In "Annals of the Bhaṇḍarkar Oriental Research Institute". Vol. XXXIV. pp. 128-165.
Reprinted as Study XX.

24. Cāṇakya's Aphorisms in the Hitopadeśa, No. 28 of the American Oriental Society Offprint Series. *Also* in JAOS 76.2, pp. 115-130; 77.1. pp. 26-31; Vol. 77. No. 2 & 3, pp. 107-115.

Reprinted as Study XXIV

25. The Mānava-Dharmaśāstra Stanzas in the Hitopadeśa. In St. Schayer Commemoration Volume. "Ŗocznik Orientalisteyzny." Vol. XX.

Reprinted as Study XXII

26. Some Dharmaśāstra Verses in the Hitopadeśa. In Dr. S. K. Belvalkar Felicitation Volume. Moti Lal Banarsi Dass, Banaras, 1957. pp. 127-148.

Reprinted as Study XXIII

27. Mānava-dharmaśāstra Verses in Cāṇakya's Compendia. In "Journal of the American Oriental Society. Vol. 79. No. 4. pp. 233-254.

Reprinted as Study XXVI

28. Two Readings of Mānava-dharmaśāstra IV 85. In "Bhāratīya Vidyā" XVIII, Nos. 3-4; pp. 64-8)

Reprinted as Study XVII

29. Cāṇakya's Aphorisms in the Pañcatantra. In the Commemoration Volume Prof. Dr. Ernst Diez", Istanbul.

Reprinted as Study XXV

OTHER JURIDICAL STUDIES

Indian Tales Interpreted from the Point of View of the Smṛtis : Pañcatantra 1.13. In "Journal of the American Oriental Society". Vol. 68. No. 2. pp. 84-91. Submitted to the 158th meeting of the American Oriental Society, 1948. New York.

Incorporated in JSAIL 20.

The Harmonizing of Law with the Requirements of Economic Conditions according to the Ancient Indian Dharmaśāstras, Arthaśāstras and Gṛhyasūtras. In "Silver Jubilee Number of the Annals of the Bhaṇḍarkar Oriental Research Institute". Vol. XXIII. pp. 528-548 Submitted to the 11th All-India Oriental Conference; Hyderabad 1941. As synopsis of lecture delivered in Mysore published by the University of Mysore.

Reprinted in Study XVI

A Sociological Study of the Forms of Marriage in Ancient India. In "Annals of the Bhaṇḍarkar Oriental Research Institute". Vol. XXII. pp. 202-219. As Synopsis of lecture delivered in Mysore published by the University of Mysore.

Partly incorporated in JSAIL 21.

Subjects of Law and Law of Family according to the Yājñavalkya-Dharmaśāstra. In "The Poona Orientalist". Vol. VII. Nos. 3-4. pp. 159-180.

Reprinted in Study XIII.

Le droit de succession dans l'Inde ancienne d'après l'Āpastambīya-Dharmaśāstra, le Baudhāyana-Dharmaśāstra, le Bṛhaspati Smṛti, le Gautamīya-Dharmaśāstra, le Kauṭilya-Arthaśāstra, le livre XIII du Mahābhārata, le Mitākṣarā, le Mānava-Dharmaśāstra, le Nārada-Smṛti, le Vāsiṣṭha-Dharmaśāstra, le Vaiṣṇava-Dharmaśāstra et le Yājñavalkya-Dharmaśāstra. In "Bulletin international de l'Academie des Sciences et des Lettres". Cracow 1938. pp. 35-46.

Prawo spadkowe w dawnych Indiach (Law of Inheritance in Ancient India). In "Polska Akademia Umiejetności. Sprawozdania z czynności i posiedzen". Cracow 1938. Vol. XI. III. Nr. 1. pp. 7-16.

Principles of Law in Ancient India. (An Extract from the Extension Lectures delivered at the Andhra University by Prof. Dr. Ludwik Sternbach on 25th November 1944). In "Andhra University College Magazine". Vol. VII. Nos. 13-14. pp. 10-12.

Similar Social and Legal Institutions in Ancient India and Ancient Mexico. In "The Poona Orientalist". Vol. VII No. 1. pp. 43-46.

India, Subcontinent of; Law (10). In "Encyclopedia Americana". Vol. XV. pp. 28d-28g.

Reprinted in Study XVIII

Chapter X entitled "Law" in "India, Pakistan, Ceylon". Edited by W. Norman Brown, Cornell University Press, Ithaca, New York 1951. pp. 116-127.

Incorporated in the previous Study.

I.

DIFFERENT TYPES OF DEPOSITS*

1. INTRODUCTION

1. *Contract of Deposit*

Deposit is a contract whereby one person delivers a movable thing to another for gratuitous safe custody. *Depositum* as well as *commodatum*, *mandatum* etc. are species of *fiducia*.

2. *Depositum Fiducia*

The *Smṛtis* very often used the word "*depositum*", whilst meaning *fiducia*. We find several sorts of deposits in the *Smṛtis*. Some of them were in reality specific varieties of deposits in the *Smṛtis* (*e. g.* sealed deposits, open deposits, etc.), but by far the greater number were not deposits from the point of view of the theory of law, but some specific contracts in which *fiducia* played a prominent role. However, since the *Smṛtis* and their commentators classed these specific agreements among contracts of deposit from the point of view of the theory of ancient Indian law, we must consider them as contracts of deposits, although from the general point of view of law these contracts have nothing to do with the contracts of deposits, or are only slightly connected with them.

3. *Synonyms*

In Sanskrit nomenclature we find three most important synonyms for the word deposit *i.e. nikṣepa*, *upanidhi* and *nyāsa*. From the legal point of view the difference between these three synonyms is very slight. Other words are also known for the designation of the deposit.

*Previously appeared as JSAIL. 10 in the "Annals of the Bhandarkaar Oriental Research Institute". Vol.XXVI, Parts III-IV, pp. 263-82. Submitted to the 8th Session of the Indian Congress, Allahabad 1945. See also Studies II and III below.

Hemacandra in Abhidhānacintāmaṇi[1] quoted these three synonyms[2]; Halāyudha in Abhidhānaratnamālā[3] quoted *nikṣepa* and *upanidhi* as synonyms[4]; and Amarakośa[5] mentioned *upanidhi* and *nyāsa* as synonyms.[6]

II

A. OPEN DEPOSITS

4. *Quotations*

The word *nikṣepa* from *ni°* (down, into)+°*kṣip* (to throw, to lay, to cast), the laid down, the delivered, the preserved, the entrusted *i. e.* a deposit, was used in Mn., N., Bṛh., Vi., Vīr., VyM. as the principal word for the designation of a deposit. *Nikṣepa* was quoted in Hem. as a synonym of *upanidhi* and *nyāsa* and in Hal. as a synonym of *upanidhi*[7].

Mn. (VIII-4) enumerating eighteen titles of law mentioned *nikṣepa* and quoting the classification of offences (XI-57) also used this word. In addition Mn. quoted *nikṣepa* in the chapter relating to deposits (VIII-179-181, 185, 186, 188, 190-192, 194, 196, 149). Mn. also used the word *upanidhi* (VIII-185, 186, 149) and considered it as another kind of deposit (VIII-196). However for a "sealed" deposit Mn. used the word *samudra* (8. 188).

Although N. (16) in enumerating the titles of law used the word *upanidhi*, and Asahāya commenting on these rules did not mention the word *nikṣepa* at all, N. in other places used the word *nikṣepa* almost exclusively (N.2.1.5 7-10, 13). N. defining the deposit also used the word *nikṣepa*; when dealing with the problem of the sale of things not from the owner he also quoted the word *nikṣepa* (N. VII-1), although repeating in I-81 the text of Mn. (VIII-149) used both the words *nikṣepa* and *upanidhi*. N. (II-14) also contained a general rule according to which the rules relating to *nikṣepa* had to be applied to *yācita*, *anvāhita*, *śilpa*, *upanidhi* and *pratinyāsa*. In

1. 870.
2. *nikṣepo'panidhi.*
3. 1.82.
4. *nikṣepaḥ syād upanidhi*
5. 2.9-81
6. *pumān upanidhir nyāsaḥ*
7. See par. 3.

the text of N., which is not published in the edition of "Bibliotheca Indica" by J. Jolly, but which is quoted by Mit. (*ad* Y. II-65), in VyM. (p. 190-10-11) etc.[8] N. distinguished between *nikṣepa* and *upanidhi* and gave excellent definitions for both these kinds of deposits.

Chapter tenth of Bṛh., which dealt with deposits, was entitled *nikṣepa*. All the other kinds of deposits were classed in Bṛh. under *nikṣepa* (10. 5, 18). However, Bṛh. seldom employed the word *nikṣepa* for the designation of the deposit (11.1) Bṛh. differentiated between *nikṣepa* and *aupanidhika* (10.6), or *nyāsa* (10.22) as well as *nyāsa* and *anvāhita* (XII-2) and expressed the opinion that all the rules contained in Chapter ten also related to *anvāhita*, *yācita*, *śilpinyāsa*, etc. (10.38-40).

Vi. quoted only the word *nikṣepa* for the designation of the deposit (V-169-171, XXXVI-3, LII-4).

Vīr. on the other hand used the words *nikṣepa* and *upanidhi* indiscriminately; Mitramiśra began the para regarding deposits (p. 493) with the word *nikṣepaṁ vivādapadamadhikṛtyāha* and concluded (p. 496) with the words *iti upanidhi-prakaraṇam*. Commenting on N. (VII-1) Mitramiśra said that the term *nikṣepa* included by implication *yācita* and other species of deposits. This statement is probably based on N. (II-14).

VyM. (p. 190/6) titled the chapter on deposits—*nikṣepa* but used as synonym of the term deposit the word *nyāsa* and understood by it all kinds of deposits.

Other sources of law considered *upanidhi* as the principal word to designate the deposit but also accepted the term *nikṣepa* meaning deposits.

Y. used the word *upanidhi* and *nikṣepa* (Y-II-25) separately; in N.-III-230, which was similar to Mn. (XI-57), the word *nikṣepa* was used; Y. did not consider the word *upanidhi* as identical with *nikṣepa* and stated (II-67) that the same rules applied to *nikṣepa* as to *upanidhi*.

Kāty. considered the word *upanidhi* as the principal word for the designation of the deposit. We read there, that *krayaproṣita-nikṣipta-bandhā'nvāhita-yācitam* were (592) identical with the

8. Vīr. *Parāśaramādhavāya*

upanidhi.[9] Kāty. indiscriminately employed the words *yācita* (595), *nyāsa* (596-7), *upanidhi* (601) *nikṣepa* (592, 593, 598, 599) in the text and concluded by saying that all the rules enumerated in this chapter referred to all sorts of *upanidhi* (602).

K. (177) also mentioned the word *upanidhi* as the principal word for the designation of deposits but extended the respective rules to *nikṣepa* (180.6).

Vās., where we find very little mention of deposits and where the rules contained in Mn. (VIII-149) and N. (I-81) were repeated, mentioned the word *upanikṣepa* for the designation of the deposit.

We also find the word *nikṣepa* in the sense of a deposit in Pañc.[10] Kath.[11] Śāk[12] and others.

5. *Definition.*

The Smṛtis did not give us a juridical definition of the *nikṣepa*. Only the unpublished text of N. quoted by Mit. (*ad* Y. 2. 65) etc. stated :

> *asaṁkhyātam avijñātaṁ samudraṁ yan nidhīyate,*
> *taj jānīyād upanidhiṁ nikṣepaṁ gaṇitaṁ viduḥ*[13].

Hence *upanidhi* was a sealed deposit, the contents of which were not counted and known, and the *nikṣepa* was an unsealed deposit, the contents of which were counted.

This definition seems to be correct. Probably, developing it, Mit. (*ad* Y. 2.67, p. 163.25) remarked : *samakṣaṁ tu samarpaṇaṁ nikṣepaḥ*. It is therefore evident that according to Mit. if delivery of the deposit was performed in the presence of the owner this kind of deposit was called *nikṣepa*; *eo ipso* in this case the deposit would be counted.

9. Prath. I, 16 etc.

10. *kraya-proṣita-nikṣipta-bandhā'nvāhita-yācitam,*
vaiśyavṛttyarpitaṁ caiva sorthas tū'panidhiḥ smṛtaḥ (Kāty. 592)

11. Tar. 7, v. 79.

12. 97-1.

13. Also quoted in Mit. *ad* Y.2.65, p. 162. 25-6, Apar. *ad* Y. 265, MMu. 8.149. SC. 14, SV. 265, VyPr. 280, VyU. 79. VyM. 84, VT. 554-5, VV 89, VyS. 87, VCi. 138, Rāgh. in MnM. *ad* Mn. 8.145.

Vīr. (p. 494/26-27), on the basis of the opinion of N. mentioned before, accepted a specific form of *nikṣepa*. This commentary was of the opinion that an article described in the presence of an artisan (*śilpine*) and handed over to him for preparation into an ornament was a *nikṣepa*. We shall see below that this was not a *nikṣepa* but a *śilpinyāsa*[14]; however, we must observe here the same *essentialia* which were found in N. and Mit. *i. e.* the handing over of the object deposited or entrusted with somebody in the presence of the owner and counted. This was also an open deposit and not a sealed one.

How obscure the definition of the *nikṣepa* is, can be seen from the fact that the two foremost experts and translators of K. understood *nikṣepa* in two entirely different ways. R. Shamashastry translated *nikṣepa* as a sealed deposit (180-6 sqq). while J. J. Meyer as an open, unsealed deposit (284-26). We do not find in K. any definition of *nikṣepa* and it is not clear from the context whether *upanidhi* or *nikṣepa* was a sealed or unsealed deposit. There is no reason for K. to be different from N., Y. and their commentators. Therefore, it would appear that J. J. Meyer's opinion that *nikṣepa* should be translated as an unsealed, open deposit is correct.

It must be assumed that the *nikṣepa* was an unsealed deposit handed over to the depositary in the presence of the owner.

It has to be pointed out that N. (2. 1) stated :

svaṁ dravyaṁ yatra viśrambhān nikṣipty aviśaṅkitaḥ,
nikṣepo nāma tat proktaṁ vyavahāra-padaṁ budhaiḥ.

(Also quoted in NMS. 3.1, Mit *ad* Y. 2.25, Apar. *ad* Y. 2.25, VyK. 130, SC.2, VRK. 83, DK. 38, VCi.36, SMC. 14, Vīr. *ad* Y. 2.67, VyPr. 279, VyM. 84, VT. 554, VV, 129, VyS. 87, VVy. 31, AP. 253.14).

'Where one entrusts his property to another in confidence and without suspicion, that is termed *nikṣepa*, a title of law''.

In N. (II-1) a very clear and exact definition of *nikṣepa* was given; however, in reality, it was the

14. See para. 17.

proper definition of the deposit in the most general sense of this word and not a species of deposit called *nikṣepa*. The best proof of that might be the fact that in the last *śloka* according to VyM. (p. 190/8-11) this general m faniengo *nikṣepa* was divided into a specified *nikṣepa* and *upanidhi*.

6. *Upanikṣepa*

Y. (II-25) enumerates in addition to *nikṣepa* the *upanikṣepa* from *upa°* (at, by, beside, near, with) *ni°* (down, into) *°kṣip* (to throw, to lay, to cast), the laid down by, the entrusted with.

Y. mentioned the *upanikṣepa* in the *śloka* identical with Mn. (VIII-149), N. (I-81), Vās. (XVI-18) and K. (191/2). All these *Smṛtis* enumerate in the respective *śloka* *nikṣepa* and *upanidhi* (*nikṣeponidhi*). Y. however uses the word *nikṣepa* instead of the word *upanikṣepa*. We read there :

> *ādhi-sīmo'panikṣepa-jaḍa-bāla-dhanair vinā,*
> *tatho'panidhi-rāja-strī-śrotriyāṇām dhanair api.*

(Also quoted in ViR. *ad* Y. 2.25, VyT. 224, SV 123, VyPr. 165, VT. 150, VV. 89, VyP. 44, VyS 47, VVCa 138, Ap. 253-4).

If we comment on this sentence, which related to the loss *inter alia* of the deposit, by adverse possession, together with identical quotations from other sources quoted above, we come to the conclusion that no difference existed between the *nikṣepa* and the *upanikṣepa* and that both meant "open deposit". This is also the opinion expressed in Mit. where we read: *upanikṣepo nāma rūpasaṁkhyāpradarśanena rakṣanārthaṁ parasya haste nihitaṁ dravyam.* (Mit. *ad.* Y. 2.25, p. 137.25-6). Consequently *upanikṣepa* was a chattel placed for self-custody in another's hand after exhibiting its quality and quantity. The same definition of *upanikṣepa* can also be found in Vīr. where we read : *upanikṣepaḥ parasya samīpe saṅkhyādinā paricchinnaṁ samarpitaṁ vastu.* (Vīr. *ad* Y. 2.25, 436. 5-6)

However, the *upanikṣepa* was defined in quite a different way in Śūlapāṇi's *Dīpakalikā* (*ad* Y. II-25). Śūlapāṇi stated that the *upanikṣepa* was a deposit placed in a vessel without mentioning details of what was deposited and sealed. Śūlapāṇi, basing himself on N., gave for the word *upanikṣepa* the definition of *upanidhi*. Possibly the preposition *upa* was misleading for Śūlapāni and, therefore, he considered erroneously *nikṣepa* as a sealed deposit. This could also be surmised from the fact that Śūlapāni referred to N. where we do not find the word *upanikṣepa* but only the words *nikṣepa* and *upanidhi*.

B. SEALED DEPOSITS.

7. *Quotations*

Upanikṣepa from *upa*° (at, by, beside, near, with)+°*ni*° (down, into)+°*dha* (to put, to lay, to bring) what was put into with somebody, a deposit, or *aupanidhika* (forming a deposit) was considered in some *Smṛtis* as the principal word for the designation of deposits.

It was said above that Hem. quoted *upanidhi*, *nikṣepa* and *nyāsa* as synonyms; Hal; *upanidhi* and *nikṣepa*; and Amar. *upanidhi* and *nyāsa*. Y., Kāty. and K. considered *upanidhi* (*aupanidhika*) as the principal word for the designation of deposits.

Y. (II-67), as was mentioned above, classed all the rules relating to deposits under the word *upanidhi*. Y. (2. 25) also used the word *upanikṣepa* and *upanidhi*.

Kāty. (592) considered several kinds of deposits as equivalent to *upanidhi*[15] and used the word *upanidhi* indiscriminately with other synonyms for this word.

In K. the heading of the respective chapter was *aupanidhika* (p. 177/12); then K. employed the word *upanidhi* (p. 177/13 sqq.) but later mentioned that the rules relating to *upanidhi* should also be applied in case of *nikṣepa* (p. 180/6). K. also used the word *upanidhi* next to *nikṣepa* (p. 191/2) in the chapter relating to prescription.

Mn. (VIII-196) differentiated between *upanidhi* and *nikṣepa* and in other places mentioned *upanidhi* as well as *nikṣepa* when stipulating that both these deposits should not be handed over to the next-of-kin (VIII-185) and when regulating the problem of prescription (VIII-149). When mentioning this last problem N. (1-81), Vās. (XVI-18), K. (191/2) and Y (II-25) also mentioned *upanidhi* next to *nikṣepa*.

15. See para. 4.

In addition *upanidhi* was mentioned in MBH. (1.126.3)[16]

8. *Definition*

We find the definition of *upanidhi* or *aupanidhika* in N. (2. 5) Bṛh. (XI-2), Y. (II-65). It must also be noted that N. (16) enumerating the eighteen titles of law mentioned *upanidhi* as one of them, although (in the second chapter) considered *nikṣepa* as the principal word for the designation of deposits. N. (quoted in Mit. *ad* Y. II-65, VyM. and others) differentiated also between *upanidhi* and *nikṣepa*.[17]

Mit. (*ad* Y. II-25 p. 136/27), Vīr, (*ad* Y. II-24/25 p. 439 and *ad* II. 65-67 p. 493-19), Śūlapāṇi (*ad* Y. II-25 and 67), Viv. (p. 26 basing the definition on Kāty., and Śukr. *aupanidhika* II-327) defined *upanidhi* and considered this word as the principal one for the designation of a deposit).[18]

The definition of the *upanidhi* or *aupanidhika* found in different *Smṛtis* is not uniform although it is admitted in the *Smṛtis* that the *upanidhi* is a sealed deposit.[19]

Vīr. stated briefly that *upanidhi* was a special kind of deposit: *tad aupanidhikaṁ nāma nikṣepa-viśeṣaḥ* (Vīr. p. 493. 19).

Exhaustive definitions of *upanidhi* can be found in N. (II-5), Y. (II-65), Bṛh. (X. 6) and N. (quoted in Mit. *ad* Y. II-25, etc.). In addition *upanidhi* was also defined in Vīr (*ad*. Y. II-24/25), Medh. (*ad* Mn. VIII-148), etc.

The *Smṛtis* state:

anyaḍravya-vyavahitaṁ dravyam avyāhṛtaṁ ca yat
nikṣipyate paragṛhe tad aupanidhikaṁ smṛtam

(N. 2.5. Also quoted in NMS. 3.2, Apar. *ad* Y. 2. 65, SC. 3, VyPr. 280, VyS 87).

vāsanastham anākhyāya hasteanyasya yad arpyate,
dravyaṁ tad aupanidhikaṁ pratideyaṁ tathaiva tat

(Y. 2.65. Also quoted in ViR. *ad* Y. 2.67, VyK. 130, GMH. 12.39, SC. 3, VRK. 83, VCi 36 SCM. 14, NṛP. 23, SV. 265, VyPr. 280, VyU. 79, VT. 557, VV, 130, VyS. 87, VVy. 31, AP. 254.25)

16. For details see para. 4
17. See par. 4.
18. Śukr. defined also deposits in a similar way.
19. It was mentioned before that K. did not give any definition of *upanidhi* and Shamashastry translated *upanidhi* as an open deposit and *nikṣepa* as a sealed deposit; differently J.J. Meyer; his translation seems to be better. See para 5.

anākhyātaṁ vyavahitam asaṁkhyātam adarśitam.
mudrā'ṅkitaṁ ca yad dattaṁ tad aupanidhikaṁ smṛtam.

(Bṛh. quoted in Apar. *ad* Y. 2.65, VyK. 130, SC. 2, 178, VRK 83, NṛP. 23, VyPr. 280, VyS. 87).

asaṁkhyātam avijñātaṁ samudraṁ yan nidhīyate,
taj jānīyād upanidhiṁ nikṣepaṁ gaṇitaṁ viduḥ.

(N. in Mit. *ad* Y. 2. 65. Also quoted in Apar. *ad.* Y. 2.65, SC. 2, MMu. 8. 149, DK. 331, SC. 14, SV. 265, VyPr. 280, VyM. 84, VT. 554-5, VV, 89, VyS. 87, VVCa. 138, Rāgh. in MnM. *ad* 8. 145).

upanidher-bhāṇḍa-sthānām aparicchinnānāṁ.

(Vīr *ad* Y. 2.24-5, p. 436. 7-8).

Hence a chattel, property (*dravya*) which being placed in a box (*vāsana* : Y. II-65) or a pot (*bhāṇḍa,* Vīr.) or hidden in another thing (N. II-5) or, as mentioned most clearly in other *Smṛtis,* under a seal (*samudra* N. in Mit. *ad* Y. 2.65), or *mudrāṅkitā* in Bṛh. XI-2) or covered with cloth and sealed (Medh. *ad* Mn. VIII-148) without being described (*anākyāya* in Y. II-65, *asaṁkhyātamadārśatam* in Bṛh. XI-2) or without being counted or known (*asakhyātamavijñatam* in N. in Mit. *ad* Y. II-65) or measured (*aparicchinnānāṁ* in Vīr) was deposited in other people's houses (*paragṛhe,* in N. II-5) or in the hands of another --was called *upanidhi.* In other words, when a chattel was given under seal to another person for deposit and if the depositary did not know what was deposited with him, this kind of deposit was known as *upanidhi.*

Some of the commentators explained what was to be understood under a sealed of hidden article in another thing. These were objects which were unknown to the depositary, *i.e.* the dipositary did not know whether it was gold, or silver, or pearls, or necklaces, etc. since the objects were tied up and secured by a private knot in order to prevent another person from taking it, or secured by the impression of a seal on which special letters were engraved (Col. p. 403/4 based on Asahāya *ad* N.).

That was one kind of definition of the *upanidhi.* However, Medh. (*ad* Mn. VIII-148), who in the beginning defined the *upanidhi* in a similar way to the definitions above, stated that it is better to take an *upanidhi* as standing for what was given for use through friendliness and favour. Most probably in this instance he based his opinion on Mn. (VIII-196). The opinion expressed in *Dīpakalikā* (*ad* Y. II-25) was similar. Śūlapāṇī stated that *upanidhi* was a deposit made over for use out of affection. This point of view completely changed the meaning of the sealed deposit, of which one of the *essentialia* was the fact that the depositary did not know what he took into deposit, and moreover, could not use it. The use of a deposited object also completely changed the character of this agreement. Therefore, Śūlapāṇi's definition was wrong. Even Śūlapāṇi, in another place, admitted that he was wrong (*ad* Y. II-25) as (*ad* Y. II-67) he expressed the opinion that the use of the deposit without the consent of the depositor was not allowed and hewho did it should be fined. It must also be borne in mind that only *Dīpakalikā* and Medh. were of the latter opinion though all the other *Smṛtis* defined *upanidhi* as sealed deposits.

C. SECRET DEPOSITS

9. *Quotations*

Nyāsa from the legal point of view was the least important synonym for the designation of deposits.

Hem. enumerated *nyāsa* as one of the three synonyms along with *nikṣepa* and *upanidhi* and Amar. as one of the two *i.e.* along with *upanidhi*.[20]

Asahāya (*ad* N. 16) also divided the deposits *inter alia* into *nyāsa*.

Kāty. (592) enumerating various kinds of deposits (*upanidhi*) did not mention *nyāsa* as one of them. This *Smṛti*, however, used this word along with *upanidhi*, *nikṣepa* and *yācita* (593, 603). Bṛh. indiscriminately employed *nyāsa* and *nikṣepa* (10.12, 40) and considered it from the point of view of law as a special kind of deposit; he gave a special definition to *nyāsa*, (Bṛh. 10.22). In addition, Bṛh. in the chapter relating to the sale of different articles by an unauthorised person, not the owner, (*asvāmin*) mentioned *nyāsa*, *nikṣepa* and *anvāhita* separately stating, in this way, that these three deposits were different from each other (Bṛh. 11.3).

Y. and N. also considered *nyāsa* as a different sort of deposit as it was stated in these *Smṛtis* that the rules relating

20. See para. 3, Hem. (870), Amar (II. 9, 81).

to *upanidhi* or *nikṣepa* applied also *inter alia* to *nyāsa* (Y. II-67, N. II-14).

It must also be added that in N., where the word *nikṣepa* was considered as the principal word for the designation of a deposit, in the chapter relating to proofs by ordeal to take place in the case of the denial of a deposit, the word *nyāsa* was used (N. I-241).

B. (II-1, 2, 3) dealing with the stealing of a deposit as an offence causing loss of caste, also used the word *nyāsa* for the designation of deposits.

Śukr. (IV-5, 310) used the word *nyāsa* in addition to *yācita* and *anvāhita*.

Generally speaking the word *nyāsa* was considered in literature, and *eo ipso* colloquially, as the principal word for the designation of deposits, although in juridical nomenclature it was a specific and rather infrequent sort of deposit.[21] And so we see in Mṛcch. that Vasantasenā entrusting the jewels to Cārudatta used the word *nyāsa* (*ṇāsa*). Similarly this word was also used by Vidūṣaka and Cārudatta.[22] In Rāj. we also find the word *nyāsa* in the chapter relating to a certain man of means who deposited a lakh of money in the house of a merchant.[23] Rāj. also preferred the word *nikṣepa* for the designation of a deposit.[24] In Śāk. (act IV-97) the word *nyāsa* was also used for the designation of deposits,[25] similarly as in Ragh[26] and Kath.[27] (when referring to the deposit of the whole

21. See para. 10.

22. *Vasantasenā : ajja aliaṁ; purisesu ṇāsā ṇikkhivianti ṇa uṇa gehesu* (Act. I, p. 69. 628-9. Cārudatta : *dhiṅ mūrkha nyāsāḥ khal vayam* (Act. I, p. 69, 633). Vidūṣaka : *ṇāso kakhu so*. Cārudatta : *kathaṁ nyāsaḥ*. Vidūṣaka : *samassadu bhavaṁ ; jai ṇāsso coreṇa avahado tumaṁ kiṁ mohaṁ upagado*. (Act III, p. 155. 282-5. Cārudatta :

yaṁ samālambya viśvāsaṁ nyāsosmāsu tayā kṛtaḥ,
tasyaitan mahato mūlyaṁ pratyaysyaiva dīyate. (Act. III, p. 161).

23. *sauhṛdā-guḍa-sadbhāve vyāpad aupayikaṁ dhanī,*
nyāsīcakāra dīnnāralakṣaṁ ko'pi vaṇig gṛhe.
(Act. VIII, 124. See also VIII. 126, 151).

24. See act VIII 147.

25. *artho hi kanyā parakīya eva tām adya samprosya parigrahītuḥ,*
jāto mamā'yaṁ viśadaḥ prakāmaṁ pratyārpita nyāsa ivā'ntarātmā.
Śāk. (Act IV. 97)

26. *sa visṛṣṭas tathety uktvā bhrātā naivāviśat purīm,*
nandigrāmatas tasya rājyaṁ nyāsam ivābhunak. (Ragh. Act. XII. 18).

27. Tar. 4.

estate with the merchant Kiraṇyadatta or Hiraṇyagupta and tricks used by Upakośā).[28] Even R. used the word *nyāsa* for the designation of the deposit[29], as well as MBh.,[30] Bhāgavata Purāṇa[31] and many others.

It must be noted that Mit. (*ad.* Y. II-67) used in addition to *nyāsa* the word *nyasta*, a special kind of deposit *i.e.* gold, etc. for preparing bracelets, etc.[32] Mit. classed this kind of deposit under "and others". From this commentary it is evident that *nyasta* was nothing more than *śilpinyasa.*[33]

10. *Definition*

From the legal point of view *nyāsa* was a deposit which was entrusted to a member of the house in the absence of the owner and without being shown to him with the mandate to be handed over to the owner of the house. Therefore *nyāsa* could be considered as a secret deposit. Its definition was absolutely identical with that found in Mit. and Vir. (*ad* Y II-67).

Mit. stated : *nyāso nāma gṛha-svāmine'darśayitvā tat parokṣam eva gṛhajana-haste prakṣepo gṛha-svāmine samarpaṇīyam iti.*

Vīr. stated : *nyāso gṛhasvāmine'darśayitvā tat parokṣam eva tadīya-jana-haste prakṣepo gṛha svāmine samarpaṇīyam iti.*

This is the correct definition of *nyāsa.* Bṛh. (XI-3) was also of the opinion that the contract of deposit (*nyāsa*) takes place in the house of another man and added the motive for the commitment of the deposit. Bṛh. states that it took place through fear of the king, robbers or other dangers or for the purpose of deceiving the heirs. We read there:

rāja-caurārāti-bhayād-dāyā-dānāṁ ca vañcanāt
sthāpyate'nya-gṛhe dravyaṁ nyāsa stat parikīrtitam. (Bṛh. 11. 3).

28. *vaṇig ghiraṇyagupto me bhatrā nyāsīkṛtaṁ dhanam,*
jihīrṣati iti vijnaptas tatra rājā tayā svayam. (Kath. Tar. 4. 72).

Kath. used also in addition *nyāsīkrta* the words : *arpidhāna, sthāpita dhāna*, etc.

29. *pāduke cā'sya rājyāya nyāsaṁ datvā punaḥ punaḥ*
nivartyayāmāsa tato bharataṁ bharatā'grajah. (R.1.1, 37).

30. 1.157, 34.

31. In Viṣṇu Purāṇa V. 8, 16, IX, 14, 20.

32. *ādi śabdena suvarṇakārādi-haste kaṭakādi nirmāṇāya nyastasya suvarṇādeḥ.* (Mit *ad* Y. 2,. 67, p. 163. 25-6). See par. 18.

33. See par. 18.

Also quoted in Apar. *ad* Y. 2.65, VyK, 130, SC. 3, VRK 83, DK. 38, NrP. 23, SV. 265, VyPr. 279, VT. 555, VV 129, VyS. 87. Identically *Dīpakalikā* (*ad* Y. II-67). Such a fear was also mentioned in K. (180/19-181/2) where, however the word *nikṣepa* was used.[34]

If we admit that the only *essentiale* of the *nyāsa*-deposit was the lodging of an object in the hands of a person for safe-keeping "in the house of another man" then we understand clearly why Mṛcch., Rāj., Kath., etc. have used the word *nyāsa* and not *nikṣepa* or *upanidhi*. However, it must be admitted (Śāk, and others) that the word *nyāsa* was principally employed, particularly in literary works, for the designation of deposits.

D. MUTUAL DEPOSITS

11. *Quotations.*

The mention of *pratinyāsa* from *brati*° (towards, over, against, in sight of)+*nyāsa* (deposit), a deposit towards another, was to be found in N. (II-14). There it was pointed out that the rules rela ting to deposits also applied *inter alia* to *pratinyāsa*.

Mit. (*ad* Y. II-67 p. 163-26) basing his opinion on this quotation also understood by "and others" the *pratinyāsa* deposit.

12. *Definition.*

The definition of *pratinyāsa* is to be found in Asahāya's commentary (*ad* N. II-14) and in VyM. (*ad* N. II-14 p. 193-3)[35] By this expression an agreement of a re-deposit or a mutual deposit had to be understood. According to this agreement both parties exchanged deposits with one another (*pratinyāsaḥ svāminā yatra nikṣipta tenā' ṣyanyatra nikṣpiptam*[36] with the words "you should keep this thing of mine, and I shall keep this thing of yours".

From the legal point of view two different contracts of deposit took place at the same time.

34. *kṛta lakṣaṇena vā dravyeṇa pratyānayane taṁ bāliśajātīyo vā rātrau rāja-dāyikā-kṣaṇabhītaḥ sāramasya haste nikṣipyā'pagacchet* (K. 180. 19-20). See also J.J. Meyer, Das altindische Buch von Welt-und Staatsleben, p. 786-8).

35. and by Nīlakaṇṭha

36. M. p. 193-3.

It must be noted that other *Smṛtis* did not mention this kind of deposit.

E. LOANS FOR USE.

13. *Quotations.*

Yācita or *yācitaka* deposit, from *yāc°* (to ask for, to request, to sue for) was classed among deposits (*upanidhi*) in Kāty (592) and in Asahāya's commentary on N. (16) when enumerating eighteen titles of law. Y. (II-67, II-14) and Bṛh (10. 39-40)[37] also stated the same; both these *Smṛtis* stated that the general rules relating to deposits had also to be applied to *yācita or yācitakā.*

Y. (II-238) quotes the word *yācita* when discussing the problem of the use by the washerman of the objects given to him and penalties to be imposed for such use (ten *paṇas*).

G. (XII-42) and Kāty. (595) use this word when dealing with the responsibility for negligence or *vis major* in the case of loss or destruction of an object which was *yācita.*

Vīr. and Smṛ. C. commenting on Kāty. (606-17) expressed the opinion that the rules of deposits apply to *yācita.*

Śukr. (IV-5, 310) used the word *yācita* in addition to *nyāsa, anvāhita,* etc.

Matsya Purāna (quoted in Dh. *ad upanidhi*) and Aparārka (p. 664) quoted *yācita* and *nikṣepa.*

14. *Definition.*

In spite of all the quotations mentioned above it was very difficult to admit from the point of view of the system of civil law that *yācita* was a deposit.

VyM. gave the following definition of the *yācita* : *yācitamudvāhādau śobhādy arthaṁ nītam alaṁ Kārādi maṁ kārādi.*

Vīr. stated : *vivāhād yutsav ārthaṁ vastrālaṅkārādikaṁ pratideyatayāṅgīkṛtya yācitvānītaṁ yācitaṁ* (*ad* Y. 2. 67, p. 494. 21-3). Similarly *Dīpakalikā* (ad Y. II-67).

Consequently, according to this contract clothes, ornaments and the like were loaned to a person on the occasion of a marriage or similar festivity for adornment purposes. These objects were given without any consideration of interest, as

37. *yācita.*

Śukr. rightly mentioned twice (II-327, 381)[38]. This opinion was also in conformity with that of Pāṇini (4, 4, 21) who said that *yācita* (*yācitaka*) were articles lent for use free of interest.

From the conclusions noted above it was evident that *yācita* (*yācitaka*) from the point of view of law were loans for use and not deposits although some *essentialia* were the same in both agreements. That was probably the reason why the *Smṛtis* classed the *yācita* amongst the *upanidhi* (Kāty., N.) and applied to these contracts the general rules relating to deposits. That is the reason why, from the point of view of the system of ancient Indian law we have to class *yācita* among deposits.

F. DEPOSITS FOR DELIVERY

15. *Quotations.*

Anvāhita from *anu°* (thereafter, afterwards, further on) +°*ā*°+ (to, upto, at)+ °*dhā* (to lay, to give) *i. e.* what was given afterwards, further on, was according to the *Smṛtis* a specific form of deposit.

Kāty. (592) classed *anvāhita* among *upanidhi* and Asahāya commenting on N. (16), when enumerating the eighteen titles of law in subdivisions of deposits, quoted *anvāhita*.

Y. (II-67), Bṛh. (XI-18) and N. (II-14) were of the opinion that the rules relating to deposits (*upanidhi*, *nikṣepa*) also applied to *anvāhita*.

Bṛh. (11.3), regulating the problem of sale without ownership, mentioned *anvāhita* in addition to *nyāsa* and *nikṣepa*.

Śukr. (IV-5, 310), discussing objects which must not be handed over to others even in time of danger, enumerated *anvāhita* along with *yācita* and *nyāsa*[39].

16. *Definition.*

None of the Smṛtis gave any definition of the *anvāhita*. We find however, some definitions in the commentaries on the *Smṛtis*.

38. *avṛddhikaṁ gṛhītāṇy ālaṁkārādi ca yācitaṁ* (2. 237. 655)
savṛddhikaṁ ṛṇaṁ dattaṁ akusīdaṁ tu yācitaṁ (2.341. 681)

39. Śukr. used also the word *nikṣepa*.

Mit. stated: *yad ekasya haste nihitaṁ dravyaṁ tenyāpy anu paścād anya haste svāmine dehīti nihitaṁ tad anvāhitam.* (*ad*. Y. 2. 67, p. 163. 22-3).

The definition found in Vīr. was almost identical. We read there : *anvāhitaṁ svāminā ekasya haste nihitaṁ dravyaṁ tenā'py anu paścād anyasya haste tasyādhātur vacanā'nnihita.* (*ad* Y. 2. 67, p. 494, 23-4).

The explanation of the *anvāhita* was clearer in the VyM., although this definition was worse from the legal point of view. We read there : *anvāhitam amukena mayi sthāpitaṁ ca svayā tasmai deyam iti puruṣāntara haste'rpitam* (VyM. p. 192. 13-4).

On the basis of these three commentaries it may be assumed that the contract of *anvāhita* took place if owner A committed to the care of B an object and B lodged it afterwards in the hands of C with the clear mandate to return it to owner A.

From the legal point of view not one but several separate contracts were performed in this case. First there was an agreement between A and B, according to which an ordinary contract of deposit took place. However, according to the contract of deposit B was obligated to return the object deposited to A. In the case of the *anvāhita*-deposit B concluded an additional agreement with C, according to which he obligated C to return the object deposited to A *i. e.* to the owner of this object. The commentators did not state whether the agreement between B and C was concluded with, without or against the will of the owner of the deposited object. As no objections were raised in the *Smṛtis* against this kind of deposit, we could admit that this agreement was concluded with or without the will of A, but never against his will.

The agreement between B and C was, above all, a contract of deposit (sub-deposit) joined with the mandate (*mandatum*) to return the deposited object not to B, but to the owner of the deposited object—A.

Therefore, the *anvāhita* was a deposit for delivery.

We find in the Smṛtis in addition to the *anvāhita* also the *anvadhi* from *anu°* (thereafter, afterwards, further on) + °*ādhi* (pledge) *i.e.* a pledge which should be given afterwards, further on. This word is found in Kāty. (611) where it was defined in the following way :

anumārgeṇa kāryeṣu ānyasmin vacanān mama,
dadyās tvam iti yo dattaḥ sa ihā'nvādhir ucyate. Also quoted in VyK. 130, VRK. 84, VV. 129, VyS. 87).

This definition was similar to that quoted above and therefore, the word *anvādhi* was indentified with *anvāhita*, which did not seem to be correct as it is composed also of *ādhi* (and not of *ā-hita*), which means a pledge.[40]

G. DEPOSITS WITH AN ARTISAN.

17. *Quotations.*

Śilpinyāsa from *śilpin°* (artisan)+*°nyāsa* (deposit) or *śilpe upanidhi* from *śilpin°* (artisan)+*°upanidhi* (deposit) or *śilpihastagata* from *śilpin°* (artisan)+*°hasta°* (hand)+ *°gata* (from *gam* being in) was according to the Smṛtis a special kind of deposit.

We find *śilpinyāsa* in Bṛh. (10.39-40)[41], Viv. (p. 25-26), VyM. (p. 193-4, 194-8, etc.) *śilpe upanidhi* in N. (2. 14) and *śilpihastagata* in Asahāya's commentary on N. (16).

Bṛh. (10. 39-40- and N. (2.14) extended the rules regarding deposits to *śilpinyāsa* or *śilpe upanidhi*. Nevertheless, Y. in *śloka* II-67, which was almost identical with the two quotations mentioned above, does not contain any mention of *śilpinyāsa*, or the like.

However, under "others" (*ādi*) this kind of deposit could be included although neither Mit. nor Vir. mentioned by name *śilpinyāsa*, or the like. Vīr. (*ad* Y. II-67 p. 494-26-27) defined deposits with an artisan calling them *nikṣepa* and Mit. (*ad* Y. II-67 p. 163-25-26) *nyasta.*[42]

Also Kāty. (592). did not mention *śilpinyāsa*, or the like, but it is evident from *śloka* 603 sqq. that this kind of deposit was known to Kāty. also. The same applied to K. where *śilpinyāsa* or the like were not mentioned in the respective chapter relating to deposits; however from another place (180-9 sqq.) it was evident that this kind of deposit was known

40. See Miśra and Bhavadeva (quoted in Col. p. 406) on 'pledge transferred.

41. See also XI. 19.

42. See par. 5 and par. 10.

to K. too. K. used in this para, for the designation of an artisan, the word *Kārava* instead of the word *śilpin*.

Asahāya (*ad*. N. 16) enumerating the eighteen titles of law mentioned as one of the kinds of deposits the *śilpihastagata* *i.e*. what has been put into the hands of an artisan.

VyM (193-4) interpreting Kāty. (603) used the word *śilpinyāsa* and then, further on, referring to some special rules connected with this kind of deposits, used also the same word.

Viv., quoting and interpreting Bṛh. (10. 39-40), used also the word *śilpinyāsa*.

18. *Definition.*

We do not find in the Smṛtis any definition of the word *śilpinyāsa*, or the like. We find it, however, in the commentaries on the Smṛtis.

We read in Viv. (p. 25) *śilpinyāse'laṅkaraṇādi-ghanā'rthaṁ śilpiṣu samarpite suvarṇādau......*

We read in VyM. (p. 192. 24-5) *śilpinyāso hemārādiṣu kuṇḍalādy arthaṁ nikṣiptam.*

Vīr., calling this kind of deposit *nikṣepa* state; *śilpine 'lakārādi-ghaṭanāya-dravya-samarpaṇaṁ ca sākṣādākhyāya samarpaṇam nikṣepaḥ*. (*ad* Y. 2.67, p. 494. 26-7) and Mit., calling it *nyāsa*, stated : *ādi śabdena suvarṇa kārādi haste kaṭakādi.nnirmāṇāya nyastasya suvarṇādeḥ*. (Mit. *ad* Y. II-67 p. 163.25-26)[43]

It is evident from these quotations that under *śilpiayāsa*, or other similar expressions, an object given to an artisn in order to perform a particular piece of work must be understood. This was *e.g*. giving of gold to a goldsmith in order to make from it earrings, necklaces etc.

From the point of view of the theory of law this conract was not *depositum* but *fiducia* because the aim of deposit was to give a movable thing for the purpose of gratuitous afe custody. In this case, however, the aim of giving a movable thing was the giving of material to an artisan for the purpose of its manufacture. The duties of such an artisan were similar to those of the depositary and probably therefore, some of the *Smṛtis* classed among deposits the giving of objects to an

43. See par. 9.

artisan for manufacturing. However, from the point of view of the theory of ancient Indian law *śilpinyāsa*, or the like, were considered as deposits. In any case we have to keep in mind that such a precise *Smṛti*, as the Y. correctly did not class *śilpinyāsa* under the contracts of deposit.

H. PROPERTY OF A MINOR.

19. *Quotations.*

Pogaṇḍa or *pogaṇḍadhāna* from *pogaṇḍa*° (a minor)+ °*dhana* (property) was according to N. 2.15) the sixth species of deposits. We read there :

pratigṛhṇāti pogaṇḍaṁ yaś ca sapradhanaṁ naraḥ,
tasyā'py eṣa bhaved dharmaḥ ṣaḍ ete vidhayaḥ samāḥ.

(Also quoted in NMS. 3.8, VyK. 134, VRK. 96),

Also Asahāya commenting on N. (16) and enumerating the eighteen titles of law mentioned *pogaṇḍadhāna*.

20. *Definition.*

The only difinition of this "deposit" could be found in Asahāya (*ad* N-II-15). We read there :

ya anāthaṁ bālaṁ sapradhanaṁ nāthābuddhyā pratigṛhṇāti yasyā'pi pūrvoktasyaiva vidhir draṣṭavyaḥ; ṣaḍ ete vidhayaḥ; ṣaḍ ete vidhayaḥ samā iti.

Hence this was the property of a minor. This kind of contract of deposit, according to N., took place when a man took a wealthy minor, who had no guardians, into his house. Then the property of the minor was subjected to the rules relating to deposits. In this case the child, whose father and mother were deceased, was "deposited" by the king or on his behalf with a man who had to take care of the orphan. As the orphan-minor could not dispose of the estate left by his father, the guardian had to take care of him similarly as an object committed to his care.

From the legal point of view in this case also, it was impossible to class this case under "deposits". This was a *tutela dativa* and the depositary was in reality a *tutor dativus* who had similar pecuniary obligations towards the minor as a depositary towards the depositror. However, here too, N. was of the opinion[44] that it is a special kind of deposit. Therefore, we have to consider it, from the point of view of the system of ancient Indian law as a species of deposits.

I. OTHER KINDS OF DEPOSITS.

21. *Krayaprosita, Bandha, Vaiśavṛttyarpita*

In Kāty. (592) we read : *kraya-aproṣita-nikṣipta-bandhā'n-vāhita-yācitam vaiśavṛttyarpitaṁ caiva so'rthastū'panidhiḥ smṛtaḥ* (Also quoted in Apar. *ad* Y. 2.65. VyK. 130, SC. 3, VRK. 84, VCi. 40, VCa. 33, VVy. 33).

We see here, that Kāty. classed, in addition to the deposits quoted above, the following contracts as deposits : *krayaproṣita, bandha* and *vaiśyavṛttyarpita.*

Krayaproṣita from *kraya°* (purchase)+*°proṣita* (from *pra°*+ *°vas* going home, going abroad) was an object sold but still in the hands of the vendor. It was not a deposit from the point of view of the theory of law, but a *constitutum possessorium.*

Bandha was a pledge, it was an article entrusted to a pledgee, but not a deposit, although the pledgee had similar duties to perform as a depositary.

Vaiśyavṛttyarpita from *vaiśya°* (merchant)+*°vṛttya* (*vṛtti*) from *vara*—to reach) + *°arpita* (from *ar*—to bring) was an object lodged in the hands of a trader. It was also not a *depositum* but *fiducia.* Here also the trader had similar duties to perform as the depositary[45]

22. *Ādi.*

Y. (II-67) and N. (II-14) used also the word *ādi i.e.* "and the like" after having enumerated *yācita, anvahita, nyāsa* (Y.), or *yācita* and *anvāhita* (N.).[46] Vīr. (*ad* Y. II-67 p. 494/27 sqq.) understood under this expression things bought but not paid for as others mentioned in G. (XII-42). G. stated there :

nidhy-anvādhi-yācitā-vakrītā-dhayo naṣṭāḥ sarvān aninditan apuruṣā parādhena.

44. ...*ṣad ete vidhayaḥ samāḥ* (N. 2.15)
45. See also a similar case of *fuducia* in K. 198.17 and many others.
46. As well as *śilpe, upanidhi, nyāsa* and *pratinyāsa.*

Therefore, these kinds of *fiducia* had also to be considered, from the point of view of the theory of ancient Indian law, as contracts of deposit.[47]

J. DIFFERENTIATION BETWEEN DEPOSITS FROM THE POINT OF VIEW OF CIVIL PROCEDURE.

23. *Deposits given before witnesses or verbally.*

From the point of view of civil procedure N. (II-6) and Bṛh. (11.6) differentiated between deposits given before witnesses (*sākṣimānita* or *samākṣita*[48]) or verbally and in private (*prokta*[49] *vahodatta*))[50]

The deposit was given verbally when the depositor had the highest confidence in the depositary. However, the depositary had to abstain from such a kind of contract; the contract of deposit before witnesses or in writing should be concluded in order to avoid any misunderstanding.

We see here that this distinction between deposits was not important from the point of view of civil law, but civil procedure; it had particular influence on possible law suits.

47. See paras 9, 11, 17, 18.

48. From *sākṣin* or *sākṣika*—witness

49. From *pra°*+*°vac.*

50. From *rāhas°*+*°datta.*

II

LAW OF DEPOSITS*

1. *Different Types of Deposits—Title of Law*

As shown in the previous study there existed in ancient India thirteen or more different types of deposit. They were : *nikṣepa*, *upanidhi* (or *aupanidhika*), *nyāsa*, *śilpinyāsa*, *pratinyāsa*, *yācita*, *anvāhita*, *pogaṇḍa*, *krayaproṣita*, *bandha*, *vaiśyavṛttyarpita*, *sākṣimanita* or *sasākṣita*), *prokta* or *rāhodatta*, etc.

In the previous study the definition of each of these different kinds of deposits has been given. It was also stated there that "deposits" were regarded as one of the eighteen (or more) titles of law (Mn. 8. 4, N. 16, Bṛh. 1.11).

2. *Special and General Rules*

The Law of deposits was based on various special rules found, in particular, in N., Mn., Y., Bṛh., G., Vi., Kāty, K, and others. These rules regulated the questions of the handing over of objects deposited, obligations and rights of depositaries and depositors, etc. These special rules should be applied to each case of the contract of deposit. If these special rules did not exist, the rules concerning debts should be applied to deposits. Probably in such a way the first sentence of K.'s Book 3.66. should be understood.[1]

3. *Definition—Confidence*

The most general and perfect definition of deposits is to be found in (N. 2.1): We read there :

> *svaṁ dravyaṁ yatra viśrambhān nikṣipaty aviśaṅkitaḥ,*
> *nikṣepo nāma tat proktaṁ vyavahāra-padaṁ budhaiḥ.*

(Also quoted in NMS. 3.1, Mit. *ad* Y. 2.25. VyK. 130, SC. 2, VRK. 83, DK. 38, VCi. 36, SCM. 14, Vīr. *ad* Y. 2.67,

* Previously appeared as JSAIL. II in the "Supplement to Bhāratīya Vidyā", Vol. VII, Nos. 3-4, pp. 1-22.

1. *upanidhiḥ ṛṇena vyākhyātaḥ* (K. 177-13)

VyPr. 279, VyM. 84, VT. 554, VV. 129. VyS. 87, VVy. 31. AP. 253. 14).

In this definition we find almost all the *essentialia* of the contract of deposit which consisted in the delivering of a movable thing by one person to another for safe custody. N. states the same. According to N.'s definition a deposit took place if one person entrusted (without suspicion) a movable thing with another person, having confidence in the latter.[2]

Asahāya (*ad* N. II-1) explained that a man who did not place confidence in another person would not deposit a single cowry even, without the guarantee of a written receipt, or of witnesses. On the other hand, he would deposit 1,000 *suvarṇas*, even without these precautions, with one in whom he had confidence.

The same idea was beautifully expressed in Mṛcch., where Cārudatta said to Vidūṣaka, referring to Vasantasenā who deposited with him some jewels :

yaṁ samālambya viśvāsaṁ nyāso'smāsu tayā kṛtaḥ,
tasyaitan mahato mūlyaṁ pratyayasyaiva dīyate,
(Act. 3.353.4)

"*She showed her trust in leaving us her treasure;*
The price of confidence has no less measure.[3]"

In another place, when Cārudatta said that his house was not worthy of the confidence placed in him, Vasantasenā handing over the jewels in deposit replied: *ojja aliaṁ; purisesu ṇāsā ṇikrikhavianti ṇa uṇa gehesu.* (Act I.628-9). "You mistake, Sir, it is to men that treasures are entrusted, not to houses.[4]"

As the handing over of deposits to a person, and not "to houses" was a matter of great confidence placed by the depositor in the depositary, the latter had to fulfil his duties personally and was not allowed to entrust the thing deposited to someone else (Śukr. IV, 5, 316).[5]

2. See also Viv. *ad* mortgages, according to which a deposit meant the act of keeping anything in the care of another.

3. According to A. W. Ryder's translation.

4. According to A. W. Ryder's translation.

5. *sāmānyaṁ yācitaṁ nyāsa ādhir dāsaś ca tad dhanam,*
anvāhitaṁ ca nikṣepaḥ sarvasvaṁ cā'nvaye sati,
āpatsv api na deyāni nava vastūni paṇḍitaiḥ. (Śukr. 4.5, 316. Also quoted in Dakṣa (Dh. 807), VyK. 144, SC. 190, VRK. 128, SCM. 19, VCa. 41, VT. 600, VV. 148, VyS. 93, VVCa. 14).

4. *Possession or Detention*

The holder of the deposit was not the possessor of the thing deposited. He had not *animus possedendi,* he had not *animus res sibi habendi,* but had *animus rem alteri habendi.* The depositary according to ancient Indian law possessed the thing deposited in subordination to the depositor; therefore, the thing deposited was in his detention only. The depositary could not alienate the thing deposited. Even in case of *traditio* of the thing deposited and of conclusion of a special contract (sale) , the person to whom the thing deposited was transferred would not become the owner of this thing, as he could not prove the *titulus acquirendi.* This rule was clearly evident from Bṛh.(XII-2).

nikṣepā' nvāhita-nyāsa-hṛta-yācita-bandhakam,
upāṁśu-jana-vikrītam asvāmī so' bhidhīyate.

(Also quoted in VRK. 100., VV. 134) Similarly N. (VII-1) and others. These sources of law expressed the opinion that contracts, effected by another than the rightful owner, did not bear consequences for the other party. In particular, this rule related to contracts of deposits (*nikṣepa, anvāhita, nyāsa,* etc.)

5. *Persons Suitable to Become Depositaries*

It was stated before that objects deposited should be handed over by the depositor into the hands of a person in whom he placed confidence, as well as in a place he found suitable. This rule, found in Mn. (VIII-179) and N. (II-2) (identically), as well as in Bṛh. (XI-4), protected the depositor. He had to choose a right man and a right place, a place where the thing deposited was safe.[6]

Mn. (8. 179) and N. (2.2) stated :

kulaje vṛttasaṁpanne dharmajñe satyavādini,
mahāpakṣe dhaninyārye nikṣepaṁ vikṣiped budhaḥ.

(Also quoted in VyK. 130, SC. 178, VRK. 85, VCi. 36,

6. Mn. and N. referred to the right man only. Bṛh. to the right man and right place.

SCM. 14, NṛP. 23, SV. 265, Vīr. *ad* Y. 2.65, VyPr. 280, VT. 554, VV. 130, VyS. 87).

Bṛh. (11.4) stated :

sthānaṁ gṛhaṁ sthalaṁ caiva tad ṛṇaṁ vividhān guṇān,
satyaṁ śaucaṁ bandhujanaṁ parīkṣya sthāpayen nidhim.

(Also quoted in VyK. 130, SC. 178, VRK. 85, SCM 14, NṛP. 23, VyPr. 280, VT. 556, VV. 130, VyS. 87).

We see that the object deposited should be entrusted by a wise man (*buddha*) (depositor), after duly considering the case, to one who was :

(1) born of a good family (*kulaja*) (kindred) *i. e.*, from an honest family; the depositor had to the consider the depositary's sons, grandsons and the rest of his family, in order to form an opinion of his kindred,

(2) endowed with good character (*vṛttasaṁpanna*) and qualities *i. e.*, whose conduct was known as good and was considered honest,

(3) truthful (*satyavādini*) or veracious as such a man would not assert a falsehood,

(4) well acquainted with *dharma* (*dharmaja*) *i. e.*, knowing the law (truthful),

(5) honourable(*ārya*)*i.e.*, plain in dealings, void of artifice,

(6) wealthy (*dhanin*) and powerful, *i.e.*, had enough means with which he was capable of protecting the effcts and possible loss of the thing deposited,

(7) had many relatives (*mahāpakṣa*), a large family, sons, grandsons, etc., who could support him.

Regarding the right place, Bṛh. (XI-4) stated only that the object deposited must be handed over to the depositary in the right place (*thāna*) and in the right house (*gṛha*). That meant that the object deposited should be kept in a town, safe, as far as its population was concerned, and in a house where it was safe from the covetousness of the depositary's wife and from fire and other calamities. The depositor, before handing over the thing deposited, had also to consider whether the master of the depositary's house was reliable (Bṛh.).

6. *Contracts of Deposit as Real Contracts*

When all these conditions, which were only advice for

the depositor, had been considered, the handing over of the thing deposited took place. This handing over could take place before witnesses, or without them, and could be either a verbal or a written contract. This contract was concluded with the handing over by the depositor of the object deposited to the depositary and, therefore, had to be considered a real contract.

7. *Depositary's and Depositor's Responsibility. General Rules*

The contract of deposit was always concluded in favour of the depositor, not the depositary. Nevertheless, if the depositary accepted the deposit he had to exercise *diligentia—diligentia quam suis rebus adhibere solet,* and if he did not, he was responsible for any damage which occurred. There existed the *presumptio juris ac de jure* that the depositary was always responsible for any damage, destruction or loss of the object deposited and that he did not exercise the *diligentia quam suis rebus*. Therefore, he had to indemnify for the damage, destruction and loss; the amount to be paid depended on the fact whether the damage, etc., were caused by *culpa levis, culpa lata,* or *dolus*. Only if the depositary could prove that the damage, destruction, or loss of the object deposited was caused by *vis major* (act of God, or king), then he was not responsible for the damage. The depositor, however, had to take back the object deposited and pay the depositary, if agreed upon, a special depositor's fee.[7]

8. *Diligentia*

That the depositary was not interested in the contract of deposit was clearly stated in Bṛh. (XI-9), where we read that it is the best course not to accept a deposit, but after taking it, the depositary should keep it carefully (Bṛh, XI-9). That means that the depositary had to exercise the *diligentia,* but only the *diligentia quam suis rebus adhibere solet.* That such a *diligentia* should be exercised was evident from the fact that N. (II-9) and Kāty. (598) stated that if a object deposited was lost together with the goods of the depositary, the loss should be that of the depositor.[8] Bṛh. (XI-6) stated that the object

7. This resulted *de contractu* but not *de jure.*

8. *grahītuḥ saha yo'rthena naṣṭo naṣṭah sa dāyinaḥ.* (N. 2.9. Also quoted

deposited had to be guarded with the same care as a son.[9] In Kath. (Tar. 7, 79)) we find also a sentence in which a daughter-in-law was given to a king in order to be protected by him "like a deposit (*nikṣepa*) should be preserved." (See also Viv. p. 24. *ad* Bṛh.)

Exercising the *diligentia quam suis rebus*, the depositary had to preserve the thing deposited from robbers, vermin, decay and the like.[10]

In addition to legal consequences the exercising of the *diligentia*, in connection with the object deposited, brought religious merit to the depositary (*i.e.* was equal to giving gifts of gold, inferior metals, clothes and the like), and the non-exercising of such a *diligentia* was a sin (*i.e.* of a woman who injured her husband or a man who killed his son or his friend.).[11]

9. *Vis Major*

A. *There existed praesumptio juris ac de jure* that the depositary was always responsible for the loss, destruction, or damage of the object deposited *i.e.*, that he did not exercise the *diligentia quam suis rebus*. Only if the loss, destruction, or damage were caused by *vis major* this *praesumptio* had not to be applied. This is clear from Kāty. (593) wher we read :

in NMS. 3.6, Mit *ad*. Y. 2.66, Apar. *ad* Y. 2.66, VyK. 131, SC. 179, VRK. 88, VCi. 37, SV. 267, VCa. 31, VyPr. 281, VT. 558, VV. 131, VyS. 87, VVy. 32) and

arāja-daivikenā'pi vikṣiptaṁ yatra nāśitam,
grahītuḥ saha bhāṇḍena dātur naṣṭaṁ tad ucyate. (Kāty. 598. Also quoted in Apar. *ad* Y. 2,.66, SC. 179, VRK. 88, VyPr. 281, VyS. 87).

J.J. Jolly in S.B.E. XXXIII p. 122 tranlated this sentence wrongly saying :
"the loss shall be the depositary's" instead of "the loss shall be the depositor's."

9. For it would be destroyed by neglect (Bṛh. XI-6).

According to Bṛh. in Viv. (p. 25) if the depositary spoiled the deposit by keeping it separate from his own articles, he was responsible for it and should make the loss good with interest.

10. Col. 416 sqq. We read there : "A deposit must be preserved from robbers, from vermin, from decay and the like; if no care be taken, and the thing be never inspected, it may decay in the ground; or be stolen by neighbouring thieves entering the house; or, if it be small it may be carried away by rats; in these and similar modes it may be destroyed."

11. *dadato yad bhavet puṇyaṁ hemakupyā'mbarādikam,*
tat syāt pālayato nyāsaṁ tathā ca śaraṇāgatam.
bhartur drohe yathā nāryāḥ puṁsaḥ putra-suhṛd-vadhe,
doṣo bhavet tathā nyāse bhakṣito'pekṣite nṛṇām (Bṛh. 11. 7-8. Also quoted in Apar. *ad* Y. 2.65 and 2.75, VyK. 131, SC. 178, VRK. 85, SCM. 15, NṛP. 23, SV. 266. VyPr. 281, VyM. 84, VT. 556, VyS. 87, VCi. 36, VV. 130).

nikṣiptaṁ yasya yat kiṁcit tat prayatnena pālayet,
daiva-rāja-kṛtād anyo vināśas tasya kīrtyate.

(Also quoted in SC. 179, VyPr. 282, VyS. 87).

The non-responsibility on the part of the depositary in case of loss, destruction, or damage of the object deposited caused by *vis major* was very clearly regulated in Y. (2.66). We read there : *na dāpyo' pahṛtaṁ taṁ tu rāja-daivika taskaraiḥ.*

(Also quoted in ViR. *ad* Y. 2,68, SC. 179, VRK. 88, NṛP. 24, SV. 266, VyPr. 281, VyU. 80, VyM. 85, VT. 558, VyS. 87, AP. 254. 26).

We find here the most typical example of *vis major i.e.* the act of king (*rājā*), the act of God destiny, fate (*daiva, deva*), and the act of thieves (*taskara*). Every plundering, by the forces of a king (foreign king), etc.—was an act of king, every cataclysm (caused by water, fire, etc.)—was an act of God, and every loss caused by the act of men (robbers, thieves)—was an act of thieves.

Some sources of law, such as N. (II-9), Bṛh. (XII-10) and Kāty, (593/4), enumerate as *vis major rājadaiva* only, others, such as Mn. (VIII-189) and almost identically N. (XII-12) mention stealing by thieves (*caura*),[12] destruction of things by water (*jala*) or burning by fire (*agni*). Certainly this, rather casuistic, enumeration, is identical with that quoted above. The most casuistic enumeration of *vis major* is found in K. (177/13-17) were we read : "Whenever forts, or country parts are destroyed by enemies, or wild tribes; whenever villagers, merchants, or herds of cattle are subjected to the inroads of invaders; whenever the kingdom itself is destroyed; whenever extensive fires or floods bring about entire destruction of villages or partly destroy immovable properties, movable properties having been rescued before; whenever the spread of fire, or rush of floods is so sudden that even movable properties could not be removed; or whenever a ship laden with commodities is either sunk or plundered (by pirates), deposits lost in any of the above ways shall not be reclaimed."[13] In reality it was not a casuistic enumeration

12. Identically also Mṛcch. act I-634, and act III-284.

13. According to Shamashastry's translation.
paracakrāṭavikābhyāṁ durga-rāṣṭra-vilope vā, pratirodhakair vā grāme-

of cases of *vis major*, but rather an interpretation of *rājadaiva*.

B. However, some exceptions exist from the rule of the non-responsibility on the part of the depositary in case of *vis major*; and so this rule does not apply if the depositary acted fraudulently (*jihwa*). In a general way this rule was stated only in N. (II-9).[14] Also Mit. interpreting Y. (II-66) states the same: *dhanina eva tad dravyaṁ naṣṭaṁ yadi jihmakāritaṁ na bhavati.* (Mit. *ad* Y. II-66 p. 163-2. Similarly Dīpakalikā and Viv., quoting N. II-9, p. 24 and interpreting Kāty. 594, p. 24 *in fine*). Such a fraudulent act took place if the depositary *e. g.*, placed the object deposited near an old wall, or the like, while he placed his own property elsewhere, or, if concealing his own property, he showed the deposit to the king (invader).[15] As far as the first example was concerned in order to do it, the depositary had to extract the thing deposited from his own property. That case was described in Mn. (VIII-189 *in fine*) and almost identically in N. (II-12).

We can admit, as a rule, that if the depositary was at fault, he was responsible for every loss, destruction, or damage of the object deposited, even if it was caused by *vis major*. In such a manner interpreting this rule G. (XII-42) stated :

nidhyan-vādhi-yācitā-vakrītā-dhayo naṣṭāḥ sarvān aninditān apuruṣāparādhena.

The consequences of the "fault" (*jihwa*) mentioned above have to be also applied in case of *vis major* which occurred after the depositary was asked to restore the object deposited. The rule was that the depositary had to restore the object deposited when asked for. If he failed to restore it, he was at fault, and if then *vis major* occurred, the depositary was responsible for the object deposited and had to restore it (*in integrum restitutio*), when lost, destroyed, or damaged (as well as pay a fine). This rule is clrearly evident from Y. (II-66) where we read : *bhreṣaścenmārgite'datte dāpyo daṇḍaṁ ca tat samam.*

(Also quoted in ViR. *ad*. Y. 2, 68, VRK. 90, NṛP. 24; SV. 267, 490, Vir. *ad* Y. 2. 68, VyPr. 283, VyU, 80,

sārthavrajāvilope. cakrayukte nāśe vā, grāma-madhyā'gny-udakā-bādhe vā kiñcid amokṣayamāne kupyam aṇirhāry avarjam ekadeśa-mukta-dravye vā jvālā-vego'-pavyṛddhevā, nāvi nimagrāyāṁ muṣitāyāṁ svayam uparūḍho no'panidhimabhyā bhavet. (K. 177. 13-7)

14. *daiva-rāja-kṛte tadvan na cettajjihma-kāritam* (N 2.9)

15. Col. 421.

VT. 558, VyS. 88, AP. 254. 26). and from Kāty (595)[16], as well as N. (II-7).[17] The same applied to the *śilpinyāsa*, *i.e.* in the case of an artisan, who retained the material handed over to him beyond the agreed period (Kāty. 603).

10. *Depositor's Fault*

On the other hand, if the loss, destruction, or damage of the object deposited was caused by the fault of the depositor, the depositary was not responsible for it. This rule was clearly stated in Kāty. (599) where we read :

jñātva dravya-viyogaṁ tu dātā yatra vinikṣipet.
sarvo-pāya-vināśe'pi grahītā naiva dāpyate.

(Also quoted in VyK. 132, SC. 179, VRK. 89, VyPr. 282, VT. 559, VyS. 88).

Ratnākara explained that if the depositor knew that the loss of the object deposited was probable, and, nevertheless, deposited it, the depositary was not responsible for any loss, destruction or damage, that meant even if it was not caused by *vis major*. However, that did not mean that the depositary was not responsible at all for the thing deposited. In any case he was responsible for *dolus*. The same rule had to be applied also in case of the *the śilpinyāsa* when the loss of the material given to the artizan was caused by the defects of the object deposited (Bṛh).

11. *Indemnification*

In the contracts of deposit, as *bonae fidei negotia*, the depositary had to indemnify for the loss, destruction, or damage resulting from his *culpa levis*, *culpa lata* and *dolus*, if he did not exercise the *diligentia quam suis rebus adhibere solet*. This rule is clear in Kāty. (596, 597). (Identically with Kāty. 597 was Vy. in Vīr. *ad* Y. II-65-67 p. 494/15-16). We read there :

16. *yācitān antaraṁ nāśe daiva-rajā-kṛte'pi saḥ,*
grahītā pratidāpyaḥ syān mūlyamātraṁ na saṁśayaḥ (Kāty. 595. Similarly Vy. in SC. 183, VyPr. 283, VyS. 88).

17. *yācyamānas tu yo dātrā nikṣepaṁ na prayacchati,*
daṇḍyaḥ sa rājñā duṣṭā'tmā naṣṭe dāpyaś ca tat samam. (N. 2.7. Also quoted NMS. 3.4, VyK. 232, VRK. 90, VCi. 38, VyPr. 283, VT. 556-7, VV. 132, VyS. 88).

nyāsādikaṁ paradravyaṁ prabhākṣitam upekṣitam,
ajñāna-nāśitaṁ caiva yena dāpyaḥ sa eva tat.
bhakṣitaṁ sodayaṁ dāpyaḥ samaṁ dāpya upekṣitam,
kiṁcin nyūnaṁ pradāpyaḥ syād dravyam ajñāna-nāśitam.

(Also quoted in VyK. 134, SC. 180, VRK. 99, VCi 40, VCa. 31, VV. 134, VyS. 88, VVy. 32,; and Mit. *ad* Y. 2 67. VyPr. 282, VyU. 80., VT. 560).

In the case of *dolus* the depositary was obliged to *in integrum restitutio* and to the payment of interests; in the case of *culpa levis*—to *in integrum restitutio*; and in the case of *culpa lata*—to the payment of little less than the value of the damage done. Similar was the opinion of N. (II-9 sqq.), Mn. (VIII-189), G.[18], Kāty, (594, 600)[19], K. (178/3)[20], Vy. (in Viv. p. 25). Bṛh. (XI-9, 12). The latter stated :

bhedeno'pekṣayā nyāsaṁ grahītā yadi nāśayet.
yācyamāno na dadyad vā dāpyas tat sodayaṁ bhavet.

(Bṛh 11.12. Also quoted in Apar. *ad* Y. 2.66, VyK. 132, SC, 180, VRK. 90, VCi. 38, SV. 267-8, VCa. 32, VyPr. 282, VyM. 84, VT. 559, VV. 132, VyS. 88, VVy. 32).

Bṛh. explained here what *deligentia quamsu is rebus adhibere solet* meant. It was declared there that if the depositary through negligence destroyed the thing deposited, while he kept his own goods with very different care,[21] he should be compelled to pay the value of it with interest. And so *e.g.*, if the depositary removed the thing deposited which was placed with his own goods, secured his own effects and neglected the

18. See Col. 425.

19. As far as *dolus* is concerned :
yasya doṣeṇa yat kiṁcid vināśyeta hriyeta vā,
tad dravyaṁ sodayaṁ dāpyo daiva-rāja-kṛtād vinā. (Kāty. 594. Also quoted in Apar. *ad* Y. 2.66, VyK. 132, SC. 179, DK. 38, VCa 31, VyPr. 282, VT. 558-9, VV. 132, VyS. 88, VVy. 32).
grāhakasya hi yad doṣān naṣṭaṁ tu grāhakasya tat,
tasmin naṣṭe hṛte vā'pi grahītā mūlyam āharet. (Kāty. 600. also quoted in VyK. 132, VRK. 89, VV. 132).

20. K. (178.5) even stated that in the case of the loss of deposits the depositary should restore four times its value and pay also a fine of five times the stipulated value (*ādhāna-vikrayā-pavyayaneṣu cā'sya catur-guṇa pañca-bandho daṇḍaḥ*).

21. *J. Jolly* in S. B. E. XXXIII p. 333 translated this word "indifference."

deposit, he did not exercise the *diligentia quam suis rebus* and was then responsible as for *dolus*.[22]

It was stated above that in case of *dolus*, the depositary was obliged to *in integrum restitutio* and to the payment of interest. In this connection it should be noted that whenever a rule was to be found in the Smṛti-s in which it was stated that the depositary had to pay interests, the rate of interests amounted to 5 per cent. This rule should be taken *per analogiam* from Kāty. where it was stated clearly :

nikṣiptaṁ...yācyamānam adattaṁ ced vardhate pañcakaṁ śataṁ (Kāty. 506)[23]

12. *Restoration of the Object Deposited*

A. The depositary's second obligation was to return the object deposited. The act of restoring the thing deposited was considered a great relief for the depositary, just as the taking of a deposit was considered a great harassment for him. This is clearly evident from Kālidāsa's Śākuntala (Act

22. Bṛh. also states that in the case of, *śilpinyāsa*, if the artist takes the deposited thing (materials of production), he is liable to pusnishment (*dolus*).

23. On this subject. H. T Colebrooke's opinion should be here quoted : "......Does interest commence from the day when the thing was deposited, from the day it was wasted, or from the day when it was demanded ? 1. To this it is answered, it shall bear interest after six months from the date of the deposit; for, the words 'after three seasons' being repeated in this text from the preceding text (*Book* I, V.LVI 1), it is proper to assume the date of the deposit, in answer to the question, from what date shall three seasons be counted ? 2. Some hold, that a deposit, not delivered on demand, shall bear interest six months afterwards, because demand is suggested by the context, where Miśra directs interest at the rate of five *paṇas* in the hundred after six months. 3. Since the wasting of the thing deposited is the cause of its bearing interest, under the authority of the text, we hold it proper that interest should commence (even earlier than six months) from the day when the thing was wasted; but the other text, ordaining interest after six months, is applicable to the case where a fraudulent depositary, though the thing has not been wasted, refuses to deliver it on demand; like the price of a commodity purchased and like a balance of interest, and so forth. What then shall be the rate of interest ? Two in the hundred, and other rates ordained by the law; because those are in their nature legal rates, and because interest is so limited by the text of Manu (*Book* I, V, XLII) : and the interest and amercement should be proportionated to the magnitude of the offence. But this does not coincide with the opinion of the author of the *Mitācsharā*; for he applies the text to a thing voluntarily wasted, and does not distinguish *payment of* interest, and exemption from interest, in cases where a thing deposited is lost by neglect and so forth......" (Col. p. 427 sqq.).

IV, 97)[24] and the Pañcatantra (Pts. 1, 14).[25]

The object deposited had to be returned in the same condition in which it was delivered—*yathā dayas tatha grahaḥ*. (Mn. VIII-180, 194, 195, N. II-3, Y. II-65); it is in the very manner and to the very man (Bṛh. XI-10). This rule was so popular that it was repeated in Mn. three times (Mn. VIII-180, 194, 195) always in different words; N. quoted the same rule (*i.e.* Mn. VIII-180) in book II-3; it was also repeated in N. (II-6). Y. (II-65) knew, the same rule but restrained its applicability to sealed deposits only; similarly Medh. *ad.* Mn., and N.

Mn. and N. stated :

yo yathā nikṣiped dhaste yam arthaṁ yasya mānavaḥ.
sa tathaiva grahītavyo yathā dāyas tathā grahaḥ

(Mn. 8.180 and N.2.3. Also quoted in VyK.131, SC.181, VRK. 86, NṛP. 23-4, SV. 269. VyPr. 285, VT. 556, VyS. 88).

nikṣepo yaḥ kṛto yena yāvāṁś ca kulasan nidhau,
tāvān eva sa vijñeyo vibruvan daṇḍam arhati. (Mn. 8. 194).
mitho dāyaḥ kṛto yena gṛhīto mitha eva vā.
mitha eva pradātavyo yathā dāyas tathā grahaḥ.

(Mn. 8.195. Also quoted in Apar. *ad* Y. 2.67, VyK.133 & 131, SC. 181, VRK. 94 &86, SCM. 15. VyPr. 284-5, VyS. 88-9).

Hence Mn. stated here that in whatever manner the depositor deposited something in the hands of the depositary—in the same manner the same objects had to be re-delivered to the depositor. If it was delivered privately it had to be re-delivered privately, but if it was delivered in the presence of a witness the proof of the re-delivery of the same quantity and quality of the object deposited was easy. Whoever, made false statements was liable to fine. Medh. gave the following commentary to the first quotation of Mn. : "In a case where it is generally known that the party concerned always keeps deposits properly sealed,—if a dispute arises, and the

24. *artho hi kaṇyā parakīya eva ṭām adya saṁpreṣya parigrahituḥ,*
jāto mamāyaṁ viśadaḥ prakāmaṁ pratyarpita nyāsa ivā'ntarātma.
(Śak. 4. 97);

25. *nikṣepe patite harmye śreṣṭī stauti svadevatām,*
nikṣepī mriyate tubhyaṁ pradāsyāmy upayācitam. (Rāgh. 12.18).

deposit is found to be unsealed, if the trustee were to say 'this man never seals his deposits, he forces them upon me and goes off,' he would be suspected of dishonesty and would lose his case; there being no room for any other evidence so far;—but when, on the seal being found broken, the question arises as to what party of the property has been extracted, the king should call other kinds of evidence; the guilty man however is to be punished in the first place, with the penalty prescribed for dishonest dealing in general;—and secondly, another penalty in connection with the 'deposit' has to be imposed after the extracted amount had been determined. 'In the case of a dishonest dealing," the man deserves to be mulcted of the entire amount involved.' True; but this is only in cases where the entire guilt is clearly indicated by proof. For instance, a certain village has been robbed,—Devadatta is accused of having colluded with other thieves and robbed the village on that day,—thereupon he pleads—'on that day I did not go to that village,'—witnesses declare that he had been seen in the village on that day, but it had not been seen that he had actually committed the robbery,—from this the deduction is that the man having denied the robbery as well as his presence in the village, since his presence had been proved, the denial of the robbery also was not true; so that when there was other evidence clearly proving the man's presence in the village, it was safe to infer that he had committed the robbery also. In the present case, however, it may be that the seal was broken through carelessness (and not necessarily intentionally), (so that the penalty need not always be severe)".[26]

This comment was very naive, but showed that Medh. referred Mn. (VIII-180) to sealed deposits, similarly as Y. (II-65)".[27]

Mn. (VIII-194 and 195)[28] did not contain anything

26. According to G. N. Jhā's translation.

27. *vāsanaṣtha-manākhyāya haste'nyasya tad arpyate,*
dravyaṁ tad aupanidhikaṁ pratideyaṁ tathaiva tat. (Y. 2.65. Also quoted in ViR. *ad* Y. 2. 67, VyK. 130, GMH. 12.39, SC. 3, VRK. 83, VCi. 36, SCM. 14, NṛP. 23, SV. 265, VyPr. 280, VyU. 79, VT. 557, VV. 130, VyS. 87, VVy. 31, AP. 254.25).

28. Mn. 8. 194-5. See above.

new and were only repetitions of the commentary on Mn. (VIII-180).

B. The object deposited had to be returned by the depositary to the depositor immediately when he asked for it, except in the case when it was taken for a definite period, or for a particular purpose. In other words, deposits given to a depositary without agreeing on the term of deposit, had to be returned immediately after the depositor asked for their return; deposits concluded on a basis of an agreement which stated the term or purpose of the contract of deposit, must be returned in accordance with the agreement. This rule was evident from Bṛh. (XI-9) and Kāty. (606).

Bṛh. stated that the depositary must restore the object deposited when asked for, even once only, and Kāty. states that if a object was taken for a particular purpose, or for a definite period of time and a demand was made in the middle and the object was not returned, the depositary was not under the obligation return it.[29] Contracts of deposit stipulating the period of time were also mentioned in K. (198/13 sqq.)

C. The object deposited must be returned to the depositor himself; if not, the depositary had to be punished (K. 180/7). In particular, it ought not be returned to the next-of-kin (son, brother, wife—Medh. *ad* Mn. VIII-185). Especially in joint families *e.g.*, the brother of the depositor could come to the depositary and ask for return, saying that it belonged to him. If this person committed a dishonest act, the depositary had no proof and lost the object deposited which then had to be restored by him; but the object deposited did not become lost if there did not occur any accident (Mn. VIII-185)[30]. However, the depositary could restore the thing deposited to the depositor's next-of-kin, if the depositor died (Mn. VIII-186 and identically N. II-10).

D. If the depositary refused to return the object deposited, or did not return it in the proper manner, he had to be compelled to restore it (Mn. VIII-184, Vi. V-178, Bṛh. XI-12,

29. Must not pay the price with interest. This rule must refer *per analogiam* to loans (Kāty. 609, 610).

30. See also similarly Bṛh. (XI-10).

Kāty. 608, K. 198/13 sqq.).[31] In addition to *in integrum restitutio*, he had to pay interest—according to Bṛh. (XI-12) and Kāty. (608),—or highest amercement—according to Vi. (V-172),—or an amercement of 12 *paṇas*—according to K. (198-13 sqq.)

If the depositary denied receiving a deposit and was convicted by witnesses or ordeal, he had to be compelled to return the object deposited (or pay its equivalent) and as a fine the amount equal to the value of the object deposited (Bṛh. XII-13). Such a denial was equal to a theft and had to be punished like a theft, according to Mn. (VIII-180 *in fine* and 181) and Matsyapurāṇa.[32]

E. In order to receive back the object deposited, some sources advised amicable action, without resorting to stratagem (N. II-11)[33], particularly, in doubtful cases (Mn. VIII-187).[34] But if this acting was in vain, machiavellian tricks could be used. As usual, the best machiavellian tricks were found in K. where we read : "When a depositary denied having received a sealed deposit which was not, however, deposited for any reasonable cause, the depositor may obtain secret permission (from the judges) to produce such witnesses as he might have stationed under a wall while depositing. In the midst of a forest, or in the middle of a voyage, an old or afflicted merchant might with confidence put in the custody of a depositary some valuable article with certain secret mark, and go on his way. On his sending this information to his son or brother, the latter may ask for the sealed deposit. If the depositary does not quietly return it, he shall not only forfeit his credit, but be liable to the punishment for theft, besides being made to restore the deposit."[35] Mn. stated similarly that the depositary could

31. If he admitted and restored it in the manner and shape in which it was deposited, then there was nothing in the charge brought against him by others (Mn. VIII-183).

32. Probably cases of refusal to restore the deposits often occurred, as we read in Raj. (VIII-128) the following aphorism: "The water which has been carried down to the ocean by the streams is received back from the cloud; but a thing deposited (*nyāsa*) in a merchant's house is never again recovered."

33. *acchalenaiva cānvicchettam arthaṁ prītipurvakam*
vicārya tasya vā vṛttaṁ sāmnaiva pariśodhayet. (N. 2.11)

34. Mn. (8. 187), same as N. (2.11) with the exception of the last word *parisādhayet* (see above).

35. According to Shamashastri's translation (p. 229).

be tried in his absence and the judge, on failure of witnesses. could deposit gold with the depositary under some pretext through spies of suitable age and appearance, and then ask him to restore it (Mn. VIII-181/2).[36]

F. The object deposited had to be taken back by the depositor at the proper time and the depositary had to avoid returning it at an improper time *e.g.*, before the cause for fear, etc. had ceased. If he did so, he should be made to pay a double fine of the value of the thing deposited[37] (Kāty. 601). K. also ruled that the depositor was not allowed to take from the depositary the object deposited at an improper time[38] *e.g.*, when he was involved in calamities (K. 178/7).

13. *Denial of Receiving a Deposit*

A. The positive obligations of the depositary were described above. In addition the question arose as to what had to be done in case the depositary denies the fact of receiving a deposit. This question could arise, and usually arose, when the deposit was made privately without any evidence (witnesses). Vidūṣaka in Mṛcch. (Act III-292) said to Cārudatta : "I intend to deny the whole thing; who gave anybody anything ! Who received anything from anybody ! Who was witness !".[39] The merchant Hiraṇyagupta (Ghiranyagupta) in Kath. (Tar. 4) also denied the fact of receiving a deposit, as it was given to him by Upakośa's husband not in the presence of witnesses.[40]

B. In case of denial of receiving a deposit, the depositor could sue the depositary. The judge (king), by the evidence of witnesses, oaths, or ordeals, could compel the depositary to give up the deposit and to pay a fine and if the depositor

36. *yo nikṣepaṁ yācyamāno nikṣeptur na prayacchati,*
sa yācyaḥ prāḍ-vivākena tān nikṣeptur-asan nidhau.
sākṣy abhāve praṇidhibhir vayo rūpa-samanvitaiḥ.
apadeśaiś ca saṁnyasyā hiraṇyaṁ tasya tattvataḥ. (Mn. 8. 181-2. Also quoted in Apar. *ad* Y. 2. 67, VyK. 133-4, VRK. 94, VyPr. 285, VyS. 89).

37. *grāhyasṭūtpanidhiḥ kāle kālahīnaṁ tu varjayet,*
kālahīnaṁ dadad daṇḍaṁ dviguṇaṁ ca pradāpyate. (Kāty. 601. Also quoted in Mit. *ad* Y. 2.67, VyPr. 282, VyL. 80, VT. 560).

38. Also when the depositary died, the depositor should not ask immediately for the return of the deposit.

39. *ahaṁ kkhu avalavissaṁ; keṇa diṇṇaṁ, keṇa gahidaṁ, ko vā sakkhi tti.* (Mṛcc. 3.292-3).

40. However Upakośā, using some tricks, described in Kath., procured witnesses.

claimed a deposit that he never deposited, to punish him. This was in particular, evident from Bṛh. (XI-14) where evidence of witnesses, or ordeal was clearly stated. Certainly the easiest way was to prove the handling over of a deposit by evidence of witnesses, where this was impossible the judge had to collect the antecedent circumstances of the deposit and the character and social position of the depositor (K. 180/7 sqq.). Then, if the object deposited was not restored precisely in the same condition as it was delivered, an ordeal had to take place (N. II-6).[41] Bṛh. (XI-15) also ruled that in case of such a dispute an ordeal was ordained for both parties, to establish the facts of the case.[42] N. (I-241) enumerated *expressis verbis*, in the chapter on ordeals the denial of a deposit as one of the events when proof by ordeal took place.[43]

In another place Bṛh. (IV-14, 15) ruled that he who did not return the deposit had to be tested by oaths or ordeals, but if the depositary appropriated the object deposited, the king should test him by ordeal even though there be witnesses. Also N. (II-4) enumerated ordeals and other modes of proof and Mn. (VIII-190) declared most generally :

nikṣepasyā-pahttāram anikṣeptāram eva ca,
sarvai rupāyair anvicchecha pathais caiva vaidikaiḥ.

(Also quoted in SC. 182, SCM. 15, VyPr. 284, VyS. 89).

Hence, Mn. stated that all methods, including oaths and ordeals, could be used in order to prove either the fact of handing over a deposit to the depositary, or of claiming by the depositor a deposit that he never deposited. To find the truth all methods were admissible.

C. The groundless denial of having received a deposit was, first of all, a crime from the religious point of view. This offence was equal to "theft of gold" (Mn. XI-57,

41. *sa punar dvividhaḥ proktaḥ sākṣimān itaras tathā,*
pratidānaṁ tathaivāsya pratyayaḥ syād viparyaye (N. 2. 6. Also quoted in Apar. *ad* Y. 2. 65, VyK. 131, SC. 3, VRK. 85, VCi. 36, SCM. 14, VV. 130, VyS. 88, VVy 31).

42. *raho datte nidhau yatra visaṁvādaḥ prajāyate,*
vibhāvakaṁ tatra divyam ubhayor api ca smṛtam. (Bṛh. 11.15. Also quoted in Apar. *ad.* Y.2.67. VyK. 134, SC. 181, VRK. 95, SCM. 15, SV. 269, VyPr. 284, BBh. *ad* Y. 2.67, VyS. 89).

43. *araṇye nirjane rātrā'vantar veśmani sāhase,*
nyāsasyā pahṇave caiva divyā saṁbhavati kriyā. (N. 1. 241).

Y. III-230, B. II-1, 2, 3,Vi. XXXVI-4) and caused loss of caste (*patanīya*) according to B. (II-1, 2, 1). B. (II-1, 2, 10) and Vi. (LII) prescribed for this offence special penalties. From the point of view of civil law, such an act was also equal to the crime of theft, and the depositary, if guilty, had to be punished as a thief (*rājñā-cauravacchāsya*—Vi. V-170[44]). The same was also Mn.'s and Matsyapurāṇa's opinion. We read in Mn. (VIII-191) :

yo nikṣepaṁ nārpayati yaś cāni 'nikṣipya yācate.
tāv ubhau cauravacchāsyau dāpyau vā tat samaṁ damam.

(Also quoted in Apar. *ad* Y. 2.67, VyK. 132, 133, SC. 181, VRK. 91, VCi. 39, SCM. 15, VyPr. 284, VyM. 84. VT. 556. VV. 133, VyS. 89, VVy. 32).

Hence Mn. ruled here that in case of such an offence as far as *nikṣepa* was concerned, the depositary[45] had to be punished like a thief (sometimes *lex tallionis* had to be applied), or be made to pay a fine equal in value to the denied deposit. In the next para (VIII-192) we read :

nikṣepasyā'paharttāraṁ sat samaṁ dāpayed damam.
tatho'panidhi-hartārām aviśeṣeṇa pārthivaḥ.

(Also quoted in VyK. 32, SC. 80; VRK. 92, VyPr. 283, VyM. 85, VT. 561, VyS. 88).

According to Mn., therefore, in case of *nikṣepa* as well as of *upanidhi* the depositary should be made to pay a fine equal to the denied deposit. These two paras are confusing. In this connection the following extracts from Medh.'s commentary on Mn. (VIII-192) should be quoted: "The preceding verse had laid down the punishment to be like that of the thief; under that rule there are two alternatives—corporal punishment and fine equal in value to the property involved—to be determined according to the caste of the accused. In the case of castes other than the Brāhmaṇa, it would be open to the king to inflict either of the two forms of punishment.... It will not be right to take the present verse as precluding corporal punishment from the case of Brāhmaṇas,

44. In M. N. Dutt's translation.
45. The depositor also had to be punished like a thief, if he was found guilty.

who also would be subject to both kinds of alternative punishment sanctioned by the preceding verse. Because corporal punishment has been already generally prohibited in the case of Brāhmaṇas; in such texts as "one shall not strike a Brāhmaṇa"[46]

Also Bṛh. (XI-14) and N. (II-4), according to Asahāya's commentary, ruled that the depositary should return the object deposited and pay a fine equal in value to the denied deposit. This commentary followed from the interpretation of N. (II-7). where it was stated that the depositor had to be punished by the king.

Mn. (VIII-193) contained a third, also confusing, para relating to the same question. We read there.

upadhābhiś ca yaḥ kaścit paradravyaṁ haren naraḥ,
sasahāyaḥ sa haṁtavyaḥ prakāśaṁ vividhair vadhaiḥ.

(Also quoted in VyK. 132, VRK. 92, VCi. 39, DV. 114. SV. 269, Vīr. *ad* Y. 2.67. VV. 133. VyS. 151, VVy. 32).

"He who by false pretences may appropriate the property of another person, shall by publicly punished along with his accomplices by various modes of corporal chastisements." It is not clear whether this para related to deposits. Taking into consideration the context and the possibility of using false pretences in case of denial of receiving a deposit, we could admit that this para could be applied to deposits if *e. g.*, the depositary should state that he did not remember where he kept the object deposited, or that it was kept by another person who left the place, and so forth. By using such false excuses the depositary could be condemned to cutting of his hands, feet, etc. (*lex tallionis*), or even to decapitation, or to another form of death (impaling, trampling to death by elephants, etc.)[47].

Similar, but somewhat different, was K.'s opinion on this subject. There it was stated that if the depositary sold the object deposited, certainly after its appropriation, he should restore four times its value and pay fine five times the stipulated value, and if it was exchanged for another one its value should be paid (K. 178/7 sqq.).

46. According to G. N. Jhā's translation (VIII 380).
47. K. (180/7 sqq.) adds that if the depositary hands over an *upanidhi* to another than the real depositor, he shall be punished.

If the depositary retained only the object deposited, he had to restore it with interest (Vi. V-169)[48].

14. *Depositor's Claims for Deposits never Deposited*

It was also stipulated that the judge (king) should by all sorts of means and oaths (that means also by ordeals) punish depositors claiming as a deposit what they never deposited (Mn. VIII-190). If it were proved that the depositor claimed an object he never deposited, he should be punished like a thief or be made to pay a fine equal in value to the object deposited, according to Mn. (VIII-191; similarly Matsya-purāṇa). Vi. (V-171) and N. (II-13) state that the depositor had to be punished in the same way as a thief; N. added that he had to be made to pay a sum equal to the value of the object deposited. These rules were quite the same as those relating to depositaries.

15. *Use of the Object Deposited*

All kinds of contracts of deposits, with the exception of the *yācita* deposit,—which, from the point of view of civil law, was not a proper contract of deposit,[49] contained the general rule that the thing deposited could not be used by the depositary without the consent of the depositor. The use of the object deposited without this consent constituted a *furtum—a furtum usus*.

This rule was clearly stated in N., Bṛh. K. Y., Vy. and others.

yaṁ cā'rthaṁ sādhayet tena nikṣeptur ananujñayā,
tatrā'pi daṇḍyaḥ sa bhaved dāpyas tac cā'pi sodayam.

(N. 2.8. Also quoted in NMS. 3.5., VyK. 132, VRK. 90., VCi. 38/9, VCa. 32, VyPr. 283, VV. 132, VyS. 88).

nyāsadravyeṇa yaḥ kaścit sādhayet kāryam ātmanaḥ,
daṇḍyaḥ sa rājño bhavati dāpyas tac cā'pi sodayam

(Bṛh. 11.13. Also quoted in VyK. 132, SC. 180, VRK. 91, VV. 133. VyS. 88).

48. *nikṣepā pahāry-artha-vṛddhi-sahitaṁ dhanaṁ dhanikasya dāpyaḥ*. Also in M. N. Dutt's edition (5. 164; see above).

49. Cf. above Study I. on Different Types of Deposits.

upanidhi-bhoktā deśa-kālā-nurūpaṁ bhogavetanaṁ dadyāt; dvādaśa paṇaṁ ca daṇḍam. (K. 178. 1-2).

ājīvan svecchayā daṇḍyo dāpyas taṁ cā'pi sodayam.

(Y. 2.67. Also quoted in SC. 180, SV. 490, VyPr. 283 VyU. 80, VyM. 85, VT. 560, VyS. 88, AP. 254.27).

All these four sources of law state the same in different words. They declared that if the depositary used (made a living *ājivati*, or the like) the thing deposited with him without the permission of the depositor (*svecchayā*, or the like) he should be punished.[50] The legal consequences of the interdiction of the use of the object deposited varied; according to N. (II-8), the depositor had to restore the profit with interest. Similarly in Bṛh. and Y. According to K., the depositary had to pay the *bhogaveteṇa* (compensation) which would be fixed after considering the circumstances of the place and time, as well as a fine of 12 *paṇas*. According to Raj., there was no compensation, but Raj. (VIII-155/6) quoted a sentence of the king who declared that the depositary who used the money deposited with him ought to pay interest on the full amount of money deposited with him from the time of its being deposited, similarly to the depositor who had to pay interest on what he had taken from the depositary (compensation). In this sentence the king took into consideration "circumstances of the place and time" and of the whole affair.

Similar to the rule found in K., and quoted above, was Mit's commentary. We read there :

ājīvan nupabhuṅkte vyavaharati vā prayogādinā labhā'rtham asāvupabhogānusāreṇa lābhānusareṇa ca daṇḍyas taṁ co'panidhiṁ sodayam-upabhoge savṛddhikaṁ vyavahāre salābhaṁ dhaniṇe dāpyaḥ.

(Mit. *ad* Y. 2.67, p. 163/12-14). Mit. also rightly interpreted the word *svecchayā*—"of his own will" as without the permission of the owner. Ratnākara *ad* Bṛh. (Col. 446) stated *a contrario*, that the depositor's consent must be attested and that with the permission of the depositor the use of the object deposited by the depositary was permitted.[51]

50. Similarly Vy. in Viv. p. 25.

51. Y. (II-238) states similarly, referring this rule to a *nejakaḥ* (washerman), that the washerman is not allowed to use any clothes given to him in deposit (*yācita*). Should he use them, then he has to pay a fine of ten *paṇas*. Similarly Mn. (VIII-396); see also N. (IX-8).

16. *Usucapio, Praescriptio, Compensatio and Other Cases*

It was explained before that, according to the ancient Indian law, the object deposited was not in the possession of the depositary, but in his detention. The depositary had only the *animus rem alteri habendi.* Therefore, even then if the object deposited was with him for several years, even twenty or thirty years, it was not liable to usucapio. The depositary could not prove his *bona fides.*

This is the explanation for almost identical rules found in Mn. (VIII-149), N. (I-81). Vās. (XVI-18), Y. (II-25), and similarly in K. (191/2). We read there :

ādhiḥ sīmā bāladhanaṁ nikṣepo'panidhī striyaḥ,
rājasvaṁ śrotriyasvaṁ ca na bhogena praṇaśyati.

(Mn. 8. 149).

Hence deposits (*nikṣepo'panidhi*, in K. *upanidhi* and *nikṣepa*, in Y. *upanikṣepa*) as well as boundaries, pledges, etc. were not lost by adverse possession, i.e. were not liable to usucapio. This rule was so clear and well-known in ancient India that in Raj. (VIII) the merchant, who used different tricks in order not to return the object deposited with him for twenty, or thirty years (VIII-126), did not object to it, and did not even try to declare the acquisition of the object deposited by usucapio. He also did not make any reservation saying that the depositor could not demand the return of the object deposited because of lapse of time (plea of limitation). That also shows that *praescriptio temporis* was unknown to ancient Indian law, as far as deposits were concerned. That seems to be also evident from the fact that the *praescriptio longi temporis* was not mentioned in the Smṛti-s. However, it is evident from Raj. (VIII-135 sqq.) that *compensatio* was admissible.[52]

Other rules, in particular, those relating to debts, could be applied to deposits when special rules relating to deposits did not exist (K. 177/13).

52. For special rules relating to *śilpinyāsa* see Kāty. (603 sqq.) and Bṛh (XI-16 sqq.). From the legal point of view, they did not have, much in common with deposits.

III

CONTRACT OF DEPOSIT IN SOME NON-JURIDICAL SOURCES IN CLASSICAL SANSKRIT*

I. MENTIONS OF CONTRACTS OF DEPOSITS IN NON-JURIDICAL SOURCES

1. *The story of the stolen jewels (Mṛcchakaṭika and Cārudatta)*

1. The subject of Śūdraka's Mṛcchakaṭika and of Cārudatta, attributed to Bhāsa (the original of Mṛcchakaṭika, or an abridgment thereof) was based on the contract of deposit. This contract formed the principal thread of these dramas.

2. The first act of Mṛ., called *alaṁkāraṇyāsa*, gave the impulse to the whole drama. Vasantasenā informed Cārudatta in this act that she would entrust[1] her jewels to his house.[2] When Cārudatta said that his house was not worthy of trust,[3] Vasantasenā replied that it was to men that treasures were entrusted[4] and not to houses[5]. Maitreya, who took the jewels, thought that they were presented to Cārudatta who lost his money, but Cārudatta made it clear that the jewels were only entrusted[6] to him[7] for a short time[8] after which he ought to restore them to Vasantasenā;[9] then Maitreya interjected that

* Previously appeared as JSAIL. 19 in the "Journal of the American Oriental Society". Vol. 72, pp. 145-54, Vol. 73, pp. 16-26. Submitted to the 162nd meeting of the American Oriental Society in Boston, Cambridge and Waltham, Mass., April 1952.

1. *Nikṣepa.*
2. *Ajja ! Jai evvaṁ ahaṁ ajjassa aṇuggejjhā, tā icche ahaṁ imaṁ alaṁkāraaṁ ajjassa gehe ṇikkhividuṁ* (Mr. 45. 8-10).
3. *Nyāsa.*
4. *Nyāsa.*
5. Cārudattaḥ—*ayogyam idaṁ nyāsasya gṛham.*
   Vasantasenā—*ajja ! aliaṁ. Purisesu ṇāsā ṇkkhiviaṁti, ṇa uṇa gehesu* (Mr. 45. 14-6).
6. *Nyāsa.*
7. Vidūṣakaḥ—(*Gṛhītvā*) *sotthi bhodie.*
   Cārudattaḥ— *Dhiṅ mūrkha ! Nyāsaḥ khalv ayam* (Mr. 45-21-2).
8. Cārudattaḥ—*acireṇaiva kālena* (Mr. 46-3).
9. Cārudattaḥ—*Niryātayiṣye* (Mr. 46.6).

thieves may take them[11] and that the jewels entrusted[12] by Vasantasenā to Cārudatta were 'ours.'[13]

3. In Cār. this problem was described in a similar manner. There Vasantasenā (the courtezan) left her jewels with Cārudatta (the hero).[14] Maitreya (Vidūṣaka) took them and gave them to Radanikā with the order to keep them till the sixth and seventh day, while he was to take them on the eighth day—a holiday.[15] Radanikā handed over the jewels to Maitreya on the eighth day.[16] Maitreya was prepared then for the actual theft.[17]

In Cār. Vasantasenā explained why she entrusted the jewels to Cārudatta. She wanted to find a reason to go to his home, since Cārudatta was shy of frequenting her home because of his loss of wealth. She left the jewels with him because if she went all of a sudden to his house and he could not give her a present, she might not be able to see him again. On the other hand, if the jewels were deposited with him, she always had a pretext for visiting Cārudatta.[18]

4. In the third act of Mṛ., Radanikā discovered that a thief cut a hole in the wall of the house and escaped. She informed accordingly Maitreya[19] who remembered that the jewels were entrusted by Vasantasenā and that he gave them to Cāru-

11. Vidūṣakaḥ—(*Apavārya*) *Jaï evvaṁ tā corehiṁ avahariadu* (Mr. 46.1).

12. *Viṇyāsa.*

13. Vidūṣakaḥ—*Eso se amhāṇaṁ viṇṇāso* (Mr. 46.4).

14. *jai me ayyo pasaṇṇo, aaṁ me aḷaṅkāro iha evva ciṭṭhadu. aḷaṅkāraṇimittaṁ pāvā maṁ aṇusaranti* (Cār. 211.21.2).

15. Vidūṣakaḥ—(*Gṛhītvā*) *Radaṇie* ! *Gahṇa edaṁ suvaṇṇālaṇkāraṁ tuvaṁ. Saṭṭhīe sattamīe a dhārehī. Ahaṁ aṭṭhamīe aṇaddhāe dhāraissaṁ* (Cār. 212. 7.8)

16. Ceṭī—*Iaṁ suvaṇṇabhaṇḍaṁ saṭṭhīe sattamīe pariveṭṭāmi* (or better *veṭṭhāmi*). *Aṭṭhamī khu ajja* (Cār. 226. 4-5) (*Ceṭī dattvā niṣkrāntā*) (Cār. 226. 16).

17. Vidūṣakaḥ—*Kā gai. Āṇehi gaṇhāmi corehiṁ gaṇhiamāṇaṁ* (Cār. 226. 14).

18. Ceṭī—*Kiṁ, vihavamandaddāe vasavāsappasaṅgakādaro dukkhaṁ tti jai ṇa āacche.*

Gaṇikā—*Naṁ ahaṁ taṁ kāmemi.*

Ceṭī—*Jai ettao bahumāṇo, kiṁ ṇābhisarīadi ?*

Gaṇikā—*Ṇa hu ṇa gacchāmi. Kintu sahasā abhisarido paccuaāraduḷḷabhadāe puṇo me duḷḷabho bhave tti viḷambemi.*

Ceṭī—*Haṁ, kiṁ, etaṇṇimittaṁ tahiṁ evva so aḷaṅkāro ṭhāvido ?*

Gaṇikā—*Īdisaṁ evva* ! (Cār. 215. 5-17).

19. Radanikā—(*Gatvā, satrāsam*) *Haddhī haddhī, amhāṇaṁ gehe saṁdhiṁ kappia coro ṇikkamati. Bhodu, Mitteaṁ gadua pabodhemi.* (*Vidūṣakam upagamya*) *Ajja Mittea* ! *Uṭṭhehi uṭṭhehi, Amhāṇaṁ gehe saṁdhiṁ kappia coro ṇikkaṁte* (Mṛ. 89. 12-5).

datta.[20] Cārudatta, absent-minded, was at first pleased that the thief found jewels to steal and did not go away disappointed.[21] However Maitreya reminded Cārudatta that the jewels constituted a deposit;[22] when Cārudatta realized this, he swooned.[23] Maitreya did not see the reason for it,[24] since he was not responsible for the objects deposited when they were stolen. But Cārudatta, coming to, said:[25]

Who will believe the truth !
Suspicion now is sure.
This world will show no ruth
To the inglorious poor.
Alas ! If envious fate before
Has wooed my wealth alone,
Why should she seek my store
Of virtue as her own ?[26]

Maitreya, recognizing Cārudatta's arguments, suggested that it be denied that the deposit was given and received by Cārudatta, since no witnesses could be summoned.[27] Cārudatta could not agree to this proposal and promised to repay Vasantasenā for the stolen deposit.[28]

20. Vidūṣakaḥ—*Bho ! Kadhaṁ taṁ jjeva corahadaaṁ aṇusocasi ? Teṇa ciṁtidaṁ mahaṁtaṁ edaṁ gehaṁ. Ido raaṇabhaṁḍaaṁ suaṇṇabhaṁḍaaṁ vā ṇikkāmissaṁ. (Smṛtvā, saviṣādamātmagatam) Kahiṁ taṁ suvaṇṇabhamḍaaṁ. (Punaranusmṛtya, prakāśam) Bho va assa ! Tumaṁ savvakālaṁ bhaṇāsi—"Mukkho Mitteao, apaṁḍido Mitteao" tti. Suṭṭhu mae kidaṁ taṁ suvaṇṇabhamḍaaṁ bhavado hatthe samappaaṁteṇa. Aṇṇadhā dāsīe putteṇa avahidaṁ bhave* (Mṛ. 91 5-11).

21. Cārudattaḥ—......*Vayasya ? Diṣṭyā te priyaṁ nivedayāmi.*
Vidūṣakaḥ—*Kiṁ ṇa avahidaṁ ?*
Cārudattaḥ—*Hṛtam.*
Vidūsakaḥ—*Tadhā vi kiṁ piaṁ ?*
Cārudattaḥ—*Yadasau kṛtārtho gataḥ* (Mr. 92. 1-6.)

22. *Nyāsa.*

23. Vidūṣakaḥ—*Ṇāso khu so.*
Cārudattaḥ—*kathaṁ nyāsaḥ ?* (*Mohamupagataḥ*) (Mr. 92. 7-8)

24. Vidūṣakaḥ—*Samassasadu bhavaṁ. Jai ṇāso coreṇa avahido tumaṁ kiṁ mohaṁ uvagado ?* (Mṛ. 92. 9-10).

25. According to A. W. Ryder's translation.

26. Cārudattaḥ—(*Samāśvasya*) *Vayasya !*
kaḥ śraddhāsyati bhūtārthaṁ sarvo māṁ tulayiṣyati.
śaṅkanīyā hi loke'sminniṣpratāpā daridratā (24).
bhoḥ ! Kaṣṭam,—yadi tāvat kṛtāntena praṇayo'rtheṣu me kṛtaḥ,
kim idānīṁ nṛśaṁsena cāritram api dūṣitam ? (25) (Mṛ. 92. 12-7).

27. Vidūsakaḥ—*Ahaṁ khu avalavissaṁ—"Keṇa diṇṇaṁ. keṇa gahidaṁ, vā sakkhi" tti* (Mṛ. 92.18-9).

28. Cārudattaḥ—*Ahamidānīmanṛtam abhidhāsye ?*
Bhaikṣyeṇāpyarjayiṣyāmi purnar nyāsapratikriyām,
enṛtaṁ nābhidhāsyāmi cāritrabhraṁśakāraṇam (26) (Mṛ. 93. 1-3).

Radanikā informed Cārudatta's wife that the jewels which belonged to Vasantasenā were stolen.[29] Cārudatta's wife, afraid that people might suspect Cārudatta of stealing the jewels, because of his poverty, offered her husband her only necklace[30] which Cārudatta reluctantly accepted, praising the generosity of his wife.[31] He then ordered Maitreya to take the necklace to Vasantasenā, to explain to her that he gambled away her jewels and to ask her to accept the necklace in the place of the deposited jewels.[32] When Maitreya suggested that Cārudatta should not give the very expensive necklace of his wife for the cheap things that were stolen,[33] Cārudatta replied : [34]

She showed her trust in leaving us[35] *her treasure,*
The price of confidence has no less measure ![36]

5. In the fourth act of Mṛ., Śarvilaka, the thief who stole the jewels from Cārudatta's house, being in love with Madanikā, Vasantasenā's maid, wanted to give the jewels to Vasantasenā as the ransom price for Madanikā, but she recognized the jewels as those which Vasantasenā deposited[37] with Cārudatta.[38] Alarmed about Cārudatta's fate, Madanikā suggested that Śarvilaka pretend he was a

29. Radanikā—*Tā jāva ajjā dhūdāe gadua ṇivedemi* (Mṛ. 93.4).

30. Ceṭī—...*kiṁ tu jo so vessājaṇakerako alaṁkarao so avahido* (Mr. 93. 10-1).
Vadhūḥ—"......*Saṁpadaṁ ujjaiṇīe jaṇo evvaṁ maṁtaissadi—daliddadāe ajjaütteṇa jjeva īdisaṁ akajjaṁ aṇuciṭṭhidaṁ" tti.* (*Ūrdhvamavalokya, niḥśvasya ca*) *Bhaavaṁ kaaṁta ! Pokkharavattapaḍidajalabiṁducaṁcalehiṁ kīlasi daliddapurisabhāagheehim. Iaṁ ca me ekkā mādugharaladdhā raaṇāvalī ciṭṭhadi* (Mṛ. 93. 17-20)

31. Cārudattaḥ—.....*kaṣṭam, idānīmasmi daridraḥ.*
ātmabhāgyakṣatadravyaḥ strīdravyeṇānukampitaḥ.
arthataḥ puruṣo nārī yā nārī sā'rthataḥ pumān (27).
athavā, nāhaṁ daridraḥ; yasya mama
vibhavānugatā bhāryā sukhaduḥkhasuhṛd bhavān,
satyaṁ ca na paribhraṣṭaṁ yaddaridreṣu durlabham (28) (Mṛ. 95. 15-21).

32. Cārudattaḥ—*Maitreya ! Gaccha ratnāvalīmādāya Vasantasenāyāḥ sakāśam. Vaktabyā ca sā madvacanāt—"yatkhalvasmābhiḥ suvarṇabhāṇḍamātmīyamiti kṛtvā visrambhāddyūte hāritam; tasya kṛte gṛhyatāmiyaṁ rāmavali" iti* (Mṛ. 95. 22.5).

33. Vidūṣakaḥ—*Mā dāva akkhāidassa abhutassa appamullassa corehiṁ avahidassa kāraṇādo catuḥsamuddasārabhūdā raaṇāvalī dīadi* (Mṛ. 96. 1-2).

34. According to A. W. Ryder's translation.

35. *Nyāsa*

36. *yaṁ samālambya viśvāsaṁ nyāso'smāsu tayā kṛtaḥ*
tasyaitanmahato mūlyaṁ pratyayasyaiva dīyate (29) (Mṛ. 96. 6-7

37. *Vinikṣipta.*

38. Madanikā—*Sa ca tassa ajjassa hatthe viṇikkhitto* (Mṛ. 107.:

servant of Cārudatta and gave the jewels to Vasantasenā,[39] since then Cārudatta would not be considered a thief and thus would have discharged his obligation and Vasantasenā would get her jewels back.[40] Śarvilaka, following that advice, returned the jewels in the name of Cārudatta.[41]

Maitreya then saw Vasantasenā so as to carry out Cārudatta's errand.[42] Vasantasenā decided to take the jewels given to her by Maitreya, and not yet to show him the stolen jewels; she then informed Maitreya that she would visit Cārudatta.[43]

6. In the fifth act of Mṛ., Maitreya, who had been under the impression that the only aim of courtezans, and thus of Vasantasenā, was to gain money irrespective of means,[44] in giving an account to Cārudatta of his errand, repeated his reservations as to the behaviour of Vasantasenā.[45] When Vasantasenā arrived in Cārudatta's house, Maitreya said again that she being dissatisfied with his wife's necklace, was coming for something more;[46] his conviction was strengthened when the maid informed him that Vasantasenā was coming to

39. Madanikā—*Tassa jjeva ajjassa kerao bhavia edaṁ alaṁkāraaṁ ajjaāe uvaṇ'hi* (Mṛ. 108- 16-7).

40. Madanikā—*Tumaṁ dāva acoro, so vi ajjo ariṇo, ajjaāe sakaṁ alaṁkāraaṁ uvagadaṁ bhodi* (Mṛ. 109. 2-3.)

41 Śarvilakaḥ—*Sārthavāhas tvāṁ vijñāpayati—"jarjaratvād gṛhasya dūrakṣyam idaṁ bhāṇḍam; tad gṛhyatām"* (Mṛ. 110. 12-3).

42. Vidūṣakaḥ—*Mae taṁ suvaṇṇabhaṁḍaaṁ vissaṁbhādo attaṇakeraketti kadua jūde hāridaṁ. So a sahiɔ rāavatthahārī ṇa jāṇīadi kahiṁ gado tti* (Mṛ. 128.5-7).

Vidūṣakaḥ—*Tā tassa kāraṇādo geṇhadu bhodī emaṁ raaṇāvaliṁ?* (Mṛ. 128. 14).

Vasantasenā—(*Ātmagatam*) *Kiṁ daṁsemi taṁ alaṁkāraaṁ?* (*Vicintya*) *Adhavā ṇa dāva.*

Vidūṣakaḥ—*Kiṁ dāva ṇa geṇhadi bhodī edaṁ raaṇāvaliṁ?* (Mṛ. 128. 16-9)

43. Vasantasenā—(*Vihasya, sakhīmukhaṁ paśyantī*) *Mittea! Kadhaṁ ṇa geṇhissaṁ raaṇāvaliṁ?* (*Iti gṛhītvā pārśve sthāpayati, svagatam*) *Kadhaṁ jhīṇakusumādo vi sahaārapādavādo maaraṁdobiṁdao ṇivaḍaṁti?* (*Prakāśam*) *Ajja! Viṇṇavehi taṁ jūdiaram mama vaaṇeṇa Ajjacārudattaṁ—"ahaṁ pi padoso ajjaṁ pekkhiduṁ gacchāmi" tti* (Mṛ. 128. 20-129. 1).

44. Cf. L. Sternbach, *Gaṇikā-dharma-saṁgraha* (Hoshiarpur 1952).

45. Cārudattaḥ—*Vayasya! Kathaya tatkāryam.*
Vidūṣakaḥ—*Taṁ khu kajjaṁ viṇaṭṭaṁ.*
Cārudattaḥ—*Kiṁ tayā na gṛhītā ratnāvalī?*
Vidūṣakaḥ—*Kudo amhāṇaṁ ettiaṁ bhāadheaṁ? ṇavaṇaliṇakomalaṁ aṁjaliṁ matthae kadua paḍicchiā* (Continued as in notes 33 and 36) (Mṛ. 132. 20-133. 12).

46. Vidūṣakaḥ—*mae jāṇidaṁ. Appamullā raaṇāvalī, bahumullaṁ suvaṇṇabhaṁḍaaṁ tti ṇa parituṭṭā avaraṁ maggiduṁ āadā* (Mṛ. 140. 8-9).

ask about the value of the necklace.[47] The maid returned the jewels to Cārudatta[48] and, when Vasantasenā reproached Cārudatta for being wrong in showing his distrust of her by sending the necklace, Cārudatta again voiced his apprehension that nobody would believe the truth, since he lost his wealth.[49]

The whole story was briefly repeated in the ninth act of Mṛ. before the judge. There, Vasantasenā's mother, in order to show Cārudatta's magnanimity, stated that when Vasantasenā left the jewels as a deposit[50] in Cārudatta's house and when they were stolen, Cārudatta gave a very expensive necklace in place of them.[51]

7. In Cār. the story was identical, though narrated more simply. Maitreya informed Cārudatta that the jewels were stolen.[52] Cārudatta, afraid that no one would believe the truth,[53] accepted a very expensive necklace from his wife which he orderd to be given to Vasantasenā to recompense her for the loss of her own jewels,[54] as the price of that great confidence which

47. Ceṭī—*esā khu ajjaā evvaṁ pucchiduṁ āadā—"kettiaṁ tāe raaṇāvalīe mullaṁ" tti.*

Vidūṣakaḥ—(*janāntikam*) *bho ! Bhaṇidaṁ mae—jadhā appamullā raaṇāvalī, bahumullaṁ suvaṇṇabhaṁḍaaṁ. Na parituṭṭā avaraṁ maggiduṁ āadā* (Mr. 149. 2-7).

48. Ceṭī—*ajja ! vaṁcidosi diṭṭīe. Taṁ jjevva edaṁ suvaṇṇabhaṁḍaaṁ* (Mr. 149. 23).

49. Vasantasenā—*ajja Cārudatta ! Juttaṁ ṇṇedaṁ imāe raaṇāvalīe imaṁ 'aṇaṁ tulaiduṁ.*

Cārudattaḥ—(*savilakṣasmitam*) *Vasantasene ! paśya paśya.*
kaḥ śraddhāsyati bhūtārthaṁ sarvo māṁ tulayiṣyati.
śaṅkanīyā hi loke'smin niṣpratāpā daridratā (43) (Mṛ. 152. 4-9).

50. *Nyāsa.*

51. Vṛddhā—........*jo tadāṇiṁ ṇāsīkidaṁ suvaṇṇabhaṁḍaaṁ rattiṁ corehiṁ ıvahidaṁ tti tassa kāraṇādo cadussamuddasārabhūdaṁ raaṇāvaliṁ dedi, so dāṇiṁ atthakallavattasa kālaṇādo imaṁ akajjaṁ karedi ? Hā jāde ! Ehi me putti !* (Mṛ. 244. 15-8).

52. Vidūṣakaḥ—*dāṇiṁ me hatthe paḍicchidu attabhavaṁ* (Cār. 232. 12).

53. Nāyakaḥ—(*ātmagatam*).
kaḥ śraddhāsyati bhūtārthaṁ sarvo māṁ tulayiṣyati.
śaṅkanīyā hi doṣeṣu niṣprabhāvā daridratā (15) (Cār. 232. 14-6).

54. Brāhmaṇī—......*mama ññādikuḷādo ḷaddhà ṣadasahassamuḷḷā muttāvaḷī. Taṁ pi ayyaütto soḍhīradāe paḍicchādi ! Bhodu, evaṁ dāva karissaṁ* (Cār. 233. 7-12.)

Brāhmaṇī—......*ayyametteaṁ saddāvehi* (Cār. 234. 1).
Brāhmaṇī—*ayyamettea ! imaṁ paḍiggahaṁ paḍiganha.*
Vidūṣakaḥ—*avatthāviruddho khu aaṁ padāṇavibhavo. kudo edassa āgamo ?*
Brāhmaṇī—*ṇaṁ saṭṭhiṁ uvavasāmi. savvasāravībhaveṇa baṁhaṇeṇa sotthi vāidavvaṁ ti eso imassa āgamo.*
Vidūṣakaḥ—*aṭṭhamī khu ajja.*
Brāhmaṇī—*pamādādo adikkamo kido. ajja pūā ṇivvattīadi.*

(Continued on next page)

inspired Vasantasenā to make the deposit[55] with him.[56] In the fourth act of Cār. Maitreya informed Vasantasenā that in gambling he lost the jewels deposited[57] with him[58] and asked her to accept instead the necklace of Cārudatta's wife[59] which she did.[60]

In Cār. the conversation between Madanikā and Śarvilaka (Sajjalaka), in which Madanikā discovered that Śarvilaka stole the jewels from Cārudatta's house, is missing, as well as the plot element in which Madanikā convinced Śarvilaka to pretend to return the jewels in the name of Cārudatta. In Cār. it was stated only that Vasantasenā accepted the stolen jewels from Śarvilaka[61] and decided to take them to Cārudatta's house.[62] The fourth and the last act Cār. ended with this story.

2. *The story of the Mice that Ate Iron* (*Pañcatantra, Kathāsaritsāgara, Śukasaptati t.s., Bṛhatkathāmañjarī.*

Vidūṣakaḥ—*aṇaṇurūvadāe padāṇassa aṇukkoso via paḍibhādi.* (*Janāntikam*) (Mṛ. 234. 7-20).
Vidūṣakaḥ—......(*Upagamya*) *bho* ! *idaṁ.*
Nāyakaḥ—*kim etat* ?
Vidūṣakaḥ—*sarisakuḷadārasaṅgahassa phaḷaṁ.*
Nāyakaḥ—*kiṁ brāhmaṇī māṁ anukampate.*
Vidūṣakaḥ—*evaṁ via.*
Nāyakaḥ—*dhig ātmānam. adya hato'smi.*
mayi dravyakṣayakṣīṇe strīdravyeṇānukampitaḥ,
arthataḥ puruṣo nārī yā nārī sārthataḥ pumān(17).
Vidūṣakaḥ—*tattahodī hiaeṇa tumaṁ yācedi. ahaṁ sīseṇa yācemi gaṇha edaṁ.*
Nāyakaḥ—*tathā.* (*gṛhītvā*) *vayasya* ! *imāṁ muktāvalīṁ gṛhītvā Vasantasenāyāḥ sakāśaṁ gaccha.*
artheṣu kāmam upalabhya manoratho me
strīṇāṁ dhaneṣv anucitaṁ praṇayaṁ karoti;
māne ca kāryakaraṇe ca vilambamāno
dhig bhoḥ ! *ku'aṁ ca puruṣasya daridratāṁ ca* (18).
Vidūṣakaḥ—*aho appamuḷḷassa suvaṇṇabhaṇḍaassa kide sadasahassamuḷḷā muttāvaḷī ṇiādaidavvā* (Cār. 235. 13-236. 8).

55 *Nyāsa.*

56. Nāyakaḥ—*vayasya* ! *mā maivam.*
yaṁ samūlakṣya viśvāsaṁ nyāso'smāsu kṛtas tayā.
tasy aitan mahato mūlyaṁ pratyayasya pradīyatām (19) (Cār. 236. 10-2).

57. *Nikṣipta* (*ṇikkhitto*).

58. Vidūṣakaḥ—*suṇādu bhodī. tattahodo Cārudattassa guṇappaccāaṇaṇimittaṁ khu tue aḷaṅkāro tahiṁ ṇikkhitto. So teṇa jūde hārido* (Car. 244 15-7)

59. Vidūṣakaḥ—*tado tassa aḷaṅkārassa muḷḷabhūdaṁ imam muttāvaḷiṁ paḍicchadu bhodī* (Cār. 244. 20-1).

60. Gaṇikā—(*gṛhītvā*) *paḍicchidaṁ tae tti ayyo ṇivededu* (Cār. 245. 4).

61. Gaṇikā—*ahaṁ jāṇāmi, tassa gehe sāhasaṁ karia āṇīdo aaṁ aḷaṅkāro. tassa guṇāṇi aṇukampedu ayyo* (Cār. 246. 15-6).

62. Gaṇikā—*ehi imaṁ aḷaṅkāraṁ gaṇhia ayyacārudattaṁ abhisarissāmo* (Cār. 247. 17-8).

8. In Pañc. we find a story called The Mice that Ate Iron. This story in all the most important versions is almost identical.[63]

According to this tale, a merchant (Nāḍuka)[64], who intended to leave his country, deposited[65] a balance made of iron which weighed a thousand *pala-s* with another merchant (Lakṣmaṇa).[66] After having returned, he asked for the balance which he deposited[67] with Lakṣmaṇa but the latter replied that the balance was eaten by mice. Then Nāḍuka hid Lakṣmaṇa's son in a friend's house[68] and, when Lakṣmaṇa inquired where his son was, Nāḍuka replied that a falcon carried him off. The case was brought by Lakṣmaṇa before the judge to whom Nāḍuka explained :

Where mice eat balance-beams of iron
A thousand palas in weight,
A hawk might steal an elephant;
A boy is trifling freight.[69]

9. The same story was repeated in Kath.,[70] Śuk. t.s.,[71] and Bṛ. Kath.[72] However, Kath. and Śuk. t.s. used other expressions[73] for the act of depositing the iron balance.[74] In

63. P. 1.15; PHT. 1.17; PHP. 1.28 ; PBK. 1.21; PK. 1.21.
64. Or merchant's son.
65. *Nikṣepa.*
66. Or merchants son. *Sa* (*cā*) *'nyasmin vaṇikputrake tāṁ nikṣipya deśāntaram* (*arthopārjanāya*) *prāyāt* (P. 1. 565). *so'nyasmin vaṇikputrake tāṁ nikṣipya deśāntaram arthopārjanāya prāyāt* (PHT. 1.17; p. 50. 20-1). *Tāṁ ca śreṣṭhi-Lakṣmaṇasya nikṣepabhūtāṁ kṛtvā deśāntaraṁ prasthitaḥ* (PHP. 1.28; p. 114.20). *tāṁ ca kasyacid vaṇijo gṛhe nikṣepabhūtāṁ kṛtvā deśāntaraṁ prasthitaḥ* (PBK. 1.21; p. 89. 10-1), In PK. (1.21; p. 99. 25-100.1) instead of *kasyacid vaṇijo—śreṣṭhinān dukasya.*
67. *Sa ca mandabhāgyālaya* (*bahunā'pi kālena*) *na kiṁcit prāpya pratyāgatas* (*tāṁ nikṣiptāṁ*) *tulāṁ tasmāt prārthitavān* (P. 1. 566). PHT. omits this passage. *bho Lakṣmaṇa, samarpaya me nikṣepatulām* (PHP. 1. 28; p. 114. 22-3). *bhoḥ śreṣṭhin dīyatāṁ me sā nikṣepatulā* (PBK. 1.21; p. 89. 13 and PK 1. 21 p. 100.3).
68. Or has thrown him in a mountain cave.
69. According to A. W. Ryder's translation.
70. Kath. 10. 60; 121. 238-55.
71. Śuk. t. s. 39; p. 117.
72. Bṛ. Kath. 16. 382-9.
73. *Nyāsya* (Kath.)
74. *ayaḥ-pala-sahasreṇa ghaṭitāṁ tāṁ tulāṁ ca saḥ kasyāpi vaṇijo haste nyasya deśāntaraṁ yayau* (Kath. 10. 60. 239) *yadā tu sa tulāmātradhano'bhyavat tadā'nya vaṇig-gṛhe tulāṁ muktvā deśāntaraṁ gataḥ. tatra dhanam arjayitvā nijanagaram āgatya taṁ vaṇijaṁ tulāṁ yayāce* (Śuk. t. s. 39. 117, 5-6).

Bṛ. Kath. Kṣemendra also used for the act of depositing the balance the word *nyāsa*;[75] but a few lines later, when mentioning the son of the man who had stolen his deposit,[76] the word *nikṣepa*[77] was used.

3. *The story of King Uccala* (*Rājataraṅgiṇī*)

10. In the eighth book of Rāj., Kalhaṇa described King Uccala and his reign in the beginning of the twelfth century A.D. (1101-11). He praised him for his ability to discern between right and wrong and for his wisdom. As an example of his wisdom Kalhaṇa narrated the story of a suit between a merchant and a depositor in which Uccala was able to remove a doubt which had puzzled, among others, learned judges.

According to this story, a certain wealthy man deposited[78] in the house of a merchant a hundred thousands *dīnnāra*[79] from which he took from time to time some small amounts of money.[80] After twenty or thirty years,[81] he asked the depositary[82] to return to him the amount which remained after deducting the sums he paid him out of his deposit.[83] However, the depositary, who wanted to embezzle the deposit[84] under various pretexts, delayed returning the objects deposited.[85] When the depositor persisted in his demands for the return of the deposit, the depositary, not having found other pretexts, displayed with anger his account-book in which it was

75. *purā lohasahasrāṅkāṁ nyāsīkṛtya tulāṁ vaṇik*
vaṇig-gehe ciraṁ bhrāntvā digantāt punar āyayau (Bṛ. Kath. 16. 383).
76. *tatputraṁ so'py athaikānte hṛtvā nikṣepahāriṇaḥ.*
śyenena te hṛtaḥ sūnur ity āha vikṛtānanaḥ (Bṛ. Kath. 16. 386).
77. This story is repeated in other, not only Sanskrit, versions; cf. W. N. Brown, JAOS 39. 18-9; Th. Benfey, *Pantschatantra*, Leipzig 1859. I Par. 101; *The Ocean of Story* ed. by N. M. Penzer, London 1926. 5.64 sqq.
78. *Nyāsa.*
79. *sauhṛdā gūḍhasadbhāve vyāpad aupayikaṁ dhanī,*
nyāsī-cākāra dīnnāralakṣaṁ ko'pi vaṇig gṛhe (Rāj. 8. 124).
80. *teno payujyamānā ca vyayeṣu vaṇijaḥ karāt,*
kiyaty api gṛhītābhūd āttamātrā ntarā (Rāj. 8. 125).
81. Cf. Stein's note to Rāj.'s translation 8.126.
82. *nyāsadhārin.*
83. *triṁśad viṁśāsu yātāsu samāsu nyāsadhāriṇam,*
gṛhītaśeṣaṁ dātuṁ sa dhanaṁ pārthaya tātha tam (Rāj. 8. 126).
84. *Nyāsa.*
85. *vaṇiktu kukṛtī tasya nyāsagrāsāya sodyamaḥ.*
kālāpahāram akarottaistaiḥ kaluṣadhīr miṣaiḥ (Rāj. 8. 127).

shown that the depositor had drawn from him various amounts of money (six hundred, hundred, three hundred, seven hundred *dīnnāra*, etc.), or merchandise (ghee, ginger, honey, etc.) for various purposes (tolls, leather-workers, potter-women, butter, rice-flower, beggars, etc.).[86] Thus he totalled different expenses which were difficult to keep in mind, added to the total his interest and deducted the expenses and interest from the deposit and then offered to return the deposit[87] to the depositor.[88]

At first, the depositor thought that the depositary was just, but, after thinking the matter over, brought it before the judge accusing the depositary of embezzlement.[89] Since the judges were not able to arrive at a decision, the matter was brought before King Uccala who, in order to pronounce judgment, ordered the depositary to produce the remaining portion of the deposited[90] money.[91] When the remaining portion was brought before King Uccala, he remarked that the coins bore his name, while the money, he remembered, was deposited[92] in King Kalaśa's time;[93] thus he came to the conclusion that the depositary had used the deposited money for his own purposes,[94] just as the depositor had used the goods which he had taken from time to time from the depositary.[95]

86. *sotha niḥśeśita miṣaḥ kruddho nirbandhakāriṇaḥ,*
gaṇanā patrikām tasya sabhrūbhaṅgam adarśayat (Rāj. 8. 135).
87. *Nikṣepa.*
88. *ityādyacintyātāyuktān parihāryavyayānasau,*
tasyaikīkṛtya gaṇanāṁ lābhe'pi śanakair vyadhāt.
varṣa māsagrahatithi pratyāvṛttiḥ punaḥ punaḥ,
saṁsā rasy eva tasyā'ntāṁ na yayau nartitāṅguleḥ.
sa mūla grahaṇaṁ piṇḍīkṛtyātha sakalā'ntaram,
prasāritoṣṭhas tan netre mīlayann abhyadhān mṛdu.
śalyamuddhara nikṣepaṁ nayojjāsadhanaṁ tv idaṁ,
viśrambha dattaṁ nirdambhaṁ dīyatāṁ sakalā'ntaram (Raj. 8. 144-7).
89. *tat sa dharmyaṁ vaco jānan kṣaṇam ucchvasitobhavat,*
kṣuraṁ kṣaudropaliptaṁ tu dhyātvā, paścādata pyata.
yuktāpahnuta sarvasvaṁ krauryān yamā athārthakāḥ
vivāde nāśakaj jetuṁ nā'pi stheyā vicārakāḥ. (Rāj. 8. 148-9).
90. *Nyāsa.*
91. *stheyair aniścitanyāyaṁ puro nyastaṁ tato nṛpaḥ,*
tad ittham iti niścitya vaṇijaṁ tam abhāṣata.
adyāpi nyāsadīnnārāḥ santi cet tat pradarśyatām,
aṁśah kiyān api tatas tato vacmi yathocitam (Rāj. 8. 150-1).
92. *Nyāsa.*
93. 1063-89 A. D. (Raj. 7. 233 sqq.).
94. *Nikṣepa.*
95. *tathā kṛte tena vīkṣya dinnārān mantriṇobravīt,*
rājabhir bhāvināṁ rājñāṁ nāmnā ṭaṅkaḥ kriyeta kim. (Continued on next page

Therefore, King Uccala ruled that if the depositor had to pay to the depositary interest on what he had taken from him from that time to the present day, then the depositary had to pay to the depositor interest on the full amount[96] deposited[97] from the time of its being deposited.[98] The story ended with the praise of the wisdom of King Uccala and the care which he had bestowed on his subjects.[99]

The story contained also two aphorisms dealing with the difficulty of regaining deposits[100] from a merchant,[101] and with the fear inspired by merchants in law-suits relating to the embezzlement of deposits :[102] they fought like tigers while putting up a show of smoothness and gentle appearance.[103]

4. *The story of Upakośā* (*Kathāsaritsāgara*)

11. In the fourth *taraṅga* of Kath., we find the well-known story of Upakośā and her four lovers. According to this story told by himself, Vararuci, before leaving the country placed with[104] the merchant Hiraṇyagupta (Hiraṇyadatta) his wealth for the maintenance of his own house and accordingly informed Upakośā.[105] Upakośā, when returning home from the Ganges, was stopped by the prince's minister, by the king's domestic chaplain and by the head magistrate respectively

na cet kalaśabhūpāla kāle nyāsikṛteṣvamī,
dinnāreṣu kutaṣ ṭaṅkā mannāmāṅkā api sthiptāḥ.
nikṣiptenaiṣa lakṣeṇa vaṇiktasmād vyavāharat,
vaṇijo draviṇenāyamapy āttenā'ntarā'ntārā (Rāj. 8. 152-4).

96. A hundred thousands *dinnāra*.

97. *Nyāsa*.

98. *tasmād yadā yad etena gṛhītaṁ dīyatāṁ tataḥ.*
tadā prabṛty adyayāval lābhosmai vaṇijorthinaḥ.
nyasanānehasaś caiṣa prabhṛty asmai prayacchatu,
lakṣādakhaṇḍital lābhaṁ kiṁ vācyaṁ maulike dhane (Rāj. 8. 155-6).

99. *paprathe pārthivasyetthaṁ niścodyaṁ tasya pālanam,*
prajāsu jāgarūkasya manor iva manasvinaḥ (Rāj. 8. 160.)

100. *Nyāsa*.

101. *śrotobhir vyastamam bhodhau labhyaṁ meghamukhaiḥ payaḥ,*
prāptir bhūyas tu nāsty eva vaṇignyastasya vastunaḥ (Rāj. 8. 128).

102. *Nyāsa*.

103. *taila snigdha mukhaḥ svalpālāpo mṛdvākṛtir bhavan,*
nyāsagrāsa vivādogro vaṇig-vyāghrād viśiṣyate (Rāj. 8. 129).

104. *Nidhā* (*nidhāya*).

105. *atha saṁjātanirvedaḥ svagṛhāsthataye dhanaṁ*
haste hiraṇyadattasya nidhāya vaṇijo nijaṁ.
uktvā tac ca upakośāyai gatavān asmi śaṅkaraṁ
tapobhir ārādhayituṁ nirāhāro himācalam (Kath. 4. 1, 26-7).

and was asked by each of them for a rendezvous. She, being confused at first, invited each of them to come to her house in the first watch of the night of the spring-festival when everybody was excited and would not observe her rendezvous. The next morning she sent her servant to Hiraṇyagupta asking for the return of some money which had been handed over to him by her husband[106] in order to entertain her guests; however, Hiraṇyagupta asked her to show him love because otherwise he would not return to her the wealth which was deposited by her husband. Upakośā, afraid of not having witnesses who could prove that her husband had placed a deposit[107] with Hiraṇyagupta, made a fourth rendezvous with him.[108] When the four men came to her home, one after the other was stripped of his clothes, rubbed with lamp-black and oil and terrified with the news of the arrival of the husband, bundled, and put in a trunk which was fastened outside with a bolt. Before Hiraṇyagupta was put into the trunk, Upakośā asked him to return the wealth entrusted[109] to him by her husband. Hiraṇyagupta, being under the impression that he was alone with Upakośā, assured her that he would return the wealth deposited[110] by her husband.[111] She called this statement of Hiraṇyagupta to the attention the three men already locked in the trunk. The next morning Upakośā went before the king and stated before him that Hiraṇyagupta was endeavouring to deprive her of the wealth deposited with him[112] by her husband.[113] The king summoned the merchant who denied that

106. *sthāpita* (*bhartṛsthāpita*).
107. *sthiti* (*bhartṛdhanasthiti*).
108 *prātar brāhmaṇapūjārthaṁ vyasarji vaṇijas tayā*
ceṭī Hiraṇyaguptasya kiṁcin mṛgayituṁ dhanaṁ.
Āgatya so'pi tām evam ekānte vaṇig abravīt,
bhajasva māṁ tato bhartṛsthāpitaṁ te dadāmi tat.
tac chrutvā sākṣirahitāṁ matvā bhartṛdhanasthitim.
vaṇijaṁ pāpaṁ ālokya khedāmarṣakadarthitā...... (Kath. 4. 1, 43-5).
109. *arpita dhana.*
110. Handed over; *sthāpita* (*dhana*).
111. *dattvā atha dīpaṁ gehe'tra Vaṇijaṁ taṁ praveśya sā,*
Upakośā avadad, dehi tan me bhartrā arpitaṁ dhanam.
tac cuhrutvā śūnyam ālokya gṛhaṁ so'py avadac chaṭhaḥ,
uktaṁ mayā dadāmy eva yad bhartrā sthāpitaṁ dhanam (Kath.4.1.64-5).
112. *nyāsīkṛta dhana.*
113. *upakośa apy atha prātaś ceṭikānugata gatā*
gurūṇām anivedya eva rājño nandasya mandiram.
vaṇig Ghiraṇyagupto me bhartrā nyāsīkṛtaṁ dhanaṁ,
jihīrṣati iti vijñaptas tatra rājā tayā svayaṁ (Kath. 4. 1. 71-2).

he was keeping anything for Upakośā's husband. Upakośā, however, referred to witnesses in the trunk who heard Hiraṇyagupta's admission of having accepted the deposit from her husband[114] The trunk was brought before the king and before him the three men, who were locked in the trunk stated that Hiraṇyagupta admitted in their presence that he had received the deposit[115] from Upakośā's husband. Then Hiraṇyagupta confessed his guilt.[116] In this way Upakośā recovered the deposit of her husband and was praised by everybody for her chastity and wisdom.

5. *The story of the courtezan Samarasundarī* (*Kathāratnākara*)

12. In KR. (1.69) we find the story of a Brāhmaṇa Gaṅgadatta who wanted to give his jewels for safekeeping[117] to a truthful person. Therefore, he went to the market-place where he found a hidden spot. The merchant who saw a stranger wanted to establish confidence in himself; therefore, he gave to a servant who came to buy some goods from him more than she was expected to receive. When the servant returned home, her mistress thought that if the merchant gave more than he was expected to give, he had a special purpose in mind. She, therefore, ordered her servant to return to the merchant the overweight received. Since the Brāhmaṇa, who was hidden near the merchant's place, saw that the servant's mistress was so conscientious that she returned the overweight, he felt that she was the truthful person for whom

114. *aṅgīkṛta dhana.*

115. *aṅgīkṛta dhana.*

116. *tena tac ca parijñātuṁ tadā eva ānayito vaṇik;*
maddhaste kiṁcid apy asyā deva na asti ity abhāṣata.
upakośā tato'vādīt, santi me deva sākṣiṇaḥ,
mañjūṣāyāṁ gataḥ kṣiptvā bhartā me gṛhadevatāḥ,
svavācā puratas tāsām anena aṅgīkṛtaṁ dhanaṁ,
tam ānayya iha mañjūṣāṁ pṛchyantāṁ devatās tvayā.
tac chrutvā vismayād rājā tadānayanam ādiśat;
tataḥ ksaṇāt sā māñjūṣā prāpitā bahubhir janaiḥ.
atha upakośā vakti sma, satyaṁ vadata devatāḥ,
yad uktaṁ vaṇijā tena, tato yāta nijāṁ gṛham.
no ced dahāmy ahaṁ yuṣmān sadasy udghāṭayāmi vā.
tac chrutva bhītabhītās te mañjūṣāsthā babhāṣire.
satyaṁ samakṣam asmākam anena aṅgīkṛtaṁ dhanam.
tato niruttaraḥ sarvaṁ vaṇik tat pratyapadyata (Kath. 4. 1. 73-9)

117. *sthita.*

he was looking and decided to give her the jewels for safekeeping.[118]

The same story was repeated with a yogi who sent back a portion of the food given him under the pretext that it was too much. The Brāhmaṇa, being under the impression that the yogi was a most truthful man, decided to give him the jewels for safekeeping. The yogi at first did not wish to accept the jewels but finally did.

When the Brāhmaṇa came back and asked the yogi to return the jewels, he refused to do so saying that he knew nothing about them. The Brāhmaṇa went to the town to request the help of the courtezan Samarasundarī, which she promised to give. Samarasundarī, dressed in clothes of a woman of good family, went with five big trunks to the yogi's house. She pretended that because of an accident at sea she could not continue her trip and asked the yogi to keep for some time the trunks for her. At that moment the merchant returned to the yogi's house and asked for the return of his jewels which he left with him. The yogi, afraid that Smarasundarī might lose confidence in him and intending to embezzle the five trunks, returned the jewels to the merchant. As soon as the merchant received his jewels, Samarasundarī's servant informed her that she could proceed to the harbour.[119] Samarasundarī,

118. *sthita.*

119. *āsāpāṭakavāsī Gaṅgadatto dvijo rohaṇācalataḥ pañca ratnānyādāya svapuramāgacchannantarāle daṁbhapuraṁ puraṁ prāpyeti dadhyau, yadetāni ratnāni kasyāpyokasi vimucya tuṁgagiriśṛṅgasthi tabaladevamūrttiṁ praṇamya kṣemeṇa gṛhaṁ yāmīti matvā kasyāpi vaṇijo haṭṭe tasmin sthite kāpi dāsī ghṛtārthamāgatā, tenā'pi vaṇıjā paradeśinastasya viśvāsārthamadhikaṁ dattaṁ ghṛtamādāya gehamāgatāṁ tāṁ tat svāminī sınāha, he putri ! Yat tenā'dhikaṁ ghṛtam adāyi, tena nūnaṁ tasya haṭṭe ko'pi paradeśī sthitaḥ syāt.*

Tenādhikaṁ ghṛtaṁ vayaṁ nādāsyāma ity abhidhāya ghṛtam idam adhikaṁ pratyar payety uktayā tayā tasmin stasthuṣy eva pratyarpitaṁ ghṛtaṁ vilokya itasyā nūnaṁ vyavahāraśuddhirasti, atho'syā gehe ratnāni muṁcāmīti ıicārya tatpṛṣṭhalagno Gaṅgadattas tadāgāramājagāma tatra tasmin sthite bhikṣārtham āgatāyaikasya yoginaḥ ṣiṣyāya tayā tad viśvāsāya bhūyasī bhikṣā dattā. Śiṣyeṇānītamadhikaṁ bhikṣāmudīkṣya gurudadhyau, dhruvaṁ tadokasi ko'pi paradeśī sthito'sti, tenādhikāṁ bhikṣāṁ vayaṁ nādāsyāma ity udīrya pratyarpitāṁ bhikṣāṁ vilokya bhojye'pi nirihasya yogino dhāmani ratnāni mıncāmīti matvā, tatra ca gatvā, muḍhaiva naneti vadato'pyasya yogino balena ratnāni datvā yātrāṁ ca kṛtvā sameto yoginaṁ ratnāni yayāce. Ko'haṁ kas tvaṁ kāni ratnānīti jalpatā yoginā nirākṛtaḥ sa muṣito'ham iti bruvāṇāḥ puraṁtar bhraman ratnādānaprajñāpaṭiyaṣīṁ Samarasundarīm nāma paṇyasundarīm śrutvā tadāvāsaṁ yayau. Tad uktam ca niśamya paravañcanacaturā sā tam abhāṇīt, he subhaga yogim aṭhikāyāṁ sthitāyāṁ mayi tvayā svāni ratnāni mārgaṇīyānīti tamanuśiṣya, karkarakapūritaṁ dattatālakaṁ bhṛśaṁ śobhanaṁ ca peṭīpañcakam ādāya svīkṛtakulakāminīvaranepathyā sā tatra gatvā yoginaṁ jagau, he nātha madīyāni pravahaṇāni payonidhau bhagnānīti vārttādya samāgatā, tena bhūribhir adhamarṇair idaṁ mama sarvaṁ dhanam ādās-

full of joy that her trick worked, began to dance, as did the yogi. Asked why he was also dancing, the yogi replied that though he lost the jewels and did not get the five trunks in deposit, he learnt a new trick from Samarasundarī and therefore was very happy.

6. *Other mentions of contracts of deposit (Raghuvaṁśa, Abhijñānaśākuntalam, Kathāsaritsāgara, Mṛchhakaṭika, Rājataraṅgiṇī)*.

From other non-juridical sources which mention the contract of deposit, Ragh.,[120] Śāk.,[121] Kath.,[122] Mṛ.,[123] and Rāj.[124] may be mentioned.

13. In Ragh., where the story of Bharata and Rāma was told, it was stated that Bharata, who did not want to reign in Rāma's place, asked him to put his shoes on the throne; he did not return to the capital but went to Nandigrāma where he enjoyed the kingdom of his brother as a deposit[125] only.[126]

14. In Śāk., Kāsyapa said that a man who gave his daughter in marriage enjoyed a pleasure such as that enjoyed by a man who restored a deposit[127] to the depositor.[128]

15. In Kath. in the story of Puṣpadanta, Gaṇa went to the king Śuśarman and said that his son had been sent away and that he was going to seek him; accordingly he deposited[129]

yate, tena kiyad vāsarāṇidaṁ mama peṭīpañcakaṁ svamaṭhikāyāṁ nidhīyatāmiti vārttāṁ vidadhatyām evatasyāṁ pūrvasaṁketitaḥ sa dvijo'py āgamya ratnāni yayāce... (KR. 212. 4-214. 4).

120. Ragh. 12. 18.

121. Śāk. 4. 21.

122. Kath. 7. 79.

123. Mṛ. 210. 21-211. 1.

124. Rāj. 8. 706-10.

125. *Nyāsa*.

126. *sa visṛṣṭas tathetyuktvā bhrātrā naivāviśat purīṁ,*
nandigrāmagatas tasya rājyaṁ nyāsamivābhunak (Ragh. 12. 18).

127. *Nyāsa*.

128. *artho hi kanyā parakīya eva tām adya saṁpreṣya parigrahītuḥ,*
jāto mamāyaṁ viśadaḥ pakāmaṁ pratyarpitanyāsa ivā'ntarātmā. (Śāk. 4.21).

A. W. Ryder translates this śloka as follows :

A girl is held in trust, another's treasure;
To arms of love my child today is given;
And now I feel a calm and sacred pleasure;
I have restored the pledge that came from heaven.

129. *Nikṣepa*

with him his daughter-in-law and asked the king to keep her safely.[130]

16. In Mṛ., in addition to the story of the stolen jewels, we find in the eighth act a mention of deposits.[131] There the *viṭa*, before leaving Vasantasenā with Saṁsthānaka, said that he entrusted her to him as a deposit for safekeeping[132] to which Saṁsthānaka replied that he would execute this deposit.[133] When Saṁsthānaka, after havings trangled Vasantasenā, was requested by the *viṭa* to return the deposit[134] (Vasantasenā), he asked what deposit was meant,[135] as if he were ignorant about the deposit to which the *viṭa* referred.[136]

17. In Rāj., in addition to the story of King Uccala, we find mention of deposits in the story of Sussala. According to this story, when Bhikṣācara, the grandson of Harṣa, in the beginning of the twelfth century A.D., entered Kaśmīr, everyone was anxious to tell and hear about him, and particularly those who entertained themselves and others with seditious tales; among them, Kalhaṇa enumerated merchants who had embezzled deposits[137] and, therefore, showed themselves eager to listen to the recital of sacred texts.[138]

130. *putro me preṣitaḥ kvāpi, tam anveṣṭuṁ vrajāmy ahaṁ,*
tan me snuṣā iyaṁ nikṣepo rājan samprati rakṣyatām (Kath.1. 7, 79).

131. Since in Cār. we do not find the eighth act of Mṛ., this story is missing in Cār.

132. *Nyāsa.*

133. Viṭaḥ—*Vasentasene* ! *Na bhetavyaṁ na bhetavyam* ; *kāṇelimātaḥ* ! *Vasantasenā tava haste nyāsaḥ.*

Śakāraḥ—*Evvaṁ*; *mama haśte eśā ṇāśeṇa cyiśṭadu* (Mṛ. 210. 21-211.1.).

Pṛthvīdhara noted that in Prākrit the word *ṇāśeṇa* was used which may derive from the Sanskrit *nyāsena* for safekeeping or *nāśena* for destruction. Saṁsthānaka probably used the word in the sense of safekeeping.

134. *Nyāsa.*

135. *Nyāsa* (*ṇaśe*).

136. Viṭaḥ—*Madīyaṁ nyāsamupanaya.*
Śakāraḥ—*Kīdiśe ṇāśe* (Mṛ. 216. 2.3).

137. *Nikṣepa.*

138. *sarit snānagṛhe sanānto vṛddhāḥ kṣiṇaniyoginaḥ,*
rājaveśmany agaṇitā nāmamātranṛpātmajāḥ.
svabhāvadurjanāḥ kecid yodhāścoc cāśvakāṅkṣiṇaḥ,
kārayantopy upādhyāyāḥ, śiṣyānsphikkaṣaṇaṁ nakhaiḥ.
vṛddhāḥ suraukonartakyo devaprāsādapālakāḥ,
vaṇijo bhukt anikṣepāḥ pustaka śruti tat parāḥ.
prāyopaveśakuśalāḥ pāriṣadyadvijātayaḥ,
śastriṇaḥ kārṣakaprāyā nagaropāntaḍāmarāḥ.
sukhayantaḥ svam anyaṁś ca kim apy utpiñjavārtayā,
ete prāyeṇa deśesmin pārthivopaplavapriyāḥ (Rāj. 8. 706-10).

II. TECHNICAL LEGAL AND COLLOQUIAL TERMINOLOGY OF CONTRACTS OF DEPOSIT

18. According to the theory of law the contract of deposit was a contract whereby one person delivered a movable object to another for gratuitous safe-custody.

In the Smṛti-s the contract of deposit was very often confused with *fiducia*, which comprised *commodatum*, *mandatum* and others. In the non-juridical sources in classical Sanskrit not only *fiducia* but also simple custody was confused with the contract of deposit.[139]

19. The Smṛti-s did not give a general definition of the contract of deposit. However, they gave several definitions of different kinds of deposits.[140]

We find in the Smṛtis the definition of (1) *open deposits*[141] (*nikṣepa*),[142] the contents of which were counted and handed over unsealed to the depositary in the presence of the owner of the object deposited;[143] (2) *sealed or closed deposits*[144] (*upanidhi*),[145] the contents of which were placed or hidden in

139. Cf. *JSAIL* 10, par. 1, 2; *JSAIL* 11, par. 6.

140. Cf. *JSAIL* 10, par. 2.

141. *asaṁkhyātam avijñātaṁ samudraṁ yan nidhīyate,*
taj jānīyād upanidhiṁ nikṣepaṁ gaṇitaṁ viduḥ (N. quoted in Mit. *ad* Y. 2. 65).
svaṁ dravyaṁ yatra viśrambhānnikṣipaty aviśaṅkitaḥ,
nikṣepo nāma tat proktaṁ vyavahārapadaṁ budhaiḥ (N.2. 1).

142. Also *upanikṣepa* (Mn. 8. 149; N. 1. 81; Vās. 16. 18; K. 191. 2; Mit. *ad* Y. 2.25; Ś. *ad* Y. 2.25.

143. Mn. 8. 4; cf. 8. 149, 179-81, 185, 186, 188, 190-2, 194, 196; 11.57; Y. 2. 25, 67; N. 16; 1. 81; 2. 1., 5, 7-10, 13, 14; 3. 230; 7.1; Mit. *ad* Y. 2.65; *ad* 1. 67; VyM. 190. 6-11; Vi. 5. 169-71; 36.3; 52.4; Bṛh. 11.1, 15, 18; 12, 1, 2; Kāty. 592-3, 598-9; K. 180. 6; 180. 19-181. 2. Cf. *JSAIL* 10, par. 5.

144. *anya dravyavyavahitaṁ dravyam avyāhṛtaṁ ca yat,*
nikṣipyate paragṛhe tad aupanidhikaṁ smṛtam (N. 2.5).
vāsanasthamanākhyāya haste'nyasya yad arpyate,
dravyaṁ tad aupanidhikaṁ pratideyaṁ tathaiva tat (Y. 2. 65).
upanidher bhāṇḍasthānām aparicchinnānām (Vir. *ad* Y. 2. 24-5; p. 436. 7-8).
anākhyātaṁ vyavahitam asaṁkhyātam adarśitam,
mudrāṅkitaṁ ca yad dattaṁ tad aupanidhikaṁ smṛtam (Bṛh. 11.2).
asaṁkhyātam avijnātaṁ samudraṁ yan nidhıyate,
taj jānīyād upanidhiṁ nikṣepaṁ gaṇitaṁ viduḥ (N. quoted in Mit. *ad* Y. 2. 65).

145. Also *śilpe upanidhi* (N. 2. 14).

a box or a pot,[146] or in another receptacle,[147] or sealed[148] without being described,[149] or counted, or measured, or kncwn[150] and handed over (in other person's house);[151] to the depositary;[152] (3) *secret deposits*[153] (*nyāsa*),[154] the contents of which were entrusted in the absence of the house-holder and without being shown to him or to a member of his family or servant with the mandate to be handed over to the house-holder;[155] (4) *mutual deposits*[156] (*pratinyāsa*) in which deposits were exchanged[157] between the depositor and depositary;[158] (5) *deposits for use*[159] (*yācita* or *yācitaka*), the contents of which, consisting of clothes, ornaments and the like, were handed over on the occasion of a marriage or similar festival for adornment purposes;[160] (6) *deposits for delivery*[161] (*anvāhita* or *anvādhi*),

146. Y. 2. 65; Vīr.

147. N. 2. 5.

148. N. in Mit. *ad* Y. 2. 65; Bṛh. 11,2; or covered with cloth and sealed (Medh. *ad* Mn. 8.148).

149. Y. 2. 65; Bṛh. 11.2.

150. N. in Mit. *ad* Y. 2. 65; Vīr.

151. N. 2. 5.

152. Mn. 8. 148, 149, 185, 196; Medh. *ad* Mn. 8. 148; Y. 2.25, 65, 67; Mit. *ad* Y. 2.25, 65, Vīr. *ad* Y. 2.24-5; *ad* 2. 65-7; Ś. *ad* 2.25, 67; N. 2.5; in Mit. *ad* Y. 2. 25, 65; Vās. 16.8; Bṛh. 11.2; Kāty. 592; K. 177.12 sqq. 180. 6; 191.2; Viv. 26. Cf. *JSAIL* 10, par 8.

153. ...*nyāso nāma gṛhasvāmine'darśayitvā tat parokṣam eva gṛhajanahaste prakṣepo gṛhasvāmine samarpaṇīyam iti* (Mit. *ad* Y. 2. 67).
Nyāso gṛhasvāmine'darśayitvā tat parokṣam eva tadīyajanahaste prakṣepo gṛhasvāmine samarpaṇīyam iti ...... (Vir. *ad* Y. 2. 67; 494. 24-6).

154. Cf. *śilpinyāsa*, deposits with artisans (cf. *JSAIL* 10, par. 17) N. 2. 14; Asahāya *ad* N. 16; Bṛh. 11. 18-9, Mit. *ad* Y. 2. 67; Viv. 25-6; VyM. 193.4; 194.8. Cf. Kāty. 592, 603 and K. 180.9.

155. Y. 2. 6; Mit., Vīr. and Ś. *ad* Y. 2. 67; N. 2.14; Asahāya *ad* N. 16; B. 2. 1, 2, 3; Bṛh. 11.3; 12. 2; Kāty. 592-3, 603; Śukr. 4.5, 310. Cf. *JSAIL* 10, par. 10.

156. *pratinyāsaḥ svāminā yatra nikṣiptaṁ tenā'py anyatra nikṣiptam* (VyM. 193. 3).

157. With the words "you should keep this thing of mine, and I shall keep this thing of yours." Cf. *JSAIL* 10. par. 11.

158. N. 2. 14; Asahāya and VyM. *ad* N. 2.14; Mit. *ad* Y. 2. 67.

159. *yācitamuddāhādau śobhādyarthaṁ nītamalaṁkārādi.* (VyM). *vivāhādy utsavarthaṁ vastrālaṅkārādikaṁ pratideyatayāṅgikṛtya yācitvānītaṁ yācitam* (Vīr. *ad* Y. 2.67, p. 494.21-3; similarly Ś. *ad* Y. 2. 67).

160. Y. 2.14., 67, 238; Vīr. and Ś. *ad* Y. 2. 67; N. 16 (Asahāya): G. 12. 42; Bṛh. 11.18 (VyM. 193.3); Kāty. 595; Vīr. and Smṛ. C. on Kāty. 606-7; Śukr. 4.5, 310. Cf. *JSAIL* 10, par. 14. Śukr. (2. 327, 381) and Pāṇini (4. 4, 21) state clearly that these objects were only lent for use free of interest. From the point of view of the theory of law it was not a contract of deposit.

161. *yad ekasya haste nihitaṁ dravyaṁ tenā'py anu paścād anyahaste*

the contents of which were entrusted to a third person with the mandate to hand them over to the depositary;[162] or of (7) other deposits like *deposits of a minor*[163] (*pogaṇḍa* or *pogaṇḍa-dhāna*) identical with a *tutela minoris*; or *vaiśyāvṛtty-arpita*,[164] identical with *fiducia*; or *krayaproṣita*,[165] identical with *constitutum possessorium*; or *bandha*,[166] identical with *pignus*.

20. The Smṛti-s consistently used technical legal terms for the designation of various types of deposits, the most important of which were *nikṣepa* for open deposits, *upanidhi* for sealed deposits, and *nyāsa* for secret deposits. However, the non-juridical sources in classical Sanskrit did not employ these terms in their technical sense; when they used them, they were without the knowledge of their special technical connotations. The non-juridical sources employed the word *nyāsa* most frequently for the designation of deposits. This term must be considered as the colloquial expression for deposits in general. It may be noted, however, that while in some cases these sources employed the word *nikṣepa*, this word was used instead of *nyāsa*.

A. Mṛ. and Cār. refer fifteen times to the expression 'deposit', 'depositing';[167] in three cases the word[168] *nikṣepa*[169] was used, and in eleven cases the word *nyāsa*[170]. No reason can be found why one or the other expression was employed.

If the authors of Mṛ. and Cār. had used technical legal

svāmine dehīti nihitaṁ tad anvāhitam (Mit. *ad* Y. 2. 67). *anvāhitaṁ svāminā ekasya haste nihitaṁ dravyaṁ tena'py anu paścādanyasya haste tasyādhāturvacanān nihita......* (Vīr. *ad* Y. 2. 67, p. 494. 23-4). *anvāhitam amukena mayi sthāpitaṁ ca tvayā tasmai deyam iti puruṣā'ntarahaster pitam* (VyM. 192. 13-4).

162. Y. 2. 67; Mit. and Vīr. *ad* Y. 2. 67; N. 2. 14; Asahāya *ad* N. 16; Bṛh. 12.2.; Kāty. 592, 611; VyM. 192. 13-4; Śukr. 4. 5, 310. Cf. *JSAIL* 10, par. 16.

163. *ya anāthaṁ bālaṁ sapradhanaṁ nāthābhuddhyā pratigṛhṇāti yasyā'pi pūrvoktasyaiva vidhir draṣṭavyaḥ. Ṣaḍ ete vidhayaḥ. Ṣaḍ ete vidhayaḥ samā iti* (Asahāya *ad* N. 2. 15). Cf. *JSAIL* 10, par. 20.

164. *ktraya-proṣita-nikṣiptā-bandhā'nvāhita-yācitam,*
vaiśya-vṛtty arpitaṁ caiva sorthas tū'panidhiḥ smṛtaḥ (Kāty. 592). Cf. *JSAIL* 10, par. 21.

165. Kāty. 592. Text quoted in fn. 164. Cf. *JSAIL* 10, par. 21.

166. Kāty. 592. Text quoted in fn. 164. Cf. *JSAIL* 10, par. 21.

167. In the *alaṁkāranyāsa*.

168. Or compounds of *nyāsa* and *nikṣepa*.

169. Cf. fnn. 2, 37, 57.

170. Cf. fnn. 4, 5, 7, 12, 22, 35, 50, 55, 132, 134, 135; the first act of Mṛ. is dalled *alaṁkāranyāsa*.

terminology for the act of handing over the jewels to Cārudatta, the correct word would have been *nikṣepa*, since the jewels were handed over by Vasantasenā, the owner of these jewels, to Cārudatta or to him through Maitreya.[171] Only later were the jewels placed into the jewel-box which was stolen by Śarvilaka.[172] Therefore, the act of handing over the jewels was not an act of a sealed deposit (*upanidhi*) and even less of a secret deposit (*nyāsa*), since Cārudatta, although he did not take over the deposited objects, was present at the act of handing them over. The jewels were shown to him and no mandate was given to Maitreya to hand over the jewels to Cārudatta; Cārudatta accepted the jewels and substituted Maitreya for himself in the act of the transfer of the possession of the jewels. The jewels were not counted before Cārudatta but that was not necessary[173] since Cārudatta and Maitreya knew exactly what the deposited objects were and what their value was. That can be seen from the fact that Maitreya clearly stated in the fifth act of Mṛ. that the necklace of Cārudatta's wife was worth more than the jewels deposited with Cārudatta by Vasantasenā.

It is clear, therefore, from the legal point of view, that the contract of deposit, as described in the first act of Mṛ. and Cār., was an act of an open deposit (*nikṣepa*); thus *nikṣepa* would be the correct term for the designation of that deposit.

B. In Rāj., in the story of the king Uccala, Kalhaṇa used the expression deposit or to depose ten times; of these ten cases, twice the word[174] *nikṣepa*[175] and eight times the word *nyāsa*[176] were used. As in Mṛ. and Cār., no reason can be found why one or the other expression was employed. If Kalhaṇa had used technical legal terminology or the fact of depositing a hundred thousand *dīnnāra* in the house of a mer-

171. Vasantasenā said : *aṇuggahīda mhi*, after, which she handed over to Maitreya the jewels (*ity alaṁkāram arpayati* (Mṛ. 45. 19-20). In Cār. Vasantasenā also handed over to Maitreya the jewels (*gaṇikā vimucy ālaṅ kāraṁ prayacchati*) (Cār. 212. 6).

172. Mṛ. act 3. 3 ; 88.2. Cf. act 3.91, 6 sqq. Cār. act 3. 226, 1. sqq.

173. It was a contract of an open deposit (*nikṣepa*)

174. Or compound.

175. Cf. fnn. 87, 94.

176. Cf. fnn. 78, 82. 84, 90, 92, 97, 100, 102.

chant he would have to use the word *nikṣepa* throughout the story. The money deposited was counted, since it is stated that a hundred thousands *dīnnāra* were deposited, and it was handed over to the depositary-merchant by the owner of the money. The merchant knew exactly the amount of money deposited with him;[177] he himself received the money deposited and there was no middleman to receive the mandate to hand over to the merchant the deposited money.[178] It is clear, therefore, from the legal point of view, that the contract of deposit was a contract of an open deposit (*nikṣepa*) and the word *nikṣepa* was the right term for the designation of that deposit.

C. In Kath., in the story of Upakośā, and in KR., in the story of the courtezan Smarasundarī we do not find the classical colloquial terms for the designation of deposits. The authors used indirect expressions for denoting deposits or intrusting the wealth with the depositary. In Kath. only once the word *nyāsa* was used[179] and once *nidhā*.[180] which is not identical with the colloquial term *upanidhi* but derives from the same word;[181] other expressions used were *sthāpita*[182] (employed twice in Kath.),[183] *sthiti*[184] (employed in Kath. and KR.), *arpita*[185] and *aṅgīkṛta*[186] (employed twice in Kath.)[187] The author or authors of Kath. (*taraṅga* 4) and of KR. used, as if purposely, expressions with no clear connotation to denote the contracts of deposit which were concluded between the husband of Upakośā and the merchant Hiraṇyagupta or Gaṅgadatta and the yogi. It is clear from both these stories

177. Hence it was not a sealed deposit (*upanidhi*).

178. Hence it was not a secret deposit (*nyāsa*).

179. *Nyāsikṛta dghana*. Cf. fn. 112.

180. *Nidhāya*. Cf. fn. 104.

181. From *ni*+√*dhā* (to put, to place) 'place'; *nidhāya* 'having deposited.' *Upanidhi* from *upa*+*ni*+√*dhā*.

182. From *sthā*, 'place, locate, deposit.'

183. *Bhartṛsthāpita*, deposited by the husband. Cf. fn. 106; *sthāpita dhana*, wealth deposited. Cf. fn. 110.

184. From *sthā*, 'standing, situated'; *bhartṛdhanasthiti* 'wealth situated with, placed with, entrusted to, the husband.' Cf. fnn. 107. 117, 118.

185. From √*ṛ* 'present, give'; 'given, entrusted.' *Arpitadhana* 'weatlh entrusted.' Cf. fn. 109.

186. From *aṅga*+√*kṛ* 'agree.'

187. *Aṅgīkṛta dhana* 'wealth entrusted'. Cf. fnn. 114. 115.

that the wealth (money), not clearly described, was counted and handed over unsealed by Upakośā's husband to the merchant Hiraṇyagupta and that the jewels were handed over by Gaṅgadatta to the yogi. Therefore, from the legal point of view, both these contracts of deposit were contracts of open deposit (*nikṣepa*) and the word *nikṣepa* was the right term for denoting the act of placing or entrusting the deposit with Hiraṇyagupta and the jewels with the yogi.

D. In Pañc., in the story of the Mice that Ate Iron, the word *nikṣepa* was used[188] for the designation of the contract of deposit. The use of this word was justified from the legal point of view, because the contents of the deposit were known to the depositor and the depositary, and the object of deposit was handed over by the depositor to the depositary. However, it should be noted that in the same story in Bṛ. Kath., first the word *nyāsa* and then the word *nikṣepa* was used.[189] There also the word *nikṣepa* ought to be used consistently throughout the whole story. The same refers to Śuk. t.s. and Kath. (taraṅga 10) where the word *nyāsa*[190] was used.[191]

E. From the legal point of view it is difficult to speak of the contract of deposit in Kath. in the story of Puṣpadanta, since the objects acceptable for open, sealed, secret, or mutual deposit or deposit for use or for delivery could only be movable things and not persons. In the story of Puṣpadanta a girl was "placed in deposit"[192] with the king for self-custody. From the point of view of the theory of law, this act was not that of placing in deposit but of entrusting the girl to the king. The word *arpita* or *sthiti*, as used in Kath. in the story of Upkośa (*taraṅga* 4), would have been better.

F. As to other excerpts dealing with deposits, it is difficult to decide the word to be employed, since the sources do not contain premises on the basis of which it would be possible to judge what type of contract of deposit was concluded. These sources (Ragh. and Śāk.) used the colloquial term for the designation of deposits, that is, the word *nyāsa*.

188. Cf. fn. 65.
189. Cf. fnn. 75, 76.
190. Cf. fn. 74.
191. Cf. fnn. 70, 74.
192. *Nikṣepa*..

21. Some of the lexicographers, e.g. Amarasiṁha,[193] mentioned *upanidhi* and *nyāsa* as synonyms, while Halāyudha[194] had *nikṣepa* and *upanidhi* and Hemacandra[195] *nikṣepa*, *upanidhi* and *nyāsa*.[196] Most of the other Kośa-s did not mention other expressions which were used in the Smṛti-s for designation of various contracts of deposits. The Kośa-s which mentioned *upanidhi*, *nikṣepa* or *nyāsa* used these expressions not as denoting specific contracts,[197] but as synonyms of the same notion (deposits)[198] and thus did not give to the Kāvya writers and other authors the technical meaning of these words. That may offer an explanation why the authors of the non-juridical sources, despite the very clear general rules determining the accurate usage of terminology, used in their *kāvya*-works instead of the technical legal terminology, colloquial expressions for the designation of deposits, while the technical expressions used in the Smṛti-s and *nibandha-s*, gave technical definitions of *upanidhi*, *nikṣepa*, *nyāsa*, *pratinyāsa*, *yācita*, *anvāhita*, etc.; they were not well-known either to the general public or even to the Kāvya writers[199].

III. CONTRACTS OF DEPOSIT IN THE SMṚTI-S AND THE NON-JURIDICAL SOURCES IN CLASSICAL SANSKRIT

In the non-juridical sources the contract of deposit and its juridical consequences were mentioned several times. Generally speaking, they conformed with the rules contained in the Smṛti-s and complemented the

193. *upanidhir nyāsaḥ* (*Amarakośa* 2. 9, 81). *Amarakośa* also mentions *yācitaka* (2. 9, 3), but in the sense of a thing borrowed for use, and not in the sense of a deposit; *anvāhita*, *anvādhi* or *poganḍa* are not mentioned at all.

194. *Nikṣepaḥ syād upanidhiḥ* (*Abhidhānaratnamālā* 1. 82).

195. *Nikṣepo'panidhī-nyāse* (*Abhidhānacintāmaṇi* 870).

196. It should be noted that some important Kośa-s, as for instance, Hemacandra's *Anekārthasaṁgraha*, *Uṇādigaṇavivṛti*, *Dhātupāṭha* and *Deśīnāmamālā*, Maṅkha's *Anekārthakośa*. or Śāśvata's *Anekārthasamu caya* did not mention *npanidhi*, *nikṣepa* or *nyāsa*.

197. With the exception of *yācitaka* in *Amarakośa*. Cf. fn. 193.

198. That is clear, for instance, from Halayudha's *Abhidhānaratnamālā* where it is stated *nikṣepa syād upanidhi*.

199. Another explanation of this not ususal phenomenon may be the fact that some Bhāṣya-s on the Smṛti-s, which gave the specific definitions of the various expressions for desiganation of deposits, were not usually accepted or were written later than some of the Kāvya-s.

legal rules contained in the Smṛti-s. Therefore, they are of the greatest importance for students of the Smṛti-s.

1. *Confidence in the depositary.*

22. N. gave the definition of the contract of deposit (*nikṣepa*) according to which this contract took place if one person entrusted (without suspicion) a movable object with another in whom he had confidence[200]. Asahāya[201], the commentator on N., added that a man who did not place confidence in the depositary would not deposit a single cowry without a guarantee of a written receipt or of witnesses. On the other hand, he would deposit great wealth[202] without these precautions with one in whom he had confidence[203].

23. This commentary of Asahāya is mirrored in Mṛ. and Cār. In both these dramas Cārudatta stressed that confidence was of the greatest importance; that was shown in Vasantasenā's act of placing the jewels in his trust, though he was a poor man[204]. The same could also be seen from Mṛ. where Cārudatta said that his house was not worthy of confidence placed in him, but Vasantasenā replied that treasures were not entrusted to houses but to men[205] and placed her jewels with Cārudatta without any guarantee of a written receipt or of witnesses.

24. Similar also was the story of the courtezan Samarasundarī in KR., which was based on the premise that the depositor (Gaṅgadatta) had to find as depositary a person whom he could trust unreservedly.

2. *Ownership of the objects deposited*

25. There was no mention in the Smṛti-s of the problem of whether the depositary gained the right of property over the objects deposited as long as he was a depositary, or whether the object deposited was in his *detentio* only. Analyzing the most important contracts of deposit from the legal point of view, it is evident that *nyāsa*, *pritinyāsa* and *anvāhita* were not

200. N.2.1. Text quoted in fn. 141. (Also quoted in VMG. 84.115).
201. *Ad* N. 2. 1.
202. One thousand suvarṇas.
203. Cf. *JSAIL* 11. par. 11.
204. Cf. fnn. 36, 56.
205. Cf. fnn. 3, 7.

different contracts of deposit but that the definition of these contracts referred to the way in which an object deposited was placed in deposit. Theoretically, *nikṣepa*, as well as *upanidhi*, could be a *nyāsa*, or *pratinyāsa*, or *anvāhita*, since an open, as well as a sealed deposit, or a deposit for use could be entrusted in the absence of the house-holder and without being shown to him, or to a member of his family, or servant with the mandate to be handed over to the householder or entrusted to a third person with the mandate to hand it over to the depositary. In the same way open as well as sealed deposits, or deposits for use, could be exchanged between the depositor and depositary. However from the point of view of the Smṛti-s, *nyāsa*, *pratinyāsa* and *anvāhita* were different kinds of contracts of deposit [206].

Analyzing the question of ownership or detention in contracts of deposits from the point of view of the theory of law, it is necessary to distinguish between contracts of deposit proper and the form of placing deposits.

In case of *nikṣepa*, the depositary could gain the right of ownership over the object deposited, particularly if it was an exchangeable object. If, for instance, coins or monies were deposited, the depositary was not necessarily obliged to return to the depositor the same coins or monies, but could return other coins or monies of the same value. That was impossible in the case of *upanidhi*, since the depositary was not supposed to know the contents of the objects that were hidden in a box or the like. The same is the conclusion in case of *yācita* : the depositary knew the objects deposited, but these things consisted of specified objects needed for a special purpose. They had to be used and returnred afterwards. It was a contract of a gratuitous loan of specified objects and the same specified objects had to be restored. These objects were, therefore, in the *detentio* of the depositary.

As stated before, the Smṛti-s did not mention whether the depositary had the objects deposited in his *detentio* or gained property over them. Only Bṛh.[207] and N. [208] stated that, in the case of *nikṣepa*, *anvāhita*, *nyāsa* and *yācita*, when the objects

206. Cf. Bṛh. 12. 2. and others.
207. Bṛh. 12. 2. *Nikṣepa*.
208. N. 7. 1. *Nikṣipta*.

deposited had been sold by the depositary, the purchaser did not become the owner (*asvāmin*) of these objects. The depositary, who sold the objects deposited, could not transfer more rights than he had; since he was not the owner of these objects the purchaser could not gain ownership over these objects.

It should be noted that Bṛh. did not mention in 12.2 *upanidhi*, though *upanidhi* was defined in 11.2 Probably the *essentialia* of this contract were so clear that it was felt that it was not necessary to emphasize this problem in 12.2.

From these extracts the conclusion can be drawn that in the Smrti-s, in the case of each contract of deposit the depositary did not gain ownership over the object deposited but that the depositor held the object deposited in *detentio*.[209]

26. This problem was touched upon in the non-juridical sources and solved in accordance with the Smṛti-s.

In Rāj., when the king passed judgment he referred to the fact that the depositary used the coins given in deposit and therefore ordered the depositary to pay to the depositor interest on the full amount deposited from the moment of placing the deposit.[210] King Uccala, who, as stated in Rāj., had a highly legal mind, decided, since the depositary used the coins deposited, that they were to be considered his, and not merely in his detention. He used them in his own interest. Therefore the contract concluded between the wealthy man and the merchant could not be considered as a contract of deposit, but as another contract—a contract of loan of exchangeable objects, a kind of loan concluded in the interest of the merchant.[211] Though the contract concluded between the wealthy man and the merchant was meant to be a contract of deposit, the judge, basing his judgment of on the *essentialia* of the contract of deposit, concluded that it was not a contract of deposit, since the merchant acted as if he were the owner of the objects entrusted to him by the wealthy man. The king based his judgment on the Smṛti-s. In this way we find in the non-juri-

209. Cf. *JSAIL* 11, par. 4.

210. Cf. fn. 98.

211. The contract of deposit was concluded in the interest of the depositor and not the depositary. Cf. below, par. 32 and fn. 232.

dical sources the confirmation of a purely legal problem, not solved directly in the Smṛti-s : in case of a contract of a deposit, the depositary held the objects deposited in detention and did not gain ownership over the objects deposited even for a short time.[212]

27. It can be also deduced from Ragh. that in the case of a contract of deposit, the depositary did not gain ownership over the object deposited. There, Bharata stated that he would enjoy the kingdom of Rāma as a deposit, that is, for a short time only and not in his own name, but in the name of the real sovereign—Rāma.[213]

28. The problem of ownership or detention of the object deposited was also raised in the first act of Mṛ. when Maitreya, forshadowing the future theft, said that the jewels entrusted by Vasantasenā with Cārudatta were 'ours.'[214] this statement could mean that by the act of placing the jewels in deposit the depositary (Cārudatta) gained ownership over these jewels; however, the statement of Maitreya was not approved by Cārudatta. In the third act Radanikā, when informing Cārudatta's wife about the theft of the jewels, clearly stated that the jewels were those belonging to (of) Vasantasenā.[215] Therefore, it is difficult to arrive at any conclusions from Maitreya's statement in the first act of Mṛ.

3. *Persons suitable to become depositaries.*

29. According to Mn.[216] N.,[217] and Bṛh.,[218] a wise man (*buddha*) could deposit a object after duly considering the

212. The Smṛti-s stated clearly that the depositor was not supposed to use the objects deposited and if he used them he had to be punished and pay an indemnification.
nyāsadravyeṇa yaḥ kaścit sādhayet kāryam ātmanaḥ,
daṇḍyaḥ sa rājño bhavati dāpyas tac cā'pi sodayam (Bṛh. 11. 13);
ājīvan svecchayā daṇḍyo dāpyas taṁ cā'pi sodayam,
yācitānvāhitanyāsanikṣepādiṣvayaṁ vidhiḥ (Y. 2. 67).
upanidhi-bhoktā deśakālānurūpaṁ bhogavetanaṁ dadyāt. dvādaśa-paṇaṁ ca daṇḍam (K. 178. 1.2). Cf. *JSAIL* 11. par. 15.
In Raj. the story was not solved in a purely legal way but it was included in order to show the wisdom of King Uccala.

213. Cf. fn. 126.

214. Cf. fn. 13.

215. Cf. fn. 29.

216. *kulaje vṛttasampanne dharmajñe satyavādini,*
mahāpakṣe dhaninyārye nikṣepaṁ nikṣeped budhaḥ (Mn. 8. 179.)

217. N. 2. 2. Identical with Mn. 8. 179 quoted in fn. 216.

218. *sthānaṁ gṛhaṁ sthalaṁ caiva tad ṛṇaṁ vividhān guṇān,*
satyaṁ śaucaṁ bandhujanaṁ parikṣya sthāpayen nidhim (Bṛh. 11.4).

case, with persons who were :

(a) born of good family (*kulaja*);

(b) endowed with good character and qualities;

(c) truthful;

(d) well acquainted with *dharma*;

(e) honourable;

(f) wealthy and powerful; and

(g) who had many relatives.[219]

All these considerations were advisory only and the non-juridical sources dealing with deposits have shown that, in all cases mentioned there, the deposits were not placed with persons having the attributes enumerated above. Because the depositors did not follow this advice they incurred difficulties. All problems mentioned in the non-juridical sources arose from the fact that the depositaries were not properly chosen.[220]

As can be deduced from the story in KR. of the courtezan Samarasundarī, the depositaries knew this advice and therefore, had done their best to convince the depositor that they had the needed 'conditions' to become proper depositaries. The mistress of the servant and the yogi in KR. tried every trick possible to convince Gaṅgadatta that they were endowed with good character and qualities, that they were truthful, acquainted with *dharma*, honourable and wealthy.[221]

4. *Vis major*

30. According to Mn.[222] Y.,[223] N.,[224] Bṛh.,[225] Kāty,[226]

219. Cf. *JSAIL* 11, par. 5.

220. In Mṛ. and Cār. Cārudatta had all these attributes, except that mentioned under (f); several times explanations were given in Mṛ. to that effect. In Pañc., the balance and in Rāj. and Kath., the money, were entrusted to unreliable people and therefore they did not want to return the objects deposited.

221. Cf. fn. 119.

222. *caurair hṛtaṁ jale nodham agninā dagdham eva vā,*
na dadyād yadi tasmāt sa na saṁharati kiṁcana (Mn. 8. 189). Cf. N. 2.12. quoted in fn. 224.

223. *na dāpyo'phahṛtaṁ taṁ tu rājadaivikataskaraiḥ* (Y. 2. 66a).

224. *grahītuḥ saha yo'rthena naṣṭo naṣṭaḥ sa dāyinaḥ,*
daivarāja kṛte tadvan na cet taj jihmakāritam (N. 2. 9.)
caurair hṛtaṁ jale magmam agninā dagdham eva ca,
na dadyād yadi tasmāt sa na saṁharati kiṁcana (N. 2. 12), Cf. Mn. 8. 189 quoted in fn. 222.

225. *daivarājopaghātena yadi tan nāśam āpnuyāt,*
grahītṛdravyasahitaṁ tatra doṣo na vidyate (Bṛh. 11.11).

226. *nikṣiptaṁ yasya yat kiṁcit tat praytnena pālayet,*
daivarājakṛtād anyo vināśas tasya kīrtyate (Kāty. 593.)
yasya doṣeṇa yat kiṁcid vināśyeta hriyeta vā,
tad dravyaṁ sodayaṁ dāpyo daivarājakṛtādvinā (Kāty. 594.)

and K.,[227] the objects deposited which were lost by the depositary because of *vis major* could not be recovered by the depositor. The depositor suffered the loss in case the object deposited was destroyed or lost because of *vis major*. The Smṛti-s considered as *vis major* any act of fate or of the king (*rāja-daiva*) and *exempli gratia* enumerated also theft, plundering, fire, flood, actions of enemies or invaders, sinking of ships, etc.[228]

31. In non-juridical sources *vis major* was very often quoted as the reason for not returning the object deposited.

A. In Mṛ. and Cār. Maitreya, anticipating the future action of both dramas, said that Cārudatta would not be obliged to return the jewels if they were stolen[229] and, with the news that the jewels were really stolen, Maitreya repeated that in these circumstances Cārudatta was not responsible towards Vasantasenā for the objects deposited.[230]

B. In Pañc., Kath. Śuk. t. s. and Bṛ. Kath., in the story of Mice that Ate Iron, the reason mentioned by the merchant for not returning the balance given to him in deposit, was that it was eaten by mice. This was another example of *vis major* which released the depositary from his obligation of returning the object deposited, irrespective of whether *vis major* mentioned was likely to occur or not. It may be noted, however, that in Mṛ. and Cār. Cārudatta was afraid that nobody would believe his story of *vis major* because of his poverty.[231]

C. In all cases where *vis major* was quoted in the non-juridical sources, that problem was solved in accordance with the Smṛti-s. The non-juridical sources even complemented the rules contained in the Smṛti-s on *vis major*.

5. *Restoration of objects deposited*

32. According to Bṛh. the contract of deposit was concluded in the interest of the depositor. The depositary who received the deposited objects for safekeeping had only obli-

227. *paracakrā'ṭavikābhyāṁ durgarāṣṭravilope vā, pratirodhakair vā grāmasārthavrajavilope, cakrayukte nāśe vā, grāma madhyā'gnyudakābādhe vā kiñcid amokśayamāṇe kupyam anirhāryavarjam ekadeśam uktadravye vā, jvālāvego'pavṛddhe vā, nāvi nimagnāyāṁ muṣitāyāṁ svayam uparūḍho no'panidhim abhyābhavet* (K. 177.13-7).

228. Cf. *JSAIL* 11, par. 9.

229. Cf. fnn. 11, 17.

230. Cf. fn. 24.

231. Cf. fnn. 26, 30, 49, 53.

gations and no rights; therefore the best course for him was not to accept any objects in deposit.[232]

33. One of the most important *essentialia* of the contract of deposit was, according to the Smṛti-s, the obligation of the depositary to return the object deposited to the depositor himself in the same condition in which it was delivered. That was stated three times in Mn.,[233] as well as in Y.,[234] N.,[235] and Bṛh. [236].

The object deposited, if no definite period of time for return was fixed, had to be returned by the depositary to the depositor whenever the depositor asked for its return. According to Bṛh.[237] and Kāty.,[238] in the case of a contract of deposit with fixed term or for a particular purpose, the depositor could not ask for the return of the object deposited before the fixed term elapsed or before the particular purpose for which the deposit was given was completed.[239]

34. These rules contained in the Smṛti-s were very well mirrored in the non-juridical sources.

A. Śāk. and Kath., for instance, completed the principle contained in Bṛh. that the contract of deposit was concluded in the interest of the depositor. In Śāk. Kāśyapa said that a man who gave his daughter in marriage enjoyed a pleasure

232. *dadato yad bhavet puṇyaṁ hema kupyā'mbarādikam,*
tat syāt pālayato nyāsaṁ tathā ca śaraṇāgatam (Bṛh. 11. 7).
bharturdrohe yathā nāryāḥ puṁsaḥ putrasuhṛdvadhe,
doṣo bhavet tathā nyāse bhakṣito'pekṣite nṛṇām (Bṛh. 11.8).
nyāsa dravyaṁ na gṛhṇīyāt tan nāśas tv ayaśaskaraḥ,
gṛhītaṁ pālayed yatnāt sakṛd yācitam arpayet (Bṛh. 11.9).

233. *yo yathā nikṣiped dhaste yam arthaṁ yasya mānavaḥ,*
sa tathaiva grahītavyo yathā dāyas tathā grahaḥ (Mn. 8. 180).
nikṣepo yaḥ kṛto yena yāvāṁś ca kula sannidhau,
tāvān eva sa vijñeyo vibruvan daṇḍam arhati.
mitho dāyaḥ kṛto yena gṛhīto mitha eva vā,
mitha eva pradātavyo yathā dāyas tathā grahaḥ (Mn. 8, 194-5).

234. *vāsanastham anākhyāya haste'nyasya yad arpyate,*
dravyaṁ tad aupanidhikaṁ pratideyaṁ tathaiva tat (Y. 2. 65).

235. N. 2. 3. Identical with Mn. 8. 180 quoted in fn. 233.
sa punar devividhaḥ proktaḥ sākṣimānitaras tathā.
pratidānaṁ tathaivāsya pratyayaḥ syād viparyaye (N. 2. 6.)

236. *sthāpitaṁ yena vidhinā yena yac ca vibhāvitam,*
tathaiva tasya dātavyam adeyaṁ pratyanantaram (Bṛh. 11.10).

237. Bṛh 11.9 quoted in fn. 232.

238. *yadi tat kāryam uddiśya kālaṁ pariniyamya vā,*
yācito'rdha kṛte tasmin naprāpte na tu dāpyate (Kāty. 606).
Cf. K. 198. 13 sqq.

239. Cf. *JSAIL* 11, par. 12, 13.

such as was enjoyed by a man who returned the object deposited to the depositor.[240]

B. In Kath., in the story of Puṣpadanta, Gaṇa clearly said that he gave his daughter-in-law to the king for safe-keeping while he was away. The king had then only obligations and no rights over Gaṇa's daughter-in-law.[241]

C. In KR. the yogi pretended to refuse to take the jewels in deposit. That showed not only that he was trustworthy but also that he was not interested in taking the jewels into deposit, since such an act was not considered as concluded in his interest.[242]

35. We also find in the non-juridical sources many instances which confirm the rule that the object deposited should be returned in the very manner and whenever the depositary was asked by the depositor to do it.

A. In KR. Samarasundarī told the yogi that she would like to deposit with him the five trunks for a short time[243] and in Mṛ. Cārudatta said that the jewels given in trust by Vasantasenā were so given for a short time after which he ought to restore them.[244] Also in the fourth act Madanikā said that, if Śarvilaka were to pretend to be Cārudatta's servant and to give the stolen jewels to Vasantasenā in the name of Cārudatta, he would discharge Cārudatta's obligation towards Vasantasenā.[245]

B. In Cār. Vasantasenā stated that the reason for which she placed the jewels in deposit with Cārudatta was the possibility of visiting him whenever she wished to do so under the pretext that she wanted the objects deposited returned.[246]

C. Rāj. completed the rules contained in the Smṛti-s, relating to the right of the depositor to ask for the return of the object deposited whenever he asked for it. It is evident from the story of King Uccala that the depositor not only asked the merchant for the return of the objects deposited, whenever he wished to do so, but even asked him for the return of small parts of the objects deposited, that is, asked him for the return of the objects in small instalments.[247] That was in accordance

240. Cf. fn. 128.

241. Cf. above par. 20 where the question was discussed whether this act could be considered as a contract of deposit. Cf. also fn. 211.

242. Cf. fn. 119.

243. Cf. fn. 119.

244. Cf. fnn. 8, 9, 10.

245. Cf. fnn. 39. 40.

246. Cf. fn. 18.

247. Cf. fnn. 80. 83.

with the Smṛti-s, since, because of the nature of the objects deposited, it was possible to make such a request.[248]

D. In Rāj. in the same story of King Uccala it was also stated that the wealthy man deposited money with a merchant some twenty or thirty years ago and after this period of time asked for the return of the objects deposited.[249] Though the merchant tried all possible tricks in order not to return the money deposited, he did not argue that it was not the right time for the return of the objects deposited.

E. Also in Pañc., Kath. Śuk. t.s., Bṛ. Kath., in the story of the Mice that Ate Iron and in the story of Upakośā, the depositaries who did their best not to return the objects deposited did not argue that it was not the right time for the return of the objects deposited.[250]

F. The transitory character of the contract of deposit was also confirmed in Ragh. where Bharata said that he enjoyed the kingdom of his brother as a deposit only.[251]

6. *Denial of restoration of object deposited*

36. According to the Smṛti-s, in the case of denial of restoration of the objects deposited, the judge decided the question. The depositary could either deny the receipt of the object deposited or deny its return for different reasons although admitting that he had received the objects deposited.

The Smṛti-s, such as Mn.,[252] N.,[253] Bṛh.,[254]

248. That would not be possible if the objects deposited were indivisible.

249. Cf. fnn. 81, 82. 250. Cf. fn. 108. 251. Cf. fn. 126.

252. *yo nikṣepaṁ yācyamāno nikṣeptur na prayacchati,*
sa yācyaḥ prāḍvivākena tan nikṣepturasannidhau (Mn. 8. 181.)
nikṣepasyāpaharttāram anikṣeptāram eva ca,
sarvair upāyair anvicchec chapathaiś caiva vaidikaiḥ (Mn. 8. 190).
teṣāṁ na dadyād yadi tu tadhir anyaṁ yathāvidhi,
sa nigṛhyobhayam dāpya iti dharmasya dhāraṇā (Mn. 8. 184).

253. *yācyamānas tu yo dātrā nikṣepaṁ na prayacchati,*
daṇḍyaḥ sa rājñā duṣṭātmā naṣṭe dāpyaś ca tatsamam (N. 2. 7.)
na ced dadyāt tu nikṣeptus tad dravyaṁ tu yathāvidhi,
upasaṁgṛhya dāpyo'sau divyādibhir vyavasthitaḥ (N. 2. 4.)
N. 2, 6 quoted in fn. 235.
araṇye nirjane rātrāv antarveśmani sāhase,
nyāsasyāpahnave caiva divyā saṁbhavati kriyā (N. 1.241).

254. *bhedeno'pekṣayā nyāsaṁ grahītā yadi nāśayet,*
yācyamāno na dadyād vā dāpyas tat sodayaṁ bhavet (Bṛh. 11.12).
gṛhītvā'pahnute yaś ca sākṣibhiḥ śapathena vā,
vibhāvya dāpayen nyāsaṁ tatsamaṁ vinayaṁ tathā (Bṛh. 11.14).
raho datte nidhau yatra visaṁvādaḥ prajāyate,
vibhāvakaṁ tatra divyam ubhayor api ca smṛtam (Bṛh. 11. 15).

Vi.,[255] Kāty.,[256] Y.,[257] and K.,[258] stated that, if the depositary denied the receipt of the objects deposited, the judge had to determine the truth using evidence of witnesses, oaths or ordeals which, according to some Smṛti-s had to be used even if witnesses could be heard.[259] If the judge asserted that the depositary had received the objects deposited he had to compel the depositary to give up the deposit, to pay a fine and to punish him. If the depositary, not denying the fact of receiving the object deposited, refused to restore it for other reasons, for instance because of some counter claims towards the depositor, the judge (the king) had to find out the truth and proclaim his judgment. If the counter-claim was not proven, the judge should order *in integrum restitutio* or the payment of the value of the object deposited in case of a guilty loss of it and repayment of interest. If the depositary refused *mala fide* to return the object deposited, the judge could consider such an act as equal to a theft and impose a fine.[260]

37. We find most of these rules mirrored in the non-juridical sources in classical Sanskrit.

A. In Kath. in the story of Upakośā, Upakośā was afraid that the merchant Hiraṇyagupta would deny that he received the money deposited by her husband and therefore, resorting to tricks, forced him to avow in the presence of witnesses that he received the money deposited by her husband in order to prepare a suit before the king. Before the king, witnesses gave evidence on the basis of which the king passed judgment and ordered the restoration of the deposit.[261]

255. *pratiśrutasyāpradāyī tad dāpayitvā prathama sāhasaṁ daṇḍyaḥ* (Vi. 5. 178).

256. *yācyamāno na dadyād vā dāpyas tat sodayaṁ bhavet* (Kāty. 608).

257. *bhreṣaś cen mārgite'datte dāpyo daṇḍaṁ ca tat samam* (Y. 2. 66b). Cf. fn. 223.

258. *nikṣepā'pahāre pūrvāpa dānaṁ nikṣeptāraś ca pramāṇam* (K. 180. 7-8). *prakīrṇakaṁ tu yācita-kāvakrīta-kāhitaka-nikṣepa-kāṇāṁ yathādeśakālam adāne yāṁ acchāyāsam upaveśasaṁsthitīnāṁ vā deśakālātipātane gulmatara deyaṁ brāhmaṇaṁ sādhayataḥ prativeśānupraveśayor upari nimantraṇe ca dvādaś-apaṇo daṇḍaḥ* (K.198. 13-6).

259. Bṛh. 4. 14-5.

260. Cf. *JSAIL* 11, par. 13.

261. Cf. fnn. 107, 109, 111, 113, 116. The king did not impose any penalty on Hiraṇyagupta, though, according to the Smṛti-s, he was entitled to do so.

B. In Mṛ., Maitreya suggested to Cārudatta that he deny having received the object deposited. He wanted to ask 'who gave anybody anything ?,' 'who received anything from anybody ?,' 'who were the witnesses?'[262] If the matter were to be brought before the judge, Vasantasenā would not be able to prove that she had placed a deposit with Cārudatta and would lose the case, since she would not have witnesses who could prove her statement.[263]

C. The same was the standpoint of the yogi in KR., though he did not say as clearly as Maitreya did that nobody could prove that the deposit had been given to him. The yogi only said 'why do you come to me ?' 'I do not know anything about your jewels ';[264] in other words, 'you cannot prove anything and therefore I shall not give you any jewels, since I took nothing from you !'

D. In other non-juridical sources we find only mention of referring the dispute to the judge (the king) who decided the case without hearing witnesses, oaths or ordeals. In the story of the Mice that Ate Iron, as narrated in Pañc., Kath. and Śuk. t.s.,[265] and in the story of King Uccala in Rāj., who used his good sense in passing judgment,[266] the disputes were referred to the judge.

E. In Mṛ. and Cār., we also find certain passages which refered to the indemnification of the loss of the objects deposited. In these cases, however, the depositary was not responsible for the loss of the objects deposited. The loss of the jewels deposited by Vasantasenā was caused by theft—a *vis major*; therefore the depositary—Cārudatta was not under the obligation to recompense for that loss, but Cārudatta afraid that nobody would believe in the theft (and because of his good character) wanted to indemnify Vasantasenā and accepted from his wife a necklace which he sent through Maitreya to Vasantasenā.[267] However, this necklace was more expensive than the objects deposited and therefore Maitreya, in accor-

262. Cf. fn. 27.

263. The plaintiff, that is the depositor had to prove that he had placed the deposit with the depositary.

264. Cf. fn. 119.

265. Cf. above par. 8-9.

266. Cf. fnn. 91, 98.

267. Cf. fnn. 43, 45, 46, 51, 54, 59, 61 62.

dance with the Smṛti-s, complained about Vasantasenā's behaviour who, as he thought from greediness proper to courtezans, accepted the necklace in place of the objects deposited. If Cārudatta had been obliged to indemnify Vasantasenā for the loss of the jewels, he would have had to give either the exact value of the jewels or similar jewels of equal value.

7. *Embezzlement of deposits*

38. As stated before, the depositary who was found guilty of not returning the objects deposited was punished like a thief, since such an act was equal to the crime of theft (Vi. [268] Mn.[269]).[270]

39. In non-juridical sources the denial of returning the objects deposited was called embezzlement, which was considered as equal to theft. From these sources, it is evident that such an embezzlement occurred frequently, since it gave rise to two aphorisms quoted in Rāj. saying : 'The water which has been carried down to the ocean by the streams is received back from the clouds; but a thing deposited in a merchant's hands is never again recovered'[271] and 'a merchant in a lawsuit relating to embezzlement of a deposit is more to be dreaded than a tiger, because he shows a face smooth as oil, uses his voice but very little, and shows a gentle appearance.'[272]

In the stories quoted in Rāj.,[273] Kath.,[274] Pañc. V.[275] and KR.,[276] the depositary used various pretexts in order not to return the objects deposited and to embezzle them. However, according to the judgment passed, the depositaries were not punished as they should be, if the rules of the Smṛti-s were to be applied.[277]

268. *rajñā cauravac chāsya* (*Vi.* 5. 170. Also in M. N. Dutt's text).
269. *yo nikṣepaṁ nā'rpayati yaś cānikṣipya yācate,*
tāv ubhau cauravac chāsyau dāpyau vā tat samaṁ damam.
nikṣpasyā'paharttāraṁ tat samaṁ dāpayed damam,
tatho'panidhi-harttāram aviśeṣeṇa pārthivaḥ (Mn. 8. 191-2)
270. Cf. *JSAIL* 11, par. 12-3.
271. Rāj. 8. 128 quoted in fn. 101. According to Stein's translation.
272. Rāj. 8. 129 quoted in fn. 103. According to Stein's translation.
273. Cf. above par. 10.
274. Story of Upakośā.
275. Story of the Mice that Ate Iron; also in Kath., Śuk. t.s. and Bṛ. Kath.
276. Story of the courtezan Smarasundarī.
277. No judgment was given in the story of the courtezan Smarasundarī.

40. Rāj. contains one more interesting mention of embezzlers of deposits for which no analogy could be found in the Smṛti-s, although Kalhaṇa mentioned them in accordance with the spirit of the Smṛti-s. Kalhaṇa mentioned embezzlers as those who were held in a very low opinion; they were on the same level as old officials out of employment, *soi-disant* princes, wicked soldiers, schoolmasters who had their buttocks scratched by their pupils' nails, aged dancing-girls of the temples, Brāhmaṇs of the Purohita corporations, Damaras from the environs of the city, etc.; all these, including merchants who had embezzled deposits and therefore showed themselves always eager to listen to the recital of sacred texts, entertained themselves and others somehow with seditious tales and were known as those who delighted in the king's misfortune.[278]

8. *Praescriptio*; *usucapio*

41. As stated before, the depositary, when taking an object in deposit, had only the *animus rem alteri habendi.* The object deposited was in his detention only. The depositary could, therefore, never prove his *bona fides.* Hence objects deposited were not liable to *praescriptio* or *usucapio.* In Mn.,[279] Y.,[280] N.,[281] Vās[282], K.,[283] and Śukr.[284] we find rules which confirm this interpretation.[285]

42. The rules refering to *praescriptio* and *usucapio* were mirrored in Rāj. There the merchant who tried different

278. Rāj. 8. 706-10 quoted in fn. 138. According to Stein's translation.

279. *adhiḥ sīmā bāla dhanaṁ nikṣepo'panidhi striyaḥ,*
rājasvaṁ śrotriyasvaṁ ca na bhogena praṇaśyati (Mn. 8. 149).

280. *ādhi sīmo'panikṣepā-jaḍa-bāladhanair vinā.*
tatho'panidhi rāja-strī śrotriyāṇaṁ dhanair api (Y. 2. 25).

281. N. 1. 81. Identical with Mn. 8. 149 quoted in fn. 279. (*var. śrotriyadravyaṁ na*).

282. *anyathā'py udāharanti :*
ādhiḥ sīmā bāladhano nikṣepo'panidhi striyaḥ,
rājasvaṁ śrotriyadravyaṁ na saṁbhogena hīyate (Vās. 16. 18). Cf. Mn. 8. 149, Śukr, N. 1. 81, quoted in fnn. 279, 281, 284.

283. *jñātayas śrotriyāḥ pāśaṇḍā vā rājñāmasānnidhau paravāṣtuṣu vivasanto na bhogena hareyuḥ.*
upanidhim ādhiṁ nikṣepaṁ striyaṁ sīmānaṁ rāja śrotriyadravyāṇi ca (K. 191. 1-3).

284. Śukr. 4.5., 225. Identical with Mn. 8. 149 quoted, in fn. 279 (*var. nikṣepo'panidhi s tathā*).

285. Cf. *JSAIL* 11, par. 4, 16.

tricks in order not to return the objects deposited, deposited with him for twenty or thirty years,[286] did not even try to declare that he acquired them by *usucapio* and did not make a plea of limitation and, thus, did not try to declare that the depositor lost them by *praescriptio*.

IV. CONCLUSIONS

Despite general rules determining the accurate usage of terminology in the Kośa-s, the non-juridical sources in classical Sanskrit, instead of using technical legal terminology found in the Smṛti-s and *nibandha-s* employed for the designation of open deposits (*nikṣepa*), sealed deposits (*upanidhi*), secret deposits (*nyāsa*), mutual deposits (*pratinyāsa*), deposits for use (*yācita*), and deposits for delivery (*anvāhita*) colloquial terms, such as *nyāsa* or *nikṣepa*, although the non-juridical sources show that the contracts of deposit narrated there were not the contracts which were described by the colloquial terms used.

On the other hand, the non-juridical sources in classical Sanskrit mirrored many legal provisions relating to the contracts of deposit as included in the Smṛti-s and even complemented them, particularly as to the ownership or detention of the objects deposited, *vis major*, *in integrum restitutio* of the objects deposited, denial or restoration of the objects deposited, etc. This shows that the rules contained in the Smṛti-s and relating to the contracts of deposit were living rules that were well known to the general public.

286. Cf. fn, 81, 83.

IV

PLEDGE*

I. NOMENACLATURE

1. *"Pledge" in Sanskrit.*

In ancient Indian law we do not find a uniform terminology for the word "pledge". The usual word used in Sanskrit texts for "pledge" is the word *ādhi*. Bṛh. (X, 38) also says that "the pledge" is termed *bandha* or *bandhaka*.[1]

Pledges were enumerated in the sources of ancient Indian law among the first titles of law *i.e.* recovery of debt *ṛṇadāna* (or debt) and according to Asahāya (*ad* N. 1.20) to the eighth of the 132 branches (divisions)[2] as *ādhibheda*.[3]

They were considered as one of the two existing guarantees which can be offered to the creditor.[4]

2. *Division of Pledges in the Sources of Law.*

From the legal point of view pledges were declared to be of several sorts. Bṛh. (X, 38-39) divides pledges into eight categories *i.e. jaṅgama* (movable) and *sthāvira* (immovable); *gopya* (to be kept) and *bhogya* (to be used) : *yadṛcchika* (with no time limit) and *sāvidhi* (with a time limit); *lekhyārūḍha* (stipulated in writing) and *sākṣimān* (stipulated before witnesses).

The first six categories related to the division of pledges from the legal point of view and the last two from the formal point of view *i.e.* the manner in which the contract of pledge was concluded.

N. (1-124) divides pledges into four categories : (1) with a time limit *i.e.* which must be redeemed within a certain period of time (*kṛtakalopaneya*), (2) those without a time

*Previously appeared as JSAIL. 17 in the "Bhāratiya Vidyā" Vol. VI, Nos. 7-8, pp. 157-64; Vol. VI. No. 9, pp. 179-94.

1. *ādhir bandhaḥ samākhyātaḥ......* (N. 1.20).
2. N. 1. 20.
3. p. 10.
4. N. 1. 117. *viśrambhahetū dvāv atra pratibhūr ādhir eva ca*

limit (*yāvaddeyodyata*), (3) to be kept only (*gopya*), (4) to be used (*bhogya*).

Y. (2.58,59,61) also divided pledges into four classes, i.e. into pledges fixed as to payment, the name of which was not given (*ādhiḥ praṇaśyed dviguṇe dhane yadi na mokṣyate*)[5] and with a time limit (*kālakṛta*),[6] as well as pledges to be kept (*gopyādhi*) and to be used (*phalabhogya*). Y. introduced another kind of pledge, viz. the *caritrabandhakṛta*, i. e. pledge based on good conduct which meant according to Mit. (*ad* Y. II-61) relying on the good faith of the pledgee or pledgor. This type of pledge was contracted either when the pledgor gave the pledgee a very valuable article as a token and took in return only a small loan, or alternatively when he gave something of purely nominal value and took a large loan in return.[7]

K. (178-8-9) distinguished between pledges to be kept and pledges to be used, although the proper definition for these two pledges cannot be found.

nādhisso'pakāraḥ sīdenna cāsya mūlyaṁ vardheta; nirupakārassīden mūlyaṁ cāsya vardheta. K. in another place (178.16) mentioning immovable property (*sthāvara*) divided it into *prayāsabhogya* and *phalabhogya*. Both these terms mean pledged immovables which should be used; the difference between these two pledges depended on whether the pledge bore fruit with or without work.

Vi. did not make any division of pledges. It is however evident from the text that a distinction between pledges existed, i.e. between pledges to be kept and pledges to be used, pledges unlimited as to time and pledges limited as to time, as well as immovable and movable pledges. Vi. in 6.5 mentioned pledges to be used (*āthyupabhoga*), in 6.8 immovable pledges (*sthāvaramādhi*) and in 6.7 pledges limited as to time (*antavṛddhau praviṣṭayām api*).

G. (12.32 and 35)[8] mentioned only loans secured by a pledge to be used (*bhuktādhirna*) and *ādhibhogaḥ*.

5. See also Y. 2. 64.

6. Mit. *ad* *ādhi* divided also pledges into kṛtakāla . nd akṛtakāla.

7. Y. connected this rule with the loan contracted without a pledge ("promised" satyaṅkārakṛt).

8. Ed. by A. F. Stenzler. Ed. by L. Śrinivasacharya (XII. 29 and 32). Ed. by M. N. Dutt wrongly *muktādhirna*.

Mn. (8.143) did not mention any distinction between pledges; it mentioned only pledges to be used (*sopakāre kausīdīm*).[9]

Kāty. (516), mentioned pledges to be used and called them *bhogyādhī*; it divided this kind of pledges into *jaṅgama* (movable) and *sthāvara* (immovable). In 518 Kāty. additionally divided pledges into documentary pledges (*lekhyakṛta*) and those made before witnesses (*sākṣyakṛta*). In 520 and 519 it introduced another distinction unknown to other Smṛtis, viz., *anirdiṣṭa* and *nirdiṣta* pledges, i.e. pledges whcih were not specified (did not exist) and specified (which existed at the time of making a pledge). It can be assumed that these last two pledges determined or described only pledges when a document was drawn up (*lekhyakṛta*)[10]

3. *Division of Pledges from the Legal Point of View.*

It is evident from the above that, from the point of view of civil law, pledges (*ādhi, bandha, bandhaka*) were divided into pledges to be kept (or pledges for custody) and pledges to be used (usufructuary pledges).

Pledges for custody were known as *gopya* (Bṛh., N), or *gopyādhi* (Y.). Usufructuary pledges were known as *bhogya* (Bṛh., N.), *bhogyādhi* (Kāty.), *bhuktādhirna* (G.), *phalabhogya* (Y., K.)[11], *ādhyupa-bhoga* (Vi), *ādhi-bhoga* (G.), or *sopakāra kausīdī* (Mn.)[12]

The second division of pledges depended on the type of the object pledged, i.e. whether it was immovable or movable. An immovable pledge was known as *sthāvara* (Bṛh., K., Kāty.) or *sthāvaram ādhi* (Vi.) and a movable pledge as *jaṅgama* (Bṛh., Kāty.).

The third division related to pledges contracted for a limited time and those not contracted for a limited time.

9. Medh. on Mn. 8.143 distinctly divided pledges into pledges to be used and to be kept.

10. See also the division of pledges into four in Parāśara-mādhavīya which quotes Bharadvāja. cf. P. V. Kane. History of Dharmaśāsta, I. 128.

11. Without or with the use of work (*prayāsabhogya*).

12. Sarasvativilasa (p. 233) quoting Vyāsa and Bharadvāja divided pledges for use *bhogyādhi* into two kinds : *sapratyaya-bhogyā'dhi* and *apratya-yogyādhi*'. In the first case interest received by use of pledge was taken by the pledgee on account of the debt of the pledgor in order to reduce the principal; the second one did not differ from the ordinary *bhogyā*. See also Mit. (*ad* Y. II-64) and P. V. Kane's Kāty. p. 218, note *ad* 51.

Pledges limited as to time were known as (*sāvadhi*) (Bṛh.), *kālakṛta* (Y.), *kṛtakāla* (Mit.) or *kṛtakālopaneya* (N.) and pledges not limited as to time *akṛtakāla* (Mit.), *yādṛcchika* (Bṛh.) or *yāvaddeyodtyata* (N.).[13] This distinction was important for the designation of the time and manner in which the pledge had to be returned or the contract of pledge annulled; it was also connected with the problem of satisfying the pledgee in case the debt was not repaid at all or not properly repaid.

As a fourth division a special kind of pledge (introduced in Y. only) should be mentioned. This was the pledge based on good faith of the pledgee or pledgor and was known as *caritra-bandhaka-kṛta*.

From the poins of view of procedure there existed a fifth division of pledges, i.e. pledges stipulated in writing or before witnesses. Pledges stipulated in writing were known as *lekhyarūḍha* (Bṛh.) or *lekhyakṛta* (Kāty.) and pledges stipulated before witnesses were known as *sākṣiman* (Bṛh.) or *sākṣyakṛta* (Kāty.).

Also from the point of view of legal procedure the last division of pledges was important *i.e.*, into unspecified and specified pledges, known as *anirdiṣṭa* and *nirdiṣṭa* (Kāty.).

II. PLEDGES TO BE KEPT AND TO BE USED

A. Pledges to be kept (Pledges for custody).

4. *Objects of Pledges to be kept.*

Objects which were suitable for this kind of pledge were numerous and were mentioned examplarily by the commentators on the sources of law or even by codifiers themselves. Mit. mentioned a copper pan, Medh. cloth, and it is evident from Kāty. that female slaves could be given by the pledgor to the pledgee. It must be admitted that every object which had a value might have been considered as a pledge to be kept.

5. *General Rules.*

Such an object which was given by the pledgor into the possession (detention) of the pledgee could have been kept

13. See also Vi. VI-7.

but not used. If the pledgee used the pledge such an act caused legal consequences regulated in the *Smṛtis*. These legal consequences were various, but, in the rule, the pledgee lost all the interest due to him or part thereof and sometimes was under the obligation to pay compensation for the use of the pledged article.

The pledgee was obliged to keep the pledged object *cum omni diligentia* and was responsible for its destruction or damage.[14]

It is, therefore, evident that the pledge for custody was equivalent to the Roman *pignus*, which was given by the pledgor to the pledgee to secure the right of the latter. The pledgee was entitled to secure payment of a claim through the medium of the object pledged.

6. *Prohibition of using Pledges for Custody.*

The rule relating to the prohibition of using the pledge for custody was expressed in the best way in N. and Mn., although both sources used the word *ādhi* instead of *gopya*.[15]

The texts of N. (1.127) and Mn. (8. 144) are identical and run : *na bhoktavyo balādā'dhiḥ* (pledge for custody must not be used by force—*bala*).

In another place N. and Mn. in almost identical words stated :

yaḥ svaminā'bhyanujñātam ādhiṁ bhuṅkte'vicakṣaṇaḥ. (N.1.128)

yaḥ svāminā'nanujñātam ādhiṁ bhuṅkte'vicakṣaṇaḥ, (Mn.8. 150. Also quoted in Apar. *ad* Y. 2.59, VyK. 112, SC. 138, VRK. 23, VCi. 15, SCM. 10, NṛP. 22, SV. 231, VCa.10, Vīr. *ad* Y. 2.59, VyPr. 236, VT. 538, VV. 16, VyP. 86, VyS. 74, VVy. 25).

That means that the pledge for custody could not be used without the authorisation of the pledgor (*ananujñāta*).

N. and Mn., as we see, differentiated as to whether the pledge to be kept was used by force or without the authorisation of the pledgor. It was a distinction between the use *vi* and *clam*.

Neither the ancient Indian sources of law nor the commen-

14. See 8 7, 32.,
15. See Col. p. 151.

tators gave an explanation of what should be understood by "using a pledge to be kept *vi* and *clam*". Was it "use" against the will of the pledgor and use without the consent of the pledgor ? Or was it "use" by force of the pledge against the will of the pledged thing or without its will and without using force ? The latter interpretation seems to be evident from Kāty. (525) where we read about the pledging of a female slave whom the pledgee could make work unwillingly (*vi*) or without the consent of the pledger (*clam*).[16]

It is clear that it was an exceptional case as it happened seldom that a living thing (a female slave) was given as a pledge.

Therefore, the legal consequences of the keeping of the contract of pledge for custody depend on the wording of the contract agreed upon between the pledgor and the pledgee. It was essential whether the object pledged was used against or without the will of the pledger. That this interpretation is correct is evident from Medh.'s commentary on Mn. VIII-144 where it is said that "others explain" that the verse 144 of book VIII refers to the case where the debtor at the time depositing the pledge distinctly said "do not use the pledge, etc.........." and yet the pledgee ignoring this did made use of the object pledged.

7. *Legal Consequences of Using a Pledge for Custody.*

(**a**) *If the Pledge did not lose its Value.*

As a rule the pledgee who used the pledge *vi* forfeited the interest due to him. *bhuñjāno vṛddhimu tsṛjet*—N. I-127. Mn. VIII-144) and the pledgee who used the pledge *clam* lost one half of his interest as compensation for such use (*tenārdhavṛddhir moktavyā tasya bhogasya niṣkrayaḥ* N. 1. 128, Mn. VIII-150.

Only N. and Mn., however, distinguished between the use of pledge *vi* and *clam*. All the other sources of law discussed the use of the pledge for custody and admitted that in case of use of this pledge the pledgee forfeited the interest due to him. This was evident from the fact that the other

16. *akāmam ananujñātam ādhiṁ yaḥ karma kārayet.* See also Vācaspatimiśra quoted in Col. p. 157.

ancient Indian sources of law *i.e.* Y., Vi. G. and others admitted that the contract of pledge to be kept itself contained the prohibition of the use of pledge; that conformed to the *essentiale* of the contract of pledge for custody.[17]

Mit. (*ad* Y. I-59) explained that although the use was slight even a large amount of interest would be forfeited, as there was a breach of contract. Similarly Medh. (*ad* Mn. VIII-144) regulated this question.[18]

The question of the use of a pledge which was unwilling to work must be described apart. This case was regulated in Kāty. (525). It referred to female slaves which were pledged by the pledgor. (Ratnākara and other commentators[19] were probably right when they said that this text did not solely concern a pledge to be kept; it also related to pledges to be used.).

According to Kāty. he who used a living pledge *vi* or *clam* should receive no interest on his loan, as well as pay the *lucrum* i.e. the fruits of labour obtained by the use of the living pledge. This was in conformity with the rule mentioned above.

Viv.[20] referring to the contexts of Mn. and N. as well as interpreting Kāty. 575 came logically to the conclusion that the pledgee who caused a living pledge to work against his/her will (*vi*) should forfeit the whole interest, but if the pledge worked voluntarily *i. e.* without the consent of the pledgor (*clam*)—half the interest should be forfeited.

This interpretation seems to be correct, provided that the living pledge was given as a pledge for custody.

In this connection it must be added that according to Kāty. (526) the pledgee who insulted or injured with words or blows the living pledge while working for him had to pay the first amercement. It is clear that the general rule regarding the loss of interest had to be applied here too and the amerce-

17. Y. II-59, Vi. VI-5, G. XII-32.

18. It must be added that Bṛh. X-39-40 mentioned in general that the creditor who used a pledge by avarice (probably a pledge to be kept) before it was payable should stop its use. It is possible, however, that this rule related also to pledges for use or to a special agreement relating to pledges according to which in spite of the prohibition of using the pledge during a certain period, it was used. An extensive comment is found in Col. (pp. 157-158).

19. Quoted in Col. p. 152.

20. Viv. p. 10.

ment introduced here was connected with the rule regarding the prohibition of abuse of a pledge.

(b) *If the Pledge lost its Value.*

The rules mentioned above related to the object pledged for custody, if by using it, the object pledged did not lose its value and did not become damaged or destroyed.

If, however, in case of a pledge to be kept, the object pledged became destroyed or damaged, in the rule, in addition to the loss of interest, *in integrum restitutio* and payment of *lucrum* —the pledgee was compelled to pay a compensation. This rule was adopted in the *Smṛtis* which admitted that the pledgee could not satisfy his claim from the pledged thing. If it were, however, admitted that the pledge could satisfy the claim of the pledgee, if the debt was not paid, in the rule, the pledgee lost his right to claim the debt and was even obliged to pay compensation in case the value of the object pledged was higher than the amount of the debt due. This rule was the same in Mn. and N., but different in K. and Bṛh.

K. which took this question into consideration stated in the most general way that the rule relating to deposits should be applied (178-7). The rules relating to deposits stated that the depositary who had made use of the deposit for his own comfort should pay compensation as well as a fine of 12 *paṇas* (K. 178-1-2). K. in another place stated.

anisṛṣṭo'pabhoktā mūlyaśuddham ājīvaṁ bandhaṁ ca dadyāt. (K. 179.1).

The pledgee in case of a pledge to be kept who enjoyed this pledge without permission should lose the principal and pay the net profit and compensation—*bandha*.

On this question Mn. and N.[21] differred somewhat. Mn. (VIII-144) stated: *mūlyena toṣayec cainam ādhisteno 'nyathā bhavet.* (Also quoted in Medh. *ad* Mn. 8.150, Mit, *ad* Y. 2.58, VyK. 112, SC 138, VRK. 24. SCM. 11, NṛP. 22, VyPr. 136, 138, VyU 73,VT. 538, VyP. 86. Vys. 74-5.)

According to these two sources of law (these rules related to the use of pledge for custody *vi*), the person who by

21. Mn. VIII-144 and N. I-127.

using the pledge destroyed or damaged it was liable for the re-establishment of the original legal position (*in integrum restitutio*). Medh. (*ad* Mn. VIII-144) explained that if a pledge was in the form of things which ceased to exist by use, the full compensation must take place. And if he was not willing to repay the object pledged he had to pay the penalty which he would have to pay if he had actually stolen an object of the same kind as the pledge.

We see that in this case Medh., commenting on Mn., differed from the text of K., but conformed to one point which, after all, emanated from the rule mentioned before *i.e.* that in addition to the restoration of the pledge the whole *lucrum* derived from the use of the pledge, had to be paid. The same point of view was also found in Nārāyaṇa (Asahāya) (*ad* N. I-127). Undoubtedly the object pledged had to be restored if the value of the pledged thing was higher than the loan.

Bṛh. (X-43), however solved this question in another manner. According to Bṛh. if the object pledged was completely destroyed by use, the pledgee was not obliged to restore it. The pledgee lost only the right to recover the debt from the pledgor. If the pledge was not commensurate with the debt *i.e.* when the object pledged was of a higher value than the debt, the pledgee not only lost the right to recover the debt but also had to satisfy the pledgor *i.e.* pay the difference between the debt without interest and the value of the damaged (destroyed) pledge.[22]

It can be said that this rule was more primitive and was connected with the rule that the pledgee could satisfy his claim from the pledge received.[23]

B. Pledges to be used (Usufructuary Pledges)

8. *Definition*

Pledges to be used consisted of an arrangement between the pledgor and pledgee whereby the pledgee not only obtained

22. It seems that Viv. remarks without foundation that this rule related to cases of loans bearing no interest.

23. For the rest of the rules regarding pledges to be kept (for custody) in particular those relating to damage of pledges not caused by its use etc. see chapter VIII. on "Duties of pledgors and pledgees."

possession with the right of sale, but also the right to use the pledge and take all the fruits and profits *in lieu* of interest.

A usufructuary pledge was nothing else than the *antichresis* of the Roman law.

The best definition of the usufructuary pledge is found in Kāty. (516) :

dravyaṁ gṛhītvā vṛddhy arthaṁ bhogayogyaṁ dadāti cet,
jaṅgamaṁ sthāvaraṁ vā'pi bhogyā'dhiḥ sa tu kathyate.
(Also quoted in SV. 234, VyS. 77).

The *bhogyādhi* was contracted when a pledgor took the loan and gave to the pledgee something movable or immovable which might be enjoyed in order to meet the interest. The next sentence : *mūlyaṁ tad ādhikaṁ dattvā sva kṣetrā'dikam āpnuyāt* explained that *bhogyā'dhi* was a real *apratya-bhogyā'dhi* and not a *sapratya-bhogyā'dhi*, *i.e.* that the fruit and profits yielded by the object pledged were not used for the reduction of the principal. The whole object pledged was to be returned to the pledgor by the pledgee.

9. *Objects of Pledges to be used.*

Kāty. (516), as has already been remarked, was of the opinion that movable as well as immovable goods *jaṅgamaṁ sthāvaraṁ*......could be pledged as a usufructuary pledge. Mit. (*ad* Y. II-58) interpreting the word *phalabhogya*) stated that where profits were to be enjoyed fields, gardens etc. might be pledged; Medh. (ad Mn. VIII-143) added milch cows and Kūll. (*ad* Mn. VIII-143) a slave.[24] From Mn. (VIII-146) it was evident that camels, oxen, and other animals used to be pledged. In any case we can say that every object which was capable of yielding fruit or producing profit could be pledged as a usufructuary pledge. Articles which were consumed when used, such as corn etc. could not be the object of a pledge to be used.

10. *Differences Between Pledges to be kept and Pledges to be used.*

The most important difference between pledges to be kept and pledges to be used lay in the fact that in the case

24. See § 6.

of pledges for custody the object pledged could not be used and in the case of the pledge for use—it could be used. The legal consequence of this difference lay in the fact that in the case of pledges for custody the pledgee received interest from the loan, and in the case of usufructuary pledges the loan did not yield any interest as fruits and profit produced by the object pledged and taken by the pledgee cancelled the right to interest. In addition, according to some sources of law, the pledge to be used never lapsed while the pledge to be kept lapsed if it was not redeemed by the time the principal debt was doubled.[25]

Therefore the definition given in K. (178. 8-9) seems to be perfect. It is stated there : *nā'dhis-sopakāraḥ sīden na cāsya mūlyaṁ vardheta*; *nirupakāras-sīden-mūlyaṁ cāsya vardheta.*

This sentence clarified the difference between these two kinds of pledges. In the case of a pledge to be used interest never had to be charged on the debt and it could never be lost to the pledgor. In the case of a pledge to be kept interest on the debt had to accrue and the object of pledge could be lost.

The rule that the loan secured by a pledge to be used yielding no interest was identically solved in Mn. (VIII-143) and N. (I-129).[26] G. solved also similarly the same question.[27] An explanation of this view was given in G. (XII-34-35) where the different types of interest were enumerated. As different types of interest *karitā* (stipulated interest), *kāyika* (corporal interest), *śikhā* (daily interest) and *ādhibhoga* (pledge to be used) were enumerated; this shows that fruits and profit yielded by the object pledged were equal to interest on the principal.

The pledge for custody could not be returned, or sold before the term fixed for its redemption.[28]; [29]

25. See below § 16.

26. *na svevādhau sopakāre kausīdīṁ vṛddhiṁ āpnuyāt*, See also K. 178. 8-9. quoted above.

27. Ed. by A. F. Stenzler (XII-32); ed. by Śrinivasacharya (X I-29); ed. by M. N. Dutt *bhuktādhir na varddhate......*

28. See § 13 and 15; Mn. (VIII-143) and N. (I-129).

29. For other rules relating to pledges to be used see below. P. V. Kane in his edition of the Kātyāyanasmṛti (*ad* 530) said that Smṛ. C. explained that "the surety in case of a *gopyādhi* was called *ādhipala* and in case of *yogyādhi* was called *yuñjāpaka* and that both were included therein."

III. IMMOVABLE AND MOVABLE PLEDGES

11. *Definition.*

The difference between movable and immovable pledges lay in the object of the pledge *viz.* whether an immovable or movable property was pledged.

N. (I-139) says that pledges are declared to be of two sorts : movable and immovable.[30] *ādhistu dvividhaḥ prokto jaṅgamaḥ sthārastathāḥ*). This is also evident from Kāty. (516), although the text related to *bhogyādhi* and not to *ādhi*.

This distinction was of no great importance from the point of view of ancient Indian civil law which does not know registers of mortgages, hypothecation,[31] etc. Therefore, the legal rules were the same for movable as well as immovable objects. There existed however, a few exceptions to this rule. These exceptions referred to immovables only.

12. *Exceptions relating to Immovable Pledges*

(**a**) *Description*

According to Kāty. (522) the boundaries of immovable properties should be clearly delineated in a document. The contract regarding the pledge of immovable property should also describe the position of the pledged immovable property.

This rule is clear, as the taking into possession of an immovable property could not be carried out by delivery. In order to avoid probable future disputes regarding the return of the whole pledged immovable property a clear description of this property and its boundaries was essential.[32]

30. Identically Vyāsa. Col. p. 205.

31. See J. Jolly's *Recht und Sitte*, p. 100 sqq. and differently P. N. Sen's *Hindu Jurisprudence*.

32. In this connection it should be noted that Ratnākara stated that if the pledgee against or even without the consent of the pledgor possessed more land or property than was expressly pledged, he shall pay the first amercement and the pledger shall get back his whole pledge. See also Kāty. (527) and § 41 and 42.

(b). *Pledging of Immovable Property to two Pledgees.*

Bṛh. (X-44) declared that a field when pledged to two pledgees at almost identical times, should belong to that pledgee by whom it was first possessed. This rule was connected with the question of whether the contract of the pledge was a real or a consensual contract.[33] Ratnākara explained that this rule was applied if the priority could not be proved. It could take place when the pledgee did not enjoy the object pledged to him and it could not be remembered to which of the pledgees it was pledged first. If the first pledgee was traced then he would be considered the right one. If it should be proved, however, that they possessed the pledgedi mmovable property for an equal period, then it should be held in common *i.e.* shared equally by them (Bṛh. X-45).[34],[35]

(c). *Enjoyment of the Immovable Pledges.*

The pledged immovable property should be enjoyed, according to K. (178-16-17) in such a manner that its value does not deteriorate. This rule, however, is a general rule which is to be applied to all kinds of pledges.[36]

(d). *Return of Immovable Pledges.*

The rules of Bṛh. X-70 and 71 applied to all kinds of pledges. According to these rules when an immovable property was pledged for use and the fixed period did not expire, the pledgor could not recover his property nor the pledgee his loan. On the contrary, when the stipulated period had elapsed the pledgor as well as the pledgee were allowed to do so, provided that they had not made another agreement before, regarding the recovery of the property and loan. The same rule is found in Vi. (VI-9).

These rules do not exceed the limits of ordinary rules concerning all kinds of pledges. Similarly, we find in Bṛh. (X-67-68) a rule relating to the pledge of an immovable pro-

33. See § 23, 24 and 25.

34. Kāty. stated that he who made a false document about the pledge of immovable property, should be deprived of his tongue, hands and toes (*lex tallionis*).

35. See §35-38.

36. See § 32-34.

perty if the term of recovery of the debt was not agreed upon, but a special agreement took place. According to this agreement the pledgor offered the pledge saying that the pledged immovable property should be enjoyed by the pledgee up to the moment when the principal had been realised together with interest (i.e. when becoming equal to the principal); then the pledge should be returned to the pledgor. According to such an agreement pledged immovable properties should be enjoyed so long as it was necessary to realise "no more than the principal" (principal and interest) and then they should be returned to the pledgor.

It should be noted that K. referred in addition to the capital and interest to the expenses incurred in maintaining the pledged immovable properties and Vi. (VI-8) also mentioned a special agreement concerning restoration of pledged immovable properties.

(e) *General Characteristics of Exceptions Relating to Immovable Properties.*

These rules, although laid down by the ancient Indian sources of a law only in connection with pledged immovable properties, were similar to other rules which did not apply to immovable properties as every agreement could be concluded between the parties regarding the restoration, time limit, etc. of the pledge.

IV. PLEDGES LIMITED AS TO TIME AND PLEDGES NOT LIMITED AS TO TIME

13. *General Remarks.*

The contract of a pledge could contain the time in which the debt and the pledge ought to be returned or did not contain this stipulation. Depending on this fact the contract of a pledge would be called limited or not limited as to time.

If the time in which the pledge must be returned was stipulated, the pledgor was obliged to return his debt to the pledgee in the stipulated time and the pledgee was obliged to return the pledge to the pledgor. Provided no other agreement was concluded, the pledgor, as well as the pledgee, were protected by the stipulation of the time in which the debt and the pledge must be returned. Accordingly, the pledgor could not be forced to repay the debt and the pledgee to accept the debt before the stipulated period.

This stipulation might be important for the pledgee too, as the giving of a loan secured by a pledge might be made for his sake in view of the interest due to him.

In the event of the debt not being repaid in the stipulated period, the question arose as to whether the pledgor was guilty of non-repayment of the debt or whether he was innocent. Depending on that fact the manner in which the pledgee could be satisfied is regulated. In particular it must be made clear whether the pledge would become the property of the pledgee or would be sold and from the price obtained, the pledgee satisfied. This question is closely connected with the problem of whether the pledge was given in order to secure, or to satisfy the pledgee's claim.

As far as the pledge not limited as to time was concerned, the question had to be solved as to when the pledgee was entitled to claim the repayment of the debt and when the pledgor was entitled to repay the debt and claim the return of the pledge. This question was closely connected with the problem of the accruing of interest and limitation of the period during which payment of interest was obligatory.[37] The problem of satisfying the claims of the pledgee in the form of sale or appropriation of the pledge was in this case similar to the identical problem in the case of pledges limited as to time.

In in the case of pledges limited, as well as not limited as to time, the legal consequences depended on the wording of the relative contracts, in particular, whether the contract related to pledges to be kept or to be used.

14. *Definition.*

N. (1.124) defined in the following manner these two kinds of pledge : *kṛtakālopaneyaś ca yāvad deyodyatas tathā* *i. e.,* pledges which must be redeemed within a time agreed upon

37. See below Study XVI on the Harmonizing of Law with the Requirements of Economic Conditions.

(*kṛta°+°kāla°+°upa°+°neya*), that is pledges limited as to time and pledges which must be returned when the debt has been repayed (*yāvat°+°deya°+°ud°+°yata*), that is pledges not limited as to time.

Asahāya stated (*ad* N. 1. 124) stated : *tatra kṛta-kālo 'paneyo-yaḥ dvi-prakāraḥ; eko dīyamāne dhane prāpta-kālā-vadhau ādhi-pālaiḥ samarpaṇīyaḥ; dvitīyas tu atipuṣyamāṇo dhaninā evaṁ vicārya gṛhyate; yathā pañca varṣāṇi daśa vā iyantaṁ kālaṁ......na mocanīyaḥ; tat parato ṛṇike.*

We see here that Asahāya divided pledges limited as to time into two subdivisions. According to the first—the pledge was given to the *ādhipāla i.e.* to the pledge-keeper who had to return it at the time agreed upon.[38] According to the second one, the pledge was delivered to the creditor on condition of its being returned after the lapse of a certain period of time, viz. after five or ten years. It is not clear whether the *ādhipāla* was a third person or the pledgee himself; in any case these two subdivisions were of no great importance from the legal point of view.

It is evident from the definition contained in N. (1-124) what the *essentialia* of both these kinds of pledges were.

In the case of pledges limited as to time :

(*a*) the time of the debt secured by the pledge was limited;

(b) after this time the pledge had to be returned.

In the case of pledges not limited as to time :

(*A*) no agreement was concluded regarding the time in which the debt and the pledge must be returned;

(*B*) as soon as the debt has been discharged:

(*C*) the pledge had to be restored.

15. *Return of Debt and Pledge in Contracts of Pledge Limited as to Time.*

As far as pledges limited as to time were concerned, the problem as to when the debt must be returned to the creditor and when the creditor had to return the pledge was not solved in the *Smṛti-s*. This question had to be solved by mutual

38. See J. Jolly's *Recht und Sitte*, p. 101 and his *Indisches Sechuldrecht*, p. 298 sqq.; J. J. Meyer's *Das altindische Buch vom Welt und Staatsleben*, p.785.

agreement which, however, could not be contradictory to the general rules regarding debts. In particular, this contract could not be concluded for a very long period of time in consequence of which the interest would more than double the principal. If such a contract should be concluded, after the principal had doubled, the interest could not continue to accrue.[39]

16. *Acts which are Contradictory to Stipulations of Contracts of Pledge Limited as to Time.*

It is evident from Bṛh. (X-71) and from the definition of pledges limited as to time that these pledges had to be restored to the pledgor after the lapse of the stipulated, period provided the debt had been repaid.[40] By mutual consent, however, it could be restored before the stipulated period, although Bṛh. did not stipulate *expressis verbis* that the period to restore the pledge might be shortened by mutual agreement.

It is clear that the whole debt had to be repaid, because when a portion only had been repaid,—regardless of whether it was a contract of a pledge limited or not limited as to time, —the pledgee was not obliged to return the pledge. This rule was the same as the rule : *pignoris causa est individua* so well known to Roman law.[41]

This rule was not exclusively introduced in order to protect the pledgee. As has already been said, the pledgee was also protected in case the pledgor wanted to return his debt before the agreed period of time and in such a way did not pay the contracted interest. On the other hand the pledgor was protected too, as the pledgee could not claim his debt before the stipulated period.

This problem was regulated in an identical manner in N., Mn. and Bṛh. Although Mn. and N. referred rather to pledges to be used and Bṛh. to immovable pledges, we can admit that the respective rules were general rules which could be applied to all kinds of pledges.

39. See note 37.
40. Vi. VI-8, K. 178-10.
41. Vi. (VI-8), Bṛh. in Col. p. 165, Nand. *ad* Vi. (VI-8) stated that the agreement concerning the restoration of the pledge should be as follows : "You shall have the enjoyment of this or that mango grove as long as interest on the principal lent to me has not ceased to accrue."

Bṛh. (10.70) stated :

yatrā'dḥikaṁ gṛhakṣetraṁ bhogena prakarṣān vitam.
tatraṇīṁ cā'pnuyād bandhaṁ dhanī caiva ṛṇaṁ tathā.

(Also quoted in VyK. 114, VRK. 32, VCi. 17, SCM. 10, VCa. 12, VyP. 89, VyS. 76, VVy. 26).

When a house or field had been pledged for use and the stipulated period had not expired, the debtor could not recover his property nor could the creditor recover his loan.

Mn. (VIII-143) and N. (I-129) stated that the pledgee could not transfer or sell the pledge before the stipulated period had elapsed.[42]

17. *Date of Payment of Pledges not Limited as to Time.*

As far as pledges not limited as to time were concerned, the ancient Indians sources of law say that whenever the debtor came and restored the debt, the pledgee had to return the pledge. This was the opinion of Y. (II-62), Bṛh. (X-66) and K. (178-10).

Bṛh. (10.66) stated :

dhanaṁ mūlīkṛtaṁ datvā yad ādhiṁ prārthayed ṛṇī.
tadaiva tasya moktavyas tv anyathā doṣabhāg dhanī.

(Also quoted in VyK. 112, SC. 146, VRK. 27, NṛP. 23, SV. 241, VCa. 13, VyPr. 245, VV, 17, VyP. 89, VyS 76.

Ratnākara commenting on this para stated that it related to pledges to be used only. Vīr. (p. 319) was also of the same opinion and stated that as the restoration of the principal was only mentioned, this rule relates to pledges to be used. In the case of pledges to be kept, interest had to be paid in addition to the principal.

This interpretation does not seem to be correct. Bṛh. stated that *na* means generally "debt" and not only "principal"; in case of pledges to be used *dhana* would be the principal only but in case of pledges to be kept *dhana* would be the principal with interest. We can admit, therefore, that Bṛh. (X-66) related to pledges to be used as well as to pledges to be kept.

Halāyudha raised another problem : what would happen in the case of pledges to be used when the pledgor came to

42. This rule is not very clear and was extensively interpreted in various ways.

repay the debt on the next day and asked for the restoration of the pledge. In this case the pledge would be *de facto* deprived of interest. The reply to this question is easy; the pledge had to be restored. The pledgee did not secure his rights by limitation of the time in which the debt had to be returned and had to bear the consequences of his act.

If the pledgee, in spite of his obligation, did not return the pledge he was considered as thief (*stena*), Y. (II-62) stated. This consideration of such a pledgee as a thief involved legal consequences *i.e.* a fine determined in Bṛh. in general terms only, and in K. (178-10) as amounting to 12 *paṇas*.

K. stated :

upasthitasyā'dhima-prayacchato dvādaśa-paṇo daṇḍaḥ.

It is the most general presentation of this problem which shows once again that these rules related to pledges to be used as well as to pledges to be kept.

18. *Repayment of the Pledged Debt if the Pledgee was Absent.*

In Y. and K. another question was also solved *i. e.* what happened in the event of the pledgee being absent and the pledgor coming to restore the debt. This problem should be enlarged. Under the word "absent pledgee" we must also understand according to Mit., Ratnākara and others, the case of the "pledgee having died."

In this case the debt should be accepted and the pledge restored. The question arose as to whom the debt should be repaid. It should be repaid to the person who was legally in charge of the pledge. Y. (II-62) stated that it should be repaid to the family (*kula*) and K. (178-11) stated to the elders of the village (*gramavṛddha*). In both these cases it was a casuistic solution. In juridical language it should be said that in such a case the debt had to be returned to the person who was legally in charge of the pledge or who was the legal successor of the pledgee.[43]

If, however, the creditor was absent or dead and there was nobody who was entitled to take the debt, the pledgor had to :

43. J. J. Meyer's *Über das Wesen der altindischen Rechtsschriften......* *Leipzig.*, 1927. pp. 181-2.

(*a*) appraise the whole of the pledge at the time of its restoration.

(b) leave the pledge *tatra* (there) *i. e.* with the pledgee.

If that had been done and

(*a*) the creditor did not return the pledge,

(*b*) the interest no longer accrued until the creditor restored the pledge, if it was a pledge to be kept; if it was a usufructuary pledge the pledgee was no longer allowed to use the pledge.

That was the opinion of Y. (II-63) and K. (178 12-13).[44]

19. *Rights of Pledgees to satisfy their Claims if the Pledged Loan had not been Repaid.*

The rules quoted above were to be used if the debt has been returned by the pledgor to the pledgee.

More important, however, was the problem of what would happen when the pledgor did not return the debt.

As far as pledges limited as to time werec oncerned this question was connected with the problem of the right of the pledgee to satisfy his claim from the pledge. This act could take place when the stipulated time had elapsed.

As far as pledges not limited as to time were concerned, the problem arose as to when the pledgee had the right to satisfy his claim from the pledge; the solution would vary in the case of pledges to be kept and pledges to be used.

The problem of the right of the pledgee to satisfy his claim from the pledge not limited as to time was solved in the *Smṛti-s* in a very unsatisfactory and confusing manner. We find contradictory rules which are very difficult to understand. They can be understood only when this problem has been solved separately for pledges to be kept and separately for pledges to be used.

As far as pledges to be kept and not limited as to time are concerned, the problem was mentioned in Bṛh (X-48 and 50) as well as in Y. (II-58) and Mn. (VIII-154,) and as far as pledges to be used and not limited as to time are concerned—

44. *tat kālakṛtamūlyo vā tatra tiṣṭhedavṛddhikaḥ.* (Y. 2. 63. Also quoted in ViR. *ad* Y. 2.65, VyK. 114, SC. 146, VRK. 28, SCM. 20, *NṛP.* 23, VyPr. 245, VyU. 74, VyM. 78, VT. 548-9, VyP. 89, VyS. 76, AP. 254.23 *nivṛtta-vṛddhiko vā'dhistat kāla-kṛta-mūlyas-tatraivā'vatiṣṭheta.* (K. 178. 12-3).

in Bṛh. (X-21), Y. (II-64), Vi. (VI-7) and Vyāsa (Col. 186).

(a) *In the case of Pledges to be kept and not Limited as to Time.*

Pledges to be kept and not limited as to time became payable when the principal amount was doubled. According to some of the *Smṛti-s* when this occurred, the pledgee was entitled to claim the payment and according to others to satisfy his claim from the pledge. According to Bṛh. (X-48) the pledgee had to wait for a fortnight, after this had occurred. After having waited for this period of time he became the owner of the pledge. According to Y. (II-58) the pledge lapsed in this case *i. e.* as soon as the principal amount was doubled, the pledgee became the owner of the pledge.

This differentiation was of no great importance from the legal point of view, because according to Bṛh, the debt became payable in a fortnight after the principal was doubled[45] and according to Y. as soon as the principal was doubled. Up to this moment the pledgor was entitled to claim the pledge given by him, provided that at the same time he repaid the principal due, as well as the interest. After this term the pledgee was entitled to satisfy his claim by the act of appropriating the pledge. The lapse of time gave to the pledgee the *titulus acquirendi* of the object pledged.

Mn. (VIII. 145) stated only that the pledge after a lapse of time became liable to appropriation. This opinion conformed with another *śloka* of Bṛh. (X-50) according to which the pledge to be kept could be used after the period, mentioned above, has elapsed.

Interpreting these various rules relating to pledges to be kept not limited as to time, we come to the conclusion that after the debt was doubled the pledgee was entitled either to appropriate the pledge or to begin to use it, in order to satisfy his debt with interest.

(b) *In the case of Pledges to be Used and not Limited as to Time.*

The situation in the case of pledges to be used and not

45. See Bṛh. 10.49.

limited as to time was quite different. It was reversed here.

During the whole time the pledge was in possession of the pledgee, it was used and the pledgee defrayed the interest and obtained a profit in using the pledge. As, up to the moment of repayment of the debt in case of pledges to be kept, the contract was concluded in the interest of the debtor, while the contract of pledge to be used was concluded rather in the interest of the creditor. Therefore, if the pledgee by using the pledge and taking fruits from it (interest) doubled the principal as well as received the principal back, he was obliged to restore the pledge to the pledgor.

Y. (2. 64) stated :

yadā tu dvīguṇībhūtam ṛṇam ādhau tadā khalu,
mocya ādhis tad utpanne praviṣṭe dviguṇe dhane.

(Also quoted in ViR. *ad* Y. 2.66, Medh. *ad* Mn. 8.151, Mit. *ad* Y. 2.64, VyK. 113, SC. 147, VRK. 28, VCi. 7, NṛP. 23, AP. 254. 24).

The opinion of Vi. (VI-7) and Vyāsa (Col. 186) was similar, Bṛh. (X-21) stated that the use of the pledge after the principal has been realised was usury and reprehensible.

(c) *Interest*

We saw that as far as pledges to be kept as well as pledges to be used were concerned, the time limit depended on the fact of whether the principal had been doubled or not. This was closely connected with the rules relating to interests. *Inter alia* the ancient Indian sources of law limited the admissibility of interest by introducing the time limit *viz.* determined up to what moment interest could accrue on the capital. There was a general rule that the principal should not double.[46] If, therefore, in the case of ordinary debts the principal should not be doubled it should also not be doubled in the case when it was secured by a pledge.

46. See note 37. It can be deduced from Kāty, 541 that "if one mortgaged or pledged with the express stipulation that when the principal doubled, he would pay double the money but would not lose the property mortgaged or pledged; then the creditor was only entitled to double the principal, but not to the property." (See Kane's Kātyāyana's Smṛti, 541).

(d) *Pledges Limited as to Time.*

As far as pledges limited as to time were concerned, Bṛh. only outlined what ought to be done in the case when the pledgor did not repay the debt. Bṛh. in book X. (48 and 50) solved this problem in a similar way as in the case of pledges not limited as to time *viz.* after the principal had been doubled the pledge could be used or the pledgee could appropriate the pledge after having waited for a fortnight. It is clear that these rules refer to pledges to be kept.

It is not very clear whether *śloka* 49 of book X. of Bṛh. (according to which such pledges on which interest have ceased became the property of the pledgee after ten days), referred to pledges to be used or whether this rule was only slightly different from that contained in *śloka* 48.

(e) *Non-Repayment of pledged Debts "Ex Causa" and "Sine Causa".*

From the remarks mentioned above it was evident that pledges to be kept, as well as pledges to be used, according to Bṛh., were not sold if the debt had not been repaid, in order to satisfy the pledgee's claim, but the pledgee became the owner of the pledge. Therefore, we could say that according to Bṛh. the pledge was given to the pledgee in order to satisfy his claim not by realising the value of the object pledged but by appropriation.

It is not clear whether the same rule applied according to Mn. and N., because both these *Smṛti-s* did not mention this problem. It might be deduced from Mn. (VIII-143) and N. (I-149)[47] that it was possible that the pledgee also satisfied his claim by realising the value of the object pledged.

These rules applied to the problem of not repaying debts by a "not guilty act".

If the debtor was guilty of not repaying his debt secured by a pledge, then according to N. (I-132, 133) the king should compel him to pay it by forcible means and should take five per cent for himself. If he acknowledged the debt, the king should take ten per cent as fine and twenty

47. Identical rules.

per cent if he was adjudged to pay after denial of the debt. This rule was repeated in Mn. (VIII-139), Y. (II-44), Vi. (VI-20-22). Bṛh. (X-93, 99), Yāma (in Vivādaratnākara, p. 78) etc. It is not clear, however, if it related to debts secured by a pledge or to debts in general.

It is clear, when interpreting the respective rules of the *Smṛti-s*, that if the debtor was not guilty of non-repayment of the debt, the pledge could not be appropriated by the pledgee but had to be sold.

Bṛh. (X-51-52) in particular stated that there was no fault on the part of the debtor, as far as non-repayment of the debt was concerned, if he was not present or had died; (in this case the heirs were not responsible for the obligations of the deceased). The same opinion was expressed in Y. (II-63 *in fine*) and Kāty. (529). G. (XII-33) added a case where a pledgor was forcibly prevented from repaying the debt *i.e.*, according to Haradatta, in the case of imprisonment by the king or others, or the like. In this case according to Bṛh. (X-51) and Y. (II-63) the pledge should be sold in the presence of witnesses even without the presence of the debtor according to Kāty. (529) by the king (identically Viv.). Bṛh. (X-52) added that the pledge could also be estimated in an assembly kept for ten days, and then sold. In any case if the pledge had been sold, the debtor could not take more than cover his demand (principal and interest). The surplus (*hyperocha*) had to be returned to the pledgor or deposited with the king (Viv.).

When this sale took place it was clear from the general rules, *viz.* as far as pledges limited as to time were concerned —after the lapse of the stipulated period of time (Y. II-62-63) and as far as pledges not limited as to time are concerned, when the debt was doubled (Bṛh. X-51).

In this connection a general rule regarding the repayment of debts should be mentioned. According to N. (I-131 and 134) when a debtor had been prevented by bad luck from repayment of the debt he should be made to repay it gradually according to his means and if it occurred through a calamity the claim of the debtor should be entered in a written bond. The first part of this rule was also repeated in Mn. (VIII-177, IX-229) and Y. (II-43). The commentators interpreted this rule applying *analogia ex maiori ad minus viz.*

if the pledgor was unable to restore a pledged loan, he had to restore it successively, as best he could.

The rule, therefore, was as follows : if the debtor did not repay the loan pledged at the moment it became payable the object pledged could be appropriated by the pledgee irrespective of its value, that means without the obligation to pay the *hyperocha*. If, however, the non-repayment of the pledged loan was caused by an unguilty act on the part of the pledgor, the object pledged could be publicly sold with the obligation to pay the *hyperocha*.

If the pledgor was guilty of non-repayment of the pledged loan he could be forced to repay it, and if he was unable to repay it without guilt, he could be ordered to restore it in instalments.

V. PLEDGES BASED ON GOOD FAITH

20. *Religious Interpretation.*

This kind of pledge is found in Y. (II-61) only. The respective *śloka* is not clear and was commented on in different ways.

caritra-bandhaka-kṛtaṁ sa vṛdddhyā dāpayed dhanam,
satyaṅkārakṛtaṁ dravyaṁ dviguṇaṁ pratidāpyet.

(Also quoted in ViR. *ad* Y. 2. 63, VyK. 11, SC. 143, VRK. 33, NṛP. 22, SV, 246, VyPr. 244, VyU. 73, VyM. 77, VT. 546, VyP. 87, VyS. 75, AP. 254. 21).

Caritra-bandhaka-kṛta was a pledge by a *caritra*. *Caritra* from *car* (to go) means foot, going, behaviour, conduct, act, practice, religious act, good faith. Should the word *caritra* be understood as a religious act then such a pledge according to some commentators, should be understood as based on the ablution in the Ganges. It would be based on the promise that the debtor had to repay the debt with the additional obligation that up to the moment of repayment of the debt he would not bathe in the Ganges (Dipakalikā). Instead of bathing in the Ganges some understood the performance of the *agnihotra*.

F. Stenzler translated this śloka as "*Verpfändung unter Lebenswandel*" which corresponds to the above mentioned interpretation. It would also be a debt contracted on the pledge of religious merits.

21. *Legal Interpretation.*

A legal interpretation of this *śloka* is found in Mit. and it seems that it was the only one which was correct. Mit. understood under the expression *caritra* a pledge relying upon "good faith." It would be either good faith of the pledgor or of the pledgee. There was good faith on the part of the pledgee if he gave a large amount as loan and took a pledge of a small value. On the contrary there was good faith on the part of the pledgor if he gave a pledge of a great value and took a small amount as loan. In other words, if the value of the pledge was not in proportion to the loan taken, then we could refer to a *caritra* pledge.

From the legal point of view there is no reason to form a special differentiation for *caritra* pledges as, this kind of pledge could be either a pledge to be kept, or a pledge to be used, or a movable or an immovable pledge; or a pledge limited or not limited as to time.

22. *Legal Consequences.*

According to Y. this kind of pledge involved other legal consequences and might be considered as an exception to the general rules which stated that a pledge to be kept lapsed if doubled.

Y. stated that a pledge of this sort did not lapse even though the amount was doubled. On the other hand the amount should be paid to the extent of twice the principal only.

It should be noted that Mit. (*ad* Y. II-61) interpreting the second part of the *śloka* stated *inter alia*: "In the context of the pledge another (kind of loan) is being described. Whatever object such as a ring etc., has been placed in the hand of another with a view to complete the agreement of sale and purchase, the double of that thing should be paid if the agreement was broken. Even there, if the person by whom the ring etc. was deposited himself broke the contract, he should give the object itself. If the other party committed a breach of the contract then a double of the ring should be returned."[48]

48. According to the translation by J. R. Ghārpure in the Collection of Hindu Law Texts No. 2, p. 95.

VI. PLEDGES STIPULATED IN WRITING AND BEFORE WITNESSES

CONTRACT OF PLEDGE AS A REAL OR A CONSENSUAL CONTRACT.

A.

23. *Real and Consensual Contracts in General.*

In order to understand the division into pledges stipulated in writing and before witnesses we must first consider whether according to ancient Indian law the contract of pledge was a real or a consensual contract.

In Roman law *pignus* was a typical example of the real contract *i.e.* a contract which was actionable on the ground of performance by one party of his *res*. By handing over the *res*, the contract was completed. "*Re contrahitur obligatio veluti mutui datione.*"

Accroding to a consensual contract the mere *consensus* was sufficient to engender an obligation.

The question arises whether according to the ancient Indian law the handling over of the pledge constituted the contract of pledge, or whether for the validity of the contract of pledge it was sufficient when the pledgor promised, with the consent of the pledgee, to hand over the pledge. Was it the act of handing over, or the act of mutual consent which created the contract ?

It is impossible to give a uniform answer to this question when basing it on the *Smṛti-s*. The sources of ancient Indian law do not give a satisfactory reply to this question since the differentiation between real and consensual contracts was not carried out in India in a very strict way.

24. *Contracts of Pledge as Real Contracts.*

It is clear that Y. (II-60) considered the contract of a pledge a real contract and understood under "contract of pledge" every kind of pledge. Y. (II-60) stated *ādheḥ svīkaraṇāt-siddhī*. The contract of pledge was valid by the performance of the act of admission. Using the general word *ādhi* Y. admited that this passage has to be used to *gopya* as well as to *bhogya i.e.* to every kind of pledge; using the words *svikaraṇa°*+°*siddhi* Y. clearly stated that the contract of pledge was a real and not a consensual contract.[49]

The point of view of N., Vyāsa and Bṛh. is not clear, but we can assume that these three *Smṛti-s* were of the opinion that the contract of pledge was a real contract.

N. (I-139) referring to the division of pledges into movable and immovable ones stated that both were valid when there was actual enjoyment and not otherwise.

ādhis tu dvividhaḥ prokto jaṅgamaḥ sthāvaras tathā,
siddhir atrobhyasyā'sya bhogo yatrā'sti nā'nyathā.

(Also quoted in NMS. 2.116, Mit. *ad* Y. 2.60, VyM. 348, Apar. *ad* Y. 2.60, SC. 143, SCM. 9, NṛP. 23, Vīr. *ad* Y. 2.60, VyU. 73, VyM. 77, VT. 116, 542, VyP. 87, VyS. 75, VVy. 19).

We see that N. admitted that the possession of the pledge was the *essentiale negotii* of the contract of pledge. A pledge which was only mentioned in a document without actually being enjoyed had no legal validity, Asahāya (*ad* N. I-139) stated.[50]

An identical point of view is also found according to Vyāsa.[51] In this connection Colebrooke said that this rule related to pledges delivered for use. This view-point was only partially correct, because we must admit that it related to every kind of pledge *i.e.* to pledges to be used, to be kept, etc., as movable and immovable pledges might be given either in order to be used or to be kept.

Bṛh. stated only that when a person neither enjoyed a pledge nor obtained it from the pledgor, nor pointed it out to others, his written contract of pledge was invalid.[52]

It is evident from these rules that the possession of a pledge was essential to a contract of pledge because without possession of the object pledged the contract of pledge was invalid. It does not mean, however, that for the validity of this contract the handing over of the pledge was essential.

25. *Contracts of Pledge as Consensual Contracts.*

If, based on the sources of law mentioned before, we

49. Identically Mit. *ad* Y. II-60.
50. P. 87, line 4, from the bottom.
51. Quoted in Col. p. 205.
52. Bṛh. X-53.

can admit that the contract of pledge was a real contract, we must add that it follows from other *Smṛti-s* that the possession was of the object pledged was of great importance, even though the contract of pledge was a consensual one.

Vi. (5.184) stated :

yayor nikṣipta ādhistau vivadetāṁ yadā narau,
yasya bhuktiḥ phalaṁ tasya balāt-kāraṁ vinā kṛtā.

(Also quoted in Apar. *ad* Y. 2. 60. VyK. 115, SC. 144, VRK. 36, VCi. 17, SV. 236, VCa. 15, VyPr. 239, VT. 542-3, VV. 19, VyP. 88, VyS. 75, VVy. 26)

It is clear that according to Vi., if two men had a dispute over a property pledged to both of them, the pledgee who proved possession without force would enjoy its fruits. If it were possible to pledge an object to two persons it would be almost impossible to hand it over to two persons, as one of them only would have it in his possession.[53]

The same doubts arose in Kāty. (517): *ādhim ekaṁ dvayor yas tu kuryāt kā pratipad bhavet* (Also quoted in VyK. 115, SC. 144, VRK. 35, SV. 237. VCa. 14, VyPr. 240, VyM. 77, VT. 545, VV. 18, VyP. 88, VyS. 75).

K. stipulated what would happen to an object pledged in the event of being pledged to two persons. K. used the word *ādhi* which shows that every thing could be pledged to two persons. Therefore, it did not concern immovable or movable pledges only, but also pledges to be kept and to be used. In particular in the case of pledges to be kept it was impossible to hand over the object pledged to another person as it was already in the possession of the first pledgee. Therefore we must admit that Kāty. was of the opinion that the contract of pledge was a consensual and not a real contract.

Kāty. considered that in the event of one object being pledged to two persons, the priority, or to be more exact, a document *i.e.* a proof of a better *titulus*—was decisive.

Vi. (V-184) stated that possession was decisive and its commentators were of the same opinion. Therefore, if even the handing over of the object pledged was not an *essentiale*,

53. This is not the only proof as this para relates to fruit, therefore, probably to immovable pledges and the handing over of a field could be only performed by symbolic means. Such a symbolic act could be performed by the pledgor with several persons as registers of mortgages were unknown in the *Smṛti-s*.

the possession of the object pledged was of great importance from the legal point of view, not only from the point of view of the civil law, but also from the point of view of legal procedure.

We must admit that Y. on one side, and Vi. and Kāty. on the other, were respectively of the opinion that the contract of pledge was a real, or a consensual contract. Based on N. and Bṛh. we could also assume that in certain cases the contract of pledge was a real one, and in other cases a consensual contract.

In any case ancient Indian law was not uniform as to defining whether the contract of pledge was a real or a consensual contract.

B.

26. *Importance of Contracts of Pledge Stipulated in Writing and Before Witnesses, from the Point of View of Legal Procedure.*

The differentiation between pledges stipulated in writing and before witnesses was above all, of importance from the point of view of legal procedure. In addition this was also important, from the point of view of civil law, when the problem arose as to who had a better claim to the object pledged, in the case of a consensual agreement regarding pledges being contracted by more than two parties.

Bṛh. (X-39) stated that the pledge could be contracted in writing or stipulated orally before witnesses.

Caṇḍeśvara (*ad* Bṛh. quoted in Col. p. 142) was rightly of the opinion that the differentiation was important from the point of view of the legal procedure. Kāty. (518) also held the same point of view; according to this *Smṛti* a pledge stipulated in writing was superior to that stipulated orally before witnesses. Therefore, if a dispute arose regarding a pledge, the party who could prove the existence of the pledge by means of a document was in a better position than the one who could prove his right by means of witnesses. This conformed with the general rules which were in force in ancient India.[54] In this case it was important that this transaction was opposed to one mode of proof only. If one party was able to produce two

54. See below Study XIV on "Legal Relations between Employers and Employees in Ancient India".

proofs, he would be in a better position from the legal point of view. Therefore if one party could prove his right by means of witnesses as well as possession of the object pledged, thus having two modes of proof in its favour, he was in a better position than the person who could prove his right by means of a document but could not prove that he was in possession of the object pledged; if, however, the latter could prove that the other party possessed the object pledged *vi* or *clam* then he would also have the same or better right to the object pledged.[55] Such an intepretation was based *per analogiam* on Vi. V-184 where we find the sentence that with regard to the greater right to an object pledged, between two parties[56] the party who could prove possession not obtained by force was considered to have the better right.

From the point of view of legal procedure the problem as to who was in a better situation in case of a pledge, the right to which was proved by means of two documents, was settled in Kāty. (519).

Kāty. stated that in this case the document which specified the object pledged was more powerful. This rule was connected with *śloka* 522 of the same source. According to this verse perfect proof was given if the written contract of pledge marked out all the details of the immovable object pledged.[57]

A similar point of view was also found in Kāty. 521 where the problem was settled as to the better right from the point of view of legal procedure—of a general pledge that belonged to a man and of a pledge of specified objects.[58]

27. *Falsification of Documents.*

In addition, general rules regarding documents and proofs had to be applied to pledges. In particular two general rules regarding proofs should be mentioned here. These rules are found in Kāty. 300 and 311. According to the latter the falsification of a document of pledge of immovable property was punishable by depriving the falsifier of his

55. See Col. p. 214 sqq.
56. Pledged at the same time.
57. See above.
58. *yas tu sarvasvam ādiśya prāk paścān-nāma-cihṇitam,*
ādadhyāt tat kathaṁ na syāc cihṇitaṁ balavattaram.
Also quoted in VyK. 115, VRK. 37, SV. 238, VyPr. 241, VyP. 88, VyS. 76, SC. 143, SV. 236, VyP. 87).

tongue, hands and toes (*lex tallionis*), provided the falsification was undeniably proved.

28. *Reinforcement of Unvalid Contracts of Pledge.*

On the other hand, although, according to the general rules, a document with some defects was not valid, it became valid when it concerned a pledge which had been undoubtedly enjoyed for twenty years.[59] This rule was probably connected with usucaption, the more so as Kāty. did not admit that usucaption could not take place in the case of pledge.[60]

Other rules regarding pledges stipulated in writing, in particular problems of enjoying pledges on the basis of a vitiated document, pledge of the same object to two or more persons etc. will be discussed in another place.

VII. SPECIFIED AND NON-SPECIFIED PLEDGES

29. *Existing and non-Existing objects at the Time of the Conclusion of Contracts of Pledge.*

This differentiation is to be found only in Kāty. (520); it was important from the point of view of legal procedure only. It is connected with the problem of the contract of pledge as a consensual or real one.

The so-called *anirdiṣṭa i. e.* unspecified pledges were those in which the pledgor pledged an object which at the time of the pledge did not exist. Therefore, such a pledge could not be described and specified and, in consequence, "resembled the sky". On the contrary the *nirdiṣṭa* pledge was a pledge specified in detail and which existed at the time of the pledge.[61]

If we admit that such a *anirdiṣṭa*-pledge was in use we must admit that this contract of pledge was a consensual contract, since it is evident from this passage of Kāty. that the contract of pledge could be concluded although the pledged object did not still exist. From the point of view of legal

59. Kāty. 300.
60. See paras 39-40.
61. *ākāśabhūtam ādadhyād anirdiṣṭaṁ ca ṭad bhavet,*
yadyattad āsya yad yeta tadādiṣṭam vinirdiśet,
(Kāty. 520 Also quoted in VyK. 115, SC. 144, VRK. 38, VyPr. 241, VyP. 88, VyS. 76).

procedure this differentiation had great importance as the *anirdiṣṭa* pledge could not be specified and the *nirdiṣṭa* was specified; we have seen before how important it was from the legal point of view, to specify clearly the object pledged.

VIII. DUTIES OF PLEDGORS AND PLEDGEES

A.

Duties of Pledgors.

30. *General Rules.*

The first duty of the pledgor consisted in giving the pledge and afterwards in repaying the debt. It is clear that the *conditio sine qua non* was the ownership of the object pledged[62] on the part of the debtor who gave the pledge. The time of handing over of the pledge to the pledgee depended on whether the contract of the pledge was a consensual or a real contract. In the case of a real contract the moment of handing over of the object pledged created the contract of pledge, but in the case of a consensual contract the debtor was obliged to hand over the object pledged at the time and place stipulated in the agreement.

The second duty of the pledgor—the repayment of the debt, had to take place also at the time and place agreed upon by both the parties, or when, according to the rules mentioned above, the debt became payable.[63] If the debt had not been repaid at that time the pledgee was entitled to claim the amount due from the pledgor or to appropriate the object pledged.[64]

31. *Restitution of the Pledge in Case of Its Depreciation.*

There existed, however, on the part of the pledgor one more duty *i.e.*, the restitution of the pledge in case of its depreciation. It was known that the pledge was above all, given in order to secure the claim of the pledgee. The pledgee was entitled in conformity with *jus cogens* to receive interest on the

62. This is evident from K. (170-5) where it was stated that in case of repairing of tanks etc., he who did it got ownership of them and as result could sell and pledge them.

63. *Viz.* when the debt has been doubled.

64. See below.

loan given by him which was, however, lower than the one paid In case of a debt not secured by a pledge, since his claim was not so endangered as an unsecured claim.[65]

In ancient India the permitted interest could amount to 240 per cent yearly and according to Y. interest from debts unsecured by a pledge to 24 per cent yearly; however, in the case of debts secured by a pledge the interest could not amount to more than 15 per cent yearly.[66] From this rule the obligation of the pledgor arose to restitute the previous value of the object pledged in the event it had depreciated, or to repay immediately the debt due. The pledgee losing the previous value of the pledge at the same time lost the security of his claim and his debt could have become endangered.

This obligation of the pledgor was stipulated in Y. (II-60), N. (I-130) and Kāty. (524).

Y. and N. in an almost identical manner regulated this obligation of the pledgor. Y. (2.60) stated : ......*rakṣya māṇo'py asāratām; yātaś ced anya ādheyo dhanabhāg vā dhanī bhavet.*

(Also quoted in ViR. *ad* Y. 2.62, VRK. 26, NṛP. 22-3, VCa. 11, VyPr. 239, VyU. 73, VyM. 77, VT. 542. VyS. 74, AP. 254.

Even when the pledge had been carefully kept and suffered deterioration it had to be substituted by another or the creditor had to receive the amount due to him.

N. (1.130) stated :

rakṣyamaṇo'pi yatrā'dhiḥ kāle neyād asāratām,
tatrā'dhiranyaḥ kartavyo deyaṁ vā dhanine dhanam.

(Also quoted in VyK. 112, SC 137. VRK. 26, VCi. 16, SCM. 10, NṛP. 22, SV. 233, VCa. 11, VyPr. 239, VV. 316, VyP. 86, VyS. 74, VVy. 26).

It is evident that N. regulated this problem in an identical manner adding, superfluously, that the deterioration of the pledge had been caused due to time. This point of view seems to be wrong, because every innocent, and more particularly

65. See note 37.

66. *aśītibhāgo vṛddhiḥ syān māsi māsi sabandhake,*
varṇakramāc-chataṁ dvi-tri-catuḥ-pañcakam anyathā. (Y.2.37. Also quoted in ViR. *ad* Y. 2.39, VyK. 106-7, GMH. 12,26,SC 155, MMu. 8.142, VRK. 7, VCi. 3, SCM. 7, NṛP. 18, SV. 221, Rāgh. in MrM. *ad* 8. 142 (8.140), VyPr. 227, VyU. 74, VyM. 75, VT. 58, VV. 3, VyP. 79, VVy. 21, AP. 253, 63).

every guilty[67] loss of value of the pledge obliged the pledgor to give another pledge or to discharge the debt. Kāty. (524) regulated this problem in a similar manner although used a different language. Kāty. stated :

na ced dhanika-doṣeṇa nipated vā mriyeta vā,
ādhim anyaṁ sa dāpyaḥ syād ṛṇān mucyeta narṇikaḥ.

(Also quoted in VyK. 112, SC. 238, VRK. 26, VCi. 17, SV. 236, VyPr. 237, VyM. 77, VT. 541, VyP. 86, VyS. 74). "Using the words *nipated vā mriyeta vā* Kāty. wanted to say : fall, or detrioration, or loss. as well as destruction or death (in case of living pledges such as cows, female slaves[68] etc.) of objects pledged".

K. (178. 13-15) solved this problem in another way. This Arthaśāstra did not say anything about substitution of the pledge; it referred only to the sale of the pledge which *in facto* was equivalent to immediate obligation to repay the debt due. K., as usual, based the obligation to sell the pledge on administrative officers.

K. stated :

anāśa-vināśa-karaṇādhiṣṭito vā dhāraṇa-san-nidhāne vā vināśabhayād udgatārghaṁ dharmasthānujñāto vikrīṇīta; ādhipāla-pratyayo vā.

We see that according to K. when it was to be feared that the object pledged could become depreciated or lost in the near future, the pledgee could ask for the permission of the judges and, if granted, sell the pledge either in the presence of the debtor or an expert. He could also sell it under the guidance of the officer or office in charge of pledges. It is clear that this would take place when the object pledged was of a greater value than the debt, because if the value were smaller, the rule regarding the duty to give another pledge should be applied *per analogiam.*

B

Duties of Pledgees.

32. *General Rules*

The duty of the pledgee consisted in the giving of a loan and the restoration of the pledge as soon as the debt which it

67. See below.
68. See J. Jolly's Recht und Sitte, p. 101.

was intended to secure, was discharged.[69] The pledgee was answerable for *omnis* or *summa diligentia*, otherwise he lost interest. In case of negligence (*culpa levis* or *lata*) in consequence of which the pledge had been injured or lost, the pledgee was liable to *in integrum restitutio* (Vi., N., Y.) or, depending on the extent of the damage done, loss of interest even of the principal. The pledgee, however, was not responsible for any damage to the object pledged, if it was caused by an unavoidable accident *i.e*, *vis. major*.

33. *Preservation of the Pledge by the Pledgee.*

Regarding the duty of the pledgee to preserve the object pledged we read in N. (I-125) and Bṛh., (X-40[70]) that the pledge ought to be kept carefully *i.e. cum omni diligentia*, Bṛh., however, added that it should be kept like a deposit. According to the rules in force for deposits, the deposit had to be guarded with the same care as a son and the sin of those who damaged the deposit by negligence was as great as the sin of a woman who injured her husband or of a man who killed his son or his friend.

In addition to sanctions from the religious point of view (a sin)—Bṛh. (X. 40) as well as N. (I-125) stipulated legal sanctions in the event of the pledgee not exercising care over the object pledged *i. e*, if he did not exercise *omnem* or *summam diligentiam*. Such a fact caused the loss of interest on the principal (N. I-125, Bṛh. X-40). If, owing to negligence (*culpa lata* or *culpa levis*), the object pledged had been rendered worthless (Bṛh. X-43) or injured (N. I-126[71]) the pledgee lost the principal itself. According to Vi. (VI-6) the creditor had to make good the loss of the pledge and according to Y. (II-59) *naṣṭo deyo vinaṣṭaś ca daiva-rājā-kṛtād-ṛte*.

It is clear that Vi. and Y. stated that in such a case *in integrum restitutio* should take place. This is also distinctly stated in Mit. (*ad* II-59) where it is said that if a pledge for use is spoiled it should be restored to the state in which it was before and

69. See above and Vi. (VI-8).

70. See also Bṛh. (XI-9).

71. *pramādād dhanina-stadvad-ādhau vikṛtim āgate,*
vinaṣṭe mūla-nāśaḥ syād daiva-rāja-kṛtād-ṛte. (Also quoted in NMS. 2. 107, Mit. *ad* Y.2.59, Apar. *ad* Y.2. 59, VyK. 111-2, SC. 140, VRK. 22, VCi, 15, SCM. 10, SV. 232, VCa. 10, Vīr. *ad* Y. 2. 59, VyPr. 235, VyU. 72-3, VyM. 76, VT. 539, VV. 15-6, VyP. 86, VyS. 74, VVy. 25).

then returned. Probably Mit. stated incorrectly that this passage related to pledges for use only (it should relate to every kind of pledge) and that if the object pledged had been destroyed *i.e.* had perished entirely, it should be recompensed by paying the full price. It is, therefore, evident from the text that it should be restored and, if it was impossible to do so, it should be paid back by returning the price.

The opinion of Vyāsa (Col. p. 146) was similar to Y.'s opinion, according to which this rule related to objects pledged such as gold and other precious objects. This point of view was also identical with Bṛh.'s (X-43) where it is stated that when a very valuable object pledged was spoiled the pledgor had to be satisfied by the pledgee.

It is, therefore, evident that according to Vi., Y., Bṛh. and Vyāsa *in integrum restitutio* took place if, owing to negligence, the object pledged had been damaged or destroyed. In the most short and clear manner this rule was stated in Vi. and Y.

34. *Vis Major*.

The rule that the pledgee was not responsible for any damage to or destruction of the object pledged, if it was caused by *vis major*, was carried out consequently.

Y., N., G., Vi., Kāty., Vyāsa and Bṛh. expressed the same opinion. This is found in the most general manner in G. (XII-42). We read there that if through no fault of the holder a pledge (as well as in case of the contracts like deposits, use, sale etc.) had been lost, the holder was not responsible for this loss.[72]

Though G. did not refer *expressis verbis* to *vis major* this follows from the context. N., Y., Vi, K., Bṛh. and Kāty. referred *expressis verbis* to *vis major*. These sources of law often used the words *daiva-rāja-kṛtād-ṛte* or *daiva-rājo'paghāttās-ṛte* (Vi. Bṛh.), *daiva-rajata* (Kāty.), etc. The words *daiva* and *rāja* (in N. *rāja* only) were here repeated. *Daiva i.e.* fate. Mit. (*ad* Y-II-59) explained that under *daiva* we must understand fire, water and generally any misfortune. Asahāya (*ad* N 1.126) understood under "fate" a pledge that has been stolen by a thief. A full explanation of "fate" is found in K.

72. Similarly Mn. (VIII-189), Y. (II-66), N. (II-12, 8-9) and others regarding deposits; these rules could be used *per analogiam*.

(177.13 *sqq.*) K. stated that under such a *vis major* destruction of the pledge by enemies or wild tribes, fire, flood, sinking or plundering of ships if the object pledged was there etc. should be understood. In another place K. stated in general that *vis major* of an object pledged occurred when it died (in case of female slaves, cattle etc.) or was involved in calamities.[73]

Regarding the fate, Mit. (*ad* Y-II-59) and Asahāya (*ad* N-1-12-6) explained that the king could cause the loss of the pledge if he confiscated the whole property of a man along with the object pledged on account of a slight offence.

It is clear that these cases were examples only and that the rule consisted in the faultless loss of the pledge caused by *vis major*.

If such a *vis major* occurred, the rules regarding *in integrum restitutio*, loss of interest or of the principal were not to be applied (G. XII-42, Y. II-59, Vi. VI-6, N. I-126, K. 177-13 *sqq.* and 178-7). This was after all, in conformity with the general rules of the ancient Indian civil law.

Kāty. (523), and almost identically Bṛh (X-41) and Vyāsa (Col. p. 160), did not state that *in integrum restitutio* or loss of interest or of the principal had not to be applied. These sources of law went further, because they stated that in this case the pledgor had either to repay the debt or deliver another pledge.[74]

These rules resulted from the general understanding that the pledge was given in order to secure the pledgee's claim. If he had lost it through no fault on his part he had to get another security, or in case of pledges unlimited as to time the debt became payable immediately. Therefore, if, because of *vis major*, the pledge was destroyed, in case of debts unlimited as to time, the debt became payable immediately, provided another agreement had been concluded[75]; in the case of debts limited as to time, the pledgor was liable to deliver another pledge to the pledgee.

73. These rules concerned deposits, but as K. (178-7) stated they held good also in the case of pledges.

74. Kāty. only referred to the repayment of the debt along with interest.

75. And another pledge given.

IX. MISCELLANEA

A.

35. *Two Contracts, General rules.*

If a dispute regarding two contracts arose and these contracts were concluded at different times, the last contract was valid. On the contrary if the contracts were concluded at the same time the contract according to which the pledgee obtained first possession over the object pledged was valid. If, however, both pledgees possessed the object pledged for an equal length of time, it had to be held jointly.

In case of competition between the acts of sale, pledge and donation of the same object on one and the same day the three parties had to divide it among themselves.

36. *Two Contracts Concluded in Different Times.*

The ancient Indian law was of the opinion that in case of dispute relating to the validity of two juridical acts the act which was concluded last was valid. (Y-II-23, N-I-97). However, with regard to pledges this rule is different.

The first act was better than the subsequent one :
ādhau pratigrahe krīte pūrvā tu balavattarā
(Y. 2.23 and similarly N. 1. 97)

This rule was connected with the principle found in Y. (II-60) that a contract of pledge was a real contract. Mit. (*ad* Y-II-23) explained rightly that when a man, after pledging his field with someone and after having obtained a loan, pledged it again with another and also obtained something, the field belonged to the first only and not to the second. A second pledge of the same object was impossible.

Kāty. (517) regulated the same problem and solved it in the same manner. Kāty. clearly asked what would happen in the event of the pledgor pledging the same object to two persons. The answer was that only the first transaction was valid and the second invalid.

Kāty. added that the person who made the two pledges was liable to a fine imposed on a thief (Kāty. 517).

A higher punishment was found in Vi. (V. 181-183) *i.e.* corporal punishment.

Viv. (p. 11-9-11) rightly came to the conclusion that the meaning of the above was that the first pledge was valid and the subsequent one inadmissible. Viv. added also that a similar opinion was maintained in the Pārijāta, Ratnākara, Smṛtisāra etc.

The fact that punishments were either a fine or corporal punishment, showed that these sources of law prohibited the pledge and sale of objects pledged as long as the debt was not repaid to the pledgee. This was clearly stated in K.

If the deposit was either pledged, or sold, or lost, the depository had to restore four times its value as well as pay a fine of five times the stipulated value. Although this para related to deposits it had to be applied to pledgees too. This was stated in K. (178-7).

This view was also expressed in Mn. (8.143) (*na cādheḥ kālasaṁ rodhān nisargo'sti na vikrayaḥ*) and Viv. (12.5 sqq.) (though Viv. did not know K.) based probably his conclusion only on Mn. and the *nibandha-s*, in particular by Halāyuddha.

37. *Two Contracts concluded at the same Time*

Bṛh. and Vi. solved the question of what would happen to the object pledged if it was pledged at the same time on the basis of different acts. This applied only to immovable pledges as it was difficult to imagine that a movable object could be taken into possession if it was pledged at the same time by two different persons. It was however, possible if the contract of pledge was a consensual contract.

According to Bṛh. (X-44) when a field was pledged to two pledgees at the same time it had to belong to that pledgee who first obtained possession of it. This rule shows[76] that according to Bṛh. the contract of pledge was a consensual contract. Therefore, this rule could also be applied to movable pledges.

When it was proved which of the pledgees obtained first possession of the object pledged, his right prevailed. The same rule is also found in Vi(V-184) where it was said only that the right of that person who possessed the object

76. See above.

pledged will be greater; on the contrary he who did not possess the object pledged had no right to it.

But what would happen when both the pledgees possessed the object pledged at the same time? This problem was solved in Bṛh. (X-45) where we read that in such a case the object pledged should be held jointly or shared equally by them. It is difficult to say when this rule could be applied. It is not clear whether in this case the priority in obtaining possession of the object pledged would be considered or not, or whether only the time of possession. Probably it would take place when one pledgor pledged an object at the same time to two pledgees, taking from them two different loans, or taking one loan from two persons simultaneously.

38. *Contracts of Sale, Pledge and Donation.*

Bṛh. (X-62-64) stated that in case an object had been sold, pledged and donated on one and the same day—the purchaser, pledgee and donee should divide the object among themselves. The donee was safeguarded, according to Bṛh., in the best way, because he had to obtain a full third part of the object or of its value. The rest *i.e.* two thirds of the object or of its value had to be divided in shares proportionate to the amount for which the object was sold or pledged.

B.

39. *Prescription of Pledges. General*

Prescription (*i.e.* acquisition of ownership by continuous possession (*bona fide*) was well known in ancient Indian laws. The period of this possession *bona fide* varied in various sources of law and was dependent on what object was subjected to usucaption. According to ancient Indian law it was necessary to take the respective object into possession and to use it in good faith.[77] This rule applied with some exceptions to all movables. One of these exceptions was the pledge, since the pledgee had no possession *bona fide* but only enjoyed detention of the object pledged.

It must be noted that this point of view was not carried out consequently in all the ancient Indian sources of law, as

77. See J. Jolly's Recht Sunditte, p. 91-92.

some of the sources were of the opinion that usucaption of pledges could take place. Probably, in practice, this problem gave rise to contrary opinions though from the theoretical point of view of civil law, the property of a pledge could not be obtained by usucaption.

40. *Usucaption of Pledges Prohibited or Admissible.*

With regard to the first group of rules Mn. (VIII-149) stated :

ādhiḥ sīmā bāladhanaṁ niksepo'panidhī striyaḥ,
rājasvaṁ śrotriyasvaṁ ca na bhogena praṇaśyati.
(See above : Study II. par. 16).

Pledges and others were not lost by adverse possession.

This problem was solved in a similar manner in N. (1-81, see also N'.s quotation VIII-12), Śukranīti, (4,5,445) and Y. (II-25); and in K. (191/1-3) where we find the rule that on the basis of mere possession and use, the ownership of a pledge[78] could not be obtained.

Y. (II-26) even stated that he who, basing his claim on usucaption, took away the pledge should be made to pay the principal amount to the owner and to the king a fine of an equal amount or according to his capacity.[79]

As far as the possibility of obtaining the property of a pledge by prescription is concerned, Vās. (XVI-16-17) stated that pledges, *ādhi* and others when enjoyed for ten years continuously were lost to the owner. However Vās. stated : *anyathāpy udāharanti* and quoted Mn. (8.149) or N. (1.81) although these quotations are corrupt.

Therefore, it is evident that in Vās,'s time, and in the regions where Vās. was applied, the principle regarding the prescription of pledges was not uniform and some codifiers were of the opinion that the usucaption of pledges was prohibited, though others were of the opinion that it was admissible after an uninterrupted possession of ten years. The same must be also applied to N. as this source of law stated (I-81) that pledges etc. could not be lost to the owner by adverse possession, but in the next *śloka* stated that pledges etc. might

78. and others.

79. *ādhyāḍīnāṁ vihartāraṁ dhanine dāpayed dhanam,*
daṇḍaṁ ca tat samaṁ rājñe śakty apekṣam athā'pi vā.

be lost if they were enjoyed in the presence of the owner for twenty years.[80]

It must also be noted that G. (XII-37-39) and Kāty. (330), where we find some rules relating to usucaption, did not mention pledges as exceptions from usucaption, although the respective rules were similar to those of Mn. (VIII-149) etc. This fact might show that according to G. and Katy. the usucaption of pledges was admissible, the more so as Kāty. (300) stated that if a pledge had been undoubtedly enjoyed for twenty years, then it became valid, although it was based on a defective document.[81]

However, even against the explicit rules found in ancient Indian sources of law, we must accept the theory that from the point of view of the system of civil law prescription of pledges was not admissible.[82]

C.

41. *Penal Rules- General*

In Vi. and Kāty. we find three penal rules. They relate to the taking by the pledgee of a greater quantity of the object pledged or to the giving by the pledgor of a smaller quantity of the object pledged than agreed upon, as well as enjoyment of the pledge under a vitiated document. In all these cases in addition to other legal consequences, a fine had to be imposed on the offender.

42. *Taking More or Giving Less than Agreed.*

According to Kāty. (527) if the pledgee forcibly or against the will of the pledgor took something which had not been pledged (namely more than agreed upon) he was liable to the first amercement and the pledgor would get back his pledge.[83] It is not clear whether the whole pledge or the additional amount of the pledge taken by the pledgee could be retaken by the pledgor, as well as whether it was a general

80. *pratyakṣa-paribhogāt tu svāmino dvidaśāḥ samāḥ,*
ādhyādiny api jīryante strī-narendra-dhanād ṛte.

81. See above.

82. With this problem the problem of the loss of property of pledges, is connected if the debt was not repaid in the stipulated period of time.

83. Identically Ratnakāra.

rule, or whether it related, as Sarasvatīvilāsa stated, to pledges for use only.

Vi. (V-182) stated that if the quantity of the pledge given by the pledgor to the pledgee was less than agreed upon, the pledgor was liable to a fine of sixteen *suvarṇas*.

43. *Enjoyment of Pledges under a Vitiated Document.*

Kāty. (528) declared that when a pledgee enjoyed a pledge from the pledgor under a vitiated document, the king should make the pledgee pay a fine and should destroy the deed of pledge.

These three rules were of no great importance from the legal point of view.

V.

SURETYSHIP*

I. INTRODUCTION

1. *Definition*

Prātibhāvyaṁ nāma viśvasā'rthaṁ puruṣā'ntareṇa saha samayaḥ. Suretyship was defined by Mit. (*ad* Y. II-53) as a contract with another person with the object of creating confidence. This definition was not detailed enough. From the point of view of ancient Indian law, the contract of suretyship should be defined in the following manner : a contract of suretyship was a contract whereby a man bound himself to be personally answerable for the obligation of another, as an accessory debtor, in addition to the person principally liable.

Later on we shall see that, contrary to Roman law, surety, according to ancient Indian law, must not be answerable for the debt of another.

The "definition" given in Mit. and quoted above only outlined the motive of this contract but did not define the contract of suretyship. The motive was rightly determined. It was a guarantee for the creditor.

N. (1.117) stated :

viśrambahetū dvāvatra pratibhū rādhir eva ca.

The guarantee to be offered to a creditor may be two-fold—a surety and a pledge. Certain other sources of law recognised other guarantees of the creditor as well *viz.* the contract of copartners whereby a man or men bound themselves to be personally answerable for the obligation of another, as a solidary debtor *sahagrahīna*[1] etc. : suretyship and pledge, however, were the most typical cases of guarantees offered to a creditor.

*Previously appeared as JSAIL. 12 in "Supplement to Bhāratīya Vidyā Vol. VII. Nos. 3-4, pp, 23-50.

1. K. 174.

The contract of suretyship was one of the eighteen titles of law known to almost all the *Smṛti-s*. According to Asahāya the contract of suretyship was one of the contracts known under "recovery of a debt" (eighth subdivision).[2]

2. *Different Kinds of Sureties*

Suretyship is called in the Sanskrit text *pratibhū* (representative) and sometimes (bail) *lagnaka*.

We find in the *Smṛti-s*[3] the description of ten kinds of suretyship *i.e.* surety for appearance, for honesty, for payment, for delivering the assets of the debtor, in litigation, for ordeal, for safety, for delivering a pledge, for a written document and for work.[4]

Vy. (Smṛ. C. p. 347) enumerated the largest number of sureties *i. e.* seven in number

(*pratibhuvo grāhyā iti śeṣaḥ*).
lekhye'kṛte ca diviye vā dāna-pratya-darśane,
gṛhīta-bandho'pasthāne ṛṇi-dravyā'raṇe tathā.

Five kinds of sureties were enumerated in Kāty. (530) :
dāno'paṣthāna-vādeṣu viśvāsa-śapathyāya ca,
lagnakaṁ kārayed evaṁ yathā-yogaṁ viparyaye.[5]

(Also quoted in Apar. *ad* Y. 2.53, VyK. 116, SC. 148, VRK. 41, VCi. 19, NṛP. 21, SV. 247, VCa. 15, VyPr. 248, VyU. 28, VyP. 89, VyS. 77, VVy. 27).

Four kinds of sureties were enumerated in Bṛh. (10.73):
darśane pratyaye dāne ṛṇi-dravyā'rpane tathā,
catuṣ-prakāraḥ pratibhūḥ śāstre dṛṣṭo manīṣlbhiḥ.

(Also quoted in Apar. *ad* Y. 2.53, VyK. 116, SC. 148, VRK. 40, DK. 37, VCi. 18, SCM. 11, NṛP. 21, SV. 246, VyPr. 247, VyU. 27, VT. 527, VV. 20, VyP. 89, VyS. 77, VVy. 27).

Other *Smṛti-s* (Y.2.53, N. 1.118, Vi. 6.31, Medh. *ad*

2. *ad* I-20 (p. 10).

3. Kāty., Hār. and others.

4. It must be added that K. (175-2 sqq.). mentioned also other kinds of *Smṛti-s*, which, however, were not defined and explained. (See note 60).

5. Seven kinds of sureties were also enumerated in Śukr. Ch. IV. Sect. V-123-4. Śukr., however, did not give the nomenclature of these sureties.

Mn. 8. 158) enumerated only three kinds of sureties, viz. for appearance, for honesty and for payment :

darśane pratyaye dāne prātibhāvyaṁ vidhīyate.

We shall see below that with the exception of Mn. these three kinds of sureties were precisely described in the *Smṛti-s* the rest, however, were only mentioned in some of the *Smṛti-s*, while they have been unknown to others.

II. VARIOUS KINDS OF SURETIES

1.

SURETY FOR APPEARANCE

3. *General Remarks*

Surety for appearance was called in the Sanskrit texts *darśaṇa* (from darś to see, to perceive, to appear), or *pradarśana* (*pra°*+*°darś*—appearance). It was also called *upasthāna* (from *upa°*+*°sthā* —to assist, to come, to appear).

Surety for appearance was mentioned in Y. (II-53), Vi. (VI-41), N. (I-118) as one of three, in Bṛh. (X-73) as one of four, and in Kāty. (530) as well as in Hār.[6] '(Smṛ. C. p. 346) as one of five kinds of sureties.[7]

This kind of suretyship consisted in the obligation of the surety to produce the debtor at the time and place agreed upon between the creditor and the debtor. If the surety failed to do so, he was obliged to pay the creditor the debt contracted by the debtor, or to pay the fine determined or to be determined.

The surety, however, was not obliged to pay the debt if the debtor was prevented from appearing by an act of king or in another case of *vis major*.

The surety was liable to pay the debt of the principal debtor not only in the case of the latter being guilty of non-appearance at the time and place agreed upon, but also in the event of his death and non-appearance.

6. It must be pointed out that Hār. (Smr. C.p. 346) mentioned separately *darśana* and separately *upasthāna*. P. V. Kane (History of Dharmaśāstra p. 246) translated, the latter "return of money lent on pledge."

7. See also Mn. VIII-158, G.XII, 41, Vās. XVI-31, Vy. (Smṛ. C. p. 352).

As, according to this agreement, the surety was only liable for the appearance of the principal debtor *darś* or *upasthā*) at the time and place agreed upon, this kind of surety was called surety for appearance.

Surety for appearance was, above all, applicable if the principal obligation consisted of the appearance of a certain person for work, or in court, etc. In this, we see the greatest difference between the surety for appearance and surety for payment.

4. *Principal Aim*

Kāty. (531) and identically Bṛh. (X-75) stated :
darśana pratibhūr-yas taṁ deśe kāle na darśayet,
nibandham āvahet tatra daiva-rāja-kṛtād-ṛte.

(Kāty, 531. Also quoted in Apar. *ad.* Y. 2. 53, VyK. 116, SC. 149, VRK, 41, VCi. 20, NṛP. 21 VyPr.240, VyU. 29, VyM. 149, VV. 21, VyP. 90, VyS. 77, VVy. 27)

If the surety for appearance did not produce the debtor at the time and place agreed upon, he had to discharge the debt due to the creditor, unless he was prevented from appearing by an act of king or in case of another *vis major*.

Bṛh. (X-74) stated that the surety bound himself by saying "I will produce (the debtor)" according to Śukr. (Ch. IV Sect. V-123) by saying "I shall produce him before you", according to Medh. (*ad* Mn. VIII-158) by saiying "I shall produce the debtor at such and such place." Mit. (*ad* Y. II-53) stated, however, that the surety bound himself by saying "I shall produce the debtor whenever his appearance is necessary" (*darśane darśanā-pekṣāyāṁ enaṁ darśayiṣyamī'ti*).

Kāty.'s opinion seemed to be the most accurate one. We see there that the obligation of the surety for appearance arose with the fact of non-appearance of the principal debtor at the time and place agreed upon. This took place if the agreement contained stipulations regarding the time and place of the repayment of the obligation. If these stipulations were lacking the general rules regarding the repayment of debts had to be applied. Then Mit.'s opinion that the obligaton of the surety arose "whenever the appearance of the debtor was necessary" had to be applied.[8]

5. *Applicability*

Such a surety had to be applied in the case of the principal contract being a contract of work. If in such a contract it had been stipulated that the debtor had to appear at the place and time agreed upon and the debtor did not appear, then the surety's obligation towards the creditor arose. It is clear that the surety was bound so long as the debtor did not really appear. The debtor could not be occupied with other matters; he had to be at leisure and amenable.[9] Indication of the whereabouts of the debtor was not sufficient.

The contract of surety for appearance took place when *viz.* an artist or a labourer had bound himself to appear at the place and time agreed upon in order to perform some work and for that appearance the surety had guaranteed. In the event of non-appearance the surety was responsible and had to pay the compensation agreed upon, or to be agreed.

6. *Responsibility*

As has already been mentioned the responsibility of the surety arose when the debtor did not appear at the time and place agreed upon.

The debtor's non-appearance might be caused through no fault of his own. And so, if he died or was prevented from appearing by an act of king or in another case of *vis major*, his non-appearance was considered faultless. The *Smṛti-s* did not define this question consistently. Kāty. (531) and Bṛh. (X-75) were of the opinion that the surety was not responsible for appearance if the debtor was prevented from appearing by an act of king or another case of *vis major*, and Kāty. (533) stated that the surety was responsible in the event of the death of the debtor. Ratnākara's[10] and Viv.'s (p. 13) opinions were the same. We must, however, interpret Kāty. (533) in another way, because the death of the debtor had to be understood as an act excluding

8. Medh.'s opinion in referring only to the place agreed upon and not mentioning the time, seems to be insufficient.

9. Col. p. 243.

10. Col. p. 242.

responsibility for the debtor and caused by *vis major*. We may also interpret this *śloka* in connection with *śloka* 532 from which it is evident that the surety might extend the term for the appearance of the debtor. He was entitled to cause the appearance of the debtor six weeks after the time agreed upon. Probably, when during this time *i.e.*, six weeks, the debtor died, the surety became responsible towards the creditor for the obligation of the principal debtor.

If we interpret these *ślokas* in such a way, the principle of the non-responsibility in the event of *vis major*, would be consistently carried out in the *Smṛti-s*.

7. *Consequences*

As far as consequences of non-fulfillment of the contract of suretyship for appearance are concerned, the *Smṛti-s* mentioned only the case of the non-payment of the debt.

Mn. (VIII-158), Kāty. (535) and Bṛh. (X-77) stated briefly.[11]

adarśayan sa taṁ tasya yateta svadhanād ṛṇam.

Hence, according to these *Smṛti-s* the surety for appearance who did not produce the debtor had to pay his debt. This problem was solved in the same way in N. (I-119). Bṛh. (X-78) and Kāty. (531) rightly added that such an obligation took place when the debtor failed to repay his debt at the time (Bṛh.), or time and place (Kāty.) agreed upon. Viv. (p. 13) added that the surety had to repay the debt with interest.

Although the *Smṛti-s* used the word *ṛṇa* (debt) and thereby confined the consequences of non-appearance of the debtor, we have to apply this rule to all kinds of non-appearance of persons who were bound to appear. Therefore, this rule had to be also applied to those who were bound to appear in court, or for work, etc. It is clear that in these cases the surety was not bound to pay the debt, as this *ṛṇa* did not exist. The surety was only bound to pay a fine, the amount of which had either been fixed before, or had to be fixed by the king in the future. Consequently, it was possible to make a contract of suretyship for appearance *viz.* in court and stipulate that in

11. Kāty. and Bṛh. unnecessarily quoted Mn. (VIII-158) as they (Kāty. 531 and Bṛh. X-78) defined the same question in their own words.

case of non-appearance of the debtor the surety would be bound to pay such and such an amount as a fine.[12]

8. *Arising of Responsibility*

As already mentioned, Kāty. (531) and Bṛh. (X-78) stated that the obligation of the surety arose at the moment when the debtor did not appear at the time and place agreed upon. Both these *Smṛti-s*, however, in other *śloka-s* stated the contrary and declared that the sureties had to have time to make inquiries regarding the whereabouts of the debtor (Viv. p. 14). Depending on the distance of the place where the debtor was supposed to be hiding the creditor had to allow time for the surety to search for the debtor who did not appear. This period of time varied according to Bṛh. from two to six weeks, but according to Kāty., the maximum period given amounted to six weeks.[13] If the debtor died during this period, the surety had to pay the debt (or fine) although this period of two, four or six weeks had not yet elapsed.

These rules rightly protected the surety and in such a way made it possible for him to cause the appearance of the debtor who could have purposely hidden.

That was one of the proofs that the ancient Indian law knew the *beneficium excussionis sive ordinis*.

2.

SURETY FOR HONESTY (CONFIDENCE, ASSURANCE)

9. *General Remarks*

Surety for honesty was called in the Sanskrit texts *pratyaya* (confidence), or *viśvāsa* (confidence) (Kāty.)

Surety for honesty was mentioned in Y. (II-53), Vi. (VI-41) and N. (I-118) as one of three, in Bṛh. (X-73) as one of four, and in Kāty. (530) as well as in Hār. (Smṛ. C. p. 346) as one of five kinds of sureties.[14]

12. This interpretation conformed with that of Medh. (*ad* Mn. VIII-158).

13. See par. 33.

14. See also Mn. (VIII-160 sqq.), G. (XII-41), Vās. (XVI-31, Vy. (Smṛ. C. p. 352).

According to this kind of suretyship, the surety assured the creditor that the debtor would not deceive him, or that he was an honest, respectable and trustworthy man who would be willing to discharge the debt at the place and time agreed upon. If the debtor failed to discharge the debt, then the surety had to pay it to the creditor.[15]

We shall see that according to the rules relating to the surety for payment *dāna*, the surety was liable to pay the original debt to the creditor if the debtor did not repay the debt at the time and place agreed upon.

It seems that in practice no difference existed between surety for honesty and surety for payment. The difference was really very small. In case of a surety for honesty, the surety assured only the creditor that the debtor was an honest man, that he was respectable, trustworthy, willing to discharge the debt, and would not deceive the creditor. Therefore, when taking the loan, the debtor was a wealthy man and, later through no fault of his own, lost his financial stability and was unable to repay the debt, although he had shown his readiness to do so, the surety for honesty would not be liable to discharge the debt; on the contrary, the surety for payment will be liable to discharge such a debt. This interpretation is, in particular, evident from N. (I-119) where we read : *ṛṇiṣv aprati kurvatsu pratyaye vā'pi hāpite.* J. Jolly rightly translated it in the following manner : "If the debtors fail to discharge the debt, or if they prove dishonest......" That shows that in the case of surety for honesty the obligation of the surety did not arise at the time of the payment of the debt, but when dishonesty was proved. In consequence the obligation of the surety did not arise if the debt had not been paid because of the lack of funds on the part of the debtor, who was willing to repay the debt, but was unable to do so.

That was probably the only difference between sureties for honesty and sureties for payment. Col.[16] tried to find other differences too. It was said there that, for instance, when the surety for honesty said "that man is trustworthy, if he punctually paid debts formerly contracted from others without

15. It seems that the suretyship for honesty implied neither a *sponsio* nor a *promissio* but, merely, in the most general way, a desire (*jussio*) that the principal debtor should be given credit.

16. Col. p. 236.

dispute, and never did a dishonest act, but subsequently practise knavery in regard to payment of this debt, the surety (for honesty) is not in that case amenable; for none can know further events." This interpretation seems to be incorrect because in this case the surety for honesty would act only as a source of information and not as a guarantor for the future, for which purpose the surety for honesty had been introduced.

Also the following opinion of Col.[17] does not seem to be correct. According to this opinion, if the surety for honesty said "that man is wealthy," and if it were proved that he was then indigent, the surety for honesty had to pay the debt, even though the debtor could not discharge if due to his inability. But if his wealth was proved, and the debtor withheld payment because of dishonesty or the like, a surety for payment would be compelled to discharge the debt, and not the surety for honesty. Here again the surety for honesty could not act as an information bureau. The word *pratyaya* or *viśvāsa* meant confidence *i.e.* confidence that the debtor was an honest man who would repay the debt.

The surety for honesty guaranteed not the estate of the debtor but his honesty, and willingness to repay the debt and, therefore, he was called surety for confidence.

10. *Principal Aim*

In N. (I-118-119) we read that if the debtor was not honest and the surety gave guarantee for his honesty, the surety had to repay the debt. Viv. (p. 13) added : with interest.

Bṛh. (X-74) states that the surety bound himself by saying "he is a respectable man". Mit. *ad* 2. 53 stated : *pratyaye viśvāse matpatyayenā'sya dhanaṁ prayaccha nāyaṁ tvāṁ vañcayiṣyate, yato'mukasya putro'yaṁ urvarā-prāyabhūrasya grāma-varo vā'stī'ti.*

From Mit.'s context it is evident that the surety for honesty convinced the creditor that he should lend money upon his assurance and that the debtor would not deceive him. He convinced him saying that he was either from a good

17. Col. p. 236.

family, or was a rich man (possessed very fertile land or an excellent village). In addition, he assured the creditor that the debtor was a trustworthy man, that he was honest and would not be adverse to discharging the debt, nor would he take refuge with the creditor's enemy (p. 235). Such a declaration caused the obligation of the debtor.

Similar to the opinion of Mit. was that of Śukr. (Ch. IV Sec. V-124) where we read that the surety for honesty declared only what the debtor's occupation was *i.e.*, means of livelihood.

11. *Consequences*

When at the appointed time (Bṛh. X-78 and Kāty. 536) the debtor failed in his engagement—that means if the notion excited by the assertion of the surety for honesty was misconceived, or proved false, in short, the debtor was dishonest—the surety for honesty had to repay the debt to the creditor.[18] That was the opinion of Y. (II-53), N. (I-119), and others.

12. *Applicability*

Although it is not stated either in the *Smṛti-s*, or in the commentaries on the *Smṛti-s*, it must be admitted that surety for honesty could also be given in cases other than repayment of debts *i.e.*, for fulfilment of certain work, etc., and even for appearance *viz.* of a person in order to perform work. Here, as well, the fact would be decisive whether this person was willing or unwilling (was honest or dishonest) to fulfil the respective obligation. Depending on that fact the obligation of the surety for honesty would arise. Hence, *per analogiam* we can apply to this case as well, all the rules regarding *vis major*, death of the debtor, etc. which were defined in the *Smṛti-s* in connection with the surety for appearance..

3.

SURETY FOR PAYMENT

13. *General Remarks*

Surety for payment was called in the Sanskrit texts *dāna* (from *dā*—repay, repayment, payment).

18. *i.e.*, although the debtor was wealthy he was not willing to repay the debt (Col. p. 238.)

Surety for payment was mentioned in Y. (II-53), Vi. (VI-41), and N. (I-118) as one of three, in Bṛh. (X-73) as one of four, and in Kāty. (530), as well as in Hār. (Smṛ. C. p. 346) as one of five kinds of sureties.[19]

This kind of surety was similar to the *fidejussio* known to Roman law. It was a contract whereby a man bound himself to be personally answerable for the debt of another. However, it was not a *vadimonium* but a *stipulatio* with *beneficium excussionis sive ordinis*. In the Roman law the creditor asked "*centum quae titus mihi debet eadem fide tua esse jubes* ?" and the surety replied "*fide mea esse i rubeo*". According to ancient Indian law the surety said: *yadyayaṁ na dadāti tadānīm aham eva dāsyanī'ti.*[20]

14. *Principal Aim*

According to Bṛh. (X-78) if the debtor failed in his engagement at the appointed time, the surety for payment was liable for the debt.

Bṛh. (X-74), and similarly Śukr. (ch. IV. Sect. V-123), stated that the surety for payment bound himself by saying "I will pay the debt" ("I will pay what is not paid by that man") and Mit. (ad Y.II-53) by saying "if he does not pay, then I, myself, will pay." In particular it was evident from this declaration that the surety for payment was not an accessory debtor in addition to the person principally liable. He was only liable in the event of the principal debtor did not repay the debt. Therefore, the surety for payment neither *conspondet* nor *conpromittit* but *praedicet* and had always the *beneficium excussionis sive ordinis*.

Hence, we see that if the principal debtor at the appointed time (Bṛh. X-78), and place (per *analogiam* from Kāty. 531) evaded payment and, as Mit. (*ad* Y. II-53) stated either fraudulently or by pleading poverty *śāḍhyena nardhanatvena*, the surety for payment was liable to repay the debt to the creditor.

That was the opinion of Y. (II-53), Bṛh. (X.-78), N. (I-119) and Vi. (VI-41).[21]

19. See also Mn. (VIII-160 sqq.), G. (XII-41), Vās, (XVI-31), Vy. (Smṛ. C. p. 352).
20. Mit. *ad* Y. (II-53).
21. See also Mn. (VIII-160)

It is clear that under repayment of the debt we must understand repayment of the debt together with interest, but nothing else. We cannot understand under surety for payment, as Col.[22] (*ad* Kāty.) stated, surety for the delivery of the mortgaged property and the like, because the latter created a new sort of surety.[23]

4.

SURETY FOR DELIVERING THE ASSETS OF THE DEBTOR

15. *General Remarks*

Surety for delivering the assets of the debtor is called in the Sanskrit texts *ṛṇidravyārpaṇa* from *ṛṇa* (debt)+ °*dravya*° (movable property)+°*arpaṇa* (delivering).

Bṛh. mentioned clearly only this kind of surety. *ṛṇidravyārpaṇa* was enumerated as the fourth kind of surety. Other *Smṛti-s* which enumerated even five or seven sorts of sureties did not mention *ṛṇidravyārpaṇa*. Kāty. (530) also did not enumerate *ṛṇidravyārpaṇa*. However Kāty. (536) quoted Bṛh. (10.78) which was closely connected with Bṛh. (10.73) and where *ṛṇidravyarpaṇa* was clearly mentioned. Therefore we can assume that this kind of surety was known to Kāty. as well.

The text of Bṛh. (10.73,74 and 78) was unclear and did not give any definition of *ṛṇidravyārpaṇa*.

That was the reason why this sort of surety was so often interpreted. Viv. (p. 12-13) rightly explained that this sort of surety was for the return and not for payment. That was the difference between these two sorts of sureties.

In the case of the *ṛṇidravyārpaṇa* the surety bound himself to deliver a movable property taken as a loan by the debtor, if the latter did not deliver it at the time and place agreed upon.

16. *Principal Aim*

We have already seen that Bṛh. (X-73) enumerated among sureties "ordained by the sages for four different pur-

22. Col. p. 239.
23. See para. 25.

poses" *ṛṇidravyārpaṇa*. In the next *śloka* we read that the surety bound himself by saying "I will deliver his assets". (...... *draviṇamarpatāmbhyapara*.) Viv. (p. 12/13) explained that *ṛṇidravyārpaṇa* was given for such articles as were taken as loan for the use and consequently for cases in which the surety undertook to recover an object taken by someone.

Sampradāya quoted in Viv. (p. 12/13) stated that the property of the debtor was to be given to the creditor.

Under *dravya draviṇa*, we understand all kinds of effects, in particular, movable property such as household property, furniture, etc.

The surety for delivering the assets of the debtor was also responsible for the destruction of the effects, if this destruction was not caused by *vis major* and if it was impossible to return them by payment of its equivalent.

17. *Repayment of Pledges*

Miśra quoted in Col. (p. 234) had a different rendering : *ṛṇedravyārpaṇa* instead of *ṛṇidravārpaṇe*. Miśra stated that according to this version the surety guaranteed the restoration of an object lent for use. An object lent for use was anything that a man asked and obtained from another, such as ornaments etc. For instance : one said, "give me ornaments for decoration on a day of festivity at my house"; the owner asked, "if you do not restore them, what shall be done" ? In such a case, the surety for delivery said, "I will restore these effects". Here, since those ornaments were the sole property of the original owner, there could be no payment; it was, therefore, said to be for delivery or restoration.[24]

Some commentators stated that *ṛṇidravyārpaṇa* had to take place when the debtor wanted to be sure that his pledged property would be returned to him. This was evident, in particular, from Śukr. (Ch. IV. Sect. V-123), according to which this surety bound himself by saying "I shall make him return the pledge." It took place, in particular, in the case of *caritra*-pledges when the value of the pledgewas much larger than the loan given. However,[25] the *ṛṇidravyārpaṇa* would very

24. Col. p. 234.
25. See above Study II on "Pledge"

seldom be used in the case of pledges, as the pledge itself was a guarantee given to the creditor, and the debtor who took the loan and gave the pledge, did not need any other guarantee. This interpretation of Miśra did not seem to be correct, as we find in Vy.[26] (Smṛ. C. p. 347) the *gṛhīta bandho'pasthāna*, i.e. surety for delivering a pledge. In any case these two kinds of sureties were connected with each other.

5.
SURETY IN LITIGATION

18. *General Remarks*

Surety in litigation was called in the Sanskrit text *vāda* (litigation, dispute).

This sort of surety was clearly mentioned in Kāty. (530) as one of five kinds of sureties. Indirectly it was also mentioned in Y. (II-10) and Śukr. (Ch. IV. Sect. V-22).

Kāty. (535)only mentions this kind of surety but did not give an explanation as to its applicability.

According to Y. (II-10) the officer presiding over the court, after laying down the rules for the plaintiff and the defendant, could order that both of them give a surety which would satisfy the object of judgment *i.e.*, the payment of the amount decreed or the payment of the fine.

This person (or these persons) *i. e.* the surety in litigation, guaranteed that the decree of the judge would be executed Y()., or the defendant would appear in court (Śukr.). In such a way the execution of the verdict and justice were secured. It was not, however, a *conditio sine qua non* in all disputes, because Kāty. (118/117) stated that if one of the parties who did not give any surety and was a *dvija*, had to be guarded by wardens; *śūdra-s* and others had to be confined and fettered whilst the plaintiff, who was guarded, had to give the guard wages at the end of the day.

19. *Principal Aim*

Kāty. (530) eumerating five kinds of sureties mentioned *vāda*. Y. (II-10), declared : *ubhayaḥ pratibhūr grāhyaḥ samarthaḥ kāryanirṇaye.*

26. See para. 25.

A surety should be taken from both in order to satisfy the object of the judgment. Mit. (*ad* Y.II-10) rightly stated :

ubhayor arthipaty arthinaḥ sarveṣu vivādeṣu nirṇayasya kāryaṁ kārya-nirṇayaḥ ; āhitāgryā'diṣu pāṭhat kārya-śabdaṣya pūrva-nipātaḥ; nirṇayasya yat kāryaṁ ca sādhita-dhana-dānaṁ daṇḍa-dānaṁ ca tasmin samarthaḥ pratībhūḥ pratibhavati tat kāryam tadvad bhavatī'ti pratibhūr grāhyaḥ sa sabhyena sabhāpatinā.

Hence it is evident that Mit. compelled the officer presiding over the court to ask both litigants (*ubhayo*) to take a surety (*pratibhū*) who would be competent (*samartha*) to satisfy the object of judgment (*kāryanirṇaya*), i.e. the payment of the amount decreed, or the fine. Such a *pratibhū* would be *vāda*.

However Kāty. declared (117-8) :

atha cet pratibhūr nā'sti vāda-yogyasya vādiṇaḥ,
sa rakṣito dinasyānte dadyād dūtaya vetanam.
dvijātiḥ pratibhū-hīno rakṣyaḥ syād vāhya-cāribhiḥ.
śūdradīn-pratibhū-hīnān bandhayen nigaḍena tu.

Thus, Kāty. considered it possible that a surety was not given either by the plaintiff or by the defendant (although he referred to the plaintiff only) and concluded by saying that if the plaintiff was a member of the three highest castes (*dvija*) he had to be guarded; for that they had to pay a special fee. If the plaintiff was a *śūdra*, etc., he had to be confined or fettered.

On the basis of these rules Col.'s interpretation was correct. It was declared there that the surety for litigation was given "for the matter in contest : a suit being instituted by the creditor for the recovery of money from the debtor, he whom the king took as a surety, lest the debtor or creditor absconded through apprehension or losing the cause, was surety for action."[27]

According to Śukr. (Ch. IV. Sect. V-122) surety in litigation was given to prevent the defendant from hiding. Śukr. stated that having noticed that the defendant, brought by the messenger, had other engagements, the king had to take suitable security for his appearance.

27. Col. p. 240.

Hence, surety in litigation could be introduced by the king non-obligatorily in order to safeguard the execution of justice.

6.

SURETY FOR ORDEAL

20. *General Remarks*

Surety for ordeal is called in the Sanskrit text *śapatha* (ordeal), or *divya* (ordeal).

Kāty. (530) only mentioned *śapatha* as one of the five, and Vy. (Smṛ. C.p. 537) *divya* as one of the seven kinds of sureties.

The surety for ordeal was connected with surety in litigation, as well as with surety for appearance.

The surety for ordeal was, in particular, applicable in litigation and, sometimes, it was sufficient if the surety in litigation stood for the performance of the ordeal. Instead of payment of the debt—the performance of an ordeal on the part of the debtor could be sufficient.

If the surety guaranteed only the performance of an ordeal by the debtor, that kind of suretyship created only a special form of surety for appearance.

The *Smṛti-s* did not give a full explanation of this kind of surety. It was also seldom interpreted by commentators.

21. *Principal Aim*

Viv. (p.13) stated generally that the suretyship for ordeal meant "observance of oath." Caṇḍeśvara (quoted in Col. p.240) stated that it was given for the performance of an ordeal.

In Col. (p. 240) we find the following explanation : "during the procedure, if ordeal must be performed by the party himself, he whom the king, under the text of Yājñavalkya, takes as a surety, suspecting the creditor's or debtor's wish to abscond, because he perceives the probable detection of his falsehood, is surety for ordeal, the fifth sort of surety. He says, 'when this debtor should pass ordeal, I will then produce him' ; or he says, 'I will perform his office'. This should be understood incidentally in the case of a surety for the creditor". We see here these two different kinds of surety for ordeal *i.e.*, a secondary form of surety in litigation and a specific form of surety for appearance.

According to Śukr. (Ch. IV. Sect. VI. 24) the surety probably did not guarantee for standing for ordeal, but for telling the truth ; Śukr. accordingly declared that the surety bound himself by saying "he does not swear falsely." If so, the surety for ordeal would be a specific form of surety for honesty.

The consequences of not standing for ordeal by the debtor at the time and place agreed upon would be the same as in the case of other sureties *i.e.*, the obligation to repay the debt, or payment of a special fine.[28]

7.

SURETY FOR SAFETY

22. *General Remarks*

Surety for safety was called in Sanskrit texts *abhaya* (assurance, security, protection, safety.)

Hār. (Smṛ. C. p. 346) mentioned only this kind of surety but did not give any explanation as to its applicability. The word *abhaya* was a synonym for *pratibhū* as both safeguarded the creditor. It is, however, evident from Y. and K. that the surety for safety was given in order to protect people against injury. On the other hand, according to K., such a surety could safeguard peace *i.e.*, save the king from another war.

Although neither Y. nor K. used the word *abhaya* (but made use of the general word *pratibhū* or *avasthā*, we come to the conclusion that the respective rules of K., as well as Y., related to surety for safety.

23. *Guarantee for Safety*

We read in Y. (II-209) :

aśaktas tu vadann evaṁ ḍaṇḍanīyaḥ paṇān-daśa,
tathā saktaḥ pratibhuvaṁ dāpyaḥ kṣemāya tasya tu.

(Also quoted in ViR. *ad* Y. 2.293, VyK. 102, VRK. 249, MR. 120, VyN. 486, DV. 211, VyPr. 383, VyU. 121., VyM. 99, VT. 729, VyS. 160, MP. 258.6).

28. Col. p. 248.

With reference to the second part of this verse Mit. added the following expalantion :

yaḥ punaḥ samarthaḥ kṣīṇaśaktiṁ pūrvadākṣi-patyasau pūrvoktaśatādi-daṇḍo'ttarakālaṁ tasyā-śaktasya kṣemā'rthaṁ pratibhuvaṁ dāpanīyaḥ.

K. (194.9) stated :

jāta-vairāśayaḥ śaktaś cā'pakartuṁ yāvaj jīvikā-vasthaṁ dadyāt.

If we interpret the rules of Y. (II-209) with the precedent *śloka*, as well as Y. and K. together, we come to the conclusion that if any one was condemned to pay a fine for injury but was in a position to threaten the wronged person, he was compelled to furnish a security[29] for the safety of the wronged person after the infliction of the fine, or rather, as K. stated, for the life-time of the wronged person.

Śukr. (Ch. IV Sect. V.-123) was of the same opinion since we read there that the surety bound himself by saying "you have no fear from him".

In the case of such a suretyship, the surety guaranteed that the respective person would not do any wrong to the intimidated, and should he do any harm to him, he would be obliged to pay a fine, or the like.[30] Therefore, this sort of surety was also a specific form of surety for honesty.

24. *Guarantee for Peace*

The obligation of a surety who guaranteed that the conditions of the contract of peace would be safeguarded, was similar to the above. K. in book VII, Ch. XVII ('Making Peace and Breaking it") referred to various kinds of guarantees for safe guarding the concluded peace. There were two schools, K. declared. One (*ācārya*) was of the opinion : *satyaṁ śapatho vā cāla-sandhiḥ; pratibhūḥ prati-graho vā sthāvaraḥ*

(K. 313.15-6). Kauṭilya, however, was of the opinion that *satyaṁ vā śapatho vā paratreha ca sthāvaras-sandhiḥ; ihārthā-eva pratibhūḥ pratigraho vā balāpekṣaḥ.* (K. 313. 17-8).

Hence Kauṭilya expressed the view that the surety (*pratibū*) was not given in order to guarantee the peace but to strengthen it.

29. *In* Y. *pratibhū;* in K. *avastha.*

30. See also K. book II. ch. VIII *in fine.*

śapathā'tikrame mahatāṁ tapasvināṁ mukhyānāṁ vā prāti-bhāvya-bandhaḥ pratibhūḥ; tasmin yaḥ parā'vagraha samarthān pratibhuvo gṛhṇāti so'tisaṁdhatte; viparīto'tisandhīyate. (K.314. 5-7)

Peace secured by the surety was made in order to avoid the contingency of violation of oath. Ascetics engaged in penance or nobles were used as sureties. In such a peace whoever took as surety a person capable of controlling the enemy, gained more advantages, whilst he who acted to the contrary was deceived.[31]

Such a surety stood for hostages but differred from them considerably. Here too, sureties, who were probably very powerful and rich, were responsible financially for the breaking of peace.

8.

OTHER KINDS OF SURETIES

Gṛhīta-bandho'pasthāṇa and *lakhye' kṛte* found in Vy. (Smṛ. C. p. 347) must be mentioned in the first place as other kinds of sureties; they were not defined and not explained properly in the *Smṛti-s*.

25. *Surety for Delivering a Pledge*

The word *gṛhīta-bandho'pasthāna* shows that this kind of surety was for delivering a pledge (*grabha*—to gripe, to seize, to take; *gṛhīta* what was taken +°*bandha*° to bind, union, connection, junction+°*upasthāna* delivering). Smṛ. C. explained that the surety in the case of a *gopyādhi* was called *ādhipāla* and in the case of *bhogyādhi* was called *bhuñjāpaka*. Smṛ. C. considered these kinds of sureties as belonging to *abhaya*. Similarly the surety guaranteed for the return of the pledge, the *gṛhīta-bandho'pasthāna* had to be considered a special sort of surety for delivering the assets of the debtor.[32]

Even Miśra mixed up these two kinds of sureties and whilst talking of *ṛṇī dravyārpaṇa* mentioned delivery of the mortgage property and stated that if the borrower contracted a debt on the mortgage of a field, the creditor asked "who

31. According to *Shamashastri's* translation.
32. See para 17.

would deliver to me the produce of that field ?" In such a case, the surety of the debtor said : "I will deliver his property"; that is, the property of this debtor, namely the produce of the mortgaged field. If the debtor would not do it, the surety would be obliged to perform the debtor's obligation, or to pay a relative fine.

26. *Surety for a Written Document*

The surety called in Vy. (Smṛ., C. 347) *lekhye'kṛte* (*lekhya*°—document+°*kṛta*—done *i.e.*, for a written document) was similar to *śapatha* (*divya*) and was probably only a specific form of this kind of surety.

27. *Surety for Work*

Śūlapāṇi (Col. 234) declared also that when an artist was required by the king for service during a long period of time, there were only three kinds of sureties for him, a surety for appearance, a surety for honesty and a surety for work. This last *i.e.*, surety for work, formed a separate kind of surety. It was also mentioned in Śukr. (Ch. IV. Sect V-124) where we read that the surety bounds himself by saying "I shall do what was not done by him". It is clear that this sort of surety would only be a specific form of surety for appearance *i.e.*, appearance for work. However, it was not identical with surety for appearance, as Śūlapāṇi and Śukr. mentioned surety for work in addition to the surety for appearance.

28. *Sureties According to the Theory of Law*

Although the *Smṛti-s* mentioned ten various kinds of sureties, from the point of view of the theory of law we find in the ancient Indian law only four kinds of sureties.

(1) Surety for appearance which would also embrace sureties for work as well as for ordeal, (2) surety for honesty which would also embrace sureties for safety and for ordeal, (3) surety for payment which would also embrace sureties for delivering assets and delivering a pledge, and (4) surety in litigation which would also embrace sureties for written documents and for ordeal.

III. PERSONS SUITABLE TO BECOME SURETIES

This question must be divided into two different groups. To the first group belonged persons who could never become sureties, and to the second only those who because of their relation to the creditor or debtor were unsuitable to become sureties. For example to the first group belonged a minor, and to the second group the brother of the debtor.

29. *Differentiation between Persons Unsuitable to Become Sureties*

As far as the first group of persons, who were unsuitable to become sureties, was concerned, the *Smṛti-s* enumerated approximately thirty such persons. They could be divided into the following five groups :

(A.) persons who did not instill confidence because of their financial position,

(B.) persons who did not instill confidence because of their state of dependence,

(C.) Persons who did not instill confidence because of other reasonss,

(D.) Persons whose right to dispose of their property was limited.

(E.) Persons of some special position.

To be second group belonged :

1. brothers among themselves,
2. husbands and wives in relation to each other,
3. fathers and sons, provided their estates were joint, and
4. co-sharers (where the joint property of their estates was evident).

It is clear that these distinction are not faultless and some other divisions could also be given.

30. *Persons Absolutely Unsuitable to Become Sureties*

Kāty., Bṛh. and K. regulated the problem of the first group of persons who were unsuitable to become sureties.

Kāty. (114-116) stated :

na svāmī na ca vai śatruḥ svāmin ādhikṛtas tathā,
niruddho daṇḍitaś caiva saṁśayasthāś ca na kvacit.
naiva rikthī na riktaś ca na caivā'tyanta vāsinaḥ,
rāja-kārya-niyuktaś ca ye ca pravrajitā narāḥ,
nāśakto danine dātuṁ daṇḍaṁ rājñe ca tat samam,

jīvaṇ vā'pt pitā yasya tathaive' cchā'pravartakaḥ,
nāvijñāto grahītavyaḥ pratibhūtva-kriyāṁ prati. (Also quoted in Mit *ad* Y. 2. 57, VyK. 116, SC. 136, VRK. 39, SCM. 12, VyPr. 255, VyU. 27, VV. 23-4, VyP. 85, VCi. 21, VT. 534).

Bṛh. (10.79) stated :
svāmī ripu-niruddhā-dhikṛta-daṇdita-saṁśayāḥ.
rikthimātrān tāvasāyi-rājavṛtta-vītarāga-vrati-
daridra-bāla-vṛddha-strī-rugṇā na pratibhūvaḥ.

K. (174.18-175.1) stated :
na prātibhāvya-manyad asāraṁ bāla prātibhāvyam[33].

(A) Persons who do not Instill Confidence because of their Financial Position

To this group were belonged : (a) insolvent persons, (b) poor persons, (c) persons whose fathers were living.

Insolvent persons were called in Kāty. (116) : *nāśakto dhanine dātuṁ daṇdaṁ rājñe ca tatsamam.*

These person were unable to pay the money due, or amount in dispute, to the creditor *dhanine* and fine equal to that (the amount in dispute—*tatsamam* to the king. Ratnakāra[34] rightly stated that by this expression we must understand "a man unable to pay the sum to the creditor", or "a man reputed to be unable to pay the sum to the creditor, or a fine of equal amount to the king". It is clear, that a person who was known to be insolvent was unable to pay for anything and, therefore, there was no reason why this person should be accepted as a surety.

For that reason Viv. (p. 14) stated that before accepting a surety it was proper for the creditor to ascertain whether the proposed surety was able to pay the debt, in the case it could not be liquidated by the debtor. The ability to pay a debt should be ascertained.

Poor persons are called in Kāty. (113) *rikta* and in Bṛh. (X-79) *daridra*. *Rikta* (from *ric*) means empty, hollow, worthless, destitute, poor; *daridra* (from *dra*) means also empty, hollow, poor. It is clear that this expressed referred only to persons who were well known as destitutes.

33. See note 60.

34. Quoted in Col. pp. 226 and 228.

Persons "whose fathers are living" were mentioned in Kāty. (114). As long as the father was living, the son, in a joint family, had no independent property (with certain small exeptions) and, therefore, was insolvent.

(B) Persons who do not Instill Confidence because of their State of Dependency

To this group belonged : *a*) employees; (*b*) persons appointed on the king's business; *c*) imprisoned persons; (*d*) endangered persons.

Employees were mentioned in Kāty. (112) and they were called *svāminādhikṛta*. Bṛh. (10.79) called them *adhikṛta*.

Persons appointed on the king's business were mentioned in Kāty. (113) only. Kāty. called them *rājakāryaniyukta* (*from rāja°—king + °kārya°—business + °niyukta*—employee.)

Col. (p. 227) explained this sentence by declaring that it would be superfluous for a servant of the king *i. e.*, one employed by the king or his minister, to become surety because the king by the nature of his trust was a universal surety. This point of view did not seem to be correct as the aim of this transaction was to safeguard the repayment of the debt by giving a surety. Therefore, it was of no interest whether the servant of the king was trustworthy or not, as even if he were a very trustworthy man, but did not give a proper surety, the debt could not be safeguarded. Probably here too the state of dependence between the employee and the king excluded the possibility of becoming a surety.

Endangered persons were mentioned in Kāty. (112) and Bṛh. (X-79). They were called *saṁśaya* or *saṁśayasta*. These were either persons whose life was in danger *i.e.*, under somebody's influence, or seriously ill, or as VyM. (p. 19) stated vicious men *i.e.*, *abhiśasta* Haradatta explained that these persons were guilty of grave sins enumerated in Āp. (1.7, 21, 8 sqq)[35].

(C) Persons who did not Instill Confidence because of Other Reasons

To this group belonged : *a*) a person who had been

35. See *P. V. Kane's Kāty.* p. 137.

fined, *b*) a banished person, *c*) a person whose antecedents were unknown, *d*) an enemy, *e*) a man guided by his own froward will.

Imprisoned persons were mentioned in Kāty. (112) and Bṛh. (X-79). They were called in both the *Smṛti-s niruddha*. These persons' liberty was restrained. Ratnākara (Col. p. 226) explained rightly the reason therefor. He declared that a man confined by the king for some offence, becoming surety for another, might later plead that he could not enforce the payment of the debt as he could not attend to the matter when contested.

Banished persons were mentioned in Kāty. (113). They were called *atyantavāsina*. However, Madanaratna, according to Vīr. (p. 58), reads it as *atyantavāsina* which was explained as exiled in a distant land, or banished from the country. Here too the banished person could not attend to the matter when banished.[36]

Persons whose antecedents were unknown were mentioned in Kāty. (114). These persons are unknown and nobody could have confidence in them.

Enemies were mentioned in Kāty. (112) and Bṛh. (X-79). They are called in Kāty. *śatru* and in Bṛh *ripu*. Ratnākara (Col. 227) rightly explained that an enemy was one whose character was ambiguous, that is, a person whom honest men suspected to be ill disposed. If his evil disposition was ascertained, he could not be accepted as a sponsor. Others expounded the term "accused".

Persons guided by their own forward were mentioned in Kāty. (114). They were called *tathaivecchāpravartaka*. Kane explaining this sentence said that it meant a person who incited the party from whom surety was demanded. In Col. (227 sqq.) it was stated that this expression meant a person who was guided by his own froward will and not by any consideration of circumstances; consequently his incapacity for civil affairs was the objection against him.

36. Regarding *anyantavāsin* (perpetual student in theology) see par. 30 D.

(D) Persons whose Right to Dispose of their Property was Limited and Persons of some Special Social Position

To this group belonged : (*a*) children, (*b*) old people, (*c*) women, (*d*) persons broken by life, and (*e*) ascetics. With the exception of the last named, these persons were all mentioned in Bṛh (X-79) only. Bṛh did not give any further explanation. We read there *bāla-vṛddha-strirugṇā na pratibhuvaḥ*. Also K. (174.19 sqq.) mentioned children *bāla* as those who were not suitable to become sureties. All these persons were unsuitable to become sureties because they were unable to dispose freely of their estates. Also ascetics *pravrajita* or *vrita* mentioned in Kāty. (113) and Bṛh. (X-79) were not suitable to become sureties as they had no estate which could be disposed of by them.

The same was the case with perpetual students of theology. If we read the text of Kāty. (113) as follows : *anyanta vasinaḥ*, then we must understand that this expression means in accordance with Mit., *naiṣṭhika-brahma-carin*.

Finally we must also mention *svāma* (Bṛh. 70-79, Kāty. 112) included in group (E).

31. *Persons Relatively Unsuitable to Become Sureties*

The persons mentioned above might be defined as absolutely unsuitable to become sureties.

To the group of persons relatively unsuitable to become sureties belonged : (*a*) brothers among themselves, (*b*) sons and fathers, and (*c*) husbands and wives. Only a certain relation of kinship among these persons rendered the contract of suretyship impossible between them.

However, according to the ancient Indian law these rules were based on other precepts. These persons were unsuitable to become among themselves sureties when they were undivided *i.e.*, in case there existed joint ownership of estates. This point of view was correct and clear because the debtor, as well as the surety, could not be responsible for the same estate.

(A) General Remarks

As far as the question of undivided brothers, fathers and

sons, was concerned, the position of the *Smṛti-s* was clear. We know, however, that according to Y. the property of consorts was separated[37]; it will be stated below that in the first stage there existed joint property of the consorts and in the last stage—separation of their estates.[37] This is evident from Mn. (VIII-416,) Āp. (II-6, 14, 16) and K. (152-8). The rules regarding the prohibition of becoming sureties between husband and wife probably related to old times *i.e.*, to the first stage of development of the property of consorts. This can also be seen from the sentence *avibhakte dravye i.e.* before the partition of the estate.

(B) Inadmissibility of suretyship among Brothers

The rules relating to the inadmissibilty of suretyship among brothers were described in the best and clearest manner in Y. (II-52). We read there :

bhrātṛṇāṁ atha dampatyoḥ pituḥ putrasya caiva hi,
prātibhāvyaṁ ṛṇaṁ sākṣyaṁ avibhakte na tu smṛtam.

(Also quoted in ViR. *ad* Y. 2.54, VyK. 116, SC. 136, 310, VRK. 39, 607, SS. 81: 151, VCi. 254, SCM.36, DT.179, SV. 352: 440, VyPr. 44, 255, VyU. 27, VyM. 10, 60, VT. 524, 534, RDhK. 399, VyP. 85, VyS. 16 VVCa. 32,104, AP. 254.12).

Hence, it is evident that among brothers, husband and wife, father and son the relation of suretyship (and others) was not allowed while they were undivided.

N. (XIII-39) also referred to brothers. We find there the following sentence :

sākṣitvaṁ pratibhāvyaṁ ca dānaṁ grahaṇam eva ca,
vibhaktā bhrātaraḥ kūryur nāvibhaktā parasparam.

(Also quoted in NMS. 24.39, ViR. in Y.2.53, Mit. *ad* Y. 2.149, DBh. 230, Apar. *ad* Y. 2. 52, VyK. 116 (162), SC. 136, 310, VRK. 40, SS. 81, MPā. 689, DK. 37, VCi. 253, SCM. 36, DT. 164, 179, SV. 347, VCa. 100, DN. 5, VyPr. 44,431 ; 255 (263), VyU. 27, VyM. 59, VT. 474, RDhK. 460, VV. 87, VyP. 85, VyS. 16, VVCa. 31, 104).

37. See below Study XVI on Reciprocal Responsibility for Debts Contracted by Married People.

Consequently, according to N., if brothers were undivided they could not become sureties.

This rule is quoted twice in Sar. (786 and 794). Sar. was also based on Vi.'s quotation : *kraya-vikraya-dāna-grahaṇa-pratibhāvya-sākṣit-vasaṁ bhūyakāritvanidhyādhānādikaṁ paraspa-rakṛtaṁ vibhā- gahetur iti.*[38] (Also quoted in SV. 440).

Vi., as we see, was of the opinion that mutual transactions of suretyship were sources of division. Therefore, the becoming of a surety was not a mutually inter-changeable affair.[39]

(C) Inadmissibility of Suretyship between Father and Son

We find also rules (N. I. 10) regarding the usuitability of a son to become a surety for his father. We read there that a son should not pay the debt of his father unless it arose out of suretyship, and provided there did not existjoint property of their estates.

(D) Inadmissibility of Suretyship among Consorts

As far as the problem of the inadmissibility of surety ship between husband and wife, we find a long discourse in Mit. (*ad* Y. II-52) and Sar. (70 sqq.). Both these sources of law their discourse on different authorities, but did not give any clear explanation of the rule found in Y.(II-52). Y.'s opinion, that there did not exist joint property of consorts, expressed the point of view that husband and wife could not become sureties among themselves. Probably the only solution to this problem could be that stated above.[40]

38. Sar. 788.

39. Sar. 789. See also Sar. 798 and 833.

Sar. 790. was of the opinion that one who had obtained the consent of the other may undertake suretyship. This does not seem right, because if brothers were undivided and there existed joint property of estates, one brother even with the consent of the other one, could not undertake any obligation for the same thing with their joint property. This would not be suretyship but *adstipulatio* or *adpromissio*.

IV. RESPONSIBILITY OF SURETIES IN THE EVENT OF NON-PERFORMANCE OF OBLIGATIONS BY THE PRINCIPAL DEBTOR

As has been mentioned before, if the principal debtor did not perform his obligation, the surety was obliged to perform it for him. This rule was applicable, in particular, in the case of the principal debtor having to repay the loan.

1
FACILITIES

32. *General Remarks*

Mn. (VIII-169) rightly stated that sureties suffered for the sake of others and, therefore, they should not be forced to perform the debtor's obligation immediately. In this connection some of the ancient Indian sources of law introduced some facilities for sureties, if they were liable to repay the debt of the principal debtor. These facilities were of two kinds :

(a) repayment of the debt by instalments,

(b) postponement of the repayment of the debt.

As the rule, both these facilities werei ntroduced in the *Smṛti-s* in order to protect the sureties for appearance only. However, probably later, these facilities were also applicable to all kinds of sureties. Bṛh. and Kāty. (both younger sources of law) mentioned these facilities for sureties for appearance only, but Viv. (p. 14) stated generally that sureties could get time for making enquiries after the debtor and should not be harassed[41] and in this connection a debt due by surety should be realised by mild measures. Although Viv. was based on Bṛh. yet it expressed the opinion that these facilities related to all kinds of sureties.

33. *Repayment by Instalments and Postponement of Repayment*

The general rule regarding the admissibility of facilities for sureties are found in Mn. (VIII-169), where we

40. See also Study XII.
41. Viv. uses the general word : *pratibhū*.

read that three persons suffered for the sake of others : witnesses, sureties and judges.[42] Medh. explained that they underwent suffering for doing the work of others and they had not the slightest selfish motive, hence, they should not be forced to do the work. A detailed commentary on this rule we find in Bṛh. (X-84)[43], where we read that sureties should not be excessively harassed.

In this connection Bṛh. (X-84) declared that sureties should be made to pay the debt by instalments; Bṛh. added however, that they should not be attacked when the debtor was present. It is evident from this rule that Bṛh. related it to sureties for appearance.

This point of view could be seen more clearly from the preceding *śloka* of Bṛh. which related to the second facility introduced for sureties, *i.e.*, postponement of there payment of the debt. Although a rule existed that if the debtor did not repay the debt, the surety had to repay it (Y. II-53 and others[44]), Bṛh. (X-76) was of the opinion that :

naṣṭasyā'nveṣaṇe kālaṁ dadyāt pratibhuve dhanī,
desā'dhva-rūpataḥ pakṣaṁ māsaṁ sardham athā'pi vā.

(Also quoted in Apar. *ad* Y. 2.53, VyK. 117-8, SC. 149, VRK. 45, SCM. 11, SV. 248, VCa.17, VyPr.248-9, VyU. 28, VT. 531, VV. 22, VyP. 90, VyS. 77, VVy. 28).

Therefore, it is evident that the creditor should allow time for the surety to search for the debtor who had absconded. This time varied depending on the distance of the place where he was supposed to be hiding. It amounted to a fortnight, a month, or a month and a half.

Kāty. (532-3), where we find the same rule, mentioned only the maximum period that should be allowed *i.e.*, three fortnights, and stated that if the surety could produce the debtor in that time he would be free from liability, but when this time had expired and he could not produce the debtor, he should be made to pay what was due. Kāty. stated explicitly that this rule related to sureties for appearance only,

42. Mn. (8.169) : *trayaḥ parā'rthe kliśyanti sākṣiṇaḥ pratibhūḥ kulam.*

43. Bṛh. (10-84) :
nātyantaṁ pīḍanīyaḥ syur ṛṇaṁ dāpyāḥ śanaih śanaih.
svasākṣyeṇa niyojyāḥ syur vidhiḥ pratibhuvāmayam.

44. See below.

as he mentioned the producing of the debtor.[45] The same was also evident, although not so clearly, from Bṛh.; both these *Smṛti-s* mentioned the absconding of the debtor.[46]

2.
RECOURSE

34. *General Remarks*

The ancient Indian sources of law admitted the right of the surety, who repaid the debt of the principal debtor, to claim from the latter the amount paid by him to the creditor. The rule was that the surety had to receive the whole amount paid by him with interest and expenses and, in the event of him having been harassed and having paid the debt of the debtor under pressure, twice the amount paid by him. This rule, however, had certain exceptions which depended on the way in which the debt had been paid by the surety. The moment of the payment of the double amount was dependent on the date when the debt of the surety became payable.

The sources defined the repayment by the principal debtor of the double amount, being probably of the opinion that the repayment of the amount really paid was too clear to be discussed in detail.

35. *Repayment of the Simple Amount*

In connection with the repayment of the simple amount paid by the surety, we find the following query in Bṛh. (X-83) :

sādhutvāc-cen-mandadhiya ṛṇaṁ dadyur abhāvitāḥ,
yad arthaṁ dāpitā'stasmān na labheran kathañcana.
(Also quoted in Apar. *ad* Y. 2.53, VRK. 46).

45. *naṣṭasyā'nveṣaṇā'rthaṁ tu deyaṁ pakṣa-trayaṁ param,*
yad yasau darśayet tatra moktavyaḥ pratibhūr bhavet.
kāle vyatīte pratibhūr yadi taṁ naiva darśayet,
sa tam arthaṁ pradāpyaḥ syāt prete caivaṁ vidhīyate. (Kāty. 532-3. Also quoted in Mit. *ad* Y. 2.57, Apar. *ad* Y.2.53, SC. 149, NṛP. 21, SV. 247-8, VyPr. 247, 249, 254, Vy. 28-9, VyM. 78, VT. 531, VyP. 90, VyS. 77, VyK. 116, VRK. 42, VCi. 20, SCM. 11, VCa. 16, VV. 21, VVy. 27)

46. See Viv. mentioned above where reference was made to all kinds of sureties.

The author asked what the "foolish" sureties, who paid the debt *bonafide* had to do, and from whom they could recover the sum paid. Ratnākara explains that this concerned the payment of the debt by a surety who acted without guile and "unbidden by the umpire". That implied that the debt should be paid by the surety.

The reply to the question contained in Bṛh. (X-83) was found in Kāty. (540) where we read :

yasyā'rthe yena yad dattaṁ vidhinā'bhyarthitena tu,
sākṣibhir bhāvite naiva pratibhūs tat sam āpnuyāt.

(Also quoted in Apar. *ad* Y. 2.56, VyK.1 18, SC. 153, VRK. 46, VCi. 21, SCM. 12, VCa. 17, Vīr. *ad* Y. 2.53, VyPr. 252, VyU. 30, VV. 23, VyP. 91, VyS. 78, VVy. 28).

Kāty. accordingly stated that whatever the surety had paid to the creditor, who legally urged it and proved the case by witnesses, should be repaid by the debtor.

Kāty. mentioned here only the repayment of what was really paid and not the double amount.

Graheśvara and Miśra on Kāty. (quoted in Col. 260) explained this sentence in the following way : "a considerable space of time having elapsed beyond the stipulated term, if the creditor resolve on recurring to the king, but the surety, apprehending punishment, pacify the creditor at a pecuniary expense, and discharge the debt, the surety shall in that case recover from the debtor the money employed in appeasing the creditor; but shall only receive back the exact sum not twice the amount." However, Viv. (p. 14) interpreted this sentence differently stating that in addition to the double amount already paid by the surety, he had to receive any expense that was incurred by him for the debtor (Kāty.).

As Kāty. (549), contrary to the preceding *śloka* and other sources (Bṛh. X-82, Y. II-54, Vi. VI-43, N. I-21), did not mention a "harassed surety" or a surety who "was made to pay" the debt (*i.e.*, payment of the debt under pressure), we must understand that this sentence related to voluntary payments of the debt by the surety in which case the non-harassed surety was entitled to claim only from the principal debtor the repayment of that amount which he had really paid.

36. *Payment of the Double Amount*

The right of the surety to claim from the principal debtor the double amount paid by him, was defined almost identically in Y. (II-56), Vi. (VI-43), N. (I-121), Bṛh. (X-82) and Kāty. (539). The texts of Vi. and N., as well as of Bṛh. and Kāty., are identical. The only difference among these sources of law consisted in the fact that Y., N., and Vi. did not mention when the surety became liable to claim the double amount; the other *Smṛti-s* determined this time.

In Y. (II-56) we read :

pratibhūr dāpito yat tu prakāśaṁ dhanino dhanam,
dvi-guṇaṁ pratidātavyaṁ ṛṇikais tasya tad bhavet.

(Also quoted in ViR. *ad* Y.2.58, VyK. 118, SC. 153, VRK. 45, SCM. 11-2, NṛP. 21, VyPr. 252-3, VyU. 30-1, VyM. 79, VT. 530, VyP. 91, VyS. 78, AP. 254. 16).

Hence, Y. stated that if the amount which (*yad*) the surety (*pratibhū*), or his son (being harassed by the creditor), was publicly (*prakāśaṁ*), i.e. in the presence of all the people, made to pay (*dāpito*) by the king (and not which he has made voluntarily by going to him out of a craving for a double amount[47], [48]), should be repaid to him by the debtors.

The opinion of N. (I-121) and Vi. (VI-43) was identical.[49]

We find the explanation of the rule *i.e.* that the surety was entitled in this case to claim the payment of the double amount) in the rule that the surety should not be harassed (see above §.32 and Bṛh. X-84). Under such a harassment we understand use of pressure on the surety by an order of an authority commanding the payment of the debt.

At what time such double amount became payable was stated in Bṛh. (X-82) and Kāty. (539).[50] We read there :

pratibhāvyaṁ tu yo dadyāt pīḍitaḥ pratibhāvitaḥ,
tripakṣāt parataḥ so'rthaṁ dvi-guṇaṁ labdhum arhati.

Hence, Bṛh. and Kāty. stated, identically with Y., Vi. and N. that the surety, when harassed, was entitled to receive

47. Mit. (*ad.* Y. II-56) *Ghārpure's* translation.

48. Mit. (*ad* Y. II-56) objects to this interpretation and then comes to the same conclusion.

49. *yam arthaṁ pratibhūr dadyād dhanikenopapīḍitaḥ,*
ṛṇikastaṁ pratibhuve dvi-guṇaṁ pratidāpayet.

50. See Śūlapāṇi (ad Y. 2.56).

from the principal debtor twice the amount paid by him to the creditor. They only added that he could ask for that after the lapse of three fortnights and not before. This meant that he could not claim the double amount until six weeks had elapsed. Therefore, in the event of the principal debtor voluntarily repaying the surety, before the lapse of his term, he was not responsible for anything else.

It is, therefore, clear that only in the case of a guilty non-repayment of the debt by the principal debtor, he was liable to pay the double amount paid by the surety. It might be said that Kāty.'s, (539) and Bṛh.'s (X-82) points of view were medial between Kāty. (540) on one side, and Y. (II-56), N. (I. 118) and Vi. (VI 43) on the other.

Viv. (p. 14) pointed out that if the principal debtor had not repaid the debt in six weeks, he was liable, in addition, for the double amount paid by the surety, to pay interest, if a previous respective agreement had not been concluded.

37. *Payment of Non-Pecuniary Debts*

Y. (II-57) only mentioned certain exceptions to the rule that the double amount had to be paid to the surety by the principal debtor.

We read there :

saṁtatiḥ strī-paśuṣv eva dhānyaṁ tri-guṇam eva ca,
vastraṁ catur-guṇaṁ proktaṁ rasaś cā'ṣṭa-guṇas tathā.

(Also quoted in ViR. *ad* Y. 2. 59, SC. 153, NṛP. 21, VyPr. 254, VyU. 31, VT. 531, VyS. 78, AP. 254. 17).

Similarly as in the case of interest[51], Y. introduced the rule that in the case of female beasts, the debtor had to give the surety its progeny, in the case of corn threefold, of cloth fourfold, and of liquids eightfold of the principal amount.

These rules related to cases when the principal agreement did not relate to the repayment of money but other goods, for instance, cattle, goats, or female slaves[52], [53] (female beasts),

51. See below Study XVI on Harmonizing of Law with the Requirements of Economic Conditions.

52. Dipakalikiā.

53. The word progeny was also indicative by amplication of labour, according to the usage of time. (Vīr. p. 480), according to *J. R. Ghārpure's* translation).

corn,[54] cloth, or liquids. We can *per analogiam* apply to this case general rules relating to the admissibility of the rates of interest to various goods, and, in connection with the rule contained in Y. (II-57), apply them in the case of the obligation of repayment to the surety of nonpecuniary debts by the principal debtor (Y. II-39).

V. RESPONSIBILITY OF SONS FOR SURETIES' OBLIGATION

38. *Development of Legal Rules*

(A) General Remarks

This question was mentioned in nearly all the ancient Indian sources of law which deal with the subject of sureties,[55] although it was not settled in a uniform way. Some of the sources, as G., Vās. and K., were of the opinion that the son was not liable to pay the surety-money; Mn., Y. and Vi. declared that the son had to pay the surety-money in the case of surety for payment only; Bṛh. and Kāty. also in the case of sureties for delivery of assets; Vyāsa's opinion was that the son was always liable to pay the surety-money.

It seems that we find here another example of the harmonising of law with the requirements of economic conditions,[56] of the dynamics of the Indian law, of development of legal institution in ancient India.

We know that G. and Vās. belonged to the oldest *Smṛti-s* and Vyāṣa to the younger ones; G. and Vās. on one side, and Vyāsa on the other side, expressed quite different opinions. It seems that in ancient times the sons were not liable to pay the debt of the surety (surety-money), later they had to pay the surety money, in the case of surety for payment only, then of every surety who was obliged to discharge any debt *i. e.*, not only money, but also all kinds of assets; at the end the sons were liable to repay the debt of every surety.

The explanation of this fact seems to be quite simple : because of changed economic conditions the legal rules changed

54. Dīpakalikā.
55. With the exception of N.
56. See below Study XVI (see fn. 51).

accordingly.[57] From the time of G. and Vās. to the time of Vyāsa the economic life and, in particular, commercial life and commercial law, developed in India. Suretyship was used in commercial life more and more often in order to safeguard the creditor's claim. The development of commerce in India necessitated the granting of loans on a greater scale, and of concluding more frequently similar agreements. Money-lenders had become more necessary, and, therefore, wanted to be better safeguarded. Hence, probably their wish that in the case of the surety's death, or departure, the contract of suretyship should not become nul, but that the obligation of the surety should devolve upon the son—*putra*.[58] It was, in particular, of great interest to them, in the case of sureties for payment, or any other discharge of a debt, as well as in the case of sureties for honesty and appearance, and so on.

(B) In the Sources of Law

Vās. (XVI-31) stated :

athā'py udā-haranti;

prātibhāvyaṁ vṛthā-dāna-mākṣikaṁ saurikaṁ ca yat,
daṇḍa-śulkāvaśiṣṭaṁ ca na putro dātur mahati.

Vās. and Mn. (8. 159). are almost identical.[59]

Vās. was of the opinion that a son did not need to pay the surety-money, anything idly promised, gambling debts, or debts contracted for spirituous liquors, and what remained unpaid of a fine or toll.

G. (12-41) declared :

prātibhāvya-vaṇik-śulkam adyadyūta-daṇḍā na putrān adhyābhaveyuḥ, hence, was of the opinion that the surety-money, gambling debts, or debts contracted for spirituous liquors, a fine, the *śulka*, and commercial debts were not to be paid by the son.

Bṛh. (X-118) stating :

saurākṣikaṁ vṛthā-dānaṁ kāma-krodha-pratiśrutam,
prātibhāvyaṁ daṇḍa-śulka-śeṣaṁ putraṁ na dāpayet.

57. See below Study XVI (see fn. 51).

58. It was clear that the word *putra* (son) meant in this context also heirs.

59. *prātibhāvyaṁ vṛthā-dāna-mākṣikaṁ saurikam ca yat,*
daṇḍa-śulkāvaśeṣaṁ ca na putro dātum arhati (Mn. 8. 159).

(also quoted in VyK. 121, SC. 169, VRK. 57, VCi. 25, SCM. 13, SV. 256-7, VCa. 17, Vir. *ad* Y. 2.47, VyPr. 265-6, VV. 28, VyP. 98, VyS. 84, VVy. 29) defined this problem in an identical manner as G. Bṛh. added only "promises made under the influence of love or wrath". This problem was similarly solved in K. (189/12-13) where we read :

prātibhāvya-daṇḍaḥ śulka-śeṣam āsthikaṁ saurikaṁ kāmadānaṁ ca nākāmaḥ putro dāyādo vā rikthaharo dadyāt.

Hence, we see that G., one of the most ancient of all the known *Smṛti-s*, expressed the opinion that *prātibhāvya* (surety-money, *i. e.*, money due by every kind of surety) had not to be paid by the debtor's heirs when the surety died. That was the general rule prevalent in G.

Vās. did not give his own opinion on this question, but quoted Mn. (VIII-159) and so was obviously of the same opinion as G. Vās. did not quote *śloka* 160 of Mn. *i.e.*, the subsequent one. Mn. (VIII-160) was completely contradictory to Mn. (VIII-159). This, probably, shows that at the time that Vās. was composed *śloka* 160 of book VIII Mn. was not in use. This can also show that this *śloka* was a later interpolation. Vās., quoting Mn., probably cited the rules which were well known and of value at the time of the composition of Vās. These rules were also relevent at the time of the composition Mn., but at that time the legal rules had probably changed because of the change and evoltuion of the economic conditions, and Mn. in addition to the archaic rule VIII-159, introduced a new and a more recent rule (*i.e.*, as recent as possible at the time of the composition of Mn.), *i. e.*, Mn. (VIII- 160) according to which in the case of surety for payment, the surety's son should be made liable for the surety-money.

Bṛh. (X-118) introduced an almost identical rule as that found in G. (XII-41). Bṛh.'s opinion is characteristic because different rules selected from various *Smṛti-s* were contained therein. They were often archaic, and no longer in use; therefore, Bṛh. contained many contradictory rules. Regarding sureties, Bṛh. (X-118) was completely different from Bṛh. (X-78). Bṛh. (X,118) contains a general rule according to which the sons did not pay for debts incurred on the basis of a contract of surety; Bṛh. (X-78) gave the third stage of development of the liability of the sureties for the surety-money *i. e.*, in the case of contracts of surety for payment, as well as for delivering assests to the debtor. We could not even say that Bṛh. (X-118) was a general rule and Bṛh. (X-78) a specific rule, and we must assume that Bṛh. in X-118 thoughtlessly copied the rule contained in Mn. (VIII-159) or G. (XII-41) or Vās. (XVI-31). Bṛh (X-118) was the only *Smṛti* in which this rule was wrongly copied, because other *Smṛti-s* as Y. (II-47) and Vi. (VI-33 sqq.), being of the same opinion that the son was responsible for some debt incurred by the father, in the respective list did not mention-contracts of suretyship incurred by the father-surety, but mentioned, idly promised gifts, gambling debts, debts contracted for spirituous liquors, and what remained unpaid of a fine or toll etc. (Y.).

K. (189/12 sqq.) inserted the rule mentioned above in Book III in the chapter entitled "Resumption of gifts, sale without ownership and ownership." Other rules which related to suretyship did not mention this question in detail[60].

60 K. (174-18-175-3) mentioned here the word *pratibhū*, but the context is not clear. K. (174-18-19) probably related to another question *i. e.* the responsibility of the surety in the event of death of the debtor. K.'s 174-19-175-1) question *na prātibhavyamanyad asāram bāla prātibhāvyam* could be understood into different ways. We can read it as one sentence only, or in the following way: *na pratibhavyam anyat*, separately from *asāraṁ bāla-prātibhāvyam*. Probably the first interpretation is more accurate in that case we must read the first part of this sentence (a minor, as surety is inefficent, no surety is admitted for him) along with *bāla*, as it is difficult to understand what *na pratibhāvyam anyat* meant, as K. 174/18-19 did not relate to the responsibility of sons after the death of the surety.

K. (175-1-2) states that the debt, the payment of which was not limited as to time or place, should be paid by the heirs of the debtor. The following sentences mentioned *pratibhū* again and were connected with the problem quoted above. In K. (175-2-3) we read : *jivita-vivāha-bhūmi-prātibhavyam asaṅkhyā-tadeśa-kalaṁ tu putrāḥ pautrā vā vaheyuḥ.*

This sentence was translated by Shamasastri, probably wrongly, in the following manner : "Any debt, the payment of which is not limited by time or place or both and for which life, marriage or land is pledged shall be borne by sons or grandsons."

No reason can be seen why *jivita-vivāha-bhūmi-pratibhāvyam* should be translated "life, marriage, or lands," for the expression "pledge" K. used the word *ādai* etc., but never *pratibhūvya* which meant surety or surety-money, etc. J. J. Meyer translated this sentence better saying. "*Etwas aber bei der Zeit und Ort nicht festgesetzt its und bei dem Leib und Leben, Heirat oder Land die Bürgerschaft bilden sollen (nur) die Sohne oder die Enkel tragen.*" It is also difficult no accept J. J. Meyer's translation as regards *Jivita* or *vivāha* as correct. *Jivita* might mean also a person, and *vivāha* does not mean marriage only, but carrying away too. Therefore, it seems that this sentence should be translated in the following manner : "The debt, the payment

Therefore, we could assume that according to K. the rule was in force that sons were not obliged to pay for the debts of their fathers which arose from the contract of suretyship.[61]

39. *Legal Rules on Obligations of Sons for their Father-Sureties.*

Y. (II. 53) declared :

darśane pratyaye dāne prātibhāvyaṁ vidhīyate,
ādyau tu vitathe dāpyāvitarasya sutā api.

(Also quoted in ViR. *ad* Y. 2.55, GMH. 12.38, SC, 150, SCM. 11, VyPr. 248, VyU. 28, VyM. 78, VT. 525, RDhK. 399, VyP. 90, VyS. 77, AP. 254. 13).

This *śloka* was repeated in Vi. (VI 41).

Hence, Y. and Vi. stated that in the case of surety for appearance and honesty, the surety was only responsible for the debt in the case of default, whilst in the case of surety for payment even the sons had top ay the surety-money. The same rule was repeated and defined in a more detailed way in the next *śloka* of Y. (II.54). We read there :

darśana-pratibhūr yatra mṛtaḥ prātyayiko'pi vā,
na tat putrā ṛṇaṁ dadyur dadyur dānāya yaḥ sthitaḥ.

(Also quoted in ViR. *ad* Y. 2. 56, Medh. *ad* Mn. 8.160, VyK. 116, SC. 150, VRK. 40, VCi. 19, SCM. 11, NṛP. 21, SV. 248, Rāgh. in MnM. *ad* 8. 160, VyPr. 250, VyU. 29, VT.

of which is not limited as to time or place, and in which (1) a person, (2) that which can be carried away, or (3) land—form surety, should be taken over by sons or grandsons." This means that in the event of death of the surety—who guaranteed with his own person, his assets, or immovable property—the sons and grandsons were responsible for the debt, if the contract was not limited as to time and place. However, what should be understood in K. under "guarantee with the surety's person, assets, or immovable property" is not clear. It was not one of the suretyships mentioned above and defined in the *Smrti-s*. Probably we must understand that the sentence related to the problem of the limited to which the surety guaranteed for the principal debtor. J. J. Meyer did not explain this sentence either. He stated only (276-43) that "*beide Sätze handeln wohl van der Vererbung der Bürgschaft.*" He did not define the "*Bürgschaft.*" In the Sanskrit text we find the most common word *i. e. pratibū*). J. J. Meyer's point of view that 175-1-2 did not relate to sureties, is not convincing, although the two sentences were joined by the word *tu* because this sentence contains the general rule regarding the transition of the obligation from the debtor to the heirs. In particular, the connection with the sentence quoted above (K. 189-12-13), it was difficult to admit that K. (175-2-3) related to the obligation of the sons for a surety, which is not well known, the more so as the transition of the obligation from the surety not only to the sons but even to the grandsons was foreseen. This opinion was unknown to all other sources of law.

61. N. (1-10) did not relate to this question.

526, RDhK. 399, VV. 21, VyP. 90, VyS. 77, VVy. 27, AP. 254.14).

"Where a surety for appearance or honesty dies the sons must not pay for the surety money. However, in the case of surety for payment—they must pay."

Mit. (*ad* Y. II-54) explained that only sons and not grandsons were responsible in the case of surety for payment, Viv.'s (p. 13) opinion was the same. Viv. quoted Y. (2.54).

Mn. (8. 160) stated :

darśana-prātibhāvye tu vidhiḥ syāt pūrva-coditaḥ,
dāna pratibhuvi prete dāyādān api dāpayet.

(Also quoted in VyK. 117, GMH. 12.38, SC. 151-2, VRK. 57, SV. 257, VyU. 30, VV. 28, VyS. 78).

Mn. referred to the preceding *śloka*, which was quoted above, and from which it is evident that the son was not liable to a the surety-money. Mn. (VIII-160) stated, however that this rule referred to sureties for appearance only and that in the case of sureties for payment the heirs should pay the surety-mney. The commentators on Mn. (VIII-160) rightly used extensive interpretation and declared that in the case of surety for honesty[62] also the sons were not liable to pay the surety-money (Medh. *ad* Mn. VIII-160). This commentary seems to be correct, as Mn. explicitly referring to the responsibility of the son in the case of death of a surety for payment, considered it as an exception to the general rule; therefore, in the case of surety for honesty the sons were not liable to pay the surety-money.

Bṛh. and Kāty., as has already been mentioned, enumerate respectively four or five kinds of sureties, contrary to the *Smṛti-s* quoted above, where only three kinds of surety were enumerated. Therefore Bṛh., where we find *ṛṇidravyārpaṇa* stated :

ādyau tu vitathe dāpyau tat kālāveditaṁ dhanam,
uttarau tu visaṁvāde tau vinā tat sutau tathā. (Bṛh. 10. 78.)

(Also quoted in Apar. *ad* Y. 2.53, VyK. 116, SC. 150, VRK. 40, DK. 37, VCi. 19, SCM. 11, SV. 249, VCa. 15, Vīr, *ad* Y.2.57, VyPr. 248, VyM. 78, VV. 20-1, VyP. 90, VyS. 77, VVy. 27). This *śloka* was repeated in Kāty. (536).

62. This kind of surety was not mentioned in Mn.

Hence, according to these two *Smṛti-s* in the case of sureties for appearance and honesty, the sons were not liable to pay the surety-money, however, in the case of sureties for payment and for delivery of the assets of the debtor, they were liable to pay, when their father died.

Kāty. (536) did not refer to the five kinds of sureties enumerated in *śloka* 530 (Kāty. enumerated in this *śloka* five kinds of sureties and first of all surety for payment), but since this *śloka* was copied from Bṛh. it referred to Bṛh., Althogh Kāty. did not determine the problem of the responsibility of the sons for obligations arising from the contract of suretyship, for which their fathers bound themselves, we must assume that Kāty., since it quoted Bṛh. (X-78), was of the same opinion as Bṛh., *i.e.*, that the sons of sureties were responsible for the debts of their fathers contracted for surety for payment, or any other surety in which the surety bound himself to discharge the debt (hence, not only monetary loans.)

Consequently, we find here the second and third stage of the development of the responsibility of sons for the obligation of their fathers contracted in suretyship. This responsibility was mainly confined to sureties for payment and secondly for delivery the assets of the debtor, *i. e.*, to suretyships in which the surety bound himself to discharge any debt. Thus, the surety for delivering a pledge[63], if this kind of surety was known in these times, would fall under the same notion; for this kind of suretyship the surety's son would be responsible.

Vy. quoted in Mit. (*ad* Y. II-54)[64] stated :

ṛṇaṁ paitamahaṁ pautraḥ prātibhāvya-gataṁ sutaḥ, samaṁ dadyāt tat sutau tu na dāpyāv iti niścayaḥ.

(Also quoted in Apar. *ad* Y. 2. 54, VyK. 117, SC. 152, VRK. 44, VCi. 20, SCM. 11, NṛP. 21 SV. 249, Vca. 16, Vīr. *ad* Y. 2.50, VyPr. 250, VyU. 29, VyM. 78, VT. 528, RDhK. 400, VV. 22, VyS. 78, VVy. 28).

Hence, Vy. clearly stated that a son should pay the father's debts resulting from the contract of suretyship to an extent equal to the principal only. The grandsons, however, were

63. *gṛhīta-bandho'pasthāna* was only enumerated in Vy. (Smṛ. C. p. 347). According to Vyāsa sons were always responsible for all kinds of sureties contracted by their fathers.

64. This sentence was also quoted in Viv.

also liable to pay this debt. Vy. used the general word *prati-bhāvya*; therefore, we could admit that this obligation was not limited to some kinds of sureties, but covered all of them.

Mit. (*ad* Y. II-54) quoted also Hār.'s text (Dh.) although did not state that this sentence was an extract from Hār.'s work. We read there :

khādako vittahīnaḥ syāl lagnakov ittavān yadi, mūlaṁ tasya bhaved deyaṁ na vṛddhiṁ dātum arhati.

This text is not very clear. Hār. stated that if the debtor had no money but the surety possessed it, the latter should be liable to pay the principal without interest.

Mit. probably rightly stated :

lagnako yadi vittavān mṛtas tadā tasya putreṇa mūlam eva dātvyam na vṛddhir iti vyākhyeyam.

If a surety *lagnaka*, who has possessed wealth, died, then only the principal amount (without interest) should be paid by his son. Although this interpretation does not result clearly from Hār.'s context, Mit.'s point of view seems to be correct, particularly in connection with Vyāsa's point of viw, quoted above.

Consequently, these two relatively young *Smṛti-s* were of quite different opinions from Vās., G., etc., and stated that the responsibility for the debts contracted bys ureties always fell on their sons.

40. *Responsibility of Sons in the Matter of Safeguarding the Surety's Obligation*

Some of the *Smṛti-s*, which did not contain the rule that the son of the surety was responsible for his father-surety debts contracted before his death, stated that in some cases, as far as sureties for appearance or honesty were concerned, the surety's son was responsible for the father's debt. This took if the surety had received from the principal debtor a security in order to safeguard his obligation with regard to the creditor; this security could be given in the form of a pledge, deposit, etc.

This rule was correct and accordingly linked the system of non-responsibility and responsibility of the sons for the obligations of their father-sureties. The giving of such a security was not necessarily notified to the creditor, and only if he was able to prove that such a guarantee had been given to the surety, he was entitled to claim his rights from the surety's son.

Kāty. (534)[65] declared that : should a person become a surety for appearance after he received a pledge as his own security, the creditor, in case the surety died, had the right to claim the repayment of the debt from the surety's son if he proved that the surety received a pledge, as his own security. This rule was also quoted in Mit. (*ad* Y. II-54).

In this connection Mit. rightly added that sureties for appearance included sureties for honesty and that the same rule had to be applied to the case of a father dying, or going abroad.

Mn. (VIII-161) asked by what means the creditor could seek to obtain his dues in the event of the death of the surety other than the surety for payment. The answer was similar to that found in Kāty. Mn. (8.162) stated :

nirā'diṣṭadhanaś cet tu pratibhūḥ syād alaṁdhanaḥ,
svadhānadeva tad dadyān nirādiṣṭa iti sthitiḥ.

(Also quoted in in VyK. 117, SC. 151, VRK. 43, SV. 250, VyP. 91, VyS. 78).

We see that Mn. was of the opinion that if money has been handed over to the surety by the debtor and the surety had enough money, the son of the person to whom it had been handed over had to discharge the debt. Hence, according to Mn., it was sufficient for the debtor to hand over to the surety certain things with the instruction to pay off the debt, should the debtor be unable to repay the debt, in order to make the surety's son liable to repay the creditor's debt if he had enough money, *i.e.*, if this "something was as large as the debt due to the debtor." That is the interpretation of this sentence, given by Ratnākara.

It was not explained in what way the surety should be secured. As Kull. rightly stated, this security was probably given in the form of a pledge, (Other commentators mentioned deposits, etc.). Halāyuddha[66] rightly stated that this circum-

65. *gṛhītvā bandhakaṁ yatra darśanesya sthito bhavet.*
vinā pitrā dhanaṁ tasmād dāpyaḥ syat tad ṛṇaṁ sutaḥ. (Kāty 534.) Also quoted in Mit. *ad* Y.2.54, VyK. 117, SC. 151, VRK. 43, VCi. 20 SCM. 11, NṛP. 21, SV. 249, VCa. 16, VyPr. 251, VyU. 29, VyM. 79, VT, 529, VV. 21. VyP. 90, VyS. 78, VVy. 28).

66. Quoted in Col. p. 250.

stance had to be known and proved by the creditor, because, if unknown, the general rules, regarding the non-responsibility of the sons for debts contracted by their father-sureties (other than those for payment), had to be applied.

Mn. using the word *pratibhū* stated more clearly than Kāty., that this rule related to all kinds of sureties known to the *Smṛti-s*.

41. *Responsibility of the Surety's Son*

It has to be emphasized that it is evident from the *Smṛti-s* and, in particular, from the commentators on the *Smṛti-s*, that when sons were responsible for their father-sureties' obligations, these obligations were binding not only when the father-sureties died or were absent, *i.e.*, when they have gone abroad to distant regions (Mit. *ad* II-54, Ratnākara)[67], but also in the case of religious seclusion of the debt[68]; this responsibility never fell on the grandsons, but on, the sons only (Mit. *ad* Y. II-54), who were obliged to pay the capital but without interest (Vyāsa quoted in Mit. *ad* Y. II-54, Hār. quoted *ad* Y. 1-54, Viv. and Ratnākara *ad* Vyāsa quoted in Col. p. 255).

The rules concerningt he responsibility of sons in the event of co-sureties would be expiained in the next chapter.

VI. RESPONSIBILITY OF CO-SURETIES

42. *General Remarks*

This problem was mentioned in Y., N. and Vi. (the texts of N. and Vi. are almost identical) as well as, in more detailed manner, in Kāty.

If suretyship with one surety was an example of a collateral obligation, so in the case of more than two sureties their obligation towards the creditor could be either a solidary obligation or a *pro rata parte* obligation. This depended on the text of the agreement concluded. Where the sureties had declared their joint liability for the whole debt, their obligation was a solidary one. Where, however, a number of sureties had each promised to pay a certain stipulated share of the debt, their liability was *pro rata parte* only.

67. Quoted in Col. p. 248.
68. Col. p, 237.

In Roman law the *Epistola Divi Hadriani* gave several co-sureties the *exceptio divisionis, i.e.*, the right to demand that the creditor divides his claim *pro rata parte* between the co-sureties. The ancient Inidian law made the responsibility of the co-sureties dependent on the agreement, but did not explain what would happen if no agreement had been concluded. The commentators, however, were of the opinion that identically with the Roman law the co-sureties had the right to the *exceptio divisionis* and expressed the opinion that they should pay equal shares only.

43. *Solidary Obligations or "Pro Rata Parte"*

In Y. (II-55), we read :

bahavaḥ syur yadi svāṁśair dadyuḥ pratibhuvo dhanam,
ekac chāyāśriteṣv eṣu dhanikasva yathāruci.

(Also quoted in ViR. *ad* Y. 2.57, VyK. 117, SC. 152, VRK. 44, VCi. 20 : 24, SVM. 11, NṛP. 21, SV. 250, VCa. 17, VyPr. 251, VyU. 30, VyM. 79, VT. 530, VV. 22, VyP. 91, VyS. 78, VVy. 28, AP. 254. 15).

N. (1.120) and indentically Vi. (6.42) stated :

bahavaś cet pratibhuvo dadyus te'rthaṁ yathā-kṛtam,
arthe viśeṣite hy eṣu dhaninaś chandataḥ kriyā.

(Also quoted in NMS. 2.103).

Hence, these sources of law were of the opinion that in the case of co-sureties they should pay in accordance with the text of the agreement concluded (share). When, however, they were bound jointly and severally,[69] *i.e.*, in the case of a solidary obligation, they had to pay according to the choice of the creditor.

Here we have to mention a co-surety who agreed only to pay a part of the principal debt, if he bound himself along with other co-sureties to pay only a part of the debt. And so, if a debt, for example, amounted to 1,000, the surety A could bind himself to pay 500, B to pay 300, and C. to pay 200 only; in this case these co-sureties, if the principal debtor did not repay the debt to the creditor, were liable to pay the debt according to the agreement (500:300:200). This liability of co-sureties to repay the debt would take place more often, for instance, if one surety was a surety for appearance, the other

69. *ekac chāyāśriteṣu pratibhūṣu ekasyādharma-ṇasyachāyā sādṛyaṁ tamāśṅtā ekac chāyā-śṇtāḥ* (Medh. *ad* Y. 2. 55)

for honesty and the third one for payment. Then they would only be liable to what resulted from the different contracts of suretyship.

Vīr. (p. 480) added that if no agreement of this kind had been concluded, the shares of the sureties should be equal (identical with the *exceptio divisionis* of the Roman law introduced by the *Epistola Divi Hadriani*).

If an agreement was concluded[70], according to which the co-sureties bound themselves jointly and severally, the obligation became solidary. Therefore, if in this case the co-sureties were sureties for appearance, for honesty and for payment, the creditor was entitled to claim his rights from all of them in the same way as in the case of several co-sureties for payment.

Kāty. solved this problem in *ślokas* 538 and 537. *Śloka* 537 was practically the same as 538 and Mit. quoted *śloka* 538. Kāty. in *śloka* 537 referred to Bṛh. but that *śloka*[71] cannot be found in Bṛh. Therefore, in the first place *śloka* 538 should be taken into consideration. In this *śloka* it was stated that the obligation of co-sureties was solidary; it also added, similarly as in *śloka* 537, that if the surety went abroad, his son had to pay the whole amount, but if the co-surety died his father's share only. This sentence is to clear ands hould be understood in the following manner ; although Kāty. did not say that the co-sureties were bound to repay the debt *pro rata parte*, the opinion is expressed there that it could take place, since it was declared that in the case of the father's death the son should pay only that share which had fallen to the deceased father.

44. *Interest*

Mit. and Vīr. were of the opinion that the payment related to the capital only, without interest.

It must be pointed out that according to Vy. monthly interest in the case of a pledged debt amounted to an eightieth part and an eighth was added in the case of a debt secured by a surety.[72] Ratnākara explains that an 8-th is added to an

70. See Viv. p. 14.
71. From Bṛh.
72. See below study XVI on the Harmonising of Law with the Requirements of Economic Conditions.

80-th part. Hence two *paṇa-s* less than two *purāṇa-s*, or one *purāṇa* and fourteen *paṇa-s* were received only if there was a surety. Vācaspati Miśra stated that the 80-th part should be divided into eight parts and one such part should be added.[73] Consequently the allowed rate of interest would not amount to 15 per cent yearly but to almost 17 per cent[74] yearly.[75]

Other rules regarding interest in the case of a contract of surety were described above in relation to the different legal regulations. Vīr. (p. 480) added only that the interest was to begin to run three weeks after the payment had been made by the sureties, and based this point of view on Bṛh. (IX-82).[76] It is, however, very difficult to prove on what basis Vīr. interpreted Bṛh. (IX-82) in such a way. Probably, Vīr. applied the general rules relating to interest.

73. Interest in the sum of 20 *pala-s* of gold was 90 *raktikā-s*.

74. Exactly 16.87 per cent.

75. If the surety died or went abroad (to a foreign country) the debts were considered as unsecured by surety and the interest would amount in this case, as a rule, to—24 per cent yearly.

76. Identically Kāty. 539.

IV

LEGAL POSITION OF PROSTITUTES ACCORDING TO KAUTILYA'S ARTHAŚĀSTRA[1]

I. SYNONYMS OF THE WORD 'PROSTITUTE' USED IN K.

1. *Different Names*

1. K. used the words *gaṇikā*, *pratigaṇikā*, *rūpājīvā*, *veśyā dāsī*, *devadāsī*, *puṁścalī*, *śilpakārikā*, *kauśikastrī*, and *rūpadāsī* in the meaning of special kinds of prostitutes. Also the words *adāsī*, *avaruddhā*, *kṛtāvarodhā* or *kṛtāparādhā*, *duhitṛkā*, *kumārī* and others are to be found in K., probably in the meaning of special kinds of prostitutes.

This list of synonyms for the word 'prostitute' is far from complete for we find more than 250 synonyms for this word in Sanskrit literary works.[2]

The word *gaṇikā* is the most frequently used word in K. to denote prostitutes. It has a specific meaning, not the same as in other Sanskrit works, particularly in Kāmasūtra-s. Vāts.[3] gives the following definition of a *gaṇikā* :

> *ābhir abhyucchritā veśyā śīlarūpaguṇānvitā*
> *labhate gaṇikāśabdaṁ sthānaṁ ca janasaṁsadi*[4]

'A prostitute [*veśyā*], who is endowed with good character, beauty, and good qualities and distinguishes herself in them, receives the title of a *gaṇikā* and a high position among the people.'

However, in K. the word *gaṇikā* meant only a government servant, similar to any other government servant, for

1. Previously appeared in the "Journal of the American Oriental Society". Vol. 69, pp. 25-60. Submitted to the All India Oriental Conference in Bombay, 1949.

2. L. Sternbach, *Veśyā*; *Synonyms and Aphorisms* (Bombay, 1945); *First* and *Second Supplements to Veśyā*; *Synonyms and Aphorisms* in *BhV* 8.256 ff., and 11.49 ff. where 330 synonyms were quoted.

3. Vāts. 41. 24-5.

4. Amar. (Nāṭyavarga 11 b; 71.2) stated : *strīveṣadhārī puruṣ* ` *nāṭyoktau ganikājjukā*.

which the *gaṇikā'dhyakṣa*, the superintendent of prostitutes, took care. Whenever the word *gaṇikā* was used in the text of K. it had this specific meaning and should not be confused with prostitutes who worked on their own account. For denoting such a kind of prostitutes K. used most frequently, the word *rūpājīvā*[5] (a woman who lived on her beauty).

2. *Gaṇikā*

A. We do not find in lexicographies and in the Kāmasūtra-s a definition of a *gaṇikā* which would fit their description in K. On the country, the lexicographers quoted the word *gaṇikā* among other *sādhāraṇastrī* or *kuṣdrā*; similarly the Kāmasūtras.

In Sanskrit literary works the word *gaṇikā* was very often used loosely with other words to denote a prostitute. However, in all the sources the word *gaṇikā* always denoted the highest degree of prostitutes—a courtesan.

B. Hemacandra in Abhidhānacintāmaṇi enumerated as *sādhāraṇastrī* : *gaṇikā*, *veśyā*, *paṇyāṅganā*, *paṇāṅganā*, *bhujiṣyā*, *lañjikā*, *rūpājīvā*, *vāravadhū* and *vāramukhyā*,[6] and in Anekārthasaṁgraha identified the *gaṇikā* with the *bhujiṣyā* and the *dāsī*.[7]

Halāyudha in Abhidhānaratnamālā enumerated as *kṣudrā* *rūpājīvā*, *veśyā*, *gaṇikā*, and *paṇāṅganā*.[8]

Amarasiṁha in Amarakośa enumerated as *ajanā* : *vārastrī*, *gaṇikā*, *veśyā*, and *rūpājīvā*.[9]

Medinī, quoted in Śabdakalpadruma, identified *bhujīṣyā* with *dāsī* and *gaṇikā*.[10]

C. As far as the Kāmasūtra-s are concerned, certainly the best source is Vāts. Vāts. generally used to denote prostitutes by the word *veśyā*; at the end of the sixth part, dealing with prostitution (*vaiśikam adhikaraṇam*) Vāts. stated that

5. K. 41. 19; 55. 11; 113. 19; 125. 12; 144. 9; 198. 17; 236. 11; 243. 11; 316. 1.

6. *sādhāraṇastrī gaṇikā veśyā paṇyapaṇāṅganā bhujiṣyā lāñjikā rūpājīvā vārāvadhūḥ punaḥ sā vāramukhyā* (ed. O. Böhtlingk and C. Rieu; Petersburg, 1847; 532-3).

7. Ed. Th. Zachariae (Vienna-Bombay, 1893); 3. 490.

8. *rūpājivā veśyā gaṇikā paṇyāṅganā tathā kṣudrā* (ed. Th. Aufrecht, Lahore, 1928; 2. 335).

9. Ed. Colebrooke (Calcutta, 1807); Nṛvarga 19a; 44. 3. Also quoted in Śabdakalpadruma, *ad veśyā*.

10. *Bhujiṣyā—dāsi gaṇikā iti Mediniye* (ed. 1808; *ad bhujiṣyā* 99).

there were different kinds of prostitutes, but according to Yaś.[11] all kinds of prostitutes fell into three categories, that is, *kumbhadāsī*, *gaṇikā*, and *rūpājīvā*. Among *rūpājīvā* Vāts. enumerated *paricārikā*, *kulaṭā*, *svairiṇī*, *naṭī*, *śilpakārikā*, and *prakāśavinaṣṭā*, so that there were nine kinds of *veśyā* : *kumbhadāsī*, *paricārikā*, *kulaṭā*, *svairiṇī*, *naṭī*, *śilpakārikā*, *rūpājīvā*, and *gaṇikā*;[12] Yaś. defined all of them with the exception of *kumbhadāsī*, *rūpājīvā*, and *gaṇikā*.[13] On the other hand Yaś. stated that all *veśyā* were considered as *kumbhadāsī*.[14]

In other places Vāts. stated that the expression *veśyā* might also include the expression *gaṇikā*,[15] or a *gaṇikā*, a *rūpājīvā*, and a *kumbhadāsī*,[16] on the understanding that each of them could be an *uttama*,[17] *madhyama*, and *adhama*.[18] Despite this last statement Vāts. mentioned that a *veśyā* could be a *gaṇikā* or a *rūpājīvā* or a *kumbhadāsī*.[19] Vāts.[20] also used loosely the words *gaṇikā* and *rūpājīvā*,[21] as well as *gaṇikā*, *rūpājīvā*, and *kumbhadāsī*.[22]

D. In Sanskrit literary works we can find hundreds of examples of the use of the word *gaṇikā*; it was indiscriminately used with other synonymous words. It is impossible to quote but a small part of them.

11. *loke sāmānyās trayaḥ prasiddhāḥ : kumbhadāsī gaṇikā rūpājīvā ce'ti* (Vāts. 363. 15-6).

12. *kumbhadāsī paricārikā kulaṭā svairiṇī naṭī śilpakārikā prakāśavinaṣṭā rūpājīvā gaṇikā ce'ti veśyāviśeṣāḥ* (Vāts. 363. 13-4).

13. Vāts. 263. 15-22.

14. *kumbhadāsī'ti kumbhagrahaṇaṁ nikṛṣṭakarmopalakṣaṇam* (Vāts. 363. 15).

15. *Veśye 'ti vaktavye gaṇikāgrahaṇaṁ yoṣid api catuḥṣaṣṭivicakṣaṇe 'ti darśanārtham* (Vāts. 189. 5).

16. *Vividhā veśyā—gaṇikā rūpājīvā kumbhadāsī ca* (Vāts. 347. 7).

17. The *uttamagaṇikā* were those who distinguished themselves with beauty and other good qualities of mistresses and the knowledge of 64 arts (*uttamagaṇikānām iti, rūpādibhir nāyikāguṇakalādibhir anvitā uttamagaṇikāḥ*); the *madhyamā* and *adhamā* had one-quarter or one-eighth of these qualities respectively (*guṇānāṁ ca pādārdhābhyāṁ madhyamādhamāḥ*) (Vāts. 347. 16-7). Cf. Śl. S. 10. 187.

18. Cf.Rudraṭa's Kāvyālaṁkāra 155; Rudraṭa's Śṛṅgāratilaka 1.154-5; Sāhityadarpaṇa 122; Bhāratīya Nāṭyaśāstra 23. 34, etc. which stated that by dividing the *nayikā* into *uttama*, *madhyama* and *adhama* their number amounted upto 380.

19. *veśyāyā iti gaṇikāyā rūpājīvāyāḥ, na kumbhadāsyāḥ* (Vāts. 184. 12-3. Yaś. is here wrong). Cf. Vāts. 363. 13; 347. 7; 348. 17.

20. *Etat sarvaṁ gaṇikānāṁ rūpājīvānāṁ cā 'sty eva* (Vāts. 348. 8-9).

21. *madhyamādhamānām apī'ti gaṇikā-rūpājīvā-kumbhadāsīnām* (Vāts. 348. 16-7).

22. Cf. Vāgbhaṭa's Kāvyānuśāsana 63.

In the Ṛgveda *vrā*, a she-elephant, denoted the same as *gaṇikā*.[23] Also Jaṭādhara in Śabdakalpadruma identified a *gaṇikā* with a *hastinī*[24] and Śaśvata with a *kariṇī*.[25]

In MBh. and R. both the words *gaṇikā* and *veśyā*[26] were used for the designation of prostitutes. *Gaṇikā*, according to these epics, were in high esteem.[27]

The Mṛcchakaṭikā and the Daridra Cārudatta referred to Vasantasenā as a *gaṇikā* but used loosely the words *veśyā*, *paṇastrī*, and *prakāśanārī*.

In Śukasaptati it was stated that there were several kinds of prostitutes, namely, *gaṇikā*, *vilāsinī*, *rūpājīvā*, *arthavṛttikā*, and *dārikā*.[28]

In Kathāsaritsāgara the word *gaṇikā* was loosely used; such words as *veśyā*,[29] or *veśyā*, *vilāsinī*,[30] or *vilāsinī* and *vāravanitā*,[31] were also used.

In the Jātaka-s the word *gaṇikā* in the meaning of a highly esteemed person, was very often used. It was used indiscriminately with *nagarasobhinī* (or *nagarasobhīnī*), *nagarasobhanī* (or *nagarasobhanā*),[32] and *vaṇṇadāsī* (*varṇadāsī*).[33]

In Milindapañha *gaṇikā*, *lāsikā*, and *kumbhadāsī* were enumerated as those coming to the town to find residence there.[34]

23. R. Pischel u. K. F. Geldner, *Vedische Studien* (Stuttgart, 1889 1901) 2. 123.

24. *Ad gaṇikā*.

25. The Anekārthasamuccaya of Śāśvata, ed. K. G. Oka (Poona, 1918) 641; also with a *veśyā*.

26. And others. Cf. Śiśupālavadha's Commentry, *ad* 11. 20.

27. Cf. J. J. Meyer, *Das Weib im altindischen Epos* Leipzig, 1915), chapter IX; R. Schmidt, *Liebe und Ehe im alten u. modernen Indien* (Berlin, 1904) 542 ff. and note 29 to chapter II.

28. *yato gaṇikādīnāṁ bahavo bhedāḥ paraṁ pañca prasiddhāḥ. Teṣu saṁlīnāḥ sarve api bhavanti. Te ce 'me pañca gaṇikā vilāsinī rūpājīvā arthavṛttikā dārikā ce 'ti. Eteṣāṁ bhedānāṁ sā sarvottamā gaṇikā.* (Śuk. t. s., *AKM* 10. 1, p. 132. 8-10). This text is also to be found in other versions of Śuk. (A., OC., LO.). When the word *gaṇikā* was mentioned Prabhāvatī asked : *Śuka kīdṛśī gaṇikā ucyate; āsāṁ bhedā bahavaḥ saṁti. Teṣu pañca bhedāḥ; gaṇikā vilāsini rūpājīvā artha vikriyā dārikā ceti bahulakṣaṇayutā bhavaṁti* (*ZDMG* 48. 608).

29. Taraṅga 12.

30. Taraṅga 38.

31. Taraṅga 61.

32. Jāt. 276, 419, 425, and others.

33. Jāt. 14, 92, 276, 318, 419, 423, 425, 487, and others.

34. *..gaṇikā lāsikā kumbhadāsiyo......taṁ nagaraṁ vāsāya upagatā nānāvisayino janā navaṁ suvibhattaṁ adosam-anavajjaṁ ramaṇīyaṁ taṁ nagaraṁ passitvā anumānena jānanti* (ed. Trenckner; 331).

However, it seems that the greatest number of synonyms for the word *gaṇikā* is to be found in Amitagati's Subhāṣitasaṁdoha, a Jain work. Amitagati, castigating prostitutes in highly inspiring words, used loosely the words *gaṇikā*, *veśyā*, *paṇyayośit(ā)*, *paṇyapuraṁdhrī*, *dārikā*, *paṇyavanitā*, *āpaṇayoṣā*, *āpaṇanārī*, and even *puṁścalī*.[35]

E. In the Sanskrit literary works we find at least 38 synonyms for the word *gaṇikā*, that is, *ajanā*, *arthavṛttikā*, *āpaṇanārī*, *āpaṇayoṣā*, *kariṇī*, *kumbhadāsī*, *kulaṭā*, *kṣudrā*, *dārikā*, *dāsī*, (*nagarasobhinī*), *naṭī*, *paṇastrī*, *paṇāṅganā*, *paṇyapuraṁdhrī*, *paṇyayoṣit(ā)*, *paṇyavanitā*, *paricārikā*, *puṁścalī*, *prakāśanārī*, *prakāśavinaṣṭā*, *bhujiṣyā*, *rūpājīvā*, *lañjikā*, *lāsikā*, (*vaṇṇadāsī*), *vāramukhyā*, *vāravadhū*, *vāravanitā*, *vāravilāsinī*, *vārastrī*, *vilāsini*, *veśyā*, *śilpakārikā*, *sādhāraṇastrī*, *svairiṇi*, and *hastinī*.[36] All of these words had different meanings, the difference being in some cases very slight, as for instance between *paṇāṅganā* and *paṇyāṅganā*, but in other very great, as for instance between *rūpājīvā*, *dāsī*, and *hastinī*; very often these words had only in special contexts the meaning of a prostitute.

K., as stated above, used the word *gaṇikā*, in one meaning only and in none of the known cases can *gaṇikā*, as used in K., be considered synonymous with any of any of the words quoted above; in K. *gaṇikā* had a special meaning, that is, of a government servant who received a monthly salary from the king's treasury.

K. used the word *gaṇikā* in chapter 27 of the second book only where the meaning is specifically defined (123. 7-125. 10) and in two more places, that is, in 2.7 and 232.8. In 2.7, in the index to the whole work, the word *gaṇikā* was used in a compound with *adhyakṣa*—*gaṇika'dhyakṣa* which occured again as the heading to chapter 27 of the second book. In 232.8 the word *gaṇikā* was used in a compound with *duhitṛ* and had the same meaning as *gaṇikā-duhitṛkā* in 124.19. From the use of the word *bhoga* in 232.9 it is evident that *gaṇikā-duhitṛ*, used there, meant a daughter of a *gaṇikā* who would become a *gaṇikā*, a government servant, as stated

35. Ed. R. Schmidt, *ZDMG* 49 and 51; chapters 24, 31 and 6.

36. This list is certainly not exhaustive. Cf. L. Sternbach, *Veśyā; Synonyms and Aphorisms* (Bombay, 1945).

in the introductory paragraph to chapter 27 of the second book (123. 8).[37]

3. *Pratigaṇikā*

K. also used the word *pratigaṇikā* twice (123. 10, 123. 12). The meaning of this word is very clear in K. *Pratigaṇikā* was a substitute *gaṇikā*,[38] that is, a government servant, with whom the contract was concluded for a short duration only, that is, for the duration of the leave of the *gaṇikā*, when she went abroad.[39] She could become in the future a *gaṇikā*, but as long as she was only a *pratigaṇikā* she received only half of the salary of the *gaṇikā* for whom she substituted.[40]

Vāts. also used the word *pratigaṇikā* (34.5. 3).[41] The whole chapter (*lābhaviśeṣāh*), where mention of a *pratigaṇikā* is made, referred, according to Yaś. to *veśyā*.[42] However, the word *veśyā* was used in Vāts. indiscriminately and was also used instead the word *gaṇikā*.

R. Schmidt understood under *pratigaṇikā* in Vāts. *eine andere Hetäre*. However, he did not know K. In view of the clear text of K. and in view of the clear meaning of *pratigaṇikā* in K., it seems that Vāts. might have used the word *pratigaṇikā* also in the sense of a 'substitute *gaṇikā*.' It should be noted that Yaś. did not comment in this context on *pratigaṇikā*.

4. *Rūpājīvā*

A. K. used frequently, in addition to the word *gaṇikā*, the word *rūpājīvā* for the designation of a prostitute. A *rūpājīvā* was a woman who lived on her beauty.

K. generally used word *rūpājīvā* for the designation of prostitutes who were not government servants, that is *gaṇikā*; K. used also the word *veśyā*, but twice only[43] for the general

37. *gaṇikān-vayām agaṇikān-vayām* (K. 123. 8).

38. J. J. Meyer translated *pratigaṇikā* 'Ersatzkurtisane.'

39. *niṣpatitā pretayor duhitā bhaginī vā kuṭumbaṁ bhareta*; *tanmātā vā pratigaṇikāṁ sthāpayet* (K. 123. 11-2).

40. *kuḍumbārdhena pratigaṇikām* (K. 123. 10).

41. *ciram ārādhito'pi tyāgī vyalikam ekam upalabhya pratigaṇikayā vā mithyādūṣitaḥ śramam atītaṁ nā 'pekṣate* (Vāts. 345. 3-4).

42. Yaś. started this chapter with the words *trividhā veśyā*......... (Vāts. 341. 25).

43. K. 60. 3; 249. 17.

designation of prostitutes. Other expressions were used in K. in a specific meaning, that is, for expressing special kinds of prostitutes.

Although K. did not state clearly that *rūpājīvā* were not government servants, this could clearly be seen from the fact that *rūpājīvā* had to pay monthly to the government a tax amounting to twice the amount of her daily earnings,[44] and, if the king was in great financial troubles, half of her wages,[45] while *gaṇikā*, on the contrary, received monthly wages from the government[46] and the *gaṇikā'dhyakṣa* had to determine her earnings, etc., check on her extravagant expenditures, and her whole earnings were taken by him for the government.[47]

The word *rūpājīvā*, which denoted in K. all kinds of prostitutes, denoted, however, the higher kinds of prostitutes, but not as high as *gaṇikā* were. *Rūpājīvā* lived to the south of the fort[48] and were even allowed to attend the harem of the king, while other women and other kinds of prostitutes (*dāsī*), were not allowed to do so.[49]

B. The lexicographers quoted the word *rūpājīvā* among *sādhāraṇastrī*,[50] *kṣudrā*,[51] and *ajanā*,[52] while Vāts. grouped all prostitutes under three categories,[53] that is *gaṇikā*, *rūpājīvā*, and *kumbhadāsī*.[54] Vāts. also used loosely the words *gaṇikā* and *rūpājīvā*[55] as well as *gaṇikā*, *rūpājīvā*, and *kumbhadāsī*.[56] Although Vāts. enumerated nine kinds of *veśyā*,[57] Yaś.[58] considered that *paricārikā*, *kulaṭā*, *svairiṇī*, *naṭī*, *śilpakārikā*, and *prakāśavinaṣṭā* were *rūpājīvā*.[59]

44. K. 125. 12.
45. K. 243. 11.
46. K. 123. 9.
47. K. 124. 6 ff.
48. K. 55. 11.
49. K. 41. 18-20.
50. Cf. note 6 to chapter I.
51. Cf. note 8 to chapter I.
52. Cf. note 9 to chapter I.
53. Cf. notes 16 and 19 to chapter I.
54. Each of them could be an *uttamā*, *madhyamā*, and *adhamā*. Cf. notes 17 and 18 to chapter I.
55. Cf. note 20 to chapter I.
56. Cf. notes 21 and 22 to chapter I.
57. Cf. note 6 to chapter I.
58. *Etāḥ ṣaḍ rūpājīvāyām evā 'ntarbhavanti viśeṣaḥ saṁpadyate* (Vāts. 363. 2.1-2)
59. Cf. paragraph 2C above.

In Yaś.'s commentary on Vāts. we find, if not a definition, at least an explanation as to the difference between a *gaṇikā* and a *rūpājīvā*. *Gaṇikā* was expected to learn sixty-four arts[60] in the same way as the king's daughters and the daughters of high king's officials,[61] while for a *rūpājīvā* the arts were unimportant;[62] she had to be beautiful only[63] and was not obliged to learn the sixty-four arts, although she too had to wear jewelry, arrange a beautiful house and furnish it beautifully;[64] this shows that *rūpājivā-s* were very wealthy women.[65]

5. *Veśyā*

As stated above, K. used the word *veśyā* twice only[66] in the most general way, that is for the designation of all persons engaged in harlotry. It was used in the same way as *veśa*[67] which was also used twice in the text.[68] This was evident from the fact that, according to K., *veśyā* as well as tolls, fines, weights and measures, the town clerk, the superintendent of coinage, of seals and passports, liquor, slaughter of animals, threads, oils, ghee, sugar, the state goldsmith, the warehouse of merchandise, gambling, building sites, corporations of artisans and handicraftsmen, superintendent of divine service,

60. The sixtry-four arts may be divided into eleven main groups, that is, general education (14), domestic science (4), toilet (4) dressing (2), music and dancing (5), fine arts (8), physical culture (3), games (4), art of entertaining (4), professional training (14), pet animals (2).

61. *santy api khalu śāstraprahatabuddhayo gaṇikā rājaputryo mahāmātraduhitaraś ca. tasmād vaiśvāsikāj janād rahasi prayogāñ chāstram ekadeśaṁ vā strī gṛhṇīyāt. abhyāsaprayojyāṁś ca cātuḥṣaṣṭikān yogān kanyā rahasy ekākiny abhyaset* (Vāts. 30. 2-3, 7-8, 13-4). See also fn. 15 above. (Cf . Vāts. 53. 9; 316. 6.

62. Also Kṣemendra in Kalāvilāsa (4. 2, 11); Kath., tar. 12; Daś. in Apahāravarmacarita, 60 ff., Śl. S. (10.70); Bhāratīya Nāṭyaśāstra (34. 112 ff.); Daśrūpa (2. 33); and others mention that a *gaṇikā* had to learn the 64 arts.

63. (*ayaṁ prakṛṣṭo lābhātiśayaḥ*; *rūpājīvānām ity uttamānām.*) *Satsu api guṇeṣu rūpājīvāyāṁ rūpasya pradhānatvāt kalās tu na santi* (Vāts. 347. 23-348. 1).

64. *sārvāṅgiko 'laṁkār ayogo gṛhasyo'dārasya karaṇam mahārhair bhāṇḍaiḥ paricārakaiś ca gṛhaparicchedasyo 'jjvalate 'ti rūpājīvānāṁ lābhātiśayaḥ* (Vāts. 347 18-9).

65. In paragraph 2D some examples of the use of the word *rūpājivā* in literary Sanskrit works were quoted. Hundreds of other examples could be quoted, as the word *rūpājivā* was very often used in Sanskrit literature. Cf. Śuk. t. s., *AKM* 10. 1, p. 45. 8-10, quoted in note 28 to chapter I.

66. K. 60. 3; 249. 17.

67. *Hurenvolk* according to J. J. Meyer.

68. K. 210. 17; 378. 12 (in the latter place in the meaning of a tavern).

taxes collected at the gates, and people known as Bāhirika[69] came under forts. K. used here purposely the word *veśyā* and not *gaṇikā* in order to show that every kind of prostitutes, who were not king's servants, came under the head of forts. The same applied when K. encumerated in another place *veśyā* along with spies, artisans, singers and aged military officers who had to examine vigilantly the pure or impure conduct of military men.[70]

The same were also the meaning of the word *veśa*, that is, every person engaged in harlotry, who along with ascetics, world-trotters, bards, buffoons, mystics, astrologers, prophets fortelling the future, persons capable of reading good or bad times, physicians, lunatics, mutes, deaf persons, idiots, blind persons, traders, painters, carpenters, musicians, vintners, manufactures of cakes, flesh and cooked rice,[71] had to be employed as spies.[72]

The general meaning of the word *veśyā* could be easily understood since not only the lexicographers[73] but also the Kāmasūtra-s considered the word *veśyā* as the most general one for the designations of all kinds of prostitutes.[74]

6. *Other Synonyms*

Other expressions used in K. for denoting prostitutes were of lesser importance. The word *puṁścalī* was used in K. three times.[75] *Puṁścalī* meant a profligate woman, a woman who ran after men.[76] In K. it was used in the sense of a

69. *śulkaṁ daṇḍaḥ pautavaṁ nāgariko lakṣaṇā'dhyakṣo mudrā'dhyakṣaḥ surā sūnā sūtraṁ tailaṁ ghṛtaṁ kṣāraṁ sauvarṇikaḥ paṇyasaṁsthā veśyā dyūtaṁ vāstukaṁ kāruśilpigaṇo devatā'dhyakṣo dvārabāhirikādeyaṁ ca durgam* (K. 60. 1-4.)

70. *sattriṇaś cā 'yudhīyānāṁ veśyāḥ kārukuśīlavāḥ*
daṇḍavṛddhāś ca jānīyuś śaucāśaucam atandritāḥ (K. 249. 17-8).

71. *samāhartā janapade siddha-tāpasapravrajita-cakracara-cāraṇa-kuhakapracchandaka-kārtāntika-naimittikamauhūrtika-cikitsako'nmatta-mūkabadhira-jaḍā'ndha-vaidehika-kāruśilpa-kuśīlava-veśa-śauṇḍikā'pūpikapākva-māṁsikau'danikavyañjanān praṇidadhyāt* (K. 210. 15-8).

72. In this connection it might be stated that K. did not use the word *gaṇikā* in connexion with spies, since *gaṇikā-s* were king's servants and enjoyed a higher position.

73. For instance Śabdakalpadruma quoted approximately 30 synonyms of the word *veśyā*.

74. Cf. Paragraphs 2C. 2D, and 2 E,as well as notes 12,15, 16, 19. 16, 26, 29, 30, 31, 35 to chapter I.

75. K. 184. 10; 214. 14; 221. 3.

76. For synonyms of the word *puṁścalī*, cf. L. Sternbach, *Veśyā; Synonyms and Aphorisms* 17 ff.

prostitute of a very inferior grade; everyone who was seen constantly in her presence was even considered to be a suspected person.[77] According to K.[78] she had to surrender her person as she agreed to to her paramour.[79] A *puṁścali* could also be used as a spy.[80]

The word *dāsī* was also used in K. in few instances to mean a prostitute of a lower degree.[81] The real meaning of the word *dāsī* was a female slave. *Dāsī* were not allowed, similarly as women of high birth, ascetics with shaved head or braided hair, and buffoons, to enter the harem of the king, while *rūpājīvā* were allowed to enter it;[82] *dāsī*[83] could also be used as spies.[84]

Once K. used also the word *devadāsī*, that is sacred courtesans, temple-prostitutes,[85] and stated that it they had ceased to attend the temples on service[86] they had to be employed, similarly as widows,[87] crippled women,[88] girls,[89] mendicant or ascetic women,[90] women compelled to work in default of paying fines,[91] and procuresses,[92] in cutting wool, fibre, cotton, panicle, hemp or flax;[93] all the persons enumerated there were those whom the king was obliged to maintain and who were, either because of their age or illness, or because of other circumstances, unable to work at all, or to work in their old profession, but were not completely unfit to work.

K. also used the word *śilpakārikā*,[94] that is a working woman, a workman's wife, and a *kauśikastrī*,[95] that is, a woman

77. K. 214. 14.
78. K. 184. 10.
79. A similar sentence is to be found in N. (6. 18-9).
80. K. 221. 3.
81. Cf. K. 146. 12; 41. 18; 21. 8; 124. 3; 125. 14; 44.6.
82. K. 41. 18-20.
83. K. 21. 8.
84. It is not certain whether *dāsi* in other contexts was used in the meaning of a prostitute or of a female slave.
85. K. 113. 20.
86. *uparatopasthāna*.
87. *vidha*.
88. *vānyaṅgā*.
89. *kanyā*; probably girls of those to whom the king had to give maintenance, possibly young daughters of a *gaṇikā*.
90. *pravrajitā*.
91. *daṇḍāpratikāriṇī*.
92. *rūpājīvāmātṛikā*, or, more likely, *gaṇikāmātṛkā*.
93. K. 113. 18-20.
94. K. 21. 7.
95. K. 380. 15.

good for sexual intercourse, in the sense of inferior kinds of prostitutes; they could be used as spies as well.[96]

Finally it should be added that K. also quoted other words which have in some contexts the meaning of a special kind of prostitute. And so K. used the words *adāsī* and *kṛtāparādhā* along with the word *dāsī*[97] in the sense of prostitutes; *adāsī* as women who stood between prostitutes and mistresses (*kṛtāvarodhā*),[98] and *kṛtāparādhā* or *kṛtāvarodhā*[99] as prostitutes who were, at the time, mistresses of one man.[100] Also the word *avaruddhā*[101] was used in K. in the latter sense.[102]

The words *duhitṛkā*,[103] a daughter, and *kumārī*,[104] a young girl, were also used in K. in the sense of young prostitutes who were to become in the future *gaṇikā*.[105] Finally, K. used once the word *rūpadāsī*,[106] a female servant of beauty, that is a person employed in making garlands, scents and the like,[107] in the sense of a lower-degree prostitute.

II COURTESANS (GAṆIKĀ)

7. *Recruitment of gaṇikā-s*

A. According to K. any woman who was beautiful (*rūpa*), young (*yauva*) and who was endowed with arts,[1] that is, the sixty-four arts (*śilpa*),[2] could become a *gaṇikā*,[3] K.[4] further stated that depending on her beauty and jewelry she

96. *kauśika* (*kaiśika*) sexual love, sexual intercourse.
97. K. 146. 12-3.
98. J. J. Meyer, *Das altindische Buch vom Welt und Staatsleben* 235. 30 ff.
99. K. 146. 13.
100. K. 124. 5.
101. K. 124. 5.
102. In K. 124.5 where the word *avaruddhā* was used, it was a *gaṇikā* who became a mistress of one man.
103. K. 124. 14.
104. K. 124. 13.
105. Many other examples might be found in Sanskrit literary works for the use of the word *duhitṛkā* or *duhitṛ* (daughter) in the meaning of prostitutes. Cf. Śl. S. 10. 160 ff., 260 ff., 274; 11. 30 ff., and many others.
106. K. 124. 19.
107. Commentary quoted by Sharma Sastry, 154.

1. Bhaṭṭasvāmin in his commentary stated that beauty and arts should be the sole consideration in the selection of courtesans.
2. Cf. note 62 to chapter I.
3. A *caṇḍālā* could not become a *gaṇikā* (c. Śuk. t. o. 27; Śl. S. 10.73).
4. *saubhāgyā'laṅkāra-vṛddhyā sahasreṇa vāraṁ kaniṣṭhaṁ madhyamam uttamaṁ vā ''ropayet. chattra-bhṛṅgāra-vyajana-śibikāpīṭhikāratheṣu ca viśeṣā'rtham* (K 123. 14-6).

was classified as of the first, middle and highest rank,[5] in order to add to her splendour,[6] (when holding the royal umbrella, the golden pitcher, and the fan, and attending the king seated on his royal litter, throne, or chariot.)[7]

K. made a general statement that *gaṇikā* had either to be born from the family of *gaṇikā* or not,[8] which shows that any woman could be chosen as *gaṇikā-s*. This sentence shows also that preferably daughters of *gaṇikā-s* became *gaṇikā-s*[9] the more so as, according to K., daughters of a *gaṇikā* and her sisters took the household of *gaṇikā-s* when they died or went abroad.[10]

We find in Sanskrit literary works many examples of daughters of prostitutes who became prostitutes.[11] In this connection we understand the statement contained in Kuṭṭanīmata, so different from the general rule,[12] in which it was said that 'only daughters are praiseworthy ; shame upon those who rejoice in the birth of a son.[13]

Particularly Vāts. and its commentators clearly stated that the daughter of a *gaṇikā* was a *gaṇikā*. Vāts. quoted Ghoṭaka-

5. Probably those girls were employed by the *gaṇikā-s* as their servants and were also used as prostitutes of lower rank. Cf. Śl. S. 10. 105 ff.; Jāt. 3. 59 (where a *gaṇikā* had a suite of 500 *vaṇṇadāsī*); 1. 270; 6. 300.

6. Cf. Kathāratnākara 176 and 223. Cf. also note 29 to chapter II.

7. Also in Śl. S. (10. 186 ff.) we find a division of prostitutes in different categories similar to that of K. ; the highest were also supposed to attend the king at the throne, to hold the royal umbrella, etc. Śl. S. stated. :

gaṇe gaṇe ca pramukhāṁ mukharābharaṇāvṛtām
anujñātāsanacchatracāmarāmakaronnṛpaḥ.
tā gaṇāntargatā yasmād anyāsāṁ ca mahattamāḥ
taṁ mahāgaṇikāśabdam alabhanta narādhipāt.
mahāguṇās tataś cānyās tato 'py anyās tataḥ parāḥ
yāvad ghaṭakasaṁghaṭṭakaṭhorakaṭayaḥ khalāḥ.
ya eṣa gaṇikābheda idānīm api dṛśyate
tataḥ kālāt prabhṛty eva bharatena pravartitaḥ (10. 186-9).

8. *gaṇikānvayām agaṇikānvayām* (K. 123. 8).

9. However, this was not obligatory. Cf. O. Stein, *Megasthenes und Kauṭilya*, Akademie der Wissenchaften in Wien, Sitzungsberichte, Philosophisch-historische Klasse 191. 1. 114 (1919).

10. *niṣpatitā pretayor duhitā bhaginī vā kuṭumbaṁ bhareta* (K. 123. 11).

11. Samayamātṛkā, Kuṭṭanīmata, Daśakumāracarita, Pañcatantra, etc.

12. Cf. Taittirīya Saṁhitā 6. 5. 10. 3 ; *avabhṛthàm àva yanti pàrā sthālīr àsyantya ùd vāyavyāni haranti tàsmāt strīyaṁ jātàṁ parā 'syanty ùt pùmāṁsaṁ haranti.* Hence, the new-born son was lifted up with joy, while the new-born girl was kept aside. Cf. below study XV *Infanticide and Exposure of New-born children.*

13. *duhitara eva ślāghyā dhig lokaṁ putra-janma-saṁtuṣṭam, jāmātara āpyante bhavādṛśā yad abhisaṁbandhāt* (Kuṭṭ. 145).

mukha when enumerating women who should be visited,[14] and Yaś.[15] explained clearly that the *gaṇikā-duhitṛ* was a prostitute.[16]

The custom by which daughters of prostitutes were destined to become prostitutes survived in India for many centuries. Western travellers who arrived in India in the Middle Ages as well as in more recent times told of daughters of prostitutes who became prostitutes, primarily temple-prostitutes (*devadāsī*).[17]

B. Prostitutes, although mostly daughters of prostitutes, were also recruited from among young girls who were given by their parents to the *gaṇikā'dhyakṣa*. K. did not explain the reason for which these girls were so given; very few reasons could be found in Sanskrit literary works.

In RV.[18] and AV.[19] reference was made to brotherless girls who were reduced to become prostitutes;[20] in Vetālapañcaviṁśati[21] the prostitute (*veśyā*) Rūpāvatī narrated that in one of her rebirths she had been taken by the enemy in battle.[22]

Some interesting explanations from Western travellers throw some light on this subject.

Strabo, quoting Aristobulos, who accompanied Alexander the Great on his eastern expedition, mentioned the display of daughters because of their poverty for sale in the

14. *gaṇikāyā duhitā paricārikā vā 'nanyapūrvā saptamī 'ti ghoṭakamukhaḥ* (Vāts. 67. 19-20).

15. *gaṇikāduhitā paricārikā ca sukhakāryatvād veśyāyām* (Vāts. 68. 19-20).

16. Cf. Vāts. 365 and R. Schmidt, *Beiträge zur indischen Erotik* (Berlin, 1920) 151-2.

17. Abū Zayd Ḥasan (10th century), ed. G. Farrand, 124; D. Paes (16th century) in R. Sewell, *A Forgotten Empire* (London, 1900) 240; and others. Cf. *Encyclopaedia of Religion and Ethics*, by J. Hastings, 10. 406 ff.

18. RV. 1. 124; 4. 5. 5.

19. AV. 1. 17. 11.

20. A. A. Macdonell and A. B. Keith, *Vedic Index of Names and Subjects* (London, 1912) 395.

21. Jambhalatta's version of the Vetālapañcaviṁśati, ed. and trans. M. B. Emeneau (New Haven, Conn., 1934), story 21, 118.

22. Cf. Rājataraṅginī 7. 520-2, and also Ibn Baṭṭūṭa in *Voyages d'Ibn Batoutah, texte arabe, accompagne d'une traduction*, by C. Defremey and B. R. Sanguinetti (Paris, 1914) 3. 235-6.

market;[23] he also mentioned the purchased of women by the king.[24] Also Pyrard de Laval[25] and Peter Mundy,[26] both in the 17th century, mentioned sale of children by their parents because of their poverty. Duarte Barbosa,[27] in the beginning of the 16th century, describing the custom of *satī* stated that those widows who did not burn themselves were held in great dishonour and became a shame to their families; because of that, they became *devadāsī*. The same was the opinion of Tome Pires[28] who wrote his Suma Oriental also in the beginning of the 16th century.

As neither K. nor any Dharmaśāstra give any explanation as to the reasons for giving daughters for prostitution, and we do not find any explanation in Sanskrit literary works in that matter, it is difficult to state with certainly for what reasons girls were given to the *gaṇikā'dhyakṣa*.

It should be born in mind that, generally speaking, prostitution was not considered as a shameful occupation; on the contrary, a *gaṇikā* was a highly esteemed person,[29] and many

23. *Ton d'en Taxilois nomimon kaina kai aethe legei; to te tus me dynamenus ekdidonai tas paidas hypo penias proagein eis agoran en akme tes horas, kokhlo te kai tympanois(oisper kai to polemikon semainusin), okhlu prosklethentos, to de proselthonti to opisthia proton anasysesthai mekhri ton omon, eita ta prosthen, aresanan de kai sympeisthei'san, ef'ois an doke, synoikein* (15.1.62).

24. *To basilei d'he men tu somatos therapeia dia gynaikon estin, oneton kai auton para ton pateron* (15.1.55).

25. *Voyage of Pyrard de Laval* (Hakluyt Society, Ser, I, No. 76) 1. 386.

26. *The Travels of Peter Mundy* (Hakluyt Society, Ser. II, No. 35) 2. 42.

27. *The Book of Duarte Barbosa* (Hakluyt Society, Ser. II, No. 44) 1. 216.

28. *The Suma Oriental of Tome Pires* (Hakluyt Society, Ser. II, No. 89) 1. 59.

29. Prostitutes, and particularly *gaṇikā-s*, enjoyed a high position at the court. They attended the court of the king, stood behind the throne, held the royal umbrella, etc. Their high esteem was evident from many literary works. See paragraph 7 and notes.

In the MBh., for instance, (4. 34. 17-8) king Virāṭa, after victory, sent messengers to the city and asked that young girls and *gaṇikā-s* meet him when he returned. (Similarly MBh. 4, 68. 21-7. Cf. MBh. 5. 85. 15 ff., R. 2. 14. 39.) In the Rāmāyaṇa (2.3.17-8), when Rāma was to be consecrated, Vasiṣṭha ordered that prosititutes attend the ceremony and when he returned from the exile *gaṇikā-s* had to honour him (R. 6. 127. 1 ff.). Also when king Kuśika returned to his home he was received by courtesans (MBh. 13. 53. 64-5). Cf. the welcome of Śuka in MBh. 12. 325. 33 sqq. and Therīgāthās (ed. Pischel) 178. When Kṛṣṇa came to the court of the Kauravas he was greeted by courtesans (MBh. 5. 86. 15). Yudhiṣṭhira, when sending greetings to the court of the Kauravas specially greeted prositutes (*veśastrī*) (MBh. 5. 30. 38).

women, if only their social status allowed them to do so, chose to be come prostitutes.

When a king entered his home after returning from a distant journey, he had first to see prositutes and other insignia of royalty (Agnipurana 230-8-12). When Gāndhārī, the wife of Dhṛtarāṣṭra, was pregnant, a prostitute (*veśyā*) waited upon Dhṛtarāṣṭra (MBh. 1. 115. 39; cf. K. 41. 19, where it is stated that *rūpājivā-s* may attend the harem; Mudrārākṣasa 117, where it is stated that prostitutes were ornaments of the roads).

In the Jāt., where prostitutes were mostly called ornaments of the town (*nagarasobhinī*), we find many examples of prostitutes attending the king's court and particularly the festivities (cf. Jāt. 545, 132, 187) during which galleries were reserved specially for them. (See also Viṣṇupurāṇa, ed. F. Hall, 5. 24-5; śl. S. 8. 1-7).

Prostitutes followed the army of the king. And so, for instance, in the army of Duryodhana there were, inter alia, *gaṇikā-s* (MBh. 5. 195. 18-9). The army of Pāṇḍavas was also accompanied by courtesans (MBh. 5. 151. 58). In R. Daśaratha ordered that the army of Rāma be accompanied by prostitutes (R. 2. 36. 3). The same is also evident from MBh. (15. 22. 21) and Śiśupālavadha (5. 27 ff.) and others.

Prostitutes also took part in hunting expeditions along with the king's cortege (MBh. 3. 239. 22 ff.), in festivals (Ratnāvalī, Act I; Pārvatīpariṇayanāṭakam 5. 2; Kalpasūtra 1. 102), in marriage processions (Mālatīmādhava 6. 4-5), in the king's cortege (MBh. 12. 326. 32-6; Bhāgavatapurāṇa 1. 11. 20, 1; Bhojaprabandha 89; Prasannarāghava 3. 11) and elsewhere.

Treatises of Indian dramaturgy give us also a clear picture of the high position of prostitutes in Indian life. *Gaṇikā-s* were mentioned as heroines of the plays. The Bhāratīya Nāṭyaśāstra mentioned as heroines the *divyā*, *nṛpapatnī*, *kulastrī*, and *gaṇikā* (34. 7), and stated that they were of a very high character (34. 10). Daśarūpa (2. 24 and 45) and Sāhityadarpaṇa (96) mentioned as heroines the hero's own wife (*svā*), the wife of another (*anyā*), and the *sādhāraṇastrī*, and Daśarūpa (2. 33) as well as the commentary on Sāhityadarpaṇa (*ad* 96) explained that it was a *gaṇikā*, skilled in arts, bold and cunning, to be addressed as *ajjukā* (Daśarūpa 2. 104; Sāhityadarpaṇa 431). (*Gaṇikā-s* were addressed also in other literary work, not only dramas, as *ajjukā*. Cf. Śl. S. 14.' 115 ff.) Bhāratīya Nāṭyaśāstra and Sāhityadarpaṇa gave also, from the dramaturgical point of view, a very positive picture of *gaṇikā-s* heroines of Sanskrit dramas (Bhār. 34. 112 ff., Sāh. 111. Cf. Sāh 210. 512 and commentaries on these texts), although they could not meet in the dramas with a *kulajā* (Daśarūpa 3. 45. Cf. Vasantasenā in Mṛcch.). *Gaṇikā-s* used Sanskrit, while other women spoke in Prakrits (cf. Daśarūpa 2. 97; H. Lüders, *Bruchstücke Buddhistischer Dramen* in *Kleinere Sanskrit Texte* H. 1. *Der Dialekt der Hetäre und des Vidūṣaka* 42-50). Vasantasenā, the heroine of Mṛcch., could be used as the best example of an idealised *gaṇikā* (the same in Daridra Cārudatta). Similarly Devadattā in the Jaina story of Mūladeva (cf. M. Bloomfield, The Character and Adventures of Mūladeva in *Proceedings* of the *American Philosophical Society*, 52. 616 ff.).

The high position of prostitutes in India was also observed by travellers who visited India. Strabo (15. 1. 48), referring to Megasthenes, stated that courtesans followed the army and that crowds of women surrounded the king; they rode in chariots or horses, and some even on elephants (15. 1. 55). Chan Ju Kwa, in his work on the Chinese and Arab trade in the 12th and 13th centuries observed that the king was escorted by a myriad of dancing girls (*chi*), three thousand of whom were in attendance daily in rotation (in the Chola kingdom). In Chaul, Pyrard de Laval noticed

Probably women taken in battle and brotherless girls were destined for prostitution; girls of poor parents were sold and became prostitutes; also widows, though *satī* is not mentioned in K. but was known in the time of K.,[30] probably gave themselves up to the *gaṇikā'dhyakṣa*.

It might be argued, however, that girls of poor parents and those taken in battle did not know the arts (*śilpa*), mentioned in K., and, therefore were not fit to become *gaṇikā*.

8. *Salary of gaṇikā-s*

As soon as the *gaṇikā'dhyakṣa* employed a girl she was entitled to a salary amounting to 1000 *paṇa* per annum;[31] this referred to *gaṇikā* of the first rank. *Gaṇikā* of the higher rank, the classification to three ranks depended on the beauty, wealth and jewelry of the (*gaṇikā*) received a higher salary. The salary of *gaṇikā* of the middle rank amounted to 2000 *paṇa* and that of *gaṇikā* of the highest rank to 3000 *paṇa* per annum.[32]

a great number of beautiful women (prostitutes) who sang and played instruments when the king took meals (2. 258). Similarly Peter Mundy des-, cribing the life in Mollinare (Malnād near Bhatkal) (3. 1, 83) and Agra (where they took part in banquets—*mihmānī*; 2. 216. 7), John Jourdain, Manucci, and Bernier describing the life in Agra (163; 1. 195; 274 respectively), Tomé Pires describing the life in Cambay (41), Duarte Barbosa discribing life in Bisnagua (Vijaynagar) 1. 225 ff.). Domingo Paes (in Sewell 240) stated that prostitutes were allowed to be in the presence of the wives of the king, to stay with them and chew betel with them (in Vijayanagar). There, they had also special galleries built for them during some festivities (270). Similar references appeared in Tomé Pires's *Suma Oriental* (65).

Courtesans who accompanied the king's army were also mentioned by Duarte Barbosa (1. 212 and 225) when describing life in Bisnagua (Vijayanagar), and by Fryer when speaking on Śivāji's army (2. 66). Courtesans who took part in hunting expeditions were mentioned, inter alia, by A. Nikitin (14).

Manucci even mentioned that Shah Jahān conveyed to one of his dancing girls (*kañcanī*) the title of his concubine.

Travels of European travellers who visited India, particularly in the 17th and 18th centuries were full of stories of the high position and wealth of courtesans in India; this shows that their position did not change through the ages.

We find, however, in Sanskrit literary works many examples of prostitutes who were described as the meanest of creatures, who should not be touched, who were suspicious and of bad fame. Cf. paragraphs 19 A and 21 and notes.

30. A very good résumé of the practice of *satī*, as described in the ancient Indian literary works, is to be found in P. V. Kane, *History of Dharmaśāstra* 2. 1. 624-36.

31. *gaṇikā'dhyakṣaḥ......sahasreṇa gaṇikāṁ kārayet* (K. 123. 8-9).

32. *saubhāgyā'laṅkāra-vṛddhyā sahasreṇa vāraṁ kaniṣṭhaṁ madhyamam uttamaṁ vā "ropayet* (K. 123. 14-5).

If we compare the salary of *gaṇikā-s* to those of other government servants, we see that their salary was comparatively high. The salary of the *gaṇikā'dhyakṣa*, as well as of all other *adhyakṣa-s*, amounted also to 1000 *paṇa* per annum;[33] this was the same salary as that of foretellers, readers of omens, astrologers, readers of Purāṇa-s, story tellers, bards, priests,[34] charioteers of the king[35] and of various kinds of spies.[36] The highest salary was paid, according to K., to the *ṛtvij*, to the *ācārya*, to the ministers, to the *purohita*, to the commander of the army, to the *yuvarāja*, to the mother of the king, and to the first wife of the king (*mahiṣī*); it amounted to 48,000 per annum.[37]

9. *Other Income of gaṇikā-s*

A. Although the salary of the *gaṇikā* amounted from 1,000 to 3,000 *paṇa* per annum, it was understood that it was not her only income. In addition, the *gaṇikā* received an extraordinary income in the form of gifts, such as garments, gold, silver, copper, brass, and iron objects, bedding, quilts, special vestments, perfumes, spices, harnesses, ghee, olives, grain, cattle,[38] etc.[39] In general terms, Yaś. stated that what exceeded the fixed price was considered as an extraordinary income.[40]

B. According to Vāts.[41] the 'fixed price' for one night was fixed in consideration of the point,[42] place, time,[43] the qualities of the prostitute, her popularity,[44] and her position

33. K. 247. 18-9.
34. K. 247. 18-9.
35. K. 248. 12.
36. K. 248. 13.
37. K. 247. 6-5.
38. Vāts. 343. 10; 15-6.
39. Cf. Vāts. 306. 20. Vāts also gave advice to prostitutes in what way they should collect this extraordinary income from their paramours (cf. Vāts. 324. 8).
40. *tasmān niyamitād adhiko yo 'nurāgāt labhyate sa lābhātiśayaḥ* (Vāts. 342. 20-1). Cf. note 45 to chapter II.
41. *deśa kālaṁ sthitim ātmano guṇān saubhāgyaṁ cā 'nyābhyo nyūnātiriktatāṁ cā 'vekṣya rajanyām arthaṁ sthāpayet* (Vāts. 342. 8-9).
42. *Deśa. Yaś.* explained : *deśaṁ saṁpannam itaraṁ vā* (Vats. 342. 10).
43. *Kāla. Yaś.* explained : *kālaṁ yatra kāma udbhūtaśaktir vā; sthitiṁ deśapravṛttiṁ yathā adhara kāyaṁ sevamānasyai 'kaguṇaḥ pūrvakāyam opi dviguṇaḥ* (Vāts. 342. 10-1).
44. Yaś. explained : *ātmano guṇān rūpavaidagdhyādīn sato 'sato vā; tathā saubhāgyam; anyābhya iti meṣyābhyaḥ sthāna-mānābhyām ātmanaś ca nyūnatvaṁ cā 'dhikyaṁ cā 'vekṣya tad anurūpaṁ rajanyām arthaṁ sthāpayet* (Vāts. 342. 12-4).

In Kuṭṭ. mention was made of the increase of the price for enjoyment fixed by the prostitute in view of a competition between two or more paramours (335).

in comparison with other prostitutes.[45] This 'fixed price' was called in K. *bhoga*, 'payment for enjoyment.'[46] *Bhoga* 'payment for enjoyment' was also clearly defined in the same manner by lexicographers.[47] A similar meaning of the word *bhoga* is to be found in K., although it did not refer specifically to *gaṇikā* but to all kinds of prostitutes, called in that context *puṁścalī*.[48] In other places, *bhoga*, in the meaning of 'payment for enjoyment' in case of *gaṇikā*[49] and *rūpājīvā*[50] is to be found in K. However, according to K., in contradiction to the statement of Vāts., *bhoga* was not fixed by the *gaṇikā* but by the *gaṇikā'dhyakṣa*,[51] as the *gaṇikā* did not take for herself the payment for enjoyment.

C. It is stated further in K. : *bhogaṁ dāyam āyavyayam āyatiṁ ca gaṇikāyāḥ nibandhayet. Ativyayakarma ca vārayet.*[52] 'He should determine the payment for enjoyment, gifts, the gross receipts and the gross expenditure, and the net income. And he shall check the extravagant expenditure.' Hence, in addition, the *gaṇikā'dhyakṣā* fixed or determined the gifts (*dāya*[53]), the gross receipts (*āya*), the gross expenditure (*vyaya*), and the net income, profit (*āyati*[54]) and was obliged to prevent *gaṇikā* from extravagant expenditure (*ativyaya*).

It is evident from this context that the *gaṇikā'dhyakṣa*, in addition to the full control over the person of the *gaṇikā*,[55] carried out also full control over her financial affairs.

45. Sometimes prostitutes received twice or three or four times the fixed price (cf. Sam. 4. 53).

46. In the Bhaṭṭasvāmin's Commentary on K. (*Journal of the Bihar and Orissa Research Society*, March, 1925) it is stated : *bhāgīyam apadiṣṭa-sāhasrādikam*. Cf. *bhāṭī* in Sam. 2. 57; 3. 26, 30; 4. 53; Kuṭṭ 335, 341, 362, and elsewhere.

47. Śabdakalpadruma *ad bhoga*; *bhogaḥ......paṇya-strīṇāṁ bhṛtir bhadiḥ*. Hemacandra in Abhidhānacintāmani: *bhogas tu gaṇikā bhṛtiḥ* (ad 363 a).

48. *labheta puṁścalī bhogaṁ saṅgamasya......* (K. 184. 10).

49. K. 125. 3; 125. 7; 230. 8.

50. K. 125. 12.

51. (*gaṇikā'dhyakṣaḥ*) *bhogaṁ......gaṇikāyāḥ nibandhayet* (K. 124. 6).

52. K. 124. 6-7.

53. *Dāya* 'gift' ; might be also inheritance. However, since the heritage of a *gaṇikā* could be inherited by her daughter or sister, who could also be a *gaṇikā* (hence *gaṇikā* had *hereditatis factio activa ac passiva* in maternal line), it seems that the *gaṇikā 'dhyakṣa* could not interfere at that stage, in the inheritance rights of the *gaṇikā*.

54. Cf. J. J. Meyer 194. 17.

55. Cf. paragraph 22.

D. The *bhoga*, although it could be collected in practice by *gaṇikā-s* themselves, had to be transferred to the *gaṇikā'dhyakṣa*, who, in turn, transferred it to the treasury of the king. The king paid a salary to *gaṇikā*, but her income belonged to him. The same referred to her other receipts, probably in the form of additional payments for enjoyment. Therefore, *gaṇikā-s* were under the obligation to inform the *gaṇikā'dhyakṣa* about each payment for enjoyment (*bhoga*) and each other receipts (*āyati*) which they received.[56] K. did not mention here *dāya* (gifts) and, therefore, it seems that *gaṇikā-s* were not necessarily under obligation to inform the *gaṇikā'dhyakṣa* about gifts received in other form than *bhoga*, that is, in the form of garments, cattle, etc., and they probably had the right to keep them for themselves.

E. Having no other regular income than the salary paid by the king, *gaṇikā-s* received, through the *gaṇikā'dhyakṣa*, all the necessities for the discharge of their duties.[57] That is evident from the fact that the *gaṇikā'dhyakṣa* had to determine the expenditure (*āyati*) of *gaṇikā-s*.[58] This expenditure, probably, comprised their garments[59] and the maintenance of their households, since we know from literary works that *gaṇikā-s* were beautifully dressed[60] and had splendid palaces.[61] Whether their maintenance was also included in these expenses is not clear from the context. However, the *gaṇikā'dhyakṣa* should not allow *gaṇikā-s* to make extravagant expenditure,[62]

56. *gaṇikā bhogam āyatiṁ......ca nivedayet* (K. 125. 8).

57. This, probably, comprised also garments which were given to men who visited them and which had to be returned when they left their houses (cf. Jāt. 4. 249).

58. K. 124. 6.

59. It is stated in Jāt. (4. 249) that out of every 1,000 received, 500 were taken by the prostitute herself and 500 were spent on garments, perfumes, and garlands. Each man who visited the prostitute's house and stayed there during the night received garments for the night which he returned the next day. (*tasmiṁ pana gaṇikāghare idaṁ cārittaṁ : ābhataṁ sahassato, pañca satāni gaṇikāya honti, pañca satāni vatthagandhamālāmūlaṁ honti, āgatapurisā tasmiṁ ghare laddhavatthāni nivāsetvā rattiṁ vasitvā punadivase gacchantā nivāsetvā ābhatavatthān' eva nivāsetvā gacchanti* (4. 249. 10-4).

60. MBh. (4. 34. 17-8; 12. 325. 33ff.); R. (2. 3. 17-8). Cf. J. J. Meyer, *Das Weib im altindischen Epos* (Leipzig, 1915), chapter IX.

61. In Mṛcch., Act 4; in Śl. S. (10. 90 ff. Lacote stated : Cette *description est ā rapprocher de celle de la maison de Vasantasenā, acte IV de la Mṛcchakaṭikā*, 119); in Kath. 7, Tar. 38. 19; 8, Tar. 124. 177 ff. Cf. Prabandhacintāmaṇī (Singhi Jaina Series) 5. 120.

62. K. 124. 7.

such as buying jewelry,[63] or to free a slave without taking the ransom sum.[64]

On the basis of the information received from *gaṇikā-s* as to her *bhoga* and *āyati*, as well as gifts which did not belong to them, that is, gross income, and on the basis of the expenditure incurred, the *gaṇikā'dhyakṣa* had to prepare a kind of balance-sheet for each *gaṇikā*; or for all *gaṇikā-s* under his care, and to determine what was the income received from all *gaṇikā-s* who were king's servants.[65]

In order to have this income,[66] which probably was considerable,[67] Kauṭilya organized a state prostitution with public houses run by the State (king). He thought that the income of the king from such enterprises would be higher than by collecting taxes from all prostitutes.[68] It should be emphasized that the only full description of such a kind of State enterprise is to be found in K.[69]

10. *Teaching of gaṇikās provided by the King*

We had seen above that *gaṇikā-s* had to be endowed with sixty-four arts (*śilpa*)[70] and that they were government servants whose ordinary payment for enjoyment was collected for the

63. They were classified as of first, middle, and highest rank according to their beauty and splendour of jewelry (K. 123. 14).

64. Mṛcch. Act 4. 913, 102.

65. K. 124. 6-7.

66. Cf. Breloer, *Staatsverwaltung im alten Indien, Kauṭalya Studien III* (Leipzig, 1934) 533; *Alberuni's India* by E. Sachau (London, 1910) 157; *Travels in India by Jean-Baptiste Tavernier* transl. by V. Ball, 2nd ed. (London, 1925) 1.128.

67. In Sanskrit literary works, we came very often across the description of the splendour of *gaṇikā-s*; cf. Mṛcch., Kath., Śl. S., etc., ; J. J. Meyer *Das Weib im altindischen Epos* (Leipzig, 1915), chapter IX; R. Schmidt, *Liebe und Ehe im alten und modernen Indien* (Berlin, 1904) 542 ff.; J. J. Meyer's translation of Daś. (Leipzig, 1902), Einleitung.

In the narrative of D. Paes (in Sewell) who visited India about 1537 A. D. we find a striking description of the wealth of courtesans in Vijayanagar. Many other western travellers also described the wealth of Indian courtesans. Cf. *Book of Duarte Barbosa* (Hakluyt Society, Ser. II., No. 44) 226.

68. *Rūpajīva* and those prostitutes who were not government servants paid a tax of twice the amount of their *bhoga* (K. 125. 13).

69. As far as it was possible to ascertain. Some references to *gaṇika-s* employed by the king, hence government servants, were made in another Arthaśāstra, that is, Śukr. (2. 202) and in Vāts. Cf. paragraph 13.

70. Cf. paragraph 7.

king.[71] The more attractive they were, the greater income could be expected by the king. In view of that the teaching of *gaṇikā-s* was provided by the king.

K. stated : *gītā-vādya-pāṭya-nṛtta-nāṭyā'kṣara-citra-vīṇā veṇu-mṛdaṅga-paracittajñāna-gandha-mālya-saṁyūhana-saṁpādana- saṁvāhana-vaiśika-kalājñānāṁ-gaṇikā dāsī raṅgopajīvinīś ca grāhayato rājamaṇḍalād ājīvaṁ kuryāt.*[72] ('Those who teach *gaṇikā-s dāsī-s*[73] and actresses[74] singing, music, recitation, dancing, acting, writing, painting, playing on the *vīṇā*, pipe, and drum, reading the thoughts of others, manufacture of scents and garlands, conversation, shampooing, skills in arts of prostitutes shall be maintained by the king's State.')

This obligation of the State to provide for special education, as described above, of *gaṇikā-s* might be considered as their additional income, particularly in view of the possibility of regaining their freedom and then gaining their livelihood by harlotry on their own account. On the other hand, this shows how far the obligation of the king went in looking after his employees; in fact, it was done in his own interest.

11. *Pension Scheme*

Gaṇikā-s being king's servants, had the right to a pension scheme in case they lost their beauty, became old, or incapable of gaining any money.[75]

K. introduced, for the first time in ancient India, a government relief and assistance scheme for some persons who were not able to maintain themselves,[76] and a widows' and orphans' scheme in case of the death of government servants.[77],[78] In this context K. introduced a kind of a pension scheme for the government officials. And so K. stated : *saubhāgyabhaṅge*

71. Cf. paragraph 9 E.
72. K. 125. 13-5.
73. In the meaning of a king's slave and not a prostitute.
74. *Raṅgopajīvinī* in the meaning of a chief actress, a king's actress, not a prostitute; she might be engaged in harlotry.
75. K. 123. 17; 124. 3.
76. K. 47. 19 ff.
77. K. 248. 19. Cf. Śukr. 2. 411.
78. See below study IX *Legal, Fiscal, Social and Penal Privileges Accan or to Infants, Diseased, Helpless and Distressed Persons according to Ancient dendiILadw.*

mātṛkām kuryāt,[79] and *gaṇikā dāsī bhagna-bhogā koṣṭhāgāre mahānase vā karma kuryāt*.[80] 'If a [*gaṇikā*] has lost her beauty[81] she shall be appointed as a procuress.'[82] 'If a *gaṇikā* or a *dāsī*[83] has become incapable of rendering service in the form of enjoyment,[84] she shall perform the work in the storehouse or kitchen of the king.'

Hence, *gaṇikā-s* who lost their beauty and popularity but were not too old, had to receive another lower office where their income was lower; they had to become procuresses in the service of the king and, if they became very old and were completely incapable of rendering any service to the king either as *gaṇikā-s* or *mātṛkā-s*,[85] they had to work in the storehouse or kitchen of the king where they received some kind of remuneration.[86] A similar rule refers to old *devadāsī-s*, *rūpājīvā-s* and *mātṛkā-s*.[87]

This rule protected *gaṇikā-s* for their whole life. However, if a *gaṇikā* paid the ransom sum of 24,000 *paṇa* she became free and then the king was not obliged to look after her any longer in her old age.

12. *Freedom of gaṇikā-s*

A girl entering the service of the king as a *gaṇikā* lost her freedom. She received a monthly salary, enjoyed security through the form of a pension scheme, but was completely dependent, as far as her personal freedom and partly her financial affairs was concerned. The king had the right to depose her, to order her to do what he found suitable for her,[88] and to order her to yield her person to anybody he wished.

And so K. stated : *rājājñayā*[89] *puruṣam anabhigacchantī*

79. K. 123. 17.
80. K. 124. 3-4.
81. *Saubhagya* (beauty and popularity).
82. *Mātṛka* : in the service of the State.
83. In the meaning of a lower kind of *gaṇikā* or 'the *gaṇikā* being a *dāsī*,' or 'remaining a *dāsī*,' or 'the *gaṇikā* will be employed in the storehouse or kitchen as a *dāsi*.'
84. *Bhagnabhoga*.
85. In the sense of a procuress.
86. K. 248. 3 ff.
87. *vidha-vanyaṅgā-kanyā-pravrajitā-daṇḍāpratikāriṇībhi rūpājīvā-mātṛkābhir vṛddhara-jdasībhir vyuparatopasthāna-devadāsībhiś ca kartayet* (K. 113. 18-20).
88. Cf. paragraph 13 and notes 110, 112, 113, and 114 to Chapter II.
89. It would be better *rajājñāya*.

gaṇikā śiphā sahasraṁ labheta; *pañcasahasraṁ vā daṇḍaḥ*.[90] 'If a *gaṇikā* does not cohabit with a man despite the orders of the king, she shall receive a thousand lashes with a whip; or pay a fine of 5000 *paṇa*.'

Hence *gaṇikā-s* government servants, had to yield their persons to anybody, if the king so ordered, and could not, as prostitutes who were not government servants could do, choose the person whom they wanted.[91]

It should be noted that this rule has nothing in common with the obligation of *gaṇikā-s* to fulfill their obligation, if they consented to yield their person to a man and, in addition, received the price for enjoyment.

Gaṇikā-s were also not allowed to become *avaruddhā-s*. In Y. a differentiation was made between an *avaruddhā* (*aparuddhā*) and a *bhujiṣyā*.[92] An *avaruddhā*, according to Mit., was such a woman who was prohibited by her master from intercourse with other men on the understanding that she stayed at home with the object of avoiding any lapse of service[93] (a harem woman).[94] Hence, such a woman, even if she was a prostitute, could not be approached by other men as long as she stayed at home with her paramour.[95] It was common in ancient India for a prostitute to become an *avaruddhā*; however, according to K., it was not permitted to a *gaṇikā*, who was a government servant, to become an *avaruddhā*. K. stated : *aviśantī sapādapaṇ avaruddhā māsavetanaṁ dadyāt*.[96] 'An *avaruddhā* who does not show up has to pay $1\frac{1}{4}$ *paṇa* and the monthly salary.' Therefore, if anybody would take a *gaṇikā* to his home for himself only, he had to pay a penalty of $1\frac{1}{4}$ *paṇa*[97] as well as the monthly salary that she received from the *gaṇikā*-

90. K. 125. 1-2.

91. Cf. Sam. (3. 26) ; Śuk. t. o. 55.

92. Y. 2. 290.

93. *gacchannityanuvartate : uktalakṣaṇā varṇastriyo dāsyas tā eva svāminā śuśrūṣāhānivyudāsārthaṁ gṛha eva sthātavyam ity evaṁ puruṣāntaro'pabhogato niruddhā avaruddāḥ* (Mit. ad Y. 2. 290; 286. 17).

94. Cf. paragraph 25.

95. According to Y. 2. 290 he who had intercourse with an *avaruddhā* (or *bhujiṣyā*) had to pay a fine of 50 *paṇa*, although, ordinarily, intercourse with them would be permissible.

96. K. 124. 5.

97. Probably to the State. According to Bhaṭṭasvāmin's Commentary $1\frac{1}{4}$ *paṇa* should be paid *per mensem* to the State.

dhyakṣa[98] in view of the fact that she was not able to earn profit for the State during the time she was kept in the house of her paramour.[99] This rule is understandable from the point of view of the State, because of the loss by the State of the income, since the government servant did not work for the State.

Although, according to Vāts., the prostitute herself fixed the payment for enjoyment, the payment for enjoyment of a *gaṇikā*, a government servant, was fixed by the *gaṇikā'dhyakśa*,[100] who had to determine the gifts, gross receipts, gross expenditure, and profit, and prevent her from extravagant expenditure.[101] The *gaṇikā'dhyakṣa* had full control over her financial affairs; on the other hand a *gaṇikā*, according to K., did not enjoy only a part of the "property" full rights of property; she could enjoy on usufructual basis.[102] Since she was not free, her offspring were also not free;[103] her daughter was supposed to take her place as a *gaṇikā* and her son became a *kuśilava*.[104]

13. *Redemption*

But, though *gaṇikā-s* lost their freedom, they did not lose it forever. If they wished, they could regain it by paying to the king, who was their master, the price for redemption (*niṣkraya*). Their sons could also regain freedom.[105]

K. stated : *niśkrayaś caturviṁśatisāhasro gaṇikāyāḥ.*[106] 'The price for redemption of a *gaṇikā* amounts to 24,000 *paṇa*.'

This price, in comparison with her yearly salary, which

98. Probably, irrespective of the fact whether she was taken away by her paramour for one month or for less.

99. It should be noted that this sentence might also mean that a *gaṇikā* who did not show up in the house of the paramour who wanted to make her an *avaruddhā*, had to pay to him the monthly salary he had given or promised to her as well as to the king a fine of $1\frac{1}{4}$ *paṇa*. It is unlikely however, that this explanation is correct, since for depriving the paramour of sexual intercourse *gaṇikā* had to pay twice or eight times the amount of her payment for enjoyment (K. 125. 3-4. Cf. paragraph 17) which is much more than the monthly salary paid or promised by the paramour and $1\frac{1}{4}$ *paṇa* as fine.

100. Cf. paragraph 9 AB and notes 40 and 51 to chapter II.

101. Cf. paragraph 9BC.

102. Cf. paragraph 15.

103. Many other examples could be quoted in order to show that *gaṇikā-s* were not free persons.

104. Cf. paragraph 14.

105. Cf. paragraph 14.

106. K. 123. 18.

amounted to 1000 to 3000 *paṇa* per annum[107] seems to be high, if paid by a *gaṇikā* herself. It could have been paid, however, by her paramour. This is evident from Vāts. where we read, in the chapter dealing with advice to prostitutes how to behave towards their paramour, that a prostitute should request her peramour to leave with her the place where they stay[108] and ransom her from the king.[109] Yaś. explained it in another way, that is, if she would leave the place where they stay, the king could bring her back.[110] Yaś. made a very important reservation, however, that is, that this rule was to be applied only in the case when the prostitute was bound to the king,[111] that is, depended upon him. A prostitute, not being a government servant, did not need to be ransomed. This rule, as described in Vāts., is in agreement with the rules contained in K.

In the Jātaka-s we find an example of the king Daṇḍaki who deposed a prostitute (*gaṇikā*) and afterwards restored her to her former position.[112] We also find there stories from which it is evident that the king had the right to summon prostitutes (*nagarasobhanī*) and to order them (*vaṇṇadāsī*) to go to the forest after their old paramours;[113] in Mahāvagga[114] we see that Ambapālikā, a young girl was made a prostitute.[115]

We also find some examples in Indian literary works about the right of the king to ransom a prostitute. In Kathāsaritsāgara, in Tar. 12, in the story of Rūpiṇikā, a prostitute was made a free woman by the command of the king.[116] Similarly in Mṛcchakaṭikā, Śarvilaka announced that the king bestowed upon Vasantasenā the title of a 'wedded

107. Cf. paragraph 8.

108. See also Daś. (78. 13 ff.) where a prostitute wished to escape her fate by marrying her lover.

109. *tena saha deśamokṣaṁ rocayed rājani niṣkrayaṁ ca* (Vāts 317. 23).

110. *rājani niṣkrayaṁ ca yadi rājapratibaddhā tadanīṁ rājñaḥ sakāśān maṁ niṣkrīṇīhī 'ti rocayet* (Vāts. 319. 8-9). We find many such examples in Indian literary works (cf. Jāt 2. 476; 5. 134; Kath. 18, Tar. 124. 201-2.) Cf. note 88 to Chapter II.

111. *rājapratibaddhā* (Vāts. 319. 8).

112. Jāt. 5. 134.

113. Jāt. 3. 426.

114. Mahāvagga 8. 1-14.

115. Cf. the story of Addhakāsī in Cullavagga (10. 22, 1).

116. *svadhīnāṁ rūpiṇikāṁ rajadeśena tāṁ cakruḥ* (Kath. Tar 12. 193).

wife,' that is, set her free;[117] similarly she has ransomed her maid Madanikā,[118] who formed part of the property of Vasantasenā. By this act Madanikā got a higher position than her previous owner, Vasantasenā.[119]

14. *Gaṇikā's Children*

A. We find in K. some mention of children of a *gaṇikā*. Although these children were mostly children born out of wedlock, prostitutes were, probably, not prohibited from marrying[120] and could also have legitimate children. However, since *gaṇika-s* were not free persons, their children, irrespective whether they were girls or boys, were also not free.

B. As far as the daughters of prostitutes were concerned, they could become *gaṇikā-s* in case their *gaṇikā*-mothers died or went abroad.[121]

However, not all daughters of *gaṇikā-s* could automatically become *gaṇikā-s* because of the conditions required of them, that is, beauty, youth and arts. Arts were taught by a *gaṇikā* or by others;[122] youth depended on the time when the *gaṇikā* died or went abroad, but it is probable that a young, beautiful daughter of a *gaṇikā* was employed by the *gaṇikā'dhyakṣa* often before the death of her mother, or before she went abroad;[123] however, beauty was out of one's control and, therefore, if the daughter of a *gaṇikā* was not beautiful, she was incapable of becoming a *gaṇikā*. What happened to

117. *ārye vasantasene parituṣṭo rājā bhavatīṁ bandhuśabdenā 'nugṛhṇāti* (Mṛcch 10.341. 9-10). Similarly Śl. S. 12. 83 :

athā'syai gaṇikādhykṣo rājādeśaṁ nyavedayt
adyārabhya kulastrītvaṁ bhavatīnāṁ bhavatv iti.

118. *sudṛṣṭaḥ kriyatām eṣa śirasā vandyatāṁ janaḥ*
yatra te durlabhaṁ prāptaṁ vadhūśabdāvaguṇṭhanaṁ (4. 24).

Cf. Mṛcch. (4. 119. 1) : *Madanike, kiṁ Vasantasenā mokṣyati tvāṁ niḥkrayeṇa.*

119. Therefore, Vasantasenā said : 'You are now the one to whom honour should be paid,' as she received the name of a wife.

120. In Jāt. 3. 59. 22-3 *gaṇikā* Sāmā asked : *kena nu kho upāyenāhaṁ imaṁ purisam attano sāmikaṁ kareyyaṁ.* Cf. Daś. (78. 13 ff.); Dhūtratasamāgama (in Lassen's *Anthologia Sanscritica* 85. 16-9), and elsewhere.

121. Cf. paragraph 2E.

122. K. 125. 13 ff.

123. Cf. Kuṭṭ., Sam., and others.

such a girl is not clear from K. K. only stated that *gaṇikā-s* and others who were incapable of rendering any service in the form of enjoyment had to work in the storehouse or the kitchen of the king.[124] That was, probably, the fate of those daughters of *gaṇikā-s* who were unsuited to become *gaṇikā-s*.

C. The son of a *gaṇikā* was not free and belonged to the court of the king. From his eighth year of age he had to work as a king's musician—a bard (*kuśīlava*)[125] and had to be taught by the same teachers as the *gaṇikā* in acting, so as to become chief actor (*raṅgopajīvin*) and in dancing, so as to become chief dancer (*tālāvacāra*).[126]

His value, because he was not a free person, if compared to that of a *gaṇikā*, was much lower, since he did not collect any money for the king's treasury but was only employed as a *kuṣīlava* at his court. (His salary[127] amounted to 150 *paṇa* per annum[128] which was a very small sum, if compared with the salary of a *gaṇikā*; the latter amounted to 1000 to 3000 *paṇa* per annum[129]). Therefore, the price for redemption of a *kuśīlava* was fixed at half of the price for redemption paid by a *gaṇikā*, that is, was fixed at 12,000 *paṇa*. However, if we compare this price of redemption with the salary received by a *kuśīlava*, we see that it was more difficult for him to collect it in order to be ransomed, the more so as his additional income, if any, was much smaller than that of a *gaṇikā*.[130]

15. *Property Rights of gaṇikā-s*

Although *gaṇikā-s* were not free persons they had full

124. *gaṇikā dāsī bhagnabhogā koṣṭhāgāre mahānase vā karma kuryāt* (K. 124. 3-4).

125. *aṣṭavarṣāt prabhṛti rājñaḥ kuśīlava-karma* (K. 124. 2).

126. *gaṇikāputrān raṅgopajīvinaś ca mukhyān niṣpādayeyuḥ sarva-tālā-vacārāṇāṁ ca* (K. 125. 15-6).

127. It might be argued that the son of the *gaṇikā*, as a person who was not free, did not receive a fixed salary from the king.

128. *kuśīlavās tv ardhatṛtīyaśatāḥ* (K. 248. 2) ('half of three times hundred'). Shama Sastry translated '250 *paṇa*' and J. J. Meyer *dritthalb hundert*.

129. Cf. paragraphs 8 and 9 A.

130. In Jāt. (4. 298) we find a story of the incarnation of the Bodhisattva in a sage who met a beautiful prostitute (*gaṇikā*) by whcm he had a son. He wanted to give him the name of his grandfather, but then upon reflection stated : 'it is not allowed to give to a son born from a prostitute (*vaṇṇadāsi*) our family name.' Therefore, he asked the mother to give to the new-born child the name of the tree under which they stood.

rights to their own property. Girls becoming *gaṇikā-s* could bring with them jewelry (they were classified according to its value[131]) and they received salary and gifts with which they could do what they wished.[132] According to Vāts., prostitutes who lived with one man had to consider their own and his property as common,[133] hence enjoyed property rights.

Gaṇikā-s bought, usually, from their salary and gifts, if not received in *natura*,[134] jewelry (*alaṁkāra*). Jewelry was one cf the objects which added to the value and esteem of the *gaṇikā-s*[135] and was considered as a tool necessary for gaining subsistence by them. Therefore, the king could not confiscate the ornaments of prostitutes.[136]

In contradiction to this statement K. 124.9 might be quoted. It is stated there : *svāpateyaṁ vikrayam ādhānaṁ nayantyās sapāda pañcaśat paṇo daṇḍaḥ.* Shama Sastry translated this passage as follows : 'If she [a courtesan] sells or mortgages her property she shall be fined 50 *paṇa*.' Similarly J. J. Meyer; he translated : '50 *paṇa wenn sie* [*die Lustdirne*] *ihren Besitz verkauft* '*oder verpfändet*.' Both translated *svāpateya* by 'own property,' that is, the property of a *gaṇikā*. If we understand this context in this sense, than *gaṇikā-s* would not have any right to any property. Everything that they possessed would be used by them on a usufructual basis; they would have the right to use it as long as they lived, but would not be entitled to inherit it, since *gaṇikā-s* would not have the ownership over it. Such an understanding seems to be incorrect, since we have a very clear ruling as to the right of inheritance of the property of the deceased *gaṇikā-s*.[137]

131. K. 123. 14. Cf. paragraph 8.

132. Cf. paragraph 9C.

133. Vāts. 319. 25. Cf. Yaś. *ad* Vāts. 320. 9-10.

134. Jewelry, elephants (cf. Kath. 9, Tar. 51. 170).

135. About stealing of jewels by prostitutes' paramours in Jāt., see Jāt. 3. 61. 436, 6. 383. Many other examples can be found in Sanskrit literary works.

136. *āyudhāny āyudhīyānāṁ śilpadravyāṇi śilpinām*
veśyāstrīṇām alaṁkāraṁ vādyātodyādi tadavidām;
yac ca yasyo 'pakaraṇaṁ yena jīvanti kāravaḥ
sarvasvaharaṇe 'py etān na rājā hartum arhati.

(N. 17. 10-1) NMS 19. 11-2, Also quoted in Mit. *ad* Y. 2. 302, Apar, 2. 301, SV 493, VyU 165, VyM 110, VT 828, VyS 70.

137. Cf. paragraphs 15, 16.

Svāpateya did not only mean 'own property', but also 'wealth, riches,' and was probably used in this context in the sense of wealth or riches given to *gaṇikā-s* by the *gaṇikā'dhyakṣa* on a usufructual basis, for the better discharge of their profession as government servants. The palace where *gaṇikā-s* (government servants) lived, garments given to them for the use of their paramour,[138] etc. might not be their property. *Gaṇikā-s* could use them during their lifetime, or as long as they worked as government servants[139] but could not sell them or pledge them.

The same interpretation should be given to the other sentence of K. (124.8) where we read : *mātṛhastād anyatrā-'bharaṇanyāse sapādacatuṣpaṇo daṇḍaḥ.* 'If [a *gaṇikā*] puts the jewelry in the hands of another person than her "mother" [procuress], the fine amounts to $4\frac{1}{4}$ *paṇa.*'

We have seen that girls entering the profession of *gaṇikā-s*, government servants, were classified as of first, middle, and highest rank, according to their beauty and the jewelry they brought.[140] It is also stated in K. that anyone who deprived a *gaṇikā* of her jewelry had to pay as a fine eight times the value of such jewelry.[141]

The whole action of the Mṛcchakaṭikā is built on the story of Vasantasenā's pledge of jewelry to Cārudatta, etc.

It is evident, therefore, that *gaṇikā-s* had the full right of ownership of jewelry and had the right to pledge it. However, some jewels might have been given by the *gaṇikā'dhyakṣa* to a *gaṇikā* on the usufructual basis in order to raise their beauty, and only then *gaṇikā-s* had no full rights to this jewelry and had no right to pledge or deposit it, even for a night, with another person other than with a procuress who took care of her.

In other words, according to K. a *gaṇikā* (a) enjoyed ownership over jewelry and other objects she brought when becoming a *gaṇikā*, as well as over those objects which she bought from her income or received *in natura*; (b) enjoyed usufructual rights over those objects which were given to her

138. Cf. note 59 to Chapter II.

139. Before she was ransomed.

140. K. 123. 14.

141. *gaṇikā"bharaṇa...apaharato 'ṣṭaguṇo daṇḍaḥ* (K. 125. 7).

for her lifetime, or as long as she was employed as a *gaṇikā*, a government servant or *precario modo* for the better discharge of her duties.

Gaṇikā-s had full right of property over the objects quoted under (a) and could alienate them, or dispose of them in whatever way they chose. These objects formed the estate which could be inherited. However, they had no property rights over the objects quoted under (b) and could not sell them, deposit them, or pledge them; if they sold, deposited or pledged them, they had to pay a fine amounting to 50 *paṇa* and even if they entrusted jewelry, belonging to group (b), to a person other than their procuresses, they had to pay a fine of 4¼ *paṇa*.

16. *Inheritance*

Since *gaṇikā-s* enjoyed property rights over some objects, K. included specific inheritance regulations relating to *gaṇikā-s*; they were completely different from those binding other persons, including women, as far as their *strīdhana* was concerned. K. excluded from inheritance the sons of *gaṇikā-s*.

K. stated that if a *gaṇikā* died, her daughter or her sister inherited her household (*kuṭumba*) and if any one of them was not available, then the king inherited from the deceased *gaṇikā*. The whole paragraph dealing with inheritance of a *gaṇikā* said : *niṣpatitāpretayor duhitā bhaginī vā kuṭumbaṁ bhareta. Tan mātā vā pratigaṇikāṁ sthāpayet. tāsāṁ abhāve rājā haret.*[142] 'When [a *gaṇikā*] goes abroad or dies, the daughter or sister should get the household. Or the mother shall give a substitute *gaṇikā*. In the absence of them the king should take it.'

This text deals with both *pratigaṇikā* and inheritance. It is evident from if that first the daughter of a *gaṇikā* and, if she had no daughter, her sister was considered as the heir to her property. However, it is not clear what the expression *tāsāṁ abhāve* ('in the absence of them') meant; did it mean a daughter or a sister of a *gaṇikā* only, or also the mother of a *gaṇikā*, or also this person whom the mother of the

142. K. 123. 11-3.

gaṇikā took as a *pratigaṇikā* and who was neither a daughter nor a sister of the deceased *gaṇikā* ? In this connexion the question arose whether the king was entitled to inherit the wealth of a *gaṇikā jure caduco* if the second, third, or fourth person, enumerated in K., did not survive the *gaṇikā* and in what order.

J. J. Meyer, translating these three sentences stated : *Ist keine von diesen Dreien vorhanden,*[143] (that is, the daughter, the sister, or the other *pratigaṇikā*), then the king inherited. Meyer seems to be right in including all kinds of *pratigaṇikā-s* as heirs of the deceased *gaṇikā* since, as he stated *die Ersatzhetäre steht......in einem nahen Verhältnis zur Haupthetäre; sie teilt wohl ihren Haushalt, ist Familienmitglied; d.h. eine Hetarenwirtschaft, ein Kurtisanenetablissement* (*gaṇikākuṭumba*) *umfasste auch die Aushilfskurtisane.*[144] It seems, however, that the *mātṛ*, if under the expression *mātṛ* the real mother and not a procuress had to be understood, was also entitled to inherit the estate of her deceased *gaṇikā*-daughter.

Inheritance in the case of the *gaṇikā* was, according to K., in the maternal line, and both descendants and ascendants seemed to be entitled to inheritance. *Mātṛ* was enumerated, in this context, on the same footing with a *pratigaṇikā*, and if we accept that a *pratigaṇikā* was entitled to inheritance, we have also to accept that the mother of the deceased *gaṇikā* had the same inheritance rights; it even seems, if we compare this system of inheritance with the general system of *dāyabhāga*, that the mother of the deceased *gaṇikā* was entitled to inheritance from the deceased *gaṇikā* in the third place, that is, after the daughter and the sister of the *gaṇikā* and before the *pratigaṇikā* who might not stand in any blood relation with the deceased *gaṇikā*.[145]

It is, however, very probable that the text of K. should not be interpreted extensively and that we should consider that

143. 192. 12.
144. 193. 16 ff.
145. According to recent Hindū court rulings the only persons that could inherit the property of prostitutes were such of her relations as have fallen into a similar position (Sivasangu v. Minal [1888]; Narasama v. Ganga [1889] or were all those who would be entitled to inherit a woman's *strīdhana* Subbaraya v. Ramaswami [1889]; Narain Das v. Tirlok [1906]; Jagannath v. Narayan (1910). Neither of these cases throws any light on the whole problem.

only daughters and sisters of the deceased *gaṇikās* were entitled to inherit from her, and in the absence of them her property belonged to the king, since K. mentioned clearly only these two persons as possible heirs.

In this connexion it might be noted that Duarte Barbosa remarked in the beginning of the 16th century, speaking about courtesans in Bisnagua,[146] that the king inherited the property of a courtesan who died without sons or daughters.[147]

Unfortunately, the Dharmaśāstra-s do not deal with this problem, so that no indication as to the manner this problem was settled can be found elsewhere and no interpretation from other sources can be applied *per analogiam* to K.

17. *Contracts between gaṇikā-s and their Paramours*

A. We have seen that the *gaṇikā'dhyakṣa* fixed the price for enjoyment for the *gaṇikā-s*. As soon as the paramour paid this price for enjoyment (*bhoga*) a contract between him and the *gaṇikā* was concluded.[148] The *gaṇikā* was then obliged to yield her person to the paramour[149] and if she should refuse to do so, she had to pay a fine amounting to twice the amount of the *bhoga* received.[150]

K. stated : *bhogaṁ gṛhītvā dviṣatyā bhogadvi guṇodaṇdaḥ.*[151] 'If [a *gaṇikā*], after having received the *bhoga* shows hatred [to the paramour], the penalty amounts to twice the amount of the *bhoga*.' K. added : *vasati bhogāpahāre bhogam aṣṭaguṇaṁ dadyāt*...........[152] 'For deprivation[153] of the sexual inter-

146. Vijayanagar.

147. *The Book of Duarte Barbosa* (Hakluyt Society, Ser. II, No. 44) 1. 226.

148. In Milindapañha we find the story of a prostitute (*gaṇikā*) Bindumatī who performed an Act of Truth (*saccakiriyā*) which nobody else could perform. By this act Gaṅga was forced to flow backwards. This Act of Truth consisted in discharging her contractual obligations in the equal treatment of any man, irrespective of whether he was a Brahmaṇ or a slave. (J. J. Meyer in the preface to his translation of Daś. 58.)

149. In Vāts. (*niṣkāsanakramāḥ*; 329. 33), Sam. (5 75-87), Kuṭṭ. (603-13), and others we find very interesting advice given to a prostitute as to the manner in which she should behave in order to disgust her paramour who had lost his money, so that he would free her from the contractual obligations.

150. Cf. paragraph 26H.

151. K. 125. 3.

152. K. 125. 4.

153. *Apahāra* 'stealing, concealment, deprivation.'

course[154] the fine amounts to eight times the amount of the *bhoga*.'

The difference between these two sentences lies in the use of the words *dviṣatyā* ('shows hatred') and *bhogāpahāra* ('deprivation of sexual intercourse'). J. J. Meyer explained that the first sentence referred to a deprivation of sexual intercourse in case an agreement was concluded for one night and the second if it was concluded for a longer period of time.[155] It seems reasonable to assume that this explanation is right.

Hence, a *gaṇikā* who deprived her paramour, with whom she agreed to live for a longer time, of sexual intercourse, had to pay eight times the received fee.[156]

It should be noted that the contractual penalty imposed on a prostitute who concluded an agreement with a paramour for one night was found also in other legal sources; it amounted to twice the amount of the *bhoga*.[157]

If we compare the two sentences quoted above with the preceding one,[158] we see that they referred only to those paramours who had not been chosen by the king, because then the penalty amounted to 1,000 lashes with a whip and a fine of 5,000 *paṇa*.

B. The contractual penalty of twice the received payment for enjoyment, was also found in N. and Y., though there instead of the word *gaṇikā*, the words *paṇyastrī* and *veśyā* were used.

N.[159] stated : *śulkaṁ gṛhītvā paṇyastrī ne'cchantī dvis tad āpnuyāt*.[160]

154. *Bhoga*.

155. '......*bei fortwährendem Diebstahl des Genusslohnes, d. h. wenn sie bei einem Engagement auf längere Zeit sich ihrer Pfficht entzieht oder auch ohne solches in hartnackigem Sträuben verharrt. Im vorhergehenden State dagegen ist von dem* einen *Nachtgenuss die Rede* (195. 23).

156. Probably to the paramour, in addition to a fine to the king. Cf. paragraph 17C.

157. Cf. paragraph 17B and C.

158. Cf. paragraph 12.

159. N. 6. 18. NMS 7. 20, Also quoted in Mit. *ad* Y. 2. 292, Apar. *ad* Y. 2.198, VyK 160,, SC 206, VRK 166, VCi. 78, SCM 27, NṛP 25. SV 300, VyPr 330, VyU 88, VT 654, VV 172, VyS 103, VVy 42 Cf. below study XIV *Lagal Relations between Employers and Employels in Ancient India*.

160. N. quoted in Mit. reads : *śulkaṁ gṛhītvā paṇyastrī ne'cchantī dviguṇaṁ vahet* (*ad* Y. 2. 292.)

Y.[161] stated : *gṛhītavetanā veśyā ne'cchantī dviguṇaṁ vāhet.*

Mit. explained. *yadā tu śulkaṁ gṛhītvā svasthā 'pi artha patiṁ ne 'cchati tadā dviguṇaṁ śulkaṁ dadyāt;*[162] Vijñāneśvara did not introduce in his commentary anything new with the exception of adding the word *svasthā*—'being in good health.' That meant that the contract concluded between the prostitute and her paramour might be broken in case of illness.[163]

K. gave also a general rule referring it to both cases[164] and stated that the contract could be broken on account of the prostitute's illness (*vyādhi*) or the paramour's deficiency (*doṣa*).[165] K. stated clearly that the deficiency could occur also on the part of the paramour, while Mit. and N. admit that the contract could be broken if the illness occurred only on the part of the prostitute.[166]

Both N. and Y. also stated that the rule as to the obligation of fulfiling the contract between the prostitute and her paramour, lay on the part of the paramour. And so, if he had sexual connection with the prostitute and refused to pay the agreed payment for enjoyment, he had to pay a fine of double the agreed fee.'[167] probably

161. Y. 2. 292.

162. *Ad* Y. 2. 292.

163. Similarly Vīramitrodaya ad N. 6. 18.

164. Agreement for one night and for a longer period of time. It might be argued that this passage referred only to the case of an agreement concluded for a longer period of time, since it was added at the end of the sentence dealing with such an agreement (K. 125. 4-5). Since Y. did not mention agreements concluded by a prostitute with a paramour for a longer time and mentioned also these exceptions, this addition could be also referred to the first sentence.

165......*anyatra vyādhi-puruṣadoṣebhyaḥ* (K. 125. 4-5).

166. Mit. stated : *yadā punas tadicchayā bhāṭiṁ dattvā paścād anicchantīm api balād vrajanti tadā teṣām adoṣaḥ. Yadi vyādhyādyabhibhavas tasyā na syāt : 'vyādhitā saśramā vyagrā rājakarmaparāyaṇā ; āmantritā cen nā 'gacched adaṇḍyā vaḍavā smṛtā' iti nāradavacanāt.* (This statement of N. is not to be found in the published text of N.) (Mit. *ad* Y. 2. 291; 287, 29-32).

167. *aprayacchaṁs tadā śulkam anubhūya pumāṁ striyam* (N. 6. 18) also quoted in NMS 7.20, SC 206, VRK 166, SV 301, VyPr 330, VyU 89, VT 811, VyS 103 Mit (*ad* Y. 2. 292) quoted this verse of N. but added a new one as the second part of N. 6. 18 which could not to be found in the printed text of N. This runs: *anicchan datta śulko'pi śulka hānim avāpnuyāt.* This verse coincided with Mit's interpretation of Y. 2. 292 reading : *tathā śulkaṁ dattvā svayam anicchataḥ svasthasya puṁsaḥ śulka-hānir eva* (*ad* Y. 2. 292; 288. 3-4); Y. (2. 292) stated : *agṛhīte samaṁ dāpyaḥ pumān apy evam eva hi.* Also quoted in VVy 2. 197, SC 203, VRK 159, VCi. 75, NṛP 25, VyPr 325, VyU 86, VT 647, VV 169, VyS 101, VVy 41, AP 257. 43.

after having been compelled to pay the prostitute the agreed fee.[168]

Although the latter rule is not to be found in K., it might be admitted that, since it was stipulated in both Dharma-śāstra-s dealing with this subject, it should be also applied to K.

C. The rule concerning the obligation of the prostitute to pay twice the amount of the agreed fee also be could found in non-legal literary works.

In the Agnipurāṇa, if the prostitute (*veśyā*), after having received her fee, went to another man for a greater profit, she had to refund to the man who paid the fee in advance a sum equal to twice the amount originally received from him and pay also a fine of twice the amount received.[169] This rule of paying a double amount to the person with whom the agreement was concluded, in addition to a fine to be paid to the king, should also be considered as generally having legal force.

Similarly in the Matsyapurāṇa, if a prostitute after having received her fee went to another person, she had to pay twice the amount received to the man who paid her fee in advance.[170]

In the Śukasaptati (t. o. No. 55) the Brāhman Viṣṇuvardhana said to a *gaṇikā* : *ratipriye tvayā 'smadīyaṁ surataṁ soḍhuṁ na śakyate. yadi tvaṁ na sahase tadā rātri-nivāsa-parimitaṁ paṇaṁ dviguṇaṁ bhavatyāḥ sakāśād ahaṁ grahīṣyāmi.*[171]

168. Cf. Matsyapurāṇa (207. 145) where it was stated :
nītvā bhogān na yo dadyād dāpyo dviguṇavetanaṁ
rājnaś ca dviguṇaṁ daṇḍaṁ tathā dharmo na hīyate (in Ān. S.S. 227. 147).
Also quoted in VyK 160, VRK 167, VCi. 78, VyPr 330, VyU 89, VT 655, VV 172. 'If a man after bringing a prostitute does not indulge with her, the king should make him pay twice as much and should levy a similar amount of fine for himself' (according to the translation by Dutt in SBH).

169. *gṛhītvā vetanaṁ veśyā lobhād anyatra gacchati*
vetanani dviguṇaṁ dadyād daṇḍañ ca dviguṇaṁ tathā
(Agnipurāṇa, in Bibliotheca Indica 227. 44-5;

170. *veśyāgāmī dvijo daṇḍyo veśyāśulkasamaṁ paṇam*
gṛhītvā vetanaṁ veśya lobhād anyatra gacchati
vetanaṁ dviguṇaṁ dadyād daṇḍaṁ ca dviguṇaṁ tathā
(Matsyapurāṇa 227. 144b-145). *ad* also as *cd* in VyK 128, VRK 408, VCi. 188, DV 190, Vīr. *ad* Y. 2. 286 and *cd* in VyK 160, SC 206, VRK 166, SV 301, VyPr 330, VyU 89, VT 654, VyS 103, AP 2.198

171. Śuk. t. o. 376. 25-6. At the end of the story : *sā ratipriyā taṁ viṣṇuvardhanaṁ kṣamasve'ti pādayor apatat. tvam ātmīyaṁ draviṇaṁ punar gṛhāṇa param asmāsu kṛpām utpādaya. ity abhidhāya tadīyaṁ draviṇaṁ punar asmai pratyarpayām āsa* (377.4-6). Similarly Śts. No. 45.

In Dāmodaragupta's Kuṭṭanīmata[172] a *bonvivant* took the double fee from a prostitute who spent a night with another person.[173]

D. It should be noted that N. stated that in case of a doubt arising in disputes about payments for sexual intercourse the chief-prostitute (*veśyāpradhānā*) had to make a decision.[174] Kuṭṭ. also stated that a *bonvivant* sued, before old, good acquainted *bonvivants*, a prostitute who spent the night with another man and received a judgment according to which the prostitute had to pay double the amount of the fee agreed upon.[175]

It is doubtful whether this rule of legal arbitration by prostitutes or *viṭa*, in case of doubtful cases about the *bhoga*, is to be applied to K., since very clear rules refer to such cases. These rules show that the decision had to be made by official means. It seems that Kuṭṭ. cannot be taken as the basis for legal considerations and the available text of N. did not contain this rule. Only some quotations, of unknown origin, are attributed to N. Therefore, it seems that this rule should not be applied to K. and that all disputes of this kind were settled in court.

18. *Offences Committed by gaṇikā-s and towards gaṇikā-s*

A. K. contains many rules concerning penalties for offences committed by a *gaṇikā* and towards a *gaṇikā*. The text is very often unclear and it is difficult to come to a conclusion whether the offences listed in K. referred to those committed by the paramour of a *gaṇikā* or by the *gaṇikā* herself.

K., not referring to the highest offences, stated : *caturviṁśatipaṇo vākpāruṣye.*[176] *dviguṇo daṇḍapāruṣye.*[177] *sapādapañ-*

172. Kuṭṭ. 341.

173. Miliñdapaṇha 6. 1, 47 ff.

174. *veśyāpradhānā yās tatra kāmukās tad gṛhoṣitāḥ tat samuttheṣu kāryeṣu nirṇayaṁ saṁśaye viduḥ*
(quoted in Mit. *ad* Y. 2. 292; 288. 9-10 not to be found in the printed text of N.). This verse with some variants is also quoted in Apar. *ad* 2. 298, VyK 160, SC 206, VRK 167, VCi 79, NṛP 27, SV 301, VyPr 330, VyU 89, VT 811, VV 172, VyS 103.

175. Kuṭṭ. 341.

176. K. 124. 10.

177. K. 124. 11.

cāśat paṇaḥ paṇo 'rdhapaṇaś ca karṇacchedane.[178] *gaṇikām akāmāṁ rundhato niṣpātayato vā prāṇavidāraṇena vā rūpam upaghnataḥ sahasraṁ daṇḍaḥ.*[179] 'For defamation 24 *paṇa*. Twice as much for assault. 50¼ and 1½ *paṇa* for cutting off the ears. For keeping under confinement an unwilling *gaṇikā*, for abducting, for disfiguring [so as to cause] hurt to her beauty, the fine is 1000 *paṇa*.'

It is evident that the second sentence refers to a *gaṇikā* who had been kept in confinement, abducted or disfigured; that is clearly stated in the text. However, it is not clear whether the defamation was cast, assault was made, and cutting off of the ears was inflicted on a *gaṇikā* or by the *gaṇikā*. J. J. Meyer expressed the opinion that this context refers to defamation, assault and the cutting off of the ears of a *gaṇikā*, while other translators interpreted as being done by a *gaṇikā*. Meyer rightly remarks : *Dass der Mann einem Weibe, besonders, wenn es ihm untreu geworden ist, die Ohren abschneidet, ist eine alltägliche Sache in der altindischen Literatur. Lustdirnen aber, die sich so an einem Besucher vergreifen, sind mir, soweit ich mich erinnere, dort niemals begegnet.*[180] It seems however, that this interpretation cannot be accepted, since K. in a few lines which follow the above stated that for disfiguring a *gaṇikā*, so as to cause hurt to her beauty, the fine amounted to 1,000 *paṇa*.[181] Cutting off the ears of a *gaṇikā* certainly would disfigure her and make her unattractive, for which offence the offender had to pay a fine of 1,000 *paṇa* and not as in the first case[182] 50¼ and 1½ *paṇa*. In any case such a fine for inflicting damage on the property of the king would seem to be too low for K., the more soas a *gaṇikā* with ears cut off wouldnot be a great asset for the king; she could not be of great use to the *gaṇikā'dhyakṣa*.

Therefore, it seems that if a *gaṇikā* should cause defamation to her paramour, she would be compelled to pay 24 *paṇa* and for assaulting him 48 *paṇa*. If she should cut off her para-

178. K. 124. 12.
179. K. 124. 15-6.
180. K. 194. 22.
181. K. 124. 15-6.
182. K. 124. 12.

mour's ears she would have to pay 50¼ *paṇa*, in addition to 1½ *paṇa* which she would have to pay to the superintendent.[183]

B. However, offences committed towards a *gaṇikā* by any person would be punished more severely, particularly if by these acts the king's interests would be violated.

And so, if somebody kept under confinement a *gaṇikā* against her will, he had to pay a fine of 1,000 *paṇa*; should she be willing, the fine would amount to her monthly salary in addition to a fine of 1¼ *paṇa*.[184] If semobody abducted her against her will, the offender had to pay a fine of 1,000 *paṇa*. K. used here the word *niṣpātayato* (from *niṣpat* 'to fly out, to rush out, to depart, to elope'). Therefore, abduction here had, probably, the meaning of eloping with an unwilling *gaṇikā* and not only of rape. In the latter case K.[185] and Y.[186] used the word *prasahya* and fixed the penalty in the amount of 12 and 10 *paṇa* respectively.

In this connexion it should be emphasized that K. did not mention the fine inflicted on a person who violated a *gaṇikā*. Reference was made however, to violation of a *rūpājīvā* and of a fine to be inflicted in this case; the penalty amounted then to 12 *paṇa*.[187]

Reference was also made to having sexual intercourse with a *kumārī* against her will. K. stated : *akāmāyāḥ kumāryā vā sāhase uttamo daṇḍaḥ; sakāmāyāḥ pūrvaḥ sāhasa daṇḍaḥ*.[188] 'Or in case of an unwilling *kumārī* the highest amercement; in case of a willing one the first amercement.'

Kumārī was a young girl, a not yet sexually mature girl. Sexual intercourse with such a girl was considered an offence[189] and not permitted ;[190] only in K., as far as it has been possible to ascertain,[191] the word *kumārī* was used in the sense

183. According to Bhaṭṭasvāmin's Commentary.

184. Cf. paragraph 12.

185. K. 236. 11; refers to *rūpājīvā*.

186. Y. 2. 291; refers to *dāsī*.

187. *rūpājīvāyāḥ prasahyo'pabhoge dvādaśa-paṇo daṇḍaḥ* (K. 236. 11).

188. K. 124. 13-4.

189. Vi. 36. 7 ff.

190. Ratirahasya, fol. 14b, quoted in R. Schmidt's *Beiträge zur indischen Erotik* 558.

191. Cf. L. Sternbach *Veśyā; Synonyms and Aphorisms, op. cit.*

of a young, not yet sexually mature girl who will become a *gaṇikā*. *Kumārī* in K. was a young, sexually immature *prati-gaṇikā* or more correctly, *gaṇikā-duhitṛkā*. If such a *kumārī* should be violated against her will, the highest amercement would be inflicted on the offender, and if she would be willing, the first amercement.[192]

However, the Sanskrit text, quoted above, is not very clear. Shama Sastry translated it differently reading *akāmāyāḥ gaṇikā* or *akāmāyāḥ kumārī*. He translated the text as follows : 'When a man has connexion with a prostitute against her will or with a prostitute girl, he shall be punished wit hthe highest amercement......' If this reading should be correct, then the question of penalty imposed for violating a *gaṇikā* would be solved. It seems, however, that it is difficult to accept such a reading and that this passage referred only to violation of a *kumārī*.

C. We have seen that the penalties for keeping under confinement, abducting, or disfiguring a *gaṇikā* amounted, according to K., to 1,000 *paṇa*. In this connexion K. said : *sthānaviśeṣeṇa vā daṇḍavṛddhir āniṣkraya-dviguṇāt paṇa-sahasraṁ vā daṇḍaḥ*.[193] 'Depending on the position and status, the fine will remain 1000 *paṇa* or will rise to double of the ransom sum.'

In this text K. stated that this penalty of 1,000 *paṇa* might either remain in the amount of 1,000 *paṇa* or rise to twice the ransom sum of a *gaṇikā*, that is, to 48,000 *paṇa*, depending on conditions accompanying the crime and the peculiar merits of the person who had been injured. And so, the penalty was lower or higher, for instance, if the disfiguration of the *gaṇikā* was greater or smaller, or if the disfiguration was the same, the penalty was higher or lower depending on the fact whether the *gaṇikā* was of the first, middle, or highest rank.[194]

D. This gradation of the penalty referred to those who harmed in any way a *gaṇikā* or, through her, the king's treasury. Another rule referred to both offences committed by a *gaṇikā* and towards a *gaṇikā*.[195] And so, K. stated :

192. *sakāmāyāḥ pūrvaḥ sāhasa-daṇḍaḥ* (K. 124. 13-4).
193. K. 124. 16-7.
194. Cf. K. 123. 14-5.
195. This is evident from the word *sarvatra*.

sarvatra prathame 'parādhe prathamaḥ; dvitīye dviguṇaḥ; tṛtīye triguṇaḥ ; caturthe yathākāmī syāt.[196] 'In every case, if the offence is committed for the first time, the first amercement; if for the second time, twice as much; if for the third time, three times as much; if for the fourth time, according to discretion [of the person who inflicts the punishment].' Hence, the penalty was twice, three, four, or more times higher than the basic penalty if it was committed more than once. A higher penalty was inflicted on a recidivist and depended on the number of times the recidivist committed the same offence.

19. *Killing of Paramours by gaṇikā-s and Killing of gaṇikā-s by their Paramours*

A. K. contains also two separate rules relating to the killing of a *gaṇikā* by her paramour and the killing of a paramour by a *gaṇikā*. In Sanskrit literary works we find many examples of killing of prostitutes by their paramours, particularly in order to rob them of their jewelry.[197] K. stated : *prāptādhikārāṁ gaṇikāṁ ghātayato niṣkrayatriguṇo daṇḍaḥ.*[198] 'For killing a *gaṇikā* who was going to the favourite place,[199] the fine amounts to three times the ransom sum.' That means that he who killed a *gaṇikā* had to pay the penalty of 72,000 *paṇa* to the king for depriving him of his government servant, through the work of whom the king gained money. That would appear to be the reason for such a high penalty.

K. mentioned in this connexion that for killing the mother (*mātṛkā*) of the *gaṇikā* (probably in the meaning of a procuress employed by the king), of the daughter (*duhitṛkā*) of the *gaṇikā* (probably in the meaning of a young prostitute who was expected to become a *gaṇikā* and, in the meantime,

196. K. 124. 20-1.

197. Cf. note 135 to Chapter II; J. J. Meyer, *Über das Wesen op. cit.* 294.

198. K. 124. 18.

199. *prāptādhikārām*. Shama Sastry translated this word by 'prostitute appointed at the court.' J. J. Meyer translated it by *eine Kurtisane, die zu bevorzugter Stelle galangt ist.* In Bhaṭṭasvamin's commentary the word *prāptādhikārā* was explained as referring to a prostitute 'who has attained majority.' Every *gaṇikā* was appointed in K. at the court, therefore, it would not be correct for the author to use the word in this sense. *Prāptādhikārām,* as J. J. Meyer rightly translated this word, was used in order to show that the killing of the *gaṇikā* was done in connection with the performance of her occupation.

was taught the sixty-four arts [a *pratigaṇikā*]), and for the killing of a *rūpadāsī* (that is, a prostitute of lower degree, who was a maid of a *gaṇikā*[200] and belonged to her retinue[201]), the offender was to be punished with the highest amercement.[202]

In this connexion it should be emphasized that, according to some of the Smṛti-s, the killing of a woman who subsisted by harlotry was not considered a sin. G. stated : *vaiśikena kiñcit.*[203] Similarly Aṅgiras.[204] This was due to the belief, expressed in a few Sanskrit sources, that whores (*kṣudrā paṇyayoṣit*) were open thieves or swindlers and were punishable (Bṛh.,[205] N.,[206] Mn.,[207] and VyM., where an unknown text ascribed to N. was quoted[208]). They were also considered as thorns in the side of the people[209] and their occupation as the meanest of all.[210] Some of the Smṛti-s stated also that a man who had sexual intercourse with a prostitute[211] had to perform a *prājāpatya* penance, or subsist for three nights on grain, etc.

200. Bhaṭṭasvāmin's Commentary explained that *rūpadāsi* was a person employed in making garlands, scents, and the like. According to J. J. Meyer a *rūpadāsī*, "*Schönheitsdienerin*" *bezeichnet hier allem Anschein nach eine niedrigere Art Lustdirne als die gaṇikā oder Kurtisane, aber eine, die ebenfalls Eigentum des Königs ist.*

201. We find in Sanskrit literary works many examples of such prostitutes who formed the cortege of *gaṇikā*. Cf. note 29 to chapter II.

202. *matṛkā duhitṛkā rūpadāsīnāṁ ghāta uttamas sāhasadaṇḍaḥ* (K. 124. 19)

203. G. 22. 27; also quoted in Mit. ad Y. 3. 268.

204. Aṅgiras's text, not found in the printed edition by Dutt, is quoted in Mit. *ad* Y. 3. 268; there it was stated that for killing a prostitute the offender should donate water only. The text quoted *vaiśya* twice instead of quoting in the first instance *vaiśya* and in the second *veśyā*; that is probably an error, as already pointed out by Haradatta (cf. *Sacred Laws of the Aryas ad* Y. 3. 268; 433. 16-8).

(*kośaṁ kūpe ca vipre vā brāhmaṇyāḥ pratipādayet; vadhe dhenuḥ kṣatriyāyā basto vaiśyāvadhe smṛtaḥ. śudrāyām āvikṁ avaiśyāṁ hatvā dadyāj jalaṁ naraḥ.*)

205. Bṛh. 22. 12 (*kṣudrā*).

206. N. Pariśiṣṭa 2 (*paṇyayoṣit*); same in VyM 101. 10 (*pāpayoṣit*) Vīr. 491 ascribed to Bṛh. (*parayoṣit*).

207. Mn. 9. 259.

208. VyM 101. 7 quoted a N. text which could not found in the printed text of N. An almost identical text is found in Bṛh. 22. 2, but there instead of the word *kṣudrā* the word *bhadrā* was used.

209. Mn. 9. 259-60.

210. Cf. Milindapañha 4. 1. 47 ff.; Jāt. 3. 436; 6. 228; 5. 425; Kath. 6. 20; Hemacandra's Pariśiṣṭaparvan 2. 288; Karpūramañjarī 1. 18 ff.

211. *Veśyā. Gaṇikā* was never quoted.

(Vi.,[212] Atri,[213] Saṁvarta,[214] Parāśara,[215] Mahānirvāṇa tantra,[216] etc.[217]), since such intercourse was compared with intercourse with an animal, cattle, a she-buffalo, a she-camel, a she-ass, a female monkey, or a sow,[218] as well as considered as most blameworthy and reprehensible.[219] On the other hand, according to other Smṛti-s, it was not permitted to have intercourse with women belonging to a higher caste than the man.[220] It was believed that prostitutes[221] were unclean persons and food given by them should not be eaten (Mn.,[222] Y.,[223] Vi.,[224] Vās.,[225] Agnipurāṇa,[226] Brahmavaivartapurāṇa,[227] and elsewhere). According to Buddhist jurisprudence, in order to guard women from falling a prey to the sensuality of the outside world, they were, *inter alia*, forbidden to bathe at those places where men and prostitutes used to bathe.[228] These rules were, however, of no legal consequence[229] and Sanskrit literary works were full of stories in which reference was to intercourse of men with prostitutes, eating food prepared by them, etc.

212. Vi. 53. 7.

213. Atri (ed. Dutt) 267.

214. Saṁvarta (ed. Dutt) 161. If it was a Brāhmaṇa, a *kṛcchra* penance had to be performed.

215. Parāśara (ed. Dutt) 10. 15.

216. Mahānirvāṇatantra (ed. Dutt) 11. 43.

217. AP. (p. 665); Saurapurāṇa 52. 24 (cf. Y. 2. 284; Mn. 8. 361-3); B. 2. 2, 4, 1-3.

218. Cf. Vi., Atri, Saṁvarta, Parāśara, Mahānirvāṇatantra quoted in notes 212-16 above.

219. Cf. Amitagati's Subhāṣitasaṁdoha, ed. by R. Schmidt in *ZDMG* 49 and 51, chapter 24 and 6. 12; 31. 88-9; 31. 21-4.

220. N. 12. 77-8. Cf. Vāts. 62. 8 ff.

221. The texts used here the word *gaṇikā* in the meaning of *paṇyastrī* or *veśyā*. Cf. Mit. *ad* Y. 1. 161.

222. Mn. 4. 209.

223. Y. 1. 161.

224. Vi. 51. 7.

225. Vās. 14. 10.

226. AP. (ed. by Dutt) 168. 3. 7.

227. Brahmavaivartapurāṇa 31. 2.

228. Cullavagga 10. 23; Vinaya 4. 278. Cf. Durga N. Bhagavat, *Early Buddhist Jurisprudence* 171.

229. On the contrary, legally, sexual intercourse with *veśyā* and *dāsī* was, in principle, permitted (N. 12. 78). Cf. B. 2. 2. 4. 1-3; Mn. 8. 362.

B. As far as the killing of the paramour by a *gaṇikā* was concerned, we find in K. the following rule : *puruṣaṁ ghnatyāś citāpratāpo 'psu praveśanaṁ vā.*[230] 'For killing a paramour she shall be burnt on alive or thrown into water.' This penalty was extremely severe; it could be considered as a preventive one, since prostitutes might kill their paramour in order to take away their money.

20. *Stealing*

K. also contains a rule according to which a *gaṇikā* was protected from unlawful dealings of her paramour, that is, if he has stolen from her her jewelry or money, or did not pay the agreed payment for enjoyment. K. stated : *gaṇikā "bharaṇā'rthaṁ bhogaṁ vā" 'paharato'ṣṭaguṇo daṇḍaḥ.*[231] 'For depriving a *gaṇikā* of jewelry, money, or payment for enjoyment the fee amounts to eight times [the value].' Thus, if a paramour who concluded an agreement with a *gaṇikā* had stolen from her her jewelry or any money, he had to pay eight times the value of the jewelry or eight times the amount of money stolen. The same rule applied if a paramour, who had agreed to pay the *bhoga*, after enjoyment, declined to pay it to a *gaṇikā*; in this case he had to pay eight times the agreed *bhoga.*[232] On the other hand a *gaṇikā* who had shown hatred to the paramour, after having received her *bhoga*, had to pay twice the amount of the *bhoga* and for depriving the paramour of sexual intercourse, eight times the amount of the *bhoga.*[233]

230. K. 125. 6.

231. K. 125. 7.

232. I have not come across a similar rule in other Smṛti-s. In this connection it might be noted that the Matsyapurāṇa (*SBH*) stated : 'If a man after bringing a prostitute does not indulge with her, the king should make him pay her twice as much and should levy a similar amount of fine for himself' (227. 147 or 145; for text see note 168 to Chapter II). Another protective measure against unlawful dealings of the paramour of a prostitute found is to be also in the Matsyapurāṇa; it is stated there :

anayam uddiśya yo veśyāṁ nayed anyasya kāraṇāt
tasya daṇḍo bhaved rājan suvarṇasya ca māṣakam (227. 146) Also quoted in AP 2. 198, VyK 160, VRK 167, VCi 78, VyPr. 330, VyU 89, VT 655, VV 172.

'If a man takes a prostitute to another person on the pretext of taking her to some particular individual should be find a *māṣā* of gold' (according to the translation by Dutt in *SBH*).

233. Cf. paragraph 17.

21. *Duty to Furnish Information about Paramours*

We have seen before that *gaṇikā-s* were under obligation to inform the *gaṇikā'dhyakṣa* about each payment for enjoyment and each additional gift which they received.[234] K. stated : *gaṇikā bhogam āyatiṁ puruṣaṁ ca nivedayet.*[235] Thus, a *gaṇikā* was not only obliged to inform the *gaṇikā'dhyakṣa* about the *bhoga* and *āyati*, but about the *puruṣa* as well, that is the man who was spending time with her, once or more frequently.

In this connexion the following verses from MBh. might be quoted which show the reason for such a rule :

pānāgāraniveśāś ca veśyāḥ prāpaṇikās tathā
kuśīlavāḥ sakitavā ye cā 'nye kecid īdṛśāḥ
niyamyāḥ sarva evai 'te ye rāṣṭrasyo 'paghātakāḥ
ete rāṣṭre 'bhitiṣṭhanto bādhante bhadrikāḥ prajāḥ.[236]

These places should be carefully watched.[237]

Also the very often repeated aphorism[238] reading :[239]

daśa-sūnā-samaṁ cakraṁ daśa-cakra-samo dhvajaḥ
dāśa-dhvaja-samā veśyā daśa-veśyā-samo nṛpaḥ[240]

shows that prostitutes[241] were considered as dangerous persons[242] with whom enemies of the king might hide.[243] For that reason, that is, for police reasons, *gaṇikā-s* had to inform the *gaṇikā' dhyakṣa* about men who were spending time with them.[244]

234. Cf. paragraph 9D.

235. K. 125. 8.

236. MBh. 12. 88. 14-5 Similarly Mn. 9. 264-6. Cf. MBh. 12. 140. 40-2; the History of Agaḍadatta in H. Jacobi's *Ausgewählte Erzählungen in Māhārāṣṭrī.*

237. Bārhaspatyasūtra (Nītiśāstara) 3. 27.

238. Cf. Mn. 4. 84 (4. 85 in the Bombay edition); Y. I. 141 quoted in L. Sternbach, *Veśyā*; *Synonyms and Aphorisms*, *op. cit.* Also see study XVII below.

239. MBh. 13. 125. 9.

240. Cf. Vivādaratnākara 335. 7; MBh. 2. 68. 1, where it was stated that gamblers had in their homes many loose women (*bandhavya*).

241. In both these contexts the word *gaṇikā* was not used.

242. Cf. Mn 9. 259; 4. 209, 219, 5. 90, Y. 1. 461; Vi. 51. 7. 63. 29; Vās 14. 10, and elsewhere.

243. Cf. below Studies VIII. *Legal Position of Physicians in Ancient Indian Law*, chapter IIIC, K. 203. 13 ff.; 144. 11 ff.

244. It should be noted that Abul Qādir ibn i Mulūk Shāh of Badāon in his *Muntakhab ut Tawārīkh*, the commentary on 'Abul Fazl 'Allani's *Āīn-i-Akbari*, mentioned that the Dāgorah (similar to the *gaṇikā' dhyakṣa*) and a clerk were also appointed to register the names of those who went to prostitutes, or wanted to take some of them to their houses; without permission no one was allowed to take dancing girls to his house. Cf. Rājataraṅginī 8. 3352, and note 262 to Chapter II.

It should be noted that Strabo, referring to Megasthenes, also stated that in India prostitutes were used as spies.[245]

22. *Gaṇikā'dhyakṣa-s*

Gaṇikā-s who were government servants were, as stated above, under the complete supervision of the *gaṇikā'dhyakṣa.*

The word *gaṇikā'dhyakṣa* was mentioned in the 'contents' of K.[246] Also the whole chapter XXVII of the second book of K. was entititled *gaṇikā'dhyakṣa*;[247] this shows that everything which was contained in this chapter related to him.

The *gaṇikā'dhyakṣa* appointed the *gaṇikā-s*, employed them,[248] classified them in the first, middle, or highest rank,[249] paid their salary,[250] supplied them with all necessities needed for the discharge of their duties,[251] fixed their payment for enjoyment,[252] determined their gifts, gross receipts, gross expenditure, and profit, checked their extravagant expenditure,[253] prepared statements based on information supplied by them, as well as payments for enjoyment and other receipts received,[254] accepted fines and ransom sums,[255] looked after them when they lost their beauty or service in the form of enjoyment,[256] etc.

The *gaṇikā'dhyakṣa* was the superintendent of *gaṇikā-s*, the minister for State-prostitution, responsible for the entire system of public houses run by the Government and State-prostitution. He was put on the same footing as other ministers —superintendents, such as the superintendents of treasury, of gold, of store-houses,of commerce, of forest produce, of armoury, of weights-and measures, of space and time, of tolls, of weaving, of agriculture, of liquor, of slaughter-houses, of ships, of cows, of horses, of elephants, of chariots, of infantry, of passports, of pasture lands, of the city, etc.

245. Strabo, Geography 15. 1, 48. Cf. note 264 to Chapter II.
246. K. 2. 7.
247. K. 123. 7.
248. K. 123. 8 ff.
249. K. 123. 14 ff.
250. K. 123. 9, 14.
251. K. 124. 6.
252. K. 124. 6.
253. K. 124. 6-7.
254. K. 125. 8.
255. K. 124. 1, 5, 8 ff.; 125. 1 ff.
256. K. 123. 17; 124. 3.

The function and position of the *gaṇikā'dhyakṣa* was a peculiarity of K., but not completely unknown to Sanskrit literary works. For instance, ŚlS. also mentioned the *gaṇikā'dhyakṣa*.[257]

The scheme of administration, as can be gathered from the inscriptions of Aśoka, did not show that in Aśoka's times the political administrative structure of the State knew such an institution as State-prostitution and a superintendent of prostitutes, who were government servants. The rock-edict of Girnār[258] mentioned the *ithījhakhamahāmāt(r)a* and the rock-edicts of Ṣāḥbāzgārhī[259] and of Mānsehrā[260] mentioned the *strī adhyakṣa mahāmātra*, but although their functions were not explained, it seems that their duty was to look after the women who were members of the king's family[261] and that they had nothing to do with prostitutes or public houses.[262]

However Strabo, referring to Megasthenes, mentioned *adhyakṣa* (*eforoi*,[263]) who had to inspect what was being done in the kingdom and report secretly to the king, using for that purpose prostitutes (*hetairai*)[264]

III. PROSTITUTES WHO WORKED ON THEIR OWN ACCOUNT

23. *Position of Prostitutes*

A. As stated before, the word *rūpājīvā* was used in K., along with other words for the designation of all kinds of pros-

257. Śl. S. 12. 83.
258. 12.
259. 12.
260. 12.
261. Cf. V. R. Ramachandra Dikshitar, *The Mauryan Polity* (Madras, 1932) 210.
262. 'Abul Qādir ibn i Muluk Shāh of Badaōn in his *Muntakhab ut Tawārīkh* (cf. fn. 244 above) mentioed the Dāgorah who had similar duties to the *gaṇikā'dhyakṣa*.
263. Arrian called them *episkopoi*, but Diodoros agreed with Strabo in calling them *eporoi*. Cf. McCrindle, *Ancient India as Described in Classical Literature*, 53.
264. *Ektoi d'eisin oi eforoi; tutois d'epopteuein dedotai ta prattomenā kai anangellein lathra tō basilei, synergus poiumenois tas heteiras tois men en tē polei tas en tē polei, tois de en stratopedō tas autothi; kathistantai d'oi aristoi kai pistotatoi.* (Strabo, Geography 15. 1. 48).

titutes who were not government servants. However, generally, this word was used for the designation of higher kinds of prostitutes but not as high as *gaṇikā-s* were.[1] The latter statement is evident, in particular, from the first book, chapter XII of K., where it is stated[2] that the king should not allow ascetics, buffoons, and *dāsī* to enter his harem, nor to women of high birth,[3] but *rūpājīvā......snānapragharṣa-śuddha-śarīrāḥ parivartita-vastrālaṅkārāḥ paśyeyuḥ.*[4] '*Rūpājīvā* may attend the harem after having cleaned themselves by bathing and rubbing, and after their garments and ornaments have been examined.'

This shows that while even women of high birth and *dāsī-s* (this word used in this context in the meaning of prostitutes of lower degree),[5] were not allowed to attend the wives of the king in the harem, this permission was granted to *rūpājīvā-s*; this shows that *rūpājīvā-s* enjoyed a higher position than other prostitutes who worked on their own account.

It should be also noted that their mothers (*rūpājīvā mātṛkā*),[6] old king's slaves (*vṛddhā rājadāsī*),[7] and temple prostitutes who had ceased to attend temples (*vyuparatopasthānā'-devadāsī*)[8] were to be employed by the *sūtrā'dhyakṣa* to cut wool, fibre, cotton, panicle, hemp, and flax,[9] in the same way as a *mātṛkā*[10] of a *gaṇikā*.[11]

1. Cf. paragraph 4 AB.

2. *muṇḍa-jaṭila-kuhaka-pratisaṁsargaṁ bāhyābhiś ca dāsībhiḥ pratiṣedhayet. na cai 'nāḥ kulyāḥ paśyeyur anyatra garbhavyādhisaṁsthābhyaḥ* (K. 41. 18-9).

3. Except when they came as midwives or in connexion with illness or medicines.

4. K. 41. 19-20.

5. Cf. K. 44. 6-8. Mention was there made of *dāsī* used to do work of bathroom servants, shampooers, bedroom servants, washermen, garland-makers. Shama Sastry translated, in this context, *dāsī* as 'prostitutes,' while J. J. Meyer as 'female slave' (*Sklavin*). It seems that Meyer's translation is more correct.

6. Procuresses.

7. The word *dāsī* was here, possibly, used in the meaning of prostitutes (old king's prostitutes) or, more likely, old king's slaves.

8. That is the only place where K. used the word *devadāsī*. About *devadāsī*, see Kath. translated by C. H. Tawney, ed. by N. M. Penzer (The Ocean of Story), Vol. I, Appendix IV, 'Sacred Prostitution'; R. Schmidt, *Liebe und Ehe im alten und modernen Indien* (Berlin, 1904) 542; J. Jolly, *Rechet und Sitte* 18 ff.; J. J. Meyer in the prefect to his translation of Daś. and in his *Sexual Life in Ancient India* (264 ff.), and many others. Some references to *devadāsī* are to be found in Sanskrit and Pāli literary works. Many references to *devadāsī* are to be found in the travel descriptions made by Western and Eastern travellers in India.

9. For text, see note 87 to Chapter II.

10. Also in the meaning of a procuress.

11. Cf. paragraph 11.

B. The word *rūpājīvā* was used in K. only nine times,[12] and once only in the chapter on the *gaṇikā'dhyakṣa* where rules concerning *gaṇikā-s* were laid down.

As seen from Vāts.,[13] the *rūpājīvā*, being wealthy persons, were not obliged to learn the sixty-four arts; they had to be beautiful only.[14]

The legal position of the *rūpājīvā-s* and prostitutes other than *gaṇikā-s* was not laid down in K. in the same way as that of the *gaṇikā-s*. There existed in K. only scattered rules which throw some light on their position, but we do not find a clear picture of their activities and position.

K. gave us some information on the dwelling places of *rūpājīvā-s*, their paramours, their protection from misuse on the part of the latter, their taxation, their position in the king's palace, their use by the king as spies, and their fate when they became old.

Some of these rules, as far as they were not in contradiction with the rules laid down for the *gaṇikā-s*, could be applied *per anologiam* to *gaṇikā-s*, particularly those which referred to the protection of the *gaṇikā-s* from misuse on the part of the paramour.

24. *Dwelling Places*

A. Concerning prostitutes' (*rūpājīvā*) dwelling places K. stated : *...nagara-dhānya-vyāvahārika-kārmāntika-balā'dhyakṣāḥ pakvā-nna-surā-māṁsa-paṇyāḥ rūpājīvās tālāpacārā vaiśyāś ca dakṣiṇāṁ diśam adhivaseyuḥ.*[15] 'The superintendents of the city, grain, transport, manufactories, and army, traders in cooked rice, liquor, and flesh, *rūpājīvā*, principal actors, Vaiśya shall live to the south (of the fort).'

It is evident from this quotation that in a model town special dwelling places were designed for prostitutes (*rūpājīvā*) in the south of the city; special quarters were destined for them.

B. In the Agnipurāṇa we find a similar rule; it was stated there that to the south of the town, dancers and pros-

12. K. 41. 19; 55. 11; 113. 19; 125. 12; 144. 9; 198. 17; 236. 11; 243. 11; 316. 1.
13. Cf. paragraph 4B.
14. They, as well as other kinds of prostitutes, could not be *cāṇḍālā*.
15. K. 55. 10-2.

titutes (*veśyāstrī*) shall live.[16] In the Milindapañha[17] it was mentioned that *gaṇikā, lāsikā, kumbhadāsī,* and others be brought to a model city;[18] in the Bṛhat-Kathā Ślokasaṁgraha, Budhasvāmin gave a splendid and lively description of the quarters of prostitutes.[19] A description of these quarters is also found in the Daśakumāracarita.[20] In the Bhojaprabandha special streets where prostitutes lived were mentioned;[21] that such special streets existed in ancient India is also evident from the Kuṭṭanīmata and the Samayamātṛkā. The inscriptions in the Tanjavur showed that temple women (*devadāsī, tanichcherippeṇaḍukan*) were those who resided in the streets near the temple.[22] We find many instances in Sanskrit literary works in which it was shown that *devadāsī-s* particularly dwelt on special streets near the temples[23] and that prostitutes occupied special quarters.

Many references to special quarters for prostitutes were also found in the journeys of European travellers to India.[24]

C. The rule concerning special quarters or streets for prostitutes had no application to the *gaṇikā-s* since they had either their own palaces or lived in houses placed at their disposal by the *gaṇikā'dhyakṣa.*

25. *Prostitutes—Avaruddhā-s*

A. In K. we find a special rule referring to prostitutes (*rūpājīvā*) who were *avaruddhā* (or *aparuddhā*). We read

16. *dakṣiṇe nṛtya-vṛttīnāṁ veśyā-strīṇāṁ gṛhāṇi ca* (Agnipurāṇa, in Bibl. Indica 107. 7).

17. For text, see note 34 to chapter I.

18. Cf. MBh. 3. 239. 22 ff., where it was stated that Duryodhana 'having reached that spot......commanded to construct pleasure-houses.'

19. *Veśa.* Śl. S. 10. 61-89; 12. 58. Cf. Śl. S. 11. 80 ff.; 10. 90-116.

20. ...*nirgatya-sva gṛhe veśavāṭe dyūta-sabhāyām āpaṇe ca nipuṇam anviṣyan no 'palabdhavān* (Daś. 80. 15-8).

21. Bhojaprabandha (Calcutta, 1883) 86. 19.

22. *Archaeological Survey of India, South Indian Inscriptions,* ed. and transl. E. Hultzsch, vol. II. part III (Madras, 1895), no. 66.

23. Cf. Jāt. 3. 463. where it was stated that prostitutes (*vaṇṇadāsī*) sat along the banks of great rivers tempting men.

24. In the 15th century 'Abd al-Razzāq (29.30). In the 16th century Domingo Paes in Darcha (Dharvar) (in Sewell, 240). In the 17th century 'Abul Qādir ibn i Muluk Shāh of Badaōn in *Muntakhab tu Tawārikh* (commentary to the '*Aīn i Akbarī* (192) ; Tavernier in Golkonda (127-8); Ovington in Surat (184); and many others, Cf. Ibn Baṭṭūṭa who mentioned special quarters for singers (prostitutes) in Dulat Ābād (4. 50) and Nicolô Conti who mentioned prostitutes in all parts of cities (23).

there :...... *rūpājīvām anyoparuddhāṁ gacchataḥ......aṣṭacatvārimśat-paṇo daṇḍaḥ.*[25] 'For sexual intercourse with a *rūpājīvā* kept by another, the penalty [amounts to] forty-eight *paṇa*.'

Y. divided women into two categories, that is, *avaruddhā* and *bhujiṣyā*.[26] Mit. gave a definition of both. And so, according to Mit., an *avaruddhā* was one who was kept in the house itself and was forbidden to have sexual intercourse with any other man; *bhujiṣyā* was one who was not kept in the house, but elsewhere, and was allowed to have sexual intercourse with a certain person only. Mit. referred this rule to prostitutes.[27]

K. stated in the context quoted above that if a prostitute (*rūpājīvā*) was kept at home and thus prohibited from having intercourse with any man other than this person who paid for her[28] (*avaruddhā*), the fine amounted to 48 *paṇa*. This fine had to be paid by the man who had sexual intercourse with such a prostitute (*rūpājīvā*) and not by the prostitute herself. That is evident *per analogiam* from Y.[29]

A prostitute (*rūpājīvā*) *avaruddhā* was a prostitute who was preferably taken by her paramour to his home, as his concubine (or harem woman) and who was paid a monthly salary.[30]

B. We find in Y. and N. similar rules. Y. clearly imposed a fine of 50 *paṇa* on a man who had sexual intercourse with either an *avaruddhā* or a *bhujiṣyā* with whom ordinarily anybody could have intercourse,[31] and N., referring the quotation to *bhujiṣyā* only, declared that sexual intercourse with

25. K. 198. 17-20.

26. *avaruddhāsu dāsīṣu bhujiṣyāsu tathai 'va ca*......(Y. 2. 290). Cf. fn. 31 below.

27. *uktalakṣaṇā varṇastriyo dāsyas tā eva svāminā śuśrūṣāhānivyudāsārthaṁ gṛha eva sthātavyam ity evaṁ puruṣāntaro'pabhogato niruddhā avaruddhāḥ. Puruṣaniyataparigrahā bhujiṣyāḥ. Yadā dāsyo 'varuddhā bhujiṣyā vā bhaveyus tadā tāsu tathā. Caśabdād veśyā-svairiṇīnām api sādhāraṇāstrīṇāṁ bhujiṣyāṇāṁ ca grahaṇam* (Mit. *ad* Y. 2. 290; 286. 17-21).

28. He paid a *vetana*, a monthly salary and not a *bhoga*, payment for enjoyment (for one or more nights). Cf. K. 118. 8; 124. 5; 243. 11; and elsewhere.

29. *gamyāsv api pumān dāpyaḥ*......(Y. 2. 290). cf. fn. 31 below.

30. Cf. paragraph 26B.

31. *avaruddhāsu dāsīṣu bhujiṣyāsu tathai 'va ca*'; *gamyāsv api pumān dāpyaḥ pañcāśat paṇikaṁ damam* (Y. 2. 290).

them was prohibited since they belonged to another man,[32] although sexual intercourse with any woman[33] who belonged to a lower caste than oneself[34] was permitted.[35] Both Y. and N. referred these rules to prostitutes also; N. stated clearly that the rule referred to *veśyā*,[36] and, though Y. did not make it clear, Mit. explained that when a *dāsī* was *avaruddhā* or *bhujiṣyā*, then, since the word *ca* was used in the context, *veśyā-s*, *svairiṇī-s* and *sādhāraṇastrī-s* were also to be included.[37]

Although K. stated clearly that the rule quoted above referred to prostitutes (*rūpājīvā*) who were *avaruddhā* only and did not mention *bhujiṣyā*, it seemed that this rule was also applicable to prostitutes who were *bhujiṣyā*, since Y., in a similar statement to that of K., mentioned both *avaruddhā-s* and *bhujīṣyā-s*, and N. mentioned *bhujiṣyā-s* only.[38]

C. The rule concerning prostitutes (*rūpājīvā avaruddhā*) was applicable to all kinds of prostitutes with the exception of *gaṇikā-s*. We have seen earlier[39] that a *gaṇikā* could not become an *avaruddhā*; she was a government servant who received a monthly salary paid by the *gaṇikā'dhyakṣa* and worked for the king and for the increase of his treasury and, therefore, the king could not be deprived of her services. If a man took a *gaṇikā* and made her an *avaruddhā*, he had to pay a fine of

32. *āsv eva tu bhujiṣyāsu doṣaḥ syāt paradāravat,*
gamyā api hi no 'peyā yat tāḥ paraparigrahāḥ
(N. 12. 79. Also NMS 13. 79). Also quoted in Mit *ad* Y. 2, 90, AP 2. 290, VyK 178, VRK 405, MR 132, DV 188, NṛP 209, VyPr. 402, VyU 138, VyM 107, VT 808, VV 277, VyS 156. This verse is also quoted in Mit. (*ad* Y. 2. 290; 286. 24-5) more correctly. The third and fourth pāda-s read there : *gamyāsv api hi no peyād dattāḥ paraparigrahāḥ.*

33. *Svairiṇī*, *veśyā*, or *dāsī*, who were *niṣkāsini*, not restrained, that is neither *bhujiṣyā* nor *avaruddhā*.

34. Or to the same caste, not to a higher caste.

35. *svairiṇy abrāhmaṇī veśyā dāsī niṣkāsinī ca yā*
gamyāḥ syur ānulomyena striyo na pratilomataḥ
(N. 12. 78 NMS 13. 78). Also quoted in Mit. *ad* Y.2. 290. VyK 128, VRK 405, MR 132, DV 188, NṛP 209, VyPr 402, VyU 138, VyM 107, VT 808, VV 277, VyS 156, AP 2. 290.

36. *Veśyā......niṣkāsinī*, as opposed to a *bhujiṣyā*.

37. Cf. note 27 to Chapter III.

38. Cf. Hemacandra's Pariśiṣṭaparvan 2. 288 ff.; Dhūrtasamāgama in Lassen's *Anthologia Sanscritica* (90. 15 ff.).

39. Cf. paragraph 12.

$1\frac{1}{4}$ *paṇa* and to the king a monthly salary of the *gaṇikā* which she used to receive from him or the *gaṇikā'dhyakṣa*.

26. *Protection of Prostitutes*

Concerning the protection of prostitutes from misuse on the part of their paramour, the following rule from K. should quoted : *rūpājīvāyāḥ prasahyo'pabhoge dvādaśa-paṇo daṇḍaḥ; bahūnām ekām adhicaratāṁ pṛthak caturviṁśati-paṇo daṇḍaḥ.*[40] 'For enjoyment of a *rūpājīvā* by the use of force the fine [amounts to] twelve *paṇa*. When many enjoy one [*rūpājīvā*] each one [has to pay] a fine of twenty-four *paṇa*.'

A. The first rule referred to violating a prostitute (*rūpājīvā*). According to K., in such a case the fine amounted to twelve *paṇa*. A similar rule is to be found in Y. where it is stated : *prasahya dāsyabhigame daṇḍo daśa-paṇaḥ smṛtaḥ.*[41] 'For sexual intercourse with a *dāsī*, by the use of force, the fine is declared to amount to ten *paṇa*.' Y. used here the word *dāsī*, while K. used the word *rūpājīvā*; however Mit. explained that under the word *dāsī* a *svairiṇī* and others[42] should be understood, that is, all kinds of prostitutes.

It is clear that according to K. and Y. a fine of 12 or 10 *paṇa* respectively had to be paid for violating an unwilling prostitute, but if she had received and taken her payment for enjoyment, then this rule could not be applied; then, there existed a *praesumptio juris ac de jure* that she was willing and had to abide by her contractual obligations;[43] that is clearly explained in Mit.[44]

B. Special rules referred to prostitutes being violated by watchmen in the towns during the night. K. stated : *striyaṁ dāsīm adhimehayatāṁ pūrvas sāhasa-daṇḍaḥ; adāsīṁ madhyamaḥ, kṛtāparādham uttamaḥ; kulastriyaṁ vadhaḥ.*[45] 'For carnal connection with a *dāsī*, first amercement; with an *adāsī*, the

40. K. 236. 11-2.

41. Y. 2. 291. Also quoted in ViR *ad* 2. 295, VyK 128, VRK 406, VCi 187-8, VyN 406, DV 190, SV 473, VyPr. 402, VyU 138, VT 810, BBh *ad* Y. 2. 134. VV. 278, VyS 155, AP 258. 73.

42. ...*dāsīṣu svairiṇyādiṣu*......(Mit. *ad* Y. 2. 291; 287. 27).

43. Cf. Dhūrtasamāgama in Lassen's *Anthologia Sanscritica* (86. 16 ff.).

44. *yadā punas tad icchayā bhāṭiṁ dattvā paścād anicchantīm api balād vrajanti tadā teṣām adoṣaḥ* (Mit. *ad* Y. 2. 291; 287. 29-30).

45. K. 146. 12-3. In other MSS *kṛtā varodhā*.

middlemost; with a *kṛtāparādhā*, the highest. With a woman of high birth—death.' K. used here the word *adhimehayatām* for denoting sexual intercourse by the use of force.[46] However, it is not clear what the meaning of the three words for the designation of the three different kinds of women was i. e. *dāsī*, *adāsī*, and *kṛtāparādhā* (or *kṛtāvarodhā*) (*kulastrī* denoted a woman coming from a good family, a woman of high birth).

Dāsī meant either female slave, or a prostitute of lower degree; a *kṛtāparādhā*, similarly as an *avaruddhā* (or *aparuddhā*), meant a woman kept in the house itself who was forbidden to have sexual intercourse with any other man.[47] that is, a harem woman; she could be either a free woman, a concubine, or a prostitute kept as a concubine;[48] *adāsī* was a person who was not a female slave.

It seems that K. made in this context a distinction between free women on the one hand (*kulastrī*), and prostitutes on the other. Thus for violating a *kulastrī* the highest existing penalty, that is, capital punishment, had to be applied; the other penalties, although high, could not be even compared with the latter.

If we admit that *dāsī*, *adāsī*, and *kṛtāparādhā* were different kinds of prostitutes, then a *dāsī* was a prostitute of the lowest rank, and a *kṛtāparādhā* such a prostitute as was kept in the house of her paramour as his concubine;[49] such a prostitute was under special protection and all penalties imposed for hurting her were higher than those applied to other prostitutes;[50] *adāsī* was, then, something between a *dāsī* and a *kṛtāparādhā*, a prostitute of a higher rank than a *dāsī*, e. g. a *rūpājīvā*.[51]

46. Literally *adhimehayati* means 'to urinate on something' but also 'to have sexual intercourse' (cf. Y. 2. 293). Comparing the two texts the the whole context in which the word *adhimehayatāṁ* was used in K., it was clear that it meant sexual intercourse without the consent of the woman, sexual intercourse by use of force.

47. Cf. paragraph 25 A.

48. Cf. paragraphs 25 and 12.

49. Cf. J. J. Meyer (234. 11-235, 2 and 235, 16-35) Meyer translated *dāsī* by *Gekaufte*, *adāsī* by *nicht Gekaufte* and *krtāparādhā* by *ständige Beischläferin, eine Mätresse*.

50. Cf. paragraphs 25B and 12.

51. Cf. the difference between *dāsi* and *rūpājīvā* in K. 21. 18-9 and K. 21.19-20. Cf. paragraph 23.

It is clear that this rule was a specific one and had to be considered applicable to watchmen only, because for violating a prostitute (*rūpājīvā*) the fine amounted to 12 *paṇa*.[52] The enactment of this rule is easily understandable since, as seen from Sanskrit literary works, in ancient India prostitutes used to walk by night to the house of their paramour and the watchmen were their only protectors during the night. If they should violate a prostitute, they would not only commit a crime against the prostitute, but also a crime against the State by not performing their ordinary duties and by violating the very existence of the institution of watchmen introduced in Kauṭilya's State. Probably, primarily because of the latter reason, the penalty imposed on watchmen was so high, in some cases as high as for violating a *gaṇikā*.

C. Other special rules referred to violating those prostitutes who were under special protection. These were *duhitṛkā-s*, that is, daughters of prostitutes who were not yet *gaṇikā-s* but who expected to become *gaṇikā-s* in the future; and not yet mature girls (*kumārī*) who were also expected to become *gaṇikā-s* in the future. Both these had to be considered as *pratigaṇikā-s* and were, therefore, under the special care of the State.[53] Also *rūpadāsī-s*, that is, those employed in making garlands, scents and the like for the *gaṇikā-s*, as well as *mātṛkā-s*, of the *gaṇikā-s* were under the special protection of the State, since they formed either the personal property of the *gaṇikā-s* or were related closely to the *gaṇikā-s*.

And so, for violating a *kumārī* by using force the highest amercement was to be imposed and for sexual intercourse with a willing *kumārī* the first amercement.[54] For violating a *mātṛkā*, *duhitṛkā*, or *rūpādāsī* the highest amercement was to be inflicted,[55] while for sexual intercourse with a *gaṇikāduhitṛ*, a fine of 54 *paṇa* was to be imposed on the offender who had also to pay to her *mātṛkā* sixteen times her payment for enjoyment (*bhoga*).[56]

D. We have seen above that according to K., he who abducted a *gaṇikā*, that is, eloped with her, had to pay a fine

52. Cf. paragraph 26.
53. Cf. paragraph 3.
54. K. 124. 13-4.
55. K. 124. 19.
56. K. 232. 8-9.

of 1,000 *paṇa* and that for violating a *kumārī* the highest amercement was inflicted on the offender.[57] Comparing these two different rules and the amount of fines imposed in both cases, we see that the social position of prostitutes (*rūpājīvā*) was very low in comparison with *gaṇikā-s* king's servants. Comparing these rules with those dealing generally with women, we see that the position of prostitutes was generally extremely low. K. stated three times that sexual intercourse with a woman against her will was forbidden.[58] For defiling a maiden of equal caste before she has reached maturity, the hand of the offender was to be cutt off or a fine of 400 *paṇa* was to be imposed;[59] if she had attained maturity, the offender's middle finger was to be cut off or a fine of 200 *paṇa* was to be imposed,[60] and even according to K., for defiling the daughter of his own male or female slave the fine, amounted to 24 *paṇa* plus an adequate nuptial fee and jewelry.[61] while for sexual intercourse with a prostitute (*rūpājīvā*) against her will the fine amounted to 12 *paṇa* only, that is, half of the fine imposed for defiling a daughter of a slave. Particularly this last example shows that the daughter of a slave enjoyed a higher legal protection than a prostitute (*rūpājīvā*).

E. The second part of the rule quoted above[62] dealt with another question. There, it was stated that if more than one man enjoyed a prostitute (*rūpājīvā*) by the use of force, each one had to pay a fine amounting to 24 *paṇa*, that is, twice the amount that one had to pay if he should commit the same offence alone.

A similar rule is to be found in Y.[63] Y. clearly stated that the fine of 24 *paṇa* was to be inflicted when the offence was committed against a *dāsī*, or any other prostitute, since this sentence formed the second part of the verse dealing with forcible sexual intercourse with prostitutes,[64] and that it could

57. Cf. paragraph 18B.
58. K. 231. 2, 12; 232. 1.
59. K. 230. 16-7.
60. K. 231. 1-2.
61. K. 232. 10-1.
62. Cf. paragraph 26A.
63. *bahūnāṁ yady akāmā 'sau catur-viṁśatikaḥ pṛthak* (Y. 2. 291) Cf. note 41 above.
64. Mit. ad Y. 2. 291. Cf. paragraph 26 and note 42 to Chapter III.

only be inflicted in case of sexual intercourse against the will (*akāmā*) of the prostitute; both these premises were lacking in K.'s text.

It should be noted that in N. we also find a similar-rule. It is stated there that if any person caused a prostitute, a harlot (*paṇyastrī*) to be approached by many, then he had to pay eight times the payment for enjoyment and a fine of the same amount.[65] N. did not use the word *pṛthak*, but it is clear that each of the offenders had to pay the same penalty. On the other hand N. made it clear, what was stated before with regard to the protection of prostitutes (*rūpājīvā*), that the penalties were imposed only in the event that the prostitutes did not receive beforehand their payment for enjoyment.

Also in the Matsyapurāṇa we find the same rule. There it was stated that in a similar case each offender had to pay twice the amount of the prostitute's payment for enjoyment.[66]

F. We do not find a similar rule in the chapter dealing with *gaṇikā-s*. It seems that the general rule of higher penalty imposed on each offender in case of forcible enjoyment of a prostitute should be applied *per analogiam* to *gaṇikā-s* also.

G. The next sentence which follows those quoted above[67] reads : *striyam ayonau gacchataḥ pūrvas sāhasa-daṇḍaḥ.*[68] 'The first amercement for having intercourse with a women outside the *yoni*.' Similarly it is stated in Y. where we read : *ayonau gacchato yoṣāṁ puruṣaṁ vā 'pi mehataḥ; catur-viṁśatiko daṇḍaḥ.......*[69]

65. *ayonau vā samākrāmed bahubhir vā 'pi vāsayet,*
śulkaṁ so 'ṣṭaguṇaṁ dāpyo vinayaṁ tāvad eva 'tu
(N. 6. 19, NSM 7. 21) Also quoted in Mit. *ad* Y. 2. 292, VyK 160, SC 206, VRK 166, VCi 78, SV 301, VyPr. 330, VyU 89, VT 654, VV 172, Vy S 103, VVy 42, AP 2.198.
The text found in Mit. *ad* Y. 2. 292; 288. 8, seems to be more correct in the first part, where it is stated :
ayonau, vā 'bhigacched yo bahubhir vā 'pi vāsayet.

66. *bahūnāṁ vrajatāṁ ekāṁ sarve te dviguṇaṁ damaṁ*
dadyuḥ pṛthak pṛthak sarve daṇḍaṁ ca dviguṇaṁ param
(Matsyapurāṇa 227. 148; in *SBH* 227. 146). Also quoted in AP 2. 198, VyK 160, VRK 167, VCi 78, VyPr 330, VyU 89, VV 172.

67. Cf. paragraph 26.

68. K. 236. 13.

69. Y. 2. 293. Also quoted in ViR 2. 296, Vy K 128, VRK 406-7, VCi 188. VyN 403, DV 179, Vy Pr 404, VyU 139, VyM 108, VT 811, VV 325, Vy S 156, AP 2. 292.

K. referred this rule to a *strī*, while Y. referred it to a *yoṣā* and Mit. commenting on this verse stated that it referred even to a *svayoṣā*. However N. had a similar rule and, though it did not refer explicitly to prostitutes, it is reasonable to assume that it referred to *paṇyastrī*. In the same verse N. mentioned sexual intercourse by many persons with one woman and the intercourse outside the *yoni* (*ayonau*); in the preceding verse (N. 6.18) N. used the word *paṇyastrī* and it seems obvious that N. 6.19 also referred to *paṇyastrī* in the general meaning of 'prostitutes.' N. stated there :

ayonau vā samākrāmed bahubhir vā 'pi vāsayet,
śulkaṁ so 'ṣṭaguṇaṁ dāpyo vinayaṁ tāvad eva tu.[70]

Since N. referred this rule to prostitutes and since in K. as well as in Y. these rules immediately followed the rules relating to prostitutes, it seems that it could be assumed that K. referred this rule also to prostitutes. Hence, according to K., for intercourse with a prostitute outside the *yoni* the offender had to pay the first amercement.

Mit. gave the following explanation for intercourse outside the *yoni* : *yas tu svayoṣāṁ sukhādav abhigacchati.*[71]

H. If we accept that this rule referred to prostitutes in general, it seems that it might be said that it referred *par analogiam* to *gaṇikā-s* also.

I. In connexion with what was said before the following verse found in K. might be quoted :

labheta puṁścalī bhogaṁ saṅgamasyo 'paliṅganāt;
atiyācñā tu jīyeta daurmatyāvīṅayena vā.[72]

'The prostitute after having surrendered her person to sexual intercourse shall take payment for enjoyment . However, any improper demand because of bad intentions or misbehaviour should be nul and void.'

The first sentence contained the well-known rule described above[73] that a prostitute, if she has received her *bhoga*, has concluded a contract according to which she was obliged to yield her person to the paramour who paid for the enjoy-

70. N. 6. 19. Cf. note 65 to Chapter III. *ayonau vā*...was also used in the text of N. quoted in Mit. (note 65 to Chapter III).

71. Mit. ad Y. 2. 293.

72. K. 184. 10-1.

73. Cf. paragraph 17.

ment.[74] Although it was not stated in this verse clearly, it was evident that the contractual penalty stipulated in K.,[75] N.,[76] Y.,[77] and mentioned in the Matsyapurāṇa,[78] the Agnipurāṇa,[79] the Śukasaptati,[80] the Kuṭṭanīmata,[81] and elsewhere, amounting to twice the agreed *bhoga*, was to be paid by the prostitute if she declined to abide by her contractual obligations. However, the second sentence of the verse quoted above, gave to the prostitute the right to decline her contractual obligation to yield her person to the paramour, if his demand was improper because of his bad intentions (foolishness, wickedness, malice—*daurmatya*) or misbehaviour (indecency, impudency, obscenity—*avinaya*). This would be the case if the paramour wanted to have intercourse with a prostitute *ayonau*,[82] or if one or more than one man wanted to enjoy a prostitute,[83] or if the paramour took her to another person on the pretext of taking her to some particular individual.[84] Also the rule of breaking the contract by the prostitute because of her or her paramour's illness[85] was admissible (*dourmatya*).

These rules were in complete agreement with the respective rules applicable to *gaṇikā-s*, and complemented these rules. The rules applicable to prostitutes (*puṁścalī*) were of a more general nature.

27. *Taxes*

Prostitutes (*veśyā* and *rūpājīvā*) had to pay taxes to the State.

A. As far as *veśyā-s* were concerned, K. stated only, in most general terms, that *veśyā-s*, as well as many others mentioned in connexion with *veśyā*, came under the head of forts

74. Cf. Śuk. t. o. 376. 25-8. Similarly Śts No. 45.
75. K. 125. 3.
76. N. 6. 18.
77. Y. 2. 292.
78. Matsyapurāṇa 227. 14-5; cf. note 170 to Chapter II.
79. Agnipurāṇa 227. 44-5.
80. Śuk. t. o. 377. 4-6.
81. Kuṭṭ. 341.
82. Cf. paragraph 26 FGH.
83. Cf. paragraph 26 DEF.
84. Matsyapurāṇa 227. 14C.
85. Cf. paragraph 17B.

(*durga*)[86] and that the Collector General should attend to the collection of revenues from forts and others,[87] since they formed the body of revenues.[88] This shows in a general way only that some income was derived by the Collector-General from *veśyā-s*.[89]

More details were found, as far as *rūpājīvā* were concerned. K. stated : *rūpājīvā bhoga-dvayaguṇaṁ māsaṁ dadyuḥ*.[90] '*Rūpājīvā* shall pay monthly twice the amount of her payment for enjoyment.' This payment for enjoyment, called in K. *bhoga*, was fixed, according to Vāts., by prostitutes in consideration of the point, place, time, their qualities, popularity, and their position in comparison with other prostitutes;[91] it was also fixed in view of competition between two or more paramours.[92]

The *rūpājīvā* had to pay monthly twice the amount of the payment for enjoyment (*bhoga*) as was fixed by her for spending a night with a paramour.

B. This rule, although contained in the chapter dealing with *gaṇikā'dhyakṣa*[93] referred to all kinds of prostitutes (called in the context *rūpājīvā*) with the exception of *gaṇikā-s*.

According to K., the government servants did not pay taxes on their salaries, and since *gaṇikā-s* were government servants, no taxes could be levied on them while *rūpājīvās* and other prostitutes who were not *gaṇikā-s* government servants, but who worked on their own, were taxable on their income; they paid twenty-four times their *bhoga* yearly.

C. K. contains an additional rule about taxation levied on prostitutes (*rūpājīvā*). This rule was also specific for all prostitutes with the exception of *gaṇikā-s* government servants.

K. states that if the king found himself in great financial trouble and needed money, he could collect it by imposing

86. *śulkaṁ daṇḍaḥ pautavaṁ nāgariko lakṣaṇā'dhyakṣo mudrā' dhyakṣaḥ surā sūnā sūtraṁ tailaṁ ghṛtaṁ kṣāraṁ sauvarṇikaḥ paṇyasaṁsthā veśyā dyūtaṁ vāstukaṁ kāru-śilpi-gaṇo devatā'dhyakṣo dvāra-bāhirikādeyaṁ ca durgam* (K. 60. 1-4).

87. *samāhartā durgaṁ raṣṭraṁ khaniṁ setuṁ vanaṁ vrajaṁ vaṇikpathaṁ cā 'vekṣeta* (K. 59. 15).

88. *ity āyaśarīraṁ* (K.60.13).

89. Niccolo Manucci in his *Storia do Mogor* stated that in the time of the reign of Shāh Jahān all prostitutes paid taxes.

90. K. 125. 12.

91. Cf. paragraph 8AB.

92. Kuṭṭ. 335.

93. That was the only rule relating to *rūpājivā-s* found in this chapter.

extraordinary taxes;[94] as far as prostitutes (*rūpājīvā*) and bards (*kuśīlava*)[95] were concerned K. stated : *kuśīlavā rūpājīvāś ca vetanā'rdhaṁ dadyuḥ.*[96] '*Kuśīlava* and *rūpājīvā* have to pay half of their salary [if the king is in distress].' K. used here the word *vetana* whereas, when the usual tax was discussed, the word *bhoga* was used. The word *vetana* was not synonymous with the word *bhoga*; *bhoga* was the payment for enjoyment paid to prostitutes, while *vetana* was the usual expression for salary or wages paid periodically to workers, employees, etc.[97] However, prostitutes (*rūpājīvā*), who were not government servants, worked on their own account and did not receive any *vetana*, only a *bhoga*; they were not employees. They could, however, receive salaries when they were either *avaruddhā* or *bhujiṣyā*.

Therefore, it seems that the sentences, in which it is stated that prostitutes (*rūpājīvā*) had to pay half of their *vetana* in the case of the king's distress, referred only to prostitutes who were either *avaruddhā* or *bhujiṣyā*, the more so as they could not receive any *bhoga*[98] and, thus, the calculation of their taxes was made impossible (*vetanārdham*).[99]

28. *Prostitutes as Spies*

A. Persons engaged in harlotry had, generally speaking, access everywhere[100] and consequently did not cause any suspicion if they were present in places usually not frequented by other women. Therefore, persons engaged in harlotry, irrespective whether they were *rūpājīvā*, *veśyā*, *dāsī*, *puṁścalī*, *śilpakārikā*, *kauśikastrī*, *bandhaki*, or others, were used, according to K., as spies; *veśā*, that is, most generally speaking, persons engaged

94. Book 5, ch. 2 (242. 5 ff.).

95. Sons of *gaṇikā-s* became automatically *kuśīlava-s* (K. 124. 2). Cf. paragraph 13.

96. K. 243. 11.

97. K. 62. 13; 69. 2; 89. 16; 101. 8; 124. 5; and many other passages. Cf. note 46 to Chapter II.

98. They were kept by one man.

99. K. did not state, however, what was the tax to be paid in normal times by *rūpājīvā*, *avaruddhā*, or *bhujiṣyā*.

100. Not all kinds of prostitutes had access to the queen's apartments. It should be noted that according to treatises on Indian dramaturgy prostitutes should never meet with highborn women (Daśarūpa 3. 45).

in harlotry, were employed in the Machiavellian system of State, in the police State of Kauṭilya.

This is the explanation for many references in K. to prostitutes who acted as spies.

In this connexion it should be emphasized that K. nowhere mentioned *gaṇikā-s* government servants, as spies, since they received their monthly salary in order to increase the king's treasury and enjoyed a special position. Their only obligation was to inform the *gaṇikā'dhyakṣa* about the man who was under their influence.[101]

B. Since persons engaged in harlotry had, generally speaking, access everywhere, including places where mendicant women (used as spies) could not have access, K. used for espionage purposes prostitutes (*dāsī*) and other persons who did not cause any suspicion, such as artisans (*śilpakārikā*)[102] or bards (*kūśīlava*).[103]

K. also used prostitutes (*puṁścalī*), persons having a similar character, story-tellers, and others, as spies on thieves, since they were often seen in their presence.[104] On the other hand K. stated that the Collector-General employed spies disguised as persons engaged in harlotry (*veśa*), different kinds of ascetics (*siddha, tāpasa, pravajita, cakracara*), of bards (*cāraṇa, kuhaka, kuśīlava*), of foretellers (*naimittika, mauhūrtika*), of cripples (*unmatta, mūka, badhira, jaḍa, andha*), of workers (*kāru, śilpin, vaidehaka*), of those who prepared food and drinks (*śauṇḍika, āpūpika, pākva, māṁsika, audanika*), and physicians (*cikitsaka*), and sent them abroad for espionage.[105]

K. also stated that different kinds of procurers (*bandhakī-*

101. Cf. paragraph 21.

102. Other kinds of prostitutes.

103. *bhikṣukī-pratiṣedhe dvāstha-paramparā, mātā-pitṛ-vyañjanāḥ śilpakārikāḥ kuśīlavā dāsyo vā gītovādya bhaṇḍagūḍhālekhya-saṁjñābhir vā cāraṁ nirhareyuḥ* (K. 21. 7-10).

104. *tulyaśīla-puṁścalī-prāpāvika-kathā-vakāśa-bhojanadātṛbhir apasarpayet; evam atisandadhyāt* (K. 221. 3-4).

105. *siddha-tāpasa-pravrajita-cakracaracāraṇa-kuhaka-pracchandaka-kārtāntika-mauhūrtika-cikitsako'nmatta-mūka-badhira-jaḍā'ndha-vaidehaka-kāruśilpa-kuśīlava-veśa-śauṇḍikā'pūpikapākva-māṁsikau'danikavyañjanān* (K. 210. 15-8).

poṣaka,[106] *plavaka*, *naṭa*, *nartaka*, *saubhika*)[107] sent very young and beautiful women[108] as spies; through them the procurers excited love among leaders of the enemy's army or chiefs of corporations and then ordered that these women should go to another man or be abducted by force by another man; if the leaders of the army or chiefs of corporations were brought by this sham-act to a quarrel, they were either made to leave the country or to proceed to help in the invasion undertaken or killed by fiery spies[109] who declared that they were killed by the other lover (in consequence of love).[110] The procurers (*bandhaki-poṣaka*) used also the king's servants (*rājapreṣyā*),[111] who were very young and beautiful, to collect taxes.[112]

We find also in K. other references to prostitutes (*kauśi-*

106. By a *bandhaki-poṣaka* ('keeper of loose women') a procurer should be understood and not a government servant, as in the case of *gaṇikā* there was a *gaṇikā'dhyakṣa*, a superintendent of prostitution. Shama Sastry translated *bandhaki-poṣaka* by 'keeper of harlots,' or'he who maintains prostitutes' and J. J. Meyer by *Hurenpfleger* or *Dirnenpfleger*. There was no place in Kauṭilya's State for another official who would look after prostitutes who were not government servants. However, a *bandhakī-poṣaka*, like all other procurers and procuresses, certainly stood at the service of the king and, therefore, if the latter needed a prostitute for espionage purposes he approached the *bandhakī-poṣaka*, as he approached a *kuṭṭinī*, or a *plavaka*, or a *naṭa*, or a *nartaka*, ot a *saubhika*, etc.

107. Cf. paragraph 30A, and notes 7 and 8 to Chapter III.

108. *puram rūpayauvanā*. The texts did not state explicity 'prostitites', but it is evident that these procurers used for this purpose either prostitutes (*bandhakī*) or their own wives or daughters, who usually were engaged in harlotry.

109. Fiery spy, *agent provacateur*, used also to cause quarrels in brothels and taverns among the chiefs of corporations, by praising those whom he disliked. *Veśa-śauṇḍikeṣu vā pratiloma-praśaṁsabhiḥ saṅgha-mukhya-manuṣyāṇāṁ tīkṣṇāḥ kalahān utpādayeyuḥ* (K. 378. 12-4).

110. *bandhakīpoṣakāḥ parama-rūpa-yauvanābhiḥ strībhis senāmukhyān unmādayeyuḥ. bahūnām ekasya dvayor vā mukhyayoḥ kāme jāte tīkṣṇāḥ kalahān utpādayeyuḥ. Kalahe 'parājitapakṣaṁ paratrāvagamane yātrāsāhāyya-dāne vā bhartur yojayeyuḥ* (K. 384. 17-20). *bandhakīpoṣakaḥ plavaka-naṭa-nartaka-saubhikā vā praṇihitāḥ strībhiḥ parama-rūpayauvanābhis saṅghamukhyān unmādayaiyuḥ. jatakāmānām anyatamasya pratyayaṁ kṛtvā 'nyatra gamanena prasabha-haraṇena vā kalahān utpādayeyuḥ. kalahe tīkṣṇāḥ karma kuryuḥ—"hato 'yam itthaṁ kāmukaḥ " iti* (K. 380. 1-5).

Cf. in Mudrārākṣasa (ed. and transl. K. H. Dhruva, Poona Or. Ser. 25; 5. 68. 5; 5. 21; 1. 14; 19; 20 (12. 18); 2. 14 (26. 18); 2. 15; 2. 16, and elsewhere) where references to poison-damsels (*viṣakanñā*, *viṣakanyakā*, *viṣāṅganā*, (*viṣamayī*, *viśakañ ñā*, *viṣakaṇṇā*) were made. Cf. also Śl. S. 10. 142. Cf. also N. M. Penzer, Poison-Damsels and other essays in Folklore and Antropology, London 1952.

111. Another kind of prosititute.

112. *bandhakī-poṣakā rājapreṣyābhiḥ parama rūpa yauvanābhiḥ kośaṁ saṁhareyuḥ* (K. 243. 16-7).

kastrī) who were used as spies; their duty was to excite love among undesirable men; to this end they made appointments with them in secret houses where the men either found death from the hands of fiery spies or were carried away in chains.[113]

Prostitutes (*rūpājīvā*, *veśyā*) were also used to spy on military men (*veśyā*)[114] and for kidnapping princes (*rūpājīvā*). In the chapter on 'Making Peace and Breaking it'[115] K. mentioned carpenters, artisans, dancers, actors, singers, players on musical instruments, and many others serving the prince as spies, who kidnapped the prince kept as an hostage,[116] and ended this paragraph by saying[117] that this explains the work of prostitutes (*rūpājīvā*) and women spies under the disguise of wives of the prince.[118]

It should be emphasized that those prostitutes (*rūpājīvā*) who were brought to the model city,[119] were brought for a special purpose, that is, to act as spies for the superintendent of the city (*nāgaraka-praṇidhi*) along with vendors of liquors, cooked rice, cooked flesh, and cooked mashed grain.[120] They, according to K., had to be visited only by such men whom they knew (*parijñāta*). The word *parijñāta* not only means 'thoroughly known' but also 'ascertained'; therefore, prostitutes and other persons enumerated there had to take in their house only those persons about whom they had the obligation to ascertain from where they came, who they were, and the like.

This rule has nothing in common with another rule referring also to a lower kind of prostitute, that is, *puṁścalī-s*, the latter rule stated that those who constantly moved with prostitutes (*puṁścalī*) were considered as suspected persons.[121]

113. *kaūśikastriyo nartakī-gāyanā vā pratipannān gūḍhaveśmasu rātrisamāgama-praviṣṭās tīkṣṇā hanyur baddhvā hareyur vā* (K. 380. 15-6).

114. *satriṇaś cā 'yudhiyānāṁ veśyāḥ kāru-kuśīlavāḥ*
daṇḍavṛddhāś ca jānīyuś śaucāśaucam atandritāḥ. (K. 249. 17-8)

115. Book VI, Chapter XVII.

116. K. 315. 15-21.

117. *tena rūpājīvā bhāryāvyañjanāś ca vyākhyātāḥ* (K. 316. 1).

118. Cf. Hemacandra, Pariśiṣṭaparvan, 1. 142 ff.

119. Cf. paragraph 24.

120. *śauṇḍika-pākva-māṁsikau'danika-rūpājīvāḥ. parijñātam āvāsayeyuḥ; ativyayartāram atyāhita-karmāṇaṁ canivedayeyuḥ* (K. 144. 9). It should be noted that K. mentioned here almost the same as those mentioned in K. 55. 10-2.

521. K. 214. 14.

Although special rules referred to the seizure of these persons who had contact with *puṁścalī-s*, and although this rule made it clear that *puṁścalī-s* enjoyed had reputation and might be used as spies, this rule did not make it obligatory for the *puṁscalī-s* to spy on their paramours.

In this connexion it should be noted that *gaṇikā-s* were also obliged to inform the *gaṇikā'dhyakṣa* about the *puruṣa* who were spending time with them, since unknown and dangerous persons could hide with them.[122] Prostitutes (*rūpājīvā*) had a spy on them and find out every thing about them; they had to know them thoroughly and inform the *nāgarakapraṇidhi* immediately about everything they knew about them.

IV. PERSONS ENGAGED IN HARLOTRY

29. *Husbands Living on Harlotry of their Wives*

Almost at the end of the chapter entitled *gaṇikā'dhyakṣa*[1] we find the following sentence : *etena naṭanartakagāyakāvādakavāgjīvanākuśīlavaplavaku saubhikācāraṇānāṁ strīvyavahāriṇāṁ striyo gūḍhājīvāś ca vyākhyātāḥ.*[2] 'By that are explained [the duties] of women making their living secretly [*gūḍhājīvā*] [such as] women of actors [*naṭa*], dancers [*nartaka*], singers [*gāyaka*[, players on musical instruments [*vādaka*], buffoons [*vāgjīvana*], bards [*kuśīlava*], rope dancers [*plavaka*], jugglers [*saubhika*] wandering bards [*cāraṇa*], and procurers [*strīvyavahārin*].

Two problems were settled in this context, that is : (a) that, in addition to procurers, other persons, such as actors, dancers, bards, wandering bards, singers, players on musical instruments, buffoons, jugglers and rope dancers lived upon the prostitution of their wives; and (b) that some rules, which were given before in K. referred to these persons.

30. *Special Categories of Persons Living on Harlotry of their Wives*

A. As far as the problem of persons living on the prostitution of their wives is concerned another sentence from K.

122. Cf. paragraph 21 and K. 125. 8; MBh. 12. 88. 14-5; Mn. 9. 259; 4. 209, 219; 5. 90; Y. 1. 161; Vi. 51. 7; 63. 29; Vās. 14.10; MBh. 13. 125. 9; Mn. 4. 84; Y. 1. 141.

1. K. book II, chapter XXVII.

2. K. 125. 9-10.

might be quoted. K. in book. in book III, chapter IV, explaining rules referring to vagrancy, elopement, and short and long sojournment, stated that if a woman left the house of her husband and went to another village she had to pay; inter *alia*, a fine of 12 *paṇa*. If, on a road or in the forest or in any other concealed place, she fell into the company of another man, or if, with a view to enjoyment, she accompanied a suspicious or forbidden person, she was guilty of elopment. But K. stated : *tālāpacāra-cāraṇā-matsyabandha-kalubdhakā-gopālakaśauṇḍikānām anyeṣāṁ ca prasṛṣṭāstrīkāṇāṁ pathy anusaraṇam adoṣaḥ*[3]. 'It is no offence to fall into the company of persons who surrender their women for sexual intercourse, such as principal actors [*tālāpacāra*], wandering bards [*cāraṇa*], fishermen [*matsyabsndhaka*], hunters [*lubdhaka*], herdsmen [*gopālaka*], and vintners [*śauṇḍika*].' K. in addition to *cāraṇa*[4] and principal actors [*tālāpacāra*][5] mentioned before, made here reference to vintners, herdsmen, hunters, and fishermen, who were also classed by K. among those who lived from prostitution of their wives. We have seen above[6] that K. included among procurers, in addition to *bandhakī-poṣaka* the following : *plavaka*, *naṭa*, *nartaka*, and *saubhika*,[7] and in different places mentioned these persons as those whose women were engaged in harlotry.[8]

B. We find similar, though not so detailed rules in Mn. and B. Mn., after having explained that no man under the penalty of one *suvarṇa*, should converse with wives of others,[9] stated :

> *nai 'ṣa cāraṇadāreṣu vidhir nā'tmo'pajīviṣu,*
> *sajjayanti hi te nārīr nigūḍhāś cārayanti ca.*[10]

3. K. 158. 11-2.
4. K. 125. 10.
5. K. mentions in 125, 9 *naṭa* 'actor.'
6. Cf. paragraph 28.
7. K. 380. 1-5.
8. *Cāraṇa, kuśīlava, śauṇḍika* were mentioned along with *veśa* in K. 210. 15-9; *śauṇḍika* along with *puṁścali* in K. 214. 14, and along with *rūpājīvā* in K. 144. 19; *kuśīlava* were mentioned along with *rūpājīvā* in K. 243. 11; in K. 55. 11 it was stated that, *inter alia*, *rūpājīvā*, *kuśīlava*, and *tālāpacāra* should live to the south of the fort; there was similar statement in the Agnipurāṇa (106. 7) where, *inter alia*, actors and fishermen were also mentioned. Also *śauṇḍika* (K. 214. 14), *kuśīlava* (K. 204. 4), *vādaka*, *gāyaka*, and *lubdhaka* (327. 19) were mentioned among undesirable persons.
9. Mn. 8. 361.
10. Mn. 8. 362. Also quoted in VyK 125 VRK 387, RDhK 130, VCi 174-5, DV 158, Vīr. *ad* 2. 285, VyPr 401, VT 801, VV 265, VyS 1,54, AP 2. 285.

'This rule[11] does not apply to wives of wandering bards or of those who live on [harlotry of] their own [wives]; for such men secretly bring their wives into contact [with other men] and tempt them on.'

An almost identical rule is found in B. where it is said :

na tu cāraṇadāreṣu na raṅgā'vatare vadhaḥ
saṁsarjayanti tā hy etān niguptāṁś cālayanty api.[12]

'But no punishment for [intercourse] with wives of wandering bards and actors, for such men carry them [to other men] or lying concealed permit them to have culpable intercourse.'

Both these texts stated the same, that is, that sexual intercourse with the wives of wandering bards (*cāraṇa*), actors, and others who lived on prostitution of their wives, was permissible. Very instructive was Medh.'s commentary on Mn. Medh. stated that *cāraṇa* meant also dancers, singers, and actors;[13] *ātmopajīviṣu* impiled 'those wives who live upon their own beauty';[14] *sajjayanti* meant 'unite their wives with other men,'[15] and *nigūḍhāḥ* meant 'not in the open market',[16] Medh. continued ; *gṛhaveṣatvād eva tāḥ, prasīddha-veśyābhyo bhidyante,* and thus explained what was the difference between these women and other prostitutes.[17] Medh. ended the commentary on Mn. 8.362 with the statement that these men not only secretly brought their wives into contact with other men but also seduced, through their wives, the wives of other men and in such a way made their wives act as prostitutes as well as procuresses.[18]

11. That is, the preceding one, Mn. 8. 361.

12. B. 2. 2. 4. 3.

13. Medh. *ad* Mn. 8. 362 (22. 3-4). Govinda in the commentary on B. explained that the wives of *cāraṇa* were *devadāsī*. Wives of *cāraṇa* were not, however, the only *devadāsi*.

14. Medh. *idem* (222. 4).

15. Medh. *idem* (222. 5-6).

16. Medh. *idem* (222. 6).

17. That is, that they were not to be found in an open market but carried their occupation within their own houses. Medh. *idem* (222. 6-7).

18. *athavā svā nārīḥ 'sajjayanti' yojayanti, anyāś ca sva strībhiś ' cārayanti' pravartayanti veśyātvaṁ kuṭṭanītvaṁ ca svadārāṇāṁ kārayantī 'ty arthaḥ* (Medh. *idem* 222. 9-10).

We also find in Śukr. and Vāts. references to wives of some of the persons enumerated in K. with the explanation that they were engaged in harlotry, or were considered prostitutes. And so, Śukr. stated that those who lived upon musical instruments lived also upon the prostitution of their wives,[19] and Vāts. stated that one of the nine kinds of prostitutes (*veśyā*) was a *naṭī*,[20] identified by Yaś. with an actress (*raṅgayoṣit*).[21] Vāts. also stated that bards (*kuśīlava*) lived upon prostitution of their wives,[22] and Yaś. identified them with wives of actors (*naṭa*) and dancers (*nartaka*) and said that they usually were prostitutes,[23] like wives of Cokṣa-s.[24] Vāts. also mentioned, *inter alia*, the wives of vintners (*saurika*), herdsman (*gopālaka*), and washermen (*rajaka*) as those with whom men about town should live on good terms.[25]

C. Very interesting statements can also be found in some of the Smṛti-s when the question of obligation of payments for debts between married people was explained. In ancient India, in principle, the husband was not obliged to pay for the debt incurred by the wife and vice-versa. However, this rule was not applied as far as debts of wives of those men who lived on their harlotry was concerned, since these husbands 'were dependent upon the earnings of their wives.' These exceptions were made for wives of vintners (*śauṇḍika*),[26] herdsmen (*gopa*),[27] hunters (*vyādha*),[28] dancers (*śailūṣa*),[29] and barbers (*nāpita*).[30] All these persons, as was stated in Y., Kāty., and N., lived on the earnings of their wives[31] who were considered in these contexts as engaged in harlotry.[32]

19. Śukr. 2. 202.
20. Vāts. 363. 13-4.
21. Vāts. 363. 20.
22. Vāts. 262. 7.
23. *Kuśīlavā-bhāryā naṭa-nartakā'dīnāṁ bharyā veśyā-prāyāḥ* (Vāts. 263. 5).
24. Vāts. 263. 22-3. Cf. Vāts. 262. 13.
25. Vāts. 72. 3-6.
26. Y. 2. 48; Mit. *ad* Y. 2. 48; Vi. 6. 37; Bṛh. 10. 119; N. 1. 19; Kāty. 568, 570.
27. Y. 2. 48; Mit. *ad* Y. 2. 48; Vi. 6.37; Bṛh. 10. 119; N. 1. 19; Kāty. 568- 570.
28. Y. 2. 48; Vi. 6.37; Bṛh. 10. 119; N. 1. 19; Kāty. 568, 570.
29. Y. 2. 48; Mit. *ad* Y. 2. 48; Vi. 6. 37.
30. Bṛh. 10. 119; Kāty. 568 (I read *nāpita* instead of *nāvika*).
31. Y. 2. 48; Kāty. 570; N. 1. 19.
32. Cf. *below study XII*; *Reciprocal Responsibility for Debts Contracted by Married Pepole.*

D. We also find in some of the Smṛti-s statements that these persons were impure and that touching their food was a sin for which a penance was foreseen. And so, Mn. stated that food of actors (*śailūṣa*), washermen (*rajaka* and *kāruka*), vintners (*śauṇḍika*), and bards (*nṛśaṁsa*)[33] should not be eaten, and Medh. explained that *śailūṣa* were identical with *naṭa*, that is, those who sold their wives to the public.[34] Vi. also mentioned actors (*śailūṣa*), washermen (*rajaka*), vintners (*śauṇḍika*), and actors (*rangāvatarin*);[35] similarly Y.,[36] adding, *inter alia*, bards (*bandin*) and those who lived from selling liquors (*surājīva*),[37] and Vās., enumerating *rajaka* and *śauṇḍika*.[38] Also *rajaka*, *śailūṣa*, and others were mentioned in the Agnipurāṇa.[39] We also find many references in minor Dharmaśāstra-s to impure food of washermen,[40] actors,[41] those who lived by singing and playing on musical instruments,[42] etc. Consequently, most of these sources stated that wives of those persons who gained their living on harlotry, were impure;[43] a *dvija* who had sexual intercourse with these women had to be purified by *taptakṛcchra*, *cāṇḍrāyaṇa*, *parāka*, or other penances.[44] These rules were introduced in the sources in consequence of the general rule that a *dvija* should not have sexual intercourse with a prostitute.[45]

These examples, taken not only from the Arthaśāstra-s, but also from the Dharmaśāstra-s and Kāmasūtra-s, made it clear that wives of different kinds of actors, bards and musicians, and acrobats, as well as wives of dancers, buffoons, vintners, herdsmen, hunters, and fishermen, enumerated in

33. Mn. 4. 214-6.
34. Medh. *ad* Mn. 4. 214.
35. Vi. 51. 13-5.
36. Y. mentioned *aṅgāvatārin* (1. 161) and *rajaka* (1. 162-4),
37. *bandin* (Y. 1. 165) and *surājīva* (Y. 1. 164).
38. Vās. 14. 3.
39. Agnipurāṇa 168. 4-5; cf. Śl. S. 20. 257-9.
40. *rajaka*. Āpastamba-Saṁhitā (ed. Dutt) 9. 31, 10. 12; Aṅgira 1. 3; Yama 1. 54; Atri 168.
41. *saliūṣa* in Atri 168. Cf. *naṭa* in Aṅgira 1. 3, Yama 1. 54, Atri 195-6 and 282.
42. Uśanas 4. 30.
43. Āpastamba-Saṁhiṭā 7.4.
44. Atri 169, 195-6, 282; Yama 1. 18-9, 55.
45. Cf. paragraph 19A, and notes 210-8 to Chapter II.

K., must be considered as engaged in harlotry and must be put on the same footing as other prostitutes.

31. *Rules relating to Prostitutes and Persons Living on Prostitution of Their Wives*

As we have seen above, K. stated : *etena naṭa nartaka-*, [etc.]......*vyākhyātāḥ*. It is not clear from the context what 'has been explained by that.' Should we understand that all preceding rules contained in the chapter entitled *gaṇikā'dhyakṣa* should apply to the persons considered as engaged in harlotry (*naṭa*, *nartaka*, etc.), or should we understand that these persons should be engaged in espionage activities like *gaṇikā-s* ?

Both translators of K., Shama Sastry and J. J. Meyer, failed to touch upon this problem, but translated this sentence as if they would be of the opinion that all the preceding rules, contained in the chapter on the *gaṇikā' dhyakṣa* referred to the persons engaged in harlotry.[46]

It seems, however, that what 'has been explained by that' referred only to the espionage activities of *gaṇikā-s* that is, their obligation to inform about the man who was under their influence.[47] The preceding sentence reads : *gaṇikā bhogam āyatiṁ puruṣaṁ ca nivedayet*, and K. continued : *etena naṭa...... vyākhyātāḥ*.[48]

It was explained above that, according to K., the *gaṇikā* was a government servant who had special rights and duties which were very specific for them and which could not be performed by other prostitutes (e. g. to hold the royal umbrella, pitcher, fan, to attend upon the royal litter, throne, or chariot, to receive a periodic salary, and many others arising from the fact that *gaṇikā-s* by entering the king's service had lost their freedom). In view of that and because the sentence beginnning with *etena* followed closely the rule stating that *gaṇikā-s* had also special espionage duties, it would seem that this rule meant that the persons enumerated in K. 125. 9-10, and, *per analogiam*, also other persons who were engaged in

46. Shama Sastry translated ; 'The same rules shall apply to an actor, etc.' J. J. Meyer translated : *Mit dieser (bisherigen Darlegung) ist auch das Nötige über die Weiber der Schauspieler......gesagt*

47. Cf. paragraph 21.

48. K. 125. 8-10.

harlotry,[49] were obliged to perform some espionage duties, particularly to inform the police officials about persons who were under their influence. This was due to the fact that persons who had sexual intercourse with prostitutes were considered to be suspected persons.[50]

It seems that this point of view is strengthened by the fact that K. in the last verse of the chapter entitled *gaṇikā-'dhyakṣa* stated :

saṁjñā-bhāṣāntarajñāś ca striyas teṣām anātmasu
cāraghāta-pramādārthaṁ prayojyā bandhu-vāhanāḥ[51]

'The wives of these persons[52] who know the signals and foreign languages, along with their relatives shall be used against the wicked ones [spies], shall spy on them, shall kill them, and shall make them incautious.' Thus, K. explained in this context that these persons were used generally as spies for many purposes. It should be also noted that we find in K. very often references to *naṭa*,[53] *nartaka*,[54] *gāyaka*,[55] *vādaka*,[56] *vāg-jīvana*,[57] *kuśīlava*,[58] *plavaka*,[59] *saubhika* or *sauhika*,[60] *cāraṇa*,[61] as well as *lubdhaka*[62] and *śauṇḍika*,[63] used as spies who had to convey special information.

32. *Taxes*

K. stated in the next sentence : *teṣāṁ tūryam āgantukaṁ pañca-paṇaṁ prekṣāvetanaṁ dadyāt.*[64] 'They bringing musical instru-

49. And encumerated in K. 158. 11-2 and maybe also in Śukr., Mn., B., Y., N., Bṛh. Kāty., Āp., Yama. Aṅg., Atri, Uś., Vāts. (Cf. paragraph 30 BCD).
50. Cf. K. 214. 14; paragraph 28 and 21.
51. K. 125. 17-8.
52. That is, those enumerated in K. 125. 9-10 quoted above.
53. E. g. K. 21. 2; 315. 17; 380. 1.
54. E. g. K. 21. 2; 315. 17.
55. E. g. K. 315. 17.
56. E. g. K. 21. 3; 315. 17.
57. E. g. K. 21. 3; 36. 11; 315. 17.
58. E. g. K. 21. 3; 249. 17; 315 17; Cf. K.44. 11; 202. 12; 248. 2.
59. E. g. K. 315. 18.
60. E. g. K. 315. 18.
61. E. g. K. 210. 15.
62. E. g. K. 390. 4, 44; 402. 10.
63. E. g. K. 210. 17; 378. 12; 379. 9; 389. 13.
64. K. 125. 11.

ments shall pay five *paṇa* as fee for public show.' K. considered these persons as nomads who did not stay always in the same place and, therefore, did not pay ordinary taxes. Thus, K. stated that they should pay a special fee to the king's treasury whenever they made a public performance. They, similarly as *rūpājīvā-s* and other prostitutes, had to pay taxes, hough not periodic taxes, while *gaṇikā-s* were exempt from taxes;[65] that seems to be one reason more for the undertanding that the preceding part of the chapter on the *gaṇikā' dhyakṣa* did not apply to them.[66]

V. CONCLUSIONS

Kauṭilya in his Arthaśāstra painted a very clear picture of the legal position of prostitutes. He divided them into two categories-*gaṇikā-s* and other persons gaining their living upon harlotry, and particularly described in detail the rights and duties of *gaṇikā-s* since he considered them to be government servants. As such, they received from the king's treasury a fixed salary and some objects for usufructual use during the performance of their duties, special training, and security in case of inability to earn their living, particularly due to age or illness; but they lost their personal freedom and freedom of disposing freely of their income which had to be turned over to the king's treasury; their children as well had no personal freedom, but both could be ransomed when they, or somebody else paid a redemption sum for them. They had also to perform special functions, such as espionage, with which they were charged. *Gaṇikā-s*, being king's servants, enjoyed also special protection against any offences committed towards them; this was introduced particularly in view of the fact that any damage caused to them injured the king's treasury. K. introduced in his Arthaśāstra a State prostitution with public houses run by the government for which a special officer, superintendent of prostitutes, a State minister of prostitutes, was responsible.

The legal position of prostitutes, as described in K., does not seem to be an abstract or theoretical picture. Sanskrit literary works, such as Budhasvāmin's Bṛhat-Kathā Śloka-

65. Cf. paragraph 27.
66. Cf. below study VII on Legal Position of Women whose Husbands live on their Earnings.

saṁgraha, Vātsyāyana's Kāmasūtra, Dāmodragupta's Kuṭṭanīmata, Kṣemendra's Samayamātṛkā and Kalāvilāsa, the Śukasaptati, Somadeva's Kathāsaritsāgara, and many others contained stories which confirmed and complemented the rules contained in K. Legal rules contained in major and minor Dharmaśāstra-s also endorsed legal implications of contractual obligations of *gaṇikā-s* who concluded agreements with their paramours.

We also find in K. rules dealing with other prostitutes than *gaṇikā-s* government servants; these rules were not so complete, since K. was more interested in *artha* than in *dharma*. However, although these rules did not give a full picture of the rights and obligations of these persons, with the exception of their obligations to serve as spies, they supplemented in some details the rules relating to *gaṇikā-s*; these rules, if not contradictory to the institution of *gaṇikā-s*, serving as king's servants, had to be applied *per analogiam* to *gaṇikā-s*.

Kauṭilya's Arthaśāstra is a unique source for the comprehension of the legal position of prostitutes, particularly from the point of view of the State and for the introduction of State prostitution in ancient India.

VII

LEGAL POSITION OF WOMEN WHOSE HUSBANDS LIVE ON THEIR EARNINGS*

1. In the ancient Indian literature we find more than 250 synonyms for the word prostitute,[1] of which some twenty are found in the Dharmaśāstra-s and Arthaśāstra-s.[2] These synonyms of the word *veśyā* denoted various kinds of prostitutes, harlots, courtesans, etc.

The Dharmaśāstra-s, and more particularly the Arthaśāstra-s, contained specific rules on the rights and duties of prostitutes, so that their legal position seems to be well defined.[3] Particularly, interesting is the legal position of prostitutes in K. It is evident from this Arthaśāstra that prostitutes, if called *gaṇikā*, were government servants, who got a fixed salary from the king's treasury, and security in the event of becoming unable to earn their living, and enjoyed special protection, but lost their personal freedom as long as they served as king's servants and were not ransomed.[4]

To the group of prostitutes, irrespective of whether they were called *veśyā*, *gaṇikā*, or *rūpājīvā*, etc., a new group might be added : a group of women whose husbands lived on their earnings, that is, gained their livelihood from their wives' prostitution.

Mn., B., K., Śukr. and other sources did not call these women prostitutes, but gave a long list of men whose wives were known to be engaged in prostitution. These were the wives of actors (*raṅgāvatārin*, *naṭa*, *tālāpacara*, *nṛśaṁsa*), wander-

*Previously appeared as JSAIL, 18 in the "Siddha-Bhāratī, being Dr. Siddheshwar Varma Presentation Volume", Part 2, pp. 295-305.

1. L. Sternbach : *First* and *Second Supplements to Veśyā*; *Synonyms and Aphorisms* in Bh. V., Bombay 1945; VIII. p. 256 sqq. and XI. 49 sqq. where 330 synonyms are quoted.
2. See above study VI.
3. Cf. fn. 1 p.
4. Cf. fn. 1; Ch. V.

ing bards or bards (*cāraṇa, kuśīlava, bandin*), dancers (*nartaka, śailūṣa*), rope-dancers (*plavaka*), jugglers (*saubhika*), singers (*gāyaka*), players on musical instruments (*vādaka*)[5], buffoons (*vāgjīvana*) fishermen (*matsyabandhaka*), herdsmen (*gopālaka, gopa*), hunters (*lubdhaka, vyādha*), washermen (*rajaka, kāruka*), vintners (*sauṇḍika, saurika, surājīvin*), and barbers (*nāpita*).[6]

The procurers *sensu stricto* were called : *strīvyavahārin, bandhakīpoṣaka, plavaka, naṭa, nartaka, saubhika*).

2. We find some specific statements in respect of these persons in Mn. B., Y., Kāty., N. and, particularly, K. and Śukr.

Mn. (8. 362), after having explained that no man, under the penalty of one *suvarṇa*, should converse with wives of others (Mn. 8.361),[7] stated:

naiṣa cāraṇa-dāreṣu vidhir nā'tmo'pajīviṣu
sajjayanti hi te nārīr nigūhāś cārayanti ca.

This rule does not apply to wives of wandering bards or of those who live on (prostitution of) their own (wives); for, such men secretly bring their wives into contract (with other men) and tempt them on.'

An almost identical rule is found in B. (2.2. 4. 3), where it was said :

na tu cāraṇa-dāreṣu na raṅgā'vatate vadhaḥ,
saṁsarjayanti tā hy etān niguptāṁś cālayanty api.

'But no punishment for (intercourse) with wives of wandering bards and actors; for, such men carry them (to other men) or, lying concealed, permit them to have culpable intercourse.'

Both these texts stated in similar words that men might have sexual intercourse with wives of *cāraṇa* (according to Medh.

5. And those who made their living by playing musical instruments, also lived on the earnings of their wives (*vādyajāyāprajīviṇaḥ, Śukr.* 2. 202).

6. Vātsyāyana (*Kāmasūtra*, 262 : 7) clearly stated that bards (*kuśīlava*) lived upon the prostitution of their wives, and Yaśodhara in his commentary identified them with actors (*naṭa*) and dancers (*nartaka*) and said that their wives, usually were prostitutes (*kusīlavabhāryā naṭanartakādīnāṁ bhāryā veśyaprāyāḥ* 263. 5) ; similarly, as wives of *Cokṣas* (263. 22-3 ; cf. 262. 13). Vātsyāyana also mentioned *inter alia* the wives of vintners (*saurika*) herdsmen (*gopālaka*) and washermen (*rajaka*) as those with whom men about the town should live on good terms (72 : 3-6). In Sanskrit literature the barber was very often mentioned in the meaning of a procurer, e.g. Sts. tale 62.

7. Also quoted in VyK. 125, VRK. 387, RDhK. 130, VCi. 174-5, DV. 158, Vīr. *ad* Y. 2. 285, VyPr. 401, VT. 801, VV. 265, VyS. 154, AP. 2. 285.

the word *cāraṇa* denoted not only wandering bards, but also dancers, actors and singers and according to Govinda also (*devadāsīs*), *raṅgāvatārin* (actors and other *ātmopajīvin* (those living on prostitution of their wives), but *nigūḍhāḥ*, that is as Medh. explained (*ad* Mn. VIII. 362, 22/4),' not in an open market.' In this lies the difference between regular prostitutes and the group of women whose husbands lived on their prostitution. The latter could not be found in the open market, but carried on their occupation within their own houses.'[8]

These women had according to the commentary by Medh., another additional duty : they had to seduce wives of other men, in order that they also act as prostitutes.[9] In that way this group of women acted as prostitutes as well as procuresses.

3. According to many Sanskrit sources, prostitutes were considered as impure persons, and food given by them had not to be eaten (Mn. 4.209; Y. 1. 161; Vi. 51. 7; Vās. 14. 10; Agn. P. 168. 3-7 and other). In conformity with this rule, the Dharmaśāstra-s and other Sanskrit sources stated that persons living on the prostitution of their wives were also, considered as impure. Thus, Mn. (4.214-6) stated that food of actors (*śailūṣa*), washermen (*rajaka, kāruka*),[10] vintners (*śauṇḍika*) and bards (*nṛśaṁsa*) should not be eaten.[11] *Naṭa-s* were also considered by Medh. as *śailūṣa*, that was those who sold their wives in public (Medh. *ad* Mn. 4. 214)[12]; Vi. (51. 13-5) mentioned, similarly, actors (*śailūṣa, raṅgāvatārin*), washermen (*rajaka*) and vintners (*śauṇḍika*).[13] Similarly Y. (1. 161-5)

8. *gṛha-veṣatvād eva tāḥ prasiddha-veśyābhyo bhidyante* (Medh. *ad* Mn. 8. 362; 222. 7).

9. *athavā svā nārīḥ "sajjayanti" yojayanti, ānyāś ca svastrībhiś; "cārayanti" pravartayanti veśyātvaṁ kuṭṭanītvaṁ ca svadārāṇāṁ kārayantī'ty arthaḥ* (Medh. *ad* Mn. 8. 362; 222. 9-10).

10. We also read in *Apastamba-Saṁhitā* (VII. 4) that washerwomen were impure.

11. *piśunā 'nṛtinoś cā 'nnaṁ kratu-vikrayakasya ca,*
śailūṣa-tunna-vāyān-naṁ kṛtaghna syān-nam eva ca.
karmārasya niṣādasya raṅgāvatarakasya ca,
suvarṇa-kartur veṇasya śastra-vikrayiṇas tathā.
śvavatāṁ śauṇḍi kānāṁ ca cailanirṇejakasya ca,
rañjakasya nṛśaṁsasya yasya co'papatir gṛhe. (Mn. 4. 214-6).

12. *śailūṣo naṭaḥ* (Medh. *ad* Mn. 4. 214).

13. *śailūṣa-tontuvāya-kṛtaghna-rajakānāṁ ca; karmakāra-niṣāda-raṅgāvatāri-veṇaśastra-vikrayiṇāṁ ca; śvājīvi-śauṇḍika-tailika-caila-nirṇejakānaṁ ca.* (Vi. 51. 13-5).

adding *inter alia* bards, (*bandin*) and those who sold liquors (*surājīvin*)[14] and Vās. (14.3) mentioned washermen (*rajaka*) and vintners (*śauṇḍika*).[15] Agn.P. (168. 4, 5) mentioned washermen and actors (*śailūṣa*).[16] The latter were also, mentioned in *Atri-Saṁhitā* (168)[17]; actors (*naṭa*) in *Aṅgiras-Saṁhitā* (1. 3).[18] *Yama-Saṁhitā* (1. 54-5),[19] *Atri-Saṁhitā* (195-6, 282)[20]; those who lived from singing and playing on musical instruments in *Uśanas-Saṁhitā* (4. 30).[21]

Since these persons were impure, a *dvija*, who had sexual intercourse with their wives, had to be purified by *taptakṛcchra cāndrāyaṇa*, *parāka*, or other penance(*Atri-Saṁhitā* 169.195-6[22]-[23]; *Yama-Saṁhitā* 1. 18-9; 55[24]-[25]).

14. *kadarya-baddha-caurāṇāṁ klība-raṅgā-vatāriṇāṁ,*
vaiṇabhiśasta-vārddhuṣya-gaṇikā-gaṇadī-kṣiṇāṁ,
cikitsakā 'tura-kruddha-puṁścalī-mattavidviṣāṁ,
krūrogra-patita-vrātya-dāmbhiko 'cchiṣṭa-bhojināṁ.
avīrā-strī-svarṇakāra-strījita-grāmayājinām,
śastra-vikrayi-karmāra-tantuvāyaś vavṛttinām,
nṛśaṁsa-rāja-rajaka-kṛtaghna-vadha-jīvinām,
caila-dhāva-surājīva-sahopapati-veśmanām.
piśunānṛtinoś caiva tathā cākrika-bandinām, ,
eṣām annaṁ na bhoktavyaṁ soma-vikrayiṇas tathā. (Y. 1. 161-5).

15. *kadarya-dīkṣita-baddhā'tura-soma-vikrāyitakṣa-rajaka-śauṇḍika-sūcakavardhuṣika-carma-vakṛntānām.* (Vās. 14. 3).

16. *rajakasya nṛśaṁsasya bandinaḥ kitavasya ca,*
mithyā-tapa-sinaś caiva caura-daṇḍikayos tathā.
kuṇḍa-golaka-strījitānāṁ veda-vikrayiṇas tathā,
śailūṣa-tantra vāyā 'nnaṁ kṛtaghnasyā 'nnam eva ca (Agn. P. 158. 4-5.)

17. *rajakaḥ śailūṣūś caiva veṇu-karmo 'pajīvinaḥ,*
eteṣāṁ yas tu bhuṅkte vai dvijaś cāndrāyaṇam caret. (Atri. 168).

18. *rajakaś-carmakāraś ca naṭo varūḍa eva ca,*
kaivarttam edabhillāś ca saptaite cā 'ntyajāḥ smṛtāḥ.
(Āṅgira 3; similarly Piṭamāha).

19. Yama 54-5. See above Āṅgira 3. Yama adds:
eṣāṁ gatvā tu yoṣāṁ vai tapta-kṛcchaṁ samācaret.

20. Atri 195-6. See Āṅgira 3 above. Atri adds :
eṣāṁ gatvā striyo mohād bhuktvā ca pratigṛhya ca,
kṛcchrā 'bdam ācarej-jñānād ajñānādaindava-dvayam.
Atri has on another place the following:
carmako rajako vaiṇyo dhīvaro naṭakas tathā.
etān spṛṣṭvā dvijo mohād ācāmet praya to' pi san. (Atri 282).

21. *paunarbhavaḥ kusīdī ca tathā nakṣatra-darśakaḥ,*
gīta-vāditra-śīlaś ca vyādhitaḥ kāṇa eva ca. (Uśana 4. 30).

22. *sarvā 'ntya jānām gamane bhojane sampraveśane,*
parākeṇa viśuddhiḥ syād bhagavān atrir abravīt. (Atri 169).

23. See fn. 20.

24. *astaṁ gato yadā sūryaś cāṇḍāla-rajaka-striyah,*
saṁspṛṣṭās tu tadā kaiścit prāyaścittaṁ kathaṁ bhavet,
jātarūpaṁ suvarṇaṁ ca divānītaṁ ca yaj jalam,
teṇa snātvā ca pītvā ca sarve te sucayaḥ smṛtāḥ. (Yama 18-9).

25. See fn. 19.

4. K. almost at the end of the Chapter (II. 27) entitled *gaṇikā'dhyakṣa* and dealing with *gaṇikās* stated :

etena naṭa-nartaka-gāyika-vādaka-vāgjīvana-kuśīlava-plavaka-saubhika-cāraṇānāṁ strī-vyavahāriṇēṁ striyo gūḍha jīvāś ca vyākyātāḥ (K. 125. 9-10).

"By that are explained (the duties) of women making their living secretly (*gūḍhajīvin*, such as), women of actors (*naṭa*), dancers (*nartaka*), singers (*gāyeka*), players on musical instruments (*vādaka*), buffoons (*vāgjīvana*), bards (*kuśīlava*), rope-dancers (*plavaka*), jugglers (*saubhika*), wandering bards (*cāraṇa*) and procurers (*strīvyavahārin*)."

It is not clear from this context what the words 'by that are explained' meant. They could either mean that to these persons all the preceding rules which refer to *gaṇikā-s* applied, or that these persons had to be engaged in espionage activities, as *gaṇikā-s* were.

Both translators of K., Shama Sastry and J. J. Meyer, did not touch upon this problem, but translated this sentence as if they were of the opinion that all the preceding rules contained in the Chapter of the *gaṇikā'dhyakṣa* referred to persons engaged in halotry.[26]

It seems, however, that words 'by that are explained' referred only to the espionage activities of these persons, that is to their obligation to inform about the men who were under their influence. The preceding sentence reads : *gaṇikā bhogam āyatiṁ puruṣaṁ ca nivedayet* and K. continued : *etena naṭa......vyākhyātāḥ* (125. 8-10).

According to K. the *gaṇikā* was a government servant, and had specific rights and duties which could not be performed by other prostitutes (e. g. to hold the royal umbrella, pitcher, fan; to attend upon the royal litter, throne or chariot; to receive a periodic salary and many other rights and duties arising from the fact that the *gaṇikā*, by entering the king's service, had lost her personal freedom). In view of that, and in view of the fact that the sentence beginning with *etena* followed closely the rule stating that the *gaṇikā* had also

26. Shama Sastry translated : 'The same rules apply to an actor...'. J. J. Meyer translated : '*Mit dieser (bisheriger Darlegung) ist auch das nötige über die Weiber der Schauspieler...gesagt.*'

special espionage duties, it seems that this rule meant that the persons enumerated in K. 125. 9-10 (including those living on prostitution of their wives and quoted above) and *per analogiam* also other persons who were engaged in prostitution and enumerated in K. 151. 11-2, such as *tālāpacara*, *cāraṇa*, *matsyabandhaka*, *lubdhaka*, *gopālaka* and *śauṇḍika*,[27] were obliged to perform some espionage duties, in particular to inform the police and city officials about persons who were under their influence. According to K. the *gaṇikā* was obliged to inform the *gaṇikā'dhyakṣa* about the *puruṣa*, that is the man who had spent time with her, once or more frequently, as well as about the payment for enjoyment and other gifts received by her.[28]-[29] This was due to the fact that the persons who had sexual intercourse with prostitutes were considered to be suspect[30] and dangerous[31] persons with whom enemies of the king might hide.[32-33]

The point of view that the sentence beginning with the word *etena* referred to the special espionage duties of persons engaged in prostitution is strengthened by the fact that

27. As well as enumerated in some Dharmaśāstra-s (see above).

28. *gaṇikā bhogam āyantiṁ puruṣaṁ ca nivedayet.* (K. 125. 8).

29. It should be noted that 'Abul Qādir Ibn i Mulūk Shāh of Badaōn in his *Muntskhab-ul-Tawarīkh*. the commentary on 'Abul Fazl 'Allani's *Aīn-i-Akbarī* mentioned that a Dārogah (similar to the *gaṇikā' dhyakṣya*) and a clerk also were appointed to register the name of those men who went to prostitutes, or wanted to take some of them to their houses; no one was allowed to take dancing girls to his house without permission.

30. Cf. K. 241. 14.

31. Cf. Mn. 11. 259., 4, 209, 219., 5. 90; Y. 1. 161 ; Vi., 51.7, 53. 29; Vās. 14. 10 and others.

32. Cf. below study *VIII Legal Position of Physicians in Ancient India*, Chapter III. C. K. 203 : 13 sqq. 144 : 11 sqq.

33. Mahābhārata (12. 88. 14-5) stated :

pānāgāraniveśāś ca veśyāḥ prāpaṇikas ṭatha,
kuśīlavāḥ sakitavā ye cā 'nye kecid īdṛśāḥ.
niyamyāḥ sarva evai'te ye rāṣṭrasyo'paghātakāḥ,
ete rāṣṭre 'bhitiṣṭanto vādhante bhadrikāḥ prajāḥ.

(Similarly MBh. 12. 140. 40-2; the hisory of Agaḍadatta in J. Jacobi's *Ausgewählte Erzahlungen in Mahārāṣṭrī*). These places should be carefully watched (Bārhaspatyasūtra (Nitiśāstra, 3. 27)).

Also the very often repeated reading :
daśa-sūnā-samaṁ cakraṁ daśa-cakra-sami dhvajaḥ,
daśa-dhvaja-sama veśya daśa-veśyā -samo nṛpaḥ. (MBh. 13. 125. 9).
(cf. Mn. 4. 84 01 85 in the Bombay edition, Y. 1. 141 and Vivādaratnākara 335. 7; MBh. 2. 68. 1). where it was stated that gamblers had in their homes many loose women (*bandhakī*), shows that prostitutes (the word *gaṇikā* was here not used) were considered as dangerous persons. See also study XVII below.

K. in the last verse (125. 17-8) of the Chapter entitled *gaṇikā'-dhyakṣa* stated :

saṁjñā'bhāṣāntarajñāś ca striyas teṣām anātmasu,
cāraghāta-pramādā'rthaṁ prayojyā bandhuvāhanāḥ.

'The wives of these persons[34] who know the signals and foreign languages as well as their relatives, shall be used against the wicked ones (spies), shall spy on them, kill them and to induce them imprudence.

Thus, K. explained in this context that these persons were used generally as spies for many purposes. It should be, also, noted that we find in K. very often various references to *naṭa*[35], *nartaka*[36], *gāyaka*[37], *vādaka*[38], *vāgjīvana*[39], *kuśilava*[40] *plavaka*,[41] *saubhika* or *sauhika*[42], *cāraṇa*[43], as well as *lubdhaka*[44] and *śauṇḍika*[45] used as spies who had to convey some special informations.

5. According to the Sanskrit sources prostitutes, who were not government servants (*gaṇikā*), had to pay taxes to the Collector-General.[46] *Rūpājīvā-s* had to pay monthly a tax twice the amount of their payment for enjoyment (*bhoga*, [K. 125. 12)])[47] and if the king was in distress he could collect from them an extraordinary tax amounting to half of their salary K. (243. 11).[48]

However, persons living on the prostitution of their wives, being considered as nomadic, had to pay not ordinary taxes but special fees for their public shows. K. (125. 11) in

34. That is those enumerated in K. 125. 9-10.
35. E. g. K. 21. 2; 315. 17; 380. 1.
36. E. g. K. 21. 2; 315. 7.
37. E. g. K. 315. 17.
38. E. g. K. 21. 3; 315. 17.
39. E.g. K. 21. 3; 36. 11; 315.17.
40. E.g. K. 21. 3; 249. 17; 315. 17. Cf. K. 44. 11; 202. 12; 248. 2.
41. E. g. K. 315.18.
42. E.g. K. 315.18.
43. E.g. K. 210. 15.
44. E.g. K. 390. 4. 44; 402 10
45. E.g. K. 210. 17; 378. 12; 379. 9; 389. 13.
46. Cf. above study VI *Legal Position of Prostitutes according to Kauṭilya's Arthaśastra*; paragraph 27.
47. The word *rūpājīvā* meant in this context all kinds of prostitutes with the exception of *gaṇikā-s*; cf. fn. 46 above
48. E.g. *vetana*. This sentence referred, probably, to *avaruddhā-s* or *bhujiṣyā-s*. Cf. fn. 46.

a sentence immediately following the word *etena* stated : *teṣāṁ tūryam āgantukaṁ pañca-paṇaṁ prekṣāvetanaṁ dadyāt.*

'Those, who bring musical instruments, shall pay five *paṇas* as fee for the public show.'

This meant that according to K. they should pay a special fee to the king's treasury, whenever they gave a public performance. They, like *rūpājīvā-s* and other prostitutes, had to pay taxes, although not periodic taxes, while *gaṇikā-s* were exempt from paying taxes ; that seems to be another reason that the preceding part of the Chapter on the *gaṇika'dhyakṣa* of K. did not apply to them.

6. Persons living on the prostitution of their wives depended on their earnings. Therefore, they were obliged to pay for the debts incurred by them. According to Y. (2.48)[49], Vi. (6.37),[50] Bṛh. (10. 119),[51] N. (1 19)[52] and Kāty. (568-70)[53] in case of *śauṇḍika* (Y. and Mit. *ad* Y., Vi., Bṛh., N., Kāty.), *gopa* (Y., Vi., Bṛh., N., Kāty.). *vyādha* (Y. Vi., Bṛh., N., Kāty.), *śailūṣa* (Y., Mit. *ad* Y., Vi.,) and *nāpita*[54] Bṛh., Kāty.) the general rule contained in the Smṛti-s about the division of the estates of married people was not applied, and the husbands of these prsons were under the obligation to pay for the debts incurred by their wives.[55]

49. *gopa-śauṇḍika-śailūśa-rajaka-vyādha-yoṣitām,*
ṛṇaṁ dadyāt patistāsaṁ yasmad vṛttis tadāśrayā. (Y. 2. 48. Also quoted in VVy. 2. 50, VyK. 122, SC. 175, VRK. 59, SCM. 14, NṛP. 20, VyPr. 174, VyM. 83, VT. 506, VV. 29, VyS. 86, AP. 254. 8).

50. *gopa-śauṇḍika-śaiūṣa-rajaka-vyādha-strīṇaṁ patir dadyāt.* (Vi. 6. 37. Also quoted in SC. 174, VRK. 55, VyS. 86).

51. *sauṇḍika-vyādha-rajaka-gopa-nāpita-yoṣitām,*
adhiṣṭhātā ṛṇaṁ dāpyas tāsāṁ bhartṛ-kriyāsu. (Bṛh. 10. 119. Also quoted in VRK. 60, VV. 30).

52. *anyatra rajaka-vyādha-gopa-śauṇḍika-yoṣitām,*
teṣāṁ tat pratyayā-vṛttiḥ kuṭumbaṁ ca tad āśrayam. (N. 1. 19, NMS. 4. 19; Also quoted in ViR. 2. 50, VyK. 122, SC. 175, VCi. 28, VyPr. 174, VT. 505, VyS. 86, VVy. 30, AP. 2. 48.

53. *śauṇḍika-vyādha-janaka-gopa-nāvika-yoṣitām,*
adhiṣṭhātā ṛṇaṁ dāpyas tāsāṁ bhartṛ-kriyāsu tat.
na ca bhāryā-kṛtam ṛṇaṁ kathaṁ cit patyur ābhavet,
āpat kṛtādṛte puṁsāṁ kuṭumbā 'rthe hi vistaraḥ.
anyatra rajaka-vyādha-gopa-śauṇḍika-yoṣitām,
teṣāṁ tu tat parā vṛttiḥ kuṭumbaṁ ca tad āśrayam. (Kāty. 568-70. Also quoted in VyK. 122, VyPr. 274; SCM. 13).

54. Not *nāvika*.

55. See below Study XII on *Reciprocal Responsibilities for Debts Contracted by Married People*, par. 7.

7. In conclusion it might be stated that in addition to various kinds of *veśyā*, *rūpājīvā*, *gaṇikā*, etc. who were considered as harlots, prostitutes or courtesans and whose legal position was quite clearly defined in the Dharmaśāstra-s, another group of persons should be added : women whose husbands lived on their earnings (prostitution). They were wives of actors, bards, dancers, jugglers, singers, etc., that was women who did not need to be necessarily their legal wives. The difference between these women and regular prostitutes lies in the fact that the first carried out their occupation in their own houses and could not be found 'in an open market', they acted not only as prostitutes but also as procusreses as they had to seduce also wives of other men. Acting in both capacities, they were considered as if they were prostitutes of the lowest class. They were, therefore, always considered as impure and a *dvija* was not allowed to have sexual intercourse with them; according to K. they had to perform espionage work, like other prostitutes.

According to K. these women were, like *gaṇikā-s*, not completely free persons. However, while *gaṇikā-s*, according to K., depended on the king, these women depended on their "husbands", and in some cases, procurers. Therefore, according to the Dharmaśāstra-s, there did not exist in their case any division of conjugal estate, or, more correctly, the husbands of these women were under the obligation to pay for the debts incurred by their wives, although, usually, they would not be under this obligation. They[56] also had to pay taxes not depending on their income but fees for each public performance.

As was said above, although women, whose husbands lived on their prostitution might be considered as regular prostitutes, the Dharmaśāstra-s and Arthaśāstra-s made some small distinctions between them and regular prostitutes.

56. These women.

VIII

LEGAL POSITION OF PHYSICIANS IN ANCIENT INDIA*

1. *INTRODUCTION*

1. It is generally accepted that the origin and growth of the science of Āyurveda and the rise of the early schools of medicine in India were as follows[1] :

(a) Primitive medicine. Very little data on this subject are now available. This period may be looked upon as a prelude to the Indus Valley Civilization and the Vedic medicine.

(b) Early Vedic medicine. Gods such as Rudra, Soma, Varuṇa, Vāstoṣpati, Ādityas, Maruts, Vāta, etc. had as one of their numerous attributes the power of causing or revealing diseases.

In the Ṛgveda (X-97, 6) the physician (*bhiṣaj*) was called *vipraḥ sa ucyate bhiṣag rakṣohāmīvacātanaḥ*.

Rudra "bearing in his hand a sharp weapon, a pure one; mighty; bearing healing medicines" was called "the best of physicians" (*bhiṣaktamo bhiṣajām*),[2] or "first divine physician",[3] or god "who has caused disease" ; he "shall perform the cure" and "prepare remedies...together with early physicians".[4]

Indra was called "restorer of limbs, sight and whole life", "releaser from the unknown disease phthisis", "releaser from influence of evil planets", "protector and granter of life". Many prayers to Indra for good health and protection from illness were contained in the Ṛgveda.

* Previously appeared as JSAIL. 14 in the "Annals of Bhandarkar Oriental Research Institute." Vol. XXIX, Parts I-IV, pp. 21-42; Vol. XXX, parts I-II, pp. 1-22.

1. D. V. S. Reddy's Indian Medicine, its Origin and the Rise of Early Medical Schools in *The Journal of the Indian Medical Association*, Volume VII. No. 11, 663.
2. Ṛgveda.
3. Yajurveda.
4. Atharvaveda.

Soma was the god who "healed whatever was sick". The fermented juice of the soma-plant (*soma rasa*) made "the blind see and the lame walk".

Varuṇa was the owner of a hundred thousand medical drugs."

Vāstoṣpati was "the deliverer from disease."

(c) The appearance of physicians among Gods (i.e. of the Aśvin twins). These twin horseman were "the divine physicians." They were the healers of the blind" (*andha*), of "emaciated" (*kṛśa*), of the lame (*ruta*, *śroṇa*, *srāma*).[5] They gave sight to Ṛjrāsva blinded by his father,[6] restored youth to Cyavāna and prolonged his life when he became old and decrepit.[7] When the beautiful maiden Viśpalā had her leg cut off in Khela's battle during the night, the Aśvins supplied her with an iron limb (*jaṅghām āyasīm*).[8] They saved Bhujyu from drowing, Atri from a fiery pit, and made the lame walk[9];

(d) Celestial physicians begun to treat or cure human beings, or appear on earth as the incarnation of Viṣṇu or Dhanvantari, to propagate the knowledge of Āyurveda, among the mortals. Āyurveda was attributed to Viṣṇu who was a teacher of medical science. He was also called Sudhāpāṇi "the carrier of nectar in his hands."

(e) Indian sages besought divine beings or incarnation of Dhanvantarī to teach them Āyurveda for the relief of ailing mankind.

5. Ṛgveda (10-39; 1-112, 8), etc.
6. Ṛgveda (1-116, 16).
7. Ṛgveda (10-39,4).
8. Ṛgveda (1-116, 15).
9. Compare R. F. G. Müller's Die Medizin in Ṛgveda in *Asia Major,* Volume VI, 4, p. 370; P. J. Sarma's The Art of Healing in Ṛgveda in *Annals of Medical History*, Volume I, 1939; H. Zimmer's *Altindisches Leben*, 397.

Of the many hymns offered to the Aśvin twins P. J. Sarma quoted the following :

Ye place the germ in female creatures,
Ye place it within all beings, the fire,
O Aśvins, mighty ones, ye set in motion,
The water and the forest trees.
Ye are physicians with your remedies
and charioteers with your chariot skill;
Ye also strong ones, bestow lordship
On him who with a sacrifice
Honours you in his heart.

(f) Bhāradvāja, Ātreya, Agniveśa and colleagues of Suśruta and his co-pupils wrote learned treatise based upon the lectures they had heard and propagated the theory and practice of medicine, among the learned classes of ancient India. There seemed to have been two principal centres of medical education, Takṣaśilā and Kāśī (Vārāṇasī), the former famous for its philosophical treatment of the subject, particularly of internal medicine, and the latter for the elucidation of the practical aspects, particularly, surgical procedures and techniques.

It is clear, therefore, that medicine and medicinal books had a very early origin. We find some mention of anatomy in the Śatapatha-Brāhmaṇa (X and XII) and the Atharvaveda. The Āyurveda contains the greatest part of the ancient knowledge of medicine.

The Buddhist literature also contains many references on medicine. In the legends, we often come across the physician Jīvaka, who studied the Ātreya medicine in Takṣaśilā. Also in Vinayapiṭaka many different types of medicines, were enumerated.

The most important medical works are, however, the Caraka-Saṁhītā, the Suśruta-Saṁhitā and the Vāgbhaṭa. When preparing this study was necessary to refer to these works, although the main sources of reference were the Dharmaśāstra-s and the Arthaśāstra-s.

It is said that Caraka lived in the time of Kaniṣka (second century A.D.). Suśruta was also an old author. Suśruta, however, lived after Caraka, probably, at the end of the second or the beginning of the third century A. D.

These are only the most important medical works. There were many others but this study does not intend to describe the medical system in ancient India, or the medical profession of 'those times, but solely the legal position of physicians in ancient India, according to the available legal Indian literature.[10]

10. It should be emphasized that in this introductory section only general reference has been made to medical literature and medicine in Ancient India. For more details see J. Jolly's *Medizin, zur Quellenkunde*; M. Winternitz's *Geschichte der Indischen Litteratur*, 3-541 sqq; A. F. R. Hoernle's *Studies in the Medicine in Ancient India* and bibliographies quoted there. It is not possible to enumerate in this short study the other numerous works on this subject.

II. MEDICAL STUDY AND PREPARATION FOR MEDICAL PRACTICE

2. *Definition of "Physicians"*

A. *In Juridical Sources*

Sanskrit words commonly used in the Dharmaśāstra-s and Arthaśāstra-s to designate physicians were : *cikitsaka*, the experienced, the physician : *bhiṣaj*, the healer ; and *vaidya*, the learned, the skilled in art of curing.[1]

The physician (*cikitsaka*) was defined in Vīr. (*ad* Y. 1-162) as one whose means of subsistance was diagnosis[2] and in Mit. (*ad* Y. 1-162) as one whose means of subsistence was medicine.[3] More specific, however, is, the definition found in Śukr. (2-183) where it was stated that a physician (*bhiṣaj*) was one who could discover the nature of diseases by a study of their causes and symptoms, and one who gave remedies and tried prescriptions after ascertaining whether the diseases were curable or incurable.[4]

B. *In Non-juridical Sources*

The non-juridical sources define the physician in more medical terms e.g. Car. (3-1. 39) stated that a physician was one who was "conversant with the tastes, all articles of food and drink, the faults, and diseases in respect to their potency." He should also know the place and time and the elements which made up the body and governed its respective functions.[5] Such a physician (i.e. who was conversant with the tastes and their use)[6] was never stupefied when ascertaining causes and symptoms, means of mitigation and cure of the many diseases which afflicted mankind (Car. I-26).

1. Āp. also used in one instance the word *śalyakṛnta*, the remover or cutter of splinters (similarly MBh. *śalyakarttṛ*). This word was used in addition o *cikitsaka* and denoted a surgeon. Amarakośa quoted in addition to *bhiṣaj*, *vaidya* and *cikitsaka—rogahārin* and *agadaṅkāra* (II-6, 2, 8).
2. *cikitsakaḥ cikitsāvṛttiḥ.*
3. *cikitsako bhiṣag-vṛtty-upajīvī.*
4. *hetuliṅgīṣadhībhir yo tryādhīnāṁ tattvaniścayam,*
   sādhyāsādhyaṁ viditvopakramate sa bhiṣak smṛtaḥ.
5. *rasān dravyāṇi doṣāṁś ca vikārāṁś ca prabhāvataḥ,*
   veda yo deśakālau ca śarīraṁ ca sa no bhiṣak (3-1, 39).
6. And with the varieties of manner in which the faults may be excited.

3. *Qualifications for a Medical Student*

According to the medical literature (the juridical sources, with few exceptions, did not contain similar rules (a person who intended to become a physician had to be well behaved, brave, clean in habits, modest, bodily strong, firm, intelligent and had to possess good memory and the desire to learn and achieve success.[7]

The external nature of a candidate for a physician also played a great role. A medical pupil had to have an honest face, nose and eyes, a thin tongue and lips, straight teeth, as well as a cheerful disposition, good address, and ability to bear trouble and pain.[8] Similar, but more detailed attributes of a medical pupil were enumerated in Car. (3.8).

Suś. (1-2) stated that if the candidate did not possess these attributes he would not be admitted as a medical pupil.

It is clear that all these "conditions" had to be considered only as advice and *eo ipso* as *lex imperfecta*.

A physician could take as a pupil a person who possessed all these qualities, provided that he was a son of a Brāhmaṇa, Kṣatriya or Vaiśya of good family, and was sixteen years old.[9] On the other hand, Vās. (3.3) stated that he who practised medicine could not be called a Brāhmaṇa.[10]

Mn. (10.47) stated that physicians belonged to *ambaṣṭha*[11] i.e. sons from a Brāhmaṇa and a Vaiśya woman.[12] In any case a physician could not belong to a Śūdra caste, or to a mixed caste in which the man or woman belonged to the Śūdra caste, although Suś. (1.2) stated that "some say a Śūdra of good family and character might be admitted as a pupil but without the recitation of the *mantra-s*."

Car. (3.8) stated generally that the pupil should belong

7. Suś. (1-2).
8. Suś. (1-2).
9. Suś. (1-2).
10. *nānṛbrāhmaṇo bhavati na vaṇiṁ na kuśīlavaḥ,*
na śūdrapreṣaṇaṁ kurvan na steno na cikitsakaḥ.
11. *ambaṣṭhānām cikitsanam.*
12. Mn. (10-8).

to a family the members of which have studied medical scriptures or followed medicine as a profession."[13]

4. *Qualifications for a Teacher*

Car. (3.8) also enumerated the qualifications of the physicians chosen as teachers of medicine. Such a physician-teacher had to know the *śāstra* i.e. the medical books and other branches of study, should possess experience and practice in surgery and the implementation of his profession, should be clever, of good conduct (pure internally and externally), without malice or wrathfulness, capable of bearing privation or pain; he should not be defective in any of the senses, he should be compassionate towards all those who approached him, well disposed towards disciples, willing to teach them and capable of imparting his ideas to them.[14]

5. *Study of Medicine*

In Car. (3.8) and Suś. (1.2) we also find very interesting and detailed information concerning the subjects which the medical student had to study and the way in which the study had to be conducted.

According to Car. (3.8) the medical pupil should select at the outset his particular treatise for study, since many treatises appertaining to the medical profession were available.

Once a pupil has been accepted bv a physician, the ceremony of initiation had to take place This ceremony was described in detail in Suś. (1.2).[15]

During apprenticeship the pupil had to "give up lust, anger, avarice, folly, vanity, pride, envy, rudeness, deception, falsehood, idleness and all other reprehensible conduct." He always had to have his "hair and nails cut short, should put on red coloured cloth, lead a pure life, avoid sexual intercourse and be ready to obey his superiors." He had to obey his teacher,--go about, lie down, sit down, eat and study according

13. Compare Dr. Cecil Webb-Johnson's Medicine in India, in *Asiatic Review*, Sar. 4., Volume 17. 245, where he stated : "Whether a man can practice Hindu medicine depends upon his caste, and invariably the profession of physician is handed down from father to son, for the Hindu physician is born, not made."

14. For details on qualifications of medical pupils and teachers see R. Roth's Indische Medizin ; Caraka, in *ZDMG* 26. 445-457.

15. And others.

to his wishes; he had also to be always ready to improve himself. If he failed in those duties his learning would not only become useless, but he would also be guilty of a sin and his teaching would be fruitless.[16]

The medical student had to study first the various *śāstra-s*. It was however, admitted that who knew only one *śāstra* could not properly understand any subject and it was desirable, therefore, that he be accquainted with many *śāstra-s*. He had to study them thoroughly before he could become a genuine physician.[17]

The second stage was the study of the treatment of diseases, the most important part of which was the study of surgery.[18] Suś. attached great importance to the practical training of the medical pupil and accordingly stated that even if the pupil was acquainted with all the *śāstra-s*, in order to take him properly qualified, the teacher had to give him practical instruction on the performance of surgical operations and the application of oils, etc. A man could not qualify for practice without practical training and repeated recitation of lessons.[19] This practical training in surgical operations had to be carried out upon "various objects," which proved that this practical training did not apply to human beings. Only then did the medical student become a "qualified operator and did not faint when he was called to perform any operation on his patient." Then also "he performed these operations in the same way as he had practiced them on the above mentioned objects, etc."[20]

6. *Graduation and Licence*

After having completed the period of apprenticeship, i.e. after having studied the *śāstra-s* and learned their meaning, after having attained the proficiency of reciting the *śāstra-s*, and after having obtained a practical knowledge of surgical treatment, the medical pupil could become a physician. Before commencing to practise, however, he had to receive a licence, i.e. the permission of the king. This permission gave him the title of a

16. Suś. (1-2); Compare Car. (3-8).
17. Suś. (1-4).
18. Suś. (1-5).
19. Suś. (1-9).
20. Suś. (1-9 *in fine*). According to U. C. Dutt's translation.

bhiṣaj and only in this way did he become a licensed and fully qualified physician.

Although this rule was not to be found in the Dharma-śāstra-s or Arthaśāstra-s, it was evident from the medical literature that such a licence was a *conditio sine qua non*.

Suś, stated clearly that "the physician should obtain the permission of the king and commence practice."[21] Such a physician was called, "a saviour of life."[22]

There existed, on the other hand, another class of physicians who were not licensed and who "followed diseases and destroyed life."[23] These men were "companions of diseases and destroyers of the life-breaths."[24] They were "ignorant" physicians.

7. *Qualifications of Physicians*

The four principal qualifications of physicians were : mastery of scriptures, experience, cleverness and purity.[25] But in order to cure a disease it was not only necessary to have a good physician. Drugs, the nurse and a good patient were also necessary.[26]

"Abundance of virtue, adaptability to the disease under treatment, capacity of being used in diverse ways, and undeterioration numbering the fourth, were the attributes of drugs.

Knowledge of the manner in which drugs should be prepared or compounded for administration, cleverness, devotedness to the patient waited upon, and purity (of both mind and body) were the four qualifications of the attending nurse.

Memory, obedience to directions (given by the physician), fearlessness and communicativeness (with respect to all that was experienced internally and all that was done by him during the intervals of the physician's visit) were the qualifications of the patient.[27]

However, the physician was "the most important of these four postulates", Car. stated, "since he recognised the disease,

21. Suś. (1-10).
22. Car. (1-29, 4).
23. Car. (1-29,5).
24. Car. (1-29, 8 sqq.).
25. Car. (1-9, 6). Compare Car. (1-9, 3).
26. *bhiṣag-dravyāny upasthātā rogī pādacatuṣṭayam,*
guṇāvat kāraṇaṁ jñeyaṁ vikāravyupaśāntaye (Car. 1-9, 3).
27. Car. (1-9, 7 sqq.). According to A. C. Kaviratna's translation.

directed the treatment and applied the remedies. The physician in this aggregate of four is the chief cause for the achievement of success. Since he is the ascertainer of the character of the disease, the director with respect to what the patient and the nurse should do, and the minister who applies the remedies that bring about the cure. As in the task of cooking, a vessel, fuel, and fire were means in the victor's hands for achieving a victory in battle; even so the patient, the nurse and drugs were objects that were regarded as the physician's means in the matter of achieving a cure. In the act of treatment, the physician was regarded as the chief cause. Like clay, stick, wheel, thread, etc. in the absence of the potter, failing to produce anything by their combination, the three others viz., drugs, nurse and patient, could not work out a cure in the absence of the physician"[28] and again "since the three requisites of treatment were completely dependent upon the physician, therefore the physician had to exert his best in the matter of these qualifications that constituted wealth."[29]

III. DUTY OF PHYSICIANS. MEDICAL TREATMENT

8. *Medical Ethics*

Medical ethics were clearly described in ancient India. Not everybody could be treated by physicians. The physician was ordered not to treat hunters, fowlers, outcasts and sinners. Suś.[1] stated that by acting in this way he made himself known as learned and attained friends, fame, virtue, wealth and everything he desired. This was understandable because under Indian social conditions, when treating the persons mentioned above, he could not give treatment to those of higher social position and might, in some cases, be considered as an outcast. In addition, he could not treat incurable diseases.[2]

9. *Medical Treatment*

A. The first duty of the physician was to treat and protect his patient, but what could he do, even if he would be a Dhan-

28. According to A. C. Kaviratna's translation.
29. Car. (1-9, 25). According to A. C. Kaviratna's translation. Compare Suś. (1-34).
1. Suś. (1-2 *in fine*).
2. See chapter 3 (B) 1.

vantari. HK asked if the patient's life was spanned.[3]

The physician (*vaidya*) always had to be friendly towards his patients, have compassion for them, and be enthusiastic in the case of curable diseases, but as was stated above, he had to refuse to treat incurable diseases, or those persons who were on the point of death.[4] He also had to be reliable and not a flatterer. In this connection HK, in a beautiful aphorism, stated :

vaidyo guruś ca mantrī ca yasya rājñaḥ priyaṁvadāḥ,
śarīradharmakoṣebhyaḥ kṣipraṁ sa parihīyate.[5]

The physician who acted "not for self-interest, neither for his own enjoyment, but out of compassion for creatures and who devoted himself to treatment excelled all (people)" was stated in Suś.[6] Car. stated that if the physician desired to win merit, he should protect his patients from diseases, as he would protect his own children.[7] Therefore, the sick man trusted the physician and was willing to place his life in the latter's care without fear, although he might fear his mother, father, children or friends.[8] Only physicians who wounded themselves in the performance of operations should be avoided,[9] and, of course, those who had no knowledge of medical treatment.[10] The talent of physicians was tested in diseases, for, H asked who was not wise when all went smoothly ?[11]

B. Before entering the patient's house, the physician had to observe the favourable and unfavourable omens. He had to

3. *prakṛtiḥ svāminā tyaktā samṛddhā'pi na jīvati,*
api dhanvantarir vaidyaḥ kiṁ karoti gatāyuṣi (HJ, 3. 147, HH. 96, 26-7, HS. 3.141, HC. 129, 6-7 and 147, 14-5, HM. 3.144, HK 3.145, HP. 3.141 and 4.62, HN. 3.141).

4. *maitrī kāruṇyam ārteṣu śākye prītir upekṣaṇam,*
prakṛtīstheṣu bhūteṣu vaidya-vṛttiś-catur-vidhā (Car. 1-9, 26).

5. A king whose physician, *guru*, and minister are flatterers, fast loses his health, his religious merits and treasure (HJ. 3.108, HH. 91-7-8, HS. 3.103, HC. 121.7-8, HM. 3.104, HK. 3.104; Cf. PS 1.85, PN 2.64, PT 1.67, PTem 1.89, PRE 1.96, PD 300.100, VCir VI. 1 [p. 34].

6. Suś. (I-10 *in fine*).

7. *bhiṣag apyāturān sarvān svasutān iva yatnavān,*
ābādhebhyo hi saṁrakṣed icchan dharmam anuttamam (Car. 6-1, 3, 56).

8. Suś. (1-25 *in fine*).

9. Suś. (1-25).

10. See above.

11. *mantriṇāṁ bhinnasandhāne bhiṣajāṁ sānnipātake,*
karmaṇi vyajyate prajñā susthe ko vā na paṇḍitaḥ. (HJ. 3.125, HH. 98.23-4, HS. 3.119, HC. 124.17-8, HM. 3.121, HK. 3.121, HP. 3.117, HN. 3.117, PS 1.125, PN 2.101, PT 1.146 PTem 1.133, PP 1.97, Pts 1.127 and 381, PtsK 1.143, PRE 1.138, BhŚ 836).

sit down and examine his patient by sight, touch and questions.[12] He had to ascertain accordingly the nature of the disease[13] and start the cure, of curable diseases only, relieving those which could be relieved, but ignoring incurable cases.[14]

C. After ascertaining the nature of the disease, the physician had first to test the longevity of the patient[15] and apply carefully selected medicines. He then had to commence "the treatment with full knowledge." "The physician who did not carefully diagnose, seldom met with success even if he was well conversant with medicines and their application. The physician who was well conversant with features of diseases, who had knowledge of the considerations dependant upon time and place, achieved success, without doubt[16] was stated in Car. 17.[17] However, Car. said that any physician who was not acquainted with the analysis of tastes, etc. was never competent to allay disease.[18]

10. *Duty of Physicians to Inform Administrative Authorities of Undertaking Medical Treatment.*

A. In K. we can find two very interesting administrative and police rules which referred to the medical treatment and the responsibility of physicians who undertook medical treatment without informing the administrative authorities.

And so we read in K.[19] *bhiṣajaḥ prāṇābādhikam anākhyāyo'-*

12. Suś (1.10).
13. According to Suś. (1.10 *in fine*)"the physician who wished to attain virtue, wealth, objects of desire and fame, had to ascertain carefully the character of the disease before undertaking the treatment of the following classes of people : Brāhmaṇa-s learned in the Vedas, kings, women, children, old men, timid people, servants of kings, cunning and weak persons,slanderers of physicians, poor, miserly or irritable people, orphans, persons who concealed their diseases, or who had control over their diseases, or who had no control over their transactions......The physician should not sit together, talk, or joke with females, and, except eatables, should not accept any other presents from them."
14. Suś. (1.10).
15. Suś. (1.35).
16. According to A. C. Kaviratna's translation.
17. *rogamādau parīkṣeta tato'nantaram auṣadham,*
tataḥ karma bhiṣak paścāj jñānapūrvaṁ samācaret,
yas tu rogam avijñāya karmāṇy ārabhate bhiṣak,
apyauṣadhavidhānajñas tasya siddhi yadṛcchayā.
yas tu rogaviśeṣajñaḥ sarvabhaiṣajyakovidaḥ,
desakāla-pramāṇajñas tasya siddhir asaṁśayam (Car. 1.20, 21, 22).
Similarly Suś. (1-10 *in fine*).
18. Car. (3-1).
19. K. (203.13-14).

pakramamāṇasya vipattau pūrvas sāhasa-daṇḍāḥ (physicians who undertake perilous medical treatment without informing (*scilo* the respective authorities), if death follows, are confined to the lowest fine).

Who has to be informed is stated in K.[20] where we read : *cikitsakaḥ pracchannavraṇapratīkārakārayitāram apathyakāriṇaṁ ca gṛhasvāmī ca nivedya* (*gopasthā nivedya*) *gopasthānikayor mucyetā'nyathā tulyadoṣas syāt* (any physician who undertakes in secret the treatment of a patient from wounds or (excess of) unwholesome food or drink, as well as the master of the house, are only innocent when they report to the *gopa* or *sthānika*; otherwise both of them are equally guilty with the sufferer).

We see here that according to K., in order to safeguard himself from a possible penalty, the physician had to inform the corresponding office (officer) i.e., the *gopa* or *sthānika* of treating a grievous case which might cause death. If he did not inform the office (officer), and death occurred, he was liable to the first amercement which amounted to 12 to 96 *paṇa*.[21] The physician had also to inform the *gopa* or *sthānika* immediately in cases when he was called to a patient suspected of concealing his whereabouts. If the physician gave medical treatment to any such patient, whether for a wound or an excess of unwholesome food, he was liable to the same penalty as the patient.[22] Anyone sheltering such a patient was also liable to the penalty.

B. This rule is well known in contemporary codes as well. These are rules which are introduced, particularly during war or in a state of emergency in order to determine the whereabouts of partisans or underground movements. The police state of Candragupta Maurya introduced in the 4th century B. C.[23] special "modern" legal rules.

11. *Other Duties of Physicians*

Another duty of the physician (*cikitsaka*), according to K.[24] was "to overcome pestilences" by using medicines.

Physicians (*cikitsaka*) had not only to give medical treat-

20. K. (144.11-13).
21. K. (203.13).
22. The diseases were enumerated only by example.
23. Kauṭilya's Arthaśāstra gave a splendid picture of a state and legal rules, probably, at the time of Candragupta Maurya and his minister Kauṭilya.
24. *auṣadhaiś cikitsakāḥ, śāntiprāyaścittair vā siddhatāpasāḥ* (K. 208, 4-5).

ment, but also prepare medicines, particularly from *arișța*[25] a kind of liquor.[26]

12. *King's Physicians*

A. The highest aim of a physician was to become the king's physician. Some physicians were skillful in diagnosis and some were skillful in treatment. However, only those who were skilful in both could become royal physicians. Car. stated, therefore, that physicians who had knowledge of symptoms of the diagnosis, the means of alleviating the disease and to cure the disease so effectually that it might not reappear, deserved to be king's physicians.[27]

In another place, Car. emphasized that the physicians who had special knowledge of conception[28] deserved to become king's physicians. This enumeration of physicians' knowledge must be considered, in the light of Car. (1-9, 19), as of lesser importance.

B. The principal duty of the king's physician was to protect the king from poison.[29] Therefore, he had particularly to inspect the kitchen (*mahānasa*). In this connexion it is understandable that Caraka, the author of the well known medical work, was the son of Nārāyaṇa, cook (*rasavatyadhikārin*) of the Bengali king Nayapāla.

We find some mention of the king's physicians in K. There they were called *bhiṣaj* and not *cikitsaka*. According to K.[30] the king's physicians capable of detecting poison had always to attend the king and had to administer medicines, liquors and other beverages to him. On the other hand, the king had to attend to the business of a *vaidya*.[31],[32]

25. *cikitsaka pramāṇāḥ pratyekaśo vikārāṇām ariṣṭāḥ* (K. 120, 12).

26. K. (120, 6). It should also be noted that we find in K. a long list of duties and rights of veterinarians, in particular, elephant doctors (*anīkastha*) (K. 50, 10; 135. 17; 138. 11. 15, 17; 139, 1; etc.) and horse doctors (*aśvānāṁ cikitsaka*) (K. 133, 13; 134, 19; etc.).

27. *hetau liṅge praśamane rogāṇām apunarbhave,*
jñānaṁ caturvidhaṁ yasya sa rājārho bhiṣaktamaḥ (Car. 1.9, 19).

28. In Sārīrasthānam, lesson 4.

29. Car. (4.4, 58, 59). Cf. L. Sternbach, Cāṇakya-rāja-nīti. Maxims on Rāja-nīti. The Adyar Library Series No. 92; Maxim 228.

30. K. (43. 19-44. 2).

31. *agnyagāragataḥ kāryaṁ paśyed-vaidya-tapasavinām.*
purohitā'cāryasakhaḥ pratyutthāyā'bhivādya ca (K. 39. 6-7).

32. In this context it is not clear whether *vaidya* means learned man or physician.

Suś.[33] described ways in which the physician had to protect the king (Yuktasena). It is stated there that "when the king, accompanied by his ministers, went out on an expedition for conquest, he should be carefully protected, especially from poison. The roads, water, shady places, food, grass and fire-wood were poisoned by enemies. They were to be checked and purified......The physician should remain in a large tent close to that of the king, equipped with all the necessary articles for treatment. Patients suffering from poison, wounds, or disease should come with confidence to the physician there located, as the banner of fame and reputation".[34]

According to K., physicians (*cikitsaka*) with surgical instruments, machines, etc. had to stand behind and encourage fighting men.[35]

(Alexander the Great, during his Indian campaign, took with him some physicians whose duty was to protect his troops from poison—serpents).

Suś.[36] also declared that "in the Atharva-veda it was stated that there were one hundred and one forms of death; of these one was owing to old age, the rest were all accidental. The physician, by his knowledge of medicines, and the priest by his knowledge of incantations, should carefully and constantly protect the king from death caused by deranged humours or accidents. For this purpose Brahmā had revealed the Āyurveda composed of eight parts which forms a portion of the Vedas. The prudent physician should always act according to the wishes of the priest."[37] Here we see the combination of the duties of a physician and a priest, the latter being considered more important than the former.

IV. SOCIAL POSITION OF PHYSICIANS

13. "*Physicians*" *in Sanskrit Vocabulary*

Differences existed between a *cikitsaka*, *bhiṣaj* and *vaidya*; one was more esteemed than the other, but from the legal point of

33. Suś. (I-34).
34. According to U.C. Dutt's translation.
35. *cikitsakāḥ śastrayantrāgadu-sneha-vastrahastāḥ, striyaścānna pānarakṣinyaḥ puruṣāṇāmuddhatṣaṇīyāḥ pṛsṭhatas tiṣṭheyuḥ* (K. 369, 1:2).
36. Suś. (I-31).
37. According to U. C. Dutt's translation.

view, as found in the Dharmaśāstra- and Arthaśāstra-texts, there was no differenced between the three expressions. These sources used the three words, mentioned above, indiscriminately; very often one of the words was defined by the other. For example Medh.[1] in defining a *cikitsaka* stated *cikitsaka vaidyaḥ*. In this way Medh, considered that a *cikitsaka* was identical with a *vaidya*.[2] The *bhiṣaj* was identified with a *vaidya* in Mit.[3] and in Vīr.[4] The comparison between Mn.[5] and Vi.,[6] where in both cases wrong action (*mithyā*) of a physician was considered punishable, shows that both these Dharmaśāstra-s identified *bhiṣaj* and *cikitsaka*. Mn. used the word *cikitsaka* while Vi. used the word *bhiṣaj*. On the other hand, it must be pointed out that Āp. (1.6, 18, 21[7] and 1.6, 19, 15)[8] when repeating twice that food given by a physician must not be eaten, used in the first instance the word *bhiṣaj*, and in the second instance, the word *cikitsaka*.[9] Āp., however, in 1.6, 18, 21 used his own words while in 1.6, 19, 15 he quoted some other authorities.[10] It can be assumed, therefore, that it was not the intention of Āp. to differentiate between a *bhiṣaj* and a *cikitsaka*.

14. *Vaidya*

Although the words *cikitsaka*, *bhiṣaj* and *vaidya* had the same meaning in the Dharmaśāstra-texts this did not mean that they had the same meaning in daily life in ancient India, or that a *cikitsaka* enjoyed the same importance and esteem as, for instance, a *vaidya*. Generally speaking, ancient Indian literary works revealed wide differences in the importance of physicians.

1. Medh. (*ad* Mn. 9-259).
2. See also Maskari *ad* G. 17.15) in Government Oriental Library Series, *Bibliotheca Sanscrita* No. 50.
3. *Vaidyo vidvān bhiṣag vā* (Mit. *ad* Y. 1.157, 158).
4. *vaidyo bhiṣak vidyāvān iti* (*kecit*) (Vir. *ad Y.* 1-157, 158)
5. *cikitsakānāṁ sarveṣāṁ mithyā-pracaratāṁ damaḥ,*
amānuṣeṣu prathamo manuṣeṣu tu madhyamaḥ (Mn. 9.284) Also quoted in Vy N. 510).
6. *bhiṣaṅ mithyā-caran uttameṣu puruṣeṣu* (Vi. 5. 175).
7. *bhiṣak.*
8. *cikitsakasya mṛgayoḥ śalyakṛntasya pāśinaḥ.*
kulaṭāyāḥ ṣaṇḍhakasya ca teṣām annam anādyam (Āp. I-6, 19, 14).
9. In addition—*śalyakṛnta*.
10. *atha purāṇe ślokāv udāharanti* (Āp. 1.6, 19, 13). The first *pāda* is identical in Āp. (I-6, 19, 15) and Mn. (4.212).

The highest importance was attributed to the *vaidya*. After gaining the knowledge of the Vedas[11] a *vaidya* was said to have three births. In the absence of this knowledge the word *vaidya* could not be applied to any man. A *vaidya*, therefore, could not be born; he had to gain the knowledge of the Vedas and then could become a *vaidya*.[12] A *vaidya* also had to know the scriptures (*śruti*) well, had to have wide experience, cleverness, and purity of both mind and body. These qualifications were regarded as the four principal ones of a *vaidya*.[13] However in order to accomplish everything a person had to possess the following six qualifications : knowledge of the scriptures on the science of life the faculty of reasoning from established proportions, acquaintance with other branches of knowledge, memory, cognisance of the treatment of disease and repeated experience in treatment. These qualifications can explain the etymology of the word *vaidya* i.e. knowledge, physician.[14] A person possessing these auspicious qualifications, in particular knowledge, deserved the designation of *vaidya*; such a person was the giver of both life and happiness.[15]

15. *High Esteem Paid tc Physicians*

A. As emphasized before, we do not find in the Ancient Indian sources any differenciation line between the three categories of physicians, although a *vaidya* was certainly the highest of all, while the word *bhiṣaj* was mostly used for the designation of a king's physician. *Bhiṣaj* and *cikitsaka* were used indiscriminately. The general belief, however, was that physicians were held in high regard. The reason for this was the devotion of the physician to human beings. Hence we read in

11. *vidyāsam āptau brāhmaṁ vā sattvam ārṣamathāpi vā.*
dhruvam āviśati jñānāt asmād vaidyastrijaḥ smṛtaḥ (Car. 6.3, 53. Compare Car. VI-1. 3, 52).

12. *vidyāsamāptau bhiṣajas tṛtīyā jātir ucyate,*
aśnūte vaidya śabdaṁ hi na vaidyāḥ pūrvajanmanā (Car. 6.3,52).

13. *śrute pary avadātatvaṁ bahuśo dṛśtakarmatā,*
dākṣyaṁ śaucam iti jñeyaṁ vaidye guṇa-catuṣṭayam (Car. 1-9,6).

14. *vidyā vitarko vijñānaṁ smṛtis tatparatā kriyā,*
yasyaite ṣaḍguṇās tasya na sādhyam ativartate.
vidyā matiḥ karmadṛṣtir abhyāsaḥ siddhir āśrayaḥ,
vaidyaśabdābhiniṣpattā-valam ekaikamapyataḥ (Car. 1. 9, 21, 22).

15. *yasya tv ete guṇāḥ sarve santi vidyādayaḥ śubhāḥ,*
sa vaidyaśabdaṁ sadbhūtam arhan prāṇisukhapradaḥ (Car. 1.9, 23).

Car. :[16] "He who thinking that compassion for creatures is the supreme virtue, devotes himself to treatment, has his ends (of life) accomplished and enjoys eternal felicity."[17]

Suś.[18] stated that the physician who gave treatment with the welfare of his patient at heart, was liked by good men, and had to attain virtue, wealth and fame, and finally heaven.

B. It follows that physicians had to be worshipped as gods were worshipped. We read in Car.[19] "those foremost of physicians, by these and diverse other acts (of success in treatment) became objects of worship the Aśvins, those celestial physicians, were worshipped with devotion by the deities with their chief (*scil.* Indra) at their head, they who were immortal, who transcend decrepitude, and who were above change. Why then should not physicians be worshipped by men, to the best of their power, who were desirous of obtaining happiness. It has been declared that one who was preceptor of the science of Life who was possessed of pure conduct, who was endued with intelligence, who was devoted (to the science be professed), who belonged to the regenerate orders, and who had thoroughly mastered the scriptures (bearing upon his science) should be worshipped by all persons even as a *guru* was worshipped......"[20]

It was also stated in Suś. that learned physicians should be respected like kings. Salutations of reverence were due to physicians who were conversant with the scriptures, possessed cleverness, were imbued with purity of behaviour and heart, skilled in treatment of disease, of practised hand, and had their souls under complete control."[21]

The high regard enjoyed by physicians was also evident from many literary works. Leumann[22] stated for instance, that a physician who had been called by a merchant was accompanied to the door of the palace. The expression *kavirāja*

16. *paro bhūtadayā dharma iti matvā cikitsayā*
vartate yaḥ sa siddhārthaḥ sukham atyantam aśnute (Car. 6. 13, 62).
17. According to A. C. Kaviratna's translation.
18. Suś. (I-25 *in fine*).
19. ...*mṛtyu vyādhijarāvaśyair duḥkhaprāyaiḥ sukhārthibhiḥ,*
kiṁ punar bhiṣajo martyaiḥ pūjyāḥ syur nātiśaktitaḥ.
śīlavān matimān yuktas trijātiḥ śāstrapāragaḥ,
prāṇibhir guruvat pūjyaḥ prāṇācāryaḥ sa hi smṛtaḥ (Car. 6.1,3, 50, 51).
20. According to A. C. Kaviratna's translation.
21. Suś. (I. 24).
22. *Die Nonne* p. 438 sqq.

(*kabirāja* of today), the king among sages, was very often used to describe a physician, shows how highly he was esteemed.

C. According to the Dharmaśāstra-s physicians were highly esteemed. This is evident, for example, from Mn. 4.179-180) and Y. (1.157-8),[23] where we read :

ṛtvik-purohitā'cāryar mātulātithisaṁśritaiḥ
bālavṛddhāturair vaidyair jñāti-sambandhi-bāndhavaiḥ
mātāpitṛbhyāṁ jāmibhir bhrātrā putreṇa bhāryayā,
duhitrā dāsavargeṇa vivādaṁ na samācaret,[24]

and

mātṛpittratithibhrātṛ-jāmisaṁbandhimātulaiḥ,
vṛddhobālāturācāryavaidyasaṁśritabhāndhavaiḥ.
ṛtvik-purohitā-patya bhāryā-dāsa-sanābhibhiḥ,
vivādaṁ varjayitvā tu sarvāṁ llokāñ jayedgṛhī.[25]

Mn. and Y. (and similarly MBh.) mentioned here *vaidya* among *ṛtvij*, *purohita*, father, mother, brother, son, wife, daughter, etc., and stated that if all worlds were to be conquered quarrels with them had to be avoided.

Mit. (*ad* Y. 1.157, 158)[26] and Vir. (*ad* Y. I-157, 158)[27] made it clear that the word *vaidya* used in Y. should be interpreted to mean *bhiṣaj*. The same might be said *per analogiam* about Mn. and MBh. Thus, it is evident that, according to these sources a physician had to be honoured and esteemed, as had to be a *guru*, *purohita*, father, etc.

This high esteem and honour attributed to physicians was probably due to the fact that they were considered useful and indispensable in a community. And so we find in H the following aphorism :

tatra mitra na vastavyaṁ yatra nāsti catuṣṭayam,
ṛṇadāta ca vaidyaś ca śrotriyaḥ sajalā nadī,[28]

and in Cāṇakya's collections :

23. Similarly MBh. (*Śāntiparvan* 249, 14-17).
24. Mn. 4. 179, 180).
25. Y. (1. 157, 158).
26. *vaidyo vidvān bhiṣag vā.*
27. *vaidyo bhiṣak vidyāvān iti* (*kecit*).
28. HJ. 1 112, HH. 22. 17-8, HC. 30. 12-3, HM. 1. 105, HK. (1. 107. Cf. MP. 34. 112b-113a and Vi. 71.66). One should not dwell there, oh friend where these four things do not exist, viz., a creditor, a physician, a Brāhmaṇa versed in the Vedas, and a river with water (ever flowing). (According to M. B. Kale's translation).

pañca yatra na vidyante na tatra divasaṁ vaset,
dhanikaḥ śrotriyo rājā nadī vaidyas tu pañcamaḥ.[29]

Vi.[30] referring the whole chapter to a snātaka also stated: *na saṁvased vaidyahīne* (and he must not live in a kingdom in which there are no physicians).[31]

K. also realised that physicians as well as veterinarians were important, and induced them to migrate to a newly formed village, by endowing them with lands."[32]

D. Kauṭilya turned the high esteem and honour attributed to physicians to his own advantage and to the better use of his machiavellian purposes. In K. we find very often mention of physicians used as spies.

Hence, we read in K. that some spies could be sent "under the disguise of physicians", etc.[33] in order to ascertain the nature of the intrigue prevalent among parties favourably disposed to his master, as well as the conspiracy among hostile factions, and in order to determine whether people were loyal or disloyal to the enemy, etc. Similarly the Collecter General could employ spies disguised as physicians and send them abroad for espionage purposes.[34]

Spies disguised as physicians, could in addition, be ordered to make a "seditious" minister, or another person "of seditious

29. One should not dwell there where five things are lacking : a wealthy man, a Brāhmaṇa versed in the Vedas, a king, a river and, as fifth, a physician. (CVND. 1. 9, CVM. 1. 8; CvW. 1. 12, CvP. IV. 1. 10, CvP. V. 1. 10, CvGt. 1. 10, CvTb. 1. 10, CvH. 1. 10, CvI. 1. 11, CvL. II. 1. 10, CvLd. 1. 10; CNJV. 36, CNS. 50, CNW. 41, CNF. 5, CNPh. 75, CNPN. 32, CNG. 292, CNŚC. 35, CNŚl 1. 35, CNŚ. 34, CNŚL. 21, CNNM. 30, CNŚT. 32, CNŚK. 35, CNL. 14, CNI. II. 6; CnT. II. 1. 9, CnT. III. 1. 9, CnT. VI. 1.9, CnT. V. 1. 10, IS. 3861 HJ 1.110, HS 1.110, HP 1.78, HN 1.80, HH. 22. 13-4, GP 1.110, 26).

30. Vi. (71. 66).

31. If this verse is compared with the foregoing and subsequent ones, the opposite might be assumed, i.e. that the physicians were considered low-class persons, since, in this context, Vi. mentioned persons to be avoided by the *snātaka* (Śudra. king—64; wicked people—65; afflicted with disease—66, etc.). The similar verses to those of Vi. (i.e. Mn. 8. 60, 61 ; B. 2. 3, 51; Āp. 16. 22, 32. 18) do not mention the physician. However it must be noted that Vi. used the word *vaidya* i.e. sage and not e.g. *cikitṣaka*, or *bhiṣaj*.

32. *adhyakṣasaṅkhyāyakādibhyo gopasthānikānīkastha cikitsckāśvadamaka-jaṅghākarikebhyaś ca vikrayādhānavarjam* (K. 46, 10-11).

33. *tayor antevāsibhiś ckitsakapāṣaṇḍavyañjanobhayavetanair vā* (K. 31 4 sqq.).

34. *samāhartā janapade siddhatāpasapravrajitacakracaracāraṇakuhaka-pracchandaka kārtāntikanaimittikamauhūrt kacikitsakonmattomūkai adhiraja ḍāndhavai-dehakakāruśilpikuśīlavaveśaśauṇḍikāpūpikapākvamāṁsikaudanikavyañjanān praṇidadhyāt* (K. 210. 15 sqq.).

character" believe to be sick, and could contrive to poison him while prescribing medicines and diet.[35]

In order "to make peace and break it." spies disguised a physicians could set fire to a building filled with valuables.[36]

These are only some examples from K.[37] in order to show that physicians were used as spies in the Mauryan machiavellian system of government, as described by Kauṭilya. In addition, these examples show that physicians (*cikitsaka*) were considered to be persons worthy of high esteem and the confidence of all.

The fact that the physician (*cikitsaka*) was considered as trustworthy was demonstrated by the fact that a physician could not be arrested for being near royal buildings or for ascending the fortifications of the capital, whereas, under the law, such an offence was punishable.[38]

E. Car. stated however, that not all physicians had to be worshipped, but only those who were characterised by equanimity, knowledge, and science.[39]

In the Dharmaśāstra-s we find some examples which also show that the physicians were not always highly esteemed. It is said, for instance, that food given by a physician should not be eaten. This was stated in Mn.[40] Y.[41] 'G.[42] and Vās.[43] which used the word *cikitsaka* to mean a physician. Āp., being of the same

35. *cikitsakavyañjano vā daurātmikam asādhyaṁ vā vyādhim dūṣyasya sthāpayitvā bhaiṣajyāhārayogeṣu rasenātisandadhyāt* (K. 240. 3-4); *cikitsakavyañjano vā gadam agadāpadeśena pratyāsanno vā dūṣyasya satrī praṇihitam abhiṣekabhāṇḍam amitraśāsanaṁ ca kāpaṭikamukhena ācakṣita'kāraṇaṁ ca brūyāt* (K. 246, 13-15 sqq.)

36. *ārakṣakaprotsāhanena vā nāgarakakuśīlavacikitsakāpūpikavyañjanā vā rātrau samṛddhagṛhānyādipayeyuḥ* (K. 316, 10 sqq.).

37. Compare K. (31, 4).

38. *rajaparigrahopagamane nagararakṣārohaṇe ca madhyamassāhasadaṇḍaḥ, sūtikācikitsakapretapradipāyananāgarakatūryaprekṣāgninimittamudrābhiścāgrāhyāḥ* (K. 146, 5-7).

39. Car. (II-8 *in fine*).

40. *matta-kruddhāturāṇāṁ ca na bhuñjīta kadācana,*
kṛśakīṭavapannaṁ ca padā spṛṣṭaṁ ca kāmataḥ (Mn. 4. 207).
cikitsakasya... (Mn. 4. 212).

41. *adattāny agnihīnasya nānnam adyād anāpadi* (Y. 1-160).
cikitsaka... (Y. 1-162).
eteṣāṁ cikitsakādinām annaṁ nāśnīyāt (Mit. *ad* Y. I-162).

42. *keśakīṭāvapannam* (G. 17. 9).
utsṛṣṭapuṁścalyabhiśastānadeśyadaṇḍikatakṣakadaryabandhanika-cikitsaka-mṛgayvaniṣucāryucchiṣṭabhojigaṇavidviṣāṇānām (G. 17. 17).

43. *cikitsakamṛgayupuṁścalīdaṇḍikastenābhiśastaṣaṇḍhapatitānām annam abhojyam* (Vās. 14. 2).

opinion, used the word *cikitsaka* and *śalyakṛnta*, as well as *bhiṣaj*[44] probably in order to avoid misunderstanding as to the meaning of a "physician." It should be emphasized, however, that Āp. did not use the word *vaidya* in this connexion. Āp. felt that the physician's food might be eaten, since he stands on a higher leval than a *cikitsaka*, *bhiṣaj*, and or *śalyakṛnta*. Vi. was also of the opinion that the food of a physician was unclean, but did not state it as clearly as other Dharmaśāstra-s did; it was said in Vi. only that he who ate the food of a physician had as a penance, to subsist upon milk for seven days.[45]

The only explanation of this prohibition of the eating of food given by physicians was given in Mn.;[46] it was stated there that the food of a physician *cikitsaka* was as vile as pus. It was unclean, since physicians were considered, in this context, unclean persons, persons of a lower degree. The same was also evident from Mn., where it was stated that food given by a physician became pus and blood,[47] Mn. used there the word *bhiṣaj* and not, like in 4.220, the word *cikitsaka*.

It must be also emphasized that according to Vās.[48],[49] he who practised medicine could not be called a Brāhmaṇa and according to Mn.[50] and Vi.[51] that the physicians had not to be invited to a *śrāddha*. Both these examples show that, in these contexts, the physician was not considered worthy of high esteem.

44. *cikitsakasya mṛgayoḥ śalyakṛntasya pāśinaḥ,*
kulaṭāyāḥ ṣaṇḍhakasya ca teṣām annam anādyam (Āp. 1. 6, 19, 14).
saṅghānnam abhojyam (Āp. 1, 6, 18, 16).
bhiṣak (Āp. 1. 6, 18, 21).

45. *gaṇagaṇikāstenagāyanānnāni bhuktvā saptarātraṁ payasā varteta* (Vi. 51. 7) ...*cikitsaka*... (51. 10).

46. *pūyaṁ cikitsaksyānnaṁ puṁśacalyās tv annam indriyam,*
viṣṭhā vārdhuṣikasyā'nnaṁ śastravikrayiṇo malam (Mn. 4. 220).

47. ...*bhiṣaje pūyaśoṇitam* (Mn. 3. 170; according to other texts 3. 180). Identically MBh. (13, 90, 13, 14).

48. Vās. (3. 3).

49. See above.

50. *cikitsakādevalakā-māṁsavikrayiṇas tathā,*
vipaṇena ca jīvanto vajyāḥ syur havyakavyayoḥ (Mn. 3. 142; according to other texts III-152).

51. *hinādhikāṅgān vivarjayet* (Vi. 82. 3).
cikitsakān (Vi. 82. 9).

V. LEGAL RESPONSIBILITY OF PHYSICIANS FOR IMPROPER MEDICAL TREATMENT

16. *Non-licensed Physicians*

As was stated above, in ancient India it was necessary for a physician to obtain permission of the king for starting medical practice.[1]

Non-licensed and ignorant physicians were called "companions of diseases".[2] They wore the robes of physicians, but were "the thorns of the world. Behaving after the manner of those whom they imitated, those persons, through the heedlessness of kings, moved about in all countries. This was their special indication, *viz.*, clad in the robes of physicians and indulging in self-praise, they walked along the public streets, in expectation of calls. When they heard of anybody's illness, they run towards his neighbourhood, and in the hearing of that person's friends loudly proclaimed their own skill and accomplishments as physicians. These men frequently proclaimed the short-comings of the person whose treatment they took up. They wished to win over the friends of the ailing person by doing what gladdened them, by stories and conversations, and various small services. They proclaimed their own disposition to be pleased with a small remuneration. Obtaining a case for treatment, they constantly kept their eye on all things, desirous of concealing their ignorance by dexterity. Unable to alleviate the disease, they accused the patient as unequipped with desirable necessities, as disposed to transgress the directions of the physician, and as having no control over his inclinations. When the last stage came, they flew away, leaving the patient. When present in assemblies of ignorant or common men, they proclaimed their own skill in treating disease, betraying their ignorance the while. Manifesting their own ignorance, they censured knowledge and wisdom of physicians that were truly wise. Beholding an assembly of men that were learned and wise, they avoided it from distance, like travellers avoiding a wilderness where there is cause of fear. If any one was ever cured, by these physicians, of any light disease, that cure was always referred to by them in cases where the treatment that

1. Suś. (I-10). See para 6. above
2. Car. (I-28, 8 sqq.).

effected the cure was inapplicable or where an altogether different kind of treatment was required. They did not desire to consult anyone (in respect of anything connected with the medical scriptures). Nor did they desire to be consulted by anyone. They feared anyone who wished to consult them as one feared death itself. No one knew who their preceptor was, or who was their fellow-student."[3]

Car. concluded this chapter with the following words : "Those men, who, wearing the garb of physicians, sought to gratify afflicted persons like fowlers seeking to capture birds in the woods by having recourse to their nets, those men who were endowed with scriptures, experience, (knowledge of) curative operations, time, measure, and place, had to be avoided. They walk on the earth like the followers (messengers) of Death. A wise patient always had to avoid those foolish men with a show of learning who, for earning their subsistence, pretended to the honour of being physicians. They were like snakes subsisting on air."[4]

The Dharmaśāstra-s and Arthaśāstra-s did not describe such ignorant, non-licensed physicians, Mn. however, stated that those who "acted improperly" (*asamyakkāriṇaḥ*) were like thorns" in the side of the people.[5]

17. *Legal Protection of the Patient*

Car. showed, although in another epoch, the true picture of the social conditions in India as far as physicians, or so-called physicians, were concerned. The same picture was also true for the epoch of the Dharmaśāstra-s and Arthaśāstra-s. The Indian society had to protect itself from such rogue physicians. That is probably one of the reasons for the introduction in the

3. Car. (1. 29, 8). According to A. C. Kaviratna's translation.

Compare P. K. Gode's "Some Estimates of the Indian Physician and his Profession between A. D. 1550 and 1820" in *The Journal of the Kaliṅga Historical Research Society*, p. 89 sqq.

4. See previous note. According to A. C. Kaviratna's translation.

5. Mn. (9. 259, 260). Also quoted in VyK. 109, MV, VRK. 291 DV. 118, VyS. 149.

asamyakkāriṇaś caiva mahāmātrāś cikitsakāḥ,
śilpopacārayuktāś ca nipuṇāḥ paṇyayoṣitaḥ.
evamādyān vijānīyāt prakāśāṁl lokamkaṇṭakān,
nigūḍha cāriṇaś cānyān anāryān āryaliṅginaḥ.

Dharmaśāstra-s and Arthaśāstra-s of special rules concerning the legal responsibility of physicians for improper medical treatment. This responsibility of physicians was dealt with only in Mn., Y., and Vi. The responsibility of physicians and veterinarians was dealt with in K.

The ancient Indian sources of law did not directly protect the patient, since the patient received no indemnity in the case of improper medical treatment. Nor did his heirs receive any indemnity in the case of the death of a patient caused by a physician, but physicians were liable to penalties for their careless medical treatment. The penalties were collected by the king (State). They were not similar to the penalty fixed in other ancient codes, e.g. the Hammurapi's Code,[6] because the Ancient Indian sources of law did not foresee in this case *lex tallionis* but imposed on the physician a fine, the extent of which varied according to circumstances.

In order to state clearly those eligible for protection the Dharmaśāstra-s made a distinction between persons—whether the patients were (a) ordinary persons, or (b) king's men (servants)—and animals subjected to medical treatment.

K. dealt separately with both persons and horses. We may generalise "horses" and presume that the rule relating to horses referred to all animals,[7] thus to veterinarians.

18. *Rules Prescribing Legal Responsibility of Physicians*

The rule concerning the responsibility of physicians for careless medical treatment is to be found in Mn. (9.284). We read there : *cikitsakānāṁ sarveṣāṁ mithyāpracaratāṁ damaḥ* (all physicians who act improperly are liable to punishment).

This responsibility for "improper action" was decreed in detail in Y. and Vi.

Y. (2.242) stated :

6. Probably the oldest code in which we can find the rule concerning the medical responsibility of physicians for their carelessness is the Hammurapi's Code of Law. According to this Code any physician who operated on a man or an animal and caused death was liable, in case of a man, to the penalty of having his fingers cut off (*lex tallionis*). The same penalty applies in the case of slaves (paragraph 218 sqq.). Cf. *R. Taubenschlag*, The Law of Greco-Roman Egypt in the Light of the Papyri, second edition, Warszawa 1955, p. 632 sqq.

7. *Pars pro toto* See K. (135-7).

bhiṣaṅmithyācaran-daṇḍyastiryakṣu prathamaṁ damam,
mānuṣe madhyamaṁ rājapuruṣeṣ ūtamaṁ damam.

(A physician who acts improperly should pay the first fine in the case of animals, the second highest in the case of men, and the highest in the case of king's men).

Vi. (5.175, 176, 177) stated :

bhiṣaṅmithyācarann-uttameṣu puruṣeṣu,
madhyameṣu madhyamam,
tiryakṣu prathamam...[8]

(A physician who acts improperly should pay the highest amercement in the case of persons of highest rank, the second highest in the case of (other) persons, the first amercement in the case of animals.[9]

It is clear that Y. and Vi. regulated this matter in an identical manner. They instituted three different penalties in three different cases.

Mn. (9.284) regulated this question in a different manner. We read there: *amānuṣeṣu prathamo mānuṣeṣu tu madhyamaḥ* (in the case of non-human beings the first, in the case of human beings the middlemost amercement).

Thus, Mn. distinguished between two different cases (human beings and animals) and ordered two different penalties (first and the second highest fine).

On the other hand, K. (203-14 sqq.) settled only one case i.e. the responsibility of physicians for their improper medical treatment of persons only. We find there the following sentence : *karmāparodhena vipattau madhyamaḥ, karma vadhavaiguṇyakaraṇe daṇḍapāruṣyaṁ vidyāt.*[10]

K. in chapter 30 of book 2, dealing with the superintendent of horses stated as follows : *kriyābhaiṣajyasaṅgena vyādhivṛddhau pratikāra dviguṇo daṇḍaḥ, tadavarodhena vailomye paramūlyaṁ*

8. Also quoted in VyK. 112. VyS. 158, VRK. 306, VT, 768, ViR. 2. 248, DV. 104; RDhK. 493, AP. 258. 36.

9. According to Dutt's edition; according to J. Jolly's edition—Vi. 5. 175, 176, 177).

10. "If the death of a patient under treatment is due to carelessness, the physician shall be punished with the middlemost amercement. Growth of disease due to negligence, or indifference of a physician should be regarded as assault or violence" (according to Shama Sastry's translation). "*Geht es schief wegen falscher Behandlung, dann die mittlere. Verursacht er einen Schaden durch Verletzung lebenswichtiger Teile dann soll man das als tatliche Beleidigung betrachten*" (according to J.J. Meyer's translation).

daṇḍaḥ.[11] The same rule applied to the treatment of cows, buffaloes, goats and sheep.[12]

19. *Meaning of Improper Medical Action*

From the above sentences the conclusion can be reached that the rule concerning the responsibility of physicians for their improper medical treatment was confirmed.

Mn. stated : *cikitsakānāṁ sarveṣām, mithyā'pracaratāṁ damaḥ.*[13] Y. (2.242) and Vi.(5.171) also used the word *mithyā* which has many different meanings ranging from "erroneously" to "wrongly" and "improperly". There is a great difference from the legal point of view in the interpretation of the word *mithyā.*[14]

Mithyā (contracted from *mithūyā*) is very often used in legal, medical, and philosophical literature.

20. *Use of mithyā in Legal Literature*

Mn. used the word *mithyā* several times. Mn. (9.284)[15] used *mithyā* as meaning "dishonest action". This is explained by Medh. as follows : *teṣāṁ mithyāpracārāṇām auṣadhadānam-ubhayathā saṁbhavati. yadi vā'vijñātaśāstraprayogatayā, śāstre paricite'pi vā'tasparatayā'rthalipsayā.* Thus, the prescribing of medicines by dishonest physicians could be done in two ways : either because of the physician's complete lack of theoretical and practical knowledge, or due to his negligence or greed even if he had sufficient theoretical knowledge.[16]

11. K. (135.4-6) "When owing to defects in medicine or carelessness in medical treatment the disease (from which a horse is suffering) becomes intense, a fine of twice the cost of the treatment shall be imposed, and, when, owing to defects in medicine, or not administering it, the result becomes quite the reverse, a fine equal to the value of the animal shall be imposed' (according to Shama Sastry's translation). "*Wenn durch Saumseligkeit in der Pflege oder in der Verabfolgung von Heilmitteln die Krankheit wächst, dann-eine Strafe, die doppelt soviel betragt, wie (die Ausgaben für die) Wiederherstellung. Wenn sie ganz unterlassen werden und es geht schief, dann ist die Strafe der Preis des Pferdes* (according to J. J. Meyer's translation).

12. K. (135-7).

13. Mn. (9.284). For translation of this passage see above.

14. In the same sense in literature e.g. Śākuntala (125); Raghuvaṁśa (17. 42); Kathāsaritsāgara (23.8, 27, 186); Pañcatantra (9.1; 9. 24); Vetālapañcaviṁśatikā (in Lassen's C. *Chrestomathia* (2.7, 17); Pañcarātra 1.6-47; (1.6-49); MBh. (13.328); Harivaṁśa (2089; 2090); etc.

15. *Ad* Mn. (3.284).

16. Kullūka did not give any explanation of the meaning of *mithyā.*

Mn. (8.59) also used the word *mithyā* as meaning "dishonestly" or "falsely"—without any legal basis.[17]

Similarly Vyāsa,[18] Yama,[19] N.[20] and G.[21].

In Mn. (8.400) *mithyā* was also used in the sense of a "false statement." It was explained by Medh. that this falsehood consisted, for instance, in counting some objects and mentioning a figure higher than the actual one, or concealment of some objects.[22]

Similar to this was the opinion of Y. (2.262) where we read about the false (*mithyā*) declaration of quantity.[23]

Y. (2.242) also used the word *mithyā* in the sense "falsely." Mit.[24] commented on *mithyā* in the following way : *yaḥ punarbhiṣak mithyā āyurvedān abhijña eva jīvanārthaṁ cikitsitajño' ham iti tiryaṅmanuṣya-rājapuruṣeṣu cikitsām ācaraty asau yathākramena prathamam adhyamottama-sāhasān daṇḍaniyaḥ*. Vir.[25] accepted the same point of view stating : *bḥiṣak mithyā caran vyādhimatsu tiryyakṣu gavādiṣu caran upacāraṁ kurvan prathamasāhasam, arājakīya mānuṣe mithyā caran madhyamasāhasam, rājapuruṣeṣu mithyā carann uttamasāhasaṁ bhiṣak, cikitsako dāpyaḥ.*

17. *yo yāvan nihnuvitārthaṁ mithyā yāvati vā vadet.* Medh. explained *mithyā yāvati viparītaṁ dhanaṁ......* (similarly Kullūka).

18. In Viv. p. 77.

19. In Viv. p. 78.

20. In Viv. p. 78.

21. *mithyā vacane yāpyo daṇḍyaś ca sākṣī* (G. 13. 23).

22. *śulkasthānaṁ pariharann akāle krayavikrayī*
mithyāvādī ca saṁkhyāne dāpyo'ṣṭaguṇam atyayam (Mn. 8. 400). Identically N. (in Apar. p. 834) (Also quoted in VyK. 110, VRK. 297, DV. 93, BBh. 2. 262, VyS. 159) Medh. explains : *Saṁkhyāne mithyāvādi—nyūnaṁ kathayati gaṇanāyāṁ. upalakṣanaṁ caitatsaṁkhyānam. tena pracchādane'py eṣu eva vidhiḥ.*

23. *mithyā vadan parīmāṇam śulkasthānād apāsaran,*
dāpyaścā'ṣṭaguṇaṁ yaś ca sa vyājakrayavikrayī (Y. 2-262). Also quoted in ViR. 267, VRK. 298, VCi. 126,, SV. 495, VT. 585, VV. 231, 321, VyS. 91, AP. 258. 52).

Vir. (*ad* Y. 2. 262) explained : *śulkavañcanārthaṁ paṇyasya vastram uktādeḥ parīmāṇaṁ mithyā vadan śulkasthānād apāsaran vā idaṁ mayā'tra sthāpyate na tu krīyate vikriīyata iti vañcayitvā krayavikrayakārī ca vaṇik paṇyād aṣṭaguṇaṁ daṇḍaṁu dāpyaḥ.* Mit. did not mention *mithyā expressis verbis* but also interpreted this word in the same way Y. (2. 262).

Compare also similar statements in Śaṅkha Likhita (in Viv. p. 298) and in Kāty. (167, 169, 189, 245, 380).

24. Mit. (*ad* Y. 2. 242).

25. Vir. (*ad* Y. 2. 242).

Y. (2-11) also used the word *mithyā* in the sense "falsely".[26]

Mithyā was also used in (Y. 3.284, 285) and its meaning there "false" is very clear.[27] Still clearer is the statement of Mit., where we read : *yas tu parotkarṣerṣyājanitaroṣakaluṣitāntaḥ—karaṇo janasamakṣaṁ mithyaiv ābhiśāpaṁ brahmahathādikam anena kṛtam ityāropayati tasya taded dviguṇaṁ bhavati...na kevalaṁ mithyābhisaṁsi dviguṅadoṣabhāk. api tu mithyābhiśastasya yadanyad duritajātaṁ tad api samādatta iti vakṣyamāṇaprāyaścitte' rthavādo na punaḥ pāpadvaiguṇyādipratipādanamatra vivakṣitam.*[28]

Kāty. used very often the word *mithyā* in the sense "falsely", particularly in so as far as testimony (proofs) was concerned.[29] Very characteristic was the statement contained in *śloka* 278 and identically in *śloka* 380, which showed that *mithyā* should be understood in this sense.[30]

Also in the same sense (regarding testimony—proofs) the word *mithyā* was used in N.[31] and Bṛh.,[32] and in the sense "wrongly", rather than "falsely," in B. and Āp.[33]

The same might be also said about K. which used the word *mithyā* only once, as far as it was possible to ascertain.[34]

26. *mithyābhiyogī dviguṇam abhiyogād dhanam vahet* (Y. 2. 11). (Y. 2. 11. Also quoted in ViR. 2. 11, VyK. 128, SC. 122, VyCi. 96, VCi. 35, VyN, DV. 350, NṛP. 17, VCa. 267-8, VySau. 92, VyPr. 279, VT. 96 : 499, VV. 38, 317, Vyp.77, VyS. 67, VVy. 31, AP. 253. 40-1). Mit. explains : *athārthī bhāvayitaṁ na śaknoti tadā sa eva mithyābhiyogī jāta ity abhiyogād abhiyuktdhanād dviguṇaṁ dhanaṁ rājñe dadyāt.* Similarly Vir. (*ad* Y. 2. 11) *mithyābhiyogakarī tu vādī abhiyogād vivādadhanād dviguṇaṁ dhanaṁ rājñe vahet.*

27. *mithyābhiśaṁsino doṣo dviḥ samo bhūtavādinaḥ,*
mithyābhiśastadoṣaṁ ca samādatte mṛṣā vadan (Y. 3. 284-285).
Still clearer is the statement of Mit., where we read : *yas tu parotkarṣerṣyājanitaroṣakaluṣitāntaḥkaraṇo janasamakṣaṁ mithyaivābhiśāpaṁ brahmahatyādikam anena kṛtam ity āropayati tasya tad eva dviguṇaṁ bhavati.......na kevalaṁ mithyābhiśaṁsī dviguṇadoṣabhāg api tu mithyā bhiśastasya yad anyad duritajātaṁ tad api samādatta iti vakṣyamaṇaprāyaścitte'rthavādo na punaḥ pāpadvaiguṇyādi pratipādanam atra vivakṣitam.* Similarly Vir. (*ad* Y. 3. 284-, p. 1031).

28. Mit. (*ad.* Y. 3. 284-285).

29. Compare Kāty. (167, 169, 189, 245).

30. *nātathyena pramāṇaṁ tu doṣenaiva tu dūṣayet,*
mithyābhiyoge daṇḍyaḥ syāt sādhyāryāc cā'pi hīyate; (Kāty. 278, 380. Also quoted in Apar. 2. 72, VyK. 49, SC. 63, 83).

31. E. g. N. *Tīkāsahitā* (2. 5).

32. E. g. Bṛh. (3. 17).

33. *mithyaitad iti Gautamaḥ* (B. 1-1, 2, 7) or *mithyaitad iti Hārītaḥ* (B. 2. 1, 2, 21), Āp. (1. 10, 28, 13; I-10, 29, 12); and *atha khalv ayaṁ puruṣo yāpyena karmaṇā mithyā vā caratyayājyaṁ vā yajayatyapratigrāhyasya vā pratigṛhṇāty anāśyānnasya vānnam aśnāty acaraṇīyena vā carati* (B. 3. 10, 2).

34. We read in the last *ślokas* of book 4 the following :
adaṇḍyadaṇḍane rājño daṇḍa triṁśadguṇo'mbhasi,
varuṇāya pradātavyo brāhmaṇebhyas tataḥ param,
tena tatpūyate pāpaṁ rājño daṇḍāpucārajaṁ,
śāstā hi Varuṇo rājā mithyā vyācaratāṁ nṛṣu. (p. 236. 16-237. 2).

These are only a few examples of the use of the word *mithyā* in the legal literature, where its meaning was either "falsely.", "improperly" or "wrongly."

21. *Use of mithyā in Medical Literature*

In medical literature the word *mithyā* was often used (in the form of compounds) generally meaning "wrongly" or "improperly."

Inter alia in Suś. we come across the word *mithyācāra* in the sense of 'improper conduct', 'wrong treatment'; *mithyo'pacāra* (*mithyā* + *upacāra*) in the sense of "improper treatment"; or *mithyo'payojita* (*mithyā* + *upayojita*) in the sense of "wrongly applied."[35]

In Car. we also come across the word *mithyārambha* in the sense of "wrong treatment."

22. *Use of mithyā in Philosophical Literature*

The philosophical literature of India[36] understands by the expression *mithyā*, *mithyājñāna*, etc. an "error," "false conception," "false apprehension."

Tarkasaṅgraha means by *mithyā*, *mithyājñāna* the cognition of a thing as possessed of an attribute which in fact it does not possess.[37]

Nyāyabodhini definitely identifies *mithyājñāna* with an error—*bhrama*.[38]

Nyāyakośa defines *mithyājñāna* in a similar way, stating that *mithyājñānam—bhramsvad...*

Nyāyasūtra[39] used *mithyā* to mean "false apprehension"; this was destroyed by the knowledge of the truth, just as the concept of an object in a dream came to an end on awakening.[40] This "false apprehension." Nyāyasūtra stated, had a twofold character because of the distinction between the essence and

35. Suś. (Calcutta edition) 1. p. 370-5; 2. p. 314-7; p. 350-7; p. 394-12; p. 368-8).

36. Including Buddhist philosophy.

37. *mithyājñānaṁ viparyayaḥ; tathā śuktau "rajatam" iti* (p. 42; Bombay edition of 1925).

38. *mithyājñānam iti—ayathārthajñnam ity arthaḥ, viparyayo nāma bramaḥ* (p. 42; Bombay edition of 1925).

39. *Nyāyasūtra* (4. 2, 35).

40. *mithyopalabdhivināśas tattvajñānāt svapnaviṣayābhimānapraṇāśavat pratibodhe.*

appearance of its object.[41] Nyāyasūtra also used *mithyājñāna* with the meaning "fault," "misapprehension."[42]

Padmapāda's Pañcapādikā[43] commenting on the first four *sūtra-s* of Śaṅkara's commentary on the Brahmasūtra-s stated that the precise meaning of *mithyājñāna* was there was a force or potency (*śakti*) of ignorance which constituted materiality (*jaḍātmikā avidyāśaktiḥ*) and that it was this potency which transformed itself into the stuff (*upādāna*) of the "world-appearance." It must be noted that Śaṅkara did not seem to go deeply into the meaning of "world-appearance" and simply passed it over in asserting that this "world-appearance" was all due to "ignorance" (*avidyā*). It was neither existing, nor non-existing; it was merely illusory, like the conch-shell silver.

Padmapāda also drew a distinction between two meanings of falsehood (*mithyā*), viz. falsehood as simple negation (*apahnavavacana*) and falsehood as the unspeakable and indescribable (*anirvacanīyatāvacana*).[44]

In Abhidharmakośa of Vasubandhu *mithyā* was often mentioned and in the commentary on *mithyādṛṣti*[45] it was explained that this expression meant "false view." Although all the "views falsely conceived" (*mithyāpravṛtta*) were "false views,' *mithyādṛṣti* alone received this name as it was the falsest of all. It was negation (*apavāda*).

Abhidharmakośa, in enumerating the seven *māna-s*, included the *mithyāmāna*, which was defined as the act of attribution to oneself of qualities (*guṇa*) which one did not possess. This *mithyāmāna* had no foundation (*nirvastuka*). It was the arrogance of a person who was void of some qualities but thought that he had them.[46] Similar was also the explanation of *mithyāmāna* in the *bhāṣya* to Vijñaptimātratāsiddhi (Triṁśikā)[47].

41. *tattvapradhānabheda ca mithyābuddher dvaividhyopapattiḥ* (4. 2, 37).

42. *duḥkhajanmapravṛttidoṣamithyājñānām uttarottarāpāye tadan antarāpāyād apavargaḥ* (1. 1, 2).

43. P. 4; Vizianagram Sanskrit Series.

44. It was probably he who of all the interpreters first described *ajñāna* or *avidyā* as being of a material nature (*joḍātmikā*) and of the nature of a power (*jaḍātmikā avidyāśakti*), and interpreted Śaṅkara's phrase *mithyājñānanimittaḥ* as meaning that it was this material power of *ajñāna* that was the constitutive or the material cause of the world-appearance.

Das Gupta's *History of Indian Philosophy*, Vol. 2. pp. 8; 105.

45. 5. 7, 3.

46. 5. 10a.

47. *Ad* 11-12, *aguṇavato guṇavān asmīti yā cittasyonnatiḥ sa mithyāmānaḥ*.

The *bhāṣya* to Vijñaptimātratāsiddhi (Triṁśikā)[48] also explained that *mithyādṛsti* meant "false view."[49]

Similar was also the conception of Dharmakīrti's Pramāṇavārttika[50] to which Manorathanandin gave the following commentary : *tatsvarūpānyabhāsataḥ.*

In the texts of Śūnyavāda Mahāyāna Buddhism, for instance, in the Laṅkāvatāra Sūtra, *mithyā* was also used to mean "false apprehension". We read in this Sūtra :

keśoṇḍuk aayṁ thā mithyā gṛhyate tai mirain janaiḥ,
tathā bhāva vikalpo'yaṁ mithyā bālair vikalpyate.[51]

Mithyājñāna was understood in the Laṅkāvatāra Sūtra as implying "wrong knowledge", "false apprehension". Later it was stated in this Sūtra :

ananyalakṣaṇābhāvāj jñānaṁ yadi na paśyati,
vyavadhānadūrasām ipyaṁ mithyājñānaṁ tad ucyate.
bālavṛddhāndhayogāc ca jñānaṁ yadi na jāyate,
vidyamānaṁ hi taj jñeyaṁ mithyājñānaṁ tad ucyate.[52]

Laṅkāvatāra Sūtra also mentioned "false illusion" rising from delusion.[53]

23. *Use of mithyā in Lexicographical Literature*

The lexicographers, such as Amarasiṁha in Amarakośa and Hemacandra in Abhidhānacintāmani identified *mithyā* with

48. *Ad* 11-12.

49. *yayā mithyādrsṭyā hetuṁ vā pavadati phalaṁ kriyām vā sad vā vastu nāśayati. Sā sarva darśana pāpatvān mithyādrṣṭir ity ucyate.*

50. *mithyāvabhāṣiṇo vaite pratyaḥ śabdanimmitāḥ* (2. 170).

51. 3. *śl.* 51. "As a hairnet is wrongly perceived by those who are dim-eyed, so existence discriminated (as real) is due to wrong discrimination of the ignorant", (according to D. T. Suzuki's translation).

52. 3.*śl.* 59, 60. "If (transcendental knowledge) fails to see, through various obstructions far and near, its own unique object that does not present itself (as an object). such is to be called wrong knowledge." "If (transcendental) knowledge fails to know, on account of defective senses such as infancy, old age, and blindness, its own object which is present such as to be called wrong knowledge" (according to D. T. Suzuki's translation).

53. *te ca kalpanti yad vastu citta gocara vibhramam,*
kalpanāyām aniṣpannaṁ mithyābhrānti vikalpitam (*Sagāthakam śl.* 51).

"When the field of mentation gets confused, they imagine that there is something (real) to take hold of; in this imagination there is no perfect knowledge, it is false imagination rising from delusion" (according to D. T. Suzuki's translation).

It should be noted that the Laṅkāvatāra Sūtra often used the word *mithyā* in the sense of "false", "falsely" as for instance in Sagāthakam *śl.* 147, 175, 427, 507, etc.

mṛṣā (from *mṛṣ*),[54] thus suggesting that *mithyā* meant "falsely", "improperly", "wrongly."

Mithyādṛṣṭi (*mithyā*+*dṛṣṭi*) was identified in Amarakośa with *nāstika* (from *na*—not) unbeliever,[55] thus indicating that *mithyādṛṣṭi* meant "a denial of God", "disbelief."

Mithyābhiyoga (*mithyā*+*abhiyoga*) was identified in Amarakośa with *abhyākhyā* (from *abhy*+*ā*+*khyā*) "to accuse falsely", and *mithyābhiśaṁsana* (from *mithyā*+*abhi*+*śaṁsana*) was identified in Amarakośa with *abhiśāpa* (from *abhi*+ *śāpa*), "to charge", "to accuse falsely."[56] Thus both these expressions meant "false accusation."[57]

Finally *mithyāmati* (from *mithyā*+*mati*) was identified in Amarakośa and Abhidhānacintāmaṇi with *bhrānti* "wandering about," "confused", "error" and *bhrama* (from *bhram*) "wandering about", "moving round", "confused", "error".[58] Thus *mithyāmati* meant "error."

24. *Interpretation of mithyā*

A. From these few, and, certainly not exhaustive examples, we see that the word *mithyā* had various meanings. It meant "dishonestly" (dishonest action) "falsely", "wrongly", "incorrectly", "improperly", and also "false apprehension", "false conception", "illusion", "error."

According to the commentaries on Nyāyasūtra[59] this error or misapprehension was like a mirage, or dream ; it consisted in imputing "that" to what was "not that" just as one might mistake a post for a man. The objects of the apprehension were however, not unreal, inasmuch as they arose from our memory and imagination. When we mistake a post for a man, our knowledge assumed the form "that is man." Our knowledge of the post, insofar as it was called "that" was a true knowledge,

54. *mṛṣā mithyā* (Amar. 3. 5, 15); Hemacandra identified *mithyā* with *mṛṣā* and *anṛta* stating *mṛṣāmithyānṛte* (1534).

55. *mithyā dṛṣṭir nāstikatā* (Amar. I.1, 4, 13).

56. *mithyābhiyogo'bhyākhyānaṁ atha mithyā bhiśaṁsanaṁ, abhiśāpaḥ* .1 1, 5, 11). Hemacandra's Abhidhānacintāmaṇi (268) stated similarly : *mithyābhiyogo'bhyākhyānaṁ......*

57. Not as Loiseleur Deslonchamps translated the first expression by "groundless demand."

58. *bhrāntir mithyā matir bhramaḥ* (Amar. 1. 1, 4, 13 and identically Abh. 1374).

59. Nyāyasūtra (*ad* 4. 2, 35 and 37).

but insofar as it was described as "man" was a false knowledge. This falsity of knowledge was due to our perception of certain properties common to the post and the man.

Thus, the question arose as to whether a physician acting *mithyā* acted either improperly i.e. dishonestly or erroneously that was falsely. In any case he was responsible for every dishonest or improper act, including carelessness, and so he was responsible for *dolus*, *culpa lata* or *culpa levis*.

If, however, his action being the sequel to misapprehension, appeared to be false or wrong, i.e. when the physician imputed "that" to what was "not that," and gave a wrong diagnosis and treated his patients according to it, in such a case there did not arise any *dolus*, *culpa lata* or *culpa levis*; consquently, it would seem that, in case of such a misapprehension the physician could not be held responsible even if his medical treatment proved to be without success.

B. However, the philosophical interpretation of the word *mithyā* might justify, in some specific cases, consideration of misapprehension as *culpa levis*. One could actually inquire into the reason for such misapprehension; whether it was caused merely by false conception i.e. error, or rather by ignorance. Abhidharmakośa and Vasubandhu and the *bhāṣya* to Vijñaptimātratāsiddhi (Triṁśikā),[60] commenting on *mithyāmāna*, false conception, stated that it had no foundation and thus identified it with ignorance, (arrogance of a person who was void of some qualities but thought he had them). Also the Jainists who recognized five different kinds of *mithyātva* false faiths i.e. *ābhigrahika*, *anābhigrahika*, *abhiniveṣika*, *sāṁśayika* and *anābhoga*, stated that the *anābhoga* was caused by ignorance i.e. through lack of ability to absorb the truth.[61]

C. The question arose as to whether the physician was responsible for every "false apprehension," however much it be "not unreal." The other alternative was to what extent the "falsity of the physician's knowledge was due to his recognition of certain properties (symptoms) common" to various diseases. It seemed that the physician could not be held responsible for every false apprehension, but only then if when misapprehension was due to ignorance, i.e. lack of medical know-

60. Cf. para 22 above.

61. H. V. Glasenapp's *Der Jainismus* (p. 180).

ledge. This type of misapprehension could be considered as *culpa levis*. This seemed also to be evident from the interpretation of Mn. (9.284) given by Medh. and of Y. (2-242) given in Mit.[62] These commentaries stated clearly that the physician was not only responsible for his negligence or greed[63] but also for being devoid of theoretical and practical knowledge.[64]

If, however, the misapprehension was due to false recognition of certain symptoms common to two or more different diseases and at the same time this false recognition was not caused by ignorance but was due exclusively to an error (misapprehension) the physician was free from responsibility for his medical treatment.

D. The word *mithyā* could be interpreted from two different points of view, since the meaning of *mithyā*, as used in the Dharmaśāstra-s and Arthaśāstra-s, was different to some degree from that used in the philosophical literature. It seems however, that both the legal and philosophical interpretations could be used in this case. A physician acting *mithyā*, would therefore not be responsible for improper or dishonest medical treatment alone, but also for an error caused by ignorance.

E. The question of the physician's responsibility for careless improper medical treatment was also solved in K. in two different places. However, K. did not use the word *mithyā*. Although neither text of K. is very clear[65] both indicate that the physician was held responsible only in the case of an improper action, or carelessness and not in the case of misapprehension, even caused by ignorance.

Two different cases were mentioned in K. They were not made *ad personam*, but *ad rem*. The penalty depended upon whether :

(a) the patient died, or
(b) his illness increased (injury to vital parts of the human body).

62. Cf. para 20 above.
63. Medh. and self-evidently also Mit.
64. Medh. and Mit.
It is clear that the mere lack of medical knowledge would not make the physician responsible. Only if his medical treatment proved useless or the patient's illness increased, the physician could be held responsible.
65. K. (203. 14-15 and 135. 4-6).

K.'s opinion was similar as far as the medical treatment of horses (animals) was concerned. The penalty depended upon whether, due to negligence (no matter whether negligence in medical treatment, default in medical treatment, or negligence in the prescription of medicines).

(a) the animal died ("the result became quite the reverse"), or

(b) the illness increased.

In both cases K. did not differentiate between the result of the physician's (veterinarian's) improper action and his fault (*culpa levis, culpa lata*, or *dolus*).

25. *Penalties for improper medical treatment*

A. As mentioned above, according to Mn., the penalty was dependent upon whether a non-human or a human suffered because of poor medical treatment. The same was true of K.'s ruling. According to this Arthaśāstra, special rules referred to human beings, and other to horses (animals).

According to Y. and Vi. the penalty was dependent upon whether he (it) who suffered loss because of medical treatment was (a) an animal,[66] (b) a middle class man, or (c) a king's man.

Although Mn. mentioned only human beings (*mānuṣa*) as victims, Y. and Vi. mentioned *rājapuruṣa or rājamānuṣa* or *uttamamānuṣa* on the one hand, and *mānuṣa* or *madhyama* on the other.

Rājapuruṣa and *uttamamānuṣa* were persons of a higher class, especially king's officials (king's person). *Madhyama* or *mānuṣa* were other common persons, persons of middle class. The fine varied in degree depending upon the category to which the victim belonged (*varṇa*). The rule was the higher the social class to which the victim belonged, the higher was the responsibility of the physician for his carelessness in medical treatment. On this subject Mn. was more "democratic", since it imposed

66. Medh. (*ad* Mn. 9. 284) included in the expression *amānuṣa* (a non-human being), cows, horses, elephants and so forth, while Mit. (*ad* Y. 2.242) used the expression *tiryañc* to mean lower animals. From the point of view of law, the expression *tiryañc*, used in Y. (2. 242) and Vi. (5. 173), was not a good expression, while the word *amānuṣa* used in Mn. (9. 284), was a much better expression because the codificators' aim was, in principle, to take under protection every living being cured by a physician or, more correctly, by a veterinarian i.e. a physician for animals (*tiryañc*) only.

the same penalty on the physician for his improper medical treatment, regardless of the social class of the victim.

B. In principle, the fine was always the same in the Dharmaśāstra-s in the case of animals : the first amercement, has to be imposed.[67] However, according to Mn. and Vi. the first amercement amounted to 250 *paṇa*[68] and according to Y. to 270 *paṇa*.[69]

According to K., however, the penalty depended upon the wrong done. If the animal died the penalty amounted to the value of the animal, and if the illness of the horse (animal) increased, but did not result in death, the penalty amounted to double the cost of the amount usually paid for the successful treatment of an animal.

In the case of human beings, regardless of their rank, Mn. imposed the middlemost amercement, i.e. 500 *paṇa*.[70] According to Y. and Vi.[71] the middlemost amercement was to be imposed in case of persons belonging to the middle class. According to Vi. this middlemost amercement amounted to 500 *paṇa*,[72] but according to Y. it amounted to 540 *paṇa*.[73] In the case of persons of the highest rank the highest amercement was to be imposed according to Y.[74] and Vi.[75] This highest amercement amounted according to Vi. to 1,000 *paṇa*.[76] and according to Y. to 1080 *paṇa*.[77]

According to K.[78] in the case of the patient's death the second highest line had to be imposed. This amercement amounted in K. to 200 to 500 *paṇa*.[79] Should the disease be prolonged (a less dangerous eventuality) the punishment fixed for injuries should be imposed. This last penalty varied in K. from 3 to 24 *paṇa*.[80]

67. Mn. (9. 284), Y. (2. 242), Vi. (5. 173).
68. Mn. (8. 138), (Vi. 4. 14).
69. Y. (1. 365).
70. Mn. (8. 138).
71. Y. (2. 247), Vi. (5. 171).
72. Vi. (4. 14).
73. Y. (1. 365).
74. Y. (2. 242).
75. Vi. (5. 172).
76. Vi. (4. 14).
77. Y. (1. 365).
78. K. (203. 13-15).
79. K. (192. 11-12).
80. K. (194-2 to 195-15).

The rule applied here was very clear and self-evident : the higher penalty had to be imposed, depending upon the class of persons wronged (Mn., Y., Vi.), or upon the value of the objects wronged (K.).

C. We do not find in the Dharmaśāstra-s and Arthaśāstra-s any rule stating that the degree of the penalty to be imposed depended upon the degree of guilt. This characteristic feature can frequently be found elsewhere in ancient Indian law.

It seems that a greater penalty had to be imposed on a physician who intentionally gave improper medical treatment, a lighter penalty on a physician who acted negligently or carelessly, and a still lighter penalty on a physician whose improper medical treatment was due to misapprehension caused by ignorance.

Although such a rule was not stated *expressis verbis* in the Dharmaśāstra-s and Arthaśāstra-s the judge (king) certainly had the right to subject his sentence, as far as the degree of the penalty was concerned, to the degree of guilt of the accused physician proved during the investigation of his case.

VI. REMUNERATION OF PHYSICIANS

26. A. It was accepted in ancient India that physicians should receive remuneration for their work.

We find a general statement in the form of an aphorism in the Vetālapañcaviṁśatikā, where we read that nobody should come empty-handed to a physician. We read there :

riktapāṇir na paśyeta rājānaṁ bhiṣajaṁ gurum,
daivājñaṁ putrakaṁ mitraṁ phalena phalam ādiśet.[1]

Another aphorism is also quoted in C; it contains a similar thought. We read there that a physician (*vaidya*) did not go away from his patient empty-handed because otherwise his visit would have been ineffective.[2]

B. In the Ṛgveda[3] it was stated that the physicians (*bhiṣaj*) and the carpenter (*takṣan*) worked in order to get re-

1. Vet. Intr. 10. Also quoted in *Lassen's* Chrestomathie 2, PT *ad* 152.1, VCsr. 7. 8, CNI. I. 36, CNG 305, CNT IV 244, IS .5786, SB. 265.
2. *devo rājā gurur bhāryā vaidya-nakṣatra-pāṭhakāḥ,*
riktahastā na gacchanti gate kāryaṁ na sidhyati CNW. 8. 8, CNPN 68, Also quoted in IS 2957.
3. Ṛgveda (9.112, 3)

muneration. Similarly, it was stated in the Ṛgveda[4] that the physician expected to receive "a horse, and an ox, and a vestment from his patient."[5]

Jīvaka Komārabhacca, who was contemporary to Buddha, used to receive very high remuneration for his splendid treatment.[6] In the Mahāvagga[7] a physician received remuneration amounting to 200,000 *kāhāpaṇa* for the healing of a *seṭṭhi*.[8]

The necessity of payment to physicians for medical treatment was also evident from Suś. There it was explained whom the physician should treat free of charge. To this category belonged all Brāhmaṇas, *guru*, poor men, friends, ascetics, neighbours, devotees, orphans and people coming from distant countries, who should be treated as if they were his own friends. By acting in this way, Suś. stated, the physician made himself known as learned, and attained friends, fame, virtue, wealth and everything he desired.[9]

C. The legal aspect of the obligation of payment to the physician was dealt with in K., where we read: *kāru śilpi kuśīlavacikitsaka vāgjīvana paricārakādirā śākārikavargas tu yathā'nyas tad vidhaḥ kuryāt, yathā vā kuśalāḥ kalpayeyuḥ, tathā vetanaṁ labheta*,[10] and *adhyakṣasaṅkhyāyakā dibhyo gopasthānikānīkasthacikitsakāśvadamakajaṅghākarikebhyaś ca vikrayādhānavarjam.*[11]

Thus, we see that K. stated clearly that physicians (*cikitsaka*) who worked on their own, had to earn as much as persons employed in a similar fashion elsewhere usually received.[12] However those (*cikitsaka* and *anīkastha*) who were induced to migrate to newly formed villages, received lands from the king. These lands could not be sold or mortgaged. It is understood that migrant-physicians received the usual wages, in addition to the land.

4. Ṛgveda (9.97, 4, 8).
5. ZDMG 25, 646.
6. Vinaya Texts, translated from the Pali by T. W. Rhys Davids and H. Oldenberg, part II, p. 173 sqq.

Compare also P. K. Gode's "Some Estimates of the Indian Physician and his Profession between A. D. 1550 and 1820" in *Journal of the Kaliṅga Historical Research Institute*, 93".

7. Mahāvagga (8-1, 16 sqq.).
8. He had to share it with the king Bimbisāra.
9. Suś. (1.2).
10. K. (184. 1-3).
11. K. (46. 10-11).
12. Cf. below study XIV. on Legal Relations between Employers and Employees in Ancient India.

Physicians-officials who served in the army received according to K., a fixed salary of 2,000 *paṇa per annum*, which was rather a small salary compared with that of ministers (48,000), Collector-Generals (24,000), Chiefs of military corporations (5,000), Superintendents of infantry and cavalry (4,000), Chariot drivers, Trainers of horses (2,000), soldiers, accountants and writers (500).[13]

If it was difficult to fix the salary to be paid to the physicians on the basis of the clause "as similar persons employed elsewhere received,"[14] experts (*kuśala*) had to be called to fix the amount of wages due.[15] In case of failure to pay wages, the patient, according to K., had to be punished with the fine of ten times the amount of wages or 6 *paṇs*.[16]

27. From the legal rules, quoted above, it is evident that physicians had the full right to remuneration for their treatment and were also legally entitled to claim it :

(A) as settled before, or agreed upon,[17] and,

(B) if not settled

  (a) in the same amount as was obtained usually by similar persons, or

  (b) in the amount to be fixed by experts.

However, the physician who wished to attain virtue, wealth and be the object of desire and fame had "not to accept (with the exception of eatables) any other presents" from the patients.[18] The same was stated in Car.[19] where we read that "those physicians who, for the sake of their living, sell treatment as (if it were) an article of trade, (may be said to) throw off heaps of gold and accept heaps of ashes in return."[20]

These rules referred, however, only to certain very learned and wealthy physicians.

13. D. V. S. Reddy's "The Physician in the Mauryan Empire in *The Indian Physician* II," No. 29, p. 372.

14. See note 12 above.

15. K. (184. 2-3). See note 12 above.

16. *vetanādāne daśabandho daṇḍaḥ ṣaṭpaṇo vā* (K. 184-5).

17. *saṁbhāṣitavetanas tu yathāsaṁbhāṣitam* (K. 183-20).

18. Suś. (1-10 *in fine*).

19. *nārtharthāṁ nā'pi kāmārtham atha bhūtadayāṁ prati*
vartate yaś cikitsāyāṁ sa sarvam ativartate,
kurvate ye tu vṛtty artham cikitsā-paṇya-vikrayam,
te hitvā kāncanaṁ rāśiṁ pāṁśurāśim upāsate (Car. 6. 1, 3, 58, 59).

20. According to A. C. Kaviratna's translation.

VII. CONCLUSIONS

A. We find, firstly in the medical literature, rules, which have to be considered as *leges imperfectae*, concerning the study of medicine, the qualifications of medical students and their teachers, and the qualifications of physicians.

B. In order to be able to practise in ancient India, a physician (*vaidya*, *bhiṣaj*, *cikitsaka*, *śalyakṛnta*) had to receive a special permission—license from the State (king). The license was an administrative act which legally entitled the physician to begin medical treatment and to accept remuneration.

C. The Dharmaśāstra-s and Arthaśāstra-s, did not contain any rules stipulating the type of medical treatment. The medical literature, however, gave a very detailed picture of the medical treatment, as well as some information on the ethics of physicians. They were not obliged to treat everybody. On the contrary, lists enumerated those persons who should not be treated by conscientious physicians. This list was a result of specific social conditions prevailing in ancient India. In addition, the physician was not allowed to treat all diseases, particularly incurable ones.

When treating serious cases, which might cause death, physicians had to inform the corresponding administrative office. The same practice applied to patients suspected of concealing their whereabouts. Violation of this rule would result in punishment for the physician, or for anyone concealing a patient. The first rule was introduced in order to safeguard the physician from misuse of the regulation relating to his responsibility for negligence in medical treatment. The second rule was introduced as a means of ascertaining the whereabouts of enemies of the State (king), partisans, etc.

D. In order to protect the ancient Indian society from rogue-physicians and negligence in medical treatment, the Dharmaśāstra-s and Arthaśāstra-s introduced rules concerning the responsibility of physicians and veterinarians for improper medical treatment, which depended on the social class of the patient. The physician was held responsible for his *mithyā* action when it was caused by *dolus*, *culpa lata* or *culpa levis*. He was also held responsible if his *mithyā* action was the result of false conception-misapprehension, but only if this misapprehension—wrong diagnosis was due to his ignorance, his lack of medical knowledge. If the false apprehension was due to false recognition of certain peculiarities (symptoms) common to different diseases and was caused purely by an error and not by ignorance, the physician was not held responsible for his medical treatment.

E. The degree of the penalty depended upon the result of *mithyā* medical treatment, and particularly upon the degree of the wrong done, i.e. whether the treatment led to death, increased illness, or proved useless. It was also dependent upon the social class of the patient.

No rule existed in the Dharmaśāstra-s and Arthaśāstra-s stating that the degree of penalty depended upon the degree of the guilt of the physician. This rule was accepted however, in the light of the general principle which gave to the king (judge) the right to use his own discretion in the imposition of penalities.

F. The rules relating to the responsibility of physicians for their improper medical treatment were not introduced primarily to safeguard the patient, but rather to safeguard the good administration of the State. There is no specific mention in the Dharmaśāstra-s and Arthaśāstra-s, therefore, of the right of the patient to an indemnity; the penalty was imposed by the State and paid to the State (king).

G. Other rules found in the medical and legal literature did not refer to the legal position of physicians. They show that physicians enjoyed a foremost position in the social structure of the ancient Indian State and that they were held in high esteem. This factor was responsible for their use as spies in the machiavellian system of Kauṭilya's state-administration.

IX

LEGAL, FISCAL, SOCIAL AND PENAL PRIVILEGES ACCORDED TO INFANTS, AGED, DISEASED, HELPLESS AND DISTRESSED PERSONS ACCORDING TO ANCIENT INDIAN LAW*

I. INTRODUCTION

Infants (*bāla*)[1], aged persons (*vṛddha*), persons afflicted with disease (*vyādhita*), and distressed persons (*ārta*)[2],[3] had a peculiar and special place in the Indian law, for according to Mn. they should be always held in respect by the king.[4] They should be honoured, treated with kindness and should be the recipient of gifts.[5]

They[6] conquered all the worlds[7] and, therefore, one[8] should not enter into a dispute with them.[9] A *snātaka*

* Previously appeared as JSAIL. 15 in the "Sarūpa-Bhāratī, being the Dr. Lakshman Sarup Memorial Volume", pp. 326-41. Submitted to the 159th meeting of the American Oriental Society, 1949, New Haven, Conn.

1. *Bāla* was one who had not reached the age of sixteen (Kull. and Nār. on Mn. 8. 27, *Śūlapāṇi ad* Y. 2. 25 and many others). Cf. below XIV study on Legal Relations between Employers and Employees in Ancient India., 3 B.

2. *Ārta* or *ārtta*. According to Medh. 'distressed by separation from his loved ones or such other causes" : *ārttaḥ priyaviyogādinā* (Medh. *ad* Mn. 8. 395).

3. As well as vedic scholars (*śrotriya*), indigent persons (*akiñcana*), persons of high birth (*mahākulīna*) and honourable persons (*ārya*).

4. *śrotriyaṁ vyādhitārttau ca bāla-vṛddāv akiñcanam,*
mahākulīnaṁ āryaṁ ca rājā saṁpūjayet sadā. (Mn. 8. 395).

5. That was the explanation given by Medh. to the word *saṁpūjana* : *saṁpūjanam anugrahaḥ...eteṣāṁ dānam ānābdibir anugrahaḥ kartavyaḥ.* (Medh. *ad* Mn. 8. 395). *Saṁ* V‾*pūj* meant also to salute deferentially, honour greatly, revere, to present respectfully with, to praise, to commend, etc.

6. Infants (*bāla*), aged persons (*vṛddha*) and persons afflicted with (*ātura*) (Y. 1. 157).

7. *mātṛ-pitra-tithi-bhrātṛ-jāmi-sambandha-mātulaiḥ,*
vṛddha-bālā-turā'cārya-vaidya-saṁśrita-bāndhavaiḥ.
ṛtvik-purohitā'patya-bhāryā-dāsa-sanābhibhiḥ,
vivādaṁ varjayitvā tu sarvān llokāñjayad gṛhī. (Y. 1. 157-8)

8. A *snātaka*.

9. *mātrādibhir vivādaṁ kalahaṁ vakṣyamāṇa-lakṣaṇaṁ vyavahāraṁ varjayan gṛhasthaḥ sarvān brāhmaṇādīn lokān jayati prāpnoti tasmād ebhir vivādaṁ nācared iti tātparyaṁ,* (Vīr. *ad* Y. 157-8).

should not quarrel with them.[10]

The rule given in the Dharmaśāstra-s that a Brāhmaṇa should without hesitation give food to these persons 'even before his guests[11],' can well be taken as an illustrative example, that they should be honoured.

The legal implication of the rule that they be 'treated with kindness'' is that these persons should be given special privileges. They were under a special protection of the State, because of their dependence and their inability to direct their own affairs.[12],[13]

These privileges were accorded in ancient India to these persons[14] in the legal, fiscal, social and penal fields. Many examples could be quoted; below only the most important privileges granted are given :

10. *ṛtvik-purohitā'cāryair mātulā-tithi-saṁśritaiḥ,*
bāla-vṛddhā'turair vaidyair jñāti-sambandhi-bāndhavaiḥ,
mātā-pitṛbhyāṁ jāmībhir bhrātrā putreṇa bhāryayā,
duhitrā dāsa-vargeṇa vivādaṁ na samācaret· (Mn. 4. 179-80).

Cf. *Mahābhārata* 12, 244-14, 15.

11. Infants or young people (*bāla*, *kumāra*, etc.) were mentioned in Mn. (3. 114), Y. (1. 105). Āp. (2. 2, 4, 12), B. (2. 7, 13, 5), G. (5. 25), *Śañkhāyaṇa-Gṛhyasūtra* (2. 14, 21), *Pāraskara-Gṛhyasūtra* (2. 9, 13), *Viṣṇu-Purāṇa* in *Parāśaramādhavīya* p. 364, M.P. (*idem*) aged persons (*vṛddha*, *sthavira*, etc.) were mentioned in Y. (1. 105), Āp. (2. 4, 12), B. (2. 7, 13, 5), G. (5. 25), *Śāṅkhāyana-Gṛhyasūtra* (2. 14, 21), *Pāraskara-Gṛhyasūtra* (2. 9, 13), *Viṣṇu-Purāṇa* in *Parāśaramādhavīya* p. 364, *MP.* (*idem*); persons afflicted with disease (*ātura*) are mentioned in Mn. (3. 114), Y. (1. 105), Āp. (2. 2, 4, 12), B. (2. 7, 13, 5), G. (5. 25); distressed persons (*dīna*) were mentioned in B. (2. 7, 13, 5), etc.

12. Infants were mentioned in Mn. (8. 163), Y. (2. 32). Bṛh. (6. 52), Vi. (7. 10), K. (184.11); aged persons are mentioned in Mn. (8. 163), K. (148. 11), Śūlapāṇi (*ad* Y. 2. 32); distressed persons were mentioned in Y. (2. 32); Bṛh. (in VyM 13. 28, VI, 42), N. (1. 41). Mention was also made of persons afflicted with disease (*unmatta*) in Mn. (8. 163), Y. (2. 32), Bṛh. (in VyM. 13. 28). etc.

13. As such they are considered as incapable to conclude any contracts. Cf. below study XIV on Legal Relations between Employers and Employees in Ancient India, 3 B.

They could not give evidence in court and be called as witnesses. Infants (*bāla*, *śiśu*) were mentioned in Mn. (8. 66, 71), Y. (2. 70), Vi. (8. 2, 3), N. (1. 187, 190, 191) because they would give fake evidence due to their ignorance, *ajñāna*), Uśanas (in VyM 17. 6); persons afflicted with disease (*ātura*) were mentioned in Mn. (8. 71), N. (1. 179); distressed persons (*ārta*) were mentioned in N. (1.178). They were also not acceptable as sureties (*bāla* and *vṛddha*) and the like. Cf. above study V. on Suretyship, in 30 D.

14. As well as to others, the most important of which were women (*strī*). In this connexion cf. A. S. Altekar, *The Position of Women in Hindu Civilisation*, Benares, 1938 ; J. J. Meyer : *Das Weib im altindischen Epos*.

II. LEGAL PRIVILEGES

1. *Protection of Property*

The most general rule, found in the Smṛti-s and Dharmaśāstra-s, stated that the property of persons incapable of transacting legal business (*aprāptavyavahāra*) had to be protected by the king.[15] *Aprāptavyavahāra* implied, in the first place, minors in law[16]; it implied also other persons incapable of transacting legal business, such as women, helpless persons, etc.

In Vi. we also find a more general rule ; it was stated there that the king was required to protect the property of infants (*bāla*), helpless persons (*anātha*) and of women.[17] In G. it was stated only that the property of infants (*bāla*) must be protected[18]; similarly Mn.[19] and AP.[20]

Special rules for the protection of property of persons incapable of transacting legal business (*aprāptavyavahāra*), in regard to inheritance law, are also to be found in Kāty.[21] K.[22], B.[23] and others.[24]

The protection of the property of infants (*bāla*), helpless persons (*anātha*), or those persons who were unfit to transact legal business (*aprāptavyavahāra*) meant the administration of their property, as long as they were unfit to transact legal business on their own. This was explained in Vās., Mn. G. in so far as it related to infants.

15. *aprāpta,vyavahāraṇāṁ.* (Vās. 16. 8). Similarly Śaṅkha-Likhita, in VCi. 598.

16. Monier-Williams : *A Sanskrit-English Dictionary.*

17. *bālā'nāthā-strī-dhanāni ca rājā paripālayet* (Vi. 3. 65).

18. *rakṣyaṁ bāladhanamā vyavahāra prāpaṇāt sagmavṛtter vā.* (G. 10. 48. Also quoted in Apar. *ad* Y. 2. 25, GMH. 10. 48-9, VyP. 460).

19. *bāla-dāyādikaṁ rikthaṁ tāvad rājān upālayet* (Mn. 8. 27. Also quoted in MV, VyK. 161, SC. 132, VRK. 598, SS. 137, VCi. 244, VyP. 83, VyS.72).

20. Rājadharma (222. 18-9).

21. *aprāpta-vyavahārāṇāṁ ca dhanaṁ vyaya-vivarjitam,*
nyaseyur bandhu-mitreṣu proṣitānāṁ tathaiva ca. (Kāty. 845. Also quoted in Apar. *ad* Y. 2. 117, VCa. 73).

22. *prāpta-vyavahāraṇāṁ vibhāgaḥ, aprāpta-vyavahārāṇāṁ deya-viśuddhaṁ mātṛbandhuṣu grāma-vṛddheṣu vā sthāpayeyur vyavahāra-prāpaṇāt proṣitasya vā.* (K. 161. 4-6).

23. *teṣām aprāpta-vyavahāṇām aṁśān so'pacyān suriguptan nidadhyurā vyavahārā prāpaṇāt.* (B. 2. 2. 3, 36. Also quoted in VyK. 161. VRK. 599, SS. 137).

24. According to some commentators Mn. (8. 27) referred to inheritance law only.

Vās., although using the word *aprāptavyavahāra*, stated that as soon as this person came of age, his property had to be made over to him.[25]

Mn.[26] and G.[27] dealing with the same rule stated that the king should protect the property of a minor until he had returned from his teacher's house or until reached the age of maturity. According to the commentators (Kull. and Nār.) a youth attained manhood upon reaching his sixteenth year, but if "an infant" finished his Veda-study before attaining sixteen years of age, he became capable of transacting legal business on his own. Medh. also explained that the first alternative was applied to *dvija-s* and the second to *sūdra-s*.[28]

It is evident from the rules quoted above that a most general protection was extended by the State to infants and helpless persons as long as they were incapable of transacting legal business. They received a legal guardian in the person of the king, or his administration unless other persons, who were nearer to the infants, or to other persons who were incapable of transacting legal business had not the right and duty to take care of them.

2. *Legal Advisers*

K. stated clearly that transactions of infants (*bāla*), aged persons (*vṛddha*) persons afflicted with disease (*vyādhita*) and helpless persons (*anātha*) had to be decided by judges themselves (K. 200 1-3).[29] That meant that these persons, being under the special protection of the State, enjoyed not only the

25. *prāptakāle tu tadyat.* (Vās. 16. 9).

26. *yāvat sa syāt samāvṛtto yāvad vā'tīta śaiśavah.* (Mn. 8. 27. Also quoted in MV, VyK. 161, SC. 132, VRK. 598, SS. 137, VCi. 244, VyP. 83, VyS. 72).

27. *rakṣyaṁ bāla-dhanamā vyavahāra prāpaṇāt samāvṛtter vā.* (G. 10. 48 Also quoted in Apar. *ad* Y. 2. 25, GMH. 10. 48-9, VyP. 460.).

28. *bālo dāyādo'sya tad idaṁ bāladāyā'dikaṁ, dāyādaḥ svām yatrocyate, bāla svāmikaṁ dhanaṁ tāvad rājā rakṣed yāvad asau samāvṛtto gurukulāt pratyāgato yāvadvā'tītaśaiśavaḥ atikrāntabālabhāvaḥ, ayaṁ ca vikalpaḥ, yo gṛhaśaiśavo bhavati tad artham atīta śaiśavam ucyate—yas tu vratakḥ sa nivṛtte'pi śaiśave ā samāvartanāpratipālya-dhanaḥ syāt, athavā dvijātīnāṁ samāvartanaṁ avadhiranyeṣāṁ śaiśavātyayaḥ.* (Medh. *ad* Mn. 8. 27).

29. *deva-brāhmaṇatapasvi-strī-bāla-vṛddha-vyādhitānām anāthanām anabhitsaratāṁ dharmasthāḥ kāryāṇi kuryuḥ, na ca deśa-kāla-bhogac-chālenā'tihareyuḥ.* (K. 200. 1-3).

special privileges in law, mentioned above, but had also in the judges their official legal advisers who had to transact without any fee, *ex officio*, all the affairs of the infants (*bāla*), aged persons (*vṛddha*), those afflicted with disease (*vyādhita*) and helpless persons (*anātha*).

3. *Statute of Limitations*

A. According to the ancient Indian law, ownership of property could not be acquired by another person through possession of the property for ten or twenty years if the owner did not object to such a possession ; possession was not a *titulus acquirendi* of ownership (Mit. *ad* Y. 2. 24).[30] However, the owner of the property could not receive it if he 'was looking quietly' that another person enjoyed his property for ten or twenty years,[31] because if a man was so foolish' that he allowed his property to be enjoyed by another person before his very

30. Different was the opinion of other schools, e.g. Asahāya on N. *ad* (1. 78).

31. *yat kiṁcid daśa-varṣāṇi saṁnidhau prekṣate dhanī,*
bhujyamānaṁ parais tūṣṇīṁ na sa tal-labdhu-marhati. (Mn. 8. 147). Also quoted in VyMā. 347, GMH. 12. 34, DK. 33, SS. 106, VyC. 67, VyT. 222, VCa. 153, VySau. 68, VyP. 157, VV. 88, VyS. 46, VVCa. 136; identical N. 1. 79, NMS 2. 70, Śukr. 4. 713-4; also quoted in VyMā. 347, VyK. 72, VyT. 222, VCa. 153, VySau. 68, VyP. 157, BBh. *ad* Y 2. 24, VV. 48, Vyp. 45).

paśyato'bruvato bhūmer hānir bhūmer viṁśati-vārṣikī,
pareṇa bhujyamānāyā dhanasya daśa-varṣikī. (Y. 2. 24. Also quoted in Apar. 253. 52-3, ViR. *ad* Y. 2. 24, Medh. *ad* MnM 8.3, VyMā. 342, GMH. 12. 34, SC. 68, 311, SS. 94, VyC. 65, VyT. 208, SV. 125, Rāgh. in MnM. 8. 148, VCa. 153, VySau. 68, VyP. 157, VT. 144, RDhK. 395, VV. 87, VyS. 46, VVCa. 136).

ajaḍā'pogaṇḍa dhanaṁ daśa-varṣa-bhuktaṁ paraiḥ saṁnidhau bhoktuḥ. na śrotriya-pravrajita-rājanya-puruṣaiḥ. paśu-bhūmi-strīṇāṁ anatibhogaḥ. (G. 12. 37-9. Also quoted in VyMā. 346, GMH. 12, 34-6, SS. 106, VyC. 67, VyT. 223, VyP. 166, 45, VV. 88, VVCa. 137, VyK. 73-4, VySau. 69).

paśyann anyasya dadataḥ kṣitiṁ yo na nivārayet,
satā'pi lekhyena bhuvaṁ na punastāmavāpnuyāt. (Bṛh. 7. 41. Also quoted in VyMā. 348, Apar. *ad* Y. 2. 25, GMH. 68, SS. 107, VCa. 156, VyP. 158, VyS. 46, VVy. 18).

yaṁ kañcid daśa-varṣāṇi san nidhau prekṣate dhanī,
bhūjyamānaṁ parair arthaṁ na sa taṁ labdhu-marhati.
varṣāṇi yiṁśatir yasya bhūr-bhuktā tu parair iha,
sati rājñi samarthasya tasya seha na sidhyati. (Śukr. 4. 5, 221-2).

Cf. also *śaktasya saṁnidhāv artho yena lekhyena bhujyate,*
varṣāṇi viṁśatiṁ yāvat tat patraṁ doṣa-varjitam. (Kāty. 299. Also quoted in VyMā. 340, 346. Mit *ad* Y. 2. 24, VyK. 66, SC. 64, VyC. 63, 67, NṛP. 9, SV. 121, VT. 145-6, VyS. 44, VVy. 16).

Cf. also Vyāsa quoted in DK. (*ad* Y. 2. 24), Vās. (16. 16-7) and Bṛh (7. 43-6).

eyes then he had no right to recover it.[32] Where, however, the owner, though unable to recover his property owing to special reasons, proffered his claim every day, or every month, or every year, it was not lost to him even after the lapse of ten or twenty years, whichever period should be applicable.[33]

Hence, according to some of the Indian juridical schools the right of ownership was lost through failure to exercise this right and according to some other schools the right of ownership was acquired by the long exercise of possession.

B. There were some exceptions from this general rule. And so, this rule could not be applied, *inter alia*, to minors (*poganḍa*),[34] since according to Mn.,[35] Y.[36], N.[37], Vās.,[38] Śukr.[39], and G.[40],[41] the property of infants (*bāla*) and other persons mentioned in the Dharmaśāstra-s and Arthaśāstra-s was not lost by adverse possession.

32. Or the goods shall belong to the possessor, even in the presence and during the lifetime of the rightful owners.

bhujyamānān parair arthān yaḥ svān maurkhyād upekṣate,
samakṣaṁ jīvato'py asya tān bhuktīḥ kurute vaśe (N. 1. 78).

33. *yadi punar deśa-kālabalā-pekṣayā svā'rthaṁ prāptuṁ na kṣamaḥ, prativacāḥ pratidinaṁ pratimāsaṁ prativarṣaṁ ca karoti, tataḥ kālāntare'pi tat tasya na praṇaśyati vyavahāra uttaraṁ labhata ity arthaḥ.* (Asahāya *ad* N. 1. 79).

34. *ajaḍaś ced apogaṇḍo viṣaye cā'sya bhujyate,*
bhagnaṁ tad vyavahāreṇa bhoktā tad dhana marhati. (Mn. 8. 148. Also quoted in Mit. *ad* Y. 2. 24, Apar. *ad* Y. 2. 24, SC. 68, DV. 292, SV. 127, VCa. 153, VyPr. 158, VT. 145, VyP. 45, VyS. 47; identically N. 180, also quoted in NMS, 2. 75, VyMā. 350, SC. 70, VyT. 226, VCa. 154, VV. 92, VyP. 45, VyS. 47, VVCa. 142, VVy. 19. Cf. Bṛh. (7. 31).

35. *ādhiḥ sīmā bāla-dhanaṁ nikṣepo'panidhīḥ striyaḥ,*
rājasvaṁ śrotriyasvaṁ ca na bhogena praṇaśyati (Mn. 8. 149. Also quoted in VyMā. 351, VyK. 74).

36. *ādhi-sīmo'panikṣepa-jaḍa-bāla-dhanair-vinā,*
tatho'panidhi-rāja-strī-śrotriyāṇaṁ dhanair api. (Y. 2. 25. Also quoted in ViR. *ad* Y. 2. 25, Subodhinī *ad* Y. 2. 24, VyT. 2.24, SV. 126, VyPr. 165, VT. 150, VV. 89, VyP. 44, VyS. 47, VVCa. 138, AP' 253. 53-4).

37. *ādhiḥ sīma-bāla-dhanaṁ nikṣepo'panidhī striyaḥ,*
rājasvaṁ śrotriya-dravyaṁ na bhogena praṇaśyati. (N. 1. 81, Also quoted in NMS. 2. 73, VyMā. 351, VyK. 74, SS. 107, VyC. 75, SCM. 50, VySau. 69, VyPr. 166, VyM. 15, VVy. 20).

38. *ādhiḥ sīmā bāla-dhano nikṣepo'panidhi striyaḥ,*
rājasvaṁ śrotriya-dravyaṁ na saṁbhogena hīyate. (Vās. 16. 18).

39. *ādhiḥ sīmā bāla-dhanaṁ nikṣepo'panidhis tathā,*
rājasvaṁ śrotriyasvaṁ ca na bhogena praṇaśyati. (Śukr. 4. 5, 225).

40. *ajaḍāpogaṇḍa-dhanaṁ daśa-varṣa-bhuktāṁ paraiḥ saṁnidhau bhoktuḥ na śrotriya-pravrajita-rājanya-puruṣaiḥ. paśu-bhūmi-strīṇāṁ anatibhogaḥ.* (G. 12. 37-9. Also quoted in VyMā. 346, VyK. 73, GMH. 12. 34, SS. 106, VyC. 67, VyT 223, VyPr. 166, VV. 88, VVCa. 137).

41. Cf. Bṛh. (7. 41) and K. 190. 17-8) quoted below.

We see here that according to the most important Dharmaśāstra-s and Arthaśāstra-s the minors (*pogaṇḍa*) or infants (*bāla*) were under the special protection of the law, since the Dharmaśāstra-s and Arthaśāstra-s considered them as exceptions and ruled that infants (minors) did not lose their rights of ownership by failure to exercise this right and could recover their right of ownership even if the possessor enjoyed before his very eyes, *in bona fide*, the possession.

C. K. went further and, quoting the same rule as that found in Mn. Y., Vās., Śukr., and G.[42], stated that forfeiture of the title of ownership, if it was used by another person during ten years, had not to be applied to infants (*bāla*) only, but also to aged persons (*vṛddha*), persons afflicted with disease (*vyādhita*) and helpless persons (*vyasanin*) who were absent from home, or who had deserted their country during national disturbances.[43]

D. K. also stated that debts neglected for ten years which, in principle, could not be recovered after that period of time might be recovered, *inter alia*, in case of infants (*bāla*), aged persons (*vṛddha*), persons afflicted with disease (*vyādhita*) and distressed persons (*vyasanin*).[44] K. stated in general, that to transactions pertaining, *inter alia*, to infants (*bāla*), aged persons (*vṛddha*), afflicted with disease (*vyādhita*) and helpless persons (*anātha*) excuses with regard to time, place or possession could not be pleaded.[45]

4. *Interests on debts*

According to K.[46] infants (*bāla*) and persons afflicted with disease (*vyādhita*) were exempt from the payment of interest on debts. Interest on debts due from these persons as well as from those engaged in sacrifices

42. Cf. paragraph 4 B.

43. *yat svaṁ dravyam anyair bhujyamānaṁ daśa-varṣāṇy upekṣeta, hīyetāsya anyatra bāla-vṛddha-vyādhitavya-saniproṣita-deśa-tyāga-rājya-vibhramebhyaḥ.* (K. 190. 17-8).

44. *daśa-varṣo-pekṣitaṁ ṛṇam apratigrāhyam anyatra bāla-vṛddha-vyādhitavya-saniproṣita-deśātyāga-rājya-vibhramebhyaḥ* (K. 174. 16-7).

45. *deva-brāhmaṇa-tapasvi-strī-bāla-vṛddha-vyādhitānām anāthānām amabhisaratāṁ dharmasthāḥ kāryāṇi kuryuḥ, na ca deśa-kāla-bhogac-chalenā'ti hareyuḥ.* (K. 200. 1-3).

46. *dīrgha-satra-vyādhi-guru-kulopa-vṛddhaṁ bālamasāraṁ vā narṇamanuvardheta* (K. 174. 14).

taking a long time, or detained in the houses of their teachers, or those who were very poor could not be permitted to accumulate. Thus Arthaśāstra-s considered that these persons were unable to pay interest and, therefore, exempted them from this obligation. The case of infants (*bāla*) and persons afflicted with disease (*vyādhita*) was probably based on the precept that they were, according to the ancient Indian law, under the special protection of the State.

III FISCAL PRIVILEGES

5. *Exemption from Taxes and Tolls*

According to Vās., *inter alia*, infants (*bāla*), aged persons (*vṛddha*) and youth (*taruṇa*) were exempt from taxes.[47] According to Āp, *inter alia*, male children before attaining puberty (*kumāra prāgvyañjana*) and persons afflicted with disease (*rogin*)[48] and, according to Mn., very aged persons, that is seventy years old (*saptatyā sthavira*)[49] were exempt from taxes.

We do not find in K. a similar rule. K. stated only that, *inter alia*, infants (*bāla*), aged persons (*vṛddha*) and persons afflicted with disease (*vyādhita*) were exempt from tolls, when crossing rivers.[50]

Both these rules show that the Dharmaśāstra-s and Arthaśāstra-s accorded to the persons who were under the special protection of the State certain fiscal privileges.

IV. SOCIAL PRIVILEGES

In Kauṭilya's Arthaśāstra we find a very interesting and progressive rules which show that the State accorded, at that time, special privileges to persons who were under the special protection of the State and that it was incumbent upon the

47. *akaraḥ śrotriyo rājā-pumān-anātha-pravrajita-bāla-vṛddha-taruṇa-prajātāḥ.* (Vās. 19. 23. Also qyoted in Vīr. 640, DV. 111).

48. *akaraḥ śrotriyaḥ. sarva-varṇānāṁ ca striyaḥ. kumārāś ca prāg vyañjanebhyaḥ. ye'ca vidyā'rthā vasanti. tapasvinaś ca ye dharma-parāḥ. śūdraś ca pādavanektā. andha-mūka-badhira-rogā-viṣṭāś ca. ye vyarthā dravya-parigrahaiḥ.* (Āp. 2. 10, 26, 10-7. Also quoted in HDh. 2. 19).

49. *andho jaḍaḥ pīṭhasarpī saptatyā sthaviraś ca yah,*
śrotriyeṣūpakurvaṁś ca na dāpyāḥ kenacit karam. (Mn. 8. 394).

50. *brāhmaṇa-pravrajita-bāla-vṛddha-vyādhita-śāsanahara-garbhiṇyo nāvadhyakṣa-mudrābhistareyuḥ.* (K. 127. 5-6).

State to take care of these persons. It might be said that these privileges had more of a social than of a legal implication.

The State, according to Kauṭilya, maintained these persons; it was a type of a Government relief and assistance scheme. The State also accorded to deceased relatives of government servants special privileges; it was a type of widows and orphans pension scheme. Finally the State accorded to those persons also the right to petition the king personally.

These special privileges were also accorded in the Dharmaśāstra-s.[51]

6. *Government Relief and Assistance Scheme*

A. According to K. the king had to provide, *inter alia*, infants (*bāla*), aged persons (*vṛddha*), persons afflicted with disease (*vyādhita*), distressed persons (*vyasanin*) and helpless persons (*anātha*) with maintenance (*bibhṛyāt*).[52] This was, as stated above, a type of Government relief and assistance scheme.

B. It is, however, doubtful whether this scheme was completely free, that is, whether the State (the king) could require from the persons, whom he maintained to do something for him. It is stated in K. that persons not related, who were not bound with anybody, (*asambandhin*)[53] and who were necessarily supported (maintained : *avaśyabhartavya*) had to study science, palmistry, sorcery etc. in order to become government spies.[54]

Persons who had to be supported always by the State were mentioned above,[55] that is, infants (*bāla*), aged persons (*vṛddha*), persons afflicted with disease (*vyādhita*), distressed persons (*vyasanin*), and helpless persons (*anātha*), as well as helpless women when they were carrying and new-born male children.[56] In the context, mentioned above, K. used the word *asambandhin*

51. With the exception of penal privileges, all the other privileges in social matters were accorded in K. only.

52. *bāla-vṛddha-vyādhitavya-sanyanāthaṁś ca rājā vibhṛyāt.* (K. 47. 19).

53. I read the text *ya cā'py asambandhino* (Shamashastry) and not *ye cā'sya sambandhino* (Gaṇapati Śāstri).

54. *ye cā'pyasam-bandhino'vaśya bhartavyāste lakṣaṇam aṅgavidyāṁ jambhaka-vidyāṁ māyāgatam āśramadharmanimitta-mantra-cakram ity ādhīyānāḥ satriṇas-saṁsarga-vidyā vā* (K. 20. 2-4).

55. K. (47. 19). See above.

56. *striyam aprajātāṁ prajātāyāś ca putrān.* (K. 47. 20).

which had a broad meaning. It can be applied to all kinds of persons who enjoyed special privileges. It is evident from the whole Chapter Twelve of the First Book of K., that the work of spies was not an easy one, and, therefore, it was difficult to admit that, for instance, aged persons (*vṛddha*) or persons afflicted with disease (*vyādhita*) would be able to become spies. However, infants (*bāla*) or new-born male children, as soon as they were capable of administering their own affairs, or women after child birth, etc., if they were *asambandhin* that is, not related, not having any relative, who had no support from any source except the State, were to study science, palmistry, etc., in order to become spies.

K., although introducing a very progressive scheme of Government relief and assistance, had also in mind the machiavellian needs of the State.

7. *Widows and Orphans' Pension Scheme*

According to K.,[57] there existed a widow's and orphans' pension scheme in case of the death of government servants. Śukr.[58] also stated that the king had to pay to the wife, well behaved daughters, as well as sons of the deceased government servant as long as they were incapable and minors, a special pension.

K. went further and stated that the same favour should be shown to infants (*bāla*), aged persons (*vṛddha*) and persons afflicted with disease (*vyādhita*), if they were related to the deceased government servant.[59] Since this sentence immediately follows the general rule as to the, widows' and orphans' pension scheme it seems to be clear that infants (*bāla*), mentioned in this context, were not minor sons (*putra*), but other infants who were under the care of the government servant so long as he was alive. Kauṭilya, introducing this new obligation of the State to take care of persons who were unable to look after themselves, granted undefined additional privileges to infants (*bāla*), aged persons (*vṛddha*) and persons afflicted with disease (*vyādhita*), who were under the care of the deceased

57. *karmasu mṛtānāṁ putra-dārā bhakta-vetanaṁ labheran.* (K. 248. 19).
58. *yāvaj jīvaṁ tu tat putre'kṣame bāle tad arddhakam,*
bhāryāyāṁ vā suśīlāyāṁ kanyāyāṁ vā svaśreyase. (Śukr. 2. 411).
59. *bāla-vṛddhavyādhitāś caiṣām anugrāhyāḥ.* (K. 248. 19-20).

government servant and so reiterated that they were under the special protection of the State.

8. *Right of Petition* :

K. clearly stated that, when in the court, the king had the duty to hear petitioners, because when the king made himself inaccessible to his subjects and entrusted his work to his immediate officers, he might engender confusion in business and cause thereby public disaffection and become himself a prey to his enemies. He had to hear all urgent calls at once and never put them off because if they were postponed they could prove too difficult or impossible to be settled.[60]

This duty of the king to hear petitions was not defined as clearly in any of the Smṛti-s or Dharmaśāstra-s,[61] as it was in K.

The king was not necessarily obliged to perform this duty personally; he could entrust this work to his immediate officers; but since doing so he could "cause public disaffection and become himself a prey to his enemies", he was advised to perform this duty personally. However, in the order of enumeration, or according to the urgency or pressure of work, the king had to attend personally to the business of gods, of heretics, of those learned in the Vedas, of cattle, of sacred places, as well as of infants (*bāla*), aged persons (*vṛddha*), persons afflicted with disease (*vyādhita*), distressed persons (*vyasanin*), helpless persons (*anātha*) and women[62]; these persons had always the right to petition the king personally. The persons last mentioned were those who were under the special protection of the State.

Here again, special privileges, in the sphere of social activities were accorded to infants (*bāla*), aged persons (*vṛddha*), persons afflicted with disease (*vyādhita*), distressed persons (*vyāsanin*) and helpless persons (*anātha*).

60. *upasthāna-gataḥ kāryārthinānam advārāsaṅgaṁ kārayet; dūrdarśo hi rājā kāryā'kārya-vipsaryāsam āsannaiḥ kāryate; tena prakṛtiko'pamari vaśaṁ vā gacchet.* (K. 38. 18-39. 1).

61. It might be only argued that Mn. (7. 146) stating :

tatra sthitaḥ prajāḥ sarvāḥ pratinandya visarjayet,
visṛjya ca prajāḥ sarvā mantrayet saha mantribhiḥ;

anticipated the existence of oral petitions before the king.

62. *tasmād devatā'śramapāṣaṇḍa-śrotriya-paśu-puṇya-sthānānām bāla-vrddha-vyādhitavya-sanyanāthānāṁ strīṇāṁ ca krameṇa kāryāṇi paśyet; kāryagaura-vādāt-yayikavaśena vā.* (K. 39. 1-3).

V. PENAL PRIVILEGES

9. *Lower Penalties*

A. Persons who were under the special protection of the State were not punished, according to Mn., in the same way as other offenders; the penalty in such cases was less severe. The king inflicted on them punishment with a whip, or a bark, or a rope, or the like.[63]

The following persons were enumerated in Mn. : women (*strī*), infants (*bāla*), men with distorted intellect (*unmatta*), aged persons (*vṛddha*), poor persons (*daridra*) and sick persons (*rogin*). J. Jolly read Mn.'s text *daridra*+*anātha rogiṇām.* G. Jhā and most of the editors of Mn. read : *daridrāṇāṁ ca rogiṇām.* Therefore, those commentators of Mn. who based themselves on the text used by Jolly included in the list of persons on whom corporal punishment should be inflicted—helpless persons (*anātha*). It seems that J. Jolly's reading is the more correct one.

Medh. *ad* Mn. (9.230) considered these persons as too poor, and as incapable of labour, and stated therefore, that this kind of punishment had to be inflicted on them.[64] However, it seems that the real reason for this less severe punishment was the fact that these persons were under the special protection of the State.[65]

B. This can also be seen from K. where it is stated that, *inter alia*, infants (*bāla*), aged persons (*vṛddha*) and persons afflicted with disease (*vyādhita*) could never be subject to tortures.[66] The explanation, given in K., was similar to that given in Medh. *ad* Mn.; these persons were considered to be

63. *strī-bālo'nmatta-vṛddhānāṁ daridrāṇāṁ ca rogiṇām,*
śiphāvidala-rajjvādyair vidhān nṛpatir-damam. (Mn. 9. 230. Also quoted in SC. 124, VRK. 658, DV. 60, NṛP. 17, BBh. 2. 203, VV. 314; VyP. 78, VyS. 67).

64. *damam; karmakaraṇe'py asamarthā daridrā eva gṛhyante; mahāpātakināṁ sāmyāt tac chiphādibhis tāḍanam.* (Medh. *ad* Mn. 9. 230).

65. It should be noted that N. (15 and 16, 11 ; 12), Bṛh. (21. 20) and Kāty. (783) also enumerated other persons on whom corporal punishment instead of a fine should be inflicted; these persons were persistent sinners. Whipping was considered more suitable for them than a fine. The reason for the imposition of such a penalty was completely different to that relating to persons under the special protection of the State.

66. *mandā'vadhānṁ bālaṁ vṛddhaṁ vyādhitaṁ mattam unmattaṁ kṣut-pipāsā-dhva-klāntam atyāśitam ātmakāśitaṁ durbalaṁ vā na karma kārayet.* (K. 221. 1-2).

too weak, too feeble (*durbala*) to be able to endure tortures and, therefore, were under the special protection of the State.

C. K. also stated that, *inter alia*, to persons afflicted with disease (*vyādhita*) mercy should be shown.[67]

This rule of special mercy to be accorded to persons under the special protection of the State, was confirmed by Kauṭilya's general statement that, in case of amnesty, infants (*bāla*), aged persons (*vṛddha*), persons afflicted with disease (*vyādhita*) and helpless persons (*anātha*) should be set free; there were no exceptions as far as these persons were concerned. Amnesty had to be accorded always to these persons who were under the special protection of the State.[68]

D. Mn.[69] also stated that, *inter alia*, infants (*bāla*) aged persons (*vṛddha*) and sick persons (*ātura*)[70] should be forgiven by the king if they abused him, that is, cast aspersions upon or cursed him.[71] In this manner the king "accomplished his own welfare".[72]

Finally Mn.[73] stated that, *inter alia*, children (*bāla*) and aged persons (*vṛddha*) should be only reprimanded when they droped filth on the king's high road and should clean the place, while all others should pay in addition, two *kārṣāpana-s* as a fine.[74]

10. *Ordeals*

The Dharmaśāstra-s accorded also special privileges to some of these persons in case of ordeals.

67. *tīrthakara-stapasvī vyādhitaḥ kṣut-pipāsādhva-klānta-stirojānapado daṇḍa-khedī niṣkiś-canaś cā'nugrāhyāḥ.* (K. 199. 15-6).

68. *bandha-nāgāre ca bāla-vṛddha-vyādhitā'nāthānāṁ ca jātanakṣatrapaurṇa-māsīṣu visargaḥ* (K. 146. 18-9).

69. *kṣantavyaṁ prabhuṇā nityaṁ kṣipatāṁ kāryiṇāṁ nṛṇāṁ,*
bāla-vṛddhā'turāṇāṁ ca kurvatā hitamāt manaḥ. (Mn. 8. 312, Also quoted in Gov. in MnM., VyK. 19, SC. 29, SCM. 5, DV. 38, VySau. 14, VyP. 18, VyS. 13).

70. If we read *bāla*+*vṛddha*+*āturāṇāṁ*; or not rich persons if we read *bāla* +*vṛddha* +*aturāṇāṁ*

71. *kasmiṁścid badhyamāne yadi tat pitā tan mātā vā rājanāṁ kṣipet kutsayet abhiśaped vā tadā kṣamā kāryā.* (Medh. *ad* Mn. 8. 312).

72. *evam ātmane hitaṁ kṛtaṁ bhavati; kṣantavyam ity etad vidheḥ phalam evātma hitam* (Medh. *ad* Mn. 8. 312).

73. *āpad gato'thavā vṛddhā garbhiṇī bāla eva vā,*
paribhāṣaṇam arhanti tac ca śodhyam iti sthitiḥ. (Mn. 9. 283. Also quoted in Apar. *ad* Y. 2. 154, VyK. 98, SC. 235, VRK. 222, MR. 117, VCi. 99, VyPr. 365, VyU. 109, VT. 707, VV. 192, VyS. 116).

74. *samut-sṛjed-rājamārge yas tvamedhya manāpadi,*
sa dvau kārṣāpaṇau dadyād amedhyaṁ cāśu śodhayet. (Mn. 9. 282).

And so, according to Kāty.[75], torture should never be administered to infants (*bāla*)[76] and, according to N.[77], to persons afflicted with disease (*vyādhita*).[78]

These were exceptional rules,[79] since other rules mentioned that the ordeal by balance should be applied to infants (*bāla*), persons afflicted with disease (*rogin*, *asamartha*) and others.

Particularly Y.[80] stated that the ordeal by balance was prescribed for infants (*bāla*), aged persons (*vṛddha*), persons afflicted with disease (*rogin*)[81], and N[82]. for infants (*bāla*),[83] aged persons (*vṛddha*)[84], distressed persons (*ātura*),[85] and others.[86] Also Vi.[87] stated that this kind of ordeal could be

75. *mātā-pitṛ-dvija-guru-bāla-strī-rāja-ghātinām,*
mahāpātaka-yuktānāṁ nastikānāṁ viśeṣataḥ. (Kāty. 427. Also quoted in VyK. 80, SC. 103, DK. 40, VyC. 87, VySau. 74, VyPr. 179, VyM. 22, BBh. 2.99, Vyp. 65).

76. And women (*strī*).

77. *sarvratānāṁ bhṛśārtānāṁ vyādhitānāṁ tapasvināṁ,*
strīṇāṁ ca na bhaved divyaṁ yadi dharmastvavekṣyate. (N. 1.256. Also quoted in Mit. *ad* Y. 2.98, VyK. 80, VyCi. 87, VySau. 74, VT. 207, VyS. 54).

78. And women (*stri*), persons engaged in the performance of a vow (*savrata*), persons afflicted with a heavy calamity (*bhṛsārta*) and ascetics (*tapasvin*).

79. N. (1.313) stated that despite the fact that according to N. (1.256) women (*strī*), children (*bāla*), persons afflicted with disease (*rogin*), aged persons (*vṛddha*, and feeble persons (*durbala*) were not to be subject to the ordeal of water. This seems to show that N. (1.256) was not always applied in practice.

80. *tulā-strī-bāla-vṛddhā'ndha-paṅgu-brāhmaṇa-rogiṇām,*
agnir-jalaṁ vā śūdrasya yavāḥ sapta viṣasya vā. (Y. 2. 98. Also quoted in ViR. *ad* Y. 2. 103, SS. 117, VyCi. 86, SCM. 51, SV. 172, Rāgh. in MnM. 8. 116, VySau. 73, VyPr. 178, VyU. 53, VyM. 21, VT. 207, RDhK. 411, VyS. 53, VVy. 8, AP. 255. 33).

81. As well as women (*strī*), blind men (*andha*), cripples (*paṅgu*) and Brāhmanas.

82. Quoted in Vīr (*ad* Y. 2. 98, p. 536), VyK. 79, SC. 103, SS. 117, VyC. 86, SV. 173, VySau. 73, VyPr. 177, VyM. 21, VT. 208, VyP. 64, VyS. 54:

klība-turān sattvahīnān paritāpārditan, narāh,
bāla-vṛddhā'turādīṁś ca parīkṣeta ghate sadā.

and in the Vulgata 1. 251 (*ad* N. 1. 256, p. 112).

agnau toye viṣe caiva parīkṣeto'rjitān narān,
bāla-vṛddhā'turāṁś caiva parīkṣeta ghaṭe sadā

83. Quoted in Vir. and in the vulgata (cf. note 82).

84. *Ibid.*, (cf. note 80).

85. *Ibid.*, (cf. note 80).

86. Women (*strī*), persons devoid of energy (*sattvahīna*), eunuchs (*kitba*) (in Vir. cf. note 80).

87. *strī-brāhmaṇa-vikalā'samartha-rogiṇāṁ tulā deyā; sā ca na vāti vāyau.* (Vi. 9. 23-4. Also quoted in VyK. 80, SC. 104, VyC. 87, VyPr. 178, VyM. 21, BBh. *ad* Y. 2. 99, VyS. 54-5).

administered, *inter alia*, to persons afflicted with disease (*rogin*), (*asamartha*).[88]

On the other hand, it is clear, according to N.[89], that the ordeal by water could never be administered to infants (*bāla*), aged persons (*vṛddha*), persons afflicted with disease (*rogin*) and others[90] and, according to Vi.,[91] the ordeal by fire could never be administered to persons afflicted with disease (*asamartha*).[92]

The reason for according these persons special privileges was however, different from that mentioned above. It was not due to granting them special protection but due to the understanding that these persons were unable to endure difficult ordeals. It was understood that these persons would perish immediately, for instance, after diving in case of an ordeal by water.[93] On the other hand the ordeal by water could not be administered to those persons who "gained their subsistance from water,"[94] for example, to divers because for them diving would not be an ordeal.

The Dharmaśāstra-s, having in mind the feebleness of the persons to whom they usually accorded special privileges, stated that these persons, if not completely exempt from ordeals,[95] should be, at least, submitted to such an ordeal in which their

88. As well as women (*strī*), Brāhmaṇas and persons devoid of an organ of sense (*vikalas*).

89. *na majjanīyaṁ strī-bālaṁ dharmaśāstra-viśāradaiḥ,*
rogiṇaś cā'pi vṛddhāś ca pumāṁso ye ca durbalāḥ. (N. 1. 313. Also quoted Apar. *ad* Y. 2. 98, VyK. 80, SC. 103, SS. 117, VyC. 86-7, SCM. 51, VCa. 163, VySau. 73, Vīr. *ad* Y. 2. 98, VyPr. 178, VyM. 21, VT. 211, BBh. *ad* Y. 2. 99, VyP. 65, VyS. 54).

90. Women (*strī*), feeble persons (*durbala*), persons afflicted by calamity (*kliṣṭa*) and other (Cf. N. 1. 314) :

nirutsāhān rujā-kliṣṭānā'rtāmś ca na nimajjayet,

sadyo mriyante majiantaḥ svalpa-prāṇā hi te smṛtāḥ. (Also quoted VyK. 80, SC. 117, VyC. 87, SCM. 51, VySau. 73-4, Vīr *ad* Y. 2. 98, VyPr. 178, VyM. 21, VT. 211, BBh. *ad* Y. 2. 99, VyS. 54). Also Vi. (9. 29) stated *na śleṣma-vyādhyarditānāṁ bhirūṇāṁ śvāsakāsināmam bujīvināṁ codakam.* (Cf. fn. 87).

91. *na kuṣṭhya-samartha-lohakārāṇāṁ agnir deyaḥ.* (Vi. 9. 25).

92. As well as lepers (*kuṣṭhin*) and others.

93. *sadyo mriyante najjantaḥ svalpa-prāṇa hi te smṛtāḥ.* (N. 1. 314). (cf. fn. 90).

94. *na śleṣma-vyādhyarditānāṁ bhirūṇāṁ śvāsakāsināmam bu'iivināṁ codakam* (Vi. 9. 29). Cf. fn. 87.

95. As ordered by N. (1. 250) and Kāty. (427).

feebleness was not a handicap, that is, to the ordeal by balance[96] which consisted in double weighing before and after exhortations.[97]

VI. CONCLUSIONS

The few examples, quoted above, indicate that accord-

96. As ordered by Y. (2. 98), Vi. (9. 23, 24), and N. (quoted in Vir. *ad* Y 2. 98, p. 536, translated by J. Jolly in N. Quotations 6. 8, in the Vulgata, 1. 258, *ad* N. 1. 256, p. 112, translated by J. Jolly in N. Quotations 6. 8, in the Vulgata 1. 158, *ad* the Vulgata, *ad* N. 1.. 256, p. 112, translated by J. Jolly in N. Quotations 6. 10).

97. A full description of this ordeal is to be found in P. V. Kane's *History of Dharmaśāstra*, Vol. III. pp. 369-370 : 'A sacrificial tree (such as *khadira* or *udumbara*) should be cut to the accompaniment of Vedic mantras (employed in making a sacrificial post). Two wooden posts made of that tree should support a transverse beam (called *akṣa*). The posts should be fixed in the ground, the part above the ground being four cubits and that below being two cubits. This frame should face the east (i.e. the posts must be in the south and north). Then the beam of the balance was to be made from the same tree and was to be suspended from the transverse beam of the frame by means of a hook. Three iron rings were to be fastened to the beam of the balance, two at the end and one in the middle for suspending the balance from the transverse beam by means of a chain or string. Two scales were to be suspended at the two ends of the beam by hooks and strings from the iron rings fixed at the ends of the beam On the two sides of the balance there should be two arches in which the scales should move and which should be ten *aṅgulas* higher than the balance. There should be two perpendicular pendants made of clay hanging down from the arches and touching the upper surface of the balance. In the pan to the west the *śodhya* should be placed and weighed against clay, bricks and stones placed in the other pan. Then traders or goldsmiths or braziers should examine the balance and bring it on a level with the two pendants hanging down from the arches and examine the perfect horizontality of the beam of the balance by spilling a little water on the beam. When the person sitting in one pan is equal in weight to the materials (clay etc). in the other, a line should be drawn with chalk by the experts on the arch (to show the exact position of the pans). Then the man is made to get down from the pan and he is to invoke the balance as stated in Y. 2. 101-102. 'O balance, you are the abode of truth, you were created by the gods for this purpose, declare the truth, free me from this (cloud of) suspicion. Mother ! if I am a sinner then take me lower, if pure take me upwards'. The person is then to hear exhortations about the result of untruth after putting the writing on his head (vide N. 6. 276 and 6, 10, 9), then he is again to be placed in the pan to the accompaniment of invocations (N. 4. 278-279, 6. 10, 10-11). A worthy *brāhmaṇa* learned in astronomy is to calculate the time of five *palas* or *vināḍīs* (A *vināḍī* is the time required for reciting 60 long syllables and 60 *vināḍīs* make one *ghaṭika*. So five *vināḍīs* will be equal to two minutes). Then his weight is again to be marked. If the person goes up (i.e. is found lighter than what he formerly weighed) he is declared innocent (according to the commentary N. 4. 283, 5, p. 60, Dipakalikā on Y. 2. 102); if he weighs the same or goes down (i.e., weighs more) he is guilty. Then the person concerned is to distribute gifts to the judge, the brāhmaṇas and sacrificial priests and take leave of the deities invoked. Bṛh. (SBE, Vol. 33 p. 317 v. 19) stated that he who weighed the same should be weighed once more. If the pan or the beam or the hooks broke or the ropes gave way owing to some visible cause then the procedure was to be repeated, but if the breaking was due to an unseen cause or accident, the person was to be declared guilty."

ing to the Dharmaśāstra-s and Smṛti-s, and, in particular, according to Kauṭilya's *Arthaśāstra*, important privileges in legal, fiscal, social and penal matters were accorded in ancient India to those persons who were considered as being under the special protection of the State. It must, however, be emphasized that not only infants (*bāla*, *pogaṇḍa*), aged persons (*vṛddha*, *sthavira*), persons afflicted with disease (*vyādhita*, *rogin*, *ātura*), helpless persons (*anātha*) and distressed persons (*vyasanin*, *ārta*) were the only persons to whom these privileges were accorded; these persons were more numerous, but those mentioned above[98] were quoted most frequently in the Dharmaśāstras and Arthaśāstras-texts.

98. In particular in addition to women (*strī*).

X

LEGAL PROTECTION OF PLANTS IN ANCIENT INDIA*

1. The ancient Indian sources of law show that the Indians believed that plants (trees) lived their own lives. They enjoyed life, felt pain and grew, although some of their parts were cut off.[1]

Trees were highly esteemed and whoever planted trees offered pious gifts. So, according to Vi. "He who planted trees would have those trees for his sons in a future existence. Even a giver of trees gladdened the gods by offering up their blossoms to them. He also gladdened his guests by giving their fruits to them, and the travellers with their shade and the manes with the water trickling down from their leaves when it rains."[2]

A Snātaka Brāhmaṇa should keep the right side towards well known and large trees.[3] Women who desired to have a son should worship trees[4],[5].

2. We find in the Dharmaśāstra-s rules, the aim of which was to protect plants. However, it is doubtful whether the respective rules were equivalent to the legal protection of nature reserves which we find in contemporary legislations.

The rules contained in the Dharmaśāstra-s should be divided into three groups :

a. Protection of plants from the points of view of religion,
b. Protection of plants which were considered *objecta sacra*,
c. Protection of plants as private property.

* Previously appeared as JSAIL.5 in the "Annals of the Bhandarkar Oriental Research Institute." Vol. XXV, Part IV, pp. 231-8.

1. See P. V. Kane, History of Dharmaśāstra, Vol. II, Part II, p. 895-6; Marco Polo B. III, ch. 30.

2. Vi. 91. 4-8. See MBh. Anuśāsana-parva 23-32; Padma-purāṇa.

3. Mn. 4. 39, Y. 1. 133, Vi. 63, 28, Mārkṇḍeya in Aparārka p. 176.

4. Kādambarī 56.

5. See P. V. Kane's, History of Dharmaśāstra, Vol. II, Part II, p. 893-896.

3. *ad a.* The protection of plants from the point of view of religion was based on the rule of *ahiṁsā*. The belief in the life and sufferings of the plants seems to confirm this statement.

This protection of the plants is based on the rule which is to be found in Vās. :

svadharmo rājñaḥ pālanaṁ bhūtānāṁ tasyā'nuṣṭhānāt siddhiḥ.

Under "all beings" we[6] shall also understand plants. According to Vās.[7] not even the king should be allowed to injure trees that bore fruit and flowers.

This rule was developed in Mn. and Yi. ; Vi. even repeated this *śloka* from Mn.

phaladānāṁ tu vṛkṣāṇāṁ chedane japyam ṛkśatam,
gulma-vallīlatānaṁ ca puṣpitānāṁ ca vīruddhām[8],[9]

"For cutting trees yielding fruit, shrubs, creeping or climbing plants or plants yielding blossoms he must mutter a Vedic text a hundred times."

Y.[10] solved this question in the same manner and also used the words : *vṛkṣa, gulma, latā, vīruchedane, japya, ṛk and śata.*

The commentators on Vi. and Y. stated that the trees must be useful because bread fruit and mango fruit[11] were "fruit bearing, trees"[12] and jasmins[13] were plants yielding blossoms. The prayers *ṛk* are Gāyatrī.[14] This meditative repetition of the *ṛk* one hundred times did refer to the case of Dvijas and not to the case of Śūdra-s and the like; for they had no right to the meditative repetition of the Mantra-s. They had to fast for two days and nights. Their penance was prescribed in proportion to their penalty.[15]

Mn.[16],[17] stated

kṛṣtajānāṁo'ṣadhīnāṁ jātānāṁ ca svayaṁ vane,
vṛthālambhe'nugacched gāṁ dinam ekaṁ payo'vrataḥ

6. Vās, 19.1.
7. Chapt. XIX.
8. Mn. XI-142. (in Mn. Jh. 11. 141).
9. Vi. L-48 is identical with Mn. XI-42.
10. Y. III-276.
11. Mit. 640.
12. Mit. 640.
13. Vi.
14. Mit.
15. Mit. 643.
16. Mn. XI-144. (in Mn. Jh. 11.143).
17. Repeated in Vi. L-50.

"If a man has wantonly cut plants, whether sown in ploughed fields or growing spontaneously in the forest, he must wait on a cow and subsist upon milk for one day."

The commentators understood as "plants which were sown in ploughed fields"—rice and barley and under "growing spontaneously in the forest"—wild rice, or better to say all the useful plants which grow wild.

Y. did not distinguish between cultivated plants and plants growing wild. Mit. took an example from Mn. and Vi. and added that it was immaterial whether the plants were growing in a village or in the forest.

According to Y. the same penance was prescribed. Mit. explained that he who had cut down plants had to follow cows for one day, that is, during the entire course of the day for the purpose of rendering them service, and drink milk at the end without having recourse to any other kind of food.

Mn.[18] added that it was immaterial whether these acts were caused willingly or unwillingly. This point of view of the Dharmaśāstra-s is comprehensible because it deals only with religious penance, and not the legal consequences of the act.

Seemingly this rule was contradictory to the rule contained in Mn. XI.144 (second part) and Vi. L.50, because the word *vṛthālambhe*-wantonly, intentionally, was used; therefore, only he who intentionally cut plants was liable to penance; but the commentators explained clearly that the word *vṛthalāmbhe* meant for purposes other than those of religious sacrifice or divine worship. Y.[19] stated it clearly saying : "for cutting down plants unless for sacred purposes one shall for one day follow cows and subsist on milk." Mit.[20] explained this rule and said that "if the cutting was for the purpose of Pañcayajña there is no violation of the rule." This resulted also *per analogiam* from the rules concerning the killing of animals for religious purposes.[21] The same rule was also found in Vi.[22] and Vās.[23]; Vās. added also "for cultivation purposes". Hence for higher purposes trees could be injured.

18. Mn. XI-146.
19. Y-III-276.
20. Mit. 640.
21. See second part.
22. Vi. LI-63.
23. Vās. XIX-12.

The principle that the cutting of tree was not permissible is based on the religious maxim that cutting down a tree (*druma*) for the purpose of getting fire wood, or injuring plants, cutting trees (*druma*), shrubs (*gulma*), creepers (*vallī*) long climbing plants (*latā*) or herbs was a minor sin (*upapātaka*).[24]

4. *ad b.* The trees as *objecta sacra* were particularly protected. The penalty was then doubled. This rule is found only in Y. and K.[25] As such trees were considered trees growing on special places such as a sacrificial place, a cemetery, a boundary, a sacred place or a temple, or well known trees,[26] which meant probably trees which were particularly revered. According to Mit.[27] the *pippala*, i.e. the holy fig tree (*ficus religiosa*)—"the lord of trees",[28] as well as palāśa also called *kiṁśuka* (*butex frondosa*) used for marking boundaries were considered as such trees.[29] As was said before, the penalty in this case was twofold. It was twice as great as the penalty for hurting a tree which belonged to a private person (private property).

5A. *ad c.* From the legal point of view the matter of injuring trees which were private property is very well solved in the Dharmaśāstra-s and shows an exceedingly high level of understanding of legal problems by the authors of the Dharmaśāstra-s.

The main principle was : he who injured the tree which was private property should pay in accordance to the damage done.[30] He should not only pay for the damage done (*damnuṁ emergens*) but also for the loss of his profit (*lucrum cessans*).

The principle was expressed as follows :

vanaspatīnāṁ sarveṣāṁ upabhogo yathā yathā,
tathā tathā damaḥ kāryo hiṁsāyām iti dhāraṇā.[31]

The rule was that a fine had to be paid for injuring all (kinds of) trees in proportion to their usefulness..

24. Mn. XI-64, Y.III-24, Vi. XXXVII-24.
25. Y-II-228, K 197, 11-12 (§ 73).
26. According to K. (197, 11-12) also trees which were grown in the king's forest.
27. Mit. *ad* Y-II-228.
28. Pitāmaha in Mit. *ad* Y. 2. 103.
29. Mn. 3. 246.
30. Amount of damage done.
31. Mn. 8. 285. Also quoted in Apar. *ad* Y. 2. 229, VyK. 108, VRK. 284, MR. 123, VCi. 122, DV. 38, SV 484, VyM. 100, VT. 744, VyS. 163.

This rule is found in Mn.[32] and was repeated word for word in Kāty.[33] Mn. used the words "all trees" which meant "all kinds of trees" which were, for instance, enumerated in Y. and Vi. "In proportion of their usefulness" meant in accordance to their products[34] and position.[35] This rule too is repeated in Vi. and Y., but these Dharmaśāstra-s went further. And so, Vi. mentioned firstly *phalopagama druma* (trees yielding fruit)[36] as the most valuable trees and imposed the highest penalty; then mentioned *puṣpopagama druma* (trees yielding flowers)[37] as less valuable, and imposed the second penalty, afterwards mentioned *valli-gulma* and *latā*[38] as much less valuable and imposed the penalty of 100 *karṣāpaṇa*, and lastly mentioned the least valuable plants, i. e. grass (*tṛṇa*)[39] ; in case of injuring them the penalty of 20 *karṣāpaṇas* was imposed.

This rule was also included in Y.[40] Vi., as well as Y. enumerated the plants. The text of the rules varied although the principle was the same; it was : the more valuable the plant, the higher the penalty.

Y. mentioned *prarohaśaktimaḥ* (trees which throw down branches having sprouts)[41] i.e. those branches which when cut off developed again at each knot of trees (*praroha*) such as the banyan and the like;[42] *śākha* (branch), *skandha* (trunk) i.e. that from which the original branches shoot out[43] and *upajivya-druma* i.e. trees which were means of livelihood, as for instance the mango tree.[44]

We should distinguish in this enumeration the degrees in injuring trees, i.e. injuring the whole tree—*prarohaśākhina* and *upajivīvya-druma* on one side, and its parts *śākhā* and *skandha* on the other. Y.2. 227 completely confuses these two different

32. See fn. 31 above.
33. Kāty. 793. See fn. 32.
34. Kullūka.
35. Medhātithi.
36. Vi. 5. 55.
37. Vi. 5. 55.
38. Vi. 5. 57.
39. Vi. V-58.
40. Y-II.227.
41. Stanzler's Translation : *Bāume deren Zweige wieder wachsen.*
42. Mit *ad* Y-II-227.
43. Mit. *ad* Y-II-227.
44. Mit *ad* Y-II-227.

notions. Here too the author or authors of the Yājñavalkya-Dharmaśāstra stated that the fundamental penalty amounted to 20 *paṇa-s* but probably the penalty could be doubled depending on the value (*viṁśator-dviguṇodamaḥ*). Mit.[45] explained this rule in the following manner : "the three fine penalties (fines) *viz.* twenty *paṇa-s*, forty *paṇa-s* and eighty *paṇa-s* are inflicted respectively for the offences of cutting of the branches and for the offences following in the order."

This sentence,[46] however, probably did not mention three but four penalties, provided it was admitted that *prarodviśākhina*, *śāsvā*, *skandha* defined only the word *upajīvya druma*; the word *ca* however does not allow such an interpretation.

If we assume that this sentence enumerated four kinds of trees we cannot accept the point of view of Mit. that the fine should be inflicted according to the list of their enumeration, because we must apply the rule that the penalty depends on the usefulness of these plants. In this case we should admit that for the cutting off of branches the penalty of 20 *paṇa-s* was to be imposed; for the complete destruction of the trunk—40 *paṇa-s*; of the trees which throw down branches having roots—80 *paṇa-s*; of the trees which are the means of livelihood—160 *paṇas*.

However, according to Y.[47] for the cutting or destruction of less valuable plants, the fine was half of that mentioned above, was 10 *paṇa-s*. To these less valuable plants belonged: *gulma* such as *mālatī* plant.[48] and the like i.e. creepers which do not develop into any considerable length,[49] *guccha* which did not have the form of creepers and were not generally smooth and straight i.e. the *kuraṇḍhaka* plant,[50] a species of amaranth,[51] *kṣupa* i.e. the *karavī* plant,[52] a kind of tree with white, red or yellow flowers and the like which are generally straight and smooth[53] *latā* i.e. the *atimukta*,[54] a creeper which developed into considerable length,[55] *pratāna*, i.e. creepers without knots of

45. Mit. *ad* Y-II-227.
46. Y-II-227.
47. Y. II-229.
48. *Echites carrgophyllata*, kind of jasmin.
49. Mit. *ad* Y. II-229.
50. *Ammania Vesicatoria.*
51. Mit. *ad* Y. II-229.
52. *Nerium odorium, oujeinensis.*
53. Mit. *ad* Y. II-229.
54. a grape *dulbergia*
55. Mit, *ad* Y. II-229.

offshoots and growing straight such as *sāri vā* and others[56], *obadhaya* i.e. plants which develop fruit such as the paddy plant, etc.[57] and *viruddha* i.e. the *gaḍūcī*[58], a plant generally growing on trees, used for medicines, a kind of plant which even when cut grows and develops in various parts.[59]

Very similar rules are to be found in K.[60] K. also distinguishes between more and less valuable plants and imposes fines according to the damage done to the plants. K. stated : *puro'pavanaspatīnāṁ puṣpa-phalac-chāyā'vatāṁ prarohac chedane ṣaṭ-paṇaḥ; kṣudra-śākhāc-chedane dvādaśa-paṇaḥ pīna-śākhāc-chedane catur-viṁśati-paṇaḥ; skandha-vadhe pūrvas-sāhasa-daṇḍaḥ ; sam ucchittau madhyamaḥ-puṣpa-phalac-chāyāvad gulma-latās-vardha-daṇḍaḥ.*[61]

So we see that for cutting sprouts of fruit trees, flower trees or shady trees in the parks near the city the fine amounted to 6 *paṇa-s*, for greater damage i.e. for cutting off of big branches the fine amounted to 24 *paṇa-s*, for even greater damage i.e. the cutting off of trunks, the perpetrator was punished with the first amercement, which amounted to 12 to 96 *paṇa-s*;[62] and in case of the greatest damage i.e. the felling of the respective trees the perpetrator was punished with the second highest fine, which amounted from 200 to 500 *paṇa-s*.[63]

On the other hand, in case of injuring of less useful plants (*gulma, lata*) which bore flowers, fruits, or provided shade, half of the above fines should be levied.

According to K. it made no difference where these trees had grown.[64]

These were the rules referring to the restitution i.e. repayment of the damage really done, which—as mentioned above—depended on the real value (*pretium affectionis* was not taken into account) of the destroyed or damaged plants which was the property of the wronged person.

56. Mit. *ad* Y. II-229.
57. Mit. *ad* Y, II-229.
58. *Cocculus cordifoleus.*
59. Mit. *ad* Y. II-229.
60. K. 197, 6-10 (§. 23).
61. K. 197, 6-9 (§,23).
62. K. 192 (§ 69).
63. *Ibid.*
64. K. 197, 10-11 (73).

B. Vi. contains also the rule concerning the loss of profit (*lucrum cessans*). We read there : *sarve ca tat svāminām̐ tad utapattim.*[65]

And all such offenders (shall make good) to the owners (of the trees or plants cut off or destroyed by them) the revenue which they yield i.e. the profit which they earned from the trees or plants being their property. In what way, however, this "profit" should be calculated was not stated. Therefore, the general legal rules should be applied to this case.

6. The Dharmaśāstra-s also contained rules relating to the prohibition of eating some plants which were considered unclean. To these plants belonged red and white garlic, onions, leeks, mushrooms, red gums from trees, exudations from trees, frumenty rice milk, fresh beans, turnips, brinjals, gourds, *kucuṇḍa, kumbhāṇḍa*, tree-roots and others, the modern equivalents of which are difficult to find.[66]

It is evident that these rules had purely religious meaning.

7. The rules which belonged to the groups I and II contained rules the aim of which was the protection of plants (trees); they were not equal to the rules concerning the protection of nature reserves which we find in civil law. The rules which belonged to the first group i.e. the protection of plants from the point of view of religion, did not have any legal sanctions. The same applied to the rules belonging to the second group.

The aim of the rules belonging to the third group was not the protection of nature reserves, but the protection of the plants; therefore, this group cannot be interpreted from the point of view of legal protection of plants.

As to the rules which belonged to the first and second group, although from the point of view of the modern system of civil law, they were *leges imperfectae*, they cannot be treated in a completely negative manner. The ancient Indian civil law is to such a great extent mixed with religious rules, that religious sanctions should, in principle, be considered as legal sanctions.

65. Vi. V-59.

66. Mn. IV-5-11, Y. I-171, Āp. I-17, 19, 26-28, G. XVII-32, Vās. XIV-33, Vi. LI-3, 34, 36, B. (Aparārka 247) and Bhaviṣyapurāṇa, Brahmapurāṇa, Taittiriya-uti, Yama, Hārīta and Devala (all in Vīra Āhnika 77 p. 511-513) etc.

On the other hand, however, it must be pointed out that the protection of animals was much better solved in the Dharmaśāstra-s and, in particular, in the Kauṭilya's Arthaśāstra. We find there special rules which concerned, for instance, the prohibition of killing or torturing animals,[67] protection in their old age and in case of disease;[68] even some kinds of national parks were mentioned there,[69] as well as prohibition against catching, killing or injuring deer.[70] It is possible that the aim of this protection of animals was merely the protection of private property, in particular the king's property, because even national parks could be created for the purpose of protecting animals (deer) for the king in order to facilitate hunting.

Although from the point of view of modern civil law we consider deer as State property or we qualify them as *res nullius*, we can assume that in ancient India legal protection of animals existed.

67. K. II-43, (the penalty of 500 *paṇa-s* is imposed for torturing to death of a calf or a milk-cow); K IV-88 prohibition of harness of oxen (vṛṣayam-ukṣāṇam) or cows which did not calve; similarly Kāty. 789 & 791; Mn. VIII-295-298, Vi. V.52-54 enumerated penalty for killing animals as example; Bṛh. XXI 16 and Kāty. 769—employment of animals at an improper time, etc.

68. K. II-47 sick and old horses get "bread of charity;" K. II-146 old and sick cattle should get from the herdsmen medical treatment, etc.

69. K. II-43 (123. 3-4) abhayavana mentioned twice.

duṣṭāḥ paśu-mṛga-vyāḷā matsyāś ca bhaya-cāriṇaḥ,
anyatra guptisthānebhyo vadhabandham avapnuyuḥ.

K. II-20 establishments of parts for game where all the animals have access etc.

70. N. 2. 43 (*nagapaśu*) birds, fish and many other animals were mentioned as examples.

XI

FORMS OF MARRIAGE IN ANCIENT INDIA AND THEIR DEVELOPMENT*

I. INTRODUCTION

1. The ancient Indian law recognised eight forms of marriage that is the *Brāhma-vivāha*, the *Daiva-vivāha*, the *Ārṣa-vivāha*, the *Prājāpatya-vivāha*, the *Āsura-vivāha*, the *Gāndharva-vivāha*, the *Rākṣasa-vivāha* and the *Paiśāca-vivāha*. When, however, these forms of marriage are closely examined the conclusion can be reached that from the legal point of view there existed in ancient India not eight but *eleven forms of marriage*. These are two forms of the *Gāndharva-vivāha* i.e. the *Gāndharva-vivāha* combined with the *Rākṣasa-vivāha* and the *Gāndharva-vivāha* not combined with the *Rākṣasa-vivāha* and a new form of marriage, the *Svayaṁvara*.

If the *Gāndharva-vivāha* would be divided into two forms of marriage and the *Svayaṁvara* regarded as a separate form, the interpretation of the respective rules, which were frequently contradictory, would be greatly facilitated, especially as far as the *Gāndharva-vivāha* was concerned.

2. The differences between the above mentioned forms of marriage were, however, as far as legal consequences were concerned, exceedingly small, so that from the legal point of view all forms of marriage could, in principle, be divided into *orthodox forms of marriage* (*Brāhma-vivāha*, *Daiva-vivāha*, *Ārṣa-vivāha*, *Prājāpatya-vivāha*) and other forms of marriage (*Āsura-vivāha*, *Gāndharva-vivāha*, *Rākṣasa-vivāha*, *Paiśāca-vivāha*). A marriage contracted according to one of the orthodox forms of marriage entailed different legal consequences than a marriage contracted according to unorthodox forms.

In ancient India the form of marriage (*vivāha*) signified in what way the marriage was contracted.

* Previously appeared as JSAIL. 21 in the "Bhāratīya Vidyā", Vol. XII, pp. 62-138.

3. Ancient Indian law is remarkable for the fact that it sought to legislate exactly for every phase of human life. Since exact rules and legal regulations treating for instance different aspects of love exist, the more so exact rules exist for such important occurrences in life, as marriage or the way in which the marriage was contracted. (*vivāha*)

4. The conclusions of this study are based on the most important Dharmaśāstras, Arthaśāstras, Kāmasūtras, Gṛhyasūtras and the Mahābhārata as well as on other sources, whenever the latter dealt with the forms of marriage from the legal point of view.

5. The aim of this study is to explain from the strictly legal point of view each particular form of marriage. The author will also try to prove that from the purely legal point of view there existed in ancient India eleven forms of marriage. Further the legal consequences of a marriage contracted in conformity with any of the forms of marriage quoted below will be discussed. Lastly an endeavour will be made to demonstrate on the basis of the existing rules and by comparison with other legislation that there existed in India some development of the institution of the forms of marriage although the rules found in the Smṛtis are rather of a static nature.

II. LEGAL ASPECTS OF THE FORMS OF MARRIAGE IN ANCIENT INDIA

A. *Rākṣasa-vivāha*

6. The *Rākṣasa* form of marriage called also *Kṣatra* was "a marriage by capture" said Śaṅkh. (4-6) briefly. What was meant by "capture" according to the ancient jurists could be seen from other Smṛtis.[1]

Capture was a "forcible abduction" said Mn. (3-34), G. (4-12), Vās. (1-34), B. (1-11-20-8), Vi. (24-25), N. (12-43), K. (3-2), MBh. (13-44), Y. (1-61), Pañcas. (by Schmidt 529) and similarly Āp. (2, 15, 12, 2), Āśv. (1-6, 8), Kām. (31,

1. See the story of Vimada in the Ṛgveda 1. 116, the story of Subhādrā and of Ambā and Ambālikā won by Bhīṣma for Vicitravīrya in MBh.

231), Hārīta (Vīra Saṁskāra 856), Devala (Vīr. Saṁs. 857). The maiden abducted [Mn. 3-33, Āp. 2, 5, 12, 2, N. 12-43, MBh. 13-44, Pañc. (by Schmidt) 529, Hār. (Vīr. Saṁs. 857), Dev. (Vīr. Saṁs. 857)] was wedded [MBh. (13-44)] ; he who took her away was her suitor (bridegroom) [MBh. 13-44, Kām. 31, 231, Vi. 24-25, Vās. 1-34, Āśv. 1-6, 8]. This suitor or bridegroom was obliged after the abduction to proceed with the marriage [Kām. (§31, 231)]. The forcible abduction could take place at night [Pañcas. (by Schmidt. 519)] from the house (home) of the maiden, or her father's house, [Mn. (3-33) and Pañcas. (by Schmidt 519)] or from a public garden, when the maiden was on her way there (Kām. §31, 231) or from a village when she was going to another village [(Kām. §31, 231); cf. the commentators on Vātsyāyana's Kāmasūtra (§31, 231)].

Those were the *essentialia negotii* of the *Rākṣasa-vivāha*. The Smṛtis often gave a commentary as to what should be understood by the expression "forcible abduction." It may be seen from these texts that the abduction had not to be symbolical act but a real one.

The captor was obliged when capturing a maiden from the house to break open the house of her kinsmen or guardians, [Mn. (3-33) and Pañcas. (by Schmidt 529)] and wage war, [Y. (1-61) and similarly Dev. (Vīr. Saṁs. §857)], or declare war on her guardians (Kām. 31, 231) that is according to Jayamaṅgalā's commentary on Vātsyāyana's Kāmasūtra the protectors of the women (Jayamaṅgalā on Kām. 31, 231). It is clear that by the expression "guardians" also the father of the girl (Āp. 2-5, 12, 2),or her kinsmen (MBh. 13-44, Mn. 3-33, Āp. 2-5, 12, 9, Vās. 1-34, Āśv. Gṛh. 1-6, 8) should be understood. The expression found in Y. (1-61) "wage war" meant, according to Āp. (2-5, 12, 2) that the captor had to overcome the guardians.[2] Vās. (1-34) was of the opinion that they i.e the guardians had to be destroyed by force of arms, (Kām. 31, 231) attacked, and according to Hār. (Vīr. Saṁs. §856) attacked and chastised. For the legislators this was not cruel enough They ruled that in this "war" the guardians in the confusion (Pañcas; Schmidt 529) should be killed,

2. Women were considered as booty.

according to Kām. (§31, 231), Mn. (3-33), Āśv. (1-6, 8), Pañcas. (by Schmidt 529) and beheaded, according to Āśv. (1-6, 8) and MBh. (13-44), or at least wounded, according to Mn. (3-21) or "violently used" according to Pañcas. (by Schmidt 529). That this capture was a real capture and not a symbolical one was clear from the fact that the girl had to cry, (Mn. 3-33) and to weep, [Mn. (3-33), MBh. (13-44) and Āśv. Gṛh. (I. 6, 8)]. It may be argued, however, that the cries of a girl might be proof that this abduction was symbolical as the cries would symbolise the resistance of the girl.

7. The *Rākṣasa-vivāha*, as well as the next form of marriage the *Paiśāca-vivāha*, were based on forcible abduction of a maiden. However, nearly all the Dharmaśāstras prohibited forcible abduction and considered such an act as a crime. We also find in the Dharmaśāstras various punishments for such a crime. In Bṛh. (22-22) he who stole a woman should be placed on a bed of hot iron or burned by fire kept up with straw. We find the same rule in Vyāsa (Vivādaratnākara p. 317) but this source added that the entire property of the thief of the maiden should be confiscated and he should be put to death. Y. (2.287) made this dependent on whether the maiden belonged to a higher caste or not. In the first case the abductor had to be condemned to death, in the second case he had to pay the lowest fine. According to K. the punishment depended on whether the maiden had gold ornaments on her person or not. In the first case the highest amercement had to be imposed, in the second case a fine of 200 *paṇas* only (K. 4. ch. 12). According to Bṛh. (23.7-8) the thief had to be executed or had to be fined. According to Mn. (8. 323) the thief had to suffer corporal punishment and according to N. (Theft 28) he had to be also deprived of his entire wealth. According to Vyāsa (Vivādaratnākara p. 318) the fine for the stealing a woman amounted to 104 *kārṣapaṇas*.

It is not the scale of the punishment which is interesting but the fact that forcible abduction was prohibited. If this forcible abduction has been prohibited and has to be considered as a crime how would it be possible to admit that the marriage based on forcible abduction was allowed. Of course it could not be allowed.

8. It is possible that the *Rākṣasa-vivāha* was only a relic in the Smṛtis of some form of marriage which had existed in primitive times. In the period of the Dharmaśāstras this form of marriage must have been considered not admissible and if we find rules dealing with it, it must be concluded that these rules were archaic, like many others found in the ancient Indian sources of law—or that the forcible abduction was only a sham abduction and the "robbery" became legalised through a solemn act i.e. the wedding ceremony. That forcible abduction without a wedding ceremony did not constitute marriage between the abductor and the abducted appears clearly from Vās. (17.73). We find there the rule that if a girl has been abducted by force and has not been wedded with the sacred texts, she could be lawfully given to another man as she was considered to be a maiden. A similar rule may be found in MBh. (Ādi Parvan 73) where we read "there is not the least doubt that......our wedding ceremony may take place."

9. It must be added that it appears from the interpretation of the relative rules that marriage contracted according to this form was always effected without the participation of the father or of the guardian of the girl. This form of marriage had no financial consequences because the fathers or the guardians did not have to give a dowry or an endowment to the girl and the suitors did not have to make any payment to the fathers or to the guardians for the girl. By the act of robbery the girl came under the power of the conqueror.

10. This form of marriage was recognised as unlawful probably for members of the Brāhma caste (N. 12.44, Mn. 3.25) but permissible to kings (MBh. Ādi Parvan 73). As permissible to kings, this form of marriage was permissible for members of the Kṣatriya caste (B. 1.11, 20, 12, Śaṅkh. 4.3, Mn. 3.24, 26, MBh. Ādi Parvan 73, Pañcas. IO, 2526).

This form of marriage had to be avoided according to Mn. (3.42) and Yama (Vīr. Saṁs. p. 865), which reproduced the words of Mn., because from blameworthy marriages blameworthy children will be born and this form of marriage was recognised as blameworthy (*nindita*). We do not find in other places in Mn. this distinction between the forms of marriage as blameworthy and unblameworthy (*nindita* and *anindita*) but only as lawful and unlawful (*dharmya* and *adharmya*) (Mn. 3.23,

25, 26) and we also see that some forms of marriage were said to be commended (Mn. 3.24).

Mn. did not give a clear answer as to which forms of marriage were lawful and which were unlawful, but gave some theories by which this question could be answered. According to Mn. (3.23) *Brāhma*, *Daiva*, *Ārṣa*, *Prājāpatya*, *Āsura* and *Gāndharva* were lawful to the *Brāhmaṇas*, and according to Mn. (3.25) only *Prājāpatya*, *Āsura* and *Gāndharva* forms of marriage. What Mn. meant by the expression "*nindita*" and "*anindita*" is not clear, but as according to Mn. (3.29) only sons born from *Brāhma*, *Daiva*, *Āsura* and *Prājāpatya* forms of marriage[3] were endowed with Brāhmaṇic glory and respected by cultured persons, these four forms of marriage could be considered as blameless forms and the other forms beginning from *Āsura* (i.e. *Āsura*, *Gāndharva*, *Rākṣasa* and *Paiśāca-vivāha*) might be considered as blameworthy forms. These four latter forms of marriage were inferior forms although according to the commentaries on Mn. 3.41 only the *Gāndharva*, *Rākṣasa* and *Paiśāca-vivāha* were considered inferior forms of marriage.

The children born in this form of marriage were blameworthy (Mn. 3.42, Yama in Vīr. Saṁs. p. 865) i.e. defective (commentaries on Mn. 3.24).

11. In all these Smṛtis in which the *Paiśāca-vivāha* was known the *Rākṣasa-vivāha* took the penultimate place in the list of the forms of marriage i.e. the seventh place (Mn. 3.21, Y. 1.59-61, Śaṅkh. 4.2, Vi. 24.19, K. 3, G. 4, B. 1.11, 20, N. 12.38/39) with the exception of Āśv. Gṛh. (1.6) where it took the place after the *Paiśāca-vivāha*. In Āp. which source did not mention the *Paiśāca-vivāha* it took the last place and in Vās. (1.29) which also did not mention the *Paiśāca-vivāha* the penultimate place i.e. before the *Āsura-vivāha*.

This form of marriage was known in Mn., Y., Śāṅkh., Vi., K., G., B., N., Yama, Hār., Dev., MBh., Kām., Pañcas., Āśv. Gṛh.

B. *Paiśāca-vivāha*

12. The *Paiśāca* form of marriage was a marriage based on deception of the girl; this was clearly stated in Y. (1.61). This form of marriage was similarly defined in Śāṅkh. (4.6)

3. Four marriages mentioned consecutively.

where it is said that the *Paiśāca* form of marriage took place by stratagem. Hār. (Vīr. Saṁs. 858) used the expression "based upon want of care". Only these sources gave such a definition of this form of marriage. All other sources, although using other words, defined this form of marriage as being based upon seduction of the girl during her insensibility or upon sexual intercourse with her during insensibility. We read about seduction of the girl in Dev. (Vīr. Saṁs. 858) and Mn. (3.34). Mn. (3.34) and K. (3.2) stated that the girl had to be seduced by stealth (Mn. 3.34). We read about sexual intercourse with the girl, under the conditions mentioned below, in N. (12.43), B. (1.1,11 20, 9) and similarly in G. (4.13), Vi. (24.26) and Kām. (§31, 230). That the seduction or sexual intercourse with a maiden had to take place during her insensibility appeared from all sources which dealt with these problems. Only G. (4.13) determined that the girl had to be deprived of consciousness. Other sources like Vi. (24.26), N. (12.43), Kām. (§31, 231), Dev. (Vīr. Saṁs. 858), Hār. (Vīr. Saṁs. 858) understood that the girl was "insensible" when she was asleep, and "unconscious" when she was asleep and intoxicated, or when she was asleep, intoxicated and out of her senses, [according to Mn. (3.34) and B. (1.11, 20, 9)], or when she was asleep, unconscious, or mad, or in distress, [according to Dev. (Vīr. Saṁs. 858)]. According to Jayamaṅgalā, the commentator on Kām. (§31, 231) this form of marriage took place when the girl who was asleep on the lap was left alone. This form of marriage was similarly determined in Āśv. (1.6, 7). There we read that the man could "carry her off, while she was sleeping or when she was not paying attention."

We see here likewise two separate *essentialia negotii*. However, the deception of the girl on the one hand and the seduction of, or sexual intercourse with, a girl during her insensibility on the other, were not two different *essentialia negotii*. We may see this when we read the commentaries on Y. In Y. this form of marriage was regulated as follows: "*Paiśāca-vivāha* took place by deceiving the girl." But what was the deception of the girl ? Mit. determined that it consisted in deceitfully and fraudulently carrying off the girl when she was asleep (Mit. on Y. 1.61), and BBh. determined that it was not by force but by fraud practised on the girl (BBh. on Y-1.61). In other words, therefore, the deception of the girl was nothing more than the abduction of the girl when she was insensible.

13. If the *Rākṣasa-vivāha* was capture or abduction of a girl by force, the *Paiśāca-vivāha* was the carrying away of (or sexual intercourse with a girl) deceitfully and fraudulently. In other words the *Paiśāca-vivāha* was a part or a special branch of the *Rākṣasa-vivāha*; it was a variant of the *Rākṣasa-vivāha* only. The difference between the *Rākṣasa-vivāha* and the *Paiśāca-vivāha* is not great. According to the *Rākṣasa-vivāha* the girl was taken away by force; in the *Paiśāca-vivāha* she was taken away by deception and fraud.

14. If we admit that the *Paiśāca-vivāha* was only a variant of the *Rākṣasa-vivāha* and that this form of marriage was also based on forcible abduction (and that seems to be undisputable) we must apply to this form all that was said about the *Rākṣasa-vivāha*. Thus, we see that this form of marriage was also not allowed. The *Paiśāca-vivāha* must be considered as disallowed even more than the *Rākṣasa-vivāha* because it was based on fraud. According to the Smṛtis all acts (documents) executed by fraud became nullified [Mn. 8.165, Y. 2.89, Vi. 7.7, N. 1.137, Bṛh. (Vy. M. p. 13), Kātyāyana in Aparārka p. 686] as well as acts executed by force [Mn. 8.168, Y. 2.89, Vi. 7.6, N. 1.137, Bṛh. (Vy.M. p. 13), Yama in Parāśaramādhava Vyavahāra p. 162]. The seduction of the girl took place in this form of marriage during insensibility i.e. when she was asleep, intoxicated or out of her senses. In the Smṛtis we very often find rules which stated that a transaction made by a person not in full control of his action was invalid (N. 1.40, K. 3, ch. 1—*apagṛhīta*). This also applied to an intoxicated person [N. 1.137, Vi. 7.10, Y. 2.32, Bṛh. (Vy. M. p. 13), K. 3 ch. 1].

This form of marriage was also based on the seduction of a girl i.e. most probably on sexual intercourse against the will of the maiden. Such sexual intercourse was a very great crime according to the Smṛtis. For this crime the capital penalty was prescribed in the Matsya Purāṇa (Vivādaratnākara p. 401), Y. (2.288) and N. (12.71) (if the girl belonged to a higher caste). According to other sources banishment was prescribed as the penalty (Āp. 2.10-26-21) or, *lex tallionis* i.e. the cutting off of the *penis* and *scrotum* (Bṛh. 24.13; or, according to Kullūka commenting on Mn. 8.364) of the hands

(Y. 2.288, K. 4, ch. 12), or of two fingers (N. 12.71, Śaṅkh. Likh. in Aparārka p. 859). Other sources stipulated as the penalty for this crime confiscation of property (Āp. 2, 10, 26, 21, Bṛh. 24.13, K. 4. ch. 12).

Thus, we find here another argument in favour of the statement that the *Paiśāca-vivāha* at the time in which the Smṛtis were in force was no longer a permitted form of marriage and that the rules which we find in the Smṛtis were archaic. Another argument for this statement is the fact that Āp. and Vās. did not mention this form of marriage at all.

It is improbable that abduction according to this form of marriage could be a sham abduction, although it could probably be so in the case of the *Rākṣasa-vivāha*.

15. It is clear that this form of marriage when it took place, was effected without the participation of the father or of the guardian of the girl and that therefore it had no financial consequences. Through this act of abduction the girl came under the power of her husband like a slave.

16. John D. Mayne in his Treatise of Hindu Law and Usage, (Madras 1900) described the *Paiśāca-vivāha* more like a sudden lust of the ourang-outang than any thing human and considered it as an unlawful form of marriage probably for the *Brāhma* caste (N. 12.44, Mn. 3.25) the more so as it should never be practised (Mn. 3.25, MBh. 13.44, Ādi Parvan 73). But this form of marriage was permissible to Vaiśyas and Śūdras according to Mn. (3.23) B. (1.11, 20, 13) and Pañcas (10. 2526). According to the same Smṛtis it was also permissible to Kṣatriyas (3.23). These conflicting opinions in Mn. were due to the commentators who tried to reconcile the various interpretations.

This form of marriage should be avoided according to Mn. (3.42) and Yama (Vīr. Saṁs. 865), because it was a blameworthy marriage. From this marriage blameworthy offspring were born (Mn. 3.42, Yama in Vīr. Saṁs. p. 865).

17. In all the Smṛtis in which the *Paiśāca-vivāha* was known, this form of marriage took the last place in the list of the forms of marriage i.e. the eighth place (Mn. 3.27, Y. 1.59-61, Śāṅkh. 4.2, Vi. 24.19, K.-3, G. 4. B. 1.11, 20, N. 12.38, 39) with the exception of the Āśv. Gṛh. where it took the penultimate place (seventh).

This form of marriage was known to Mn., Y., Śāṅkh., Vi., K., G., B., N., Dev., Hār., Kām., Āśv. Gṛh.

C. *Āsura-vivāha*

18. The *Āsura-vivāha*, called also *Mānuṣa*, was defined clearly and in few words only in Vi. (24.24). We read that "if a girl was sold to the bridegroom" it was called an *Āsura*-marriage. In other words this form of marriage was based upon the purchase of the maiden by the suitor.[4]

In this form of marriage the maiden (bride) [Mn. 3.31, Vās. 1.35, B. 1.11, 20, 7, Śāṅkh. 4.5, Āśv. 1.6,6, Vi. 24.24, N. 12.42, K. 3.2, Paiṭh. (Vīr. Saṁs. 853, MBh. 13.44 and 1.102, Pañcas in Schmidt 527] could be married or wedded [Mn. 3.31, Āp. 2.5, 12, 6, Vās. 1.35, B. 1.11, 20, 7, Paiṭh. in Vīr. Saṁs. 858, MBh. 13.44, Āśv. 1.6, 6] when the bridegroom (suitor) [Āp. 2.5, 12, 1, Āśv. 1.6, 6 etc.] gave money or other valuable goods [Mn. 3.31, Āp. 2.5, 12, 1, G. 4.11, Vās. 1.35, B. 1.11, 20, 7, Śaṅkh. 4.5, Vi. 24.24, 12.42, K. 3.2, Y. 1.61, MBh. 13.44, 1.102, Pañcas in Schmidt 527, Paiṭh. Vīr. Saṁs. 858] to her father or her kinsmen [Āp. 2.6, 13, 12, N. 12.42, B. 1.11, 20, 7, Mn. 3.31, MBh. 13.44] or, as G. (4.11) clearly stated, to those who had authority over the girl.

We know that the woman could never be independent; she had to be protected by her father in her infancy, by her husband, during her youth, by her son during her seniority [Mn. 9.3, 5.148, MBh. 13.46, 14, Y. 1.85, 86, B. 2.3, 45, Vās. 5.3, Vi. 25.13, Apar. 109 and others]. For that reason it must be understood that the designation of the persons to whom the bridegroom or suitor gave money for the maiden was "those who had authority over the maiden."

The most difficult question regarding this form of marriage was the question of how much the suitor had to pay for the girl. We do not find a clear answer to this question. We find in MBh. (1.102) the statement that a fixed amount had to be paid for the girl whereas Āp. (2.5, 12, 1) stated that the suitor had to pay according to his ability; similarly Mn. (3.31), where we read that the suitor had to pay as much as he could afford.

4. The marriage of Kaikeyī, Gāndhārī and Mādrī (in the epics), Isidāsī (in the Pāli literature) etc.

We see here for the first time that the price of the maiden had to be high and that the bridegroom had to make an effort to pay this price. A similar definition of the amount to be paid for the maiden is found also in K. (3.2) where we read that plenty of money had to be received (*scillicet* by the persons who had authority over the maiden). Similarly Y. (1.64) designated this form of marriage as marriage in which money was largely given (see Mit. *ad.* 1.61). BBh. gave a philological explanation for the word *ādānāt*. According to him this word meant the giving (*dāna*) of a large quantity (*ā*). [Also in MBh. (13.44) and in Pañcas (Schmidt 527) we read that the price paid for the maiden must be high].

The precise amount which had to be paid for the bride could be found in Vās. (29. 21) where we read "if a gift of one thousand oxen fit to draw a carriage (has been bestowed) according to the rule on a perfectly worthy man, that is equal to giving a maiden." It may be seen from this passage that the price of a maiden amounted to 1,000 oxen and a carriage. But in the same Dharmasūtra we find in another place that 100 cows besides a carriage should be given (Vās. 1.36). That is a quotation from the Vedas and we find the same (only enlarged) in Āp. (2.16, 13, 12). Neither of the quotations was absolutely binding but these quotations gave an idea of the amount of payment for the girl; this amount was, of course, very high.

Vās. (1.35) mentioned that the suitor made a bargain with the father. (See also B. 2.1, 2, 27).

It must be pointed out that according to Mn. (3.31) and Pañcas. (in Schmidt 527) the bridegroom had to give wealth for his future wife not only to her kinsmen i.e. to "those who had authority over the maiden", but also "according to his own will to the bride herself." He had to give according to Pañacas (in Schmidt 527) vestments, jewels, and gold (similarly Āśv. 16-1, 6).[5]

19. Since the girl was an article of merchandise, all her defects had to be mentioned by the person who gave her in marriage (Mn. 8.205, Y. 1.66, N. in Aparārka p. 95). If this person gave away the girl without mentioning her defects he

5. Concerning the *Āsura-vivāha* recorded in ancient Indian tradition see Dr. A. S. Altekar : "The Position of Women in Hindu Civilisation" p. 47-48.

was liable to punishment at the highest amercement (Y. 1.66, N. in Aparārka p. 95) but if he mentioned her defects he was free of punishment (Mn. 8.205). These defects were madness (Mn. 8.205), chronic and loathsome disease (N. in Aparārka p. 95), like elephantiasis (Mn. 8.205) and shortness of limbs (N. in Aparārka p. 95), loss of virginity (Mn. 8.205, N. in Aparārka p. 95) or immodesty or attachment to another man (N. in Aparārka p. 95). Doubtless, these "defects" were mentioned in the sources as examples only. Although it was not mentioned clearly that these rules were applicable to the *Āsura-vivāha*, it should be accepted that they were applied to this form of marriage because they were placed amongst the rules, which related to merchandise (Mn.).

The preceding sentence in Mn. related to the sale of merchandise other than that which was chosen. We read there that, after one girl has been shown another was given to the bridegroom, he may marry both of them for the same price (Mn. 8.204). In other word, if he who concluded an agreement concerning the sale of the girl gave a girl other than the one promised, he had to give the promised girl as well as an amercement. This rule found only in Mn. is very strange, since this Dharmaśāstra in other places did not allow the practice of marriage by purchase. Therefore, it must be admitted that this rule, like other rules in Mn. concerning the *Āsura-vivāha*, was an archaic one.

Another very interesting case was discussed in Mn. i.e. what occurred if the buyer died after having paid the price but before the girl has been given away by her father or guardian. Some commentators like Kull. (on Mn. 9.97) added "before the consummation of the marriage". According to Mn. if after the nuptial fee paid for a maiden the giver of the fee died, the girl, if she consented, had to be given in marriage to his brother (Mn. 9.97). This rule was a consequence of the fundamental notion found in Mn. 9.69; according to this rule if the bridegroom died after the girl had been promised to him she had to be given in marriage to his brother (See Vās. 17.72, Kāty. in Vīr. Saṁs. p. 739).

The difference between these two rules is considerable. Although it is a case of marriage by purchase the girl had to give her consent to her marrige to the brother of the buyer.

From the interpretation of these two rules (Mn. 9.97 and 9.69) we see, probably, in the Mānava-Dharmaśāstra, the first stage of restriction of this form of marriage, since according to other sources the girl belonged to the father (Vās. 17.72) or should wait for three menstrual periods and then marry another person (Kāty. in Vīr. Saṁs. p. 739).

20. It must be pointed out that the *Āsura-vivāha* could be divided into two groups. One group, although it contained the rules relating to the *Āsura-vivāha*, said that the sale of a daughter was a crime and that for that reason this form of marriage should not be contracted; on the other hand the second group, which was based on the Vedas and on other sources, considered this form of marriage as permissible. To the first group belonged : Āp., B. and Mn.; to the second group : Vās. Other sources did not discuss this case.

There seems to be no doubt that the rules which stipulated that this form of marriage was non-permissible belonged to the more advanced and more recent rules although the sources of law in which they were found sometimes belonged to the oldest sources of law. Knowing the history of the origin of the Smṛtis this could be easily understood.[6]

Concerning the first group of sources of law, we find in Mn. (3.51) a sentence which stated that the father of a girl who knew the law should not accept even a small consideration i.e. nuptial fee (*śulka*). By accepting a consideration, through avarice, he became a child-seller i.e. committed a sin. That this was a great sin appeared for instance from B. (1-11, 21, 3) where we read : that those wicked men who, seduced by avarice, gave away a daughter for a fee, who (thus) sold themselves and committed a great crime, fell (after death) into a dreadful place of punishment and destroyed their family down to the seventh (generation). Moreover they would repeatedly die and be reborn again. All (this) was declared (to happen) if a fee (was taken). We read also in B. (1.1, 2, 27) that he who gave away his daughter, making a bargain, sold a portion of his spiritual merit. Even Āp. clearly declared that the acceptance

6. For instance in the Dekkan and Gujarāt manuscripts we do not find the rule B. 1.11, 21, 3 (see below). See Dr. A. S. Altekar, "The Position of Women in Hindu Civilisation p. 42-43.

7. K. stated that the father and the mother received money (K. 3.2).

of a gift and the right to sell (or buy) a child were not recognised (Āp. 2.6, 13, 11) i.e. not allowed. The same could be seen from another passage of Mn. i.e. from 3.52. This sentence cannot be easily understood. According to Medh. Nār. and Nandana, commentators of Mn., this passage should be understood in the following manner : those (male) relations who in their folly lived on property obtained by (the sale) of women, (i.e.) carriages or beasts of burden and clothing (received in exchange for) females, committed a sin. Also in the ninth book of Mn. we read "Even a Śūdra ought not to take a nuptial fee when he gives away his daughter, for he who takes a fee sells his daughter, covering the transaction by another name (9.98). If a member of the lowest caste could not sell his daughter, still more so a member of a higher caste could not do so. "Nor, indeed,"—Mn. concluded—"have we heard, even in former creations of such (a thing as) the covert sale of a daughter for a fixed price called a nuptial fee" (9.100).

But not only did he who sold his daughter commit a great sin; it was also said that a female who had been purchased for money was not a wife; she could not assist at sacrifices offered to the gods or the manes (B 1.11, 21, 2). Kāśyapa has stated that she was a slave (B. 1.11, 21, 2); Atri (384) that the girl would remain in her father's *gotra* and her sons would not be entitled to offer oblations to the ancestors of her husband. According to the Padma Purāṇa (Brahma-Khaṇḍa 24, 26) even the face of the seller should not be seen.

These rules made it clear that these sources were of the opinion that the sale of a daughter by her father or guardian was not allowed and in consequence that the form of marriage by purchase was not allowed.

But contrary to these rules we find quite a different opinion in Vās. where we read that the purchase of a girl was mentioned in the following passage of the Veda : "Therefore one hundred (cows) besides a chariot should be given to the father of the bride" (Vās. 1.36). In the next sentence the author of Vās., in reference to Cāturmāsyas, stated : "She, who has been bought by her husband commits a sin as afterwards she unites herself with a stranger" (Vās. 1.37). In these two sentences the author of Vās. stated clearly that the form of marriage by purchase could be contracted.

But the author of Vās. only cited other authorities (Vedas, Cāturmāsas) and did not give his own opinion on this question.

The author of Āp. evidently knew the same sentence from the Vedas when he stated : "It is declared in the Vedas that at the time of marriage a gift, for the (fulfilment of) his wishes should be made (by the bridegroom) to the father of the bride in order to fulfil the law 'Therefore one hundred (cows) besides a chariot should be given' ". But the author of Āp. gave his own opinion, his own point of view on this question. His opinion belonged to the time of the origin of this Dharmasūtra that is to a period later than the Vedas. We read in Āp. "In reference to those (marriage rites), the word 'sale' (is only used as) a metaphorical expression; for the union (of the husband and wife) is effected through the law." This "sale" was a metaphorical expression—said the author of Āp. because of the fact that the "gift" had to be returned to the giver, and the marriage had to be effected through the law i.e. through an action not being in accordance with the legal rules. As contrary to the archaic rules of the Vedas, at the time of the legal validity of the Smṛtis, the act of selling the daughter was not recognised (Āp. 2. 6, 13, 11); the form of marriage by purchase was not allowed.

This interpretation of the legal rules could be used as the basis for the statement that all the Smṛtis (although—like Vās. they recognised the admissibility of the form of marriage by purchase) contrary to the ancient rules (found, for instance, in the Vedas) did not admit the form of marriage by purchase as legal. Though the author of Vās. stated that this form of marriage was admissible, he did not give his own opinion, but only that of the Vedas; *per analogiam* it must be accepted that this rule from the Vedas had to be interpreted in Vās. in the same manner as in Āp. i.e. that the form of marriage by purchase was not allowed. We find in Vās. another example of the existence of archaic rules in the Smṛtis which were not in use at the time of the legal validity of this Smṛti.

So, we can admit that according to all the Smṛtis, although many of them gave a different opinion or did not deal with this question, the father or the guardian should not sell a girl, because by selling her, he committed a sin, and the girl did not become a legal wife of the buyer.

21. This form of marriage was similar to the Roman *coemptio* especially *coemptio uxoris*. The initiative for a marriage of this form lay with the suitor and the girl had no right to choose her husband for herself; those who had authority over the girl had to undertake the choice on her behalf (the father, mother or guardian). This choice did not depend on the good qualities of the suitor but primarily on his financial position and on the price he was prepared to pay.

The fact that the agreement was concluded between the suitor and the person who exercised power over the girl—was not considered sufficient to make the marriage complete. It is very probable that the marriage was concluded only after the marriage ceremony had taken place, although, as it appears, the participation of the priest was not necessary.

22. The *Āsura-vivāha* was considered as an unlawful (unrighteous, improper) form of marriage probably for the Brāhmaṇs caste (N. 12.44, MBh. 13.44, Ādi. Parvan 73); it was so unlawful that it should never be practised (MBh. 13-44, Ādi Parvan 73, Mn. 3.25). On the other hand (in another place in Mn.) it was considered as lawful, probably for the Brāhmaṇs (Mn. 3.23). According to G. some said that even this form of marriage was lawful for the Brāhmaṇs (G. 4.15). But this form of marriage was permissible to Vaiśyas and Śūdras according to B. (1.11, 20, 13, Mn. 3.34 and Pañcas. 10. 2526), and to Kṣatriyas, Vaiśyas and Śūdras according to the Smṛtis last mentioned (Mn. 3.23) and to Kṣatriyas according to MBh. (Ādi Parvan 73). And here again the author of Mn. gave some theories on the same subject. These conflicting opinions were an attempt to reconcile the various interpretations.

The *Āsura-vivāha* had to be avoided according to Mn. (3.42) and Yama (Vīr. Saṁs. 865) because it was a blameworthy marriage.

From this marriage blameworthy offspring were born (Mn. 3.42, Yama—Vīr. Saṁs. 865).

23. This form of marriage—according to the rules—took the rst or the second place in the list of the forms of marriage outside the orthodox forms. It took the fifth place in the general list of the forms of marriage (Mn., 3.21, Y. 1.59-61, Śāṅkh. 4.2, Vi. 24.19) after *Brāhma, Daiva Ārṣa* and *Prājāpatya* and in Āp. (3.5, 12) the fifth place after *Brāhma*, *Ārṣa*, *Daiva* and

Gāndharva. According to other Smṛtis, the *Āsura-vivāha* took the sixth place after *Brāhma*, *Prājāpatya*, *Ārṣa*, *Daiva* and *Gāndharva* (K. 3, G. 4, B. 1.11, 20, N. 12.38, 39. Āśv. Gṛh. 1.6) but only according to Vās. the sixth and last place in the list of the forms of marriage, after *Brāhma*, *Daiva*, *Ārṣa*, *Gāndharva* and *Rākṣasa* (Vās. did not mention Prājāpatya and Paiśāca). (Vās. 1.29).

This form of marriage was known to Mn., Y., Śāṅkh., Vi., K., G., B., N., Āśv. Gṛh., Āp., Vās., Yama, Paiṭh., and MBh.

24. We may note that a completely different definition of this form of marriage can be found in Hār. This definition, given probably in more recent times, had nothing to do with the classical definitions of this form of marriage. We find there the following sentence. "When the girl is given away to a man who is suspected by other people of hypocrisy and deceit, it is *Āsura-vivāha*". (Vīr. Saṁs. p. 853).

D. *Ārṣa-vivāha*

25. This form of marriage was concluded by the gift of a bull and a cow.

It may be said that the marriage was concluded according to this form when the father [Āp. 2.5, 11, 18, K. 3.2], or, more correctly speaking, he who had authority over the maiden [G. 4.8, B. 1.11, 20, 4] gave his daughter in marriage [Mn. 3.29, Āp. 2.5, 11, 18, Śāṅkh. 4.4, K. 3.2, Y. 1.59, MBh. Ādi Parvan 112, Dev. Vīr. Saṁs. 851] or approved of the marriage after receiving [Mn. 3.29, Āp. 2.5, 11, 18, G. 4.8, N. 12.41, Y. 1.59, MBh. Ādi Parvan 112] from the bridegroom [Mn. 3.29, Āp. 2.5, 11, 18, Dev. Vīr. Saṁs. 851] who should be praiseworthy and not belonging to the same *gotra* [Dev. Vīr. Saṁs. 851], (these reservations must be understood more as a counsel than an order), a cow and a bull [Mn. 3.29, Āp. 2.5, 11, 18, G. 4.8, Vās. 2.32, B. 1.11, 20, 4, Śāṅkh 4.4, Āśv. Gṛh. 1.6, N. 12.41, and similarly Dev. in Vīr. Saṁs. 851, Vi. 24.21, Śāṅkh. Likh. Vīr. Saṁs. 851, K. 3.2, Kām. 23, Y-1.59].[8]

Sometimes we find in the Smṛtis other expressions for instance in Y. (two cows), but always the Smṛtis meant a cow and a bull. The two well-known commentators on Y.—Mit. and BBh. explained that the term "two cows" must be understood

8. For the purpose of getting milk for religious sacrifices.

as "a cow and a bull". But sometimes instead of a cow and a bull "a suit of clothes" could be given for the maiden (Śāṅkh. Likh. in Vīr. Saṁs. 851) or in addition to a cow and a bull a dress (N. 12.41) or generally speaking—wealth (Kām. 23).

This present of a bull and a cow had to be given "for the fulfilment of the sacred law" (Mn. 3.29) i.e. according to the commentators of Mn. 'pronouncing the words prescribed for making a gift' (commentators *ad* Mn. 3.29). It had to be offered "after the first of the burnt offerings of parched grain which were prescribed for weddings". (commentaries on B. Gov. cited in S.B.E. 14, *ad* B. 1.11, 20, 4).

26. There is no doubt that the price paid for the maiden amounting to a cow and a bull and sometimes to a cow and a bull and of other goods was not the real price of the maiden. This price, being always the same and not high, in comparison with the price paid according to the *Āsura-vivāha*, could not be the real price for the girl. Therefore it could be said, that this form of marriage was based on sham-purchase.

That this form of marriage was based on sham-purchase and was not the purchase of a girl by a man is evident from the following words which we find in Mn. (3.29) : "When the father gives away his daughter according to the rule after receiving......a cow and a bull". These words are understood by the commentators or Mn. as follows : "it is not with the intention of selling his child". The commentators went further when they said that the bridegroom should give to him who had authority over the maiden a bull and a cow and receive them back along with the bride (Gov. *ad* B. 2.11, 20, 4 in S.B.E. 14 *ad* B. 2.11, 20, 4, MBh. Anuś. 81, 1.2, 13.46 1.2); therefore, if the bridegroom received his "price" for the girl from the person who had authority over the maiden it could not be said that the maiden was sold by this person or purchased by her future husband. The price that was given was returned probably in the form of a dowry, and therefore could not be considered as a price nor the marriage as a marriage by purchase, but only by sham-purchase.

It must also be pointed out that according to Śāṅkh. Likh. in addition to the gift of a cow and a bull or of a suit of clothes, ornaments and a dowry had to be given (Vīr.

Saṁs. 851); this could be taken as proof that not only the commentators but also the later Smṛtis were of the opinion that this form of marriage was not a marriage by purchase but only a marriage by sham-purchase.

It was pointed out, when interpreting the *Āsura-vivāha*, that the selling of a girl was a sin. The question was whether a pair of oxen given to the father or guardian of the girl and accepted in this form of marriage was to be regarded as a "consideration" (*śulka*) or a "sale" (*vikraya*). According to Mn. 3.53 it was a *vikraya*—a sale, because it made no difference if the gift was small or large (identically MBh. 13.80, 20-21, 13.45, 20).

But this would only be the case if the value of the girl did not exceed the value of one cow and one bull i.e. if it were a real marriage by purchase (*Āsura-vivāha*). In this connexion we find in the next *śloka* of Mānava-Dharmaśāstra the following sentence : "In the case of girls whose relations do not appropriate the bride's gift, it is not a 'sale'. It is only a means of honouring the maidens and is entirely harmless" [Mn. 3.54, identically MBh. Anuś. 81, 1.2, and 13.46, 1-2]; this meant that there was not the slightest taint of sin in this act [Commentary on Mn. 3.54].

We have seen that the price given for the girl was, according to Mn. and other sources of law, returned to the bride or bridegroom, therefore, this gift was "only a means of honouring the girl" but not a sale. The words "means of honouring" were interpreted by the commentators on Mn. (3.54) in the following manner: "The receiving of presents on behalf of brides was a means of honouring them; it raised the girls in their own estimation; they came to think that 'we are so good that we are being married after receiving proper presents'. They rose in the estimation of the people also, who looked upon such brides as very handsomely fortunate."

We find the same opinion in MBh. (13.45, 2) where we read "that a girl, in respect of whom nothing is taken by her kinsmen in the form of dower, cannot be said to be sold...... Her sire and brothers and father-in-law and husband's brother should show her every respect and adorn her with ornaments if they be desirous of reaping benefits, for such conduct on their part always leads to considerable happiness and advantage.

If the wife does not like her husband or fails to gladden him, from such dislike and absence of joy, the husband can never have issue for increasing his race". This adorning of the girl with ornaments was the dowry. So we can see in this quotation of MBh. the development from the marriage by purchase to the marriage by sham-purchase and then to the marriage in which the dowry was to be given to the future husband of the girl. This dowry was the *essentiale negotii* of the orthodox forms of marriage to which this form of marriage also belonged.

27. As in the *Āsura-vivāha*, in this form of marriage also the marriage depended not on the choice exercised by the girl, but on the choice exercised by her father or her guardian. This form of marriage differed from the other orthodox forms of marriage: in the other orthodox forms of marriage, the marriage always depended on the father or guardians and sometimes on the fathers and guardians of both parties (for example in the case of the marriage of children), while in the marriage concluded according to this form of marriage, the first stage was the choice made by the suitor and the next stage was the supplementary consent on the part of the father or guardian.

As in the *Āsura-vivāha*, in this form of marriage too, the matrimonial ceremony did not take place before the act of sham-purchase, although it was likely that the participation of a priest was not necessary.

28. Because this form of marriage was considered as praiseworthy (Āp. 3.5, 12, 3) it was considered also as lawful (*dharmya*) and righteous, probably for members of the Brāhma caste (G. 4.14, B. 1.11, 20, 10, N. 12.44, Vi. 24.27, Kām. 23, MBh. Ādi Parvan 73 and 13.44 Pañcas 10,2526, see Śāṅkh. 4.3). According to Mn. (3.23), which source of law gave some theories on this subject, there could be found two expressions i.e. that this form of marriage was lawful for Brāhmaṇas and commended (approved for) for them (3.24), since Mn. gave the points of view of many law-teachers on this subject. According to MBh. (Ādi Parvan 73) this form of marriage was proper also for a Brāhmaṇs and a Kṣatriyas.

29. The sons born in this form of marriage were endowed with Brāhmaṇic glory and were respected by cultured persons. Endowed with beauty and the quality of goodness, possessing wealth and fame, with full enjoyment and righteousness they lived for a hundred years (Mn. 3.39-40, Yama in Vīr. Saṁs. p. 865, see B. 1.11, 21, 1, Āp. 2.5, 12, 4).

A son born of a wife married according to this form of marriage saved three generations from hell (G. 4.30) and according to Y. (1.59) six men; Mn. explained that he purified three ancestors and three descendants i.e. six men. According to Vi. he purified seven men (24.31) and according to Āśv. Gṛh. (1.6-1) and Śaunaka (Vīr. Saṁs. p. 863) seven men on the father's and seven on the mother's side, i.e. altogether 14 men. According to Śāṅkh. Likh. (Vīr. Saṁs. p. 865) only five men on the father's side and five on the mother's side and himself, i.e. altogether 11 men. This was purely laudatory exaggerations.[9]

30. The father or the guardian who gave the girl in marriage according to the *Ārṣa-vivāha* gained merit for himself and for the girl. We read in Vi. (24.34) : "(He who gives a girl in marriage) according to the *Ārṣa* rite (brings her) into the world of Viṣṇu (and enters that world himself)."

31. Because this form of marriage was considered as praiseworthy on account of the fact that it was not based on purchase but on sham-purchase, it took a high place in the list of the forms of marriage in ancient India. It took the third place after *Brāhma*, and *Daiva* [Mn. (3.21), Y. (1·59-61), Śaṅkh. (4.2), Vi. (24.18) and Vās. (1.29)] and the second place after *Brāhma* and *Prājāpatya* [G. (4), B. 1.11, 20), N. (12.38, 39), K. (3) and Kām. (23)]; it took the second place after *Brāhma* [Āp. (3.5, 12)] and the fourth place after *Brāhma*, *Daiva* and *Prajāpati* [Āśv. Gṛh. (1.6)].

The *Ārṣa-vivāha* was considered an orthodox form of marriage.[10]

This form of marriage was known to all the Smṛtis. We find it Mn., Y., G., N., Āp., Vās., Śāṅkh., Dev., K., Āśv. Gṛh., Kām., MBh.

E. *Brāhma-vivāha*

32. The voluntary giving away of the girl to an honour-

9. See Commentaries on Mn. 3.37 cited below (*Brāhma-vivāha*).
10. See below.

able man after having decked her with ornaments was the *Brāhma-vivāha*.

According to this form of marriage the maiden (daughter, bride, damsel, girl) was given away [Mn. 3.27, Āp. 2.5, 11, 17, G.4.6, Vās.1.30, B. 1.11, 20,2, Śāṅkh. 4.4, Āśv. Gṛh. 1.6, 1, Vi. 24.19, N. 12.40, K. 3.2, MBh. 13.44, Ādi Parvan 112, Y. 1.58, Devā., Samvarta and Vyāsa in Vīr. Saṁs. 487, Brahmapurāṇa and Śāṅkh. Likh. and Paiṭh. in Vīr. Saṁs. 848] to a suitor [Vās. 1.30, Śāṅkh. 4.4] by her father or, more correctly speaking, by the person who had authority over her [Mn. 3.27, Āp. 2.5, 11, 17, Vās. 1.30, K. 3.2, MBh. 13.44, Samvarta in Vīr. Saṁ. 847]. The Smṛtis had a more explicit description of the person to be taken as husband by the girl and demanded that he possesses some special qualities. If the Smṛtis did not describe exactly the qualities with which the suitor had to be endowed they determined that he had to be a suitable (fit, accomplished, deserving qualified) man [Vi. 24.19, MBh. Ādi Parvan 112, Dev. Vīr. Saṁs. 847, Samvarta in Vīr. Saṁs. 847, Brahmapurāṇa Vīr. Saṁs. 848]. Those Smṛtis which described more exactly the qualities of the suitor demanded sometimes that the father or the person who had authority over the maiden enquire regarding the qualities of the suitor [Āp. 2.5, 11, 17, B 1.11, 20, 2, MBh. 13.44]. These qualities were good (virtuous) conduct [Mn. 3.27, G. 4-6, MBh. 13.44; this expression according to Har., commentator on G. (S.B.E. 2 to G. 4.6) meant "performance of the acts prescribed in the Vedas and Smṛtis"], good character [Āp. 2.5, 11,7, B. 1.11, 20, 2, MBh. 13.44, G. 4.6) which expression according to Har., commentator on G. (S.B.E. 2 to G. 4.6) meant : "faith in the ordinances of the law"], good actions and acquirements [MBh. 13.44], learning in the Vedas [Mn. 3.27, Āp. 2.5 11, 17, G. 4.6, MBh. 13.44, B. 1.11, 20, 2; this expression according to Gov., commentator on B. (S.B.E. 14 to B. 1.11, 20, 2), had a double sense of "a student of the Veda" (it is he who had not broken his vow of chastity) and "chaste"], descent from a good family [Āp. 2.5, 11, 17, MBh. 13.44, Śāṅkh Likh. in Vīr. Saṁs. 848; this expression according to Śāṅkh. Likh. (Vīr Saṁs. 848) meant "descending from the same caste and well-known" to the bride's father (guardian], good health [Āp. 2, 5, 11, 17], having relatives [G. 4.6], well armed [B. 1.11, 20, 2];

some more recent Smṛtis added—probably incorrectly that the suitor had to have one final quality i.e. he had not yet have reached puberty. One of these Smṛtis declared also incorrectly, that when one offers a pair of clothes to a man and gives his girl to him "without deprecating him, directing him to jointly carry on *Dharma*—this is Brāhma-Vivāha" [Hār. in Vīr. Saṁs. 848].

On the other hand some of the Smṛtis demanded that the maiden be decked with ornaments (endowed, dressed and adorned) [Mn. 3.27, G. 4.6, Āśv. Gṛh. 1.6, 1, N. 12.40, K. 3.2, Y. 1.58, Āp. 2.5,11,17, MBh. Ādi Parvan 112, Dev. in Vīr. Saṁs. 847, Vyāsa in Vīr. Saṁs. 847, Samvarta in Vīr. Saṁs. 847, Brahma-Purāṇa in Vīr. Saṁs. 848, Paiṭh. in Vīr. Saṁs. 848, Kām. 23]. She had to be decked with ornaments [Mn. 3-27, K. 3.2, Samvarta in Vīr. Saṁs. 874] i.e. with gold [Paiṭh. in Vīr. Saṁs. 848] or endowed with wealth (Śāṅkh. Likh. in Vīr. Saṁs. 848). She had also to be honoured by many valuable presents such as jewels [MBh. Ādi Parvan 112, Mn. 3.27] and wear new bangles [Dev. in Vīr. Saṁs. 847]. The dressing (endowment) had to be carried out according to the best ability of the person who was obliged to supply these ornaments (endow the girl). This was very well expressed by Āp. [2.5, 11, 17] and Brahmapurāṇa [Vīr. Saṁs. 848]. According to Hār. [Vīr. Saṁs. 848] a set of clothes had to be offered to the suitor with the girl. According to some more recent Smṛtis it was understood that the girl had to be endowed with good qualities [Dev. and Samvarta in Vīr. Saṁs. 847].

According to this form of marriage the initiative for the marriage was taken by the father or the person who had authority over the girl. That is stated *expressis verbis* (contrary to the *Prājāpatya-vivāha*) in Mn. (3.27), B. (1.11, 20, 2) Vi.(24.19), N. (12.40), Y. (1.58), MBh. (Ādi Parvan 112), similarly in Śāṅkh. (4.4). Differently Kām. (23).

The giving away of the girl took place after going round the fire three times, and after having pronounced the name of the *gotra* [Vyāsa in Vīr. Saṁs. 848] or after pouring out a libation of water [Vās. 1.30, Āśv. Gṛh 1.6, 1. See Yama in Vīr. Saṁs. 848].

The purpose of this form of marriage was the performance of the rites that had to be performed together [Āp. 2.5, 11, 17].

33. We have seen from the interpretation of the *Ārṣa-vivāha* that it required that the gift given to the father by the suitor be returned to the girl. It has been pointed out that this gift constituted a dowry and that the dowry was the *essentiale negotii* of the orthodox forms of marriage to which the *Ārṣa-vivāha* belonged.

The *Brāhma-vivāha*, like the *Daiva-vivāha* and the *Prājāpatya-vivāha*, belonged to the orthodox forms of marriage. In the case of these three forms, contrary to the *Ārṣa-vivāha*, the obligation to give a dowry was clearly expressed. So we may say that the bestowal of the dowry was the essential point in these three orthodox forms of marriage (*Brāhma*, *Daiva*, *Prājāpatya*) and that they and the *Ārṣa-vivāha* were the highest and the most esteemed forms of marriage.

In Mn. we find the reason why it was advisable to give a dowry to a girl. We read in Mn. (3.56) that "Where women are honoured, there the gods rejoice; where on the other hand they are not honoured, there all rites are fruitless." Commentators on Mn. (3.56) explained that a girl was honoured by the giving of gifts (see also commentators on Mn. 3.54). The same passage can also be found in MBh. (13.46, 5-6).

We read also in Mn. "The houses where female relations are not duly honoured, are accursed, they perish completely, as if destroyed by magic. Hence men who seek (their own) welfare, should always honour women on holidays and festivals with (gifts of) ornaments, clothes, and dainty food. In that family, where the husband is pleased with his wife and the wife with her husband, happiness will assuredly be lasting." [Mn.3. 58-60, similarly MBh. 13.46, 7, 15]. We find the full explanation of the necessity of giving a dowry in the next *ślokas* of Mn. (3.61-62) and in MBh. (13.46-4 which contained the same words as those found in Mn.). "For if the wife is not radiant with beauty, she will not attract her husband; if she has no attraction for him, no children will be born. If the wife is radiant with beauty, the whole house is bright; but if she has no beauty, all will appear dismal."

34. According to this form of marriage the girl was given no part in the choice of the man, because the choice of a husband depended on the will of the father or guardian only.

The initiative for the marriage lay with the father or guardian and with the suitor. Herein we find the greatest difference between this form of marriage and the *Prājāpatya-vivāha.*[11] Probably the participation of a priest in this form of marriage was not necessary because the final act of the delivery of the girl to the suitor by the father or guardian completed the marriage. Possibly, the execution of some ceremonial acts completed the marriage. In ancient Germanic Law the case was almost the same.

35. Because this form of marriage was considered praiseworthy (Āp. 3.5, 12, 3) it was considered also lawful (*dharmya*) and righteous for the Brāhma caste (G. 4.14, B. 1.11, 20 10, N. 12.44, Vi. 24.27, Kām. 23, MBh. Ādi Parvan 73 and 13.44 Pañcas. 10. 2526 see Śāṅkh. 4.3).

According to Mn. (3.23), which source included some theories on this subject, two expressions could be found i.e. that this form of marriage was lawful for and commanded (approved) for Brāhmaṇs (3.24) (Mn. gave the point of view of many law-teachers on this subject). According to G. Banerjee (The Hindu Law of Marriage and Strīdhana, being the Tagore Law Lectures for 1878 p. 79) this form of marriage was called the Brāhma form because it was the form particularly fit for Brāhmaṇs. It must be noted however that according to MBh. (Ādi Parvan 73) this form of marriage was proper also for Kṣatriyas.

36. Sons born in this form of marriage were endowed with Brahmaṇic glory and were respected by cultured person. Endowed with beauty and the quality of goodness, they possessed wealth and fame and with full enjoyment and righteousness they lived for a hundred years (Mn. 3.30, 40, Yama in Vīr. Saṁs. p. 865, see B. 1.11, 21, 1, Āp. 2.5, 12, 4).

A son born of a wife married according to this form saved or purified (liberated from sin) twenty-one men (Vi. 24.29, Y. 1.58) i.e. ten ancestors, ten descendants and himself as the twenty-first (Mn. 3.37, G. 4.33) and according to Āśv. Gṛh. (1.6, 1) and Śaunaka (Vīr. Saṁs. p. 863) twelve descendants and twelve ancestors on both sides (the husband's and the wife's side).

11. Cf. A. S. Altekar's "The Position of Women in Hindu Civilisation" p. 55.

Medh. on Mn. 3.37 added very correctly that this verse was a "purely laudatory exaggeration". Hence the question needed not be raised how a man could save from sin his descendants, who were not yet born. For ancestors, freedom from sin was actually brought about by the proper performance by the son of *śrāddha* and other rites. The assertion that "he absolved from sin ten descendants" meant that in his family ten lines of descendants were born sinless.

37. Also the father or the guardian who gave the girl in marriage according to this form gained merit for himself and for the girl. Therefore we read in Vi. 24.33 "he who gave a girl in marriage according to the Brāhma rite brought her into the world of Brāhmaṇ (after her death, and entered tha world himself)." It was the highest and the best world.

38. This form of marriage was considered in all the Smṛtis as the highest of all and always took the first place in the list of the forms of marriage (Mn. 3.21, Y. 1.59-61, Śaṅkh. 4.2, Vi. 24.13, Kām. 23, K. 3, G. 4., B. 1.11, 20, Āśv. Gṛh. 1.6, Āp. 3.5, 12, Vās. 1.29).

The *Brāhma-vivāha* was known to all the Smṛtis which dealt with the forms of marriage (Mn., Y., Vi., G., B., N., Āp., Vās., Śāṅkh., Dev., Samvarta, Vyāsa, Paiṭh, K., Kām., Āśv. Gṛh., MBh., Brahma Purāṇa etc.).

F. *Daiva-vivāha*

39. To give a girl to a *ṛtvij*, while he was officiating at a sacrifice consituted the *Daiva-vivāha*.

According to this form of marriage one[12] gave away the girl [Mn. 3.28, Vās. 1.31, Āp. 2.5, 11, 19, G. 4.9, B. 1.11, 20, 5, Śāṅkh. 4.4, Āśv. Gṛh. 1.6, 2, Vi. 24.20, N. 12.41, K. 3.2, Y. 1.59, Dev. and Yama in Vīr. Saṁs. 849] decked with ornaments [Mn. 3.28, G. 3.9, Vās, 1.31, Āśv. Gṛh. 1.6, 2, Mit. to Y. 1.59, (the text does not mention that the ornaments must be given to the girl. BBh. added that the words from Mn. 3.28 i.e. from the *Brāhma-vivāha* "decked with ornaments, according to his ability" should apply to all kinds of marriages". Similarly B. 1.11, 20, 5, Dev. Vīr. Saṁs. 849),

12. According to A. S. Altekar (The Position of Women in Hindu Civilisation) it was the sacrificer. (p. 53).

i.e. duly decked (Āśv. Gṛh. 1-6, 2) with gold (Dev. in Vīr. Saṁs. 849)] to an officiating priest (*ṛtvij*) [Mn. 3.28, Āp. 2.5, 11, 19, G. 3.9, Vās. 1.31, B. 1.11, 20, 5, Śāṅkh. 4.4, Āśv. Gṛh. 1.6, 2, Vi. 24.20, N. 12.41, K. 3.2, Kām. 23, Y. 1.59, Dev. in Vīr. Saṁs. 849. Ya. in Vīr. Saṁs. 849], while he was officiating at a sacrifice Mn. III-28, Āp. II-5, 11, 19, Vās. I-31, B. 1.11, 20, 5, Śāṅkh. 4.4, Āśv. Gṛh. 1.6, 2, Vi. 24.20, K. 3.2, Kām. 23, Y. 1.59].[13]

According to Āp. (2.5, 11, 19) it had to be a *śrauta*-sacrifice, according to Āśv. Gṛh (1.6, 2) a sacrifice with three *śrauta*-fires, and according to BBh., (*ad* Y. 1.59) and commentators on Mn. (3.28) an important sacrifice like *jyotiṣṭoma*.

This form of marriage differred little from the *Brāhma-vivāha* (instead of a suitor having some special qualities he was an officiating priest at the moment at which he was officiating at a sacrifice). This could be well understood after the commentaries of the Smṛtis have been studied.

According to BBh. (*ad* Y. 1.59) "when a person commenced the performance of any important sacrifice, like *jyotiṣṭoma* etc., he could give his daughter in marriage to the officiating priest, in consideration of his finishing the sacrifice, which could last for several days."

Therefore we could admit that the giving of a girl to the *ṛtvij* was in consideration of his fee (BBh. *ad* Y. 1.89, Mit. *ad* Y. 1.89). The girl was given as part of the sacrificial fee (*dakṣiṇā*) to one of the priests after a sacrifice has been completed. Gov., commentator on B. (S.B.E. 14. *ad* B. 1.11, 20, 5), added that the recipient had to accept the gift with the six *mantras* (*prajāpati striyāṁ yaśaḥ*:; Taitt. Brāhm. 3.4, 6, 5).

13. A. S. Altekar in his "Position of Women in Hindu Civilisation" stated "Vedic sacrifices, which were quite popular down to the 4th century B.C. often lasted for several weeks. The sacrificer had to invite a large number of priests to perform various duties in their connection. During this close and prolonged association, he would often be favourably impressed by the culture, education and attainments of some one among the priests, and would decide to solve the marriage problem of his grown-up daughter by offering her to him. These were the days of post-puberty marriages; owing to the close association during the sacrifices, daughters also could get an opportunity to form an estimate of their future husbands and guide their parents in the choice. Daiva marriages disappeared with Vedic sacrifices. Later tradition has not preserved any instances of the earlier period. The case recorded in the Bṛhaddaiva is not really an instance of this marriage; for there the sage Śyāvāsva does not himself marry the sacrificer's daughter, but selects her for his son (V, 54-55)." (p. 53-54).

It must be pointed out that according to Dev. (Vīr. Saṁs. 849), the *Daiva-vivāha* took place "when the girl was given within the altar to the bridegroom after having presented to him a pair (a cow and a bull)". It is evident that Dev. was mistaken and that the form of marriage described in such a manner in Dev. was not the Daiva-vivāha but the Ārṣa-vivāha.

Moreover, according to J. Jolly (Hindu Law and Custom, p. 116) "The sacrificial priest is, as is often the case, inferior in position to a virtuous and learned Brāhmaṇ; on the other hand his position is raised if he is just at that time engaged in a sacrifice just as the murder of a man in the act of performing a sacrifice is a still more heinous crime (Vi. 50, 7)."

40. In the *Daiva-vivāha* which also belonged to the orthodox forms of marriage, the girl, as in the *Brāhma-vivāha*, had no influence in the choice of her husband; this choice depended on the will of her father or guardian. The participation of a priest in this form of marriage was probably not necessary and it was certain that the participation of a priest was not an *essentiale negotii* in the matrimonial act, because the act of the delivery of the girl to a *ṛtvij*, actively engaged in sacrifice, was tantamount to marriage although it is possible that it was necessary to execute a ceremony such as *saptapadī* (seven steps). This form of marriage was therefore very similar to the ancient Germanic forms of marriage, where the participation of a priest was not necessary for the validity of the marriage.

41. Because this form of marriage was considered as praiseworthy (Āp. 3.5, 12, 3) it was considered also as lawful (*dharmya*)) and righteous for the Brāhma caste (G. 4.14, B. 1.11, 20, 10, N. 12.44, Vi. 24.27, Kām 23, MBh. Ādi Parvan 73 and 13.44, see Śāṅkh. 4.3 Pañcas. IO 2526). According to Mn. (3.23), which source of law gave some theories on this subject, two opinions may be found i.e. that this form of marriage was lawful (for Brāhmaṇs) and commended (approved) for Brāhmaṇs (3.24). Mn. gave the point of view of many law-teachers on this subject. According to MBh. (Ādi Parvan 73) this form of marriage was proper for the Brāhmaṇs and Kṣatriyas.

42. The sons born in this form of marriage were endowed with Brāhmaṇic glory and were respected by cultured persons. Endowed with beauty and the quality of goodness, they possessed wealth and fame with full enjoyment and righteousness and they lived for a hundred years (Mn. 3.39-40, Yama in Vīr. Saṁs. p. 865, see B. 1.11, 21, 1, Āp. 2.5, 12, 4).

A son born of the wife married according to this form of marriage saved seven men i.e. three ancestors and descendants and himself (Śāṅkh. Likh. Vīr. Śaṁs. p. 865); according to G. (4.31), ten ancestors; according to Vi. (24.31) and Y. (1.59) fourteen men; and according to Āśv. Gṛh. (1.6,1) and Śaunaka (Vīr. Saṁs. p. 863) ten ancestors and ten descendants altogether twenty persons. Śaunaka (*ibidem*) added that the purified persons could belong to the father's or mother's side.[14]

43. Also the father or the guardian or he who gave the girl in marriage, according to the *Daiva-vivāha* gained merit for himself and for the girl. We read in Vi. (24.34): "(He who gives her in marriage) according to *Daiva* rite (brings her) into *svarga* (or heaven) (and enters *svarga* himself)."

44. This form of marriage generally took the second place after *Brāhma-vivāha* in the list of the forms of marriage in ancient India (Mn. 3.21, Y. 1.59-61, Śāṅkh. 4.2, Vi. 6.24.18, Āśv. Gṛh. 1.6 and Vās. 1-29). According to Āp. this form of marriage took the third place after the *Brāhma-vivāha* and the *Ārṣa-vivāha*, and according to Kām. (23), K. (3), G. (4), B. (1.11-20) and N. (12.38-39) the fourth place after the *Brāhma-vivāha*, *Prājāpatya-vivāha* and *Ārṣa-vivāha*.

The *Daiva-vivāha* was known to all the Smṛtis which dealt with the forms of marriage (Mn., Y., Vi., G.,B.,N., Āp., Vās., Sāṅkh., Dev., Yama., K., Kām., Āśv. Gṛh., MBh.).

G. *Prājāpatya-vivāha*[15]

45. The giving of a girl to a suitor by saying that both should perform together their duties was the *Prājāpatya-vivāha*.

According to this form of marriage the father, or he who had authority over the girl, had to give away the girl [Mn. 3.30, B. 1.11, 20, 3, Sāṅkh. 4.5, Y. 1.60, K. 3.2, Dev. in Vīr Saṁs. 851] to a suitor i.e. to a person who solicited her hand [Mn. 3.30, Śāṅkh. 4.5, Vi. 24.22, N. 12.40, Y. 1.60] by saying a formula such as "may both of you perform together your duties'

14. See Commentators on Mn. 3.37.

15. This form of marriage is still in use and is considered a legal form of marriage.

[Y. 1.60, Mn. 3.30, G. 4.7, 1.11, 20, 3, Āśv. Gṛh 1.6. 3, N. 12.40, K. 3.2, Kām. 23, Dev. in Vīr. Saṁs. 851]. This formula had to express that the husband and the wife had to co-operate in the performance of their duties. According to BBh. (*ad* Y. 1.60) this form of marriage was meant for monogamous couples only. A person married by this rite of *Prājāpatya*, could not take another wife, during the lifetime of his first wife. This was the force of the marriage address "may both of you perform together your duties." In other forms of marriage, the married couple had to perform their duties together, but in this form they were specially enjoined to observe their duties to each other, so that the husband could not renounce his wife and take to the order of *sanyāsa* or *vānaprastha*,[16] nor could he take another wife as long as she lived (Nṛsiṁha and Haradatta *ad* G. 4.7).[17] According to B. (1.11, 20, 3) and Dev. (Vir. Saṁs. 851) the girl had to be decked with ornaments as in the other forms of marriage. (See also Mn. 3.30).

The difference, which appears from the texts, between this form of marriage and the *Brāhma-vivāha* was as follows : in this form of marriage, contrary to the *Brāhma-vivāha*, the bridegroom was the suppliant and was not invited by the father of the bride. The *Prājāpatya-vivāha* was probably used only for monogamic marriages.

46. According to G. Banerjee (The Hindu Law of Marriage and Strīdhana being the Tagore Law Lectures for 1878), in this form of marriage the bridegroom was an applicant for the bride's hand. That was the distinction of this form from the *Brāhma-vivāha*, and made it inferior to the latter in which the bride-groom was voluntarily invited by the father to accept the bride. Marriage, being according to Hindū notions a gift, lost a portion of its merit if the gift was not voluntary, but had to be applied for. A.S. Altekar in his "The Position of Women in Hindu Civilisation" came to a different and, it seems, unfounded conclusion that the *Brāhma* and *Prājāpatya* were synonymous words and that it was possible that the *Brāhma* marriage was originally identical with the *Prājāpatya*. This con-

16. Without her consent or her company.

17. It could be said that this form of marriage rendered polygamy impossible.

clusion was supported, according to A. S. Altekar, by the fact "that two of the early writers, Vāsiṣṭha and Āpastamba, did not mention *Prājāpatya* marriage at all; they referred to only three approved forms, *Brāhma*, *Daiva* and *Ārṣa*. *Prājāpatya* was added later, probably, in order to reach the number eight. Smṛti writers therefore naturally fail to bring out the difference between the two."

47. In this form of marriage, called also *Kāya-vivāha*, the delivery of the girl to the wooer by the father or guardian was probably held to be equivalent to the wedding ceremony (similar to the ancient Germanic law), so that it was not necessary to perform a further ceremony in the presence of a priest. The *Prājāpatya-vivāha* belonged to the orthodox forms of marriage.

48. This form of marriage was considered as lawful (*dharmya*) and righteous for the Brāhma caste (G. 4.14, B. 1.11, 20, 10, N. 12.44, Kām. 23, Vi. 24.27, MBh.-Ādi Parvan 73, Pañcas 10. 2526, see Śāṅkh. 4.3). According to Mn. 3.23, which source of law gave some theories on this subject, two opinions can be found i.e. that this form of marriage was lawful (for a Brāhmaṇ) and commended (approved) for a Brāhmaṇ (3.24); Mn. gave the point of view of many law-teachers on this subject. According to MBh. (Ādi Parvan 73) this form of marriage was proper for a Brāhmaṇ and a Kṣatriya.

In another place MBh. (Ādi Parvan 73) stated that this form of marriage was improper. Probably this was only a point of view of one author who did not realize the importance of this form of marriage.

49. The sons born in this marriage were endowed with Brāhmaṇic glory and were respected by cultured persons. Endowed with beauty and the quality of goodness, they possessed wealth and fame with full enjoyment and righteousness and lived for a hundred years (Mn. 3.39 40, Yama in Vīr. Saṁs. p. 865, see B. 1.11, 21, 1, Āp. 2.5, 12, 4).

A son born of a wife married according to this form of marriage saved four ancestors from hell (Vi. 24-32) and, according to Y., six men as well as himself (Y. 1.60); according to G. (4.32) ten persons; according to Mn. (3.38) twelve persons, i.e. six ancestors, and six decendants; according to Śāṅkh. Likh. (Vīr. Saṁs. p. 865) fifteen persons i.e. seven ancestors and seven descendants and himself; and according to Āśv. Gṛh. (1.6) and Śaunaka (Vīr. Saṁs. p. 864) sixteen persons i.e. eight ancestors and eight descendants. These statements were also purely laudatory exaggerations.[18]

50. Also the father or the guardian who gave the girl in marriage according to the *Prājāpatya-vivāha* gained merit for himself and for the girl. We read in Vi. (24.36) : (He who gave a girl in marriage) according to the *Prājāpati* rite (took her) into the world of the gods (and entered that world himself).

51. This form of marriage usually took the fourth place in the general list of the forms of marriage in ancient India (Mn. 3.21, Y.-1.59-61, Śāṅkh. 4.2, Vi. (24.18) i.e. after the *Brāhma*, *Daiva*, and *Ārṣa*, but also took the second place after the *Brāhma* (K. 3, G. 4, B. 1.11, 20, N. 12.38, 39) and the third place after the *Brāhma* and *Daiva* rites (Āśv. Gṛh. 1-6).

The *Prājāpatya-vivāha* was known to all the Smṛtis which dealt with the forms of marriage, with the exception of Āp. and Vās (Mn., Y., G., B., N., Śāṅkh., Dev., K., Kām., Āśv. Gṛh.).

H. *Gāndharva-vivāha*[19]

52. The union of a willing maiden and a lover constituted the *Gāndharva-vivāha*.

This form of marriage was a voluntary (or spontaneous) [Mn. 3.32, K. 3.2, Kām. 26 G. 4.10] union (*saṁyoga*) [Mn. 3.32, Āp. 2.5, 12, 20, G. 4. 4.10, B-1, 11, 20, 6, Śāṅkh. 4.6, Vi-24.23, N. 12.42, K. 3.2, Kām. 26, Dev. in Vīr. Saṁs. 855] of a loving (willing) [G. 4.10, Vās. 1.33, B. 1,11, 20, 6, N. 12-42] maiden (bride, virgin (*kanyā*), damsel, woman) [Mn. 3.32, Āp. 2.5, 12, 20, Vās. 1.33, B. 1.11, 20, 6, Śāṅkh. 4.5, Aśv. Gṛh. 1.6-5, N. 12-42, K. 3.2, Dev. (Vīr. Saṁs. 855, Hār. Vīr. Saṁs. 856)] with her lover (bridegroom) [Mn. 3.32, Äp. 2.5, 12, 20, G. 4.10, Vās. 1.33, B. 1.11, 20, 6, Śāṅkh. 4.5, Āśv. Gṛh. 1.6, 5, N. 12.42, K. 3.2, Dev. in Vīr. Saṁs. 855, Hār in Vīr. Saṁs. 856]. Vi. (24.23) defined this form of marriage as a union

18. See Medhātithi's commentary on Mn. 3.37.

19. A more detailed analysis of the *Gāndharva-vivāha* appeared as No. 9 of the author's JSAIL in "the Poona Orientalist", Vol. 10, Nos. 3.4, pp. 69-78 entitled "Juridical Aspects of the Gāndharva Form of Marriage."

between two lovers. Āśv. (1.6, 5) added that this form of marriage took place after a mutual agreement has been made. Similarly Dev. (Vīr. Saṁs. 855). This mutual consent or reciprocal attachment was the *essentiale negotii* of this form of marriage, according to Y. (1.61). For the better understanding of this form of marriage some Smṛtis added that this form of marriage took place through love [Āp. 2.5, 12, 20, Śāṅkh. 4.5, Dev. (Vīr. Saṁs. 855)], or that it sprang from desire and had sexual intercourse for its purpose [Mn. 3.32]. According to Vās. the lover had to take (Vās. 1.33) a girl of equal caste (Vās. 1.33); according to Vi. (24.23) without the consent of the mother and father and according to Dev. (Vīr. Saṁs. 855) to a sacred place.

Commentators on Mn. (3.32) entered into a discussion of the question whether the prescribed offerings and wedding ceremonies were to be performed in the case of the *Gāndharva-vivāha*, *Rākṣasa-vivāha* and *Paisāca-vivāha*. Relying on a passage of Devala and of the Bahṛka Gṛhyapariśiṣṭa (Śaunaka) we find that the *homas* had to be performed, at least in the case of Āryan couples. But they held with Manu's *dictum* (8.226) which restricted the use of the *mantras* to women, married as virgins, saying that the Vedic nuptial texts could not be recited. From the comment of Medh. on verse 34 it would appear that opinions on the subject were divided, and that some held weddings with the recitation of *mantras* to be permissible while other thought that no wedding was permissible.

BBh. (*ad* Y. 1.61) stated that in the case of the *Gāndharva-vivāha* and other rites of marriage, in order to constitute the legal status of husband and wife, the ceremonies of *homa* and all the rest up to *saptapadī* had to be performed. According to some texts the *Gāndharva-vivāha* was a marriage which was consummated before the due performance of the sacred rituals.

In this connexion, the definition of this form of marriage which we find in the Kāmasūtras should be quoted. We read there: that a yonug man behaves in public towards a girl who has been courted by him and is entirely his, as if she were his wife. He obtains consecrated fire from a Brāhmaṇ, strews the ground with holy grass, makes an oblation before the fire, and, thus, is married according to the religious regulations relative to this form of marriage. There are no witnesses.

After the ceremony the man informs the girl's parents of the accomplished fact. Such a marriage before consecrated fire is indissoluble. All the other relations are also advised and their consent solicited.

Thus, it is evident that the marriage of the *Gāndharvas* was a form of concubinage till the formal wedding ceremony, which took place without the consent of the girl's parents (See Vi. 24-23). For instance in the Pañcatantra *textus ornalior* 1.8) we read that sexual intercourse with a married woman (adultery) was "a marriage contracted according to the *Gāndharva-rite*" (Similarly Pañc. *ibid.* 2.5). In the ancient Indian Literature we can find many such examples.

53. Quite a different point of view is found in MBh. (13.44); we read there : "when the father of the girl disregarding his own wishes, bestows his daughter upon a person whom the daughter likes and who reciprocates the girl's sentiments, the form of marriage, O Yudhiṣṭhira, is called *Gāndharva* by those are conversant with the Vedas." We see that according to MBh. it was a real form of marriage; it was one of the highest forms of marriage, where the father (guardian) had no influence in the choice of a husband for the girl.

In Mn. 3.26 we find the following sentence:

pṛthak pṛthag vā miśrau vā vivāhau pūrvacoditau,
gāndharvo rakṣasaś caiva dharmyau kṣatrasya tau smṛtau.

"The *Gāndharva* and the *Rākṣasa*, the two *vivāhas* mentioned above have been declared to be lawful for the Kṣatriyas whether separate or combined" (identically MBh. Ādi Parvan 73.12 13).

We can see from this sentence that there existed two subdivisions of this form of marriage i.e. the *Gāndharva-vivāha* combined with the *Rākṣasa-vivāha* and the *Gāndharva-vivāha* not combined with this form of marriage i.e. a "separate *Gāndharva-vivāha*".

An excellent explanation of the *Gāndharva-vivāha* combined with the *Rākṣasa-vivāha*[20] can be found in Medhātithi's commentary on Mn. 3.26, where we read "A girl living in her father's house, happens to see a boy living in the same house and having heard praises from messengers, falls in love with him, but not being mistress of herself she cannot meet him,—

20. It is a blameworthy form of marriage, but should not be confused with the *Rākṣasa-vivāha*.

and then she enters into a compact with her lover, requests him to take her away by some means or other, and gets herself carried away; the bridegroom, being possessed of great strength, carries her away after having 'killed and wounded' (her guardians). Now in this case, since there is 'voluntary union between the two' it fulfils the conditions of the '*Gāndharva*' form; while, since he has carried her away, after 'having killed and wounded', the conditions of the 'Rākṣasa' form are also fulfilled." Such a *Gāndharva-vivāha* combined with the *Rākṣasa-vivāha* ("a blameworthy *Gāndharva-vivāha*) was nothing but a specific form of the *Rākṣasa-vivāha* and had to be interpreted according to the rules prescribed for the *Rākṣasa-vivāha* (See in the Bhāgavata-Purāṇa the story of the marriage of Rukmiṇī).

On the other hand we find quite a different form of marriage called also *Gāndharva-vivāha* (separated from the *Rākṣasa-vivāha*, i.e. the separate *Gāndharva-vivāha*). It is this form of marriage which we find in MBh. 13.44.6[21] and which has to be considered as one of the highest forms; there the father (guardian) had no influence in the choice of the bridegroom for the girl.

Concerning the first kind of *Gāndharva-vivāha* we find the following sentence in the Hindu Law of Marriage and Strīdhana, being the Tagore Law-lectures for 1878 by G. Banerjee p. 85, although the author did not mention the division of the *Gāndharva-vivāha* into two sub-divisions : "Marriages in this form, which depend merely upon the agreement of the contracting parties, resemble to some extent what are called Gretna-Green marriage—that is run-away marriages by persons governed by the English law, at Gretna-Green and elsewhere in Scotland, to evade the provisions of the law against ill-advised and clandestine marriages." This kind of the *Gāndharva-vivāha* was contracted "for the purpose of amorous embraces proceeding from sexual inclination" (John D. Mayne : A Treatise on Hindu Law and Usage, Madras 1900. par. 79).

The second kind of the *Gāndharva-vivāha* was contracted for the happiness of the girl and was a real marriage in which the consent of the father was not an *essentiale negotii*. But the father (guardian) of the girl was obliged—irrespective of

21. See above para 53 below.

whether the suitor was acceptable to him or not to give the daughter to the suitor. He had to act only for the happiness of his daughter and not to look for his own advantage.

If the *Gāndharva-vivāha* would be divided into these two forms of marriage we could understand the contradictory conceptions and rules of the *Gāndharva-vivāha* found in the Smṛtis, for example the rules concerning the admissibility of this form of marriage to members of different castes etc.

54. The "blameworthy *Gāndharva-vivāha*" had to be avoided according to Mn. (3.42) and Yama (Vīr. Saṁs. p. 865) because it was a "blameworthy marriage."[22]

From this marriage blameworthy offspring were born (Mn. 3.42, Yama, Vīr. Saṁs. p. 865).

This kind of the *Gāndharva-vivāha* was fit for the Kṣatriyas, Vaiśyas and Śūdras (Mn. 3.23) and according to other sources of law permitted to the Kṣatriyas (Mn. 3.26, MBh. Ādi Parvan 73, Vi. 24.27, B. 1.11, 20, 12, Pañcas. IO. 2526. See Śāṅkh. 4.3).

The second kind of the *Gāndharva-vivāha*, i.e. the *Gāndharva-vivāha* separated from the *Rākṣasa-vivāha* was lawful for members of the Brāhma caste (Mn. 3.23, 25, N. 12.44, G. 4.15).[23] On account of the general character of this form of marriage, based on love, which did not know any caste differences some Smṛtis[24] recommended the *Gāndharva-vivāha* for all castes (B.1.11, 20, 16, N. 12.44).

55. According to the sources of law the "blameworthy *Gāndharva-vivāha*" was the rule; that was the reason why the *Gāndharva-vivāha* took a low place in the list of the forms of marriage. It took the first place after the orthodox forms of marriage i.e. the fourth[25] place in the general list of the forms of marriage according to Āp. (3.5, 12) (after the *Brāhma*, *Ārṣa* and *Daiva*) and Vās. (1.29) (after the *Brāhma*, *Daiva* and *Ārṣa*) and the fifth place according to G.

22. See paragraphs 6-11 (*Rākṣasa-vivāha*).

23. The sources of law say "some say that........." (Mn. 3.23, G. 4.15). It is another proof that there existed two kinds of the *Gāndharva-vivāha*.

24. This is another example for the high position of this form of marriage, although from the Indian view-point it was rather a humiliation.

25. Āp. and Vās. did not mention one of the orthodox forms of marriage (Prājāpati).

(4), B. (1.11, 20), N. (12.38, 39), K. (3) (after the *Brāhma, Prājāpati, Ārṣa* and *Daiva*) and Āśv.-Gṛh. (1.6) (after the *Brāhma, Daiva, Prājāpatya* and *Ārṣa*). According to other sources it took the second place after the orthodox forms of marriage i.e. the sixth place in the general list of the forms of marriage [Mn. (3.21), Y. (1.59-61), Śāṅkh. (4-2), Vi. (24.9) (after the *Brāhma, Daiva, Ārṣa, Prājāpati,* and *Āsura*)].

In the Kāmasūtra of Vātsyāyana, this form of marriage was considered the best form of marrtage, although it was not enumerated as the first one. It was the best form of marriage because "the ultimate object of the different ceremonies is after all the mutual love between man and the woman...This ceremony does not require too much effort, nor does it involve the various stages of wooing and is based on mutual love" (Vāts. 5, 3, 29).

This form of marriage was known to all the main sources of law.

I. *Svayaṁvara*

56. *Svayaṁvara* was the self-choice.

In Sanskrit sources we come across the festive *svayaṁvara* which we find in the ancient Indian literature and the ordinary *svayaṁvara*, which we find in the Smṛtis.

Three kinds of festive *svayaṁvara* may be distinguished. The *svayaṁvara* of Sāvitrī was a unique instance of the absolute freedom of a princess to choose her husband. Alone Sāvitrī travelled through various countries in quest of a husband and at last met Satyavān. But it is hardly probable that a princess of a proud and noble family already shackled by fetters of long standing tradition should be allowed to proceed in this way and Hopkins was very probably right when he said that this was the earliest form of *svayaṁvara* (JAOS 13, 168 f.f., 357 ff.). Another form of *svayaṁvara* was that the bride was *vīryaśulkā* i.e. was to be won by a feat of prowess as in the case of Sītā and Draupadī. The usual form was well-known but it was hardly possible that the bride could follow her own inclinations in a festive gathering dominated by her father (J. Jolly: Hindu Law and Custom p. 111).

This festive *savayaṁvara* has always been a favourite theme, eagerly utilised by poets. That *svayaṁvara* was well-known specially from the episode of Nala and Damayantī.[26] It was also known in the Rāmāyaṇa (Rāma got Sītā), the Mahābhārata (Arjuna got Draupadī), Purāṇas, the Raghuvaṁśa, the Vikramāṅkadevacarita of Bilhaṇa, Vātsyāyana's Kāmasūtras and others.

In the case of a festive *svayaṁvara*—as described in the epics—the father of a marriageable princess arranged that princes of his own standing should present themselves at the *svayaṁvara* of his daughter and in the festive assembly the *patiṁvarā* as a sign of her choice put the garland round the neck of the chosen bridegroom. A fine example of a festive *svayaṁvara* can be found in the story of Nala and Damayantī. We read there :

"When the lord of earth his daughter saw in blooming youth mature,
"Knew he for the *svayaṁvara* Damayantī's time was come.
"Straight the lord of many peasants summoned all the chiefs of earth,
" 'Come ye to the *svayaṁvara* all ye heroes of the world !'
"Damayantī's *svayaṁvara*, soon as heard the kings of men,
"All obeyed king Bhīma's summons, all to Bhīma's court drew near;
"Elephants, and steeds, and chariots, swarmed along the sounding land;
"All with rich and various garlands, with his stately army each,
"All the lofty-minded Rājas, Bhīma with the arm of strength,
"As beseemed, received with honour, on their thrones of state they sat."

....

"Came the day of happy omen, moonday meet, and moment apt;
"Bhīma to the *svayaṁvara*, summoned all the lords of earth,
"Once and all, upon the instant, rose the enamoured lords of earth,
"Suitors all to Damayantī in their loving haste they came.
"They, the court with golden columns rich, and glittering portal arch,
"Like the lions on the mountains entered they the hall of state.

26. According to some authors it was not a *Svayaṁvara*, because the selection of the husband in these cases depended not on the choice of the girl but on the ability of the suitor to satisfy the specific conditions previously laid down.

"Shone the faces of the Rājas like the radiant stars in heaven.
"As with serpents, Bhagavatī, the wide hall was full of kings;
"As the mountain-caves with tigers, with the tiger-warriors full.
"Damayantī in her beauty entered on that stately sence,
"With her dazzling light entrancing every eye and every soul.
"O'er her lovely person gliding all the eyes of those proud kings;
"There were fixed, there moveless rested, as they gazed upon the maid.

....

"And of right king Bhīma's daughter named Niṣadha's king her lord.
"Modestly the large-eyed maiden lifted up his garment's hem,
"Round his shoulders threw she lightly the bright zone of radiant flowers.
"So she chose him for her husband, Nala, that high-hearted maid".

(Story of Nala, Book II).

75. But this festive *svayaṁvara* was quite different form the ordinary *svayaṁvara* which correctly speaking was not a special form of marriage. In some cases the girl had the right to choose a husband for herself. For this reason the *svayaṁvara* was closely connected with the *Gāndharva-vivāha*.

The ordinary *svayaṁvara* took place when the maiden had attained her puberty in her father's house. After a period had passed, the maiden could choose a bridegroom for herself.

According to this form of marriage if a maiden had passed her monthly periods [Mn. 9.20, B. 4. 1, 14, Vi. 24.40, G. 18. 20 Vās. 17.67] defined in the Smṛtis [Mn. 9.20, B. 4.1, 14, Vi. 24.40, G. 18.90, Vās 17.61], had attained puberty [Mn. 9.90, B. 4.1, 14, Vās. 17.67] and if her father (and in his absence he who had the right to give her in marriage i.e. the guardian) had not married her during this period of time [Y-1. 64, G. 18.20] she could choose a bridegroom [Mn. 9.90 Y. 1.64, B. 4.1, 14, Vi. 24.40, G. 18.20, Vās. 17.68] for herself [Mn. 9.90, Y-1.64, B. 4.1, 14, Vi. 24.40, G. 18.20, Vās.17.68].

This period of time which had to pass after the maiden has attained puberty was either one of three years (*varṣa*) [Mn. 9.90, B. 4.1, 14, Vās. 17.67] or one of three monthly periods (*ṛtu*) [Vi. 24.4, G. 18.20]. The difference in the duration of time was undoubtedly great. According to Nanda the commentator on Vi. the expression *ṛtu* could be used as *varṣa* and vice-versa. It did not seem that Nand. was right. Probably the expression *ṛtu* was the better one; in ancient times it was sufficient that the girl received the right of self-choice if she was not married by her guardian during the first three monthly periods. The first duty of the young couple was to bear children. Therefore immediately after the monthly period the *ṛtu-gamana* (*coitus*) had to take place. This was of great importance for the marriage and therefore the time of three monthly periods was completely sufficient. Only with great liberality was it possible for the later commentators to extend this period.

The man in this case to be chosen by the girl had to be a proper man or a blameless man or a man of equal caste and rank (Y.1.64, G. 18.20, Mn. 9.90, Vās. 17.67). But this rule was of course a *lex imperfecta* although we find in the Smṛtis such a sentence : "The maiden, though marriageable should rather stop in (the father's) house until death than to be given to a man destitute of qualities" (Mn. 9.89). This last sentence was based on the principle that a girl should be given in marriage before puberty to a man who had not broken the vow of chastity [B. 4.1, 11], who possessed good qualities [B. 4.1, 11, Śatatapa in Vīr. Saṁs. 755], i.e. good character [Lalla and G. in Vīr. Saṁs. 754, B. 4.1, 11, Śatatapa in Vīr. Saṁs. 755], family [Yama, G., Lalla in Vīr. Saṁs. 754, Śatatapa in Vīr. Saṁs. 754], age [Yama in Vīr. Saṁs. 754, Lalla in Vīr. Saṁs. 754, Śatatapa in Vīr. Saṁs. 755], beautiful body [Yama in Vīr. Saṁs. 754], learning [G., Yama, Lalla in Vīr. Saṁs. 754, Śatatapa in Vīr. Saṁs. 755], guardians [Yama and others in Vīr. Saṁs. 754, 755], health [Lalla in Vīr. Saṁs. 754, Śatatapa in Vīr. Saṁs. 755], wealth [Lalla in Vīr. Saṁs. 754] etc.

But if a girl not without defects had to choose a bridegroom after reaching puberty it was not probable that she would find a proper bridegroom. Only B. (4.1, 14) admitted therefore that "if no man of equal rank was available i.e. one who did not have the qualities mentioned above, the maiden could even take one destitute of good qualities" (identically Nīlakaṇṭha).

If the girl acted in such a manner she incurred no guilt (Mn. 9.91, Vi. 24.40) because if he whose duty was to marry the girl failed to give her in marriage he incurred the sin of killing the embryo at every menstruation (Mn. 1.64). But the maiden who chose a man for herself should not take with her any ornaments given by her father or her mother or her brother. If she carried them away it would be a theft (Mn. 9.92, G. 18.20).

On the other hand the man who had been chosen in such a manner was not obliged to pay a fee to the father of the girl because through his negligence the father lost his authority over the daughter. That was the reason for which the Brāhmaṇs did not consider the ordinary *svayaṁvara* as one of the forms of marriage.

That was the description of the ordinary *svayaṁvara* in the Smṛtis. Very interesting are the rules concerning the ordinary *svayaṁvara* in the Kāmasūtra (Ch. 4. § 29). We read there that the girl had to choose a man whom she loved and that she had to try to make him fall in love with her. She had to show herself to him, to come in to the house in the evening with flowers, perfumes and betel; she had to show him her accomplishment in the arts, in massage, in the touch of his head, she had to narrate stories to him and to act according to the rules contained in Chapter 3 § 26 of Vātsyāyana's Kāmasūtra. If he desired to kiss her, she had only to allow him to do so by force, and if he desired to have sexual intercourse with her she had to allow him to touch only the *yoni* with great difficulty. If she was kissed she should not show that she was satisfied by it and yet if she fell in love she should never act in a manner that would enable him to perceive it. (Compare Yaśodhara to Vātsyāyana's Kāmasūtra Ch. 3. § 26.)

J. *Legal Consequences of the Forms of Marriage*

58. The above-mentioned forms of marriage were more or less systematically tabulated in the sources although some authors deviated in their order. There was, however, a certain stability in the tabulating system. It is obvious from the general list of the forms of marriage according to the sources of law that Mn., Y., Vi., and Śāṅkh. showed the same method in the system of the forms of marriage. An almost identical order was to be found in B., G., N., K. and Kām. while we meet with another order in Āp., Vās. and Āśv. Gṛh. One absolute regularity may be observed in all the ancient Indian sources viz. *Brāhma*, *Daiva*, *Ārṣa* and *Prājāpatya-vivāhas* occupied always the first four places and *Āsura*, *Gāndharva*, *Rākṣasa* and *Paiśāca-vivāhas* occupied the next four.

The order of the particular forms of marriage in the general list of forms was not insignificant. A rule is to be found in three sources, namely in B., Āp. and Kām. that each preceding form of marriage was better than the following one (Āp. 2.5, 12, 3, B. 1.11, 20, 10) and that each succeeding form was more sinful than the preceding one (B. 1.11, 20, 11) as the modes of marriage were given in a descending scale of worthiness (Kām. P. 3. Ch. 5).

59. From the purely legal point of view the forms of marriage should be divided into the orthodox forms of marriage and other forms of marriage. That such a division existed may be learned from the fact that the so-called orthodox forms of marriage (*Brāhma*, *Daiva*, *Ārṣa*, *Prājāpatya*) always, though sometimes not in the same sequence, occupied the first four places in the general list of the forms of marriage. This division was of some importance according to Y. and Vi. and to a certain extent also according to Mn. We read in Vi. (17.19, 20) as well as in Y. (2.145) that if a woman married according to the *Brāhma*, *Daiva*, *Ārṣa* or *Prājāpatya-vivāha* died childless her property i.e. the *strīdhana* belonged to her husband and if she was married according to one of the other four forms of marriage the *strīdhana* belonged to her father. The same point of view was also expressed in Mn. (9.196.197) with the sole distinction that the *strīdhana* belonged to the husband not only in the case of the orthodox forms of marriage but also in the case of the *Gāndharva-vivāha* (probably the *Gāndharva-vivāha* not combined with the *Rākṣasa-vivāha*); in the case of a marriage concluded according to the three lowest rites the property belonged not to the father but to both the parents of the dead woman. (It must be pointed out that K. (3.2) was of the opinion that, in particular, irrespective of the manner in which the marriage was concluded, the *strīdhana*, if the women died without leaving sons, belonged to the husband.)

60. According to K. the manner in which the *strīdhana* was used depended on the form in which the marriage was concluded.. According to K., the woman should be able to make use of the *strīdhana* if she required it, that is, in the case that she was a widow and had no sons. She was further able to make use of the *strīdhana* to maintain a son, daughter-in-law or herself, should an absent husband have made no provision for her maintenance. The husband could make use of the *strīdhana* in the event of calamity, disease or famine, to ward off danger and for charitable purposes. These were exceptional occasions. Another exceptional activity permitted the use of the *strīdhana*. It could be used by "mutual consent" by a couple that had brought forth twins. Yet another exceptional case depended on whether or not the marriage had taken place according to one of the orthodox forms of marriage.

There "shall be no complaint" if the *strīdhana* "has been enjoyed for three years by those who are wedded in accordance with the customs of the first four kinds of marriage." Therefore, if the marriage was concluded according to the *Brāhma-vivāha*, *Prājāpatya-vivāha*, *Ārṣa-vivāha* or *Daiva-vivāha* the married couple were themselves able to agree upon the use of the *strīdhana*, but not for longer than three years. If, however, the marriage was not concluded according to one of the orthodox forms of marriage the couple had no right to such an agreement. In the case of a marriage contracted according to the *Gāndharva-vivāha* or the *Ārṣa-vivāha*—they were obliged "to restore the *strīdhana* together with interest" and in the case of marriage contracted according to the *Rākṣasa-vivāha* or *Paisāca-vivāha* the use of the *strīdhana* had to be dealt with as theft."[27]

These were the only cases in which, according to the Smṛtis, some of the forms of marriage had any legal consequences.

61. Another rule concerning the consequences arising from the form in which the marriage was contracted is found in K. (3.2). According to K. if the marriage was contracted according to one of the orthodox forms (*Brāhma*, *Prājāpatya*, *Ārṣa* or *Daiva*) "as an ancestral custom of old", the marriage was valid after the approval by the father, the rest were to be sanctioned by both the father and mother "for it was they that receive the money (*śulka*) paid by the bridegroom for their daughter". This sentence is quite clear as far as the orthodox

27. See above study XII on "Reciprocal Responsibility for Debts Contracted by Married People."

forms of marriage are concerned but is unintelligible in the cases of the *Gāndharva-vivāha*, *Rākṣasa-vivāha* and *Paiśāca-vivāha*, because according to these forms the consent of the father was not necessary, much less than of the father and the mother. But it was possible, and this rule may be interpreted in such a manner, that as far as *Āsura-vivāha* was concerned, in which case both parents received the money (*śulka*) paid by the bridegroom for their daughter, the consent of both was necessary. This interpretation could be based on the argument used by the author of the rule "for it was they that received the money paid by the bridegroom for their daughter."

62. In any case it appears from these considerations that the division of the forms of marriage into 8 or 11 forms had no special meaning from the legal point of view and all the forms of marriage could be divided into righteous forms i.e. orthodox forms of marriage (*Brāhma*, *Daiva*, *Ārṣa*, *Prājāpati* with the exception of the only case Mn. 9.196-7 also *Gāndharva*) and the blameworthy forms of marriage i.e. the non-orthodox forms of marriage (*Gāndharva*, *Āsura*, *Rākṣasa*, *Paiśāca*).

63. It must further be pointed out that according to Āp. and B. "the quality of the offspring depended on the quality of the marriage rite" (Āp. 2.5, 12, 4, B. 1.11, 21, 1) i.e. from praiseworthy marriages virtuous children were born, and from blameworthy marriages bad children (Mn. 3.39-42). These virtuous children were radiant with knowledge of the Vedas and were honoured by the Śiṣtas.

To the first group of children belonged those born in orthodox forms of marriage and to the second group those born in non-orthodox forms of marriage.

III. SOCIOLOGICAL ASPECTS OF THE FORMS OF MARRIAGE

64. All the forms of marriage that we find in the ancient Indian sources were described together. That is to say that in every source of law we find simultaneously all the above mentioned forms of marriage. On considering and interpreting the forms of marriage from this point of view it could be said that the authors of the ancient Indian sources considered all the forms of marriage as being in contemporary use at the time of the validity of the individual Smṛtis.

After having acquainted oneself with the problem in question, this standpoint seems to be not completely correct. In all probability the forms of marriage had passed through the same evolution in Ancient India as, in general, they developed elsewhere and in consequence the non-orthodox forms of marriage did not exist at the time of the validity of the above mentioned sources of law, though they were known by name; the rules contained in the Smṛtis were only archaic. Although a marriage might perhaps be contracted in one of the superseded forms it could not be considered legal and the persons who contracted a prohibited marriage of the sort were even punished.

65. When we study law from the sociological point of view and consider examples found among the peoples of antiquity and the peoples of the so-called lower stage of civilization, we can establish the principal stages of the development of the forms of marriage; they are as follows :

1. marriage by capture,
2. marriage by purchase (or by consideration),
3. marriage based on the choice of a husband by the girl's father independently of her consent.
4. marriage based on the free consent of the bride and bridegroom.

In the second or in the third stage, we can observe the development of the dowry. We very often find between the second and the third stage, the marriage by sham purchase.

However, frequently some of the stages are absent, and other stages of the development of the forms of marriage take their place or are added.

Besides the above mentioned development of the forms of marriage, there existed another development; polygamous marriage among people living at a so-called lower stage of evolution, in course of time, lost its characteristics in favour of monogamous marriage. At the highest stage of culture only monogamy exists.

E. Westermarck rightly maintains in his "History of Human Marriage" (Vol. III, p. 105); "No superstitious beliefs keep civilised men apart from their wives during pregnancy and for a long time after childbirth. The desire for offspring has become less intense. A large family instead of being a help in the struggle for existence is often considered an insufferable burden. A man's kinsfolk are no longer his only friends, and his wealth and influence do not depend upon the number of the wives and children. A wife ceases to be a mere labourer, and manual labour is to a large extent replaced by work of domestic animals and the use of the implements and machines. The sentiment of love has become more refined and, in consequence, more enduring. To a cultivated mind youth and beauty are by no means the only attractions of a woman, and besides, civilisation has given female beauty a new lease on life. The feelings of the weaker sex are held in higher regard, and the causes which may make polygamy desired by women themselves no longer exist. Better education bestowed on them, and other factors in modern civilisation, enable them to live comfortably without the support of a husband." The development of marriage must be traced from polygamy, some times polyandry to monogamy.

A. *Marriage by Capture*

66. At the so-called primitive stage of civilisation the family or clan was the sole unit of social life. This family or clan was endogamic. Women were at that time the common possession of all the members of the family or clan and no one of these members had the individual and exclusive right over one woman. Probably later the right of one individual member of the family or clan over a woman, if she was captured by him from another family, was recognised. Recognition of this first right by capture formed the earliest basis of individual marriage.

In this way marriage by capture became the first form of marriage, that is the first form of individual marriage.[1]

In this way, marriage which was formerly endogamic became exogamic. The wife was no longer taken from the same

1. Concerning the origin of the practice of marriage by capture great diversity of opinion prevails. Thus G. Banerjee in "The Hindu Law of Marriage and Stridhana" stated (p. 28) that Mr. Lennan assumed that this form of marriage originated from female infanticide, leading to scarcity of women within the tribe which compelled its members to obtain wives by capture from neighbouring tribes. According to Sir John Lubbock, this view was erroneous. and the practice really owed its origin to the fact that forcible possession would be the only mode by which individual marriage—that is the appropriation of a woman by a single man—could arise out of communal marriage (p. 95, 97). But Spencer has shown that the practice must have originated from a number of concomitant causes, such as the hostile relations of primitive neighbouring groups, resistance from female coyness, and opposition of parents to the taking away of daughters "Sociology" page 649-655).

family or clan but from another. Thus could be traced the first development of the institution of marriage.

67. The taking of a woman by a man by force without her consent and without the consent of her kindred was marriage by capture.

The practice of capturing wives prevailed in nearly all parts of the world, and traces of it are met with in the marriage ceremonies of several peoples, indicating that it occurred more frequently in past ages. In the ancient civilized world marriage by capture was prevailing in Greece, Rome, Arabia etc. In India it was represented by the *Rākṣasa-vivāha* and the *Paiśāca-vivāha*.

In Japan marriage by capture is said to have been common in ancient days, but from the time of Taiho-ryo (701-1192) this custom was gradually abandoned according to Nakajima ("*Marriage*" Japanese and Korean in Hastings *Encyclopaedia of Religion and Ethics*, 8.460). The capture of women for wives prevailed among the ancient Semites, according to Robertson Smith ("*Kinship and Marriage in Early Arabia* pp. 72 sq.) and Wellhausen "*Die Ehe bei den Arabern*" in "*Nachrichten von der kōnigl. Gesellschaft der Wissenschaften zu Göttingen*" (1893 p. 435). In Arabia it was common before Muhammad.

Among the Hebrews members of the military class were allowed to marry foreign women taken in war contrary to the law which forbade intermarriage with the Gentiles (*Deuteronomy* 21.10). According to Dionysus of Halicarnassus (*Antiquitetum Romanorum quae supersunt* 2.30. 5) marriage by capture at one time existed throughout Greece, and according to Sakellarios (*Die Sitten und Gebräuche der Hochzeit bei den Neugriechen* p. 61) it occurred there occasionally even in quite recent times. "*Les premiers Romains*" says M. Ortelan (*Historie de la législation romaine* p. 81) *d'après leurs traditions hèroiques, ont été obligès de recourir à la surprise et à la force pour enlever leurs premières femmes.*

68. The ancient Teutons evidently captured women for wives, according to Dargun (*Mutterrecht und Raubehe und ihre Rechte im germanischen Recht und Leben* p. 111). Of the Scandinavians Olaus Magnus said that they were constantly at war with one another "*propter raptas virgines aut arripiendas*" (*Historia de gentibus septemtrionalibus* p. 328). In the earliest Teutonic laws though marriage by rape was a punishable offence, it was admissible as marriage (Pollock and Maitland's *History of the English Law before the time of Edward I, II.* 364). In the Irish Nennius we read of the rape of wives by the Picts from Gael (Wood-Martin *Traces of the Elder Faiths of Ireland* II, 35, 37). Marriage by capture also occurred among the Slavs in early times, according to Maciejowski's *Slavische Rechtsgeschichte* (2.189). The Cossacks of Little Russia and the Ukrainians practised it still in the 17th century (Kowalewski : *Modern Customs and Ancient Laws of Russia* p. 24) and many Southern Slavs in the beginning of the 19th century or later (Krauss: *Sitte und Brauch der Südslaven* p.245). In High Albania the forcible capture of a girl occasionally occurs to this day, according to Durham (*High Albania and its customs in* 1908). The same is the case among the Caucasian mountain tribes who consider that a captured girl becomes the wife of her captor by being deflowered by him (see Darinsky's *Die Familie bei den caukasischen Völkern* der *Zeitschrift. f. vergl. Rechtswiss.* 14, 198).

69. Marriage by capture still exists even in modern times among certain so-called primitive people. In Tierra del Fuego marriage by capture sometimes occurs both among the Yaghans and the Onas (see Hyades's *Ethnographie des Fuegiens* in *Bull. Soc. d'Anthr.* Paris 3. Vol. 20.334). Of the latter it is said that when they make war on a neighbouring tribe they kill off the men and marry the women, whereas in times of peace, when they take wives from their own tribes, marriages are arranged by peaceful negotiations between the father of the parties (see Gallardo's *Tierra del Fuego Los Onas* p. 214). In many Brazilian tribes also, women are captured from other tribes and married to the captors (see Martius's *Beiträge zur Ethnographie Amerikas* 1. 107, 372, 620); among the Karaya, wars seem to have been waged solely for this purpose (see Krause's "*In den Wildnissen Brasiliens*" p. 320); but among the Bororo marriage by capture occurred even within the tribe (see K. von den Steinen's *Unter den Naturvölkern Zentral-Brasiliens*, p. 500). The same mode of marriage is found among the Indians of Equador.

The Macas Indians acquire wives by purchase if the women belong to the same tribe, but otherwise by force (See Buckley, quoted by Lubbock, *Note on the Macas Indiens*, in *Jour. Anthr. Inst. iii.* 30). The Jibaros frequently make war only in order to procure wives (See Rivet's *Les Indiens Jibaros* in *l'Anthroplogie*,

8. 605, 615). The Zaparo Indians in many cases take forcible possession of women, the men running away with their neighbours' wives; and though the women may sometimes object, they make no virtual difficulties, but, apparently, "rather like being run away with." (See Simson's *Travels in the Wilds of Ecuador*, p. 172 sqq.) The Caribs married female captives of war who pleased them (see de Poincy's, *Histoire naturelle et morale des Iles Antilles de l'Amerique*, p. 545). Among the Comanche marriage by capture occurred now and then (See ten Kate's *Reizen en onder-zoekingen* in *Noord-Amerika* p. 390). Among the Luiseño Indians on the coast of California one method of marriage is said to have been "for a man and several of his friends to carry off by force the woman he wished to marry, even from the house of her parents." (See Sparkman's, *Culture of the Luiseño Indians* in *University* of *California Publications in American Archeology and Ethnology* 8.214). Among the Aht a man occasionally steals a wife from among the women of his own tribe, (See Sproat's *Scenes and Studies of Savage Life*, p. 98). On the east coast of Greenland the men not infrequently abducted other men's wives, sometimes at the request of the woman's own family, in order that she should be better supported. (See Holm's, "*Konebaads editional til Grönlands Östkyst* 1883-85, in *Geografisk tidskrift*, 8.92). The inhabitants of Unimak invaded the other Aleutian lands chiefly for the purpose of carrying off women. (See Coxe's *Account of the Russian Discoveries between Asia and America*," p. 257.)

Among the Chukchee, Dr. Bogoras was told that, in olden times "a company of young men would seize a young girl in the open, bind her hands and feet, and carry her to the house of one who wanted to have her for a wife. Not only the men of other families, but even the relatives and cousins, acted so, after having been refused by the girl's father. The assault and ravishing, however, were not considered as a reason for implacable hatred and feuds. The parents would come afterwards and ask for ransom, which was paid, not in reindeer, but one woman for another......Even at present a case of ravishment may happen now and then. (See Bogoras's *Chukchee* p. 590). The great wars of the Gilvak, very often served the object of carrying off women; and even now marriage by capture occurs among them, when a man lacks the means of buying a wife, although such an act usually followed by blood revenge (See Sternberg reviewed in *L'Antopologie* v. 343. Schrenk quoted by Miss Czaplicka's *Aboriginal Siberia*, p. 101).

In New Caledonia "*les enlevements de femmes mariées ne sont ...pas rares, et souvent ils attirent des guerres entre les tribus ou les familles, à moins que celui qui a fait le rapt ne soit un chef ou relativement un grand personage.*" (See Brainne's *La Nouvelle-Caledonie*, p. 251 sq.). On the larger islands of the Fiji Group the custom of seizing upon a woman by apparent or actual force in order to make her a wife was often found. (See William's and Calvert's *Fiji and Fijians*, p. 149). Among the Maori, female prisoners of war were generally appropriated by members of the victorious party and taken as inferior or slave wives (See Best's, *Maori Marriage Customs* in *Trans. and Proceed. New Zealand Institute*, 36, 63). Of the same people we are told that "an ancient and favourite way of marriage was to get up a war-party (or mimic war-party) and carry off the bride by force. There were so many relatives to be consulted, some of whom would be sure to feel aggrieved if their consent was not obtained, that abduction was easiest. There was often feigned abduction and feigned defence, but it was at times very hard on the girl (See Tregear's, *The Maori Race* p. 293. See also Talyor's *Te Ika a Maui*, p. 336.)

The Tasmanians captured women for wives from alien and hostile tribes (See Milligan, quoted by Nixon in *Cruise of the Beacon*, p. 29). In Australia marriage by capture has been found in all parts of the continent (See Hodgson's, *Reminiscences of Australia*, p. 243). Mathew said that "marriage by capture takes place between members of hostile communities. Sometimes a surprise party will be organised to attack a camp, slaughter the males and abduct and appropriate the females. The wholesale abduction is paralleled by individual cases of forcible abduction, on which occasion the woman, if resisting, will be cruelly beaten" (See Mathew's *Eaglehawk and Crow* p. 113 sqq.). Speaking of some Central Australian natives Willshire observed that if a man does not succeed in securing a wife in the formal and regular fashion, he is driven to the hazardous course of stealing one (See Willshire's, *Aborigines of Central Australia*, p. 13). Spencer and Gillen, however, said that capture was the "very rarest way in which a Central Australian secured a wife (See Spencer's and Gillen's *Native Tribe of Central Australia*, p. 104, 554 sqq.). Contrary to some statements made by early observers in New South Wales, it was usually reported to be merely an exceptional or occasional mode of contracting marriage in Australia. (See Malinowski's, *The family among the Australian Aborigines*, p. 53 sqq.).

Of the Sakalava in Madagascar we are told that every year they steal many women of other tribes, and that some of their wives Hova and Basileo women from the interior were eagerly sought after by the cattle-lifters (See McMahon's, *Sakalava and their Customs*' in *Antananarivo Annual* and *Madagascar Magazine*, 4. 391 sqq.). Anderson states that among the Bushmen women is only too often "*belli teterrima causa*". (See Anderson's, Oka-*vango River* p. 143). Among the Auin who belong to the Kalahari Bushmen, women and girls who were captured in war were adopted and maried into the tribes of the captors (See Kaufman's, *Die Auin* in *Mittheil. d. Deutsch. Schutzgeb*. 23. 154). Concerning the Hottentots—whose marriage customs generally required that cattle should be given by the bridegroom to the nearest relatives of the bride we read that "one of the principal objects in their wars with each other was to take females as prisoners who were generally regarded as mere concubines, but were sometimes, raised to the dignity of wives. The difference ...involved a right over the distribution of the milk, and upon it depended the inheritance of the children" (See Theal's, *Yellow and Dark-skinned People of Africa south of the Zambesi* p. 85). So also it is the custom among the Fingu a kafir tribe, that a girl who has been captured in war could be legally married to the captor, if only he publicly declared that she was his wife, although otherwise a woman whom a man took to his hut without paying anything for her was regarded was a concubine or as a prostitute (See Kropf's, *Das Volk der Xosa-Kaffern im östlichen Südafrika* p. 138 sqq.). In the different groups of the Ababua, Babati and Baieu (Bantu-speaking) tribes along the Upper Wele Bokandi and Upper Rubi rivers, according to Grenfell, "marriage by capture is of common occurrence, but frequently results in war between the two villages; properly the husband ought to buy his wife, her consent not being absolutely necessary". So also marriage by capture is said by the same writer to exist among the forest tribes in the north-eastern part of the Mongala basin:

"A man carries off a wife by force, betakes himself with her to the forest, lives there by hunting, and only return to the village when the wife has a child and it is weaned. Returned home, he quits his temporary wife, and gives her half the proceeds of their hunting in exchange for the child. (See Johnston's *George Grenfell and the Congo* 2, pp. 676, 674). Many other examples could be quoted.[1]

70. There are many kinds of marriage by capture and various kinds of marriage co-exist sometimes in one nation. We find it not only in India (*Rākṣasa-vivāha*, *Paiśāca-vivāha* and *Gāndharva-vivāha* combined with the *Rākṣasa-vivāha*) but also with other nations. And so with Galela and Tobelorese we distinguish a marriage by capture (like the *Rākṣasa-vivāha*), a marriage by secretly creeping into the house of a woman (like the *Paiśāca-vivāha*) and a marriage by abduction (like the *Gāndharva-vivāha* combined with the *Rākṣasa-vivāha*). The Slavs of the South distinguish between a girl captured against her will (*otkradnota*, *moma-kradena*, or *ugrabljena*, *obeta djevoyka*) (like the *Rākṣasa-vivāha*), a girl captured against the will of her parents but with her connivance (*prestanka*, *moma priestanola*) (like the *Gāndharva-vivāha* combined with the *Rākṣasa-vivāha*) and a girl who ran away of her own will from her father's house to that of her lover (*bjegunica*, *ubjeglica*, *podijegnola moma*) (like the *Gāndharva-vivāha* combined with the *Rākṣasa-vivāha*). (See Kraus's *Sitte und Brauch bei den Südslaven* p. 245). Among the Galla there existed a symbolical marriage by capture, and a marriage constituted by a girl's flight or elopment in agreement with her lover, without her father's permission from his house to that of her lover (like the *Gāndharva-vivāha*).

The marriage by capture may be a real capture or a symbolical act. Real capture would consist of the capture of a woman during war or her capture by a wooer or his relations. The symbolical act of capture is to be found with many variants. Among the Gallas there existed two kinds of marriage by capture. One named *ananota* and the other *buta*. The first is real capture,

1. Among the Samoyeds, Votyaks, Ostyaks, Voguls, Cheremisses, Mordvins, Tartars of Crimea, Yakuts, Kalmuks, Esthonians, in Purang, among the Bhotias, among many tribes in India (Sikhs, Malayalis etc.) in Malai Archipelago, in the Philippines, in New Guinea, among the Aruntas, in Central Africa, among the Berbers of Morocco and many others. Quoted from Westermarck II, ch. XXI.

the second symbolical capture; by this last "capture" the wooer captured the girl with the consent of her parents; after this capture he received from his father-in-law oxen and cows.

There is no doubt that the capture of a woman became with the development of human civilization the regular form of marriage. Marriage by capture was based upon the violation of the existing (international) law because it was based upon robbery. This violation of existing (international) law often caused a war between one family or clan and the other. The families or clans would, however, often not go to war. It could be avoided by an agreement between the two families or clans when it was stipulated that instead of war the wooer paid the penalty.

In this way, probably, first as an alternative and afterwards in place of the marriage by capture a new form of marriage, marriage by purchase came to existence.

71. According to Westermarck marriage by purchase grew out of marriage by capture. We read "...It has been suggested that the transition from marriage by capture to marriage by purchase was brought about in the following way: abduction, in spite of parents, was the primary form; then there came the offering of compensation to escape vengeance; and this grew eventually into the making of presents or paying a sum beforehand." (See Kōnigswarter's, *Etudes historiques sur le developpement de la société humaine*, p. 53; Spencer's *Principles of Sociology* I. p. 625 and others).

The same can be observed in ancient India. Marriage by capture, irrespective of the manner, either capture by force (*Rākṣasa-vivāha*) or by cunning (*Paiśāca-vivāha*) was a marriage prohibited by law, for capture was considered as a crime (Mn. 8.323, Y. 2.282, Bṛh. 22.12, K. 4.12, Vyāsa. Viv. 318, and others), and a crime of such a degree as to be threatened with capital punishment. Therefore it is difficult to believe that as these marriages were described in the Smṛti-s as avoidable they could exist as legal marriages at the time of the validity of the Smṛti-s although they are mentioned therein. This is a typical example of an act non existent in practice and in course of time prohibited which remained in the Smṛti-s as an out of date and archaic law. Although there is no actual proof of this, it is probable that marriage by capture was the most primitive form of marriage in ancient India. Comparison with general sociological literature points to this form of marriage, especially explained in MBh. (Arjuna, Bhīṣma, Duryodhana) as being the proper form for the Kṣatriya-s. When the so-called Aryas came to India from the North, they were likely to capture women of the country, which would bring about marriage by capture. These so-called Aryas were warriors and the prototypes of the Kṣatriya caste. That this form of marriage had already lost importance at the time of the validity of the Smṛti-s may be concluded from the fact that Āp. and Vās, did not mention the Paiśāca-vivāha.

Probably this primitive form of marriage disappeared in India and marriage by purchase came into being along side or in its place.

B. *Marriage by Purchase*

72. The marriage by purchase was based on an agreement between two families or two tribes. That would appear to be so from the fact that with some nations the blood friends of the bridegroom were obliged to share in paying the price for the girl and that on the other hand the blood friends received part of the purchase-money. Probably the purchase of the woman was an intertribal agreement. Later the rights and the duties of the members of the tribe were eliminated and one person undertook the duties and also obtained the rights formerly pertaining to the copartners; that existed in patriarchal times.

73. The foundation of the marriage by purchase was a family with a definite head. This head had to have the right over other members (copartners) of the family, especially over women, of an owner over objects which could be purchased by him. Having acquired the right of purchase and of disposal of an object, that object could be handed over to another at the price determined by the owner.

In practice the head was the *pater familias*, the father, and the object which could be sold by him was his daughter who was considered by him as a piece of merchandise. He who bought this object from the owner became its sole owner and had the same right over it, as his property, as had the previous owner. In other words the girl became the property of her future husband instead of that of the previous owner, her father. The husband would exercise the same right as was hitherto exercised by her father.

This was apparent in ancient India. It is well known that in ancient India at the head of the family stood a principal —*the pater familias*—who had extensive rights over the whole family and a girl who was *sub patria potestate*; she came after marriage *sub manu mariti* (Mn. 9.3, 5.148, MBh. 13.46, 14, Y. 1.85, 86, Vās. 5.2, Vi 25.13, B. 2.2, 3, 45, N. in Viv. 410, 411, Smṛtyantara, Aparārka p. 109). The father had the right to sell his daughter. Thus, this marriage in ancient India was represented by the Ārṣa-vivāha.

74. The purchase of a girl from her family for a price to be fixed that was the marriage by purchase.

That was the rule, but by paying the purchase price the bridegroom received in some nations extensive rights and in others his rights were curtailed. These rights depended on the degree of independence the woman obtained from her former family. When she became quite independent she was as a rule—the property of her husband. If she was not quite independent of her former family her husband, as a rule, gained only limited rights over her, her former family kept also the right and the duty to protect her.

75. Marriage by purchase was known more or less to all nations of the ancient civilised world and to races at the so-called primitive stage of development, sometimes also at a higher stage of civilization, living in the new world.

In Japan marriage by purchase is said to have been common in ancient days, but from the time of the Taiho-ryo (701-1192) this custom was gradually discarded, according to Nakajima's Marriage (Japanese and Korean in Hastings's, *Encyclopoedia of Religion and Ethics*, 8.460).

Marriage by purchase was the first form known to the Semitic races. In Babylonia a suitor had to give to the father of the intended wife a bridal price or present (*tirḥātum* or *terḥatu*), the amount of which varied, according to the rank of the parties; and if the young man did not himself possess the sum which was required, his parents were expected to provide him with it. (See Koschaker's, *Rechtsvergleichende Studien zur Gesetszgebung Hammurapis* p. 130 sqq., Meissner's *Beiträge zum altbabilonischen*

Privatrecht p. 13 sqq.). But from the Laws of Hammurapi we learn that although it was the general custom for a man to pay a bridal price to his father-in-law, this payment was not universal (see *Laws of Hammurapi*, para. 138 sqq., John's translation, p. 27). Koschaker (in *Rechtsvergleichende Studien zur Gesetzgebung Hammurapis* p. 153 sqq.) explains this by suggesting that marriage by purchase had ceased to exist according to Sumerian law, whereas it was retained in Babylonian law. The bridal price was also reverted to the husband if the wife died without having given him children. (See *Laws of Hammurapi* para 163 sqq.—John's translation p. 32 sqq.). In Genesis we read that Jacob served Laban, his mother's brother, for seven years for each of his cousins Leah and Rachel. (*Genesis*, 29.20 sqq.); but the usual method of obtaining a wife in ancient Israel was by paying a bride price, called *mohar* or *mahr*, (See Ewald's *Antiquities of Israel* p. 200, Gans's *Das Erbrecht in weltgeschichtlicher Entiwicklung*. 1.128, Robertson Smith's, *Kinship and Marriage in early Arabia*" p. 70. *Wellhausen's Die Ehe bei den Arabern* in *Nachrichten der königl. Gesellschaft der Wissenschaften zu Göttingen*, 1893, p. 433. Benzingers, *Hebräische Archaologic* p. 106. Nowak's, *Lehrbuch der hebräischen Archäologie* 1. 155). According to Talmudic Law the mutual consent of the parties to marry each other had to be legally manifested with a special formality, which gave validity to the marriage contract. The usual formality was that called *kaseph*, or "money". In the presence of two witnesses the man gave to his chosen bride a piece of money —even a *perutta*, the smallest copper coin used in Palestine, was sufficient for the purpose—or object of equal value, with the words, "be thou consecrated to me"; but during the Middle Ages it became customary for the act of betrothal by *kaseph* to be performed by means of a plain ring, instead of a piece of money, and this custom has ever since prevailed up to our time (See Mielziner in *Jewish Law of Marriage and Divorce in Ancient and Modern Times*; p. 77 sqq.) The betrothal by *kaseph* may be a survival of the old marriage by purchase, but it has also been supposed to be an imitation of the roman *coemptio*.

Among the ancient Arabs a bridal price, *mahr*, was given by the bridegroom to the father or guardian of the bride; and this bridal price has survived in Muhammadan law, where it has been confused with the *ṣadāq*, which was a gift offered to the bride by the bridegroom in Early Arabia. (See Robertson Smith's *Kinship and Marriage* (p. 76-78, 91) Although the Koranic law presumes that the *mahr*, or *ṣadāq*, shall be the property of the bride, this rule was not always followed in practice.

Aristotle tells us that in Greek primitive times men bought their wives (*Politica* 2.8). In heroic times a suitor gave *hedna* consisting of cattle, to the father of the bride elect, and a maiden was called *alfesiboia*, that is, one who brings her parents many oxen as presents from her suitor according to Ilias (18.593), or by some other name compounded from the Greek word for an ox, the gold currency of the time (See Murray's *Rise of the Greek Epic*, p. 86). Contrary to other writers, Hruza maintains that the *hedna* was not the price of a bride, but merely a *douceur* intended to prevail upon the father; but he admits that in a yet earlier age marriage by purchase existed in Greece, although, as he rightly points out, the transaction could not have been the purchase of a chattel but only of the rights of a husband. (See Hruza's *Beitr.̄ge zur Geschichte des griechischen und römisehen Familienrechtes*, 1.8 sqq.).

Marriage by purchase cannot with equal certainty be established as a form of marriage on Roman soil; but a reminiscence of it is supposed to have been preserved in the symbolical process of *coemptio*, which was the ordinary form in which any Roman citizen, whether patrician or plebeian, might contract a marriage. It was a traditional ceremony representing the purchase of a bride, the intending husband "purchasing" the bride from the person under whose authority she was, with a view to thereby acquiring that marital power without which marriage as a legal relationship was considered impossible. (See Rossbach's "*Untersuchungen über die rōmische Ehe*," pp. 80, 87 sqq., Sohm's "*Institutes*" p. 452 sqq. and others). On the other hand there are also writers who deny that *coemptio* can be regarded as a survival of ancient bride purchase. Marquardt maintains that it was an artificial and comparatively late form of marriage, whilst *confarreatio*, the specifically patrician kind of marriage which suggested no idea of purchase, was the oldest form of marriage in Rome (See Marquardt's *Das Privatleben der Rōmer*" p. 38). Karlowa thinks that if marriage by purchase prevailed in ancient Rome or among the ancestors of the Romans, a survival of it remained not in the *coemptio* but in the *arrha sponsalitia,* which in historical times was given to the bride. (See Karlowa's "*Römische Rechtsgeschichte*", 2.166).

Marriage by purchase was a custom of all Teutonic peoples. There is a kind of marriage by service in the "Eyrbyggja Saga" : Vigstyr says to the berserk Halli, who asked for the hand of his daughter Āsdī: "As you are a poor man, I shall do as the ancients did and let you earn your wife by hard work." (See Weinhold's *Altnordisches Leben*, p. 22). But the general consideration given for a bride was money paid down by the bridegroom. Originally, we may presume, that the amount of it depended on agreement, but during the period of the law-books, both in England, and on the Continent, it was generally fixed by custom or by statute. (See Sohm's *Das Recht der Eheschliessung*, p. 23 sqq.). The bridal price was called *wittum* or *widem*, the Anglo-Saxons called it *weo tuma*, the Longobardians *meta* or *mundium* the Frisians *mundsket*, the Scandinavians—*mundr*, and in Latin it was termed *pretium nuptiale* or *pretium emptionis*. (See Schröder's *Lehrbuch der deutschen Rechtsgeschichte* pp. 70, 299, V. Amira's *Recht* in *Pauls Grundriss der germanischen Philologie* 3.161). Betrothal was *mercatio*, and to marry was *uxorem emere* or *feminam vendere*. (See Brunner's *Deutsche Rechtsgeschichte*, 1.14, Schrôder's *Lehrbuch der deutschen Rechtsgeschichte* p. 299). The Kentish law of King Aethelbirht speaks of a man buying a maiden with cattle, and the transaction is called a "bargain", (See *Laws of King Aethelbirht*, ch. 77). In Germany the expression "to purchase a wife" was in use till the end of the Middle Ages. (See Laband's *Die rechtliche Stellung der Frauen im altrömischen und germanischen Recht*", in *Zeitschrift für Völkerpsychologie und Sprachwissenschaft*, 3. 154) and we find the same term in Christian IV.'s Norwegian Law of 1604. (See Olivecrona's *Om makars giftoraett i bo*, p. 150). In Holland the bride is still, in the language of the common people, represented as *verkocht*, that is "sold". (See Brunner's *Deutsche Rechtsgeschichte* p. 74). But here again we should notice that marriage by purchase did not imply the purchase of a piece of property; the ancient Teutons bought the *mund* or protectorship over the woman. (See Friedberg's *Das Recht der Ehe-schliessung in seiner geschichtlichen Entwicklung*, p. 18) and other rights which marriage conferred on the husband.

Marriage by purchase prevailed among the early Slavs

(See Ewers's *Das älteste Recht der Russen* p. 226; Maciejowski's *Slavische Rechtsgeschichte* 2. 195). The bride price was called *veno*, in Polish *wiano* (See Piprek's *Slavische Brautwerbungs- u. Hochzeitsgebräuche* p. 151) and in old Russia a marriageable girl was called a *kunka*, from *kuna* "marten" because her parents might exchange her for marten skins, the usual medium of payment in ancient Russia (See Schrader's *Family Teutonic und Balto-Slavic*; *Encylopoedia of Religion and Ethics* 5.750). "To this day among the Russian peasantry" says Schrader, "the first act of the nuptials is the suit or proposal, *svátanie*, which is a purely commercial transaction. The father of the suitor usually accompanied by a relative visits the girl's parents and says, "We have a purchaser, you a commodity: will you sell your ware ?' Then follows the bargaining, which differs in no respect from a negotiation about the sale of a cow." In Serbia at the beginning of the nineteenth century the price of girls reached such a height that Black George limited it to one ducat (See Kraus's *Sitte und Brauch der Südslaven* p. 275). In High Albania "marriage was entirely by purchase, except for the occasional forcible capture of a girl" (See Miss Durhan's, *High Albania and its Customs* in 1908, in *Jour. Roy. Anthr. Instit.* XL 59).[1]

The Ancient Celts paid a price for their brides. In Ireland it consisted of various objects, such as articles of gold, silver or bronze clothes or horse-bridles, cattle or swine, land or houses. (See Sullivan's *Introduction in O'Curry's, Manners and Customs of the Ancient Irish* Vol. I. p. 174 sqq.). It often had the form of a yearly payment from the husband after marriage, and we find it laid down in the Brehon Law that the woman's father was entitled to the whole of the first year's bridal price. (See *Ancient Laws and Institutes of Ireland* 2.347, 3.315). In Ireland it was called *coibche*, though there were also other names for it (See Joyce's, *Social History of Ancient Ireland* 2.4). and in Wales *gober* (*gobyr*) or *amober* (*amobor, amobyr*) (See *d'Arbois de Jubainville's Cours de la literature celtique* 7.234. *Venedolian Code* 2.19, 1 and others).[2]

Marriage by purchase exists also recently among peoples at the so-called primitive stage of civilization. Many examples could be quoted.

1. Quoted from Westermarck II. p. 413.
2. Quoted from Westermarck II. pp. 407 spq.

76. Marriage by purchase was also known in ancient India and was represented by the *Āsura-vivāha*. It was similar to the marriage by purchase of the Batans, among the people of the island of Nias etc., where an actual contract of purchase took place. In this agreement the girl was considered solely as a merchandise and the price given for her depended on the circumstances of the parties.

C. *Marriage by Sham-Purchase*

77. The amount given for a wife varied greatly among different proples. In the lowest tribes it amounted to very little. Among the Veddas of Ceylon some food was presented to the parents of the girl, (see Hartshorne's "*Weddas*", in *Indian Antiquary*, 8. 320) or nothing at all, apparently, could be given for her. (See Le Mesurier's *Veddas of Ceylon*, in *Jour. Roy. Asiatic Soc. Ceylon Branch*, 9.340). Among the Sakai of Perak the bridegroom made a present to his prospective father-in-law of certain specified articles, for example, knife, or hatchet, or yams, "according to his means." (See de Morgan's *Moeurs, coutumes et langages des Negritos de l' interieur de la presquile Malaise*, in *Bull. Soc. normande de Geographie*, 7.421); whilst among the Orang Sletar of the Orang Laut a mouthful of tobacco and one *chupah* of rice handed to the mother of the bride confirmed the hymenal tie. (See Thomson's *Remarks of the Sletar and Sabimba Tribes*, in *Jour. Indian Archipelago*, 1.341). Among some Australian tribes, where the exchange of females was customary the bridegroom supplied his father or parents-in-law with game, or in addition presented the former with boomerangs and other weapons. (See Howitt's *Native Tribes of South-East Australia*, p. 220). Concerning the Central African Pygmies, Grenfell said that marriage among them "is little else than the tendering of a gift of arrow, heads or knives or other objects of local value to the father of the girl, who is thereby acquired by the purchaser; though no doubt inclination counts for much in the bargain." (See Johnston's *George Greenfell and the Congo* 2.674. See also Casati's *Ten Years in Equatoria*, 1.157). According to Hutereau, again, a man acquired a girl for wife by offering to her father two animals killed in the chase and to her mother a dog. (See Hutereau's *Notes sur la vie familiale et juridique de quelques popula-*

tions du Congo Belge, p. 4). Among the Namib Bushmen some food, blankets, and furs were given to the prospective parents-in-law. (See Trenk's *Die Buschleute der Namib* in *Mittheil. Deutschen Schutzgeb*. 23.168).

With the development of civilization the girl, probably, ceased to be an object of merchandise and the practice of purchasing wives was gradually abandoned and came to be looked upon as infamous. The wealthier classes took the first step, and poorer and humbler persons subsequently followed their example.

This above mentioned condition existed at the time when the patriarchal organisation disappeared and was replaced by the system of State.

We meet with the same evolution in India. There too the purchase of a girl became an infamous act (Mn. 9.100, 9.98, 3.51), a sin (Mn. 3.52) and even according to some sources a prohibited act (Āp. 2.6, 13, 11) or a great crime (B. 1.11, 21, 3) and a woman married according to this form of marriage was not considered as a wife (B. 1.11, 21, 2).

It may be deduced from the rules contained in sources of law that this form of marriage was out of date in the Smṛti-s, and though it cannot be maintained that it was absolutely archaic, it must be considered as slowly disappearing.

78. We may discern two different ways in which this gradual disappearance of marriage by purchase had in general, taken place. On the one hand, the purchase became a symbol and appeared as a sham purchase in the marriage ceremonies, or as an exchange of presents; on the other hand, probably in the second stage of the development of marriage by sham-purchase the purchase-sum was transformed into the morning gift and the marriage portion, a part —afterwards the whole—was given to the bride either directly by the bridegroom or by her father. These changes in marriage by purchase have taken place not only in the history of the so-called civilised nations but also among several peoples who are still in the so-called semi-civilised state; and in few instances it is expressly stated that they consider marriage by purchase a disgraceful practice.

79. We see the same development of symbolical purchase in many nations. And so in the ancient civilised World the Roman *coemptio* (a kind of a marriage with *manus*), was a real purchase. The woman there declared she would be sold in order to become a *mater familias* in return for which the husband took her hand and said : *ego ex iure Quiritum matem familias meam esse ajo*. The piece of ore reputed to be the purchase price was then weighed out. In pre-historic times the purchase was probably accomplished on the principle of the "gens". Regardless of the real value of the merchandise *i.e.* the girl, the price was a piece of ore. According to Salic law the guardian of the girl rceived an *arra, a solidus* and a *denar* for his consent to the marriage, a symbolical price as compared with the former real price of purchase.

80. Among many tribes at the so-called lower stage of civilisation the price paid for the girl was only symbolical.

Among the Angmagsaliks on the east coast of Greenland, according to Holm, (*Ethnologisk Skizze af Angmaksalikerne in Meddeleser om Groenland* 10.96) the young man gave to the father a harpoon or some similar articles to get his daughter in marriage, but it also happened that good hunters were paid by fathers to marry their daughters. Among the Eskimo of the Ungava district, Hudson's Bay Territory, "the sanction of the parents is sometimes obtained by favour or else bought by making certain presents of skins, furs, and other valuables to the father and mother." (See Turner's *Ethnology of the Ungava District, Hudson Bay Territory* in *Ann. Rep. Bur. Ethn.*" 11.188). Among the Eskimo round Repulse Bay the father who selected a little girl for his young boy to be his daughter-in-law paid her father something—perhaps a snow-knife or a sled or a dog or, in later days, a handful of powder and a dozen percussion caps. (See Gilder's *Schwatka's Search* p. 249 sqq.). Of the Central Eskimo Dr. Boas simply says that the bride must be bought from the parents with some presents. (See *Boas's Central Eskimo* in *Ann. Rep. Bur. Ethn* 6.579).

Among the South American Indians the consideration, if any, given for a wife likewise varied greatly among different tribes. A Huitoto bridegroom gave a small quantity of cocoa or tobacco to the *capitan*, or chief of the subtribe, to obtain his approval, and cut a supply of firewood for his future mother-in-law; and shortly afterwards the girl was given to him. (See Hardenburg's *Putumayo* p. 154). Among the Puris, Coroados, and Covoapos some game and fruit were given by the bridegroom for his bride immediately before marriage, whereas the more civilized tribes of the Brazilian aborigines carried on an actual trade in women. (See v. Martius's *Beiträge zur Ethnographie und Sprachenkunde Amerikas zumal Basiliens* 1.109 sqq.). The price paid for a Goajiro girl chiefly consisted of cattle. (See Simon's *Exploration of the Goajiro Peninsula, U.S. of Colombia* in *Preceed. Roy. Geograph. Soc. N. S.* 7.792). Among the Mocobis in the southern part of the Gran Chaco a girl was given in marriage either for some tiger-skins or for one or two horses, a cow, and a few ornaments. (See Kohler's *Pater Elorian Baucke* p. 315). The Patagonians gave mares, horses, silver ornaments for their brides; even a hundred mares have been paid for an heiress who had animals of her own. (See Muster's *On the Races of Patagonia* in *Jour. Anthr. Inst.* 1. 201[1]). Many other similar examples could be given.

81. The same also occurs in ancient India with the *Ārṣa-vivāha,* where the price did not correspond to the real value of the purchased merchandise. The price paid for the girl consisted of a cow and a bull and a dress (N. 21.41) or of suit of clothes (Śaṅkh. Likh. in Vīr. Saṁ. 851) and afterwards permanently of a cow and a bull (Mn. 3.29, Āp. 2.5, 11, 18, G. 4.8, Vās. 2.32, B. 1.11, 20, 4, Śaṅkh. 20.4, Āśv. Gṛh. 1.6, 4, and other). The price was paid probably in the first stage of the development of this form of marriage to the father (Āp. 2.5, 11, 18, K. 3.2) or to him who had authority over the girl (G. 3.8, B.1. 11, 20, etc.).

D. *Dowry*

82. It seems that the development of marriage by sham-purchase has not come to an end but the purchase price has been transformed into the morning gift or a marriage portion.

And so from marriage by purchase or a symbolic marriage by purchase, in which the price paid for the girl did not correspond to the real value of the girl, we come to the practice of dowry, which is apparently the very reverse of marriage by purchase. But whilst the marriage portion partly derives its origin from the purchase of wives, it does not so in every case. It serves different ends, often indissolubly intermingled. It may have the meaning of a return gift. It may imply that the

1. Quoted from Westermarck II. p. 375 sqq.

wife as well as the husband is expected to contribute to the expenses of the joint household. It is also very often intended to be a settlement for the wife in case the marriage was dissolved through the husband's death or otherwise. In the social history of the civilised races the marriage portion had played so prominent a part, that, as we have spoken of the state of marriage by purchase, we may speak of another and later stage where fathers were bound by custom or law to portion their daughters.

We see the limitation of the form of marriage by purchase by the fact that the parents of the woman more or less lost the economic advantages they derived from her marriage, and that greater regard was paid to the interests of the contracting parties. We meet here with the practice of offering a return gift.

83. We can find many such examples in the ancient civilised World. In China the parents of the bride, or her guardian, accepted only a part of the presents, returning the balance, to which they added some articles for the parents of the bridegroom; but they accepted all the money, and all the silks and satins designed for the use of the girl (See Doolittle's *Social Life of the Chinese* 2.71). The exchange of presents formed in fact, the subject of a long section in the old penal code; for "the marriage articles and betrothal presents once exchanged, the parties are considered irrevocably engaged" (See Medhurst's *Marriage, Affinity and Inheritance in China*" in *Trans. Roy. Asiatic Soc. China Branch*, 4.11). As to the presents exchanged at the time of sending the engagement cards without which no betrothal was regarded as binding, it was said that in the Chinese view they were "omens of good to the parties most intimately concerned" (See Doolittle's *Social Life of the Chinese* 2.66 sqq.).

In ancient Greece there were at the conclusion of a marriage not only the *hedna* given for the bride but also the *meilia* or presents given by her father to the bridegroom (see Hruza's *Beiträge zur Geschichte des Griechischen und Römischen Familienrechtes*" 1.11). Tacitus, after speaking of the gifts by which a German obtained his wife, said in his *Germania* (Ch. 18) that the wife "in her turn brings her husband some gift of arms. This, he added, "represents to them our marriage bond, the mystic celebrations, and all the gods of matrimony." The Welsh *agweddi* was, strictly speaking, a payment made by the kindred or parents of the bride to the bridegroom, although the word sometimes seemed to have been used to include the marriage portion of the bride as well. (See Rhys's and Brynmor-Jones's *The Welsh People* p. 211). The dowry which the bride brought with her may also be partly regarded as a return gift to the husband. (See Meissner's *Beiträge zum altbabylonishen Privatrecht* p. 14).

Among the Teutoniç peoples a similar process of development took place. At the time of the folk-laws, from the sixth to the ninth century, the bridal price was no longer paid to the father or guardian of the bride, but to the bride herself. (See Grimms' *Deutsche Rechtsaltertümer*, p. 423), the right of the guardian being practically limited to the receipt of the *Handgeld* that is, to a merely formal gift, (see Sohm's *Das Recht der Eheschliessung* p. 33) a *solidus* and a *denarius* according to Salic Law. (See Grimm's *Deutsche Rechtsaltertümer* p. 427)[1].

84. The same can be observed among the peoples at the so-called lower stage of civilisation. For instance with Bugines and Makassars the bridal price was balanced by return presents and the bride did not leave her family, according to Wilken, (*Over de Verwand.* p. 72). With the Mongols the bridegroom bought his bride but his father was obliged to replace the value of his daughter with the dowry, according to Klemm (*Kulturgeschichte* 3.165). Just so with the Tehuenchens the bridegroom gave mares or silver ornaments but he received back gifts of the same value, according to Sohler (Z. f. v. R. S.353).

Sometimes a part of the bridal price or even the total sum was employed for the dowry, which was given either to the bride or to the bridegroom. In this manner separate property belonging to the wife or a common matrimonial fortune resulted. This group of customs always appeared at the time when the institution of purchase of the maiden was dying.

Sometimes the father-in-law returned a part of the bridal price paid by the bridegroom, for example, among the Afghans. Among the Makassars and Bugines a part of the bridal sum was returned to the bridegroom, for example : 4 Reals from the bridal price of 12 Reals, from the bridal price of 20 Reals— 5 Reals and so on (See Wilken's *Over de Verwand.* p. 72).

Among the Bagobos of South-Mindanao the father of the bride returned to the husband half of the bridal price paid when

1. Quoted from Westermarck II. p. 414 sqq.

the married couple were satisfied (see Schadenberg's *Die Bewohner Von Süd-Mindanao.*) Among the Agahrs (Dinka) the father of the bride usually returned ten of the horned cattle paid for the bride as an act of generosity and as a contribution to the new household (see Schweinfurth p. 336). It may also happen that the bride sum belonged in part to the family of the bride and in part to the bride herself. Among the Makassars and Bugines a Real as a part of the bridal sum was returned in favour of the bride and the remainder was distributed among her blood-relations (see Wilken's *Over de Verwand.* p. 72.).

In many places in Ancient Serbia (now Yugoslavia) they paid one to ten ducats to the father of the bride at home (*u kucu*) or on the table (*na siniju*) sometimes more whereas the girl agreed with the "apple" (*jabuku*) or the change (*pare*). This earnest money, was given to the girl either in cash or single pieces were put in an apple (see Kraus's *Sitte and Brauch bei den Südslaven* p. 275, 276).

Sometimes the total bridal price belonged to the bride, for example with the Dajaks, the Arabs of Ahl el Shemal (see Wilken's *Over de Verwand.* p. 87 and Burckhardt *Bem rk. uber die Beduinen* p. 88).

The same is to be found in ancient India. There the price (which, as a matter of fact, was a symbolical one) was paid—it is true—to the father but it was only a return gift because the father had lost the right of retaining the "price" (Mn. 3.43, MBh. 13. 81, 1.2, 13;46, 1-2, Gov. *ad* B. 2.11, 20, 4).

85. With the form of marriage begun the duty on the part of the father of giving a dowry to the girl (MBh. 13.45,2).

In this way we are likely to meet in ancient India with the second phase of the development of marriage by sham purchase when the symbolical price paid to the father fell as a return gift to the girl's or her future husband's share. In this way the duty of giving a dowry to the girl arose. This duty of giving a dowry to the girl became afterwards the *essentiale negotii* of the orthodox forms of marriage. The fact alone that the "price was returned to the giver, buyer i.e. to the intended husband pointed to the origin of the dowry. This form of marriage was however, not likely to disappear with the development of the forms of marriage in ancient India, since it belonged to the orthodox forms of marriage and it was not mentioned whether this form was commendable, or not. In addition to this form a new form arose *i. e.* on the choice of a suitable husband by the father of the girl independently of her consent.

E. *Marriage based on the Choice of a Husband by the Father of the Girl Independently of Her Consent*

86. The duty of the father to give a dowry was not the only *essentiale negotii* of the newly formed form of marriage. The second *essentiale negotii* of this form of marriage lay in the consent of the principal of the family, that is, as a rule, of the father.

This *essentiale negotii,* the consent of the principal of the family, was also known in the forms of marriage by purchase. It was, however, a *conditio sine qua non*, as the seller was the father, and not an *essentiale negotii.*

It may be observed that by introducing marriage by purchase, marriage which depended on the choice of a suitable husband by the father of the girl independently of her consent, was created.

What was the *raison d'etre* of that kind of marriage? We find the answer in the "History of Human Marriage" by Westermarck (2. p. 283): "Marriage brings together strange families or large groups of kindred, or constitutes a new tie between friendly ones. It is therefore not surprising that the fathers or parents or other relatives of the parties want to have a voice in the matter". Speaking of the careful supervision of marriages among the Maori, Mr. Best observes, as Westermarck further stated, "to a great extent it was caused by tribal anxiety to avoid a *mêsalliance*, to prevent a person of—good birth from marrying into a family of *ware*, or low born people, to keep unmixed the blood of the *rangantira* class, to uphold the rank, fame, and dignity of first-born lines of descent and hence to prevent all *tipuheke*, or degeneration, of blue-blooded lines." (See Best's *Maori Marriage Customs* in Trans. and Proceed. New Zealand Institute, 36.50). The power of interference depended of course, upon the authority which the families or their heads possessed over the individual members of the family. Among the Xosa Kafirs, for example, the father ruled as long as he lived over the whole of his family, including the married sons. (See Kropf's p. 134 *Das Volk der Xosa Kaffern im Östl.-Süd-Africa*). Among the Kandhs, in each family absolute authority rested with the house-father: the sons had no property during his lifetime, and all the male children, with their wives and descendants, continued to share the father's meal, prepared by the common mother. (See Hunter's *Rural Bengal*, 3.72). The father chose a full-grown woman as wife for his young son. 'In the superior age of the bride,' said Colonel Macpherson, in the *Memorials of Service in India* (p. 70 sqq.) is seen but a proof of the supremacy of the paternal authority amongst this singular people. The parents obtained in the wives of their sons during the years of their boyhood very valuable domestic servants, and their selection was avowedly made with a view to utility in this character.' (See Macpheson's *Memorials of Service in India*, p. 70 sqq.)." Much more frequently than the young man, the young girl was dependent upon somebody else's will in the choice of a partner", according to Westermarck. Although the subject of family authority among the lower races required much further investigation, it can be safely admitted that among most of them a girl was in her father's power till she married, whilst in some instances his authority over her continued after her marriage. (See Westermarck's *Origin and Development of the Moral Ideas*. 1.601[1]). Yet among various peoples the consent of the mother, brother or maternal uncle was regarded as particularly essential to a girl's marriage, and in such cases the father could even have little or nothing to say in this matter. But according to Westermarck (2.284), the necessity of the father's or somebody else's consent, however, by no means implied that the girl was or could be, given in marriage against her own will. And even where her wishes were not consulted she could know how to make her influence felt. He further said that it was a mistake to suppose that among the lower races women were, as a rule, married without having any voice of their own in the matter. In many cases, their liberty of selection was, on the contrary, very considerable, apart from those already noticed in which they were actually the courters.

87. We find innumberable examples of the absolute power of the father upon his children.

And so in Ancient Chaldea the father, as in China and Japan, had great power over his children. According to Meissner

1. Quoted from Westermarck's "The History of Human Marriage" II. p. 284.

(*Beiträge zum altbablylonischen Privaterecht* p. 14[1]) a daughter was given away in marriage by her father without being able to raise any objection to his choice. According to Koschaker (*Rechtsvergleichende Studien zur Gesetzgebung Hammurapis*, p. 119) a Babylonian woman was said not to marry, but to be married).[2] And also the bride usually brought a dowry from her father's house according to Kohler and Peiser (*Aus dem Babylonischen Rechtsleben* 4.11).

The importance which the ancient Hebrews attached to the duties of a child to its parents can be seen from the placing of the law on the subject among the Ten Commandments, and from its position there in the immediate proximity to the commands relating to the duties of men towards God. (See Ewald's *Antiquities of Israel* p. 188). A father might sell his child to relieve his own distress, or offer, it to a creditor as a pledge (See Ewald's *Antiquities of Israel* p. 190). He had not only unlimited power to marry his daughters (See Benzinger's *Hebräische Archäeologie* p. 107), but even to sell them as maids into concubinage, though not to a foreign people (*Exodus* 21.7). He also chose wives for his sons (*Genesis*, 24.4, 28.1, 38.6, Exodus 34.16, *Deuteronomy* 7.3), the selection, however, sometimes being made by the mother (*Genesis* 21.21); there is no indication that the subjection of sons ceased after a certain age. (See Michanelis's *Commentaries on the Laws of Moses* 1.144).[3]

Of the ancient Arabs Wellhausen says that a woman was betrothed by her *wali*, or guardian, that is, her father, brother or cousin; but "of course, the daughter is often asked, by affectionate parents, whether she wants to have the suitor" (*Die Ehe bei den Arabern* in *Nachr. v.d. Kön. Gesell. der Wissenschaften zu Göttingen*, 1893, p. 431). According to Muhammadan law, the woman's consent was not required if she was still under her father's authority. Among the Hanafīs and the Shīa'hs the father's right to carry his daughter without her consent came to an end when she arrived at puberty. (See Ameer Ali's *Mahommadan Law* 2.335).[4]

Among the ancient Romans, in relation to the father of

1. Quoted from Westermarck II. p. 284-286.
2. Quoted from Westermarck II. p. 329.
3. Quoted from Westermarck II. p. 330.
4. Quoted from Westermarck II. p. 331.

the house, "all in the household were destitute of legal rights—the wife and the child no less than the bullock or the slave". (See Mommsen's *History of Rome* 1.74). The father not only had judicial authority over his children—implying the right of inflicting capital punishment on them, though not without just cause, (see Westermarck's *Origin and Development of the Moral Ideas* 1.393, 611)—but he could sell them at discretion (see Dionysius's of Halicarnassus's, *Antiquitates Romanae* 2.27). Even the grown-up son and his children were subject to the father's authority (*Institutions* 1.9, 3), and in marriage without *conventio in manum* a daughter remained in the power of her father or tutor even after marriage. The consent of the *pater familias* was indispensable to the marriage of children, sons and daughters alike (*Institutions* 1.10); and so strict was this rule that down to the reign of Marçus Aurelius the children of a *mente captus* could not contract a legal marriage while in the power of their father, when the latter was incapable of giving his consent (See Mackenzie's *Studies in Roman Law* p. 104 n. 4). In Rome the marriage portion became a mark of distinction for a legitimate wife. A woman had the legal right to demand a *dos*, or *dowry*, from her father but it was to be given to her husband, not to herself, as a contribution towards the defrayal of the expenses of the joint household—*ad matrimonii onera ferenda*—although it was also intended as a provision in the interests of the wife. (See Sohm's *Institutes* p. 465 sqq.).

Among the Greeks and Teutons the father had the right to expose his children in their infancy, to sell them in case of urgency as long as they remained in his power, (See Grimm's *Deutsche Rechtsaltertümer* p. 461 and Leist's *Graeco-italische Rechtsgeschichte* p. 60), and to give away his daughters in marriage without consulting their wishes (see Hruza's *Beiträge zur Geschichte des griechischenund römishen Familienrechtes* 1.9 and others).

Caesar stated that in Gaul the father had the power of life and death over his wife and children (see Caesar's *Commentarii de bello Gallico* 6.19, 3). M. d'Arbois de Jubainville maintained that according to early Celtic law, as in Rome, the authority of the father lasted till his death; but this is not quite borne out by the facts. (See *Cours de littérature Celtique* 7.244 sqq.). In Ancient Ireland the son was under the father's control till formally emancipated; but it is not known at what age the emancipation took place. (See Joyce's *Social History of Ancient Ireland* 2.13). The Welsh laws referred to the giving of a daughter in marriage by her indred as well as by her father. She did not seem to have been entirely at the disposal of the latter, not to have been, in theory, entirely free. (See Rhys's and Brynor-Jones's *The Welsh People* p. 209).[1] When marrying the daughter it was the father's duty to give her a dowry.

A great many such examples may still be quoted among the ancient civilized peoples as well as the peoples of our times.

88. We also meet in ancient India with a marriage based on the choice of a suitable husband by the father of the girl independently of her consent and connected with the duty of giving a dowry on the part of the father or the guardian of the girl. To this form of marriage in ancient India the *Brahma-vivāha* with two variants, i. e. the *Daiva-vivāha* and the *Prājāpatya-vivāha* belonged. The characteristic feature of this marriage was that the father, or some other person under whose protection the girl was, chose a husband for her and gave her a dowry. What the husband was like, when the girl was married and whose was the initiative for such a marriage was of no importance. To the same group belonged also the festive *svayaṁvara* which we find in Sanskrit literature; it is true that the girl here had some influence in the choice of her future husband but this influence was limited by the number and sort of the suitors invited by her father to the *svayaṁvara* as well as by chance (that is who would win the tournament). The above mentioned three or four forms of marriage were probably the highest forms of marriage which were liely to be originated at the same time as marriage based on sham purchase *i. e.* the *Ārṣa-vivāha*, or superseded it.

F. *Marriage based on Free Consent of the Bride and the Bridegroom*

89. Of various peoples we learn that it was a common custom for women to run away from men who have been forced upon them by their parents. (See King's and Fitzroy's *Narrative of the Surveying Voyages of the "Adventure" and "Begle"* 2.153. Patagonians *Dobrizhoffer's Account of the Abipones*, 2.207.

1. Quoted from Westermarck II. p. 283 sqq.

Brett's *Indian Tribes of Guiana* p. 254—Garib's, Fries's *Gronland*, p. iii Greenlanders). In Pentecost, of the New Hebrides, when a woman has left her husband several times and repeated beatings have not changed her mind, "her parents paid back the money and the husband gave up his wife." (See Speiser's *Two Years with the Natives in the Western Pacific*, p. 234 sqq.) Among the Bogos of North-Eastern Africa a woman who has been compelled to marry a man against her will could dissolve the union by three times running away from him (See Munzinger's *Über die Sitten und das Recht der Bogos*, p. 64).

A very common method by which a woman could obtain the husband she desired without the consent or against the will of her parents was to elope with him. Whilst this practice indicated that the mutual consent of the parties was not always sufficient for the conclusion of a marriage, it also provided a remedy in case of poverty. It was resorted to when the young man was too poor to pay the price asked for the girl or otherwise when from no fault of hers, he was unable to marry her in the ordinary way. Sometimes sham elopements were arranged with the consent of the bride's parents in order to save the expenses of a regular wedding (see Blau's *Nachrichten über kurdische Stämme*, in *Zeitschr der Deutsch. Morgenländ. Gesellsch.* xvi. 624; Ahmad Shah's *Four Years in Tibet*, p. 57, Schotter's *Notes ethnographiques sur les tribes de Koytcheou Chine* in *Anthropos*, vi. 320) or, when the bridegroom was too poor to pay the required price, "to save the credit of the bride's family in not having received a sufficient price for her." (See Biddulph's *Tribes of the Hindoo Koosh*, p. 81). Among many peoples elopement was a veritable institution, recognised by custom as a method of contracting a marriage or at least as a preliminary to it. Frequently the lover had to pay later for his bride or to conciliate her people with some gift (Plains Indians, Pawnee Siksika, Cheremiss of Oufa Ostyaks, people of Purang, Gonds of the Eastern Ghats, Kochān's natives of Bali and Tenimber, Roro and Mekeo tribes and Mafulu of British New Guinea, Jabim, people of Songa in Vellalavella, Banks Islanders, Thonga, Basoga, Lautuka, Nandi, Pangwe, Baya). Among the Pawnee and Siksika, in case of elopment, the subsequent presentation of gifts legitimised the marriage and removed the disgrace which otherwise was attached to the girl and her family.

90. Among various peoples elopement was by itself sufficient to make the runaway couple husband and wife. Among the Havasupai of Arizona, if parents refused to sell their daughter to a suitor and the couple eloped 'this ended the matter.' The ethics of the tribe were such that cohabitation once entered upon, the parents had no authority to declare the marriage void. And, as a further penalty for his obdurate obstinacy, the father lost the ten dollars or its equivalent he might have had by being kind and complaisant to the desires of the young couple." (See James's *Indians of the Painted Desert Region* p. 228 sqq). Among the Thompson Indians, even if the father of a girl who has eloped with her lover brought her back, "he could only deliver her up to the young man, as custom declared them already married." (See Teit's in *Memoirs of the American Museum Nat. Hist* vol. II. Anthropology 1324). The Dakota Indians, according to Mary Eastman, p. 103, had two kinds of marriages, buying a wife and runaway matches; for "it is an understood thing that, when the young people run away, they are to be forgiven at any time they choose to return, whether it should be the next day, or six months afterwards," (see Eastman's *Dahcotali or Life and Legends of the Sioux around Fort Snelling* p. 103.)

That was probably the first stage of the development of the marriage based on the free consent of the bride and the bridegroom.

91. In the second stage of the development of this form of marriage the consent of the bride and the bridegroom was essential, whilst the consent of the *pater familias* was not essential.

Nowhere was marriage by elopment more frequent, and indeed more needed, than among many Australian tribes. (See Malinowski's *The Family among the Australian Aborigines* pp. 36-47, 55 sqq. and others). Among the Kurnai according to Horwitt, a man, with rare exceptions, "could acquire a wife in one way only, namely, by running off with her secretly and with her own consent. Marriage, therefore, was by elopment." It was the business of the *bunjilyenjin*, a medicine-man, to aid the elopment of young couples, and this gave sanction to the practice, which arose from the difficulty of finding a wife. (See Howitt's *Native Tribes of South-East Australia* pp. 273, 274, 279). If the parties were prohibited from intermarrying on account of the relationship in which they stood to each other, the elopement was punished with great severity, whereas otherwise the lover could, at least in certain circumstances, retain the woman with whom he eloped. In many cases he had to fight the man to whom she has been promised or, if she was already married, her husband, or a more general struggle ensued in which kindred were involved; and in either case the issue of the fight decided whether he would be allowed to keep the woman or not. (See Howitt's *Native Tribes of South-East Australia*, pp. 216, 222, 258, 194, 236 sqq., Petrie's *Reminiscences of Early Queensland*, p. 60, Roth's *Ethnological Studies among the North-West-Central Queensland Aborigines* p. 181, and others). Among the Wūmbai "the girl was persued by her father and brothers, and the man she had eloped with would have to allow them to strike him on the head with a club, after which in some cases he would retain her. But in other cases there was a fight between her kindred, male and female, and those of the man she went off with." (See Howitts *Native Tribes of South-East Australia*, p. 194).[1]

It appears from the above examples that there arose a new form of marriage by elopement from the person who had authority over the girl. Such a marriage could be concluded with the consent of their parents (guardians). This form of marriage may also be connected with the capture of the girl.

In the latter stage of the development of the forms of marriage even the *pater familias* or a member of a family lost his right over his children especially his right to interfere, in anything concerning their marriage, so that the young man as well as the young girl, had the right to decide if they wanted to marry, and whom they wanted to marry. This form of marriage became the highest form of marriage, that which depended only on the free consent of the contracting parties. This form of marriage is pre-dominant in our times.

92. The same two stages of the development of marriage by the free consent of the bride and bridegroom can be found in ancient India.

The ordinary *svayaṁvara* was probably the most primitive form of marriage based on the free consent of the bride of and

1. Quoted from Westermarck II. p. 318 sqq.

bridegroom as it was in reality a form of punishment imposed on the person obliged to protect the girl because he did not choose a husband for her at the proper time.

We find that a woman could obtain the husband she desired without the consent or even against the will of her parents by eloping with him (in ancient India *Gāndharva-vivāha* combined with the *Rākṣasa-vivāha*). This elopment actually prohibited and punishable, like the *Rākṣasa-vivāha,* was probably the first stage in the development of marriage by free consent of the bride and bridegroom for it was a spontaneous elopment of the girl with the intended husband chosen by herself; this was considered in ancient Indian literature as concubinage. The second stage of marriage by free consent of the bride and bridegroom was probably the *Gāndharva-vivāha* not combined with the *Rākṣasa-vivāha* and this was the highest form of marriage as it could be contracted even without the consent of the father or the guardian of the girl.

The high place given to this form of marriage in the general list and even its inclusion in Mn. (IX-196-197), among the orthodox forms recorded in the Ancient Indian Sources of law, marked the first stage of the development of this form, the evolution of which has been so existensive.

G. *Polygamy and Monogamy*

93. In the general development of the forms of marriage we meet with another development *i.e.* with the transition from polygamy to monogamy. In this matter we read in Westermarck's *History of Human Marriage* (3. p. 104); "The examination into the causes of monogamy and polygamy makes it possible to explain why progress in civilization up to a certain point has proved favourable to polygamy whilst in its highest forms it leads to monogamy. The first tendency is largely due to economic and social circumstances—the accumulation and unequal distribution of wealth and increasing social differentiation; but it should also be noticed that the considerable surplus of females which among many of the higher savages is caused by their wars is not found at the lowest stages of civilisation, where war does not seriously disturb the proportion of the sexes. The retrograde tendency towards monogamic in the highest grades of culture, may again, be traced to a variety of causes......"

94. We find a great many examples of the transition from the system of polygamy to that of monogamy.

We see it in Babylon where the foremost Code of Hammurapi assumed that marriage should be monogamous. Among the Hebrews Deuteronomy (21.15) certainly presupposed that a man would often have two wives and the law of Exodus (20.7 sqq.) took it for granted that female slaves would become the concubines either of their owner or of his sons. The provisions of the Talmudic Law frequently refered to cases where one man contracted marriage with more than one wife (See Mielziner's *Jewish Law of Marriage and Divorce* p. 30). On the other hand from certain passages of Genesis (2.24, 4.19) and the Proverbs (31.10) and from the general tendency of the Song of Songs (by Harper 34) it has been argued that monogamy was the Biblical ideal. The same was apparent with the Ancient Greeks (Hruza: *Beiträge zur Geschichte des Grienchischen und römischen Familienrechtes*), in Rome (Willmowitz-Mollendorf's *Staat und Gesellschaft der Griechen und Romer*), among the Slavs (Ewer's *Das älteste Recht der Russen*), in Ancient Scandinavia (Weinhold's *Alt-Nordisches Leben*), Germany (*Tacitus*) and so on."[1]

95. In Ancient India too the same development can be perceived. In the *Prājāpatya-vivāha* the formula "may both of you perform together your duties" indicated that this form of marriage was in use only for monogamous marriages.

From the fact that this form of marriage was not known to Vās. and Āp. and occupied an unimportant place in the general list of the forms of marriage and as it was rarely found in the literature, it may be admitted that the monogamic idea was in ancient India still in the beginning, although it must be admitted that this form of marriage was gaining an importance as N., K., and Kām[2]. already mentioned *Prājāpatya-vivāha* in the second place of the general list of forms of marriage.

IV. CONCLUSIONS

96. Although the development of the forms of marriage quoted above cannot be proved, owing to the lack of sources,

1. Quoted from Westermarck III. p. 31.
2. From the older sources G. and B.

the impression can be reached that, per anologiam with the general development of the institution of marriage according to sociological literature and taking into account certain rules which did not recognise some forms of marriage and even prohibited them as archaic, the development of the forms of marriage from marriage by capture (*Rākṣasa-vivāha*, *Paiśāca-vivāha*), to marriage by purchase (*Āsura-vivāha*) and the marriage by sham-purchase (*Ārṣa-vivāha*), further to marriage based on the choice of a husband by the father of the girl independently of her consent (*Brāhma-vivāha*, *Daiva-vivāha*, *Prājāpatya-vivāha*) and lastly to marriage by free consent of the bride and the bridegroom (*Gāndharva-vivāha* and ordinary *svayaṁvara*) is likely to have occurred in ancient India. In the same manner we can also observe the development of the institution of dowry in ancient India as that in other countries and among other nations as well as the slow transition from the unlimited polygamic to the limited polygamic or even monogamic system.

BIBLIOGRAPHY

Adam (W), Consanguinity in Marriages ; in The Fortnightly Review. Vols. II-III. London 1865-66.

Aethelbirht (King), The Laws of ; in Ancient Laws and Institutes of England. London 1840.

Altekar (A. S.). The Position of Women in Hindu Civilisation. Benares Hindu University, 1938.

Ameer Ali (Syed), Mahommedan Law compiled from Authorities in the original Arabic. Vol. II. Containing the Law relating to Succession and Status. Calcutta 1908.

Ancient Laws and Institutes of England. London 1840.

Ancient Laws and Institutes of Ireland. Dublin and London 1865-79.

Ancient Laws and Institutes of Wales. London 1841.

Anderson (John W.), Notes of Travel in Fiji and New Caledonia, London 1880.

Andersson (C. J.), Lake Ngami. London 1856.

Do. The Okavango River. London 1861.

Aṅgira-Dharmaśāstra, text and transl. by Dutt. Calcutta 1908-09.

Āpastamba-Dharmaśāstra, Govt. Oriental Library. Mysore 1898.

Do. ed. G. Bühler, Bombay 1868-1871.

Do. ed. and transl. by Dutt. Calcutta 1908-09.

Do. transl. by G. Bühler in S.B.E. III. Oxford 1879.

Āpastamba's Aphorisms on the Sacred Law of the Hindu by G. Bühler. Bombay 1894, 1932.

Āpastamba-Gṛhyasūtra, ed. Govt. Orient. Lib. Ser., Mysore 1893.

Do. ed. M. Winternitz. Wien 1887.

Do. ed. Sudarsanacarya (Kāśi Sk. Sr. 59).

Do. Transl. by H. Oldenberg in S.B.E. XXX. Oxford.

Arbois de Jubainville (H. d'), Cours de littérature celtique, 12 vol. Paris 1883-1902.

Do. Le droit du roi dans l'épopée irlandaise, in Revue archéologique, vol. XIII. Paris 1881.

Do. La famille celtique. Paris 1905.

Arner (G.B.L.), Consanguineous Marriages in the American Population. (Studies in History, Economics, and Public Law edited by the Faculty of Political Science of Columbia University, Vol. XXXI. No. 3). New York, 1908.

Ashton-Rigby (L. E.), Marriage Customs in Cromarty ; in Folk-lore, Vol. XXVII. London 1916.

Āśvalāyana-Gṛhyasūtra, ed. Haradattacarya (T.S.S.)

Do. ed. and transl. by A. F. Stenzler, Leipzig 1864-65.

Do. transl. H. Oldenberg in S.B.E. XXIX, Oxford.

Atri-Dharmaśāstra, ed. and transl. by Dutt, Calcutta 1908-09.

Avebury (Sir John Lubbock, Lord), Marriage, Totemism, and Religion, London 1911.

Do. Note on the Macas Indians ; in Jour. Anthr. Inst. Vol. III. London 1874.

Do. The Origin of Civilisation. London 1912.

Do. On the Customs of Marriage and Systems of Relationship among the Australians ; in Jour. Anthr. Inst. Vol. XIV. London 1885.

Bachman de Mello (H.). On the Concept of Woman and Mother in the Folklore of Konkan. In Secção-Etnografia-(Folklore). n. d.

Bader, La femme dans l'Inde ancienne. Paris 1867.
Bālambhaṭṭa, being a commentary on the Mitākṣarā of Vijñānesvara, ed. by J.R. Gharpure. Bombay 1914-24.
Banerjee (Gooroodass, Sir), The Hindu Law of Marriage and Strīdhana, (Being the Tagore Law Lectures for 1878). Calcutta 1913.
Bandopadhyaya, Kauṭilya. Calcutta 1927.
Barton (H. O.), Marriage (Semitic), in Hastings, Encyclopaedia of Religion and Ethics, Vol. VIII. Edinburgh, 1915.
Barua (H. C.), Notes on the Marriage Systems of the Peoples of Assam. Sibsagar, 1909.
Bastian (A), Der Mensch in der Geschichte, 3 vols. Leipzig 1860.
Do. Die Rechtsverhältnisse bei verschiedenen Vōlkern der Erde. Berlin 1872.
Do. Über die Eheverhältnisse ; in Zeitschr. f. Ethnol., Vol. VI. Berlin 1874.
Baudhāyana-Dharmaśāstra, ed. by E. Hultzsch in Abhandlungen fur die Kunde des Morgenlandes. Leipzig 1884.
Do. transl. by G. Bühler in S.B.E. XIV. Oxford 1882.
Beaman (G. B.) On the sources of the Dharma-Śāstras of Manu and Yājñavalkya. Leipzig 1895.
Bebel (August). Woman in the Past, Present and Future. Trans. London 1885.
Bentham (Jeremy), Theory of Legislation. Trans. from the French of E. Dumont. London 1882.
Benezinger (I.), Hebräische Archāologie. Tübingen 1907.
Bergel (J.), Die Eheverhältnisse der alten Juden im Vergleiche mit den Griechischen und Rōmiṣchen. Leipzig 1881
Bernhöft (France), Altindische Familienorganisation; in Zeitchrift für Vergleichende Rechtswissenschaft. Vol. IX. Stuttgart 1890.
Best (E.), Maori Beliefs concerning the Human Organs of Generation in "Man". Vol. XIV. London 1914.
Do. Maori Marriage Customs in Trans. and Proceed. New Zealand Institute 1903. Vol. XXXVI. Wellington 1904.
Bhagwan Das, The Science of Local Organisation or the Laws of Manu, 1932-35.
Biddulph (J.), Tribes of the Hindoo Koosh. Calcutta 1880.
Billington (M. F.), Woman in India. London 1895.
Bishop (J. P.), New Commentaries on Marriage, Divorce, and Separation. 2 vols. Chicago 1891.
Blau (C.), Nachrichten über kurdische Stämme ; in Zeitschr. der Deutsch. Morgenl. Gesell. Vol. XVI. Leipzig 1862.
Bloch (I.), The Sexual Life of Our Time in its Relations to Modern Civilisation. Trans. by M. Eden Pail. London 1908.
Bloomfield (M.), 'Das Gṛhyasaṁgrahapariśiṣṭa des Gobhilaputra'; in Zeitschr. der Deutsch. Morgenl. Gesellsch. XXXV. Leipzig.
Boss (F.), The Central Eskimo; in Ann. Rep. Bur. Ethnol. VI. 1884-85. Washington 1888.
Do. The Social Organisation and the Secret Societies of the Kwakiutl Indians'; in Smithsodian Report, 1895. Washington 1897.
Bogoras (W.), The Chukchee. (Publications of the Jesup North Pacific Expedition, Vol. VII.), Leiden and New York 1904-09.
Bonwick (J.), Daily Life and Origin of the Tasmanians, London 1870.
Bradtke (P. V.), Über das Mānava-Gṛhya-Sūtra ; in Zeitsch. der Deutsch. Morgenl. Gesellsch. XXXVI. Leipzig.
Brainne (Ch.), La Nouvelle Calédonie. Paris 1854.
Breloer, (B.) Kauṭalya-Studien. Bonn 1927-34.
Do. Zum Kauṭalīya Problem. in XII 7. 1929.
Brett (W. H.), The Indian Tribes of Guiana. London 1868.
Bṛhaspati-Smṛti, ed. and transl. by Dutt. Calcutta 1909-09
Do. transl. by J. Jolly, in S.B.E. XXXIII. Oxford. 1889.
Brunner (H.), Deutsche Rechtsgeschichte. 2 vols. Leipzig 1887-92.

Do. Grundzuge der Deutschen Rechtsgeschichte, München und Leipzig, 1913.

Bruns (C.G.), Fontes juris romani antiqui. Ed. by Th. Mommsen and O. Gradenwitz. Friburgi i. B. & Lipsiae, 1893.

Bukhārī (El-), Les traditions islamiques, trad. by O. Houdas and W. Marcais. 4 Vols. (Publications de l'Ecole des langues orientales, ser. IV. Vols. III-VI). Paris 1903-14.

Burckhardt (J. L.), Arabic Proverbs. London 1830.

Burdach (C.F.), Die Physiologie als Erfahrungswissenschaft. 6. Vols. Leipzig 1832-40.

Caesar (C.J.), Opera omnia. 5 Vols. London 1819.

Caland (W.), Altindischer Ahnencult, Leiden 1893.

Cambridge History of India (Rapson etc.), Vol. I. Cambridge.

Campbell (J.), Short Summary of a paper 'On Polygamy: its Influence in determining the Sex of our Race and its Effects on the Growth of Population' read by : in The Anthropological Review, Vol. VIII. London 1870.

Cauvet, (J.), De l'organisation de la famille à Athénes; in Revue de legislation et de jurisprudence, Vol. XXIV. Paris 1845.

Chandrasekhar (S.). The Hindu Joint Family, in "Social Forces", 21,3, 1943.

Chatterjee, (H.), A critical Study of Svayaṁvara Form of Marriage, Calcutta Review, Vol. 143, June 1957, pp. 281 sqq.

Do. A Study of the Prājāpatya form of Marriage, Indian Historical Quarterly, Vol. 32, March 1956, pp. 44 sqq.

Chervin (N.), Recherches médico-philosophiques sur les causes physiques de la polygamie dans les pays chauds. Paris 1812.

Clavigero (F.S.). The History of Mexico. Trans. 2 Vols. London 1807.

Colberg (H.), Über das Ehehinderniss der Entführung. Halle. 1869.

Colebrooke (H.T.), Two Treatises of the Hindu Law of Inheritance, Calcutta 1810.

Do. A Digest of Hindu Law on Contracts and Successions, 1897-98.

Do. Miscellaneous Essays, 3. Vols. London 1873.

Conybeare (F.C.), A Brittany Marriage Custom ; in Folk-Lore, Vol. XVIII London 1907.

Corin (J.). Mating, Marriage, and the Status of Women. London & Felling-on-Tyne. 1910.

Cornish. The Hindu Joint-Family, London 1915.

Coxe (W.) Account of the Russian Discoveries between Asia and America, London 1804.

Crasselt (F.), 'Die Stellung der Ehefrau in Japan'; in Anthropos Vol. III. Wien 1908.

Crawley (A.E.), 'Exogamy and the Mating of Cousins'; in Anthropological Essays presented to E. B. Tyler, Oxford 1907.

Cunow (H.), Zur Urgeschichte der Ehe und Familie ((Ergānzungshafte zur Neuen Zeit No. 14). Stuttgart, 1912.

Do. Die Verwandtschafts-Organisationen der Australneger, Stuttgart, 1894.

Czaplicka (Miss M.A.), Aboriginal Siberia, A Study in Social Anhropology Oxford 1914.

Do. My Siberian Year. London 1914.

Dahlman (J.), Das Mahābhārata als Epos und Rechtsbuch. Berlin 1895.

Dakṣa-Dharmaśāstra, ed. and transl. by Dutt, Calcutta 1908-09.

Dargun (L.), Mutterrecht und Raubehe und ihre Reste im germanischen Recht und Leben, Breslau, 1883.

Do. Mutterecht und Vaterrecht, Leipzig 1892.

Darinsky (A.), Die Familie bei den kaukasischen Völkern. in Zeitschr. für Vergl. Rechtswissenschadt. Vol. XIV. Stuttgart 1899.

De-Marchi (Attilio), Il culto privato di Roma antica, I. Religione nella vita domestica. Milano 1896.

Deuteronomy

Dionysious pf Halicarnassus, Antiquitatum Romanarum quae supersunt, Paris 1886.

Doolittle (J.), Social Life of the Chinese, 2 Vols. New York 1867.

Durham (M.E.), High Albania, London 1909.

Dutt (R.C.), 'The Social Life of the Hindus in the Rig-Veda Period'; in the Calcutta Review, Vol. LXXXV, Calcutta 1887.

Eastman (Mrs. M.), Dahcotah; or, Life and Legends of the Sioux around Fort Snelling; New York 1849.

Ehrenfels (O.R. Baron von,) The Dual System and Mother-right in India, in Anthropos. 25-6, pp. 655-80.

Ellis (Havelock), Man and Woman, 5th ed. London & Felling-on-Tyne 1914.

do Studies in the Psychology of Sex. Vol. I. The Evolution of Modesty. The Phenomena of Sexual Periodicity. Auto-erotism. Philadelphia 1910.

do do Vol. II. Sexual Inversion, Philadelphia 1915.

do do Vol. III. Analysis of the Sexual Impulse. Love and Pain. The Sexual Impulse in Women. Philadelphia 1908.

do do. Vol. IV. Sexual Selection in Man. Philadelphia 1906

Erman (A.), Life in Ancient Egypt. Trans. London 1894.

Ewald (G.H.A. von), The Antiquities of Israel. Transl. by H.S. Solly. London 1876.

Ewers (J. Ph. G.) Das älteste Recht der Russen in seiner Geschichtlichen Entwicklung. Dorpat & Hamburg, 1826.

Exodus

Farrer (J.A.), Primitive Manners and Customs. London 1879.

Feer (L.), Le marriage par achat dans l'Inde āryenne, in Journal Asiatique, Mai-juin 1885.

Fick, Die Sociale Gliederung im nordöstlichen Indien zu Buddhas Zeit. Kiel 1887.

Formichi, Salus populi, Torino 1908.

Do. Indiani e la loro scienza politica, Bologna 1899.

Fey, Die Königliche Gewalt nach den altindischen Rechtsbüchern Leipzig 1895.

Frazer (J. G. Sir) The Golden Bough, London 1922.

Friedberg (E.), Das Recht der Eheschliessung in seiner geschichtlichen Entwicklung, Leipzig 1865.

Fries (Th. M.), Grönland, dess natur och innevanare. Upsala 1872.

Callardo (C.R.), Tierra del Fuego-Los Onas. Buenos Aires 1910.

Gans (E.), Das Erbrecht in Weltgeschichtlicher Entwickelung. 4. Vols. Berlin, Stuttgart & Tübingen, 1824-35.

Guatama-Dharmasūtra, ed. by Śrinivasacharya, Mysore 1917.

Do. ed. by A.F. Stenzler, London 1876.

Do. ed. in Poona 1910.

Do. ed. and transl. by Dutt, Calcutta 1908-09.

Do. transl. by G. Bühler in S.B.E. II. Oxford 1879.

Geary (N.), The Law of Marriage and Family Relations. A Manual of Practical Law, London & Edinburgh 1892.

Geiger (W.), Civilization of the Eastern Irānians in Ancient Times. Trans. 2. Vols. London 1885-86.

Genesis

Ghani (M.A.), 'Social Life and Morality in India'; in International Journal of Ethics, Vol. VII. London 1897.

Ghārpure (J.R.), The Rights of Women under the Hindu Law, University of Bombay, 1943.

Giddings (F.H.), The Principles of Sociology. New York 1896.

Gilder (W.H.), Schwatka's Search. London 1882.

Giraud-Teulon (A.), La Mére chez certains peuples de l'antiquité. Paris 1874.

Giraud-Teulon (A), Les Origines du mariage et de la famille. Genéve & Paris, 1884.

Gobhila-Gṛhyasūtra, ed. by Tarkalankar in Bibliotheca Indica.
Do. ed. Bhattacharya in Pal. S. Sr. 1936.
Do. transl. by H. Oldenberg in S.B.E. XXX. Offord.
Gomme (Sir G. L.), 'Exogamy and Polyandry'; The Archaeological Review. Vol. I. London 1888.
Gray (J.H.), China : A History of the Laws, Manners, and Customs of the People. 2 Vols. London 1878.
Greenstone (J. H.), 'Polygamy': in Jewish Encyclopaedia, Vol. X, New York & London, s.d.
Grimm (J.), Deutche Mythologie, 2 Vols. Göettingen 1844.
Do. Teutonic Mythology. Trans. by J.S. Stallybrass, 4 Vols. London 1880-88.
Do. DeutscheRechtsalterthümer, Ed. by A. Heusler and R. Hübner, 2 Vols. Leipzig 1899.
Gumplowicz, (L.), Zasady Sociologii, Werszawa s.d.
Haas (J.), 'Die Heirathsgebräuche der alten Inder'; in Weber, Indische Studien, Vol. V. Berlin 1862.
Hamilton (Lady A.), Marriage, Rites, Customs and Ceremonies, of the Nations of the Universe, London, 1824.
Hammurapi, The Code of Laws promulgated by.........Trans. by C. H. W. Johns. Edinburgh 1903.
Do. Die Gesetze Hammurabis in Umschrift und Übersetzung. Ed. by Hugo Winckler, Leipzig, 1904.
Hārīta-Dharmaśāstra, ed. and transl. by Dutt, Calcutta 1908-09.
Harper (A), The Song of Solomon. With Introduction and Notes by. Cambridge 1902.
Hartshorne (B.F.), The Weddas'; in The Indian Antiquary, Vol. VIII. Bombay. 1879.
Hellwald (F. von), Die menschliche Familie, Leipzig, 1889.
Hildebrand (R.), Recht und Sitte auf den verschiedenen wirtschaftlichen Kulturstufen. Vol. I, Jena 1896.
Hillebrandt (A.), Altindische Politik, Jena 1923.
Do. Über das Kauṭilya Śāstra und Verwandtes, Breslau 1908.
Do. Aus Alt- und Neu-Indien. Breslau 1922.
Do. Alt-Indien. Breslau 1899.
Do. Rituallitteratur, Vedische Opfer und Zauber, Strassburg 1897.
Do. 'Eine Miscelle aus dem Vedaritual'; in Zeitschr. der Deutsch. Morgenl. Gesellschaft. Vol. XL. Leipzig 1886.
Hiraṇyakeśi-Gṛhyasūtra, ed. by Kierste, Wien 1889.
Do. transl. by H. Oldenberg in S.B.E. XXX, Oxford.
Hodgsen (C. P.), Reminiscences of Australia, London 1846.
Holm (G.), 'Ethnologisk Skizze of Angmagsalikerne'; in Meddelelser om Grönland. Vol. X. Kjöbenhavn 1888.
Do. 'Konebaads-Expeditionen till Grönlands Östkyst 1883-85'; in Geografisk Tidskrift, udgivet af Bestyrelsem for det kongelike danske geografiske Selskab. Vol. VIII. 1885-86. Kjöbenhavn 1886.
Holtzmann (A.), Zur Geschichte und Kritik des Mahābhārata.
Hopkins (E. W.), The Religions of India. London 1896.
Do. 'The Social and Military Position of the Ruling Caste in Ancient India, as represented by the Sanskrit Epic'; in Jour. Amer. Oriental Sec. Vol. XIII. New Haven 1889.
Do. India old and new. New York 1901.
Horner (I. B.), Women under Primitive Buddhism, London 1930.
Howard (G. E.). A History of Matrimonial Institutions. 3 vols. Chicago and London 1904.
Howitt (A. W.), The Native Tribes of South-East Australia, London 1904.
Do. The Native Tribes of South-East Australia, in Jour. Roy. Anthr. Inst. Vol. XXXVII. London 1907.

Do. The Native Tribes of South-East Australia in Folk-lore. Vol. XVII. London 1906.
Hruza (E.) Beiträge zur Geschichte des griechischen und römischen Familienrechtes, 2 vols. Erlangen & Leipzig 1892-94.
Hunter (W. W.), The Annals of Rural Bengal, 3 vols. London 1868-72.
Hutereau (A.), Notes sur la vie familiale et juridique de quelques populations du Congo Belge. (Annales du Musée du Congo Belge. Ethnographie et Anthropologie. Ser. III. Documents ethnographiques concernant les populations du Congo Belge. Vol. I. fasc. 1). Bruxelles, 1909.
Hyades (P.) Ethonographie des Fuégiens ; in Bull. Soc. d'Anthr, Paris. Ser. III. Vol. X. Paris 1887.
Imperial Gazetteer of India. Oxford 1907-09.
Jacobi (H.), Über die Echtheit des Kauṭilya, SKPAW, 1912
Do. Kultur-Sprach-und Literarhistorisches aus dem Kauṭilya SKPAW 1911.
Jahn (W.), Über die kosmogonischen Grundanschauungen im Mānava-Dharmaśāstra, Leipzig 1894.
James (G. W.), The Indians of the Painted Desert Region, London 1903.
Jayaswal (K.P.), Manu and Yājñavalkya, Calcutta 1930.
Jha (G.), Hindu Law in its sources, 1930.
Johaentgen, (F.) Über das Gesetzbuch des Manu. Berlin 1863.
Johnston (Sir H. H.), British Central Africa. London 1897.
Do. George Grenfell and the Congo, 2 vols. London 1908.
Do. The River Congo. London 1884.
Jolly (J.), Recht und Sitte. Strassburg 1896.
Do. Staatliches und Soziales Leben in Indien. Stuttgart-Berlin 1922.
Do. Eine indische Rechtsquelle, in Zeitschr. fuer Vergl. Rechtsverhaeltnisre XXXVII.
Do. Beiträge zur indichen Rechtsgeschichte in Zeitschr. der deutsch. Morgenl. Gesellschaft Vol. XLIV. Leipzig 1890.
Do. Kolektaneen zum Kauṭiliya-Arthaśāstra in Zeitschr. der deutsch. Morgenl. Gesellschaft 1914.
Do. Verhandlungen der I. Hauptversammlung der Internat. Vereinigung fur vergleichende Rechtswissenchaft, Berlin 1912.
Joyce (P. W.), A Social History of Ancient Ireland. 2 vols. London 1903.
Justinian, Codex Justinianus, ed. by P. Krueger. Berolini 1888.
Do. Digesta, ed. by Mommsen, in Corpus Juris Civilis. Berolini 1889.
Do. Institutions, ed. by B. Krueger, in Corpus Juris Civilis, Berolini 1889.
Kaegi (A.), The Rig-veda : the Oldest Literature of the Indians. Trans. Boston 1886.
Kane (P. V.), History of Dharmaśāstra. Poona 1930-1941.
Kanjilal (K. C.) Hindu Early Marriage ; in The Calcutta Review. Vol. CXXVIII. Calcutta 1909.
Karandikar, Hindu Exogamy, 1929.
Karlowa (O.), Römische Rechtsgeschichte, 2 vols. Leipzig 1885-1901.
Kate (H.F.C. ten), Reizen en onderzoekingen in Noord-Amerika, Leiden 1885.
Kāthāyana-Dharmaśāstra, ed. and transl. by Dutt, Calcutta 1908-09.
Kaufmann (H.), 'Die Auin, Ein Beitrag zur Buschmannforschung'; in Mittheil. Deutsch. Schutzgeb. Vol. XXIII. Berlin 1910.
Kauṭilīya-Arthaśāstra, ed. by J. Jolly and Schmidt. Lahore 1924.
Do. ed. by Shamasastry. Mysore 1924.
Do. ed. by Ganapatisastri. Travandrum 1924.
Do. ed. by Karmarkar. Karjat 1927.
Do. trans. by Shamasastry Mysore 1924.
Do. übers, von J. J. Meyer, Leipzig.
Do. trad. M. Vallauri, in Rivista degli studii Orientali. Vol. VI. Roma 1915.
Do. Artha-Śāstrapadasūrī by Shamasastry. Mysore 1925.

Kautsky (C.), Die Entstehurg der Ehe und Familie, in Kosmos. Vol. XII Stuttgart 1882.
Keith (A. B.), Marriage (Hindu) ; in Hastings, Encyclopaedia of Religion and Ethics. Vol. VIII. Edinburgh 1915.
Keith (A.) The Antiquity of Man. London 1915.
Khādira-Gṛhyasūdra, ed. in Mysore Sanskrit Series.
Do. transl. by H. Oldenberg in SBE. XXIX. Oxford.
King (P. P.) and Fitzroy (R.). Narrative of the surveying Voyages of the "Adventure" and "Beagle." 3 vols. London 1839.
Klemm (G.). Allgemeine Cultur-Geschichte der Menschheit. 10 vols. Leipzig 1843-52.
Koenigswarter (L. J.), Etudes historiques sur le développement de la société humaine. Paris 1850.
Kohler (J.), Recht der Inder; Kultur der Geganwart; Teil II, Abt. VII, 1 Allgemeine Rechtgeschichte, 1, hälfte 1914.
Do. Indisches Gewohnheitsrechte in Z.f.v. R. VIII Stuttgart 1889.
Do. Indisches Ehe-und Familienrecht in Z. f.v. R.III, Stuttgart, 1882.
Do. Ein Beitrag zur Ethnologischen Jurisprudenz, in Z. f. v. R. Vol. IV. Stuttgart 1883.
Do. Das Recht der Australneger, in Z. f. v. R. Vol. VIII. Stuttgart 1887.
Do. Das Recht der Herero, in Z. f. v. R. Vol. XIV, Stuttgart 1900.
Do. Das Recht der Hottentotten, in Z. f.v. R. Vol.XV, Stuttgart 1901
Do. Das Recht der Marschallinsulaner, in Z.f. v. R. Vol. XIV, Stuttgart 1900.
Do. Das Recht der Papuas, in Z. f. v. R., Vol. XIV. Stuttgart 1900.
Do. Das Recht der Papuas auf Neu-Guinea, Z. f. v. R., Vol. VII, Stuttgart 1887.
Do. Die Rechte der Urvölker Nordamerikas, in Z. f. v. R. vol. XII. Stuttgart 1897.
Do. Rechtsphilosophie und Universalrechtsgeschichte, in F. von Heltzenderff, Enzyklopädie der Rechtswissenschaft in systematischer Bearbeitung, ed. J. Kohler, vol. I. München, Leipzig & Berlin 1915.
Do. Studien über Frauengemeinschaft, Frauenraub und Frauenkauf, in Z. f. v. R., Vol. V. Stuttgart 1884.
Do. Zur Urgeschichte der Ehe, in Z. f. v. R. Vol. XII. Stuttgart 1897.
Do. and Peiser (F.E.), Aus dem Babylonischen Rechtsleben. 4. Vols., Leipzig 1890-98.
Koschaker (P.), Rechtsvergleichende Studien zur Gesetzgebung Hammurapis. Leipzig 1917.
Kovalewsky (M.), Coutume contemporaine et loi ancienne. Paris 1893.
Do. La famille matriarcale au Caucase, in L'Anthropologie, vol. IV. Paris 1893.
Do. Marriage among the Early Slavs. in Folk-Lore, Vol. I. London 1890.
Do. Modern Customs and Ancient Laws of Russia, London 1891.
Do. Tableau des origines et de l'évolution de la famille et de la propriété, Stockholm 1890.
Krause (F.), In den Wildnissen Brasiliens, Leipzig 1911.
Krauss (F. S.). Sitte und Brauch der Südslaven, Wien 1885.
Kropf (A.), Das Volk der Xosa-Kaffern im östlichen Südafrika, Berlin 1889.
Laband (P.), Die rechtliche Stellung der Frauen im altrömischen und germenischen Recht; in Zeitschr. fuer Völkerpsychologie und Sprachwissenschaft. Vol. III. Berlin 1865.
Landa (D.), Relacion de las cosas de Yucatan, Ed. with French translation by l'Abbé Brasseur de Bourbourg. Paris 1864.
Lang (A.), The Origin of Terms of Human Relationship ; in Proceedings of the British Academy, Vol. III. 1907-08. London.

Do. Theory of the Origin of Exogamy and Totemism; in Folk-Lore. Vol. XXIV. London 1913.
Do. Totenism and Exogamy; in Folk-Lore, Vol. XXII. London 1911.
Do. and Atkinson (J. J.), Social Origins and Primal Law. London 1903.
Lassen (Ch.), Indische Altertumskunde, 4 Vols. Leipzig, Bonn. & London 1867-74.
Law, (B.C.), Studies in Ancient Hindu Polity, London 1914.
Do. Interstate Relations of Ancient India, Calcutta 1920.
Leist (B. W.), Alt-Arisches Jus Civile, 2 Vols. Jena 1882-96.
Do. Alt-Arisches Jus Gentium, Jena 1889.
Do. Graeco-Italische Rechtsgeschichte, Jena 1884.
Le Mesurier (C. J. R.). 'The Veddas of Ceylon'; in Jour. Roy. Asiatic Soc. Ceylon Branch, Vol. IX. Colombo 1887.
Letourneau (Ch.), L'evolution du marriage et de la famille. Paris 1888.
Do. Sociology based upon Ethnography. Trans. London 1881.
Liebich (B.), Verhüllung der jungen Ehefrau, Wiener Zeitschrift fur die Kunde des Morgenlandes, 1913, p. 474 sqq.
Maciejowski (W. A.), Slavische Rechtgeschichte. German Trans. 4 Vols. Stuttgart & Leipzig. 1835-39.
Mackenzie (Th), Studies in Roman Law, Ed. by John Kirkpatrick, Edinburgh 1886.
McLennan (J.F.), The Levirate and Polyandry: in The Fortnightly Review, new ser. Vol. XXI. London 1877.
Do. The Patriarchal Theory. London 1885.
McMahon (E.O.), 'The Sakalava and their Customs'; in Antananarivo Annual and Madagascar Magazine, Vol. IV. Antananarivo 1889-92.
Macnaghten (W. H.), Principles of Hindu Law, Calcutta 1880.
Macpherson (S. Ch.), Memorials of Service in India, London 1865.
Mahābhārata, Ed. Calcutta 1834-39.
Do. Transl. by Dutt, Calcutta 1895-1905.
Do. Transl. by P. Chandra Roy. Calcutta 1883-96.
Maine (Sir H.S.), Ancient Law, London 1885.
Do. Dissertations on Early Law and Custom, London 1883.
Do. Lectures on the Early History of Institutions, London 1875.
Major (R.H.), India in the Fifteenth Centiry, Trans. and Ed. by. London 1857.
Malinowski (B.), Baloma: the Spirits of the Dead in the Trobriand Islands. in Jour. Roy. Anthr. Inst. Vol. XLVI. London 1916.
Do. The Family among the Australian Aborigines. London 1913.
Do. Zycie dzikich, Krakôw, 1937.
Mānava-Dharmaśāstra, Ed. by W. Jones, London
Do. Ed. by V.N. Mandlik, Bombay 1886.
Do. Ed. by J. Jolly, London 1887.
Do. Ed. and Transl. by Dutt. Calcutta 1908-09.
Do. Transl. by W. Jones, London 1869.
Do. Transl. by A.C.Burnell and E.W.Hopkins, London 1884.
Do. Transl. by G. Bühler in S.B.E. XXV. Oxford.
Do. Trad. par Leiseleur Deslongchamps, Paris.
Do. Trad. par G. Strehly, Paris 1893.
Do. Transl. and notes by G. Jha, Calcutta 1920-29
Marquardt (J.) Das Privatleben der Romer. Vol. I. Ed. by A. Mau, Leipzig 1886.
Martius (C. F. Ph. con). Beiträge zur Ethnographie und Sprachenkunde Amerika's zumal Brasiliens. 2 Vols. Leipzig 1867.
Mathew (J.), 'The Australian Aborigines'; in Jour. and Proceed. Roy. Soc. New South Wales, Vol. XXIII. London & Sydney, 1889.
Do. Eaglehawk and Crew. London and Melbourne, 1899.

Mayne (J.D.), A. Treatise on Hindu Law and Usage, Madras 1900, and 10th edition by J. J. Iyengar, Madras 1938.
Mayr (A.), Das Indische Erbrecht, Wien 1873.
Medhurst (W. H.), Marriage, Affinity, and Inheritance in Chinao; in Trans. Roy. Asistic Soc. China Branch, Vol. IV. Hongkong 1855.
Meissner (B.), Beiträge zum altbabylonischen Privatrecht, Leipzig 1893.
Meyer (J. J.), Das Weib im altindischen Epos, Leipzig 1915.
Do. Über das Wesen der altindischen Rechtsschriften. Leipzig 1927.
Do. Sexual Life in Ancient India, 2 Vols., London 1930.
Do. Isoldes Gottesurteil, Berlin 1914.
Michaelis (J. D.), Commentaries on the Laws of Moses, Trans. 4 Vols., London 1814.
Mielziner (M.), The Jewish Law of Marriage and Divorce in Ancient and Modern Times, Cincinnati 1884.
Milliot (L.), La Femme musulmane au Maghreb, Paris 1910.
Mitākṣarā, ed. in Kāśi, Sk. Sr. 48.
Do. ed. in Chowk, Sk. Sr. 1914.
Do. ed. in Ben. Sk. Sr. 20.
Do. ed. in Bib. Ind. 1907.
Do. transl. in SBH with Yājñavalkya's Smṛti, Vol. II. XXI.
Do. trad. par G. Orianne, Paris, 1845.
Mommsen (T.), The History of Rome, Trans. by W. P. Dickson, 5 Vols., London, 1908.
Do. Römische Forschungen, 2 Vols., Berlin, 1864-79.
Do. Römisches Strafrecht, Leipzig 1899.
Monier-Williams, Brāhnamism and Hinduism, London, 1887.
Do. Buddhism, London 1893.
Do. Indian Wisdom, London 1893.
Moore (Th.), Marriage Customs, Modes and Courtship, and Singular Propensities of the various Nations of the Universe, London 1814.
Morgan (H. D.), The Doctrine and Law of Marriage, Adultery, and Divorce. 2 Vols., Oxford 1826.
Morgan (J. de), Moeurs, Coutumes et langages des Négritos de l'interieur de la presqu' ile Malaise ; in Société normande de Géographie, Bulletin de l'anée 1885, Vol. VII, Rouen 1885.
Moszkowski (M.), Auf den neuen Wegen durch Sumatra, Berlin 1909.
Munzinger (W.), Ostafrikanische Studien, Schaffhausen 1864.
Do. Über die Sitten und das Recht der Bogos, Winterthur 1859.
Murray (G.), The Rise of the Greek Epic, Oxford 1911.
Musters (G. C.), At Home with the Patagonians, London 1873.
Do. On the races of Patagonia ; in Jour. Anthr. Inst. Vol. I, London 1872.
Nag. Arthaśāstra et les théories diplomatiques de l'Inde ancienne. Paris 1923.
Nakajima (T.), Marriage (Japanese and Korean); in Hastings, Encyclopeadia of Religion and Ethics, Vol. VIII. Edinburgh, 1915.
Nārada-Smṛti, ed. by J. Jolly, Calcutta 1885.
Do. transl. by J. Jolly in S.B.E. XXXIII, Oxford 1899.
Nixon (F.), The Cruise of the Beacon, London, 1857.
Nowack (W.), Lehrbuch der Hebräischen Archaeologie. 2 Vols. Freiburg i.B. & Leipzig 1894.
O'Curry (E), On the Manners and Customs of the Ancient Irish. Ed. by W.K. Sullivan, 3 Vols, London & Dublin 1873.
Olaus Magnus. Historia de Gentibus Septentrionalibus. Romae 1555.
Oldenberg (H.), Das Mahābhārata, Göttingen 1922.
Do. Zur Geschichte des Indischen Kastenwesens, in Zeitschr. der Deutsch. Morgenl. Gesell. LI. 1897.
Olivecrona (S.R.D.K.), Om makars giftorätt i bo. 4th edition, Stockholm.
Ortolan (J.), Histoire de la legislation Romaine, Paris 1876.
Padfield (J.E.), The Hindu at Home, Madras 1908.

Pal (Dh. N.), Hindu Philosophy of Law in Vedic and Post-Vedic Times, 1926.
Do. The Hindu Science of Marriage, n. p., 1909.
Pāraskara-Dharmaśāstra, ed. and transl. by Dutt. Calcutta 1908-09.
Pāraskara-Gṛhyasūtra, ed. by Bohre, 1917.
Do. transl. by H Oldenberg in S.B.E. XXIX, Oxford.
Paul (H.), Grundriss der Germanischen Philologie, ed. by......3 Vols. Strassburg 1900-1907.
Petrie (T.), Reminiscences of Early Queensland (Dating from 1837). Recorded by his daughter. Brisbane 1904.
Piprek (J.), Slawische Brautwerbungs- und Hochzeitsgebräuche (Ergänzungsheft X zu Band XX der Zeitschrift für österr. Volkskunde), Stuttgart 1914.
Pischel, (R.), The Races of Man, London 1876.
Poincy (L.), Histoire naturelle et morale des Iles Antilles de I'Amérique (Ed. by C. de Rochefort, Rotterdam 1681.
Pollock (Sir F.), and Maitland (F.W.), The History of the English Law before the Time of Edward I. 2 Vols. Cambridge. 1898.
Post (A. H.), Die Anfänge des Staats und Rechtslebens. Oldenburg 1878.
Do. Studien zur Entwicklungschichte des Familienrechtes. Oldenburg & Leipzig 1890.
Do. Die Geschlechtsgenossenschaft der Urzeit und die Entstehung der Ehe. Oldenburg 1875.
Do. Bausteine für eine allgemeine Rechtswissenschaft auf vergleichend-ethnologischer Basis, 2 Vols., Oldenburg 1880-81.
Do. Der Ursprung des Rechts. Oldenburg 1876.
Do. Die Grundlagen des Rechts, Oldenburg 1884.
Do. Grundriss der ethnologischen Jurisprudenz. 2 Vols., Oldenburg & Leipzig 1894-95.
Do. Afrikanische Jurisprudenz, 2 Vols. Oldenburg & Leipzig 1887.
Pramnath Sarasvati, Hindu Law of Endowments, in Tag. Law Lectures.
Prasad, The State in Ancient India, Allahabad 1928.
Do. The Theory of Government in Ancient India, Allahabad 1927.
Rapson (E.J.), Ancient India, Cambridge 1914.
Rawlinson (H.G.), Intercourse between India and the Western World, Cambridge 1916.
Rhys (Sir J.), & Brynmor-Jones (Sir D.), The Welsh People, London 1906.
Risley (Sir H.), The People of India, Ed. by W. Crooke, London 1915.
Do. Tribes and Castes in Bengal. Ethnographic Glossary. 2 Vols., Calcutta 1891.
Rivers (W.H.R.), Kinship and Social Organisation, London 1914.
Do. Marriages (Introductory and Primitive), in Hastings, Encyclopaedia of Religion and Ethics, Vol. VIII, Edinburgh, 1915.
Do. Sociology and Psychology; in The Sociological Review, Vol. IX. London 1916.
Rivet (Dr.), Les Indiens Jibaros ; in L'Anthropologie, Vol. XVIII. Paris 1907.
Do. Review of Guevara's Psicolojia del pueblo Araucano; in L'Anthropologie, Vol. XXI, Paris 1910.
Rossbach (A.), Römische Hochzeits- und Ehedenkmäler. Leipzig 1871.
Do. Untersuchungen über die römische Ehe, Stuttgart 1853.
Roth (W. E.), Ethnological Studies among the North-West-Central Queensland Aborigines, Brisbane & London, 1897.
Sachau (E.), Muhammedanisches Recht nach Schafitischer Lehre. Stuttgart u. Berlin, 1897.
Sakellarios (Ph.), Die Sitten und Gebräuche der Hochzeit bei den Neugriechen verglichen mit denen der alten Griechen, Halle a. S. 1880.
Samuelson (J.), India, Past and Present, London 1890.
Saṁvarta-Dharmaśāstra, ed. and transl. by Dutt, Calcutta 1908-09.
Sanskaran Sastri, Fictions in the development of the Hindu Law-texts, 1926.

Śaṅkha-Dharmaśāstra, ed. and transl. by Dutt, Calcutta 1908-09.
Śāṅkha- Likhita, ed. by P.V. Kane, Poona 1926.
Śāṅkhāyana-Gṛhyasūtra, herausgegeben und übersetzt von H. Oldenburg, in Indische Studien XVI.
Do. transl. by H. Oldenberg, in S.B.E. XXIX, Oxford.
Sarkar, The Political Institutions and Theories of the Hindus, Leipzig 1922.
Śātātapa-Dharmaśāstra, ed. and transl. by Dutt, Calcutta 1908-09.
Schadenberg (A.), Die Bewohner von Süd-Mindanao und der Insel Samal, in Zeitschr. f. Ethnol., Vol. XVII, Berlin, 1885.
Schlagintweit (E.), Indien im Wort und Bild, 2 Vols., Leipzig 1880-81.
Schmidt (R.), Beiträge zur Indischen Erotik, Berlin 1922.
Do. Das Liebesleben des Sanskritvolkes, Berlin 1922.
Do. Liebe und Ehe im alten und modernen Indien, Berlin 1904.
Schotter (P.A.), Notes ethnographiques sur les Tribus de Kouytcheou (Chine); in Anthropos, Vol. VI, Wien 1911.
Schrader (O.), Family (Teutenic and Balto-Slavic); in Hastings, Encyclopaedia of Religion and Ethics, Vol. V. Edinburgh. 1912.
Do. Prehistoric Antiquities of the Aryan Peoples, Transl. by F.B. Jevons, London 1890.
Do. Reallexikon der Indogermanischen Altertumskunde, Strassburg, 1901.
Schroeder (L.), Indiens Literatur und Cultur in historischer Entwicklung, Leipzig 1887.
Do. Mysterium und Mimus im Rigveda, Leipzig 1908.
Do. Die Hochzeitsgebräuche der Esten und einiger underer finnisch-Ugrischer Völkerschaften in Vergleichung mit denen der indogermanischen Völker, Berlin 1888.
Schroeder (R.), Lehrbuch der deutchen Rechtsgeschichte, Leipzig 1902.
Schweinfurth (G.), Im Herzen von Afrika, 2 Vols. Leipzig 1874.
Do. The Heart of Africa, Trans. 2 Vols., London 1873.
Sellami (M.S.), La femme musulmane; in Revue Tunisienne, Vol. III, Tunis 1896.
Sen, Hindu Jurisprudence, general principles, in Tagore Law Lectures.
Shamasastry, Evolution of Indian Policy, Calcutta 1920.
Simons (F.A.A.), An Exploration of the Goajira Peninsula, U.S. of Colombia; in Proceed. Roy. Geog. Soc. new ser. Vol. VII. London 1885.
Simson (A.), Travels in the Wilds of Ecuador, London 1886.
Smith (V. A.), Early History of India, 1908.
Do. Oxford History of India, Oxford s.d.
Smith (W. Robertson), Kinship and Marriage in Early Arabia, Cambridge 1885.
Sohm (R.), Instytucje Prawa Rzymskiego, tlum. Taubenschlag i Koztlowski, Kraków 1926.
Do. Das Recht der Eheschliessung aus dem deutschen und canonischen Recht geschichtlich entwickelt, Weimar 1875.
Solotaroff (H.), On the Origin of the Family ; in American Anthropologist, Vol. XI,] Washington 1898.
Sorabji, Some Notes on the Adhyaksha Book II of the Kauṭilyam Arthaśāstram, Würzburg 1914.
Sparkman (Ph. St.), The Culture of the Luiseño Indians; in University of California Publications in American Archaelogy and Ethnology, Vol. VIII, Berkeley 1908.
Speiser (F.), Two Years with the Natives in the Western Pacific, London 1913
Spencer (H.), Descriptive Sociology, 8 Vols., London 1873-81.
Do. Essays: Scientific, Political, and Speculative, 2 Vols., London 1883.
Do. The Principles of Psychology, 2 Vols., London 1890.
Do. The Principles of Sociology, 3 Vols., London 1882-96.
Steele (A.), The Law and Custom of Hindoo Castes. London, 1868.
Steinen (K.), Durch Central Brasilien. Leipzig, 1886.

Do. Unter den Naturvölkern Zentral-Brasiliens, Berlin, 1894.

Sternbach (L.) Le droit de succession dans l'Inde Ancienne d'aprés l'Apastambīya-Dharmasūtra, le Baudhāyana-Dharmaśāstra, le Bṛhāspati Smṛti, le Gautamīya-Dharmaśāstra, le Kautilīya-Arthaśāstra, le livre XIII du Mahābhārata, le Mitākṣarā, le Mānava-Dharmaśāstra, le Nārada-Smṛti, le Vāsiṣṭha-Dharmaśāstra, le Vaiṣṇava-Dharmaśāstra et le Yājnavalkya-Dharmasāstra, in Bull, Intern. de l'Academic Polonaise des Sciences et des Letters, Krakòw 1938.

Do. Prawo Spadkowe w dawnych Indiach in Sprawozdania z czynności i posiedzen Polskiej Akademii Umeiejetności Krakòw 1938.

Do. 'Subjects of Law and Law of Family according to the Yājnavalkya-Dharmaśāstra' in Poona Orientalist, Poona 1941.

Do. Juridical Studies in Ancient Indian Law; 1-21, ABORI 24, 25, 26, 29; PO 8. 9, 10, 13; NIA 6, 7,; Bh. 6, 7, 11, JAOS 71, 73.

Do. Similar Social and Legal Institutions in Ancient India and in Ancient Mexico. in Poona Orientalist, Poona 1941.

Sternberg (L.), Die Giljaken ; in Verhandl. Berliner Gesellsch. Anthr. 1901 Berlin.

Strabo, Geographica, Trans. into German by C. G. Groskurd, 4 Vols, Berlin & Stettin, 1831-34.

Tacitus (C. C.), Libri qui supersunt. Ed. by C. Halm, 2 Vols., Lipzig1850-2.

Teit (J. A.), The Thompson Indians of British Colombia; in Publications of the Jesup North Pacific Expedition, Vol. I, (Memoirs of the American Museum of Natural History, Vol. II, Anthropology, Vol.I), New York 1900.

Theal (G. M.), History of the Boers in South Africa, London 1887.

Do. The Yellow and Dark-skinned People of Africa south of the Zambesi, London 1910.

Thomson (J. T.), Remarks on the Sletar and Sabimba Tribes ; in Jour. Indian Archipelago, Vol. I, Singapore 1847.

Tiller (L.), Le marriage; sa genése, son evolution, Paris 1898.

Tregear (E.), Easter Island; in Jour. Polynesian Soc. Vol. I. Wellington 1892.

Trenk (O.), Die Buschleute der Namib, ihre Rechts-und Familienverhältnisse ; in Mittheil, Deutsch. Schutzgeb. Vol. XXIII. Berlin 1910.

Trevelyan (E. J.) Hindu Family Law as administered in British India, London 1908.

Tripathi, Marriage Forms under Ancient Hindu Law, Bombay s.d.

Tupper (C.L.), Punjab Customary Law, 3 Vols., Calcutta 1881.

Turner (L. M.), Ethnology of the Ungava District, Hudson Bay Territory; in Ann. Rep. Bur. Ethnol, Vol. XI, Washington, 1894.

Uśanas-Dharmaśāstra, ed and transl. by Dutt, Calcutta 1908-09.

Vāsiṣṭha-Dharmaśāstra, ed. by A.A. Führer, Poona, 1930.

Do. ed. and transl. by Dutt. Calcutta 1908-09.

Do. transl. by G. Bühler in S.B.E. XIV, Oxford 1930.

Vātsyāyana's Kāmasūtra, ed. by Durgaprasad, Bombay 1891.

Do. tlum. na polskie, Lwow 1922.

Do. übers. von R. Schmidt, Berlin 1915.

Do. trad. par Lamairesse s.d.

Venedotian Code (the); in Ancient Laws and Institutes of Wales, London 1841.

Vidyaranya, A catechism of Hindu Dharma.

Vīramitrodaya, transl. by Gopalchandra Sarkar Sastri, Calcutta 1879. (Texts see *sub* Yājnavalkya-Dharmaśāstra).

Viṣhṇu-Dharmaśāstra, ed. by J. Jolly, Calcutta 1881.

Do. ed. and transl. by Dutt, Calcutta 1908-09.

Do. transl. by J. Jolly in S.B.E. VII, Oxford 1890.

Vyāsa-Dharmaśāstra, ed. and transl. by Dutt, Calcutta 1908-09.

Vyavahāra-Mayūkha, ed. by P.V. Kane, Bombay 1879.
Do. ed. by J.R. Gharpure, 1914-24.
Do. ed. and transl. by Vishvanath Narayan Mandlik, Bombay 1880.
Wake (C. S.), The Development of Marriage and Kinship, London 1889.
Ward (W.), A view of the History, Literature, and Religion of the Hindoos, 4 Vols., London 1817-20.
Watson (F.J.) and Kaye (J. W.), The People of India, 6 Vols., London 1868.
Weber (A.), Vedische Hochzeitspruche ; in Indische Studien, Vol. V. Berlin 1861.
Do. Über die Königwaihe, des Rājasūya, Berlin 1893.
Do. Indische Skizzen, ed. by.........
Do. Indische Studien, ed. by.........Berlin, Leipzig.
Weinhold (K.), Altnordisches Leben, Berlin 1856.
Do. Die deutschen Frauen in dem Mittelalter, 2 Vols., Wien, 1882.
Wellhausen (J.) Die Ehe bei den Arabern ; in Nachrichten von der kön. Gesellsch. der Wissenschaften und der Georg Augusts-Universität zu Göttingen, 1893, Göttingen.
Do. Reste des arabischen Heidentums. Berlin 1897.
West and Bühler, A Digest of Hindu Law, Bombay 1884.
Westermarck (E.), The History of Human Marriage, 3 Vols., London 1925.
Do. The Origin of Human Marriage, Helsingfors 1889.
Do. The Origin and the Development of the Moral Ideas, 2 Vols. London 1912-17.
Do. Marriage Ceremonies in Marocco, London 1914.
Do. L'ār, or the Transference of Conditional Curses in Morocco in Anthropological Essays presented to E.B. Tylor, Oxford 1907.
Wheeler (J. T.), The History of India, 4 Vols., London 1867-74.
Wilamowits-Moellendorff (U. von) and Niese (B.), Staat und Gesellschaft der Griechen und Römer (Kultur und Gegenwart II pt. IV. 1). Berlin, 1910.
Wilken (G. A.), Over de verwandschap en het huwalijks- en erfrecht bij de volken van het maleische ras. (Reprinted from De Indische Gids, 1883, May), Amsterdam.
Williams (Th.), and Calvert (J.), Fiji and the Fijians; and Missionary Labours among the Cannibals, London 1870.
Willman-Grabowska (H.), l'Idée de l'état dans l'Inde Ancienne, Warszawa 1933.
Willshire (W. H.), The Aborigines of Central Australia, Adelaide, 1891.
Wilutzky (P.), Vorgeschichte des Rechts. 3 Vols. Breslau 1903.
Winternitz (M.), Geschichte der Indischen Litteratur, 3 Vols. Leipzig 1909-22.
Do. Das Altindische Hochzeitsrituell nach dem Āpastambiya-Grihyasūtra und einigen anderen verwandten Werken; in Denkschriften der kaiserlichen Akademie der Wissenschaften. Philosophisch-historische Classe, Vol. XL, Wien 1892.
Do. On a Comparative Study of Indo-European Customs, with special reference to the Marriage Customs in Transactions of the International Folk-Lore Congress, 1891, London 1892.
Do. Notes on the Mahābhārata, with special reference to Dahlmann's Mahābhārata ; in Jour. Roy. Asiat. Soc. 1897, London.
Wood-Martin (W. G.), Traces of the Elder Faiths of Ireland, 2 Vols, London 1902.
Yājnavalkya-Dharmaśāstra, ed. by Vidyarnava, Allahabad 1918.
Do. ed. by Khiste and Hoshing, Benares 1886.

Do. ed. Poona 1903-04.
Do. ed. by Babu Rama, Calcutta 1869.
Do. ed. by Babu Shastri Moghe, Bombay 1892.
Do. ed. by Ganapati Sastri Trivandrum 1922.
Do. ed. by Narayana Sastri Khiste Sahityacharya, Benares 1924-29.
Do. ed. mit Transkription von H.Losch,Leipzig1927.
Do. ed. and transl. by Dutt, Calcutta 1908-09.
Do. herausg. und übersetzt von F. Stenzler, Berlin 1949.
Do. transl. by Chandra Bhasa Vidyarnava, in SBH. II, XXI and SBA III, Allahabad 1913-27.

Yama-Dharmaśāstra, ed. and trans. by Dutt, Calcutta 1908-09.

Zachariae (Th.), Zum altindischen Hochzeitsritual in Vienna Oriental Journal, Vol. XVII. Wien 1903.

Zimmer (H.), Altindisches Leben, Berlin 1879.
Do. Das Mutterrecht der Pikten und seine Bedeutung fur die arische Althertumswissenschaft in Zeitschr. der Savingny-Stiftung für Rechtsgeschichte, Vol. XV. Weimar 1894.

Zmigrodzki (M. von), Die Mutter bei den Völkern des arischen Stammes. München 1886.

XII

RECIPROCAL RESPONSIBILITY FOR DEBTS CONTRACTED BY MARRIED PEOPLE*

1. The development of women's rights to their personal property can be traced in the Indian legal literature, in the Smṛtis and in the *nibandha-s.* In Ancient India a woman was a subject which could be captured and become the property of the man who captured her (Mn. 7.96), and a wife had no right to possess her own property. According to Mn. 8.416 three persons were said to be without property : a wife, a son, and a slave; whatever property they acquired belonged to the person under whose protection they were. This rule however, is not to be found in the other Dharmaśāstra-s. Only in MBh. was this question mentioned in three or four passages, but Mn. expressly mentioned the *strīdhana* (that is a woman's property which she could freely dispose of) in 9.194 etc.[1] These two contradictory rules show once more that there existed in the Dharmaśāstra-s archaic rules of no legal value and that with the development of life and culture women in ancient India acquired for some time the right of owing property i.e. property which her husband had no right to dispose of during the marriage. That would be equivalent to the institution of separation of properties of consorts. This principle existed in the Dharmaśāstra-s, but there probably existed one exception which is to be found only in K. (152.8 sqq.). According to K. if the marriage took place in accordance with the customs of one of the lawful kinds of marriage the property of the woman could be enjoyed by the husband for three years, but if the marriage took place according to the *Gāndharva* or the *Āsura* forms of marriage the husband was obliged to return the wife's property with interest (K. 152.9); if the marriage

* Previously appeared as JSAIL. 1. in the "Annals of the Bhandarkar Oriental Research Institute". Vol. XXIV, Part III, pp. 165-74.

1. See G. Banerjee, The Hindu Law of Marriage and Strīdhana, Calcutta, 1913.

was contracted according to the *Rākṣasa* or the *Paiśāca* form of marriage the use of this property should be dealt with as theft (K.152.10).

In other words K. stated that, if the marriage was concluded according to the *Brāhma*, *Prājāpatya*, *Ārṣa* and *Daiva* forms of marriage, the wife did not have the exclusive right to dispose of her property but her husband was also entitled to make use of her property for the first three years of marriage. Only when three years of marriage had elapsed did the principle of separate property for husband and wife come into force. This can be considered as the second stage in the development of the property rights among married people. In the third stage there existed full separation of property of consorts. This rule can be found for instance in Y., N., Kāty. and others. The wife was then not obliged to pay a debt incurred by her husband and the husband that of his wife. This general principle is to be found in Y. (2.46) as well as in Vi. (6.31-2). An identical point of view is found in Kāty. (Vivādaratnākara p. 573), quoted by G. Jhā (Manu Smṛti, Notes) where it is pointed out that the husband had no right to take away or to spend a woman's *strīdhana*. Even if he took away the *strīdhana* by force he could be made to repay it with interest and in addition could even be made to pay a fine.

2. As said before, K. (152.9-10) stated that if the marriage took place according to the *Gāndharva* and the *Āsura* forms of marriage, the husband was obliged to return the whole amount with interest; if the marriage took place according to the *Rākṣasa*-and *Paiśāca-vivāha* the use of the wife's property should be considered as a theft. The distinction of the responsibility of the property of the husband and the wife seems to be quite justified. Firstly, because some Sanskrit sources condemned marriages concluded according to the *Rākṣasa* and *Paiśāca* forms of marriage and secondly, because marriages concluded according to the *Rākṣasa* or *Paiśāca* forms of marriage were based upon capture or robbery, consequently, all actions having their source in this act had also to be considered as robbery i. e. a crime. K. is the only source of law which solved this question in such an accomplished manner.

Of the other sources, Devala (quoted in VyMGh. Ch. IV. see 10, 10) mentions only briefly that "the husband had no right to enjoy the *strīdhana*. In case of improper alienation or appropriation he must repay it to the wife with interest."

3. In Ancient India, similarly, as in the Roman law, in marriage without *manus*, the principle of the separation of property was strictly applied in more progressive Dharmaśāstra-s. This principle is an indication of the highly developed juridical sense of the Indian legislators and also of the high status of women in Ancient India. Even the Code of Napoleon of 1804, did not know the principle of separate property among husband and wife.

4. It is understood that the principle of separation of property had to be applied only if the property of the married people was undivided. If the properties of the married persons were separated, the wife had the right to possess and dispose of her own property i.e. the *strīdhana*. She also had the right to lend money to her husband who was obliged to return it with or without interest in conformity with the respective agreement. This appears not only from the general structure of the *strīdhana* but also *a contrario* from Y. 2.52 which stated "that among husband and wife lending has not been allowed while the estate is undivided." The same point of view is found in Kāty. (Vivādaratnākara p. 573) which remarked that "if the husband made use of the *strīdhana* with his wife's permission and in a manner agreeable to her, he should repay it."

5. The ancient Indian sources of law also recognise certain exceptions from the principle of separate property of husband and wife. These exceptions could be divided into three categories :

1. cases where the obligation of paying for the debts existed independently of the fact which conjugal partner contracted them,
2. cases where the husband had to pay for the debts contracted by his wife,
3. cases where the wife had to pay for the debts contracted by her husband,

6. *ad* 1. When the debt was contracted for family purposes :—the first part of Y. (2.46)[2] was not to be applied; in this case a woman had to pay the debts incurred by her husband or son, a father those incurred by the son and a husband those

2. *na yoṣit-pati-putrābhyāṁ na putreṇa kṛtaṁ pitā.*

of the wife[3] because *kuṭumbā'rtho hi dustaraḥ* (household expenses are indispensable—N. 1.18). However in this sentence (as it was explained by Mit. *ad* Y. 2.46) the words "except when it is contracted for family purposes" could be understood as relating to the last half-verse : the "head of the family should pay the debt incurred for family purposes." The word *kuṭumba* means not only "family" but also "household", therefore, the expression *kuṭumbā'rtha-dṛte* should be understood as debts contracted for the household i.e. for the common housekeeping, hence conjointly responsible debts. The same opinion which was to be found in Y. 2.46 was also expressed in N. (1.12) where we read "what has been spent for the household (*kuṭumba*) by a woman (*strī*) must be paid by the head of the household (*kuṭumbin*)." The same opinion was further expressed in Vi. 38-39 where we read that "a debt which was contracted by any person (*kasyacit*)—(which might be the wife) for the benefit of the family (*kuṭumba*) must be paid by the head of the household (*kuṭumbin*)" The same opinion is to be found in Bṛh. 10.121.

7. *ad* 2. An exception to the principle that each marriage partner paid only his or her individual debts existed in the case when the husband was obliged to pay for the debts contracted by his wife. So, according to Kāty., the husband should pay a debt contracted by his wife if it was contracted for his sake when he went abroad after telling her of his intentions (Kāty. 578). Kāty. expressed the right point of view that the husband leaving his wife with her permission in order to transact some important business had to consider that the debts contracted then by his wife were his personal debts. *Conditio sine qua non*, however, was that debts contracted by the wife were for the sake of the husband and only for such debts was the husband responsible to other persons. This was the only exception of a real nature, for the other exceptions regarding the husband's duty to pay for the debts contracted by his wife were more of a personal nature. There were however some cases when the debts contracted by the wives of certain persons were paid by husbands. These were debts of a wife:

3. *na yoṣit pati-putrābhyāṁ na putreṇa kṛtaṁ pitā; dadyāt ṛte kuṭumbā'rthān na patiḥ strīkṛtaṁ tathā.* (Y. 1.46).

a. of a herdsman (*gopa*) i. e. cowherd (Mit. *ad* Y. 2.48, Y. 2.48. Vi. 6.37, Bṛh. 10.119, N. 1.19, Kāty. 568, 570).

b. of a vintner (*śauṇḍika*) i. e. a liquor-manufacturer (Mit. *ad* Y. 2.48, Y. 2.48, Vi. 6.37, Bṛh. 10.119, N. 1.19, Kāty. 568, 570).

c. of a dancer (*śailūṣa*) i. e. an actor (Mit. *ad* Y. 2.48, Y. 2.48, Vi. 6.37).

d. of a washerman (*rajaka*) i. e. a dyer of clothes (Mit. *ad* 2.48, Y. 2.48, Vi. 6.37, Bṛh. 10.119 N. 1.19, Kāty. 570).

e. of a hunter (*vyādha*)—(Y. 2.48, Vi. 6.37, Bṛh. 10.119, N. 1.19, Kāty. 568, 570).

f. of a barber (*nāpita*)—(Bṛh. 10.119) or the son of a sailor *nāvika* (Kāty. 568).[4]

These rules are explained, sometimes in a different manner, in Y., N., Bṛh. and Kāty. They could be understood in two different ways. Either the husband had to pay for the debts of the women mentioned above because the debts were contracted in his own interest (Kāty. 568, Bṛh. 10.121) i. e. in his benefit, or, because the husbands were dependent on their wives i. e. on the maintenance given by the women mentioned above (Y. 2.48, Kāty. 570, and identically N. 1.19).

It is well known that persons like herdsmen, vintners, dancers, washermen were living on the earnings of their wives[5], therefore, there was no reason to state specifically that these persons, as husbands, were not obliged to pay for the debts of their wives especially as in any case these wives maintained their husbands. It is clear that if a husband was dependent for his maintenance on his wife's earnings, then he ought to be liable for any debts incurred by her. (See Mit. *ad* Y. 2.48). Therefore, in addition to the wives of men engaged in the occupations quoted above there should be included also the wives of oilpressers (see Vīr.) and the wives of men who depended

4. Only Kāty. and Bṛh. mentioned this category of persons. Bṛh. makes use of the word *nāpita* and Kāty. of the word *nāvika*. It seems that the word *nāvika* was distorted and in both cases the expression *nāpita* would be correct. This appears also from the fact that distorted expressions were very often found in Kāty.; the "barber" belonged to a group of persons who were not much esteemed (see below).

5. See above Study VII on legal Position of Women whose Husbands live on their Earnings, par. 6-7 and Study VI on the Legal Position of Prostitutes according to Kauṭilya's Arthaśāstra, par. 29C.

upon the labour of their wives independent of their caste and occupation. This covers the wives of actors, singers, dancers, rope-dancers, mimic-players, players on musical instruments, buffoons, wandering bards, jugglers etc. because they lived on their intrigues i. e. they lived on the earnings of their own wives (K. 129.9, Mn. 3.162, Kām. 263.22-23).

8. *ad* 3. In this case the following questions must be asked : whether the debt had its origin in a specific legal action (A) or whether the distinction was inherent in the nature of the debt (B).

A. With regard to the debt which originated in a specific legal action Y. (2.49), Kāty. (546-547) and N. (1.16) were of the opinion that the wife was obliged to pay the debt incurred by her husband if :

a. the debt was contracted by herself alone,
b. the debt was contracted by her jointly with the husband,
c. the debt was agreed to by her.

From the legal point of view this rule should be considered as superfluous, since it follows from the general rules; as far as the debt mentioned *ad* (a) is concerned the obligation had its source in the general structure of the *strīdhana*. A woman possessing her own property had the right to dispose of it and to undertake obligations which would be payable from her estate. This rule resulted *a contrario* from the general principle that the wife was not liable for the debts of her husband and the husband was not liable for the debts of his wife (Y. 2.46, Vi. 6.31-32 and others). For this reason N., although aware of the cases mentioned above *ad* b and c, did not mention that the wife had to pay for the debts incurred by herself alone.

Concerning point b, there is no doubt that a debt incurred by the wife jointly with her husband had to be paid by her. For every obligation could be undertaken conjointly and the words *patyā vā saha yat kṛtaṁ* could also mean a joint liability undertaken by the husband and wife together. The obligation jointly undertaken by the husband and wife was also mentioned in N. 1.16, Kāty. 546 and K. 152.7-8. The latter Arthaśāstra contained a rule concerning the wife's obligation to pay for the debts incurred by a couple "who have brought forth twins". The qualification "who have brought forth twins", was rather superfluous, but it is possible that this phrase meant on the one hand that the wife was jointly and separately responsible for her husband's debts contracted jointly with him and on the other hand that she was responsible for her husband's debt if she gave birth to twins. Hence, in the latter case the separation of the properties of the married people should not take place.

The last half verse of Y. 2.49 and Kāty. 546 gave us an answer to the question as to whether all debts contracted by the wife jointly with her husband had to be paid by the wife. For the text runs : "A woman is not bound to pay any other (*nāmyāt*) debt". Probably the correct point of view is found in Mit. (*ad* 2.49); the opinion was there expressed that this half verse referred to the text quoted above, therefore it had to be interpreted as "except any other bad debt, i. e. incurred for spirituous liquor, vice or gambling". *Per analogiam* the same could also appear from Y. (2.47) where we read that "the son should not pay any paternal debt which was contracted for the purpose of indulging in spirituous liquor, lust or gambling."

Point c can be found in Y. (2.49) and N. (1.16). It is stated there that the wife had to pay for the husband's debt if she had agreed to it (*pratipanna*); this debt was incurred in the first instance by the husband,subsequently the wife accepted the liability for it. From the text the motive for accepting the liability is not clear, nor is the time of such acceptances fixed. Such a rule was superfluous and Mit. (*ad* Y. 2.49) affirmed that by saying : "a debt which was agreed to (*pratipanna*) on being charged or enjoined by the husband who was either dying or proceeding on a journey, such a debt of the husband should be paid." A better rendering of Mit. would seem to be "that which was assented to by the wife acting under the wish of her husband who was either dying or about to set out on a journey." Strictly speaking such as interpretation did not result from this rule, but Mit. was probably correct in using such a wide interpretation. Furthermore the rule contained in Y. 2.49 and N.1.16 was also to be found in verses546 and 547 of Kāty. Points a and b are found in Kāty. (546) and point c is found in Kāty. (547) where we read: "A wife who was told by her dying husband 'you should pay my debts' should be made to pay". It is true that Kāty. mentioned only death and not "dying as well as going abroad", but since the going abroad of the husband involved almost the same consequences as his death (see rules concerning the Law of Marriage) Kāty.'s opinion was probably correct. In any case it is probable that the husband gave orders to his wife to take over his liabilities. That would be justified as material benefits were connected with the dying or going abroad of the husband i. e. the wife would take over the estate of her husband. Kāty., however, asserted that the wife even though she did not consent to the order had to pay these debts if she had the wealth (of her husband) in her possession. Though verse 547 of Kāty. was probably an interpretation of the rule contained in N. (1.16), Y. (2.49), it seems to be consistent and can be considered as a legal interpretation of the rule contained in N. and Y.

B. More interesting, however, are the cases where the wife was obliged to pay for the husband's debts because of their nature.

That occurred when the husband used his wife's property "in case of distress" (*āpad*). This rule is found in N. 1.18 as well as Devala quoted in VyM. (Ch. IV see 10, 10.). The meaning of the word *āpad* "distress" was explained only in Y., K. and Kāty. (Vivādaratnākara p. 573).

And so the husband could make use (*gṛhita*) of the *strīdhana* (Y. 2.147) :

1. in case of famine, (*durbhikṣa*) (Y. 2.147 and K. 152.7) which meant according to Mit. (*ad* Y. 2.147) "for the maintenance and preservation of the family";

2. for duties prescribed in the Dharma-s (*dharmakārya*) (Y. 2.147 and K. 152.7) which (according to Mit. *ad* Y. 2.147) had to be performed;

3. in case of illness (*vyādhi*) (Y. 2.147 and K. 152-7);

4. in the event of being just under restraint (*samprati-rodhaka*) (Y. 2.147) or under restraint (*pratirodhaka*) (K. 152.7) which meant according to Mit. (*ad* Y. 2.147) "being under restraint or confined to prison or undergoing corporal penalties" (ident. Vīr. *ad* Y. 2.147), whilst Śūlapāṇi explained this sentence as : "what was taken by one of a higher *varṇa* causing obstruction for meals etc." (*ad* Y. 2.147) :

5. in case of need of safety measures (*pratikāra*) (K. 152.7); or

6. in case of being harassed by creditors (Kāty. Vivādaratnākara p. 573).

Y. and K. and to some degree also Kāty., quoted in Vivādaratnākara, gave an excellent explanation of the word "*āpad*"; the respective passage has to be understood in the light of this interpretation because all the cases mentioned above indicated a difficult situation for the husband, who, for want of adequate property of his own, was compelled to make use of his wife's estate.

9. The Smṛtis and Dharmaśāstras did not mention whether the husband was obliged in these cases to inform his wife of the use of her property or not, but it could be assumed that in certain cases information was not given, as for example in the event of famine; the wife was however most probably obliged to give her property to her husband if he was in prison.

The rule mentioned above indicates the highly developed legal sense of the author or authors of the Smṛti-s and Dharmaśāstra-s and relevant to certain additional duties of the wife towards her husband. In other words, if the husband had no estate of his own, the wife was obliged to maintain her husband out of her own property.

In the rule mentioned above one could see a connection with the rules contained in different Smṛti-s according to which "a debt incurred by the head of the family when unable to maintain the family or when suffering from a disease, and for the purpose of meeting a calamity (such a debt is known as *āpatkṛta* that is incurred in distress), or a debt incurred for the expenses of a daughter's marriage, or for meeting funeral expenses had to be paid by the family" (Kāty. 542.3, Mn. 8. 166, N. 1.13, Vi. 6.34). As the above mentioned rules were in principle identical, it seems that debts incurred for the expenses of a daughter or funeral expenses etc. also belonged to those obligations for which the wife had to pay from her own property, if the husband did not possess his own estate.

XIII

SUBJECTS OF LAW AND LAW OF FAMILY ACCORDING TO THE YĀJÑAVALKYA-DHARMAŚĀSTRA*[1]

I. The *Yājñavalkya-Dharmaśāstra* also called *Yājñavalkya Smṛti* is next to the *Mānava-Dharmaśāstra* in importance, authority and origin.

Compared with the *Mānava-Dharmaśāstra* the *Yājñavalkya-Dharmaśāstra* is more advanced and the legal rules are as a whole dealt with in much a shorter, clearer and more systematic way. The *Yājñavalkya-Dharmaśāstra* is closely connected with the white *Yajurveda.*

It is not possible to establish exactly where and when the *Yājñavalkya-Dharmaśāstra* was written. Various scholars give different dates for the origin of the *Yājñavalkya-Dharmaśāstra.* Some of them maintain that the *Yājñavalkya-Dharmaśāstra* was written in the third or fourth century B.C; other scholars place the date of its origin at the sixth century A.D.

It must be pointed out that it is probable that the *Yājñavalkya-Dharmaśāstra* of to-day is not a uniform work, but that various portions of it have been added later. The *Yājñavalkya-Dharmaśāstra* contains many archaic rules which perhaps had the full force of law at the time of the origin of this work but had lost force when they came to be written down and existed by side of quite advanced rules; in these rules we can perceive a considerable progress of the development of Indian law. It would also be difficult to suppose that one person could be the author of this *Dharmaśāstra* except perhaps of the second book where some system and continuity of legal thoughts is noticed. It is possible also that the second book was

* Previously appeared in the "Poona Orientalist", Vol. VII. No. 3-4, pp. 159-80. Resume of a large work left behind in Poland, in 1939, due to World War II.

1. Resume of a large work left behind in Poland in 1939 on account of war.

written down later than the first and third books in spite of the fact that we sometimes meet in the second book with many archaic rules and subsequent interpolations. We can accept that the *Yājñavalkya-Dharmaśāstra* was written down within the first six centuries. A.D.

The *Yājñavalkya-Dharmaśāstra* contains three books:—The first deals with custom, the second with law and the third with penance.

The entire material of law that we find in the *Yājñavalkya-Dharmaśāstra* is divided in manner similar to the *Mānava-Dharmaśāstra* viz., into eighteen or twenty subjects; the subjects include the following : introduction, matrimonial law and personal relations between married people, civil procedure and law of things, law of obligation and mortgages, witnesses, law of inheritance, disputes regarding boundaries, disputes regarding the owner of cattle and his servants, sale without ownership, donations, loans, slaves, corporations, conditions of employment or service, law of gambling and betting, defamation and threats, protection of nature and animals, various transgressions, other conditions of loans and selling, terms of agreement of individuals in associations, robbery, murder, incendiarism, sexual offences and adultery, miscellanea, fraud, forgery, responsibility for animals, criticism of the king, improper appeals etc. The author (or the authors) of the *Yājñavalkya-Dharmaśāstra* distinguished himself by a lucid and laconic style. He has excluded the needless padding of casuistry and has tried to avoid all the misunderstandings in interpretation and has shown an exact and systematic understanding of the conditions existing in ancient India, in spite of the fact that this exactness and systematic treatment leaves much to be desired according to modern ideas. It must be pointed out as a high merit that the author of the *Yājñavalkya-Dharmaśāstra* collected, with very small exceptions, the entire material of law in one place, that is in the second book of his work.

No *Dharmaśāstra* has had so many commentaries, and by such eminent scholars, as the *Yājñavalkya-Dharmaśāstra*. The *Mitākṣarā* stands at the head of all commentaries and law-books relating to the *Yājñavalkya-Dharmaśāstra*.

2. It has to be pointed out that the *Yājñavalkya-Dharmaśāstra*, like the other ancient Indian *Dharmaśāstra-s*, contains a great number of religious precepts, and when it contains legal injunctions they are so entwined with religious injunctions that generally it is very difficult or even often impossible to separate the legal from the religious rules. The author undoubtedly intended to regulate the religious problems first and then other problems of law.

With regard to the juridical problems, the *Yājñavalkya-Dharmaśāstra* contains a collection of customs, i. e. of rules that were more or less in use, and the practice of which was connected with the *opinio necessitatis*. These rules existed with legislative sanction ; the sanction was based neither upon civil law nor upon criminal law, but only upon religious precepts; however in the case, where law is most closely connected with rules of a religious nature, the religious sanctions must be considered as legislative orders. These rules were published. The legislator's will was announced, by the Yoga *Yājñavalkya*. Hence the *Yājñavalkya-Dharmaśāstra* should be considered from the juridical point of view, with regard to the rules regulating juridical problems, as a collection of orders with full legal authority.

According to the author's wish the rules of this *Dharmaśāstra* ought to have the force of law everywhere i. e. throughout the entire known territory of India.

3. The sixth verse of the first book of the *Yājñavalkya-Dharmaśāstra* contains the definition of 'law'. Generally speaking there is only a roll of events which are able to cause sequences and therefore can be considered as cases in law. The *Yājñavalkya-Dharmaśāstra* mentioned as sources of law many *Dharmaśāstra-s* and explained in the seventh verse of the first book how an edict of the law arose. It could be seen that in this verse the author intended to show—from the point of view of the philosophy of law—the genetic development of the law. According to this verse each idea of the law sprang from the manifestation, or Revelation, or judgment—*śruti*. The Vedas had the highest value in *śruti*. Custom was higher than tradition, but custom was understood as an event which had value from the point of view of non-sacred law. If the custom should change in a lawful rule, it had to deal with good things; the law therefore had to be *jus bonum*. That this was understood by *jus bonum* follows from the last portion of the seventh verse of the first book of the *Yājñavalkya Dharmaśāstra in fine* where it is stated : what

someone desires and which springs from a good resolution.' These words have to be understood to mean : 'That which an average educated man considers as right'. As such a man the *Yājñavalkya-Dharmaśāstra* most probably meant an educated Brāhmaṇ. It seems to proceed from this verse that the *Yājñavalkya-Dharmaśāstra* recognised the nature law (*jus bonum*) which was closely connected with an individual comprehension. According to the view of the *Yājñavalkya-Dharmaśāstra—jus bonum* differed from the nature law by reason of the fact that the former could alter according to the epoch and on the opinion of those men who influenced the sources of customs. In the ninth verse of the first book we find the following sentence concerning the legislative authority : Four persons—who know the Vedas and the *Dharma* or who know only the three sciences constituted a *Parṣat* or a *Traividya* (a legal assembly).

4. According to the *Yājñavalkya-Dharmaśāstra* there existed two kinds of persons in the sense of private law i.e. natural persons and juristic persons. A man who possessed the power of acting in his own capacity in the sence of private law was considered to be a natural person. According to the *Yājñavalkya-Dharmaśāstra* every man did possess this capacity for acting independently. This capacity depended on the caste of the man, on his age, sex, conditions of dependence and other conditions.

Corporations, unions, associations etc. i. e. a subject which possessed a similar power in acting in his own private capacity in the sense of private law but which was not a living personality, was considered as a juristic person.

5. In addition to such persons possessing full rights under civil law which depended on the caste, the *Yājñavalkya-Dharmaśāstra* recognised other persons who had no rights in law. These were slaves. Such persons could not be subjects of law of property. All that they possessed and all that they have earned during their lifetime was considered in principle the property of that person whom they were subject.

6. We find in the *Yājñavalkya-Dharmaśāstra* juristic persons of public and civil law. To the first category belonged corporations founded by the king for religious purposes. These corporations possessed their own property which did not belong to the members of the corporation. Each member of these corporations retained property previously possessed by him although he belonged to the corporation. These corporations possessed their own power of administration and were to be represented by their administrative bodies. The corporation as a whole was protected by a special set of rules.

The second kind of corporations were professional unions which possessed their own property and their own administration. The protection of the private interests of the members of these unions was the aim of these juristic persons.

7. According to the *Yājñavalkya-Dharmaśāstra* the family power covered not only obligation but also subordination to which were subject not only the minors but also those adult persons who with regard to their nature were not equal to the persons who possessed family power. Internal family relations had a great influence on the property rights of the persons who were subject to family power.

The ancient Indian law based upon the *Yājñavalkya-Dharmaśāstra* knew two kinds of family power. The paternal power which was connected with guardianship and marital power. These two powers were connected with financial responsibilities; for this purpose the *Yājñavalkya-Dharmaśāstra* recognised separately the father's financial rights and matrimonial financial rights.

8. The head of the family was the father; he was the chief of the family. The power over the children was gained either *ipso jure* on the basis of a legal act. The chief of the family gained his power over the children *ipso jure* through birth, irrespective of the fact whether the children were born in wedlock or out of wedlock. The ancient Indian law did not know the right of the father of denying the conjugal (legitimate) birth of the child born by his wife. Dependent on circumstances under which a child was born, it was placed into the relative class i. e. to one of the classes to which the children and especially the sons could, according to a schematic division be placed. To this schematic division belonged (1) legitimate sons, (2) sons born *per procura*, (3) adopted sons, and (4) sons born out of wedlock. Since according to the ancient Indian law, the principle existed *pater est quem nuptiae demonstrant*, it must be accepted that the chief of the family gained his power over the sons born out of wedlock *ipso jure*. The single exception, (but which was an apparent exception only), included children born by an unmarried girl *kānīna* because they did not fall under the power of their father but under the power of their grandfather on the side of their mother according to the principle, which could be used here by analogy, that the increase from the land belonged to the proprietor. Because the unmarried daughter was the property of her father, her son too, who had no legitimate father—was his property. The father automatically obtained the power over such a child i. e. over his grand-child.

On the basis of a legal act the power of the chief of the family was also established in two cases i.e. in the way of *niyoga* (levirate) and in the way of adoption. Therefore, the sons who were born *per procura* or who were adopted sons must be regarded as sons over whom the father gained his power by a legal act. In the first case this legal act was based on the grant of a power of attorney to a woman to bear one son for the holder of the original right (i.e. for the chief of the family); in the second case this legal act was based on the act of adoption. The power of the chief of the family extended not only to the sons but also to the wife or wives as well. The number of wives was limited and dependent on the caste of the chief of the family. The power of the chief of the family extended probably to ascendents and eventually more distant descendents and relatives. The power of the chief of the family was not illimitable. He had not the right of life and death over his 'subjects' ; he had not the right to sell these 'subjects' and even his sons and wives could own property and could dispose of it. The chief of the family exercised over his 'subjects' the power of guardianship. It was a *tutela legitima* which was connected with the financial rights of the 'subjects'.

9. The *Yājñavalkya-Dharmaśāstra* did not refer to the institution of polyandry. Yet polygamy was well known. Polygamy depended principally on the existence of caste.

The most important aim of the ancient Indian marriage was the procreation of sons.

10. We find in the *Yājñavalkya-Dharmaśāstra* twelve kinds of sons. These sons could be divided into four groups :

(A) Legitimate sons : To this category belong the *aurasa* i. e. legitimate sons and the *paunarbhava* i.e. sons of a woman who was married for the second time.

(B) Sons born by *niyoga* (*per-procura*) i. e. sons born through a third person for the chief of the family. To this category belonged the *kṣetraja* the son of the mother and the *putrikāputra* the son of the daughter.

(C) Adopted sons whose status was acquired by an act of adoption irrespective of the fact as to whether the agreement was made without payment (*dattaka*), or with payment (*krīta*) and irrespective of the fact as to whether the son was adopted with his active consent (*svayaṁdatta*) or without his consent (*apaviddha kṛtrima*).

(D) Sons born out of wedlock irrespective of the fact as to whether they were born before the marriage of the mother (*kānīna*) or after her marriage (*sahoḍha*), or were conceived before the marriage ceremony of the mother and born after the marriage ceremony (*gūḍhaja*).

Sons born *per procura* and some adopted sons could be by law sons of two fathers i.e. the real (physiological) and the legal father (*dvyāmuṣyayāṇa*).

A son had duties of religious and of legal nature. As the father had the duty of taking care of his sons, so the son had the duty of taking care of his father in such cases in which he might need this care. The same applied to the duty of the son with regard to his mother.

Not much attention was devoted in the *Yājñavalkya-Dharmaśāstra* to daughters. According to the legal rules there was no difference between daughters; Daughters, like sons, were under the power of their father and were mainly considered as their property.

In addition to sons and daughters wives were other members of the family over whom the *pater familias* extended his power.

11. We find in the *Yājñavalkya-Dharmaśāstra* a spontaneous emancipation. The *patria potestas* over the son could end by spontaneous emancipation in case the son was of age (adult) or if he married. The *patria potestas* came also automatically to an end by the death of the father. The end of the *patria potestas* over the daughter followed her marriage, since in this case the power over the girl went over from the father to her husband. *Sub patria potestate* the girl passed to *sub manu mariti*.

12. Although the son was *sub patria potestate* he had the right to have a certain private property which he could have acquired through his own action without making use of the property of his father or which he had received as a gift. The dependence of the property of the son continued chiefly till the moment of his emancipation. After that, if the father has made a division of his estate among his sons during his life-time, he freed them from his *patria pot.stas* and the sons, gained through such a division their shares of the father's own property. The sons became in this way the owners of the property assigned to them by the father and also owners of any estate which they might have acquired subsequently by their individual efforts. If the son was capable of supporting himself, and if he had no desire to share in his father's estate, the father had the right to emancipate him without making any division of his estate. In that case the father had the duty to give his son 'something'. This 'something' was the beginning of the son's private property. In this case all that the son earned after his emancipation became his private property which he had the right to dispose of, as he pleased.

Those persons who had complete control over their own property could also lose this right. This took place if these persons re-united themselves. By the act of reunion the joint-family was formed. The joint-family rested on the community of living together, of having meals together, of sharing religious observances, of sharing property together, etc.

We must understand by the expression community of property, the community of estate which became the property of every co-heir who gave his share to the joint-family. The estate became the exclusive property of all co-heirs who then had the right to utilise this estate in common.

This community of estate meant that all the members of the reunited famity should dwell in the same house, take their meals together, perform their divine service at the same time, and enjoy their property in common.

The individual property became property of all the members of the community i. e. the property of the joint-family. All property acquired subsequently by any member of the joint-family did not become the property of the person who had earned it but the property of the joint-family as such. On the other hand all individual expenses of the members of the joint-family became expenses of the whole joint-family.

13. It is probable that a woman could not have a private property until she got married. The woman was always and exclusively *sub patria potestate*, *sub manu mariti*, or under the guardianship of her sons, but could have a private fortune after marriage. Then the *strīdhana* came into existence.[2]

14. The legal position of women was not fully clarified in the *Yājñavalkya-Dharmaśāstra*. During the life of her husband she was under his power; although the mother was a dependent person her position was very high, specially if she bore sons. Many legal acts could be concluded only with her consent; she, like the father, had to be esteemed and honoured. It was probably not necessary that the mother should automatically lose her position as regards her children in the case of the death of her husband and especially when the children were not adults. But if the children were adults the mother automatically lost her power over them and she came under the power of her sons. Yet the children were obliged to honour her and eventually to support her.

15. According to the *Yājñavalkya-Dharmaśāstra* some persons who were free persons could come under the control of another person i.e. of the curator. This applied to the *tutela* of a *mente captus* or of a cripple.

16. The marriage which was according to the *Yājñavalkya-Dharmaśāstra* principally polygamic and exogamic had as its aim procreation of sons. The persons in the sequence set forth in the *Yājñavalkya-Dharmaśāstra* had the power over unmarried girls but had also the duty of arranging for her marriage.[3] In the event of their failure to do so, the girl could marry on her own initiative.

17. The agreement of the betrothal which was in principle concluded between the father of the girl on one side, and probably with the father of the boy on the other side, was nothing more than a solemn promise to carry out the marriage at some time in the future; this promise was not unconditionally

2. Compare paragraph 23 below.

3. Father, grand-father, brother, *sakulya* and mother. In fault of these persons the king could have the power over the girl.

binding. There existed a possibility of breaking this agreement and the consequences of such a break were regulated by law. Only if the agreement of the betrothal was broken *ex injusta causa* some compensation or penalty were attached to such an act. The conclusion of the agreement of betrothal did not bind both parties to the future marriage.

The father was however obliged at the time of the agreement to state any defects existing in his daughter, because if he did not do so he was liable to pay a penalty which was equivalent to giving a reward to the discoverer of the defects. These defects could cause an *error in qualitate in personam.* This error was considered as a *justa causa* for breaking the agreement.

According to the *Yājñavalkya-Dharmaśāstra* the agreement of the betrothal could be broken *ex justa causa* also in the case when the father found a 'better' suitor for his daughter. It was understood that a 'better suitor'; was a boy who had better qualities than the first suitor who might have faults or whose conduct might be considered as not being good.

The consequences of the breaking off of the agreement by the father or guardian *sine causa* or *ex iniusta causa* were that in addition to the penalty (which was the same as the penalty in the case of theft[4]) another penalty was to be paid i. e. the duty of compensation for the financial loss and psychical damage or compensation for expenses incurred by the other party etc.

It must be admitted *per analogiam* that the duty to compensate for the damage to pay the penalty; etc. was not only imposed on the father or guardian of the girl who has broken the agreement (as it was stated in the *Yājñavalkya-Dharmaśāstra* probably for simplification) but also on the suitor who *sine causa* or *ex injusta causa* has broken the agreement.

If neither of the parties was culpable for not completing the marriage after the conclusion of the agreement of the betrothal the two parties concerned were obliged to return the gifts received in connexion with the agreement.

18. It is difficult to find in the *Yājñavalkya-Dharmaśāstra*, regular *impedimenta matrimonii.* All legal rules which we find in this *Dharmaśāstra* only give counsels either for the bride or

4. *Mutilatio* joined with the duty to render the stealed objects.

for the bridegroom, such as what kind of boys and what kind of girls should not be married. The *Yājñavalkya-Dharmaśāstra* did not know sanctions in the sense of private law in case of non-observance of these 'counsels'. But in some cases sanctions did exist, but not in the sense of private law; they existed in the form of religious orders. Only these 'counsels' could be considered as *impedimenta matrimonii*, because according to ancient Indian law the rules in the sense of private law were closely connected with the rules in the form of religious orders. In this way we find in the *Yājñavalkya-Dharmaśāstra impedimenta impedientiae* i.e. such *impedimenta* which did not cause the invalidity of the marriage, but which imposed (on the persons who did not observe these *impedimenta*) the duty to give sacrifices, or penances etc. Following *impedimenta matrimonii* could be recognised as *impedimenta impedientiae* : *impedimentum consanguinitatis* (of consanguinity of close blood relationship), *impedimentum castae* (of caste), *impedimentum prioritatis castae mulieris* (of the priority of the caste of the woman), *impedimentum impotentiae* (of impotence), *impedimentum aetatis* (of age), *impedimentum deficientis virginitatis* (of the lack of virginity on the part of the girl), *impedimentum prioritatis aetatis in familia* (of the priority of the age in the family).

Some *impedimenta* could be considered as *impedimenta dirimentiae* but the existence of such *impedimenta* could cause rather the dissolution of the marriage but not effect the invalidity of the marriage. Probably the dissolution took place on account of the following *impedimenta* : *impedimentum consanguinitatis*, *impedimentum impotentiae* and *impedimentum deficientis virginitatis*.

It is not possible to divide the *impedimenta matrimonii* into *impedimenta publica* and *impedimenta occulta* or into *impedimenta dispensabilitia* and *impedimenta indispensabilia*. But it is possible to divide the *impedimenta* into *impedimenta relative* and *impedimenta non relative* and into *impedimenta minoris gradus* and *impedimenta majoris gradus*. This last division could be particularly noted in the case of *impedimentum consanguinitatis*.

As regards other 'counsels' it ought to be admitted that the non-observance of these 'counsels' had not caused any legal consequences. In this case the *Yājñavalkya-Dharmaśāstra* must be considered as a book of counsels for marriage ; it was very pedantic and perhaps the most pedantic book of admonition on marriage of all the *Dharmaśāstra-s.* The counsels could be divided in counsels regarding the external faults of the parties and regarding other faults; the first mentioned kind of faults was more often mentioned.

To the *impedimenta relativa* belonged the *impedimentum consanguinitatis*, *impedimentum castae* and *impedimentum prioritatis aetatis in familia.*

To the *impedimenta non relativa* belonged the *impedimentum deficientis virginitatis* and the *impedimentum aetatis.* The *impedimentum impotentiae* was principally an *impedimentum nonrelativum* but it ought to be admitted that the *impedimentum impotentiae* over a certain woman was also *impotentia* which caused an *impedimentum matrimonii.* For this reason the *impedimentum impotentiae* could be also grouped among the *impedimenta relativa.*

In the case of the *impedimentum consanguinitatis* the parties could not be both *sapiṇḍa* or *asamānārṣa gotrajam.* The *Yājñavalkya-Dharmaśāstra* recognised by the word *sapiṇḍa* or by persons joined by. the relationship called *sapiṇḍa,* all these persons who were descended from one ancestor, irrespective of whether the relationship was direct or collateral. The relationship was up to the fourth degree (inclusive) or up to the sixth degree (inclusive) in the case of male ancestry. By the expression *asamānārṣa gotraja* the *Yājñavalkya-Dharmaśāstra* understood such persons who were descended from a common *ṛṣi* or were descended from the same *gotra.* In the first case this *impedimentum matrimonii* was equal to the Roman *impedimentum consanguinitatis maioris gradus,* and in the second case to the Roman *impedimentum consanguinitatis* or better *affinitatis minoris gradus.*

The *impedimentum castae* ought to be divided into separate two *impedimenta* i.e. (a) the *impedimentum prioritatis castae mulieris* (of the order of the priority of the caste of the woman) and (b) the proper *impedimentum castae.* The *impedimentum prioritatis castae mulieris* rested on the inadmissibility of marriages in which the woman belonged to a higher caste than the man. The proper *impedimentum castae* rested on the inadmissibility of marriages between a *dvija* (i.e. a member of the *Brāhmaṇa, Kṣatriya,* or *Vaiśya castes*) and a *Śūdrā*-woman.

The *impedimentum prioritatis aetatis in familia* rested on the interdiction of marriage of a younger brother before his older brother.

If a man was impotent even though his impotence was in regard to a certain woman, the *impedimentum impotentiae* was recognised. Impotence should have existed before the marriage and should be an *impotentia generandi*.

The *impedimentum aetatis* could be also divided into two kinds. It could be either an *impedimentum prioritatis aetatis* on the part of the bride or on the part of the bridegroom. In the first case the bride was older than the bridegroom, in the second the bridegroom has not reached the minimum age necessary for the marriage which was set forth in the *Dharmaśāstra-s*.

The *impedimentum deficientis virginitatis* could be considered rather as a counsel than as an *impedimentum matrimonii*. This *impedimentum matrimonii* rested on the principle that only a girl who had not previously belonged to another man could be married.

The *impedimentum exterioris et interioris defecti* (of physical and non-physical defects) should also be regarded as a counsel rather than a prohibition. The *Yājñavalkya-Dharmaśāstra* gave rather a description of an ideal woman and of an ideal man for marriage than set forth *impedimenta defecti*.

19. The forms of marriage (*vivāha*) depended on (1) the circumstances which accompanied the marriage; (2) the participation of the parents or guardians of the two parties in the marriage; and (3) some financial conditions. The forms of marriage described in what manner the marriage was concluded. We find in the *Yājñavalkya-Dharmaśāstra* similarly as in other *Dharmaśāstra-s* eight or nine forms of marriage. The differences between these forms of marriage were very slight and the marriage produced in each case almost the same legal consequences. The division of the forms of marriage into eight or nine was not essential according to the *Yājñavalkya-Dharmaśāstra*. From the purely legal point of view the *Yājñavalkya-Dharmaśāstra* distinguished only two forms of marriage i.e. the orthodox forms of marriage and other forms of marriage.

The historical development of the forms of marriage cannot be clearly seen from the *Yājñavalkya-Dharmaśāstra*. We find there first the form of marriage by capture; it was the *rākṣasa-vivāha* and the *paiśāca-vivāha*. The *Yājñavalkya-Dharmaśāstra* distinguished in this case between girls captured against their will (1) by the use of force only, or (2) by the use of cunning. In the first case the *rākṣasa-vivāha* and in the second the *paiśāca-vivāha* occurred.

The forms of marriage by purchase were represented by the *āsura-vivāha* (pure purchase) and the *ārṣa-vivāha* (sham purchase). In the second case it was a sham-purchase because the price paid for the girl bore no relation to her value (the price paid was symbolical and was always the same—an ox and a cow). In addition, the price had to be "repaid" to the buyer, i.e. to the suitor. The father or the guardian of the girl had to repay the price received as if he himself gave a dowry; in reality this dowry was given for that purpose by the future husband (son-in-law) himself.

Those forms of marriage which included (1) the choice of a husband for the girl by the father or by the guardian, and (2) the duty to give to the girl a dowry or endowment—were divided into three different forms of marriage. These depended on the fact as to who took the initiative with respect to the marriage. The following forms of marriage belonged to this group of forms of marriage : the *Brāhma-vivāha*, the *Daiva-vivāha* and the *Kāya-vivāha*. The *Brāhma-vivāha* was the highest form of marriage not only in this group of forms of marriage, but in general.

The last group of forms of marriage was that in which there existed a free agreement between the girl and the man without the participation of the parents or guardians. This form was represented in the *Yājñavalkya-Dharmaśāstra* by the *Gāndh rva-vivāha*. As predecessor of this form of marriage the *Svayaṁvara* (self-choice) could be recognised.

The *rākṣasa-vivāha* depended on the forcible rape of a girl by a man who intended to take her as his wife. The rape was understood to have taken place against the will of the father, or of the guardian with whom the suitor had to fight. Naturally, according to this form of marriage the marriage was carried out without the intervention of the father or of the suitor.

According to the *paiśāca-vivāha* the suitor profited by the unconsciousness of the girl, had sexual intercourse with her, in principle, against her will and afterwards captured her. The marriage concluded according to this form took place without the consent of the girl and of her father (guardian). Because this form of marriage was based on a crime it was considered as a prohibited form of marriage.

The *asura-vivāha* depended on an agreement of purchase made between the suitor and the person who exercised the actual power over the girl. Therefore this form of marriage was similar to the Roman *coemptio uxoris*. The initiative for this form of marriage lay in the hands of the suitor; the girl had no right to choose her husband for herself. The choice did not depend on any good qualities of the suitor but primarily on his financial position and on the price he was prepared to pay for the girl. This form of marriage was considered as an illegal form of marriage.

In the *ārṣa-vivāha* the suitor gave to the person who exercised the power over the girl a gift, in order that this gift be returned to the girl. In this form of marriage, therefore, a sham purchase took place. The gift consisted principally of a cow and an ox. In this form of marriage the marriage depended not on the choice exercised by the girl but on the choice of the suitor; it was concluded with the agreement of the father or of the guardian of the girl. In the first place the conclusion of the marriage depended on the choice by the suitor and afterwards on the consent given by the father or by the guardian. In this form of marriage an agreement of purchase was not concluded.

The *brāhma-vivāha*, the *daiva-vivāha* and the *kāya-vivāha* were along with the *ārṣa-vivāha* the orthodox forms of marriage. In these forms of marriage the choice of a suitor for a girl depended on that person in whose custody she lived; this person had the duty of endowing the girl. The difference between these three forms of marriage was very slight. In the *brāhma-vivāha* the suitor ought to be a member of the Brahma-caste and ought to have the best qualities. The initiative for the marriage lay with the father and not with the suitor. On the contrary in the *kāya-vivāha* the initiative for the marriage lay with the suitor but the conclusion of the marriage depended on the consent of the father or of the guardian of the girl. It was necessary to pronounce a special formula in which the parties were summoned to share in common joy and mourning as well as to execute religious duties. In the *daiva-vivāha* the suitor had to be a *ṛtvij* i.e. a sacrificer.

According to the *gāndharva-viv āha* the persons of different sexes who loved each other made a joint union by their own choice. In other words this form of marriage depended on the understanding between a man and a woman who loved each other. This form of marriage was concluded after a solemn wedding ceremony without the agreement of the parents and could be performed against their will.

The *svayaṁvara* (self-choice) depended on the right of the girl alone to choose a husband for herself ; the declaration of the will of the person who had custody over the girl was not necessary because she received the right of self-choice, as if a penalty, on account that her father or her guardian had not accomplished their duty i.e. to marry her after her puberty. The *svayaṁvara* was, properly speaking, not a special form of marriage, and the permission given in some cases to the girl to choose a husband for herself was probably contained in the *Yājñavalkya-Dharmaśāstra* in order to show in what cases a girl could legally marry according to the *gāndharva-vivāha*.

20. The wedding-ceremony was described in the *Yājña-valkya-Dharmaśāstra* only occasionally. Its nature depended on the caste of the parties concerned.

21. It is very difficult to give on the basis of the rules found in the *Yājñavalkya-Dharmaśāstra* as well as those found in the all ancient Indian *Dharmaśāstra-s* a proper legal definition for the dissolution of the marriage. As a rule the dissolution of the ancient Indian marriage took place by the abandonment or expulsion of the wife. This was equal to the Roman legal institution of *repudiatio uxoris*. Such a *repudiatio uxoris* took place without any special ceremony.

It appears from the rules found in the *Yājñavalkya-Dharmaśāstra* that not in every case did the proper *repudiatio uxoris* take place; in some cases the husband had the right to discard his former wife and to marry another girl, in consequence of such an act the first wife lost her privileged position.

Although the dissolution of the marriage by *repudiatio uxoris* was not made difficult it was not often used. The principal reason for this was the institution of polygamy. Thus, the husband could, instead of repudiating his first wife, take another woman as his wife. This act could be more advantageous to him, since in the case of the *repudiatio uxoris* he was obliged to support his first wife and to give her a special share of his estate.

We find in the *Yājñavalkya-Dharmaśāstra* cases of the dissolution of the marriage *ex justissima causa*, *ex justa causa* and *sine causa*. Adultery of the wife was considered as a motive for the dissolution of the marriage *ex justissima causa*. The *justae causae* which caused the dissolution of marriage could be divided into (1) motives independent on the will of the wife, and (2) motives dependent on the will of the wife. To the first group of motives belonged : (1) sterility, (2) bearing of daughters only and (3) illness. To the second group; (1) drinking of liquor, (2) sly character, (3) prodigality, (4) harsh manner of speech, and (5) misogamy. The dissolution of the marriage *sine causa* occurred in cases when the woman did not possess those attributes which caused the dissolution of marriage, or rather in cases when the marriage was dissolved by the husband neither *ex justa causa* nor *ex justissima causa*.

The consequences of the dissolution of the marriage depended on, whether this act took place *ex justissima causa*, or *ex justa causa*, or *sine causa*. If the dissolution of the marriage took place (1) *ex justissima causa* the woman had to receive the most essential necessities of life only, if (2) *ex justa causa*—common, necessities of life, if (3) *sine causa* the husband had to give his former wife a third part of his estate, and if he had no estate he had to provide for her in a suitable manner.

If the husband had married another woman in addition to his first wife he was obliged to give the abandoned wife as much as he spent on the new marriage, even if the dissolution of the first marriage did not take place.

The *Yājñavalkya-Dharmaśāstra*, differently as the *Mānava-Dharmaśāstra*, *Nārada-Smṛti* and *Kauṭilīya's Arthaśāstra*, set forth that the wife had the same right as the man to demand the dissolution of the marriage in the case of the common antipathy of the husband and wife.

22. The relations between the husband and the wife could be divided into (1) duties of the husband and the wife towards each other, and (2) common relations of husband and wife towards each other.

The *Yajñāvalkya-Dharmāśastra* regulated this problem from the point of view of the husband. The husband was the lord of his wife ; he had the right to abandon her *sine causa*. We do not find in the *Yājñavalkya-Dharmaśāstra* this principle which can be found in the *Mānava-Dharmaśāstra* and *Bṛhaspati-Smṛti* that the wife was the half of her husband, and therefore that she possessed the same rights as her husband. The *Yājñavalkya-Dharmaśāstra* did not describe the rights of the wife, but on the contrary almost exclusively her duties. The first duty was the duty to be chaste; this duty did not apply to the husband. This duty of the wife was so strict that during the absence of her husband the wife was not permitted to amuse herself and to dress herself; she was even prohibited from laughing, from going to foreign houses and from joining gatherings of other people; after the death of her husband she was prohibited from marrying again, while the husband was advised to marry a second wife after the death of his first wife. The problem of the deplorable position of widows was connected in the *Yājñavalkya-Dharmaśāstra* with the wife's duty to be always faithful to her husband. The legal position of widows in the *Yājñavalkya-Dharmaśāstra* was however not so deplorable as was the case in the *Viṣṇu-Smṛti* (20.39, 25.14), in the *Bṛhaspati-Smrti* (25.14), or in many other sources of law.

The duties of the wife towards her husband could be classified into the following groups : (1) the duty of being faithful to the husband, (2) the duty of obedience, (3) the duty of housekeeping, (4) the duty of esteeming the husband and his kinsmen, (5) the duty of being of good conduct and of making the life of her husband pleasant.

Besides these "duties" the wife had other duties (and rights) of a religious nature, especially the duty of performing religious ceremonies.

In the *Yājñavalkya-Dharmaśāstra* we do not find similar rules about the duties of the husband to the wife. The existence of such duties could be seen only from the rules which we find in the chapter which deal with dissolution of marriage. Upon dissolution of marriage the wife lost these previleges to which she had the right during the time of her marriage ; these rights or these duties of the husband to the wife could be classified into following three groups i.e. (1) the duty of protection, (2) the duty of support, and sometimes (3) the duty to be faithful to the wife ; this last duty was in principle not obligatory.

23. As regards the personal property of the consorts we should distinguish whether the property belonged to a joint-family or not.

If the family was joint and there was no partition of the estate, then the matrimonial community of personal property existed.

If the family was not joint, the matrimonial property was —as a rule—separated. At this time the wife had the right to her own personal estate (*strīdhana*); she had the right to administer it. This *strīdhana* after her death automatically belonged not to her husband, but to her own progeny, and in the case of lack of descendents (in some cases only) to her husband.

The *strīdhana* was made up of what the girl has received as matrimonial gifts, and what she received subsequent to her marriage from a line of persons given in the *Yājñavalkya-Dharmaśāstra*, or from her husband (for instance, as compensation for his abandoning her, or in case of *repudiatio uxoris*). This *strīdhana* could include the estate obtained by inheritance, the *śulka* etc. The *strīdhana* as represented in the *Yājñavalkya-Dharmaśātra* was at the highest stage of development because it could consist in the greatest number of objects; in addition, the husband had no right (subject to exceptional cases) to use the *strīdhana* or to administer it, because the wife had an unlimited and a limitless right i. e. the right of property. This *strīdhana* was protected by law, it could not be acquired by long possession.

The wife was not under the obligation to use her private estate for her living expenses and she was not under the obligation to contribute towards the living expenses of her husband or of her children. How widely the exclusive right of property of the wife was extended, can best be seen from the sentence which we find in the *stanza* 147 of the second book of the *Yajñavalkya-Dharmaśāstra*. According to this *stanza* (1) the husband had—as a rule—no right to the use of the *strīdhana* and if he has used the *strīdhana* against these rules he was obliged to repay or to restore it.

The last rule did not apply in the case of *vis major*, or if the husband did not possess his own private estate which was sufficient to meet the extraordinary cases. These cases included the following : (1) provision in the case of famine, (2) execution of religious acts, (3) supply of expenses in the case of an illness, (4) own maintenance during his stay in a jail, (5) the maintenance of the family.

Debts had to be repaid only by the party who has incurred the debts. Only if the debts were incurred by the husband and wife together was the duty of repaying it a joint one. For this reason the husband had no obligation to repay the debts incurred by his wife, and vice versa, provided that the debts (1) were not incurred together, and (2) were not incurred for the whole family or on behalf of the whole family.

XIV

LEGAL RELATIONS BETWEEN EMPLOYERS AND EMPLOYEES IN ANCIENT INDIA*

I. INTRODUCTION

1. A. Ancient India is a country of contradictions. The sources of law on which this study is based were written down probably between the fifth century B.C. and the fourth century A.D.[1] They give us a contemporary description of several worlds, perhaps of several epochs, probably a contemporary picture of oldest, old and actual epochs, ('actual epoch' relating to the life-time of the authors of these sources). As far as, for example the forms of marriage were concerned, every source described at the same time all its forms—the most primitive ones (capture), the later ones (purchase), the more advanced ones (sham purchase), and the most advanced ones (contracted with the mutual agreement of the parties).

In a similar manner the sources described the working conditions in ancient India. The sources of law treated in this study contain only sporadic and chaotic laws and rules concerning the working-rates and, especially, the agreements between employers and employees.

As an employee one might consider e.g. a building contractor and as a worker a carpenter, or a qualified worker who brought timber to the building place. Employers and employees were only rarely mentioned in the sources of law.

The aim of this study is to collect the different rules, dispersed and scattered at various places and to present to the reader a juridical system concerning the working condi-

* Previously appeared as JSAIL. 2 in the "Poona Orientalist", Vol. VIII, Part I-II, pp. 100-9; Vol. VIII, Parts III-IV, pp. 1-24.

1. Āpastambīya-Dharmasūtra, Bhaudhāyana-Dharmaśāstra, Bṛhaspati-Smṛti, Gautamīya-Dharmaśāstra, Kauṭilīya-Arthaśāstra, Mānava-Dharmaśāstra, Nārada-Smṛti, Vāsiṣṭha-Dharmaśāstra, Viṣṇu-Smṛti.

tions, as they are reflected in ancient Indian Dharmaśāstra-s and Arthaśāstra-s.

B. The Dharmaśāstra-s and Arthaśāstra-s knew five kinds of persons obliged to serve (*śuśruṣaka*). These persons were classified according to whether the *śuśruṣaka* performed pure or impure work. N.[2] considered as impure work the following—sweeping the gateway, the privy, the road and the place for rubbish, shampooing of the private parts of the body, gathering and putting away food scraps, ordure, and urine, rubbing the master's limbs, when desired. All other kinds of work were considered as pure work.[3] Impure work was done by "slaves". Nevertheless the slaves could not be considered as employees. Slaves evidently could neither conclude a contract with his master nor agree upon the reward, because according to the ancient Indian sources of law, the slave was not able to command himself and never received a reward ; a slave was not his own master.[4,5,6]

It appears from the sentence[7] cited below, that the main contents of the working-agreement was : the determination of the scale of the reward the worker had to receive from the employer. It is also clear that such an agreement between the proprietor as an employer and the slave as an employee could not be concluded. The pure work was done by the real workers, and the ancient Indian sources of law knew four kinds of those workers. The workers were named *karmakara* that is workers for another person. We find in N.[8] a statement concerning them : "A Veda student, an apprentice, a hired servant and fourthly : an official, these must be regarded as labourers (i.e. who work for salary) : *bhatar*..."

We find a more precise classification of the workers[9] in Bṛh.[10] We read there : 'They are pronounced to be of many sorts : according to their particular caste and occupation; and fourfold,

2. N. 5. 6-7.
3. N. 5, 7.
4. See K. 3. ch. 13.
5. N. 1.29.
6. Therefore this classification is valueless from the legal point of view.
7. See below.
8. N. 5.3.
9. *Pars pro toto.*
10. Bṛh. 15.4.

according as they serve for science, human knowledge (or skill), love or gain.' This division has probably to be understood that the workers were particulary divided according to their caste and employment ; within this classification the workers were again divided according to their general knowledge of special sciences, their predilections and abilities. Only the first classification had importance from the legal point of view, while the subdivisions could have consequences only for the wages due for their work.[11]

As regards the *karmakara*, the statement of dependence was the characteristic criterion for all those "who were working in favour of another person."[12] Neither a Veda student, nor an apprentice could be considered *sensu stricto* as a worker. The fact that the worker received the reward from the employer was the indispensable criterion for the quality of a worker. In consequence neither the Veda student, nor the apprentice nor other persons mentioned in some Dharmaśāstras, such as a *ṛtvij* or a *guru* or a merchant etc. could be considered workers from the legal point of view. Therefore the rules found in the Dharma- and Arthaśāstra-s concerning such persons are not discussed in this study.[13] This is also the case with regard to courtezans, who were often mentioned in the sources of law as workers. As it appears especially from K.[14] courtezans[15] could not be considered free persons who were able to dispose of that which they earned.[16] Therefore they could not be counted as workers.[17] Evidently the agreement concerning the salary could not be considered as a contract of service[18] despite the agreement concerning the salary mentioned in the sixth book of N., where

11. N. 5.22.

12. See par. 2.

13. Concerning *ṛtvij* see : K. 3. ch. 14; concerning *guru* : N. 5.8. 21; Vi. 18; concerning the trader : K. 3. ch. 13, N. 22; concerning the carrier : Y. 2. 197-8 and other.

14. K. 2. ch. 27.

15. See above study VI on Legal Position of Prostitutes according to Kauṭilya's Arthaśāstra, par. 1-6.

16. It results from that, that they were obliged to announce their earnings to the *gaṇikā'dhyakṣa* and that he was obliged to enter the earnings in the books. See fn. 15.

17. However some characteristic peculiarities concerning the contracts with courtezans will be discussed below, because sometimes they could be applied *per analogiam* to general contracts of service.

18. N. 6.20-22.

the cases of the non-payment of wages were enumerated;[19] all the criteria of a contract of service were missing there.[20]

According to the Dharmaśāstra-s there were three categories of *bhatar* : the highest, the middlemost and the lowest.[21] The Kṣatriyas belong to the highest class,[22] the cultivators of the soil to the middlemost,[23] and the porters to the lowest class.[24] By reason of what was said before, the Kṣatriyas can hardly be considered workers from the legal point of view, so that only the cultivators of the soil, the watchmen and the porters, in addition to the specifically mentioned herdsmen,[25] had the quality of true workers.

We find in the Indian sources of law only some kinds of enumerated workers; these enumerated workers were not the only ones known to ancient Indian law. It appears firstly from the rules contained in Bṛh. that servants employed in household work were workers,[26] and secondly from N. that the *kauṭumbika* i. e. the general family servants were appointed to manage the property of the family and to superintend the household;[27] for that reason they must be regarded also as labourers. Several sources of law mentioned different persons engaged in different occupations as workers. Not only those persons mentioned in the sources, but also those not mentioned therein ought to be considered as workers when they were in a state of dependence and if they were obliged to work for reward paid by the employer. In this study only such employees of such a kind will be discussed.

2. "The sages have declared that the state of dependence is common to all these, (i.e. labourers); but that their respective position and income depends on their particular caste and occupation" (N. 5, 6).

19. This chapter is called "Non-payment of Wages."
20. Deficiency of the state of dependence, of work and salary.
21. N. 5.22, Bṛh. 15.13
22. N. 5.23., Bṛh. 15.13.
23. N. 5.23, Bṛh. 15.13.
24. N. 5.23, Bṛh. 15.13.
25. We find in the sources special regulations concerning the contracts and the reciprocal relations between the owner of the herd and the herdsman. Because these contracts are special contracts, the respective rules will be discussed in the second part of this article.
26. Bṛh. 15.13.
27. N. 5.24.

This also is the principal idea of the ancient Indian law, from which the characteristic criterion of the contract of service in ancient India mostly proceeded. The rule contained in N. that 'the state of dependence is common to all workers' is also authoritative for the legislation of present times.

The state of dependence was the essentiale negotii of the contract of service according to ancient Indian Law.

The second part of the above mentioned sentence of N. has to be understood in such a way that their respective position depended on their particular caste, whilst their income depended on their occupation. This distinction of caste and occupation is due to the social organisation of ancient India. Nevertheless it cannot be overlooked that various services could be done exclusively by members of certain castes.

3. A. Before work begun, both parties were obliged to conclude a formal contract of service, because the labourer had to do the work which he promised to do, and had to receive the stipulated fee.[28] The contract of service had, therefore, to regulate two principal questions : the kind of the service the labourer was obliged to do and the scale of the wage the employer was obliged to pay. The labourer rendered service and the employer paid the stipulated fee for the service rendered. Because the salary scale gave more often occasion for disagreement than the kind and manner of the service to be done, the scale of the reward had to be fixed above all in the contract of service. This transpires clearly from the tennor of the title of the sixth book of N.[29] and from the contents of the first sentence of this book,[30] as well as from the third stanza of the fifteenth book of Bṛh.[31] These chapters mainly regulated the question of 'Payment and non-payment of wages' due to the employee.

B. It is certain that the contract of service had to correspond with all the general conditions and stipulations of contracts. Therefore the contract of service had to contain also the following stipulations : the date[32] i.e. the year, season,

28. Bṛh. 13.9
29. 'Non-payment of wages'.
30. We find there rules concerning the non-payment of wages.
31. Bṛh. 15.3.
32. N. 1.71, 233, 238.

month, half year, day;[33] the place where the contract was concluded[34] i.e. the village and region;[35] determination of the contracting parties and their names, castes, *gotra*,[36] the designation of the matter[37] i.e. the extent of the special specifications, the description, contents, form and kind of the service to be done;[38] the scale of the stipulated wages;[39] the duration of contract[40] and probably the reciprocal conditions between the parties,[41] as well as the additional stipulated reservations.[42]

This contract could not be concluded in contradiction with the rules of *jus cogens*[43], the special local customs[44] and especially with the current general local customs.[45]

Such a contract could not be concluded with a person incapable of acting either on the side of the employer or on the side of the employee. The following persons were considered as incapable of acting :

(a) Women,[46] unless the relative agreement was ratified by their husbands,[47] or in his absence by her son,[48] and in absence of both by the king,[49] i.e. by the existing guardian.[50]

(b) Minors. Minors were considered children[51] until the eighth year of age, and were compared with embryos,[52] young men[53] (*pogaṇḍa*) between the

33. K. 3. ch. 1.
34. N. 1.71, 233, 238.
35. K. 3. ch. 1.
36. K. 3. ch. 1.
37. N. 1.71, 233, 238.
38. K. 3. ch. 1.
39. K. 3. ch. 1, N. 1.71, 238.
40. N. 1.71.
41. N. 1.238.
42. K. 3. ch. 1.
43. Mn. 8.163, N. 1.136.
44. Vi. 7. 11.
45. Mn. 8.164, N. 1.136.
46. Vi. 17.10, N. 1.23, 137, Y. 2.31, Bṛh. in VyM p. 13.
47. N. 1.27.
48. N. 1.27.
49. N. 1.27.
50. Mn. 5.148, 9.3, Vās. 5.2, B. 2.3-45, Vi. 25.13, Y. 1.85. 66, MBh. 13.46, 14, Vās. 5.3, Nār. (Vivādaratnākara 410, 411), Smṛtyantara, (Aparārka 109).
51. Vi. 17.10, Mn. 8.166, N. 1.35, 36, 39, Y. 2.32, Bṛh. in VyM p. 13.
52. N. 1.35.
53. N. 1.35, 137.

ninth and the sixteenth year of age,[54] were also considered minors and also people of full age[55] as long as the parents were alive[56] because the son during the lifetime of his father was like a slave[57] who was not able to command himself.[58]

(c) Dependent persons,[59] i.e. already dependent persons or subsequently dependent persons,[60] for example attendants,[61] slaves,[62]—provided that the transactions of slaves were ratified by the owner of the slave,[63] or were contracted on behalf of the family of his master.[64] N. acknowledged as independent only three persons i. e. the king, the spiritual teacher, and a householder in his own household.[65] All other persons were dependent on the kings,[66] although this had no influence on their capacity of acting.

(d) Persons, who although independent had lost control over their actions,[67, 68] as persons attracted by love,[69] or anger,[70] tormented by illness,[71] distressed by calamity,[72] persons who were under the influence of friends or enemies,[73] tortured by pains or dying,[74]

54. N. 1.35.
55. K. 3. ch. 1, N. 1.36-38, 30-31.
56. N. 1.36-38, see N 1.31.
57. N. 1.30.
58. N. 1.29.
59. Vi. 7.10, N. 1.29, 48; see Mn. 8.163.
60. K. 3. ch. 1.
61. N. 1.34.
62. N. 1.29.
63. N. 1.30.
64. Mn. 8.167, Vi. 6.39.
65. N. 1.32.
66. N. 1.33.
67. N. 1.40-41, K. 3. ch. 1, Vi. 7.10.
68. N. 1.41.
69. N. 1.41.
70. N. 1.41, K. 3. ch. 1.
71. N. 1.41, Vi. 7.10, Mn. 8.163 (not wholesome and very ill), K. 3. ch. 1 (cripple), Y. 2.32.
72. Bṛh. in VyM p. 13.
73. N. 1.41, see Y. 2.31, Bṛh. in VyM p. 13.
74. K. 3. ch. 1 (unhappy), Bṛh. 8.23.

intoxicated,[75] mad,[76] idiots,[77] bashful[78] or very old.[79]

(e) Persons on whom force had been used or acted upon (intimidation,[80] fear,[81] or deception.[82]).

(f) Unauthorised persons.[83]

(g) Persons charged with a crime (criminals).[84]

(h) Ascetics.[85]

The contract had neither to be concluded *in fraudem* of the other party,[86] nor to be attested by the signature of a witness bribed by the other party,[87] nor to be written by a scribe[88] of bad character.[89]

Apart from these general conditions of contract, which are to be found in all the agreements (*jus cogens*) the contract of service could also contain other special stipulations mentioned in the sources only accessorily (*jus dispositivum*). We read for example in K.[90] that the following stipulation could be contained in the contract of service : 'You shall not employ another servant to execute the work, nor can I give the execution of this work to another person.' By such a reservation the employee was unconditionally obliged to do his work in person; should a reservation of this kind not have been put, the employee had the right to cede the execution of the work to another person.

In another passage of K.[91] it is learned that especially with regard to contracts of service, the neighbours (*āsanna*) had to know its contents.[92] This passage of K. deals probably with

75. K. 3. ch. 1, Vi. 7.10, Mn. 8.163, N. 1.137, see Y. 2.31 Bṛh. in VyM p. 13.
76. K. 3. ch. 1, Y. 2.32, Bṛh. 6.52.
77. Bṛh. 6.52.
78. Bṛh. 6.52.
79. Mn. 8.163.
80. N. 1.137, Vi. 7.10, Bṛh. 6.52, differently K. 3. ch. 1.
81. N. 1.137, Mn. 8.168, Bṛh. in VyM p. 13, differently K. 3. ch. 1.
82. N. 1.137, Y. 2.31.
83. Mn. 8.163, Y. 2.32.
84. K. 3. ch. 1. N. 1.137.
85. K. 3. ch. 1.
86. Vi. 7.7, Mn. 8.163.
87. Vi. 7.8.
88. Vi. 7.9.
89. Vi. 7.8.
90. K. 3. ch. 14.
91. K. 3. ch. 13.
92. *āsanna.*

a verbal and not with a written contract of service, because as regards the contents of a written contract no doubt could arise whether the contract was authentic. This is seen from the following passage found in N.[93] 'Writing is an excellent eye (as it were), because it solves all doubts which may have arisen as regards, to place, time, profit, matter, quantity, or stipulated period.

C. The contract of service could have been concluded either for an exactly fixed period of time, or for an indeterminate period, or for executing a certain work.

That a contract of service could have been concluded for an *exactly fixed period* of time emerges especially from verses 153 and 157 of the fifth book of Vi. We read there. 'A hired workman who abandons his work before the expiration of the term...,'[94] or 'if an employer dismisses a workman (whom he has hired) before the expiration of the term...'[95] The period of time fixed in the contract of service could contain the designation of day, month, half-year, two months, or year.[96] It must be understood that this stipulation described the periods only by way of example and that the contract of service could be concluded for any period, say of three or four months. This is seen from the general conditions regarding the conclusion of agreements on the whole. The reservations referring to the terms of the contract of service belonged to *jus dispositivm* and not to *jus cogens*.

The admissibility of a contract of service concluded for an *indeterminate term* did not result *expressis verbis* from the rules found in the Dharmaśāstra-s and Arthaśāstra-s. Indirectly the admissibility of such a contract could be deduced from the rules regarding shepherds according to which a herdsman of a hundred cows at the end of the year had to get as wages a calf and a herdsman of two hundred cows a milch-cow, or has the right to milk all the cows every eighth day.[97] Admissibility of such a contract resulted also from the contents of a contract of "manag-

93. N. 1.71.
94. Vi. 5.153.
95. Vi. 5.157.
96. Bṛh. 15.10.
97. N. 6.10 etc.

ing the property of the family" and of "superintending the household."[98]

On the contrary the admissibility of a contract of service for executing *a certain work* emerged from various rules contained in the Dharmaśāstra-s and Arthaśāstra-s. To this category belonged impure works as for example : rubbing of master's limbs,[99] sweeping the road, shampooing the private parts of the body, gathering and putting away food scraps, ordure and urine.[100] Also the following services belonged to this category: conveying merchandise to its destination,[101] and an agreement between a man and a courtezan regarding sexual intercourse.[102]

The Dharmaśāstra-s and Arthaśāstra-s distinguished employees who worked for themselves independently (individual employees) and such ones who formed associations and therefore worked in favour of the association for the total gain in which they participated.[103]

II. CONTRACTS OF SERVICE BETWEEN EMPLOYERS AND INDIVIDUAL EMPLOYEES

4. A. It was mentioned above that according to the general rules contained both in the Dharmaśāstra-s and Arthaśāstra-s, the service to be done by employees could be of different kinds, and therefore it was not to be limited to field-labour, to carrying things and so on.

Regarding the wages due to the employees, special rules existed which regulated this question, if the contract of service did not contain precise stipulations. Firstly the stipulations contained in the contract were decisive. That was expressed clearly in K.[104] twice.[105] The contract could also contain stipu-

98. N. 5.24.
99. N. 5.7.
100. N. 5.6, see par. 1. B.
101. N. 6.6 and other.
102. N. 6.18 and other, see par. 1. B.
103. Bṛh. 15.9, 14.
104. K. 3. ch. 13.
105. See N. 6.2 and other.

lations regarding the time in which the wages were to be paid. According to this rule the parties were able to determine, whether the wages were to be paid in the beginning, in the middle or at the conclusion of the work agreed upon.[106]

The Dharmaśāstra-s and the Arthaśāstra-s also contained rules concerning the scale of wages due to the employees for the service done by them, when the contract did not contain any stipulation about this question. In this regard we find two answers : one general rule and the other a special and rather a casuistic one. According to K. and Y.[107] the amount should be fixed in proportion to the work done and the time spent in doing it.[108] A similar rule about the wages due for the labour of the workmen (when there was no stipulation in the contract) is found in N.[109] According to N. wages due to the servants, were fixed in proportion to the skill and to the value of their services. It is obvious from these passages that—although K. and N. made use of different expressions—the sources of law mentioned above regulated the wages for the labour done according to the principle : "As much work a man did so much will be his wages."

B. As already mentioned, the sources of law regulated casuistic cases also where the wages due were *a priori* stipulated in controversial questions. There was the question of cultivators of the soil, of herdsmen and of traders.[110] According to K. the cultivator had to obtain one tenth of the crops grown[111] An identical stipulation is found in N.[112] However, Bṛh. first generally stated that the cultivator should receive a share of the grain,[113] but indicated in another passage more precisely that a third or a fifth of the produce should be awarded to the cultivator of the soil as his share.[114] The cultivator to whom food and clothing were given received a fifth of the crop and he who served in consideration of the profit alone received a third part of the

106. N. 6.2.
107. K. 3. ch. 13, Y. 2.196.
108. See K. 2. ch. 24.
109. N. 5.22.
110. See Bṛh. 15.14.
111. K. 3. ch. 13.
112. N. 6.3.
113. Bṛh. 15.14.
114. Bṛh. 16. 1-2.

D. It can be concluded from the exceptional rule concerning the wages that wages due to watchmen of kitchen-gardens and of produces of fields[133] were paid in cash with the exception of field-workers and herdsmen.[134] Only in K.[135] we find a rule that bad liquor could be given to workmen in *lieu* of wages, but this rule must be considered as a quite remote exception; this results from the relative passage concerned.[136]

A quite modern rule showing great progress is found in K. i. e. a rule concerning the reciprocal demands of the employers and employees. K.[137] ruled that compensation was admissible; in the case when an employee was deprived of the wages by the employer, the latter had to pay as a penalty five-fold of the loss suffered by the employee or a fine of six *paṇa-s*. It seems that this rule had to be so interpreted as meaning that the employee had the right either to prove the amount of the loss suffered by him and to demand its five-fold compensation, or to ask the lawful penalty of six *paṇa-s*. It must be pointed out that this rule could be interpreted in another way too i.e. that the failure to pay wages should be punished by a fine of ten times or five times the amount of wages, or six *paṇa-s*.

5. A. Wages had to be paid regularly, N.[138] stated. But what happened in case the employer did not pay the rightful wages belonging to the employee despite his duty to do so ? Replies to this question are found in N., Bṛh., and K., but they are not of the same character.

According to N. an employer who did not pay the wages which he had agreed to give, should pay them together with interest.[139]

On the contrary according to Bṛh. in this case the employer should be compelled to pay the wages due in addition to the fine.[140]

In a similar manner this question was explained in K.

133. K. 2. ch. 24.
134. See par. 13.
135. K. 2. ch. 25.
136. K. 2. ch. 25.
137. K. 3. ch. 13.
138. N. 6.2.
139. N. 6.26. (Nepālese manuscripts N. 6.7).
140. Bṛh. 15.9.

where we read that the employer causing delay had to pay a fine of 12 *paṇa-s* or five times the amount of the wages as indemnity.[141,142]

In other words in all the cases of delay on the part of the employer, the latter had to pay the wages due for the service done and in addition according to Bṛh. a fine, and according to K. a fine and an indemnity amounting to five-fold or ten-fold of the wages due. *Per analogiam* from the last sentence in Y. 2.198 it could be admitted that when the master compelled the servant to stop working while the latter was not giving it up, the master was compelled to pay wages to the servant.

The scale of wages for carriers was prescribed in Y. (2. 197-8).

B. The protection of the interests of the employee rested with the court and property with the king, to whom the supreme juridical power belonged. The injured party had to address himself to the king and the king according to Bṛh.[143] would compel the employer to pay the wages due and probably also impose further financial obligations.

The question as to whether the employee could address himself to the king for wages due to him depended on whether the payment of the wages was agreed upon by the parties or not.

In the first case it was stipulated that the wages were to be paid in the middle of the work done;[144] the employee would have the right to address himself to the king, although the work was not quite finished. For the payment of wages the conditions agreed upon by the parties were decisive.

In the second case i. e. when the time of the payment of wages due to the employee was not fixed, he had the right to address himself to the king only after he had performed his service or finished his work. Indeed, this did not emerge from the sources of the law *expressis verbis*, but this point of view should be accepted on the grounds of general principles. This

141. K. 3. ch. 13.

142. A special rule was applied to courtezans. According to N. 6.18 "a man who does not pay the stipulated fee, after having had intercourse with a courtezan, shall pay twice the amount of the fee" probably as an indemnity. According to Vīramitrodaya p. 422, and other commentaries : illness, was considered as a legitimate reason for breaking an engagement of this sort.

143. Bṛh. 16.11.

144. See N. 6.19.

seems to be partly justified by the following sentence : "When a master does not pay wages for the labour stipulated after the work has been performed he shall be compelled by the king to pay it."[145] This rule had to be interpreted as meaning that the legislator[146] did not intend to adjudicate the right to go to law to the *negotiorum gestor* for claiming wages; the above rule, could be as well applied to the case when the contract of service was concluded, as also to the case when the contract of service was not stipulated. But it is more probable that the above rule applied exclusively to the case when the contract of service was not concluded, because the wages, as regards the time of payment, the kind of payment, and their scale, were regulated by *jus dispositivum* and not by *jus cogens*. Therefore, the parties were able to act as they had stipulated. The correctness of this interpretation could be seen from the rule found in N.[147] We read there "a master shall regularly pay wages to the servant hired by him, whether it be at the commencement, at the middle, or at the end of his work, just as he had agreed to do."

C. It may be pointed out that the employer was obliged to treat the employee with due respect and not to abuse him. We do not find in the sources of law such a rule; we may apply by analogy the rule contained in N., which related to courtezans to whom the Dharma-and Arthaśāstra-s attributed the quality of employees, though—as already mentioned—they did not belong to this category of persons. The fact that the courtezans were considered as employees by ancient Indian law made possible the application of the respective rules to other employees. According to one of such rules[148] "should a man unnaturally abuse the person (a courtezan) or cause her to be approached by many, he had to pay eight times the amount of the stipulated fee, and a fine of the same amount." Thus it may be concluded that the employer who ill-treated the employee or abused his person was obliged to pay him a certain indemnity in addition to a fine to be paid to the king. It must be pointed out that "bad treatment", did not mean "corporal punishment," because such a

145. Bṛh. 16.11.
146. It is doubtful if this expression is exact (legislators).
147. N. 6.2.
148. N. 6.9.

chastisement was expressly admissible, although in exceptional cases only.[149]

6. The question of non-observance of the stipulated contract of service on the part of the employer was much better regulated in the sources of law. J. Jolly in his work *Recht und Sitte* devoted to this question one sentence only.[150]

A. Firstly, it must be considered what the expression: "non-observance of the contract of service" on the part of the employee meant. An implicit and exceptionally strict reply to this question is to be found in N.[151] A rule there stipulated that "if a man has promised to render service and failed to render it, it was termed breach of a contract of service." The performing of a work in an improper way i.e. not in such a manner as was promised, had to be considered as "non observance of the contract of service."[152] In connexion with this, the following questions have to be solved : what consequences arose from the non-observance or from the improper observance of the contract of service (if the non-observance of the contract of service was rightly justified), what consequences resulted in the last case, etc.

B. In the majority of the Dharma- and Arthaśāstra-s there were only general rules concerning the consequences of the non-observance of the contract of service on the part of the employee.[153]

According to some of the sources of law, consequences of the non-observance depended on whether the stipulated wages were paid or not. The employee had the right to break the contract of service when he was sick or if there was another incapacity in his person.

The consequences of the non-observance of the contract of service on the part of the employee were fully discussed in Mn.,[154] where a rule is to be found according to which the employee who, although not sick, did not perform work he has promised

149. See above and Āp. 2.11-28-213.
150. Four lines; p. 107.
151. N. 5.1.
152. See N. 6.5.
153. Special rules concerned carriers : Y. (2.197, 198), N. (6.9) etc.; but it could be hardly admitted that from the strict legal point of view carriers were employees.
154. Mn. 8.215, See also Bṛh. 16.7-8.

to do, had no right to ask for wages; on the contrary he had to pay eight *kṛṣṇala-s* as a fine. Medhātithi and Govindarāja[155] commenting on this rule expressed the opinion that the fine mentioned above amounted to eight gold or bronze *kṛṣṇala-s*—as the case may be, whilst Kullūka[156] stated that the fine always amountted to eight gold *kṛṣṇala-s*. In K.[157] a rule is to be found that the employee who did not perform the stipulated work had to pay as fine 12 *paṇa-s*. K. did not mention in this connexion whether the employee had to get the stipulated wages or not. Logically the employee could not have any right to his wages as he had not done the service, but we do not find such a rule in K. This logical conclusion, however, is to be found in another passage in K.[158] which contained the rule that the wages have to be paid only for services rendered. Applying this general rule to all the contracts of service we come to the conclusion that the question of the non-observance of the contract of service[159] on the part of the employee was regulated in the same way in Mn. and in K. although the scale of the fine was different in both the sources. But the difference was of a quantitative, and not of a qualitative nature. The fine had probably to be paid not to the king—as in the case of the non-observance of the contract of service on the part of the employer—but to the employer to whom the indemnity was due. This appears also from another rule found in K. We read there that a cultivator who arriving in a village for work, did not work, should pay double the amount of the wages received for the work promised. It is understood that he had to pay this amount to the employer.[160]

However, this casuistic rule differed quantatively from the general rule mentioned above.[161,162] It must also be admitted that the case was regulated in a similar manner when

155. See S. B. E. 25. p. 293 *ad* Mn. 8.215.

156. See S. B. E. 25. p. 293 *ad* Mn. 8.215.

157. K. 3. ch. 14.

158. K. 3. ch. 14.

159. As far as no lawful reason existed for the non-observance of the contract of service.

160. K. 3. ch. 10.

161. Instead of the fine of eight or twelve *kṛṣṇala-s* twice the amount of the stipulated wages should be paid.

162. See also N. 6.6.

the employee intentionally made the observance of the contract of service impossible. That is seen from a passage found in K.[163]

Only Āp. contained a single rule that servants in villages and herdsmen, who abandoned their work, had to be flogged (corporal punishment).[164]

C. It has been mentioned above that the consequences of the non-observance of the contract of service on the part of the employee—according to sources of law—depended on whether the employee received wages or not. From the legal point of view such a differentiation was quite necessary, because the ancient Indian legislator certainly was anxious to come to a decision as to what had to happen to wages received by the employee.

This question was solved in Y.[165], Vi.[166] and Bṛh.[167]

According to Y. one who, having received his wages, abandoned the work must pay twice the amount of the wages; and if none was received he should be made to pay an equal amount (of the wages).

According to Vi. a hired workman who abandoned his work before the term has expired had to pay the whole amount of the stipulated wages to his employer and 100 *paṇa-s* to the king. Also Vi. did not mention *expressis verbis* that he should pay this amount after having received his wages; this results *per analogiam* from the sentence of Bṛh. quoted below.

This question was solved in the best manner in Bṛh. which contains a rule that when a servant did not perform his work after having received his wages, though able to do the work, he should be compelled by the king :

(a) to restore the wages,

(b) to pay a fine (to the king),

(c) to pay twice the amount of his wages to his master.[168]

In this rule the accurate and exact solution of the above question was found. All the doubtful details—except one that will be discussed later—were clearly and plainly regulated. It is quite clear from that rule that the point at issue was

163. K. 3. ch. 13, see also Mn. 8.217.
164. Āp. 2.11-28-213.
165. Y. 2.193.
166. Vi. 5.153-154.
167. Bṛh. 16.5.
168. To the employer; it did not result *implicite* from this rule.

(whether the employee did perform his work having received his wages), what was the condition of the employee (whether he was able to do work), what steps have to be taken (shall be compelled), as well as of what kind were the employer's claims (as above under (a), (b) and (c), Bṛh. also discussed the case of the non-observance of the contract of service on the part of the employee who did not receive the wages. This question was settled in Bṛh. in one of the next verses[169] where we read that the servant who has promised to do the work but did not perform it should be compelled to do so (even by forcible means). When the servant refused to do the work for which he was not engaged, through obstinancy, he should be fined eight *kṛṣṇala-s* and his wages should not be paid to him. That the above mentioned rule of Bṛh. (16.18) had to be interpreted in connection with the preceding sentence, results *a contrario* from Bṛh. (16.5) where the case was regulated as to when the employee had received his wages, while Bṛh. (16. 7-8) did not expressly mention if this rule related to the above case, or to a different case. Probably Bṛh. (16. 7-8) did not mean to be a continuation of Bṛh. (16.5). In addition to the often mistaken *argumentum a contrario*, the above supposition is proven by the fact that the legislator of Bṛh. certainly did not intend to solve the same question twice and in a different manner. A confirmation of this interpretation of Bṛh. (16. 5-8) can be found in N.[170] where we find a rule that if a man, after having received the wages due, failed to perform such work as he has promised to do, he should be compelled to perform it; if he did not perform it after having taken wages, he must pay back twice the amount of his wages. It could be concluded that sentences 7-8 of the sixteenth book of Bṛh. formed a continuation, or a supplement of the rule contained in sentence 5 of the same book. However, this argument cannot debilitate the considerations mentioned above so that it can be admitted that Bṛh. 16.7-8 referred to the case of the non-observance of the contract of service on the part of the employee after he has received wages, while sentence 5 of the same book of Bṛh. related to the case

169. Bṛh. 16. 7-8.
170. N. 6.5.

of the non-observance of the contract of service on the part of the employee who did not receive his wages.

Unjustly, as was mentioned above,[171] the ancient Indian sources considered courtezans as employees. In this regard special rules were to be found, which, however, resembled the above mentioned ones. If a courtezan declined to receive a man after having received her fee, she should pay twice the amount of the fee,[172] provided that—as Vīramitrodaya, Nārada's commentator, quite rightly remarked[173]—an important reason for breaking a contract of this sort existed; illness was considered as such a reason.

D. Above, cases were considered where the contract of service was not observed on the part of the employee on the whole. The Dharma- and Arthaśāstra-s also discussed cases where the service agreed upon was only partially performed by the employee.

According to K. wages were to be paid for the work done but not for the work that was not done; according to Bṛh. should a hired servant fail in the performance of ever so small a part of his master's work, he forfeited his wages, and could be sued in court for his offence.[174] The above-mentioned principle was not to be used in the case when the employee begun at an improper time, or improper place, or did not perform his work in due form. K. remarked that the employer, who was in this case unwilling to pay the agreed wages to the employee, was not obliged to pay them.[175] In other words the employer had the right to pay or not to pay wages to the employee for the service done, if the employee was at fault regarding the non-performance of the work promised.

In connexion with this rule it should be pointed out that it resulted from K.[176] that the work could be performed by a third person[177] in case of an illness of the employee, unless an agreement to the contrary was concluded,[178] and that in this case

171. See above par. 1. B.
172. N. 6.18.
173. N. 6.18, S. B. E. 33. p. 1, 43.
174. Bṛh. 16.3.
175. K. 3. ch. 14.
176. K. 3. ch. 14.
177. See K. 3. ch. 14.
178. K. 3. ch. 14.

if the employee received the wages due to him he had to indemnify his substitute.[179] But when the employee malevolently[180] did not perform his work, and did not entrust a third person with the performance of the work, he forfeited completely the wages for the service performed partially.[181,182]

K.[183] further contained a rule that when the employee—without assent on the part of the employer—performed more than it was agreed upon, he had no right to demand wages for the additional work. Although this rule could be considered as contradictory with the general rule,that wages had to be paid for services done,[184,185] it is an apparent contradiction only. The basis for the last rule was the fact that the service done by the employee should have some value for the employer. Therefore, when the additional performance according to the concluded agreement ought not to be done, the *presumptio juris ac de jure* existed that such an additional performance could not have any value for the employer. That question was differently solved in Y.[186] According to the rule contained in this Dharmaśāstra, "when one disregards the place and the time, as also where one otherwise causes a reduction in profits, in such a case, the will of the master shall prevail ; but more shall be paid if more be made." The author (or authors) of Y. wanted to say, contrary to opinion mentioned above, that if a worker by reason of a special knowledge as to time and place, made more profit for his employer, an amount exceeding that fixed before, should be paid by the employer to the employee.[187]

An employee, however, who did not sell a commodity at the proper time or in a proper place, and thus disregarded these conditions through insolence or the like, or one who at the same time or place brought in less profit than has been reaped by an extensive sale of the merchandise i. e. when the emoplyer

179. See J.J. Meyer: Das Altindische Buch vom Welt-und Staatalebn, Leipzig 1926. p. 291-40.

180. *āttaḥ sustho* That when these words are placed together it appears that the author intended to define "not very ill."

181. He lost it partially too,

182. Mn. 8.217 .

183. K. 3. ch. 14.

184. K. 3. ch. 14.

185. See par. 4. A.

186. Y. 2.195.

187. Mit. *ad* Vīramitrodaya *ad* Y. 2.195.

suffered a loss in his profit on account of the fault of the employee by the non-observance of the contract of service, the employer had the right to pay as much as he wished and not the entire wages.[188]

E. The question of the non-observance of the contract of service on the part of the employee who was not at fault was discussed in N.[189] Mn.[190], Y.[191] and especially in K.[192] According to this last Arthaśāstra the employee had the right to give up the concluded agreement[193] or to cede the performance of the work to a substitute[194] and this without any unfavourable consequences for himself in following cases:

(a) if he was incapable to complete the work,
(b) if it was a contemptible work,
(c) if he was suffering from disease,
(d) if he was involved in calamities.

To cede the performance of the work to a substitute was however inadmissible where the parties have excluded this possibility *expressis verbis*.[195]

The cases quoted sub (a) to (d) were only mentioned by way of example. From the point of view of law these cases could be considered as "important motives for giving up the contract of service" on the part of the employee. Vīramitrodaya especially considered disease as an important case for giving up the contract of service on the part of the employee;[196] this results from the commentary to N. (6.10). The same question was also solved in Mn. This Dharmaśāstra pointed out that when a sick employee after his recovery performed his work, he should receive his wages with delay.[197] In other words Mn. stated that in case of justified delay (caused by the illness of the employee) the work could be performed at a later period. According to K. each alteration of the contract of ser-

188. Mit. *ad* Vīramitrodaya *ad* Y. 2.195.
189. Vīramitrodaya *ad* N. 6.17.
190. Mn. 8.216.
191. Y. 2.196.
192. K. 3. ch. 14.
193. K. 3. ch. 14.
194. K. 3. ch. 14.
195. K. 3. ch. 14.
196. Concerning courtezans see S. B. E. 33. p. 143.
197. Mn. 8.216.

vice even though it concerned only the kind of work to be performed, as well as prohibiting the employee from coming to the workshop, formed an important cause for the employee to demand the payment of wages, or to retain the received wages, although the service was not even partially performed by the employee. K. contained a rule that when the employer asked the employee to perform another work, than the one stipulated, the employee was not obliged to repay the wages received if he was not willing to do the new service.[198] And so K. stated that when the employer was at fault, in consequence of which the employee did not perform his work, or the performance of the work was made difficult, the employee had to receive his wages; especially it was then assumed that when the employee was not able to perform the work which he begun, in consequence of the fault on the part of a third person, the work had to be considered as performed.[199] We find here again an example of the social position of employees and how far their legal protection was extended.

Y.[200] regulated in a similar manner another casuistic example which gives, however, an idea on the general rule that the employee, who did not observe the contract of service without fault on his part, should receive the agreed wages, Y. regulated a problem of the non-observance of the contract of service by more than one employee. And so Y. stated : "If the work cannot be accomplished by both, the wages should be paid for the work done according to the agreement." This sentence must be understood in the following manner : If the work which was contracted could not be accomplished by two or more workers on account of illness or any other impediment but not due to the fault of the employee, the employees had the right to demand wages which must be paid proportionately to the work done.[201] It is unclear if in this case the work was contracted with more than with one worker, or if it was contracted with one worker only who afterwards gave one or more substitutes. Mit.[202] added

198. K. 3. ch. 14.
199. K. 3. ch. 14.
200. Y. 2.196.
201. Mit. *ad* Y. 2.196.
202. Mit. *ad* Y. 2.196.

that the wages which should be paid proportionately to the work done should be determined by an arbitrator. It is possible that this occurred when the contract of service did not mention *expressis verbis* the scale of wages; it must be admitted that in this case, too, workers had the right to demand proportionate wages. These proportionate wages had to be paid, according to the work done, to all the workers who have worked for the observance of the contract of service.

F. In the same way the Dharmaśāstra-s solved the question whether wages belonged to the employee when the service was not done by him, due to the fault of the employer. Only Vi. solved the case of dismissal of a workman before the expiration of the term concluded. In that case the employer was obliged to pay the entire wages to the employee,[203] and in addition a fine of 100 *paṇa-s* to the king,[204] unless the employee has been at fault.[205,206] Applying the *argumentum ex minori ad majus* a general principle could be accepted that an employee who was unable due to the fault of the employer to perform his work, though he was willing to do it, should receive the entire wages as if he had performed his work. *Per analogiam*, the same principle was applied in the case when the parties concluded an agreement concerning the performance of a fixed work. Controversial questions regarding the period of time necessary for the performance of the work had to be decided in Court. Most probably the same principle had to be applied in case the parties concluded an agreement for an indeterminate period of time, because the Dharma and Arthaśāstra-s did not solve this question. Therefore, the general rule had to be applied that all the controversial questions arising from the contract of service had to be decided in Court.[207]

7. Employers were exclusively responsible for any guilty act committed by the employee by order of the employer and for the benefit of the latter.[208] This, as far as penal law was concerned, was a strange rule, and sheds a ray of light on the

203. Vi. 5.157.
204. Vi. 5.158.
205. Vi. 5.159.
206. *i. e.* that he performs the entrusted work not in due form.
207. See par. 5, B.
208. Bṛh. 16.9.

legal position of the employee. Therefore, it appears that, as long as the employee was in condition of service to his employer he (the employee) *quasi* lost his ability of action and should be considered as if a tool in the hands of the employer. This rule stipulated that when a servant, commissioned by his master, did any improper act (such as theft) for the benefit of his master, the latter should be held responsible for it. On the contrary, the employee was exclusively and personally responsible for guilty acts committed by him, due to his own fault, during the course of service.[209]

8. Workers could engage themselves as ordinary day-work-men; in that case they did nothing more than their daily work; they could also engage themselves to do service with their own instruments. This results *a contrario* from N.[210] In the first case the employee was obliged to employ and supervise with due care the implements of work entrusted to him.[211] It also appears from the general rules that in the case of negligence as far as the instruments entrusted to the employee were concerned, the latter had to indemnify the employer.

9. Performance of work could replace a fine.[212] Therefore, the person who was not able to pay the fine inflicted on him by the king (by the Court), could do service on account of the king instead of paying the fine.

The above rules which were contained in the Dharma-and Arthaśāstra-s related to employers and independent employees who concluded a contract of service for themselves.

Other rules however referred to :

III. CONTRACTS OF SERVICE BETWEEN EMPLOYERS AND ASSOCIATIONS OF EMPLOYEES

10. This apparently quite contemporary institution, i. e. the employee-co-operative society, with whom as the representative of all the employees, the contract of service was to be concluded, was not only well known in ancient India but was in

209. N. 6.4.

210. N. 6.4.

211. K. 3. ch. 13.

212. See J. J. Meyer : Das altindische Buch vom Welt—und Staataleben, Leipzig 1926, Zus. *ad* 288-18-288-39-42.

practice widely used. Although from the legal point of view, important differences are found between the structure of the modern and the ancient Indian co-operative societies as regards the rights of the members etc., nevertheless there are many rules, which resemble the rules of the recent co-operative societies..

It must be noted that in many cases it is doubtful if the society, from the legal point of view, has to be considered a co-operative society or a civil-law partnership.

According to N. a partnership arose when traders or *others*[213] carried on business jointly[214] for the purpose to gain,and to contribute their funds towards the common stock of the association.[215] This joint contribution of funds must be considered as the basis of all partnerships (according to N.).[216] Therefore each member was obliged to contribute his proper share towards the common stock.[217,218] The chief-design and the chief-condition of the existence of an association, however, rested on the joint performance of work by all the members of the society.[219] That was the chief principle which is also found in contemporary co-operative societies.

It does not appear from Jolly's *Recht und Sitte*[220] that Jolly shared the view that the personal co-operative societies could also be employers' cooperative societies. At any rate, Jolly did not express such an opinion. The admissibility of employees' co-operative societies resulted indirectly from N. and Y.[221] while the Dharmaśāstra-s mentioned partnerships not only of traders but also of "others" (hence partnership of employees too). Also from Bṛh.[222] the admissibility of such employees' co-operative associations resulted indirectly. But Kauṭilya's Arthaśāstra, which was unknown to Jolly, expressly mentioned such employees' co-operative associations. K. contained explicit rules about employees' associations[223] as well as about the rights

213. Also employees.
214. N. 3.1, 2.
215. N. 3.2. See Y. 2.259.
216. N. 3.2.
217. N. 2.2.
218. It refers more likely to a society of civil law
219. See Mn. 8.211, Y. 2.259.
220. Par. 33.
221. N. 3.1, Y. 2.192.
222. Bṛh. 15.6.
223. K. 3. ch. 14.

and the duties of their members. That results also directly from Y.[224] Therefore, it seems to be certain that the rules contained in the Dharmaśāstra-s, as regards the associations, were also of value for the employees' associations.[225]

11. Accrding to the advice found in Bṛh.[226] persons of noble parentage, clever, active, intelligent, familiar with coins, skilled in revenue and expenditure, honest and enterprising, had to be admitted as members of partnerships. It is understood that this sentence could not be considered as a rule of any value, but, as it often happened in the Dharmaśāstra-s, as an advise to the members of the partnership. The same concerned the advisers of the general body (knowing *dharma*, pure, unavaricious).[227]

12. Each member of such a partnership was able to act only according to the instructions laid down by all the members, or only on the authority of the other partners.[228] From that it is evident that from time to time meetings of members of the partnerships took place, where all members were consulted as regards the representation of the partnership.[229] If a partner was sent to do business for the partnership (*gaṇa*), he had to deliver to the *gaṇa* whatever he received and he should be compelled to pay elevenfold the amount received if he did not deliver it.[230,231] This was the consequence of the general rule found in Y.,[232] that duties arising from any *dharma* should be carefully observed by members of the partnership (*gaṇa*), as also the duties imposed by the king.

13. Each member of the employees' society was obliged to have his proper share.[233] These shares could be equal or un-

224. Y. 2.265.
225. *Per analogiam.*
226. Bṛh. 13.1.
227. Y. 2.191. See Y. 2.188.
228. N. 3.5, Bṛh. 13.9.
229. See Y. 2.60.
230. Y. 2.190.
231. The question was regulated in another manner in Y. 2.255, where a cheat (*jihyaḥ* a man of crooked ways) should be expelled and deprived of all profits.
232. Y. 2.190.
233. It may be doubtful if Bṛh. 13.39 referred to the employee. According to this rule four shares should be awarded to the chiefs; he who was specially valiant should receive three shares ; one particularly able should take two ; and the remaining associates should share alike.

equal. In a partnership with unequal shares members possessed normal equal shares, or greater or lesser shares.[234] The scale of the shares depended above all on the funds contributed to the common stock; in this stock the members participated in ideal portions.[235] Supposing that Bṛh. (13.39) could be applied to the case, it could also be advocated that the scale of the share could depend on the personal qualities of the members ; then the chiefs would receive four shares, the valiant ones—three shares and the particularly able ones two shares, whilst all the remaining partners would share alike.[236]

Money,[237] grain,[238] liquids, condiments,[239] or the like formed the common property of the society, resulting from the shares contributed by the members. In proportion to the contributed shares the partners had to perform work, and to obtain profit or to bear losses and expenses.[240,241]

14. As N. expressly stated the terms of the agreement were decisive for the rights and duties of the employees (partners).[242] Stores, food, charges (for tolls and such alike), losses, freights and expenses of keeping valuables had to be duly paid for by each of the several partners, in accordance with the terms of their agreements. It appears, therefore, from this rule that, above all the agreement, i. e. the statute of the society, was decisive as regards the rights belonging to the employees and the duties imposed on them ; in the absence of such an agreement the principle quoted below should apply. The same was evident also from Y. Supposing that Bṛh. (13.32) was not to be applied, that rule would often be contained in the terms of the agreement. because according to the agreement unequal rights and duties could belong to each of the several partners. In addition, this appeared from the rule quoted above and found in N., that the partners could participate in the common

234. N. 3.2, Bṛh. 13.4-5.

235. Y.

236. See note 241.

237. Gold.

238. Grain.

239. Bṛh. 13.4.

240. Bṛh. 13.5. N. 3.3.

241. These rules pointed at the fact, that such associations were not co-operatives, but associations of civil law, the members of which were employees.

242. N. 3.4.

stock by apportions, and such apportions were stores,[243] food,[244] liquids,[245] condiments[246] and the like.

15. The limit of the responsibility of the partner towards the partnership for his acts was regulated in N. (3.5). A rule is found there that each partner was responsible to offer co-partners for what has been lost by his want of care, or in consequence of his acting against the instructions of, or without authority from all the other co-partners.[247] From the legal point of view that meant that each of the partners was responsible for the damage inflicted to the society due to his own fault, irrespective whether it was due to *culpa levis* or *culpa lata*. This rule was more clearly expressed in Bṛh. (13.9) and in Y. (as far as the existence of *culpa levis* or *culpa lata* was concerned). According to this rule, when a single partner acting without the assent of the other partners, or against their express instructions, injured their joint property through his negligence, he had to give compensation to all his partners. From this formulation of the text of this rule it could be admitted that according to N. an employees' cooperative society was not considered as a juristic person, but that the individual partners were regarded as subjects of law. In consequence, the society as a whole had no right to demand compensation from the guilty partner, but this right belonged to each of the partners in proportion to the scale of their shares, or share.[248] Such a supposition could result also from the interpretation of this rule together with Bṛh (13.3)[249] where we read that the single partner had to defray charges and obtain profit in proportion to the shares contributed.

When, however, a loss or diminution has occurred without guilt on the part of a single partner, for instance by *vis major* (fate or action of the king)[250]this damage had to be borne by all partners in proportion to their respective shares.[251] The interpretation of this rule shows that the society was not a juristic

243. Y. 2.187.
244. N. 3.4.
245. N. 3.4, Bṛh. 13.4.
246. Bṛh. 13.4.
247. Y. 2.260.
248. Bṛh. 2. 9-10.
249. and N. 3.3.
250. Bṛh. 13.8.
251. Bṛh. 13.8.

person, because all the partners were personally obligated to compensate for the damage which had occurred without guilt on the part of any partner. This rule has to be considered as *jus cogens* and could not be changed in the terms of the statute. It is curious that a rule of such a kind is not found in N., all the more so because this source regulated the question of partnerships in a similar manner. Both the Dharmaśāstra-s, however, contained the same rule, that when the property of the partnership was in danger through fate or through the action of the king,[252] the tenth part of the goods belonged to the partner, who has preserved them through his own effort.

When, however, a partner acted intentionally against the interests of the society or its members, or if he committed a theft, thus inflicting loss to his co-partners or to the society, he should, according to Y. and K.,[253] be excluded *ex offo* from the partnership. Such a person lost all the rights belonging to him as a partner, according to the terms of the statute of the society, or according to the general rules regarding partnerships. (Analogy from the principle mentioned below). In a similar, but somewhat different manner this question was regulated in Bṛh.[254] According to this Dharmaśāstra, a partner who has practised deceit in a purchase or sale—and, therefore, has acted against the interests of the society, or his co-partners—had to be purified by an oath or ordeal. An unable partner could have his work done by another (partner).[255]

16. K. also regulated the case when one of the partners abandoned his work or behaved unfairly towards the partnership as a whole, or towards other partners.[256] Therefore, when some work incumbent on the partnership was in progress and one of the partners abandoned his work though he was able to do it, the fine amounted to 12 *paṇa* and in addition, such a part-

252. N. 3.6, and adds very rightly : "through a gang of robbers, or...", and Y. 2.260.

253. Y. 2.268. K. 3. ch. 14 etc. We find there also other reservations and punishments. Concerning the property of *gaṇa* see : Y. 2.187. Mn. 8.219 etc.

254. Bṛh. 13.6-7.

255. Y. 2.265.

256. It may be doubtful if these rules referred to the associations or to individual workers. It seems from the context that the author (or the authors) of K. intended to regulate here the question of associations.

ner losts all the privileges belonging to him.[257]It is not clear what was to be understood by the expression "loss of all the privileges." Probably there was the question of those rights which belonged to the single partner according to the terms of the agreement,[258] or according to the general rules regarding partnerships. Especially those rules should be applied which regulated the case of the partner's leaving partnership. Therefore a partner spontaneously leaving his partnership had the right to demand the delivery of his apportion or his share from the society or from the co-partners. But in case of misbehaviour he would not have this right.

17. The Dharma-and Arthaśāstra-s regulated or discussed the case of the loss of the membership of the society if the partner went abroad or died. This question was clearly regulated in Y. and N.[259] which contain a rule that, should one partner meet with an accident, his heir should replace him, and failing an heir[260] another man (*dāyādas bāndhavas* of his *jñātis*),[261] or all the partners should replace him if they were capable of doing so. It is doubtful what the words "if they are capable" meant. In the translation of the Nārada-Smṛti,[262] Jolly amplified these words by the additional words "if they are capable of becoming his substitute." Interpreting the above rule in connexion with general rules, it seems that only such a partner could be considered "capable" who was capable of acting i. e. was able to be the subject of rights and duties, to whom especially the *factio hereditatis passiva* belonged. It seems that this case was regulated in Bṛh. in a similar manner.[263] According to the respective rules, which principally related to the deceased traders,[264] who at the same time were members of a partnership,—the right to the share of the deceased partner belonged to his heir, after the latter has proven by witnesses his right to be the heir.[265] But if no one came forward claiming the pro-

257. K. 3. ch. 14.
258. Of the statute.
259. N. 3.7. Y. 2.264.
260. Or of an other person who has rights in this case.
261. Y. 2.264.
262. S. B. E. 33. p. 125.
263. Bṛh. 13.14-8.
264. See Bṛh. 13.14.
265. See Bṛh. 13.15.

perty as heir, the king had the right to take that property.[266] This rule was in accordance with the general principles, which referred to the heirless wealth, in which case the heirless property devolved *jure caduco* on the king, or the Brahma-caste as a whole. On the contrary, the personal ceremonies—as it seems—had to be performed in the last case too by the members of the partnership.[267]

It appears also from the rules quoted above that all doubtful cases between the partnership as a whole and its members, or between the partners among themselves, had to be arbitrated by the partners themselves.[268] Each partner by his entry into partnership signed *quasi* an agreement of arbitration.

266. See Bṛh. 13.17, Y. 2.264.
267. See Bṛh. 13.18.
268. Bṛh. 13.6.

XV

INFANTICIDE AND EXPOSURE OF NEW-BORN CHILDREN IN ANCIENT INDIA*

1. The problem of the exposure of new-born children is closely connected with infanticide[1] and foeticide. These last two problems were described not quite correctly by E. Westermark in his "*Origin and Development of Moral Ideas*" Vol. I. (1906) pp. 393-413, and "*History of Human Marriage*" Vol. II. p. 162 *sec.* as he did not know the Sanskrit texts and based his remarks on McLennan's "*Studies in Ancient History*" who for his part based his remarks on H. Zimmers" *Altindisches Leben*" and B. Delbruck's "*Die Indogermanischen Verwandschaftsnamen*" p. 196. Similarly A. Weber, "9. *Indische Studien*" p. 481.

2. In the Ṛgveda (II, 29.1), we read "Upholders of the Law, you strong *Ādityas*, remove my sin like her who bears in secret ; you *Varuṇa*, *Mitra* and all-Gods who listen, I call to help me, I who know your goodness...."[2] That did not mean, as E. Westermarck stated infanticide of new born girls.

It probably referred to the exposure of a child by an unmarried woman, clandestinely practised[3].

3. It was stated in the *Avesta* "*Aśvattha* mounted on the *Semi* : there the procreation of a male-child took place; so, one

* Previously appeared as JSAIL 8 in the "Poona Orientalist" Vol. XIII. Nos. 1-2, pp. 79-87.

1. Two forms of infanticide are usually described, viz., infanticide by omission and infanticide by commission. Homicide is destroying life of a human being. Popularly the term "infanticide" is used to denote homicide where the human being killed is a newly-born infant. The law however, draws no such distinction. In law, infanticide is homicide, and the provisions of the law which apply to homicide apply equally to infanticide... Legally there is no distinction between murder of a new-born child and of an adult, and both are crimes. But although the law draws no distinction between infanticide and homicide, the subject of infanticide requires special consideration on account of—(1) the frequency with which cases occur, and (2) the special nature of the medicolegal questions which arise, (Outlines of Medical Jurisprudence for India by Lt. Col. P. Hebir and J. D. B. Gribble, Madras 1098).

2. *āre matkarta rahasūriv āg.*

3. P. V. Kane. "*History of Dharmaśāstra*" Vol. II., pt. I. p. 509.

gets a son ; so we give it up to women (6.1). *Prajāpati*, *Anumati*, *Sinīvālī* put the thing in order. She ought to bring birth of a female-child elsewhere, here she ought to give birth to a male-child" (6.11).

In *Kāṭhaka* (27.9) we read:

tasmāt striyaṁ jātāṁ parāsyanti; na pumāṁsam.

In *Taittirīya Saṁhitā* (6.5, 10, 3) we find the following passage :

tasmāt striyaṁ parāsyanty utpumāṁsaṁ haranti.

Similarly *Maitrāyaṇī Saṁhitā* (4.6, 11).

As far as the *Kāṭhaka* and *Taitirīya Saṁhitā* are concerned both these texts used the word *parāsyanti* from *parā*°,+°*as*. The *prefix parās* means—away, off, aside, along, on and *as* to throw, to cast. Therefore, *parās* must not only mean to expose a new-born-child[4]) or to throw away or down, to abandon, to reject, to leave, but also to keep aside.

If we admit that *parās* meant to cast aside, the last quoted para from *Taittirīya Saṁhitā* should be translated in the following way: They go to the *avamṛta* (the final sacrificial bath); they keep aside the *sthālī* (pots) and take up the vesels for *vāyu*; therefore, they (the people) keep aside the girl when she is born and lift up (*i. e.* greet with pride and joy) the son.

The German Indologists before 1890 translated *parās*—to expose and came to the not correct conclusion that exposure of new born girls was known in ancient India.

First O. Böhtlingk in "*Vermischtes, 3 Pflegten die Inder Töchter auszusetzen*" ZDMG., Vol. 44 p. 494 remarked : —"As I came across the exposure in question in the book of Delbrück, I immediately acquainted my friend with my doubts, I felt it difficult to believe that the ancient Indians could have been capable of carrying on such barbarity (*i. e.* exposure) and then I thought that the whole thing is very improbable as, without a girl, it would have been impossible, to achieve the greatest happiness of an Indian, *i. e.*, the procreation of a son."

In 1920 M. Winternitz in "*Die Frauen in den indischen Religionen.*" (*I Teil*, Leipzig 1920 p. 22) remarked that O. Böhtligk has already proved that this para could no longer be interpreted as relating to the custom of exposure of girls.

4. Monier-Williams "*Sanskrit English Dictionary.*" Oxford 1899. p. 59.

Dr. A. S. Altekar in "*The Position of Women in Hindu Civilisation.*" (Banares 1938, p. 8 *scc.*) also stated that this para merely refers to the traditional habit of Hindu midwives of keeping the child aside on the ground if it was a daughter; and of lifting it up in joy if it was a son[5]. The passage has no reference to the abandonment of unwanted daughters."

Also P. V. Kane in "*History of Dharmaśāstra*", Vol. II., part I (Poona 1941, p. 509 sqq.) referring to the passage quoted above, stated that this "simply refers to the fact that a daughter was not greeted as joyfully as a son[6]. It had nothing to do with exposure or infanticide. That passage only expressed the sentiment contained in the *Aitareya Brāhmaṇa* (33.1) that "the wife is indeed a friend, the daughter is distress (or humiliation), the son is light in the highest heaven." P. V. Kane quoted also other sources which showed that although in ancient India a daughter was not greeted at birth with joy she could not be killed or exposed[7].

It is undoubtedly certain that the point of view of scholars of recent times is correct. In ancient India foeticide and exposure of new-born children (girls) was unknown.

4. In the *Pañcatantra*, in the recension called *Pañcākhyānaka* of the Jain monk Pūrṇabhadra (ed. by J. Hertel in Harward Oriental Series, Vol. XI.), in the tale of the blind man, hunchback and the three-breasted princess (book *V. kathā* 10, *p.* 285, vv. 4.8) we find the following passage : *asty uttarāpathe madhupuraṁ nāma nagaram; tatra madhuseno nāma rājā; tasya kadācit tristanī kanyā jajñe; atha tāṁ tristanīṁ jātāṁ śrutvā rājā kañcukinam āhūya provāca; bhoḥ tyajyatām iyam araṇye, yathā na kaścid eva jānāti.* A. W. Ryder translated this passage as follows : "In the north country was a city called Honey Town where the king was named Honey-Host. And once there was born to him a daughter with three breasts. As soon as he learned of the birth of a three-breasted girl, he summoned the chambermaid and said: 'Sir let this girl be exposed in the forest so that not a single soul may learn the fact." This is a very good example

5. See also Hiraṇyakeśi-Gṛhyasūtra II, I. 3, 2.
6. See also Zimmer's Alt-indisches Leben p. 320.
7. See p. 510 f.

of the exposure of new-born girls. However, on the basis of this tale we should not come to the conclusion that exposure of new-born girls was allowed in ancient India, the more so as first, it concerned an abnormal child (three-breasted girl) who used to bring misfortune[8].

Secondly, even though an abnormal girl used to bring misfortune it was not stated in this tale that this particular girl was actually exposed by her father. On the contrary, it is clear from its contents that she was not exposed. It must be also noted that this story is contained in the *Pañcatantra*, a collection of imaginary tales[9].

8. Cf. below Study XVIII on the Pañcatantra and the Smṛti-s, par. 43. sqq.

9. *Hīnāṅgi vādhikāṅgī vā-bhaved ya kanyakā'tra sā, bhartus ca śyād vināśāya svaśīlanidhanāya ca, yāpunaș tristanī kanyā yāti locanagocoṛam, pitaram nāśayaty eva sā drutam nātra samśayaḥ.* (P. 5. 10)

A. W. Ryder translated these śloka-s as follows

A daughter fitted out with limbs
Too numerous or few
Will lose her character, and will
Destroy her husband, too.
But if the father sees a girl
With triple breast about
She dooms him to a speedy death
Without a shade of doubt,

Compare also KN (9.66) quoted in Böhtlingk's *Indische Sprüche* 6196: *viśrambāt priyatān eti viśrambhāt kāryam ṛcchati, viśrambhena hi davendro ditergarbhan aghātayat.*

"It is worth to quote here from the "Outlines of Medical Jurisprudence for India" by Lt. Col. P. Hehir and J. D. B. Gribble (Madras 1908) the following passage based on Lyon's Medical Jurisprudence for India pp. 151 sqq.

The frequency of infanticide in India was "specially affected by certain social customs viz., (a) early marriage, which tends to diminish the frequency of the crime, and (b) prohibition-especially among higher caste Hindoos of widow-remarriage, which tends to increase its frequency. As a consequency, therefore, while in European countries the accused is most frequently an unmarried female in India the accused is very frequently a Hindoo widow. The second form of infanticide may be said to be special to the East. In India the motives leading to female Infanticide are—(a) family pride among certain divisions of the warrior Kṣatriya caste, notably the Rajpoots and Thakoors and consequent fear that a husband of suitable rank and position may not be found for the girl; (b) the extravagant expenditure entailed by custom on the parent at the marriage of a daughter; and (c) the disgrace which, by social custom, is attached to the father of a girl who attains puberty unmarried. Not withstanding the fact that in India, owing to the exertions of the British Government, this second form of infanticide had been rendered much less prevalent, it was considered necessary in 1870 to pass a special Act for its repression and even now the crime is far from rare. Some idea of the extent to wbich it was practised may be formed from the facts which came out in the course of an inquiry ordered by Government previous to the passing of the act. It was found, for example, that in many villages of the Benares district there were no girls at all. In Mynpoory, again out of thirty

5. Foeticide was considered as one of the greatest sins, the more so as the son was necessary in order to maintain the family; in case an embryo was killed no one could know whether a future son and heir was killed[10].

According to Y. (1.72)[11] a woman who committed foeticide could be repudiated by the husband (*repudiatio uxoris*).

According to Mn. (5.89)[12] and similarly according to *Vṛddha Manu* (in *Aparārka* p. 876) liberations of water should not be offered to those who have committed foeticide.

There also exist other examples which showed that foeticide was legally prohibited. Foeticide was also considered as an act for which penance should be performed. And so Āp. (1.9, 24, 7.10) stated :
brāhmaṇamātraṁ ca; garbhaṁ ca tasyā-vijñātam, ātreyīṁ ca striyam; tasyā nirveṣaḥ.

It should also be remembered that the Viṣṇu Purāṇa states that Diti having lost her children, begged of Kaśyapa a son of irresistible prowess, who should destroy Indra. The boon

villages, in eleven there were no girls, and in the whole thirty only; 37 girls to 329 boys. Again, in the North-Western Provinces, in seven villages inhabited by Rajpoots, there were 104 boys to one girl, and in nine other villages 71 to seven girls. In Kathiavar and Kutch also the practice largely prevailed. In the latter province, 1840, there were only 335 females to 4,912 males of pure Jadeja (Rajpoot) blood. Further it was shown that where measures for the repression of the crime had been adopted, the result was to greatly increase the number of female children. In Mynpoory, for example, the number of Rajput girls rose in thirteen years from nil to 250, and in the Agra district the number of girls was doubled in few years.

In par. 381 the authors also stated : "Infanticide is a crime which is still very common in India. It is of two kinds: female infanticide, as practised among some of the still almost savage hill tribes, and īnfanticide of illegitimate children. The former offence is gradually being stamped out, though there are occasionally instances of it brought to light; but the latter offence still prevails to a very large extent, and will probably continue as long as there exists a prohibition against the remarriage af widows. This kind of crime is generally committed by the mother immediatelly after the birth, and the body of the child is then concealed and secretly disposed of, the punishment for which is provided in the Indian Penal Code."

10. See *Nṛsiṁha Tāpnīya Upaniṣad* (1, 5, 4, 1) ed. by A. Weber in "Indische Studien," Vol. 9, p. 117 *sqq*. and as (quoted there) Kāṭh. 31,7. Taittir Br. 2, 8, 12 Taittir. Ār. 10, 38-40; 2, 7, 3; Ṛg. 10,155, 2 and others See also below Study XVIII on the Pañcatantra and the Smṛti-s, par. 43 sqq. *tasnād garbheṇā'vijñātenn bhrūṇahaḥ.* By killing an unknown (as far as sex is concerned) fruit, one becomes a killer.

11. *vyabhicārā-dṛtau śuddhir garbhe tyāgo vidhīyate, garbha-bhartṛ-vadhādau ca tathā nahati pātake* (Also quoted in VyK. 132, VRK. 425).

12. *pāṣaṇḍam āśritānāṁ ca carantnīnāṁ ca kāmataḥ, garbha bhatṛ druhaṁ-caiva surāpīnāṁ ca yoṣitāhm.*

was granted, but with this condition : "If, with thoughts wholly pious and person entirely pure, you carefully carry the babe in your womb for a hundred years." She assiduously observed the condition; but Indra knew what was preparing for him. So he went to Diti and attended upon her with the utmost humility watching his opportunity. In the last year of the century, Diti retired one night to rest without washing her feet. Indra then with his thunderbold divided the embryo in her womb into seven portions. Thus mutilated, the child cried bitterly, and Indra being unable to pacify it, became angry, and divided each of the seven portions into seven, thus forming the swift moving deities called Maruts, from the words "Mārodīḥ."

6. Exposure of new-born children was not legally prohibited *expressis verbis*. Exposure of male children was certainly, punished as the birth of a son was the greatest happiness for the consorts. Generally speaking children (*bāla*) were looked upon as "rules of the middle sphere"[13] and had to be protected. Infanticide was legally prohibited[14].

Hence slayers of infants (*bāla* or *vāla*) and others were to be put to death by the king. It seems that the *Gṛhyasūtra-s* were the best sources for showing whether the exposure of new born children, of girls, in particular, was known in ancient India. They did not contain any mention of exposure of new-born children, or of new born girls, although they contained many rules[15] regarding the *jātakarman*. They contain, however, almost exclusively the description of rites regarding male children. This fact resulted from the belief that the birth of girls could not be greeted with such a joy as the birth of sons[16]. Without doubt, this did not give any cause for the assumption that, according to the *Gṛhyasūtra-s* new-born girls could be exposed. The best example to the contrary is the fact that we read in the *Āśvalāyana-Gṛhyasūtra* : *āvṛtaiva kumāyai*............i. e.

13. *klībā tyā modakaṁ kuryuḥ stenāvrātyā vikarmiṇaḥ, garbha-bhartṛ-druhas caiva surāpyaś caiva yoṣitaḥ.*

14. *ākāśeśā tu vijñeyā bāla-vṛddha-kṛśāturāḥ, bhrātā jyeṣṭhaḥ samaḥ pitrā bhāryā putraḥ svakā tanuḥ.* (Mn. 4. 184. See also Y.I. 72, MBh. 13. 244, 19 sqq.)

15. See Mn. (9. 232) : *kūṭa-śāsana-kartṝṁś ca prakṛtīnāṁ ca dūṣakān, strī-bāla-brāhmaṇaghnāṁś ca hanyād dviṭsevinas tathā.* (Also quoted in VyK. 122 SC. 324, VRR. 370, VCi. 162, VyN. 504, 508. DV. 266, 317, SV. 475, VV. 307, VyS. 157, AP. 2. 294).
Also Vi. (5. 9-11) : *kūṭaśāsanakartṝṁś ca rājā hanyāt. kūṭalekhya kārāṁś ca, garadā'gni daprasahya taskarān strī-bāla-puruṣa ghātInhś ca.* (Also quoted in VyK. 122, AP. 2. 294).

16. Unless girls were daughters of a prostitute.

that the rite without the *mantras* had to be performed in case of new-born girls. Gārgya Nārāyaṇa's commentary on it added: *kumāryās tu amantrakaṃ kuryād iti, anantarasya cāyaṁ śeṣa ity eke; anantarasya jāta-karmaṇaś cety apare*[17].

Also in the Gobhila-gṛhyasūtra (2.8, 25) it was stated: *striyās tūṣṇīṁ mūrddhany abhijighnaṇaṁ yūrddhanyābhijighnaṇam.* In the Āpastambiya-gṛhyasūtra (6.15, 13) we read, *kukumārī-yuttareṇa yajuṣā'jhimantrayate,* and *ibid.* (2. 15, 11). *āyujāṣakṣraṁ kumāryaḥ.* These quotations show how the father should act towards his new-born daughter when he went abroad and then returned and what name has to be given to a female child.

7. All these quotations show that in ancient India foeticide, infanticide and exposure of new-born boys were prohibited, and certainly unknown; the same referred to new-born girls, prohibited but, perhaps, secretly practised[18]. The custom of infanticide of girls and their exposure became known and practised in mediaeval India. We find some details on this subject in Dr. John Wilson's "*History of the Supression of Infanticide in Western India*" (1885), J. G. Browne's "*Indian Infanticide*" (1857), Tod's "*Annals and antiquities of Rājasthan*" (Vol. I. pp. 659-665), Dr. A. S. Altekar's "*The Position of Women in Hindu Civilisation*" (pp. 9-10), as well as in H. D. Griswold's *The Religion of the Ṛgveda* (p. 7 sqq.), J. R. Ghārpure's *Rights oj Women under the Hiudu Law,* University of Bombay, 1943 (pp. 19 sqq.) M. W. Pinkham's *Woman in the Sacred Scriptures of Hinduism,* New York, 1941 (pp. 3, 26, 27, 199); J.N. Farquhar's *A Primer of Hinduism* (pp. 18.22) and in *Buddhist India,* I. B. Horner's *Women under Primitive Buddhism,* London 1930 (pp. 23 sqq.) and many others.

Because infanticide had become a custom in India, by 1873 the British Government introduced the so-called "Female Infanticide Prevention Act VIII[19]".

17. See Śaṅkhāyana (1, 24), Āśvalāyana (1.15), Pāraskara (1.16) Khādira (2.2 and 3.1) Gobhila (2.7 and 2.8), Hiraṇyakeśin (2.3), Āpastamba (6.15), etc.

18. Also see Āśv.-gṛh. (1. 15, 7) : *yugmāni tv eva puṁsāmayujāṁ strīṇām* and Pāraska-gṛhyasūtra (1. 17, 3) : *ayujākṣara-ṁākārāntah striyai taddhitam.*

19. Dr. A. S. Altekar in his work *The Position of Women in Hindu Civilisation* (p. 9) also very rightly emphasized that since the *Smṛti-s* prohibited the selling of daughters in marriage and the embryo-killing, the more they had also prohibited the exposure of new-born children.

XVI

THE HARMONISING OF LAW WITH THE REQUIREMENTS OF ECONOMIC CONDITIONS ACCORDING TO THE ANCIENT INDIAN DHARMAŚĀSTRA-S, ARTHAŚĀSTRA-S AND GṚHYASŪTRA-S*

1. The particular rules of the law are always changeable. The history of Law shows that the change in the particular rules depends on the change of circumstances prevailing between one period and another and that this change of circumstances is to be found in the first place in the change of the economic situation. Depending, as they do, on the economic changes the legal rules have to be changed, or rather have to be harmonised with the changed economical circumstances. This phenomenon is to be found in all laws in which one can trace the development of legal rules. To trace the rules concerning the harmonising of the Law with the requirements of economic conditions according to the ancient Indian Dharmaśāstra-s, Arthaśāstra-s and Gṛhyasūtra-s is not an easy task. No chronology exists in India. The whole problem becomes complicated because the sources were not written down in the same place and they were applicable in different parts of India. Although it is possible to assign probable dates and place to the composition of these sources we can never rely on these a hypotheses. Probably the greater part of the rules which we find in the sources of law had been transmitted by oral tradition before they were written down by a compiler. One of the compilers may have written down all that he heard on the subject, although some of the rules which he gave were archaic and of no value. Another compiler sometimes gave his own views, sometimes the views of other savants and law-schools and sometimes he combined his views with those of the savants and different law-schools. On the basis of the ancient Indian sources of law it is not possible to

* Previously appeared in the "Silver Jubilee Number of the Annals of the Bhaṇḍarkar Oriental Research Institute." Vol. XXIII, pp. 528 548. Submitted to the 11th All India Oriental Conference; Hyderabad 1941.

ascertain that the laws which were valid at the time they were written down, had not been progressively evolved. Therefore, from the point of view of law, the Indian system of law can be discussed only as a static and not as a dynamic law, although, no doubt, the Indian law, like all other laws, had its gradual development. Only the stages of the development are in the majority of cases not known. Therefore, it is necessary to restrict the scope of this study. But in ancient Indian law which contained the germ of all modern institutions of law, we could find some examples of the harmonising of law with the requirements of economic conditions, e. g. in the institution of interests. In no other system of law do we find so many important facts bearing upon this problem.

2. Although Megasthenes had stated that the notion of interest was unknown in ancient India[1] there is no doubt that such a notion prevailed in ancient times. This can be deduced from the fact that the most ancient sources of law contained not only a mention of this institution but devoted much space to it.

The opposite of wealth (*dhana*) was debt (*ṛṇa*). Its development is similar to that of the Roman *debitum*. The general meaning of 'obligation' is still preserved in the books of law through the doctrine of the three debts which consisted of sacrifices, generation of a son and the recitation of the Vedas; they had to be dedicated to the gods, ancestors and *ṛṣis*. On the contrary the Vedas knew already the word '*ṛṇa*' as meaning 'obligation of payment' just as Indian arithmetic expressed the term of 'minus' by '*ṛṇa*', plus by '*dhana*' or '*sva*'. The recovery of a debt *ṛṇādāna* is the first of eighteen titles of law and in the majority of prescriptions concerning the legal proceedings the action for debt occupied the first place. Even the entire legal proceeding in the Mānava Dharmaśāstra and the Nārada Smṛti formed only one part of the law of debt. Accordingly J. Jolly correctly stated that the ancient age of the latter institution was manifested in the strong emphasis on religious motive, viz. that the unpaid debts pursued the debter in his successive existence and that he would be born again as a slave in the house of his creditor in order to repay the debt by his labour.[2] Else-

1. *Ute daneizusi ute isasi daneizesthai.* Fr. 27. B.
2. N. I-8.

where it was stated, from a strictly religious point of view, that the profession of a money-lender *kusīdin*, and especially of an usurer *vārdhuṣin* was not moral[3]. The usurer was compared with a thief.[4]

A. In India the caste-system has always been of great importance in the formulation of legal rules. It is the same in the case of interests. The Brāhmaṇs and in some cases the Brāhma·s as well as the Kṣatriyas were not allowed to lend money on interests[5]. This was not permitted even in case of need. It is so stated in the Mānava-Dharmaśāstra[6]. But the Yājñavalkya-Dharmaśāstra, a slightly more advanced law-book was in this instance in favour of the harmonising of law with the requirements of economic conditions and partially broke the religious rules by determining that the lending of money on interest was for a Brāhmaṇ a kind of maintenance in case of need[7]. According to the Yājñavalkya-Dharmaśāstra a Brāhmaṇ as well as a Vaiśya could in case of need lend money on interest for the purpose of gain.

According to some law-books there existed six categories of interests[8].

Kāyikā corporal interests i.e. the interests connected with manual labour or that which arose from the use of a pledged female quadrupede to be milked or of a male out to carry burdens[9];

kālikā periodical interests i. e. the interests which are due every month[10];

cakravṛddhi i.e. interests on interests[11] (compound interests);

kāritā stipulated interests i. e. the interests promised by the borrower[12]. It had to be paid always and was stipulated by

3. J. Jolly. Recht u. Sitte p. 97
4. Y. I-123, vido Vās. II-41.
5. Vās. II-40
6. Mn. X-117.
7. Y. III-41 42
8. Bṛh., G.
9. Bṛh 10-10, G. XII-35.
10. Bṛh 10. 9-10
11. Bṛh.
12. Bṛh 10-12, G. XII-35, Kāty. 498.

the debtor himself, over and above the ordinary rate of interests and was promised in times of distress[13].

sikhāvṛddhi hair interests i.e. interests which grew every day[14]. This interest was named 'hair interest' because it grew constantly like hair and did not cease growing except on the loss of the head that is to say, on payment of the principal.[15]

bhopalābha interests by enjoyment i.e. the use of a mortgaged house or the produce of a field[16].

It is obvious from these six categories of interests that even when only one kind of interests was known it was necessary to adapt the rules to the economic conditions. As long as the institution of interests was not widely spread it was enough to have one general term : interests. Economic conditions, commerce, economic life, etc. created the distinction between 'stipulated interests', 'hair interests' and 'corporal interests'. The problem of the determination of the day of payment and of a higher rate of interests which ordinarily were admitted in the law-books[17] also arose.

B. The rate of interests was determined differently when a pledge was given and differently when it was not given[18].

Generally the law-books referred to the Vasiṣṭha's.[19,20] quotation[21]. There it was reported that the legal interests for money lent was at the rate of five *māṣa-s* a month for twenty *kārṣāpaṇa-s*[22]. According to other law-books the rate of interests amounted monthly to 1-80th part of the capital[23]. According to all law-books the rate of interests in case of a pledged loan amounted monthly to one and a quarter per cent that is yearly to 15 per cent yearly.

There are many exceptions from this rule which as in the Roman Law referred to the harmonising of law with the requirements of economic conditions.

13. Bṛh. 10-12
14. Bṛh. 10.13, Kāty 499.
15. Bṛh. 10-14
16. Bṛh. 10-14, Kāty. 500.
17. Vi.
18. Y. II-37, Mn. VIII 140.
19. Vās. II 51.
20. Vide G. XII 29.
21. Mn., N., and others.
22. Twenty *kārṣāpana-s* are equal to four hundred *māṣa-s*.
23. Y. II 39, Mn. VIII 140, N.I 99, K. III. Ch. 3. Bṛh. 10.44.

And so, although the rate of interests paid per month was in Kauṭilya's Arthaśāstra[24] considered just, we find there the following sentence; 'five *paṇa-s* per month per cent is commercial interests, ten *paṇa-s* per month per cent is permissible in business which takes one across forests. Twenty *paṇa-s* per month per cent is permissible among sea-traders[25]. We read also in the Yājñavalkya-Smṛti that he whose trade took him across the forest had to pay ten per cent and sea-traders twenty per cent[26].

It is clear that the rate of interest which in normal circumstances amounted to fifteen per cent per year was much higher in cases when the borrower was exposed to greater risk or danger. The increase in the rate of interests depended upon the risk taken. If it concerned commercial enterprises in which the debtor or his merchandise had to travel through a forest, the rate of interests amounted to hundred and twenty per cent per year and if it concerned commercial enterprises in which the debtor or his merchandise had to travel by sea—two hundred and twenty per cent per year[27]. In these cases it was permissible to agree voluntarily upon the term of interests[28].

Therefore in such enterprises where the capital appeared to be endangered it was not possible to advance loans with a fixed rate of interests which amounted to one and a quarter per cent per month because the lender realised that in such a contract he was running too great a risk.

Therefore the law harmonised with the requirements of economic conditions permitted in such cases to receive or to agree to higher rates of interests.

The same applied to the higher rates of interests in trade and commerce; here the capital appeared to be more endangered than in normally pledged loans; it was however, connected with the rates of interests concerning the not pledged loans.

Normally in the case of a commercial or trade loan the rate of interests amounted to two per cent per month i. e. twenty-four per cent per year[28]. However, this principle was not clearly

24. K. III. Ch. 11.
25. K. III, Ch. 11.
26. Y. II 38.
27. It ought to be noted that in ancient India the danger by travelling by sea was greater than the danger in travelling through forests.
28. Y. II 38.

determined but followed from the Yājñavalkya Smṛti[29]. Most of the ancient commentators agreed with this viewpoint[30]. Thus, we can see here another example of the harmonising of Law with the requirements of economic conditions. A not pledged loan was more exposed to danger than a pledged loan. In order to make it possible that not pledged loans be granted, the ancient Indian Law allowed higher rates of interest, that is, instead of one and quarter per cent per month—two per cent per month.

C. According to some ancient Indian law-books no interests was raised on some loans and interests could be raised only at a lower rate than the ordinary rates of interests as for example in "loans out of friendship.' A *praesumptio juris* existed that interests accrued on such loans only after the lapse of half a year, but after this lapse of time the debtor had to pay the normal rates of interests as prescribed in the Smṛti, the lender had however the right to conclude an agreement in which any rate of interests could be stipulated[31], however as a rule, it was not allowed to stipulate the rates of interests higher than was permitted in the Smṛti-s. When the creditor claimed back the capital with or without the interests and the debtor refused to repay it on demand, the creditor who advanced the loan out of friendship, was entitled to claim along with the capital interest at the rate of five per cent per month[32]. This rule is a further proof of the harmonising of Law with with the requirements of economic conditions. We find here a kind of a conventional penalty which was introduced because of economic conditions (loans made out of friendship).

D. In case of a pledge to be used by the creditor no interests could be asked[33]. This rule was connected with the harmonising of Law with the requirements of economic conditions. According to Medh., Gov., Nār., and Rāgh[34], the Smṛti-s

29. Mn. VIII 141, N. I.101.

30. Vide Y. II 37, Mn. VIII 142, N. I-100,VI.2, Vās. II.48 in which according to the order of the castes two, three four and, five per cent monthly could be taken as interests.

31. N. I 108, 109. See also Kāty. 505.

32. N. I 109 Cf. above following.

33. Y. II 59, Mn, VIII 143, Vi. VI 5, G. XII 32.

34. Vide S. B. E. XXV. p. 278; Loiseleur Des Longchamps Lois de Manou, ad VIII 143.

understood by pledge, that was being used, the field, the cattle and the slave. The field could be cultivated and the products of the field could be collected by the creditor. The cattle and the slaves could be usufructed. Instead of paying interests it was more convenient, because of the existing economical conditions, to agree to the use the pledge.

E. Because of the economic conditions Kauṭilya declared that 'interests on debts due from persons who were engaged in protracted sacrifices or who were suffering from a disease, or who were detained in the house of their teacher for studies or who were either minors or too poor, should not accumulate[35]. It is a debatable point whether the author had here in mind compound interests or simple interests. However, for the purpose of the harmonising of Law with the requirements of economic conditions this is immaterial. Even the most ancient law-books do not contain a similar rule. In order to avoid any insecurity this rule was probably incorporated into Kauṭilya's Arthaśāstra. Indeed the conviction existed that a sick man who could not earn was not liable to pay interests or compound interests[36].

F. The ancient Indian law-books have limited the possibilities of a usurer not only by the determination of the admissible scale of the rates of interests but also by the determination the duration of the obligation of paying interests. According to the Smṛti-s books the maximum duration of the obligation of paying interest varied. And so, for example, the duration of the obligation of paying interest on corn ended in some instances after half of the capital was received, in others after five times the capital was received[37].

N. rightly stated that in some countries the loan could grow till twice the amount of the principal had been reached. In other countries it could grow till it became three or four, or

35. K. III. ch. 11.

36. It is of great interest that K. further stated that debts neglected for ten years, except in the case of minors, aged persons, sick persons, persons involved in calamities or persons who were sojourning abroad or have left the country except in the case of disturbances in the kingdom should not be received back. We read here about the rules of debts and of exceptions from these rules which were very characteristic and throw light on the application of Law to the economic conditions. Cf. also Vās. 2.49.

37. K. & Bṛh.

eight times the principal.[38] The difference depended on the customs existing in various parts of the country.

For the problem of the harmonising of Law with the requirements of economic conditions these rules were of importance because the limitation of possibilities of a usurer emphasised the application of Law to the economic condition. They were also important because the duration of the obligation of paying interest to the creditor depended also on the importance of the respective objects in the economic life. For example the capital which consisted of gold could be only doubled while the capital which consisted of spirituous liquors could be increased eightfold[39].

We also find other examples in the Smṛti-s, e.g. interest on gold could be doubled[40] on clothes and base metals trebled[41] and according to other Law-books fourfold,[42] on grain it was allowed to raise the original amount four times. The same applied to edible plants,[43] beasts of burden and wool[44] though, according to other Law-books, it only trebled.[45] After the debthas been doubled or trebled etc. no further interests could accrue on the capital. Concerning the interests on stocks K.[46] regulated that interests on stocks could amount to one half of the profit if it remained on the same place and had to be paid as each year expired. Borrowed money, which was lent for a long time abroad or was joined with the capital of the contractor had to give double of the contributed capital. We find here another good example of the harmonising of Law with the requirements of economic conditions; it is similar to the rule of the higher rate of interests by travelling by sea, etc. It also shows that the capital, which was more endangered i.e. which was sent for a long time abroad earned more interests than an ordinary loan. According to some Law-books, a loan of grain could rise four times[47] or

38. N. I-106.
39. Bṛh.
40. Y. 2-30, Mn. 8.151, Bṛh. 1a.18, Vi. VI. 11, Vās. II-44, N, I-107.
41. Such as tin or lead. Bṛh. 10-17.
42. Clothes. Y. 2.39, Vi. VI.13, Vās. II-44, N. I. 107.
43. or fruit
44. Bṛh. 10.17.
45. Y. 2.39, Vi VI.12, Vās. II.44, N. I.107.
46. K. III. ch. 11.
47. Mn. VIII.151, 153

five times[48]. According to K.[49] interests on grain had to be paid after the ripening of the crops. It could rise to a minimum of half the loan dependent on the prices. In other words the scale of the amount of the grain, to be paid, depended on the market price of the grain. Therefore, when the grain was cheaper at the time of harvest, than at the time of sowing, the debtor had to pay the difference in the price of the grain.[50] For this purpose the interests had not to be paid until after the harvesting of the grain. This rule can be found in Kauṭilya's Arthaśāstra only.

The interests on the produce of a field should not increase more than five times the value of the object and[51] on rice and edible plants[52] not more than four times.[53]

The interests on clothes could not increase more than three times the capital according to Bṛh.[54] while many objects like wool could increase fourfold[55] or fivefold[56]. On cotton[57] thread,[58] leather[59] the interests were unlimited or no interests could be exacted[60].

On base metals,[61] flavouring substances,[62] roots[63] interests could treble the capital.

According to some Law-books the interests on flowers could not increase more than treble[64] ; according to other Law-books, in such a case no interests could accrue[65].

Interests on fruits could not increase the capital more than three times;[66] according to other Law-books not more than

48. *vide* Mn. VIII-153.
49. Bṛh. 10.17.
50. K. III. ch. II.
51. J.J. Meyer, Das altindische Buch vom Welt-und Staatsleben, Leipzig p. 275.
52. G. XII,-36.
53. Bṛh. 10.17
54. Bṛh. 10.17.
55. Bṛh. 10.17.
56. G. XII-36, Mn. VIII-151.
57. Vi. VI-16.
58. Vi. VI-16, Bṛh. 10.23.
59. Vi. VI-16, Bṛh. 10.23.
60. S. B. E. XXXIII, ad Bṛh 10.23.
61. Bṛh. 10-23
62. Vās. II-45.
63. Vās. II-46.
64. Vās. II-46.
65. Bṛh. 10.23.
66. Vās. II-46.

four[67] or five-times[68], or no interests could accrue.[69]

Interests on beasts or beasts of burden,[70] as well as products of animals[71] could not increase the capital more than four times and, according to other Law-books, more than five times.

Interests on salt,[72] oil,[73] sugar,[74] honey,[75] in other words on all what was sold by weight[76] could not increase more than eight times.

On spirituous liquor[77] the debt could increase eightfold, while in the case of a loan on substances from which spirits could be extraced[78] no interests was allowed or the interests was unlimited.[79]

On grass and wood no interests was allowed,[80] also on bricks no interests was allowed[81] or interest was unlimited.[82] On weapons and char-coal interests were unlimited.[83]

The offspring had to be taken as interests,[84] from female slaves and cattle.

We see here that the possibilities of a usurer were limited:

(a) by the determination of the admissible scale of the rates of interests;

(b) by the determination of the duration of the obligation of paying interests.

G. But life was stronger than legal codes. For the ancient Indian conditions the rates of interests determined by the ancient Indian Law-books were too low. Under such circumstances the real economic conditions were an obstacle for the

67. Bṛh. 10.17.
68. Mn. VIII.151.
69. Bṛh. 10.17.
70. Bṛh. 10.17.
71. G. XII.36.
72. Bṛh. 10.18 Kāty. 510-512.
73. Bṛh. 10 18. Kāty. 510-512.
74. Bṛh. 10.18. Kāty. 510-512
75. Bṛh. 10.18.
76. Vās. II-47.
77. Bṛh. 10.18, Y. II.39, N. I.107, Vi. VI.14. Kāty, 510-512.
78. Bṛh 10.23
79. Vi. VI-16.
80. Brh. 10.23.
81. Brh. 10.23.
82. Vi. VI.16.
83. Vi. VI.16.
84. Y. 2.39, Vi. VI.15, N. I.107.

granting of a loan. Therefore, it was necessary to find another solution.

The solution was as follows : If a person could not repay the capital on the date due, he could conclude in writing a new agreement and take a new loan if he paid all the interests which he was in arrears,[86] or if he could not pay all the interests, he could in the newly concluded agreement add the interests to the capital.[87] (Capitalisation of interests.) Through this capitalisation of interests it was possible to receive higher interests than was allowed by law. In this way the grant of such loans, which, according to the Law, had to remain without interests was made easy and yielded larger and larger interests. It was only necessary to conclude a new contract in which the amount of the loan consisted of the original amount of the loan plus the additional interests.

In such a manner the rule of the determination of the duration of payment of interest was made null and void.

3. We find another example of the harmonising of Law with the requirements of economic conditions in Kauṭilya's Arthaśāstra. Kauṭilya even regulated the price for merchandise which was produced in the country and that which was imported from abroad. In ancient India, some foreign merchants and therefore some foreign merchandises were considered necessary[88]. Sometimes this was not so much for economic reasons as for political reasons, as this made it possible for the king to receive import taxes on foreign merchandise. But this consideration of no value for us, because here we are not concerned with the motive, but the principle; the fact remains that such merchandise was not available in the country.[89] The economic conditions of that time which were joined inseparably with the interests of the king necessitated the granting of privileges to foreigners.

However, according to the local economic conditons it was not desirable that prices for the merchandise should fluctuate. That was the reason for the introduction of special regulations.

86. Mn. VIII.154.
87. Mn. VIII.155.
88. J.J. Meyer Das altindische Buch vom Welt-und Staatsleben, Leipzing, p. 149.42 V.
89. K. II. ch. 16.

We read in Kauṭilya's Arthaśāstra that "the Superintendent of Commerce shall ascertain demand or absence of demand for, and rise or fall in the price of, various kinds of merchandise which may be the products either of land or of water and which may have been brought in either by land or by water centralisation path. He shall also ascertain the time suitable for their distribution purchase and sale.[90]

We find there further the following sentence: "That merchandise, which is widely distributed shall be centralised and its price enhanced. When the enhanced rate become popular, another rate shall be declared.

"That merchandise of the king which is of local manufacture shall be centralised; imported merchandise shall be distributed in several markets for sale. Both kinds of merchandise shall be sold to the people at favourable rates.

"He shall avoid such large profits as will harm the people.

"There shall be no restriction as to the time of sale of those commodities for which there is frequent demand; nor shall they be subject to the evils of centralisation.[91]

"The superintendent shall show favour to those who import foreign merchandise. They shall be favoured with remission of the trade-taxes, so that they may derive some profit.[92]

It results from Kauṭilya's Arthaśāstra that the bestowal of privileges on foreigners, who have imported merchandise was made for the purpose of obtaining foreign merchandise which was necessary for the daily use and therefore for the purpose of regulating the economic conditions. We find in Kauṭilya's Arthaśāstra the following sentence: "As regards the sale of the king's merchandise in foreign countries : having ascertained the value of local produce as compared with that of foreign produce that can be obtained in barter, the superintendent will find out by calculation whether there is any margin left for profit after meeting the payments to the foreign king such as toll, road-cess, conveyance-cess, tax payable at military stations, ferry-charges subsistence to the merchant and his followers and the portion of merchandise payable to the foreign king. If no profit can be realised by selling the local produce

90. K. 11. ch. 16. According to the translation by Shamasastry.
91. K. II. ch. 16. According to the translation by Shamasastry.
92. K. II. ch. 16. According to the translation by Shamasastry.

in foreign countries, he has to consider whether any local produce can be profitably bartered for any foreign produce."[93]

We also find in Kauṭilya's Arthaśāstra, what the superintendent of Commerce had to do in order to amass and to preserve foreign merchandise.[94]

The prohibition of import and export with reference to the economic conditions was treated also in Kauṭilya's Arthaśāstra and some other Dharmaśāstra-s.[95]

Principally they dealt with the question of the exclusion from import merchandise which caused harm or was useless to the country and of import of merchandise which was useful. Such a merchandise had to be imported free of duty.[96]

As it was necessary for the normal economic life that commodities of daily use be sold at a fixed price, the ancient Indian law-books regulated the prices of such merchandise by fixing them. We read in the Yājñavalkya's Smṛti that the sale and purchase shall be conducted daily according to the value fixed by the king.[97] It was even punishable to demand a higher price. For such people who agreed upon the determination of the price to the disadvantage of the workmen and artists, although the fluctuation of the price were known to them, the highest fine was applicable.[98] The same punishment was to be applied also those merchants who did not purchase the foreign articles at the price fixed by the king and who bought them cheaply and to those who sold them at a higher price.[99]

4. The economic life in ancient India needed foreign merchants; therefore special privileges were accorded to them. Similarly, the economic life in ancient India needed an incentive for construction of reservoirs and irrigation-dams; therefore the state granted special tax-exemptions and tax-facilities to those who constructed such reservoirs and irrigation dams.

That the irrigation-dams, tanks etc. were of great importance to the economic conditions of Ancient India is obvious

93. K. II. ch. 16. According to the translation by Shamasastry.
94. K. II. ch. 16.
95. K. II. ch. 21. Vide Mn. III.399, Y. II.261, Vi. V.130.
96. K. II. ch. 21.
97. Y. II-251. Vide Mn. VIII-402.
98. Y. II-249. Vide K. II. ch. 6.
99. Y. II. 250.

from Kauṭilya's Arthaśāstra,[100] and also indirectly from Yājña-valkya's Dharmaśāstra.[101]

We find particularly in Kauṭilya's Arthaśāstra that, in the case of construction of new works such as tanks, lakes etc., taxes on the land below such tanks were remitted for five years. For reparing neglected or ruined works of similar nature, taxes were remitted for four years. For improving or extending water-works, taxes were remitted for three years. In the case of acquiring such newly started works by mortgage or purchase, taxes on the lands below such works were remitted for two years.[102]

These laws concerning the reduction of taxes are similar to the exemption from taxes of new buildings, known in recent times. Because of economic conditions then prevailing special facilities for payment of taxes were granted in ancient India and are even at present granted for the purpose of economic welfare. Now-a-days the construction of new buildings is intended to prevent the hoarding of money; in ancient India it was intended to build new irrigation works for the purpose of improving the fertility of the fields; that was the highest aim of the economic policy of the ancient Indian State.

That this was the true aim could be seen from the fact that the duration of the exemption of taxes depended on the scale ofexpenses.

5. We have seen that the motive for the bestowing of facilities on foreign merchants was the need of foreign merchants for the economic life in Ancient India. The case was similar where the formation of villages was concerned. A deserted land was from the point of view of ancient Indian economics—a negative entry in the balance of the ancient Indian State, or better to say of the ancient Indian kings. Kauṭilya's Arthaśāstra understood well that an increase of the wealth of the citizens increased the universal prosperity and therefore increased also the wealth of the State i. e. of the king.[103] Therefore,

100. K. V. ch. 6.
101. Y. II. 157.
102. K. III. ch. 9. according to the translation by Shamasastry.
103. K. II. ch. 1.

Kauṭilya's Arthaśāstra tried—although from a machiavellistic point of view to enrich the king especially by populating the deserted land. The suggestion for such a colonisation was supported by the introduction of special laws, which once more pointed to the harmonising of Law with the requirements of economic conditions.

As regards the colonisation of a deserted land, Kauṭilya's Arthaśāstra asked what land had to be colonised : a plain or watery land ?[104]

The answer was: 'A limited tract of land with water is far better than a vast plain.[105] Plains, which are suitable for the growth of both, early and late crops, and which require less labour and less rain for cultivation are better than the reverse of these.[106] Waterly lands, that are suitable to the growth of grains are better than those which are suitable for crops other than grains.[107]'

'Of two waterly tracts, one of limited area and suitable for the growth of grains, and another, vast and suitable for crops other than grains, the latter is better, inasmuch as its vast area may not only be used to grow spices and other medicinal crops, but also to construct forts other defensive works in large numbers : for fertility and other qualities of lands are artificial.[108] Of the tract of land with forts and that which is thickly populated, the latter is better; for that which is thickly populated is a kingdom in every sense. What can a depopulated country like a barren cow be productive of ?[109]

'Such a land which was recognised as most suitable for colonisation has to be colonised by the king either by inducing the inhabitance of other tracts to immigrate or by causing the thickly-populated centres of his own kingdom to send forth their surplus population.[110]"

By trying to attract people in "such a country" we see how the Law was applied to the requirements of economic conditions. Kauṭilya's Arthaśāstra determined: 'Those who perform sacrifices, spiritual guides, priests, and those

104. K. VII. ch. 11.
105. K. VII. ch. 11 according to the translation by Shamasastry.
106. See Note 105.
107. See Note 105.
108. See Note 105.
109. See Note 105.
110. See Note 105.

learned in the Vedas shall be granted Brahmadaya lands yielding sufficient produce and exempted from taxes and fines. Superintendents, Accountants, Gopa-s, Sthānika-s, Veterinary surgeons, Physicians, Horse-trainers, and Messengers shall also be endowed with lands which they shall have no right to alienate by sale or mortgage.[111]'

When the colonisation took place the king had to grant exemption from taxes. He should regard with fatherly kindness those who have passed the period of exemption from taxes[112]. The king should carry on mining operations and manufacture, exploit timber and elephant forests, offer facilities for cattle-breeding and commerce, construct roads for traffic, both by land and water, and set up market towns. He should also construct reservoirs[113].' The king had to regulate also the internal conditions of a colonised village. 'Owing to the fact that the newly colonised villages had to look after their own interest and the men found pleasure in the fields, the king's treasury, free labour, commodities, grain and liquids have became enriched[114].'

It ought to be noted that the land may be confiscated from those who did not cultivate it and given to others. Lands prepared for cultivation should be given to tax-payers only as personal property[115]. Unprepared lands should not be taken away from those who were preparing them for cultivation[116]. Lands which were not cultivated could be given for cultivation to village labourers and traders; owners of lands which were not quite suitable for cultivation could pay less to the government. Those owners had to be favourably supplied with seeds, cattle and money[117]. Kauṭilya's Arthaśāstra stated also that the king had to give the cultivators seeds, cattle and money[118].

It is to be noted that the aim of Kauṭilya's Arthaśāstra was; to increase the king's treasure.

111. See Note 105.
112. K. II. ch 1.
113. K. II. ch. 1, according to the translation by Shamashastry.
114. K. II. ch. 1.
115. K. II. ch. 1.
116. K. II. ch. 1.
117. K. II. ch. 1.
118. K. V. ch. 2. & V. ch. 3.

In connexion with the kings duty to support the cultivators, Kauṭilya's Arthaśāstra stated that 'the king shall bestow on cultivators only such favour and remission as will tend to swell the treasury, and shall avoid such as will deplete it. A king with depleted treasury will eat into the very vitality of both town and country people[119]. This principle we find in recent times too.

According to this principle the conquered country was exempt from taxes[120]. The same applied to a poor country and country in great danger. It applied especially to people who had to suffer much from hostile neighbours, i. e. people 'who lived on the border of the kingdom or who had not enough subsistence[121]' This is another example of the harmonising of Law with the requirements of economic conditions.

6. Above, some examples of the exemptions of taxes were given . These exemptions of taxes could be divided into personal and not personal exemptions. These exemptions which point to the harmonising of Law with the requirements of economic conditions were introduced not for the purpose of protecting the subjects, but for the purpose of enriching the treasury of the king. In the epics and in these law-books, which were free from the Machiavellism of Kauṭilya's tax-policy, we could find rulings on tax-policy of the king, which were not only very praiseworthy but were also very suitable. These rulings took into consideration the economic condition of the tax-payers i. e. the king's subjects. Below some such examples from the Mānava-Dharmaśāstras, Mahābhārata etc. are quoted.

'Out of affection for his subjects, he must not bring about his own ruin by forswearing to collect his revenue from them, nor cause their ruin by his greed; by so bringing about his own ruin will become an oppressor of his own self, as well as of his subjects.'[122].

'As leeches, calves and bees, little by little draw their respective sustenances, so the king shall draw his revenue from his realm little by little, each year[123].'

119. K. II. ch. 1. according to the translation by Shamasastry.
120. K. XIII. ch. 5.
121. K. V. ch. 2.
122. Mn. VII-13, See Y, I-338-339.
123. Mn. VII-129. See Mārkaṇḍeya (Parās. p. 404).

'The king has to milk the cow as a bee collects honey from the flowers. He has to do what a herdsman, who receives the milk from his cow, does. He neither harms the udders nor lets the cow go hungry[125].'

'A good king has to milk his country as a calf sucks the milk of the cow. Because, when the calf sucks from the cow it becomes strong and can bear burdens[126].'

'But if it is otherwise and the cow is milked to excess, the calf becomes meagre and useless for the owner[127].'

'It is said that an avaricious king who imposes unjust taxes which are not sanctioned by law on his subjects causes damage to himself[128].

'The king shall never exact taxes from those, who cannot pay. He has to get them gradually, with goodness, and by lawful methods[129], [130].'

Many things can easily be acquired by a king 'who supports his country and grants facilities to his subjects and is satisfied with that which is within easy reach[131]. If the king does not receive enough of wealth to satisfy his claims, then his whole land will be his treasury and his treasury his bed-room.'[132]

'Like he who needs milk, never gets it, if the udders of his cow are cut, so the king will never be in a position to use his kingdom if he does not impose taxes in a legitimate manner.'[133]

"The king has to be clever and should milk the country every day like a cow, but he should not cut the cow's udders[134]. 'He who treats the cow well, will always receive fresh milk; in the same way it will be possible for the king to enjoy the fruits of his country. If he reigns over his country in an orderly manners.'[135] 'The country which is protected by the king bears fruits and money like a mother who willingly gives her breast to her child.'[136], [137]

125. MBh. XII.88—4.
126. MBh. XII.87—20.
127. MBh. XII.87—21.
128. MBh. XII.7—15.
129. Righteous rules.
130. MBh. XII.88—12.
131. MBh. XII.87—22.
132. MBh. XII.87— 3.
133. MBh. XII.71,16.
134. MBh. XII.120.33.
135. MBh. XII.71,17.
136. MBh. XII.71,19.
137. *Vide* MBh XII. 8, 15, 17, 18, NV 61.12, SS 6.2, 220-240.

Those rules are not only found in the Mānava-Dharmaśāstra and the Māhabhārāta but also in Kauṭilya's Arthaśāstra;[138] they were applicable only if the king possessed a treasure. However, a king who found himself in great financial trouble and needed money could collect taxes in another way[139]. The economic situation did not allow him to act in a manner in which a good king ought to act. On account of the economic situation the king had to act like a thief, in the manner prescribed by the machiavellistic school of Kauṭilya. The motive,[140] 'the enrichment of the treasure of the king', allows the king to act in the following manner not only against traitors and the godless but also against his subjects[141].

The examples quoted here, found in Kauṭilya's Arthaśāstra, are a good examples of the harmonising of Law with requirements of the economic conditions, especially when they are compared with the above mentioned rules about the correct way of collecting the taxes.[142]

It was not advisable to inflict taxes twice. But, the Collector General shall seek subscriptions from citizens and country people alike under false pretences of carrying this or that kind of business. Persons taken in concert shall publicly pay handsome donations and with this example, the king may demand donations of others among his subjects. Spies posing as citizens shall revile those who pay less. Wealthy persons may be requested to give as much of their gold as they can. Those who, of their own accord or with the intention of doing good, offer their wealth to the king shall be honoured with a rank in the court, an umbrella, or a turban or some ornaments in return for their gold. Spies under the guise of sorcerers, shall, under the pretence of ensuring safety, carry away the money not only of the society of heretics and of temples, but also of a dead-man and of a man whose house is burnt, provided that it is not enjoyable by Brāhmaṇs.

The Superintendent of Religious Institutions may collect in one place the various kinds of property of the gods of fortified

138. K. II. ch. 1.
139. K. V. ch. 2.
140. K. II. ch. 2 *in fine*.
141. *vide* K. V. ch. 2. and K. II. ch. 1.
142. K. V. ch. 2 according to Shamashastry's translation.

cities and country parts and carry away the property to the king's treasury.

"Or having on some night set up a god or an altar, or having opened a sacred place of ascetics or having pointed out an evil omen, the king may collect subsistance under the pretence of holding processions and congregations to avert calamities.

"Or also he shall proclaim the arrival of gods, by pointing out to the people any of the sacred trees in the king's garden which has produced untimely flowers and fruits.

"Or by causing a false panic owing to the arrival of an evil-spirit in a tree in the city, wherein a man is hidden making all sorts of devilish noises, the king's spies, under the guise of ascetics, may collect money with a view to propitiate the evil-spirit and send it back.

"Or spies may call upon spectators to see a serpent with numberless heads in a well, connected with a subterranean passage, and collect fees from them for the night. Or they may place in a borehole made in the body of an image of a serpent, or in a hole in the corner of a temple, or in the hole of an ant-hill, a cobra, which is, by diet, rendered unconscious, and call upon credulous spectators to see it on payment of a certain amount of fee. As to persons who are not by nature credulous, spies may sprinkle over or give a drink of such sacred water as is mixed with anaesthetic ingredients and attribute their insensibility to the curse of the gods. Or by causing an outcast person (*adhityāktā*) to be bitten by a cobra, spies may collect revenue under the pretext of undertaking remedial measures against *ominous phenomena*.

"Or one of the king's spies in the garb of a merchant, may become the partner of a rich merchant, and carry on trade in concert with him. As soon as a considerable amount of money has been gathered as sale-proceeds, deposits and loans, he may cause himself to be robbed of the amount.

"Or else a spy, in the garb of a rich merchant, or a real rich merchant famous for his vast commerce, may borrow or take on pledge vast quantities of gold, silver, and other commodities, or borrow from corporations bar gold, or coined gold for various kinds of merchandise to be procured from abroad. After having done this he may allow himself to be robbed of it the same night.

Prostitute spies under the garb of chaste women, may cause themselves to be enamoured of persons who are seditious. No sooner are the seditious persons seen within the abode of the female spies than they shall be seized and their property confiscated by the Government. Or whenever a quarrel arises between any two seditious parties of the same family, poisoners, previously engaged for the purpose, may administer poison to one party ; and the other party may be accused of the offence and deprived of their property.

"An outcast, under the guise of a high-born man, may claim from a seditious person a large amount of money professed to have been placed in the latter's custody by the claimant, or a large debt outstanding against the seditious person; or a share of parental property. An outcast may pretend to be the slave of a seditious person ; and he may represent the wife, daughter, or daughter-in-law of the seditious person as a slave-woman or as his own wife : and when the outcast is lying at the door of the seditious person's house at night or is living elsewhere, a fierce spy may murder him and declare:—'The claimant of his own property or wife has been thus killed. And for this offence others i. e., the seditious person and his followers shall be deprived of their property.

"Or a spy, under the garb of an ascetic, may offer inducements to a seditious person to acquire more wealth by taking in aid the art of witchcraft, and say:—'I am proficient in such witchcraft as brings inexhaustible wealth, or entitles, a man to get admission into the king's palace, or can win the love of any woman, or can put an end to the life of one's enemy, or can lengthen the duration of one's life, or can give a son to any one, if desired.' 'If the seditious person shows his desire to carry on the process of witchcraft securing wealth, the spy may make rich offerings, consisting of flesh, wine, and scent to the deity near an altar in a burial-ground wherein a dead body of a man or of a child with a little quantity of money has been previously hidden. After the performance of worship is over, the hidden treasure may be dug out and the seditious person may be told that as the offerings fell short, the treasure is proportionately small, that the richest of offerings should be made to acquire vast amount of treasure, and that he may purchase with the newly-acquired wealth rich offerings. Then he may be caught in the very act of purchasing commodities for offering.

"A female spy, under the garb of a bereaved mother, may in connection with the above case, raise an alarm crying that her child was murdered for the purpose of witchcraft.

"When a seditious person is engaged in sorcery at night or in a sacrificial performance in a forest, or in sports in a park, fiery spies may murder him and carry away the corpse as that of an outcast.

"Or a spy, under the garb of a servant of a seditious person, may mix counterfeit coins with the wages he has received from his master and pave the way for his arrest.

"Or a spy, under the garb of a goldsmith, may undertake to do some work in the house of a seditious person, and gather in his employer's house such instruments as are necessary to manufacture counterfeit coins.

"A spy, under the garb of a physician, may declare a healthy person of seditious character to be unhealthy and administer poison. Or a spy, attending as a servant upon a seditious person may not only call for an explanation from another fraudulent spy as to how certain articles necessary for the installation of a king and also the letters of an enemy came into the possession of his master, but also volunteer an explanation himself.

XVII

TWO READINGS OF MĀNAVA-DHARMAŚĀSTRA IV.85.

1. Mānava-dharmaśāstra (Mn.) IV 84 states that none should accept gifts from: (1) a king not born from a Kṣatriya caste, (2) keepers of slaughter-houses, (3) keepers of oil-presses, (4) keepers of liquor-seller's shops, and (5) those who live on *veśa* (*veśenaiva ca jīvatām*). In the next verse Mn. quotes an aphorism reading:

daśa-sūnā[1]*-samaṁ*[2] *cakraṁ*[3] *daśa-cakra-samo*[4] *dhvajaḥ*[5],
daśa-dhvaja-samā veśyā daśa-veśyā-samo nṛpaḥ.

In some Mn. texts *cd* of this aphorism reads:

daśa-dhvaja-samo veśo daśa-veśa-samo nṛpaḥ.

2. As can be seen from the above, the texts of Mn. IV.85 are not identical; some texts have in *cd* ·*samā veśyā daśa-veśyā* (called here first version), while others have ·*samo veśa daśa-veśa* (called here second version). In the first version the meaning of this aphorism is : "one oil-press is as bad as ten slaughter-houses, one liquor-seller's shop as bad as ten oil-presses; one prostitute as bad as ten liquor-seller's shops, one king as bad as ten prostitutes"; in the second version the meaning of this aphorism is: "one oil-press is as bad as ten slaughter-houses, one liquor-seller's shop as bad as ten oil-presses; one brothel as bad as ten liquor-seller's shops, one king as bad as ten brothels."

The second version is quoted in all Mn. editions which quoted the Manvarthamuktāvali, the Commentary by Kullūka Bhaṭṭa (e. g. in the Kāśisaṁskṛtasīrjapustakamālāyāḥ 114;

* Previously appeared in the "Bhāratiya Vidya" Vol. XVIII. Nos 3-4, pp. 64-8.

This paper was presented to the 170th meeting of the American Oriental Society in New Hayon, March 1960.

1. *śūnā* Mn Loiseleur Deslongchamps' and Haughton's editions.

2. *śamaṣ* Smṛtimuktāphalam.

3. *cckrī* Smṛtimuktāphalam, MS 1518a in India Office Library in London of Cānakya (305).

4. *cakrī* Smrtimuktāphalam, MS cakri 1518a In India Office Library London of Cānakya.

5. *dhvajī* Smṛtimuktāphalam.

Nirṇaya Sāgara Press, Śaka 1809 & 1946, etc.). as well as in A. Loiseleur Deslongchamps' edition, (Paris 1830); V. N. Mandlik's edition, (Bombay 1886); G. Jhā's edition (in Bibliotheca Indica 256); G. Ch. Haughton's edition based on William Jone's edition (London 1825).

The first version is quoted in all Mn. editions which were based on Govindarāja's commentary and in the critical J. Jolly's edition, London 1887 in Truebner's Oriental Series). It is also quoted in V. N. Mandlik's edition in the footnote, as j. jh, ṭ, ṭh, ḍ and ḍh, J. Jolly states in the notes that Medhātithi's[6], Govindarāja's, Rāghavānanda's (R.), Nandana's, Sarvajña-Nārāyaṇa's (N.) and the Kaśmīrian commentaries give the first version of Mn. IV. 85, while Kullūka's Rāghavānanda's (Rā), *varia lectio* of Sarvajña-Nārāyaṇa's (N.) commentaries and the Vulgata (*editio princeps* with Kullāka's commentary, Calcutta 1813, 1830 and 1874, Haughton's and Loiseleur Deslongchamps' editions) give the second version of Mn. IV. 85, J. Jolly added that the latter reading was wrongly referred to Medhātithi's commentary by Kullūka. However J. Jolly is not right, since G. Jhā's edition which is based on Manubhāṣya of Medhātithi has also the second version.

3. As can be seen from the above some commentators and editors of Mn. accepted the first, while others accepted the second version of Mn. IV. 85.

Kullūka in his commentary referred to Govindarāja's and Medhātithi's views and stated: *Govindarājas tu "deśa-veśyā-samo nṛpaḥ" iti paṭhati; Medhātithi—prabhṛtayaḥ prāñco "daśa-veśa-samo nṛpaḥ" iti paṭhanti.* Govindarāja[7] did not comment in detail on this point but referring to Mn. IV. 85 gives only the text in its first version. Rāghavānanda[8] in his commentary stated inter alia: *tad daśa guṇaś ca kriṇi tad daśa guṇaḥ śauṇḍika tad daśa guṇo veśyāyām; tad daśa guṇo nṛpa iti...*

4. Stanza Mn. IV. 85, which can be considered as an aphorism, is very seldom quoted in the *nibandha-s* or Sanskrit literary works. None of the important subhāṣitasaṁgraha-s cite it. It is not quoted in the Paddhati of Śārṅgadhara (ŚP), the Subhā-

6. See below. Medhātithi belongs to the other group.

7. The commentary of Govindarāja on Mānava-dharmaśāstra ed. with notes by V. N. Mandlik, Bombay 1886.

8. Quoted in Mandlīk's edtion of Mn.

ṣitāvalī of Vallabhadeva the Subhāṣita-ratna-bhāṇḍāgāra (SR), the Subhāṣita-ratnākara, the Sūktiratnahāra, the Sūktimuktāvalī of Bhagadatta Jalhaṇa, nor even in Bōhtlingk's Indische Sprüche and what is most strange it is not even found in L. Jośī's Dharmakośa, where most Mn. stanzas are quoted. However one of the Cāṇakya's compendia belonging to the Cāṇakya-nītiśāstra version,[9] viz. MS. 1518a (Eggeling 3990) in the India Office Library, London contains this aphorism, as stanza.[10]

Yājñavalkya-smṛti (Y.) contains a very similar stanza, viz. I. 141[11] which was undoubtedly based on Mn. IV. 85 and the Medhātithi's *bhāṣya*.[12] Y. states there :

pratigrahe sūni-cakri-dhvaji-veśyā-narādhipāḥ;
duṣṭā daśa-guṇaṁ pūrvat pūrvād ete yathākramam.

"As far as receiving of gifts is concerned (the following five should be avoided): a butcher, an oil-presser, ali quor seller, a prostitute and a king. Each succeeding is ten times worse than the one preceding."

Mitra Miśra, commenting in his Vīramitrodaya on this Y. stanza quotes also Mn. IV. 85 in its first version. Similarly also Bālambhaṭṭī in the *Snātaka-prakaraṇa* (401. 6) and Vaidyanātha Dīkṣita in the Smṛtimuktāphala (Dharmaśāstra granthamālā 25. 1; p. 55. 20) commenting on Y. I. 141, quotes Mn. IV. 85 in the first version. As far as it could be ascertained these are the only cases where the Mn. stanza were quoted in *nibandha-s*.[13]

5. Medhātithi in his *bhāṣya* to IV.85, referring to the preceding stanza, explained that it meant that the receiving of gifts from the one mentioned later is worse than that from the one mentioned before it. This is exactly the same explanation as that given in *cd* of Y. I. 141.

As was explained before, according to Mn. IV. 84, the worst of all was the king not born of the Kṣatriya caste, then came

9. Proceedings of the XXIV International Congress of Orientalists in Munich.

10. Recently I found this stanza in the first version in the Padmapurāṇa, Sṛṣṭikhaṇḍa 19. 236 and the Bhaviṣya-purāṇa, Uttaraparva 19 and a similar stanza 14 ŚP 2086 and SR 145.114.

11. In Gaṇapati Śāstri's edition (TSS 74) I 140.

12. Cf. L. Sternbach, The Hitopadeśa and its Sources in American Oriental Series 44, par. 26.

13. Even Aparārka's (ĀnSS 46) and Bālakriḍa of, Viśvarūpacārya's (TSS 74) commentaries do not quote Mn. IV. 85. Aparārka quotes however Mn. IV 86-91 and the Bālakriḍa Mn. IV 84.

the keeper of slaughter-houses (a butcher), than the keeper of oil-presses (oilpresser), than the keeper of liquor-seller's shops (a liquor seller) and than he who lived on *veśa*. *Veśa* generally means a place of prostitutes, a district in a town for prostitutes and more particularly, a brothel. Amarasiṁha cited in Śabdakalpadruma (*ad veśyājanasamaśraya*) identifies the word *veśa* with the words *pura*, *veśyā-śraya* and *veśyālaya* (See also Hemacandra's Abhidhānacintāmaṇi 1003a) and Medini cited in Śabdakalpadruma (*ad veśa*) with *veśyāgṛha* (see also Amarakośa; ed. by Colebrooke, Calcutta 1807; 24. 4). *Veśa* is also used in the meaning "brothel" in Mn. IX. 264, Mṛcchakaṭika, act IV (p. 107), Daśakumāracarita (228. 111, etc. See also Hemacandra's Anekārthasaṁgraha; Vienna-Bombay 1893; II, 541).

In this particular context the word *veśa* was explained by Medhātithi (*ad* Mn. IV. 84) as meaning: *paṇya-vṛttiḥstayā yo jīvati-strī vā pumān vā* and by Kullūka (*ad* Mn. IV. 84) as meaning: *paṇyastriyā bhṛtiḥ tayā yo jīvati strī pumān vā sa veśavān*. The word *veśa* does not need to mean only ""brothel" but also "wages of prostitutes" or "gain of prostitutes" (see: Revised and Enlarged Edition of V. S. Apte's Sanskrit-English Dictionary; p. 1496 *ad veśaḥ*. 9 with reference to Mn IV. 84). It was also so translated in Mn. IV. 84 by Sir William Jones (Calcutta-London 1796; Haughton, London 1869) and G. Bühler in SBE XXV, while G. Jhā, Loiseleur Deslongchamps and Strehly (Les Lois de Manou; Annales du Musée Guimet II) translated it as "brothel". Strehly, who based his translation of Mn. on J. Jolly's edition, went even so far as to reject Jolly's first version of Mn. IV. 85; basing himself on Mn. IV. 84 he stated: *Jolly imprime* veśyā *au lieu de* veśa *'un roi est l'égal des prostitués'*; *mais la gradation est plus réguliére avec* veśa.

6. When recapitulating, we see that Mn. IV. 85 has two different meanings in *cd*. Some texts have *samā veśyā daśa-veśyā-samo*, while others have *samo veśo daśa-veśa-samo*. The text based on the commentaries of Govindarāja (as well Rāghavānanda's (R), Sarvajña-Nārāyaṇa's, Nandana's and the Anonymous Kaśmīrian) uses the first version; however the text based on the commentaries of Kullūka. Medhātithi (as well as *varia lectio* of Sarvajña-Nārāyāṇa, of Rāghavananda's (Rā) commentaries and the Vulgata) uses the second version.

The commentaries quoting the Mn. (Vīramitrodaya, Smṛtimuktāphalam, Bālaṁbhaṭṭī) use also the first version. They quote Mn.'s text in conjunction with a similar stanza as the Mn. IV. 85 viz. Y. I. 141. Although the Y.'s text is similar to the Mn.'s text it contains an important change; it uses instead of places—persons. And so, it does not speak about slaughter-homes (*sūnā*) but about butchers (*sūni*); it does not speak about oil-presses (*cakra*) but about oil-pressers (*cakri*); it does not speak about liquor-shops (*dhvaja*) but about liquor-sellers (*dhvaji*); it also speaks clearly about *veśyā* and not veśa[14]. Probably, therefore the commentators on Y.'s text used Mn.'s text as found in the Govindarāja's commentary,[15] since it was better suited to Y.'s text.

Since, however, Mn. IV. 85 should be read in conjunxion with the preceding stanza where the words *sūnā*, *cakra*, *dhvaja* and *veśa* were used, the same expressions were used throughout in the subsequent stanza. All versions use in Mn. IV. 84 *sūnā*, *cakra*, *dhvaja* and *veśa*, therefore the proper use of the words in IV. 85 seems to be also *sūna*, *cakra*, *dhvaja* and *veśa*. Another argument for the use of *veśa* instead of *veśyā* in Mn. IV. 85 is that the whole aphorism deals with places and not persons; no reason, therefore, is seen while the word *veśyā* and not *veśa* should have been used in *cd* of Mn. IV. 85. It seems that there cannot be any doubt that the proper reading of Mn. IV. 85 is as follows:

daśa-sūnā-samaṁ cakraṁ daśa-cakra-samo dhvajaḥ,
daśa-dhvaja-samo veśo daśa-veśa-samo nṛpaḥ.

14. The Smṛtimuktāphalam and the Cāṇakya MS. quoted above, where the first version of Mn. is quoted, went even so far, as to change in Mn. IV. 85 places into person. SMPh. and C. have *cakri* (*ī*) and SMPh. *dhvaji*.

15. And connected with it texts.

XVIII

SHORT OUTLINE OF LAW IN INDIA*

1. By Paragraph 18(3) of the Indian Independence Act (10 and 11 Geo. 6., Ch. 30) of July 18, 1947, in the two independent dominions of India and Pakistan then being created, the laws of British India and of the several parts thereof existing immediately before the appointed day, so far as applicable and with the necessary adaptations, were to continue as the law of each of the new dominions and the several parts thereof until other provision should be made by laws of the legislatures of the two dominions. On Nov. 26, 1949, the Constituent Assembly of India adopted a new constitution, which became formally effective on Jan. 26, 1950, and superseded the previous arrangement. In Pakistan a new constitution had not yet been drafted.

In undivided India personal law in matters of succession, marriage, divorce, adoption, gifts, and charitable endowments differed for Hindūs and Moslems (Muslims), conforming in general principle to traditional law. In all other fields the statutory law applied to all persons irrespective of their religious faiths. Both systems of personal law claim divine origin and are interwoven with religion; both are based on custom and often originate from custom. But even personal law is suspended in certain agricultural tribes by customary law. A judicial decision on a customary practice is a binding authority.

1 HINDŪ LAW

2. In India, as in other countries of the Orient, law is an integral part of religion and ethics, and the books dealing

* Previously appeared in "India, Pakistan, Ceylon" edited by W. Norman Brown, Cornell University Press, 1951, chapter X on Law, pp. 116-27, being a reprint from the "Encyclopedia Americana", Vol. XV, pp. 28d—g.

In this article entitled "Law", the author gave only a very short outline of selected aspects of law in India.

with these subjects, called *Dharmaśāstra-s*, therefore offer us overwhelming data about religious purification and penance, prayer and sacrifice, prohibitions on food and drink, punishment in hell and rebirth, philosophy, eschatology, creation, funeral ceremonies and sacrifices to the dead, the study of the Vedas and ascerticism, the manner of living and customs of Brāhmaṇs and kings, and other subjects which we do not generally expect to find treated in such books. Many of them say nothing at all about law proper, and only a few later compilations may be called purely juridical works.

According to the *Dharmaśāstra-s*, the Veda-s should be regarded as the first and foremost source of ancient Indian law. In a narrow sense, the Vedas contain much data about sacrifices, penances, and prayers, as well as ethics, which are important for the history of customs, but they refer only occasionally to legal matters.

In the older books known as the *Dharmasūtra-s*, so far as they have been preserved, there are always found special sections on the law of inheritance, the law of government, legal procedure, and other features of law proper as it was taught and handed down traditionally in the oldest schools of the Brāhmaṇs.

The second stage of the legal literature is represented by the very numerous metrical works which have come down to the present time under the name of *Dharmaśāstra-s* or *Smṛti-s*. They differ from the *Dharmasūtra-s*, which are composed partly, or wholly in prose, in being written entirely in verse. Yet these works, to which the *Mānava-Dharmaśāstra*, the most esteemed authority, belongs, appear partly to have originated out of older *Dharmasūtra-s* and are therefore at least connected with the Vedic literature.

The latest stage of Indian legal literature is formed by the commentaries--*nibandha-s*, and systematic works which have been developed from the *Dharmasūtra-s* and *Dharmaśātra-s* since early mediaeval times. As the products of a new age, inspired by powerful princes and ministers, these extensive compilations gradually displaced the *Dharmasūtra-s* and *Dharmaśāstra-s* to the extent that at the time of the establishment of British rule in eastern India, the Mitākṣarā, a law compendium of the 11th century, was the standard work in the greater part of India. For the historical study of Indian law, for which clarification of the beginnings is of particular importance, this very large group of works is indispensable, especially since they are helpful in understanding the original sources.

In addition to the traditions contained in the Vedas, *Dharmasūtra-s*, and *Dharmaśāstra-s*, the Brāhmaṇical authors recognize as a third source of law the way of life and teachings of pious men, such as the *sadācāra* and the *śiṣṭāgama*. In connection with law proper, particular customs and manners of various countries, castes, and families are often emphasized as standard, though of course only so far as they are not opposed to the sacred law. The important position given in this respect to customary law is thoroughly in conformity with facts and renders it obligatory for those who deal with the history of law to search for traces and survivals of Indian customary law.

The most important sources of ancient Indian law are the *Āpastamba Dharmasūtra*, *Gautama Dharmasūtra*, *Vāsishṭha Dharmasūtra*, *Viṣṇu Smṛti*, *Mānava Dharmaśāstra*, *Yājñavalkya Dharmaśāstra*, and *Nārada Smṛti*.

The number of authors and works on the *Dharmaśāstra-s* is legion. All of them were actuated by the most laudable motives of regulating Hindū society in all matters—civil, religious, and moral—and of securing for the members of that society happiness in this world and the next. They laid the greatest emphasis on the duties of every man as a member of the whole Hindū society and of the particular class to which he belonged, and very little emphasis on the privileges of men. They created great solidarity and cohesion among the several classes of Hindū society in India in spite of conflicting interests and inclinations and enabled that society to hold its own against foreign invaders.

3. Today Hindū law is applied to: (I) Hindūs by birth and by religion, including those who after renouncing Hindūism have reverted to it; (2) illegitimate children both of whose parents are Hindūs; (3) illegitimate children in cases in which the father is a Christian and the mother a Hindū, provided the children are brought up as Hindūs; (4) sons of Hindū dancing girls of the Naik caste converted to Islam, in cases in which the sons are taken into the family of the Hindus grandparents and are brought up as Hindūs; (5) Jains, Sikhs, Nambudri Brāhmaṇs.

Hindūs are in theory divided into four major castes : Brāhmaṇs (Brāhmaṇas), Kshatriyas (Kṣatriyas), Vaiśyas (Vaiśyas), and Śūdras (Śūdras). Each of these is in turn subdivided into a number of subcastes, the latter being regarded by sociologists as the true castes. The first three of the major castes are *dvija*, or twice born. Through investiture with the sacred thread they have the right to study the Vedas and perform the saṁskara (Sanskrit : *saṁskāra*), or sacraments. All of these rights except the samskara of marriage are denied to Śūdras.

4. Today, as in ancient times, the main sources of Hindū law are found in: (1) *Śruti*, that is, divinely inspired works, including the mass of material known as the Veda; (2) the *Smṛti*; (3) customs which are based on lost or forgotten *Śruti* and *Smṛti*; and (4) judicial decisions.

The three principal *Smṛti* texts which are still considered sources of present day law are: (1) the Code of Manu (the *Mānava Dharmaśāstra*), compiled some time between 200 B.C. and 100 A. D.; (2) the Code of Yājñavalkya, written some time between 100 A. D. and 300 A. D. (the *Mitākṣara*, composed in the 11th century, is the leading commentary upon this code); and (3) the Code of Nārada, written some time between 100 B. C. and 400 A. D. In addition, there are more than 100 other *Dharmaśāstra-s* of greater or lesser importance.

The *Smṛti* texts do not agree with each other in all respects. The conflict between them gave rise to commentaries which often have been accepted as authoritative, even if they appear to scholars to proceed by wrong interpretation. Clear proof of usage outweights the written text of the Hindū law.

5. In regard to succession and inheritance, there are in principle only two schools of law, the Mitākṣarā and the Dāyabhāga. (The latter is a digest of codes on division of inheritance, written between the 13th and 15th centuries A. D.). The difference between these two systems on the subject of inheritance arises from the fact that, while the doctrine of religious efficacy is the guiding system under the Dāyabhāga school, there is no such definite guiding principle under the Mitākṣarā school. Sometimes, consanguinity is regarded as the guiding principle; at others, religious efficacy. Succession to strīdhana (Sanskrit: *strīdhana*), or property held absolutely by a female, is governed by rules different from those which govern inheritance to the property of a male. The Mitākṣarā school recognizes two modes of devolution of property: survivorship and succession. The rule of survivorship applies to joint family property; the rules of succession apply to property held in absolute severalty by the last owner. The Dāyabhāga recognizes only one mode of devolution: succession. It does not recognize the rule of survivorship even in the case of joint family property. The reason for this is that, while every member of a Mitākṣarā joint family has only an undivided interest in the joint property, a member of a Dāyabhāga joint family holds his share in quasi severally, so that it passes on his death to his heirs as if he were absolutely seized thereof, and not to the surviving coparceners as under the Mitākṣarā law.

6. The joint family is a striking feature of Hindū society and Hindū law. A joint Hindū family consists of all males lineally descended from a common ancestor and includes their wives and unmarried daughters. A daughter ceases to be a member of her father's family on marriage and becomes a member of her husband's family. The joint and undivided Hindū family is ordinarily joint not only in estate. but also in food and worship. Hindū coparcenary is a much narrower body than the joint family. It includes only those persons who acquire by birth an interest in the joint or coparcenary property. The essence of a coparcenary under the Mitākṣarā law is unity of ownership. Joint family or coparcenary property is that in which every coparcener has a joint interest and a joint possession; it devolves by survivorship, not by succession, and is property in which the male issue of the coparceners acquire an interest by birth. (In some cases the widow takes a share equal to that of her husband or son.) Property acquired in business by members of a joint Hindū family through their joint labour and with the aid of the joint family property becomes joint family property, and where it has been acquired without the aid of ioint family property the presumption is that it is the joint property of the joint acquirers. Generally speaking the normal state of every traditional Hindū family is joint, and in the absence of proof of division such is the legal presumption. All the legal rules applied according to Hindū law depend on whether the person to which the law is being applied belongs to a joint family or not. There are therefore separate rules on alienation, debts, partition, gifts, and other subjects which are applied differently to members of a joint family and to those who are not members of such a family.

7. A Hindū who is of sound mind and not a minor may dispose of his property by gift or by will for religious and charitable purposes, such as the establishment and worship of an idol, feeding Brāhmaṇs and the poor, performance of religious ceremonies, and the endowment of a university or a hospital. The moment the endowment is made, all rights pass from the dedicator. Where property is devoted absolutely to religious purpoes, the possession and management of the property belongs in the case of a *devasthāna* (temple) to the manager of the temple, and in the case of a math (Sanskrit : *maṭh*), or abode for students of religion, to the head of the math, who is called a mahant. Temple managers and mahants form a continuous representation of the property of the idol or of the math.

8. Marriage[1] is a holy union for the performance of religious duties, not a contract. In principle, a Hindū may marry any number of wives, but a woman cannot marry another man while her husband is alive. Legislation in modern times has in some provinces and states changed this general rule. The historic practice has been that the parties to a marriage must both belong to the same major caste; otherwise the marriage is invalid. But a marriage between persons belonging to different subdivisions of the same caste is not invalid. For the purposes of marriage converts to Hinduism are regarded as Śūdras. Therefore, the marriage of a Śūdra with a Christian woman converted to Hinduism before marriage is treated as a marriage between two Śūdras and is valid. A man cannot marry a woman of the same gotra or *pravara*; that is, he cannot marry a woman if his father and the woman's father are both descendants of a common ancestor in the male line. Similarly, a man and a woman cannot marry if they are sapinda (Sanskrit: *sapiṇḍa*), or persons having a common ancestor within a prescribed degree. There are two schools of thought as to who are sapinda for marriage.

According to Hindū law, the wife is bound to live with her husband and to submit herself to his authority. The hus-

1. After this article appeared the Hindū Marriage Act, 1855 was enacted (The *Gazette of India* No. 35 of 18, 1955).

band is bound to live with his wife and to maintain her. Divorce is not known in general Hindū law; a marriage creates an indissoluble tie between the husband and the wife. Judicial separation, however, is admissible.

9. Adoption is widely practised and recognized in Hindū law. The objects of adoption are to secure spiritual benefits to the adopter and his ancestors, and to secure an heir and perpetuate the adopter's name. Adoption has the effect of transferring the adopted child from his natural family into the adoptive family. In principle, it confers upon the adoptee the same rights and privileges in the family of the adopter as those of a legitimate son. On the other hand, the adopted son loses all the rights of a son in his natural family but does not sever the tie of blood between himself and the members of his natural family. For this reason he cannot marry in his natural family.

Select Bibiliography—Jones, Sir William, *Institutes of Hindu Law* (Calcutta and London 1796); Colebrooke, H. T., *A Digest of Hindu Law*, vols. 1-3 (Calcutta and London 1801); Jolly, Julius, *Outlines of an History of the Hindu Law of Partition, Inheritance and Adoption* (Calcutta 1885); West, Sir Raymond, and Bühler, J. G. *A Digest of the Hindu Law of Inheritance, Partition, and Adoption*, 4th ed. (Bombay 1921); Mayne, J. D. *A Treatise on Hindu Law and Usage*, 9th ed. (Madras 1922); Jolly, Julius, *Hindu Law and Custom* (Calcutta 1928); Jha, Ganganatha *Hindu Law in its Sources* (Allahabad 1930); Mulla, Sir D. F., *Principles of Hindu Law*, 9th ed. (Calcutta 1940); Kane P. V., *History of Dharmaśāstra*, vols. 1-5 (Poona 1930-53.

II MOSLEM LAW

10. Moslem personal law has been applied in modern India to Moslems in some matters only, that is: (I) in those which have been expressly directed by the Legislative Assembly to be applied to Moslems, such as rules of succession and inheritance; and (2) to those which are applied to Moslems as a matter of justice, equity, and good conscience, such as the rules of the Moslem law of pre-emption.

A Moslem is considered to be any person who professes that: (1) there is but One God, and (2) that Mohammed (Muhammad) is His prophet.

Moslems are divided into two main divisions, namely the Sunnites and the Shi'ites. The Sunnites are in turn divided into four sects: the Hanafi, the Maliki, the Shafi'ites, and the Hanbalites. The Shi'ites are divided into three sects: the Itha'ashriya, the Isma'ili, and the Zaydites. Moslem law applicable to each division or sect prevails for litigants of that division or sect.

11. There are four sources of Moslem law: (1) the Koran (Qur'ān); (2) *ḥadīth*, that is, precepts, actions, and sayings of the Prophet Mohammed not written down during his lifetime, but preserved by tradition and handed down by authorized persons; (3) *ijmā*, that is, consensus of Moslem scholars; and (4) *qiyās*, analogical deductions derived from a comparison of the first three sources when they do not apply to any particular case.

12. The whole estate of a Moslem who dies intestate, or so much of it as has not been disposed of by will, devolves on his heirs at the moment of his death. The heirs succeed to the estate as tenants in common in specific shares. Each heir is liable for the debts of the deceased to the extent only of a share of the debts proportionate to his share of the estate. There is no distinction of inheritance between movable and immovable property, or between ancestral and self-acquired property.

When the members of a Moslem family live in commensality, they do not form a joint family in the sense in which that term is used in Hindū law. There is not, as in Hindū law, any presumption that acquisitions by several members of a family living together are for the benefit of the family. If during the continuance of the family, however, properties are acquired in the name of the managing member of the family, and it is proved that they are possessed by all the members jointly, the presumption is that they are the properties of the family. If after the death of a Moslem his adult sons continue their father's business and retain their assets in the business, they are deemed to stand in a fiduciary relation to the other heirs of the deceased and to be liable to account as such for the profit made by them in the business. Similarly, members of a Moslem family carrying on business jointly do not constitute a joint family firm in the sense in which that expression is used in Hindū law.

13. In principle, every Moslem of sound mind and not a minor may dispose of his property by will (*waṣīyah*), which may be made either verbally or in writing. He cannot dispose of more than a third of the surplus of his estate after payment of funeral expenses and debts. Bequests in excess of the legal third cannot take effect unless the heirs consent thereto after the death of the testator. The Sunnites and the Shi'ites differ widely on other more detailed rules of succession.

An important feature of Moslem law is *waqf*, the permanent dedication by a person professing Islam of any property for any purpose recognized by Moslem law as religious, pious, or charitable. The moment the *waqf* is created, all rights of property pass out of the *wāqif*, or dedicator, and vest in the Almighty. The mutawalli (Arabic : *mutawalli*), or superintendent of the religious beneficiary, has no right in the property belonging to the *waqf*. In principle, *waqf* property cannot be alienated and is not liable to attachment and sale in execution of a personal decree against the mutawalli, nor can the rents and profits derived from such property be seized by execution.

The right of *shuf'a*, or pre-emption, is a right which the owner of an immovable property possesses to acquire by purchase another immovable property which has been sold to another person. The right of pre-emption is recognized by custom among Hindūs of some parts of India and is governed in principle by the rules of the Moslem law of pre-emption.

14. Marriage is a contract which has for its object the procreation and legalization of children. Every Moslem of sound mind who has attained puberty may enter into a contract of marriage. A Moslem may have as many as four wives at the same time, but it is not lawful for a Moslem woman to have more than one husband at a time. A Moslem male may contract a valid marriage not only with a Moslem woman, but also with a *kitābīya* (that is, a Jewess or a Christian), but not with an idolatress or a fire worshiper; a Moslem woman cannot contract a valid marriage except with a Moslem. She cannot contract a valid marriage even with a *kitābi* (Jew or Christian). If such a marriage is contracted, however, it is not void, but only irregular.

The husband is bound to maintain his wife so long as she is faithful to him and obeys his reasonable orders. If he neglects or refuses to maintain her, the wife may sue him for maintenance. A woman after divorce, but not after the death of her husband, is entitled to maintenance during the period of iddat (Arabic *'iddah*) or the period during which a divorced or widowed woman must remain in seclusion and abstain from remarriage.

Dower or mahr is a sum of money or other property which the wife is entitled to receive from the husband in consideration of the marriage. If the amount of dower is not fixed, the wife is entitled to "proper" dower. The wife may refuse to live with her husband and admit him to sexual intercourse so long as the dower is not paid.

The contract of marriage may be dissolved; (1) by the husband at his will, without the intervention of a court; (2) by mutual consent without the intervention of a court; and (3) by a judicial decree at the suit of the husband or wife. The wife is entitled to sue for a divorce on the grounds that her husband is impotent or that he has falsely charged her with adultery.

Select Bibliography.—Wilson, Sir R. K., *A Digest of Anglo-Muhammadan Law*, 6th ed. (Calcutta 1930); Fyzee, A. A. A., *An Introduction to the Study of Mohamedan Law* (London 1931); Mulla, Sir D. F. *Principles of Mohamedan Law*, 10th ed. (Calcutta 1933); Saksena, H. P., *Muslim Law as Administered in British India*, 2d ed. (Allahabad 1940); Fyzee, A. A. A., *Outlines of Muhammadan Law* (London 1950).

ERRATA

Page	*For*	*Read*
21 line 40	VRV	VRR
26 „ 40	2 & 3, pp. 107-115.	2& 3, pp. 107-115 and 166-183.
27 „ 4	Orientalistcyzny	Orientalistyczny
„ after line 20 add :		

30. Mahābhārata Verses in Cāṇakya's Compendia. In JAOS 83.1, pp. 30-67. Not reprinted.

31. Rāmāyaṇa Verses in Cāṇakya's Compendia. In Mm. Pt. Gopinath Kaviraj Commemoration Volume. Not reprinted.

29 line 8	*depositum*	*Depositum*
„ „ 9	*fiducia*	*Fiducia*
36 „ 13	and considered	; they considered
„ „ 14	deposit)	deposit
40 fn. 28 line 2	*vijnaptas*	*vijñaptas*
42 line 29	*Kārādi*	*kārādi*
46 „ 2	*Kārava*	*kārava*
„ „ 24	*śilpiayāsa*	*śilpinyāsa*
„ „ 25	artisn	artisan
55 „ 16	*There existed*	There existed
59 fn. 20 line 3	*catur-guṇa pañca-bandho*	*catur-guṇa-pañca-bandho*
65 line 1	witnesses.	witnesses,
„ „ 24	Upakośa's	Upakośā's
„ fn. 37 line 1	*ṭūtpanidhiḥ*	*tūtpanidhiḥ*
66 line 22	*pathais*	*pathaiś*
73 fn. 17 line 1	*gai*	*gaī*
75, fn. 31 line 1	*idānimasmi*	*idanīmasmi*
„ „ 6	*indent this line*	
77 fn. 53 line 2	*bhūtārthaṁ*	*bhutā'rthaṁ*
„ „ 54 „ 2	*ütto*	*utto*
79 „ 74 „ 2	*kasyāpi*	*kasyā'pi*
„ „ „ „ 2& 3	*deśāntaraṁ*	*deśā'ntaraṁ*
80 „ 80 „ 2	*āttamātrā ntarā*	*āttamātrā'ntarā*
81 „ 88 „ 4	*ṭasyā ntāṁ*	*tasyā'ntāṁ*

Page	*For*	*Read*
83 fn. 111 line 1	*Vaṇijaṁ*	*vaṇijaṁ*
84 „ 116 „ 13	*aṅgikṛtaṁ*	*aṅgīkṛtaṁ*
85 „ 119 „ 14	*nirihasya*	*nirīnasya*
„ „ 119 „ 15	*muncāmīti*	*muñcamīti*
86 „ 129 „ 1	*Nikśəḍa*	*Nikṣepa*
87 „ 138 line 6	*bhukt anikṣepāḥ*	*bhukta-nikṣepāḥ*
88 „ 144 „ 3	*vāsanasthamanākhyāya*	*vāsanatham anākhyāya*
„ „ „ „ 9	*nidhiyate*	*nidhīyate*
90 „ 164 „ 1	*-bandhā'nvāhita-yācitam*	*-bandhā'nvāhitā-yacitam*
92 „ 185 „ 1	From *Vṛ* 'present, give';	From 'present, give';
98 „ 218 „ 2	*parikṣya*	*parīkṣya*
104 „ 258 „ 4	*dvādaś-apaṇo*	*dvādaśa-paṇo*
106 line 23	Pañc. V.[275]	Pañc.[275]
114 „ 14	depend	depended
„ „ 27	*vṛddhimu tsṛjet*	*vṛddhim utsṛjet*
116 „ 35	Vys.	VyS.
120 „ 7	*ādhistu*	(*ādhistu*
„ „ 8	*sthārastathāḥ*	*sthāras tathāḥ*
„ „ 22	of an	of
123 „ 27	in the	the
130 „ 20	similar,	similar.
132 „ 20	debtor	debtor;
140 „ 3	*Unvalid*	*Invalid*
„ fn. 61 line 2	*tadādiṣṭam*	*tad ādiṣṭam*
143 line 33	*Duties of Pledgees*	**Duties of Pledgees**
154 „ 26	*manīṣlbhiḥ*	*manīṣibhiḥ*
„ fn. 5 line 2	nomenclature	terminology
155 line 13	darś	*darś*
156 „ 20	in case of another *vis*	in another case of *vis*
160 „ 22	will be	would be
161 „ 12	if	it
170 „ 32	*ihārthā-*	*ihārtha*
171 „ 16	*Gṛhīta-bandho'pasthāṇa*	*Gṛhīta-bandho'pasthāna*
174 „ 13	were belonged	belonged
„ „ 35	expressed	expression
175 „ 4	exeptions	exceptions
„ „ 6	**Dependency**	**Dependence**
182 „ 17	payable.	due.

Page	*For*	*Read*
187 line 33	*vṛthā-dānaṁ*	*vithā dānaṁ*
188 „ 24	composition	composition of
189 fn. 60 line 7	accurate in that case	accurate; in that case
„ „ „ 21	*-pratibhāvyam*	*-prātibhāvyam*
192 line 22	delivery	delivery of
193 „ 31	This took	This took place,
194 „ 23	had been	had
„ „ 25	to hand over	to have to hand over
„ „ 26	to pay off	to pay
197 „ 29	*Interest*	*Interests*
199 „ 1	**IV**	**VI**
200 „ 11	*kuṣdrā*	*kṣudrā*
212 fn. 23 line 4	*to*	*ta*
„ „	*anasysesthai*	*anasyresthai*
213 „ 29 „ 11	*śl.*	*Śl.*
214 line 13	the classification	(the classification
„ 14	(*gaṇikā*)	*gaṇikā*)
220 fn. 87 line 2	*vṛddhara-jdasībhir*	*vṛddharaja-dasībhir*
222 lines 14-15	enjoy only......basis.	enjoy full rights of property; she could enjoy only a part of the "property" on usufructual basis.
228 line 31	if	it
230 „ 21	*bhogadvi guṇodaṇḍaḥ*	*bhogadviguṇo daṇḍaḥ*
232 „ 2	*artha*	*artha-*
233 fn. 169 line 2	*vetanani*	*vetanaṁ*
236 line 24	*sāhasa daṇḍaḥ*	*sāhasa-daṇḍaḥ*
241 „ 4	burnt on alive	burnt alive
242 fn. 244 line 2	Badāon	Badaōn
244 line 19	(*hetairai*)	(*hetairas*)
246 „ 25	*pakvā-nna*	*pakvānna-*
248 fn. 31	*ca'*	*ca*
256 line 19	(*dourmatya*)	(*daurmatya*)
258 „ 27	*bandhaki*	*bandhakī*
259 fn. 103 line 2	*-saṁjnābhir*	*-saṁjñābhir-*
„ 105 „ 1	*kārtāntika-*	*-kārtāntika-samāhartā-janapade*

Page	*For*	*Read*
259 fn. 105 line 2	*mauhūrtika*	*naimittika-mauhūrtika*
263 line 9	*-matsyabandha-kalubdhakā-*	*-matsyabandhaka-lubdhakā*
,, ,, 14	[*matsyabsndhaka*]	[*matsyabandhaka*]
,, fn. 8 line 2	*puṁścali*	*puṁścalī*
271 line 25	wives	"wives"
272 fn. 6 line 9	Sts.	Śts.
276 ,, 29 line 3	*Aīn-i-*	*Āin-i-*
,, ,, 31 ,, 1	Mn. 11.259	Mn. 9.259
277 line 8	them imprudence	them to imprudence
282 ,, 22	study was	study it was
289 fn. 3 line 1	*samṛdḍhā' pi*	*samṛddhā'pi*
,, ,, 5 ,, 3-4	PT 1.67, PTem 1.89, ...VCir VI.1	PT 1.89, PTem 1.67 ... VCjr VI.1
290 ,, 17 ,, 4	*apyauṣadhavidhānajñas*	*apy auṣadhavidhanajñas*
292 line 7	skilful	skillful
295 ,, 14	cognisance	cognizance
,, ,, 22	differenciation line between	differenciation between
296 ,, 25	physicians	"physicians
298 fn. 29 line 8	HS 1.110	HS 1.100,
,, ,, 34 ,, 2	...*hūrt kacikitsa*...	...*hūrtikacikitsa*...
299 ,, 35 ,, 4	*ācakṣita'*	*ācakṣita,*
,, ,, 38 ,, 2	...*pretapradipāya*...	...*pretapradīpāya*...
301 line 15	run	ran
304 ,, 2	*rājapuruṣeṣ ūtamaṁ*	*rājapuruṣeṣ ūttamaṁ*
305 ,, 18	*teṣāṁ*	*teṣaṁ*
306 fn. 23 line 2	*dāpyaścā' ṣṭaguṇaṁ*	*dapyaś cā'ṣṭaguṇaṁ*
312 line 37	then if when	then when
315 ,, 25	line	fine
316 fn. 2 line 2	8.8	88
318 ,, 19 ,, 1	*kāmārtham*	*kamā'rtham*
323 line 16	to be found	found
324 ,, 6	until reached	until he reached
330 ,, 16	*Widows*	*Widows'*
331 fn. 62 line 2	*kāryagaura-*	*kārya-gaura-*
332 ,, 63 ,, 2	*vidhān*	*vidhyān*
334 ,, 75 ,, 2	*nastikānāṁ*	*nāstikānāṁ*

Page	*For*	*Read*
334 fn. 78 line 1	(*stri*)	(*strī*)
„ „ 83 „ 1	82	80
336 „ 96 „ 1	Vir.	Vīr.
344 line 19	in case of the greatest	in the case of greatest
346 fn. 68 line 1	K. II-146	K. II.46
358 line 18	word	words
„ „ 31	fee paid	fee was paid
359 line 25	(*śulka*).	(*śulka*).[7]
373 „ 29	*yaśaḥ*:;	*yaśaḥ*;
374 „ 11	sacrifice just	sacrifice, just
375 „ 12	*Daiva-vivāha* gained	*Daiva-vivāha*, gained
380 „ 18	those are	those who are
384 „ 4	Kāmasūtras	Kāmasūtra
385 „ 18	**75**	**57**
394 „ 12	this day,	"this day",
„ „ 17	der *Zeitschrift.*	*Zeitschrift.*
411 „ 24	S. 353).	5.353).
412 „ 20	*Bem rk. uber*	*Bemerk. über*
435 „ 42	Koztlowski	Kozlowski
437 „ 30	and	und
„ „ 44	Āpastambiya-	Āpastambīya
440 „ 27	interest	interests
465 „ 34	deal	deals